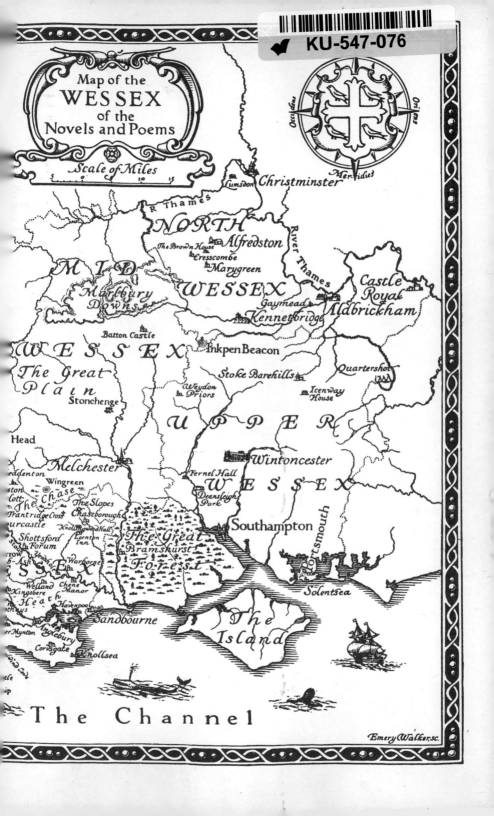

A HARDY COMPANION

A HARDY COMPANION

A guide to the works of Thomas Hardy
and their background

F. B. PINION

First edition 1968
Reprinted (with alterations) 1974
Reprinted (with alterations) 1976

Published by
THE MACMILLAN PRESS LTD
London and Basingstoke
Associated companies in New York
Dublin Melbourne Johannesburg and Madras

SBN 333 07290 1

Printed and bound in Great Britain by
REDWOOD BURN LIMITED
Trowbridge & Esher

To the memory of
CARL J. WEBER
(1894–1966)

Contents

List of Illustrations

The author and publishers wish to thank the following, who have kindly given permission for the photographs to be reproduced facing the pages quoted:

Aerofilms: p. 142 (lower)

Barnaby's: p. 175 (upper)

Canon E. B. Brooks: p. 495 (lower)

City of Birmingham: p. 495 (upper)

Country Life: p. 462 (lower)

Dorset County Museum: pp. 14 (both), 46 (upper) 111 (upper), 142 (upper), 206 (upper), 207 (lower), 239 (both), 270, 271 (lower), 303 (upper), 334 (both), 335 (lower), 366 (upper), 463 (both), 494

Eagle Photos: pp. 366 (lower), 430 (upper)

A. F. Kersting: pp. 79 (upper), 335 (upper), 431, 462 (upper)

All the other photographs were taken by the author and the copyright in them is his.

LIST OF MAPS

Preface

THIS work is intended as a reference book for the Hardy student and reader rather than as an introduction for the uninitiated. Its principal purpose is to direct attention to Hardy's writings, and present relevant information and guidance for a more accurate impression of their background, and of Hardy's views, aims, and achievement as a whole. The short stories have been summarized for recall and reference because, in general, from the brevity of their impact, they are less likely to leave as lasting and defined an impression of character, incident, and setting as the novels; three, which are not available to the general reader, have been presented in greater detail than is necessary for the others.

The largest section comprises a dictionary of people and places in Hardy's works. From this, the historical characters of *The Dynasts* have been omitted, since they belong rather to history than to the world of Hardy's creation. It includes real as well as fictitious persons, but those of no significance or special interest, such as the anonymous groups of doctors, lovers, husbands, coachmen, cottages, inns, churches and clerks which are to be found in Saxelby's *A Hardy Dictionary*, have been excluded. Everything relevant, as far as is known, is provided to enable the reader who is interested in the Wessex background to visit the settings which Hardy had in mind for his stories and a very large number of his poems.

A century has brought many changes. Most of Egdon Heath by Rainbarrow and Alderworth is no longer wild but afforested; Mellstock Lane has been denuded of trees; buildings have disappeared or been modernized. For this reason, illustrations from the past have been included wherever possible. Where the original buildings remain, parked cars and modern accessions such as television aerials introduce anachronistic elements which the photographer cannot always avoid. The Hardy enthusiast need not be deterred, however; there are few parts of England where so much of the country and so many ancient monuments and buildings remain characteristically unchanged.

Preface

It is hoped that this book will commend itself to Hardy readers in general. It provides material on a variety of topics to which one can turn and re-turn. Most references are set apart to hamper reading as little as possible. There are a few sections or sub-sections which are almost wholly referential; these are intended for students, and may be by-passed without consequent handicaps, since cross-references enable the reader to pursue the less obvious implications wherever he chooses to start.

Critical appraisal is not a major aim; it enters certain sections, notably on Hardy's novels, drama, and poetry. The general purpose is to help the reader to gain a more accurate knowledge of Hardy before making or accepting critical judgments. Inadequate attention to all the relevant facts weakens or vitiates critical as well as biographical interpretations. Detective-biographers, in particular, can be wildly imaginative, ignoring relevances in fact and fiction, or interpreting the fiction to support claims for which no valid evidence exists.

Although few authors have revealed more about themselves and their works, there is much that remains unknown in Hardy. How far the publication of his letters would help is conjectural. We cannot always know where uncertainty exists with reference to his life, yet we can recognize the problems it creates in his works. There are a few poems on the origin and background of which little if anything is known; how far invention and disguise enter some of the stories in *A Group of Noble Dames* remains largely to be discovered; a knowledge of the sources of untraced quotations and allusions might lead to a better appreciation of Hardy's thought, and throw light on unsuspected places in his works.

My interest in Hardy and Wessex has extended over a period far too long for me to trace my indebtedness. I owe much to Hermann Lea's *Thomas Hardy's Wessex* (though it is impossible to accept the view that all his identifications were authenticated by Hardy), and more than I can express to the friendship, encouragement, and writings of the late Carl J. Weber. R. L. Purdy's *Thomas Hardy, a Bibliographical Study* has been of invaluable assistance. During 1965–6 it was my good fortune to meet Professor J. O. Bailey several times; we have exchanged information on numerous occasions, particularly with reference to the poems. His generous help at several points has been too itemized for adequate acknowledgement. I am most grateful to the Curator of the Dorset County Museum, Mr R. N. R. Peers, and his staff for their courtesy and assistance on several occasions; to Mr F. R. Southerington for calling my attention to an unpublished passage from the typescript of Hardy's *Life*, the substance of which I have given in my commentary on *The Hand of Ethelberta*; to Mr H. P. R. Hoare and the National Trust for permission to refer to some of Florence Hardy's letters to Lady Alda Hoare; to John D. Gordan, Curator of the Berg Collection, New York, Mrs June Moll of the University of Texas Library, and Professor R. L. Purdy for information on the present whereabouts of some of Hardy's manuscripts; to the Dorset County Council, the Home Office, and others for kindly allowing me to take and publish photographs; and to many, among whom I should like to mention Mrs Gertrude Bugler, Miss May O'Rourke, Mr A. O. Hulton, and Mrs A. M. McTaggart, for assisting me in various inquiries. A grant from the Research Fund of the University of Sheffield is gratefully acknowledged. In the preparation of this book, I owe much to Mr T. M. Farmiloe for his encouragement and ready assistance; in its production, I am also indebted to Mr Richard Garnett and Miss Susan le Roux for their presentation respectively of the text, and the maps and illustrations. My indebtedness to my wife is too extensive to be acknowledged briefly; but for her critical appraisal of the text, its shortcomings would have been immeasurably greater.

Abbreviations for References

(*a*) 'Tony Kytes, the Arch-Deceiver' (*b*) 'The History of the Hardcomes' (*c*) 'The Superstitious Man's Story' (*d*) 'Andrey Satchel and the Parson and Clerk' (*e*) 'Old Andrey's Experience as a Musician' (*f*) 'Absent-Mindedness in a Parish Choir' (*g*) 'The Winters and the Palmeys' (*h*) 'Incident in the Life of Mr George Crookhill' (*i*) 'Netty Sargent's Copyhold'

MC	*The Mayor of Casterbridge*
MV	*Moments of Vision*
OMC	'Old Mrs Chundle'
PBE	*A Pair of Blue Eyes*
PPP	*Poems of the Past and the Present*
PRF	'The Profitable Reading of Fiction'
QC	*The Famous Tragedy of the Queen of Cornwall*
RN	*The Return of the Native*
SC	*Satires of Circumstance*
SF	'The Science of Fiction'
TD	*Tess of the d'Urbervilles*
TL	*Time's Laughingstocks*
TM	*The Trumpet-Major*
TT	*Two on a Tower*
UGT	*Under the Greenwood Tree*
W	*The Woodlanders*
WB	*The Well-Beloved*
WP	*Wessex Poems*
WT	*Wessex Tales*

(1) 'The Three Strangers' (2) 'A Tradition of Eighteen Hundred and Four' (3) 'The Melancholy Hussar' (4) 'The Withered Arm' (5) 'Fellow-Townsmen' (6) 'Interlopers at The Knap' (7) 'The Distracted Preacher'

WW	*Winter Words*

Hutchins	John Hutchins, *The History and Antiquities of the County of Dorset*, 3rd ed. in 4 vols., London, 1861–73.
Life	Florence Emily Hardy, *The Life of Thomas Hardy, 1840–1928* (*The Early Life* and *The Later Years* in one volume), Macmillan, 1962; St Martin's Press, New York, 1962.
Purdy	Richard Little Purdy, *Thomas Hardy, a Bibliographical Study*, Oxford University Press, 1954.

Sequence of Hardy's Works

The sequence followed for reference series (with some exceptions) is chronological as far as it can be ascertained. This must be conjectural to some extent. Where other evidence is missing, we must rely on dates of first publication. These, it should be noted, are the dates appended to the short stories. One discrepancy occurs: Hardy gives 'December 1899' for 'Enter a Dragoon' (*CM*. 5) where 'December 1900' could be expected.

The dates given below are for composition *except where italicized*.

Sequence of Hardy's Works

* 'An Imaginative Woman' was added to *Wessex Tales* in 1896, and transferred to *Life's Little Ironies* in 1912, when 'A Tradition of Eighteen Hundred and Four' and 'The Melancholy Hussar' were included in *Wessex Tales*.

Hardy's Life

1840   Thomas Hardy was born on 2 June in the house at Higher Bockhampton which was built for his grandfather 'Thomas the First' in 1801. The fortunes of the Hardys, who had owned extensive properties in Dorset, had declined; yet, among the collateral descendants of the Hardys who had first settled in England from Jersey centuries earlier, there was one who was famous. This was Admiral Hardy, who had been captain of Nelson's flagship at the battle of Trafalgar, and whose monument on Blackdown was something more than a landmark for Thomas as he left the Higher Bockhampton lane to follow the track across Kingston eweleaze for Stinsford or Dorchester on numerous occasions from 1849 to 1862 and later.

'The Heath' sloped down to the back of Hardy's birthplace. His paternal grandmother, who lived with the family until her death in 1857, talked of her early days at Higher Bockhampton, when the house was lonely and the 'heathcroppers' or ponies were often her only friends. Her reminiscences awakened his interest in the war against Napoleon and in dying local customs, superstitions, and unusual events. At one time the house had been used for hiding smuggled spirits.

One bitterly cold day, he and his father noticed a half-frozen fieldfare in the garden. His father threw a stone at it; instead of flying away, the bird fell dead. Thomas picked it up, and found it as light as a feather, nothing but skin and bone. At an early age, he had begun to realize 'the Frost's decree' or the cruelty of Nature; the incident haunted his imagination for the rest of his life.

Hardy's mother was unusually well-read, and loved to recite ballads. It is clear that his interest in stories began very early. He learned to read 'almost before he could walk', and the lady of Kingston Maurward House, Julia Augusta Martin, claimed to have taught him his letters (Evelyn Hardy, *Thomas Hardy's Notebooks*, 127).

1

His father and grandfather were stone-masons, and their business might have expanded had his father been more ambitious. For almost forty years the Hardys had been leading members of the village choir, which provided its own string music and played in the gallery of Stinsford Church. Hardy learned to play the violin, and loved music and dance before he went to school. His early ambition was to become a parson, and his mother did not neglect his education.

1848   Hardy became a pupil at the new school which Mrs Martin had established at Lower Bockhampton; he is said to have been so weak physically that he was never allowed to walk there (see *Life*, 16, however). His father did repairs on the Kingston Maurward estate, and owned a small farm called Talbothays on the other side of the Frome valley. 'About this time' Hardy's mother 'gave him Dryden's *Virgil*, Johnson's *Rasselas*, and *Paul and Virginia*. He also found in a closet *A History of the Wars* – a periodical dealing with the war with Napoleon, which his grandfather had subscribed to at the time, having been himself a volunteer.' About this time Hardy made his first train journey when he accompanied his mother on a visit to an aunt in Hertfordshire. (The railway linking Dorchester with Southampton and London had been opened in 1847.)

1849   Hardy was transferred to a school in Dorchester, principally because the headmaster was an excellent teacher of Latin. The walk to and from the new school helped to make him strong. Mrs Martin was aggrieved at not being consulted over this move; she was childless, and had shown 'Tommy' a great deal of affection, which he reciprocated. About the same time, whether before or after is not known, Thomas's father lost his work on the manor estate. The two events may have been related. Some time later, Thomas was taken by a young woman to witness the harvest-supper and dance in Kingston Maurward barn. The harvesters included Scotch Greys from Dorchester, but he longed, above all, to see 'the landowner's wife, to whom he had grown more secretly attached than he cared to own'. The reconciliation with the lady, whom he was not to meet again until he went to London in 1862, remained vividly in his memory in association with the red-uniformed soldiers, the dancing, and the singing of old ballads by the farm-women (see p. 383). Other memorable boyhood impressions were provided by the performance of Christmas mummers, the spectacle of village-dancing round the maypole, and the sight of a delinquent in the stocks at Puddletown.

1852–4   Hardy began learning Latin at school, played the fiddle at local weddings and dances, taught in the Sunday School, and acquired a taste for the romances of Dumas *père* and Harrison Ainsworth. He talked to local survivors of Waterloo, and acted as amanuensis for village girls who wished to write to their sweethearts in India. His attachment to Louisa Harding (see p. 395) was never forgotten.

1856   Hardy left school and was articled to John Hicks, a Dorchester architect and church-restorer, for whom his father had worked as a builder. The offices were in South Street, next door to the school kept by William Barnes, the Dorset poet. Hardy's study of the Latin classics continued. Much of his reading took place between five and eight in the morning, when he left home for the office. He began to study Greek, and discussed his 'construings' with Hicks; when a knotty point in grammar arose between him and a fellow-pupil at Hicks's, he often sought the advice of the great scholar William Barnes. On 9 August he stood close to the gallows outside Dorchester County Gaol to witness the execution of Martha Brown for the murder of her husband at Birdsmoor-gate, near Broadwindsor. Two or three years later he remembered, when he was about to sit down to breakfast, that another execution was due, and rushed out with a telescope to an eminent part of the heath from which he could see the gaol two or three miles off. He had just lifted the telescope to his eye, when the white figure of the murderer dropped; the sensation was such that he seemed to be alone on the heath with the hanged man. These two executions were the only ones he witnessed; they were unforgettable, and contributed to the story and final scene of *Tess of the d'Urbervilles.*

1858–61   He was now much stronger physically, and could maintain his studies in the early morning, his architectural employment during the day, and 'dance-fiddling' many an evening, without ill effects. He began writing poems at this time, among them 'Domicilium', the earliest of his poems to be preserved. In his Greek he was assisted by Horace Moule, the son of a distinguished minister at Fordington, the large parish adjoining Dorchester. Moule was eight years Hardy's senior, and a fine Greek scholar; he had been to Queens' College, Cambridge, after three years at Trinity College, Oxford. The two became friendly; Moule lent Hardy books, discussed classical literature with him, and advised him to give up the study of Greek plays if he wished to become an

3

architect. Moule himself was just beginning practice as an author and reviewer, at a time when scientific thought and critical research were making their early undermining impacts on the foundations of established beliefs. Hardy was 'among the earliest acclaimers of *The Origin of Species*' (1859), and was much impressed by *Essays and Reviews* (1860) by 'The Seven against Christ', as its authors were called.

1862–7 In April 1862 he went to London to pursue 'the art and science of architecture on more advanced lines'. (At this time his sister Mary was at Salisbury Training College, preparing to qualify as a teacher. Later she became a headmistress in Dorchester; her younger sister Katherine was to teach in the same school.) Hardy was soon engaged by Arthur Blomfield, an eminent restorer and designer of churches. His work was not confined to the office or to London; he travelled about the country 'very considerably' and worked for a time at the Radcliffe Infirmary Chapel, Oxford.

In London, he danced at famous ballrooms, attended operas and productions of Shakespeare's plays, and researched at the South Kensington Museum in preparation for an essay, 'On the Application of Coloured Bricks and Terra Cotta to Modern Architecture', which was awarded the Royal Institute of British Architects prize. He also won the Sir William Tite Prize, which was offered by the Architectural Association. For a term or two he attended classes in French under Professor Stièvenard at King's College. In 1865, to amuse his fellow-pupils at Blomfield's, he wrote 'How I Built Myself a House'; it was published in *Chambers's Journal*. He had the opportunity of going to Cambridge, but gave up the idea since he could no longer conscientiously prepare for Holy Orders. Hardy's reading of Spencer, Huxley, and John Stuart Mill had made him an independent thinker, and the complete overthrow of his faith may be seen in some of the poems which he wrote before he left London in 1867. He read poetry extensively, made a close study of the *Golden Treasury* and the works of Shelley and Browning, and was unusually impressed by Scott, preferring his poetry to his novels, and coming to the conclusion that *Marmion* was 'the most Homeric poem in the English language'. Swinburne's *Atalanta in Calydon* and the first volume of *Poems and Ballads* appeared in 1865 and 1866. When Swinburne died in 1910, Hardy recalled walking down a terraced street one summer morning and reading with 'a quick glad surprise' the perfervid eloquence of this great rebel against convention and God. He often lunched at a coffee shop in Hungerford Market which Dickens frequented. For many months he spent twenty minutes after lunch every day the National Gallery was open, 'studying the paintings of the masters, confining his attention to a single master on each visit, and forbidding his eyes to stray to any other'. He read incessantly every evening, often from six to twelve. The result of this ceaseless round of activities was a serious decline in his health, and advice from Blomfield that he should return to the country to recover. Like his father, Hardy lacked the ambition to be a careerist; he was beginning to feel that he would prefer the country altogether to London. He was critical of much he observed in society: 'The defects of a class are more perceptible to a class immediately below it than to itself,' he wrote. He was a shrewd and satirical observer, and claimed to know 'every street and alley west of St Paul's like a born Londoner, which he was often supposed to be'.

1867–70   In July 1867 the opportunity to work near home came when Mr Hicks wrote asking him if he could recommend someone to assist with church-restoration. Hardy volunteered to go himself, soon recovered his health at home, and once more resumed his walks to and from Dorchester. Almost immediately, he felt the urge to write, and embarked on his first novel, *The Poor Man and the Lady*. He lost little time, for the first draft was completed by January 1868. The novel contained 'original verses', probably some of the unpublished poems he had written in London.

Tryphena Sparks, Hardy's sixteen-year-old cousin, lived three miles away at Puddletown. How often they met and whether they fell in love are questions which cannot be answered with any degree of assurance. When she died in 1890, Hardy regarded her as his 'lost prize', but he entertained similar retrospective sentiments towards other women. In any estimate of their relationship, the wisdom of hindsight should not be discounted. There is no evidence to prove a passionate engagement or a separation which was a major disaster in Hardy's life. The poems which he had written in London show that, if his animadversions on Providence proceeded from personal disappointment or suffering, such experiences belong to an earlier period. Hardy never penned a stronger or more striking indictment of 'Crass Casualty' than in the poem 'Hap', which was written in 1866. It is likely that such poems were the outcome of speculations at a time when Hardy was influenced by contemporary scientific philosophy and the poetry of Swinburne. The Tryphena question is too conjectural at present to have much biographical validity (see pp. 435–40).

The Poor Man and the Lady was submitted for publication in the summer of 1868. Hardy's talents were recognized, particularly in the rural scenes, and he was given much consideration and advice, but the book was never published. The more important scenes were set in London, but Hardy's tone was too Radical and satirical for publication. Ultimately he was advised to write a novel with a more complicated plot.

In the meantime Hicks had died, and his business had been taken over by the architect Crickmay of Weymouth. Here Hardy worked for several months. He was very active, bathing at seven in the morning and rowing in the bay almost every evening in the summer; in the winter he joined a quadrille class. He wrote several poems and began *Desperate Remedies*, a compact novel of the thriller type, with a complicated plot in the Wilkie Collins manner.

1870–1   He returned to Higher Bockhampton in February, and within a week was asked by Crickmay to visit St Juliot in Cornwall to make plans of the church, which was to be rebuilt. He set out on Monday, 7 March, and stayed at St Juliot rectory, where he was received by Miss Emma Lavinia Gifford, the rector's sister-in-law. He found time to join in excursions to Boscastle, Tintagel, and Beeny Cliff. By Saturday he was back in Weymouth, at the end of the most critical week in his life. He and Miss Gifford were of the same age, and were already in love with each other.

At Weymouth Hardy worked on the church-restoration plans for St Juliot. In April he heard that *Desperate Remedies* had been rejected by publishers who disapproved of some of the incidents. Another firm expressed interest, and in May Hardy went to London, where he worked for a while at Blomfield's and then with another well-known 'Gothic architect', Raphael Brandon. Horace Moule was in London, and the two friends met frequently. In August Hardy left for a stay of two or three weeks at St Juliot. During the autumn Miss Gifford re-copied chapters of *Desperate Remedies*; the concluding chapters were written, and the novel was accepted. When it appeared in March 1871, its reception by the reviewers was mixed. One review was so damning that when Hardy read it 'on his way to Bockhampton' he wished he were dead. He was in

Cornwall again in May. During the summer he wrote most of *Under the Greenwood Tree*. A misunderstanding of a letter from the publishers to whom he had sent it made him decide to concentrate on architecture for a career. Miss Gifford encouraged him to write, and in October, when he was on his fourth visit to St Juliot, he began making notes for *A Pair of Blue Eyes* (Purdy, 331).

1872   He returned to London, and assisted the architect T. Roger Smith in making plans for schools. By chance he met the publisher of his first novel, and the result was .the appearance of *Under the Greenwood Tree*. It was favourably received. Hardy agreed to write a serial for the same publisher, and began the full-length composition of *A Pair of Blue Eyes* in July. In August he was in Cornwall again; he and Emma journeyed to Kirland, near Bodmin, to stay with her father. They were dismayed to find that he disapproved of the match and spoke of Hardy in the most opprobrious terms (see pp. 24, 353). Late in September, Hardy decided to leave London to finish his novel at home.

1873   Early in the year he made 'a flying visit' to St Juliot. In the spring he was in London, where he was joined by his brother Henry for a few days in June. Afterwards he spent two days at Cambridge with Horace Moule. It was the last time he saw him. Within a few days he was travelling to Bath to meet Miss Gifford, who was staying there with a friend. On 2 July he travelled home via Dorchester to start *Far from the Madding Crowd*. In September he was shocked to hear of the suicide of Horace Moule at Cambridge; he attended his funeral at Fordington. On the last day of the year, when he was returning from Cornwall, he was astonished to find that the first instalment of his new novel had been given pride of place in *The Cornhill Magazine.**

1874–6   By July 1874 *Far from the Madding Crowd* was finished. Hardy had found it a great advantage to be at home among the people he wrote about. The success of the novel seemed sufficient assurance for the future, for in September Hardy and Miss Gifford were married. We can assume that Mr Gifford was not reconciled to the marriage; it did not take place in Cornwall but at St Peter's, Paddington; Emma's uncle, afterwards Archdeacon of London, officiated at the ceremony. After a short

---

* Hardy did not recall all his visits to St Juliot. He came 'two or three times a year' (Emma Hardy, *Some Recollections*). See p. 354.

Continental tour, the married couple took rooms in Surbiton. Leslie Stephen asked Hardy for another serial, and Hardy, remembering that *Far from the Madding Crowd* had been ascribed to George Eliot by one critic, and resolved to show that he did not need to imitate anyone, began *The Hand of Ethelberta*. The repeated change of themes and backgrounds for his novels may have arisen from the need for a new subject to challenge his powers, but at this time it was simply a means of discovering the kind of fiction most in demand. He was married, had given up what might have been a profitable career, and could not afford to neglect popularity. Hardy's experimental novel was finished at Swanage, which, with its vicinity, provided the setting for the closing chapters.

1876–8   In March 1876 the Hardys moved to lodgings at Yeovil. At the end of May they set out for Holland and the Rhine Valley. At midsummer they entered the first house they had to themselves. It stood on the outskirts of Sturminster Newton, overlooking the River Stour in the Vale of Blackmoor. Here they spent their happiest days. Looking back at the end of their stay at 'Riverside Villa', Hardy noted in March 1878 'End of the Sturminster Newton idyll' and, later, 'Our happiest time'. His principal literary achievement during this period was *The Return of the Native*.

1878–81   Rightly or wrongly, Hardy had come to the conclusion that it was necessary for a novelist to live in or near London. His next move was to Upper Tooting. In particular he wished to work on the historical background for a novel set in 1804–5, when the French invasion of the south coast was expected. For this he did research in the British Museum and visited south Dorset. The result was *The Trumpet-Major*, which appeared in serial form in 1880. Hardy was becoming famous; he dined at clubs, and met distinguished people, including Tennyson and Browning. He had joined the Savile Club, where he made the acquaintance of Edmund Gosse, a writer and critic who was to become a lifelong friend. He had begun *A Laodicean*, an ingenious modernization of what was essentially a Gothic plot. In the summer, he and his wife made a tour of Normandy. After visiting Dorset and Cambridge, they returned to London in October. Almost immediately it was found that Hardy was suffering from an internal haemorrhage. He had to lie in bed for months, but insisted on finishing his novel, partly to fulfil his contract, but also from anxiety lest he should die and his wife be left poorly provided for.

The remainder of the novel was dictated. He did not go outside until April 1881. In May he and his wife looked for a house in Dorset, and eventually found one at Wimborne Minster.

1881–2   In August they visited Scotland. On his return he set to work on his next novel, *Two on a Tower*, the setting for which was a few miles west of Wimborne. The Hardys found time for visiting and excursions, as they had done at Sturminster Newton, and took part in private readings of Shakespeare. He joined the Dorset Natural History and Antiquarian Field Club; some of its members are to be found in the setting for the narration of *A Group of Noble Dames*. In the autumn of 1882 the Hardys visited Paris.

1883   The plight of the Dorsetshire agricultural labourer engaged Hardy's attention at this time, and an article he wrote on the subject was published in July 1883. In May and June he and his wife were in London seeing pictures, plays, and friends. Hardy met Browning again, at Lord Houghton's and Mrs Procter's, attended the dinner to mark the departure of the actor Irving for America, and met the American novelist W. D. Howells at the Savile Club. He was in London for a few months nearly every year, and became known to many distinguished people.

In June the Hardys went to live in Dorchester. The main reason for this move was no doubt Hardy's wish to superintend the building of his house Max Gate on the Wareham Road.

1884–5   'Off and on' he wrote *The Mayor of Casterbridge* for weekly serial publication.

1885–7   In June the Hardys moved into Max Gate. R. L. Stevenson was almost the first visitor. *The Woodlanders* was finished by February 1887, and soon afterwards the Hardys began their journey to Italy, where they visited Genoa, Florence, Rome, Venice, and Milan. They arrived in London in April, and Hardy met Lowell, Browning, and Matthew Arnold. By August they were back in Dorchester.

1888–92   Next spring they were in London again, and in June visited Paris. They returned home in July, and it is clear from Hardy's outing of 30 September (*Life*, 214) that he was already planning *Tess of the d'Urbervilles* in the autumn of 1888. This was set aside or interrupted for the writing of short stories. Among them was a series, forming the

9

majority of *A Group of Noble Dames*, which originated from the study of famous families in his four volumes of the third edition of John Hutchins's *History and Antiquities of Dorset*. Amputating and modifying *Tess of the d'Urbervilles* in preparation for a serial publication designed not to offend magazine-readers took up a great deal of his time. It was a process he was to repeat with *Jude the Obscure*. He performed the operation with cynical amusement, but the attempt to cater for readers who could not face the issues of life gradually sapped his enthusiasm for writing fiction. More and more he looked forward to a work on a subject which had engaged his attention for many years, and in which he could express his views without pandering to popular tastes. His plans were slowly evolving, but it was not until he had given up the writing of novels that he had time to turn to his major work, *The Dynasts*. 'The highest flights of the pen are mostly the excursions and revelations of souls unreconciled to life,' he wrote towards the end of 1891. The writing of a series of short rustic stories, now known as 'A Few Crusted Characters', came no doubt as a relief after *Tess of the d'Urbervilles*. Several other short stories, which appeared eventually in *Life's Little Ironies*, were undertaken in 1891, and another diversion, *The Well-Beloved*, was written in the interval between *Tess* and *Jude the Obscure*. In September, the Hardys enjoyed a memorable visit to the Scott country. Hardy was in London a great deal, but he was back in Dorset in the summer of 1892, when his father died. In October he visited Fawley in Berkshire; he was preparing for *Jude the Obscure*.

1893-6   The Hardys were in London again in the spring, and for the first time occupied a whole house, bringing up their servants from Dorchester. In May they travelled to Dublin, where they met Mrs Henniker, an authoress whom Hardy advised for several years and with whom he collaborated in writing a short story, 'The Spectre of the Real!'. There is reason to think, from some of his poems, that Hardy was attracted by her; he found her 'a charming *intuitive* woman'. His own domestic affairs were, to say the least, a strain. He owed much to his wife. She had encouraged him and assisted him in his writings, but was obsessed with her social superiority and at times possessed with the idea that she was a writer of genius. Occasionally her eccentricities reached a point which it was difficult not to label 'insanity'. *Jude the Obscure* aggravated dissension, and she did everything to prevent its publication. Encouraged by 'Ibscene drama' and the recollection of J. S. Mill's counsels on integrity and independence of thought, Hardy had refused to compromise. 'Never retract. Never explain. Get it done and let them howl.' These were the words addressed to Jowett, one of 'The Seven against Christ', by a very practical friend, he noted, adding significantly: 'On the 1st November [1895] *Jude the Obscure* was published.' This was the full text in volume form. Domestic disapproval and public criticism were mainly responsible for the depression voiced in the three poems, 'In Tenebris'. He felt as he had done when his first published novel had been mauled; he wished he had never been born. In addition to the various public and domestic strains which he endured, Hardy had the task of revising his novels and writing new prefaces for a uniform edition. It is surprising that he was able to accomplish so much. He recovered. As on previous occasions, he attended concerts with his wife at the Imperial Institute; in August they were at Malvern, Worcester, and Stratford; in September they visited Belgium. Hardy was making final plans to start *The Dynasts*, and spent 2 October walking about the field of Waterloo.

1897–8   After their usual London visit, the Hardys went to Switzerland. He was at Lausanne, in Gibbon's old garden, towards midnight on 27 June, the 110th anniversary to the minute of the conclusion of *The Decline and Fall*. At home he went over his old poems and wrote others in preparation for his first volume of poetry, *Wessex Poems*, which appeared with Hardy's own illustrations in 1898. He wrote poems for his own pleasure. He could easily have been an affluent author had he debased himself by writing best-sellers. As a professional writer, he wanted to be popular; but his genius rebelled against self-immolation. At one time he had seriously thought that he would have to write 'society novels', and had prepared numerous notes and sketches from his social engagements in town and country in readiness for such an emergency. All these were burnt, but we can judge them by notes in his *Life* and a scene or two in *The Well-Beloved*.

1899–1901   The next volume of poems which Hardy prepared, *Poems of the Past and the Present*, is remarkable for several poems on the universe, Nature (the great Mother) and the First Cause. Ideas or impressions in them may be found in the later novels, but they are stepping-stones towards *The Dynasts*. Although he had been preparing it for many years, this work involved Hardy in immense and protracted historical research.

1902   He began the composition of *The Dynasts* during the second half of the year. (It appeared in three volumes, successively in 1904, 1906, and 1908.)

1904   His mother died in April.

1905   Hardy received the honorary degree of LL.D. at the University of Aberdeen. In June he visited Swinburne, who 'spoke with amusement of a paragraph he had seen in a Scottish paper: "Swinburne planteth, Hardy watereth, and Satan giveth the increase."' They laughed and condoled with each other on being the two most abused of living authors.

1907   On 8 February Mrs Hardy went to London to walk in a suffragist procession. In June the Hardys were guests at King Edward's garden party at Windsor Castle.

1908   Hardy completed his work as editor of a selection from the poems of William Barnes.

1909   He was invited by the University of Virginia to attend the centenary celebrations of the birth of Edgar Allan Poe. This was not the only invitation Hardy received from the United States; as usual, he declined. At the same time, he became a governor of Dorchester Grammar School (endowed by one of his collateral ancestors in 1579), a position he held until 1925. He succeeded George Meredith as President of the Society of Authors, and his third volume of poetry, *Time's Laughingstocks*, was published at the end of the year.

1910   Hardy received the Order of Merit in June. In November he was accorded the freedom of Dorchester.

1912   In the early part of the year he was busy making his final revision of the Wessex novels; as a *story*, *The Woodlanders* was his favourite. He received the Gold Medal of the Royal Society of Literature. Suddenly, on 27 November, his wife died.

1913   Hardy's grief was great. He was conscious of his neglect and of her loyalty. Numerous poems bear witness to his 'expiation'; they express feelings which had been pent up, and prove that, though Hardy continued to write poems on miscellaneous subjects, he rarely had one to call forth his highest powers after the completion of *The Dynasts*. In 'Poems of 1912–13', which appeared in *Satires of Circumstance* (1914), the true voice of feeling is heard. Many more poems inspired by *veteris vestigia flammae* and regrets were to follow. On 6 March, 1913, 'almost to a day, forty-three years after his first journey to Cornwall', he started on a penitential pilgrimage to St Juliot, afterwards visiting his wife's birthplace at Plymouth. In June he received the honorary degree of Litt.D. at Cambridge. Twelve stories which had appeared in periodicals were collected for publication in the Wessex edition under the title of *A Changed Man*.

1914   In February he married Miss Florence Dugdale, who had been at Max Gate since 1912, organizing the household and protecting the aged author from the intrusions of numerous visitors. After the outbreak of the First World War, Hardy joined a band of leading writers who pledged themselves to write for the Allied Cause; his 'Poems of War and Patriotism' were included in *Moments of Vision* (1917). The war 'gave the *coup de grâce* to any conception he may have nourished of a fundamental ultimate Wisdom at the back of things'. He said that he would not have ended *The Dynasts* on an optimistic note had he foreseen what was to happen.

1915   Hardy's sister Mary died in November at Talbothays.

1920   He received the honorary degree of D.Litt. at Oxford.

1922   *Late Lyrics and Earlier* was published with 'an energetic preface', in which he defended his views and rebutted the charge of pessimism. He and his first wife had been great cyclists – at the age of eighty-two, Hardy could cycle to visit his brother Henry and sister Katherine at Talbothays, the house which had been built on the site of their father's farm after their mother's death.

1923   The first draft of *The Famous Tragedy of the Queen of Cornwall* was completed in April; and the Prince of Wales was received at Max Gate on the occasion of his visit to Dorchester to open a drill-hall for the Dorset Territorials.

1924   For the first time since his childhood, Hardy visited the old barn at Kingston Maurward where he had heard the village girls singing old ballads.

1925   'A deputation from Bristol University arrived at Max Gate to confer on Hardy the honorary degree of Doctor of Literature.' *Human Shows* was published in November.

1926   On 1 November Hardy visited his birthplace for the last time.

1927   He laid the foundation-stone of the new Dorchester Grammar School buildings. On the fifteenth anniversary of his wife's death, he worked 'almost all the day, revising poems'. His strength was failing rapidly at this time. He had insisted on examining a Roman pavement at Fordington before its removal to the County Museum. A cold wind blew, and soon afterwards he fell ill. The weather was bitterly cold after Christmas.

1928   On 10 January he seemed to rally. In the evening he asked that 'Rabbi Ben Ezra' should be read aloud to him. 'While reading it his wife glanced at his face to see whether he were tired . . . and she was struck by the look of wistful intentness with which Hardy was listening. He indicated that he wished to hear the poem to the end.' As it was growing dusk the following afternoon, he asked her to read the verse from 'The Rubáiyát of Omar Khayyám' beginning 'Oh, Thou, who Man of Baser Earth'. She read:

> Oh, Thou, who Man of Baser Earth didst make,
> And ev'n with Paradise devise the Snake:
>   For all the Sin wherewith the Face of Man
> Is blacken'd – Man's forgiveness give – and take!

'He indicated that he wished no more to be read.' In the evening he had a sharp heart attack. The doctor was called. Hardy remained conscious until a few minutes before the end. Shortly after nine he died.

His ashes were buried in Westminster Abbey; the pall-bearers included the Prime Minister, the Leader of the Opposition, Sir James Barrie, John Galsworthy, Sir Edmund Gosse, Professor A. E. Housman, Rudyard Kipling, and Bernard Shaw. At the same hour, 'the heart of this lover of rural Wessex was buried in the grave of his first wife among the Hardy tombs under the great yew-tree' near the entrance to Stinsford churchyard.

His last volume of poems, *Winter Words*, was published the same year, in October.

...ardy's birthplace (see Reuben Dewy and Higher Bockhampton)

...igher Bockhampton lane from the Heath (1850), showing Hardy's birthplace on ...e left (see Fairland, Lewgate, and Mellstock). From a painting by Emma Hardy

The old manor, Kingston Maurward (above), *and Kingston Maurward House* (*see Kingston Maurward, Knapwater House, and Tollamore*)

THE NOVELS

THE POOR MAN AND THE LADY

Hardy's first novel was written in the second half of 1867, after his return to Dorset from London. The first draft was completed in January 1868; the revised copy was finished by the early part of the following June. Initially described as 'A story with no plot, containing some original verses', it was never published. Portions of it survive, with modifications, in Hardy's other works; the manuscript was lost or destroyed.

The best idea of its substance and quality can be obtained from

1. Professor Carl Weber's introduction to Hardy's *An Indiscretion in the Life of an Heiress*, Russell & Russell, New York, 1965.

2. Alexander Macmillan's letter to Hardy on the manuscript, in Charles Morgan's *The House of Macmillan*, Macmillan, 1944.

3. Chap. iv of *The Life of Thomas Hardy* (ostensibly by Florence Emily Hardy, though all but the concluding chapters were carefully prepared by Hardy himself).

The most important scenes of the novel were laid in London, where Hardy had lived from 1862 to 1867 while working for the architect Arthur Blomfield. The hero, Will Strong, was an architect. Satirical representation of the squirearchy and London society suggested dangerous radical tendencies; 'the vulgarity of the middle class, modern Christianity, church-restoration, and political and domestic morals in general' were underlined; and the book, like Hardy's last novels, was obviously written with 'a passion for reforming the world'. Whereas Thackeray's satire meant 'fun', Alexander Macmillan wrote, Hardy's meant 'mischief'. Looking back, Hardy expressed the view that the satire had been 'pushed too far', and that it had resulted in an inventiveness in the action which defied probability. John Morley, Macmillan's reader, noted 'queer cleverness and hard sarcasm', but thought 'the opening pictures of the Christmas Eve in the tranter's house' were 'really of good quality'.

The opening Christmas Eve scenes at the tranter's were easily accommodated to the love-story of *Under the Greenwood Tree* (cf. *Life*, 86).

Modified to form a self-contained story, the main theme in very simple and economical outline was published in 1878 as 'An Indiscretion in the Life of an Heiress'. Here we have a very close approximation, to the 'affected simplicity of Defoe's' style which Hardy ascribed to the original story. Many scenes were shed, but the country and London settings were retained. Some of the class resentment, cynicism,and social satire remain.

More material found its way into *Desperate Remedies*. The same quotations from Shelley, Browning, and Dryden's translation of Virgil are found here as in 'An Indiscretion', and even some of Hardy's sentences. The opening paragraph of 'An Indiscretion', describing the congregation as it sings and sways in church, is found, with slight modification, in *Desperate Remedies*, xii 8. The class resentment of a poor man of genius and sensitivity is expressed once again. Some of the London vignettes, especially the more satirical, may have been recollected from the first novel, as well as the Knapwater setting.

The same social sentiments and satire are to be found to some degree in scenes and comments in later novels, e.g. *A Pair of Blue Eyes* (the scene in Rotten Row which Alexander Macmillan praised was almost certainly adapted for chap. xiv) and *The Hand of Ethelberta*.

A link with one episode is preserved in the poem, 'A Poor Man and a Lady' (*HS*); the scene is a Mayfair church in London. The novel also contained scenes in famous London ballrooms, such as Almack's, the Argyle, and Cremorne (cf. *Life*, 42–3); and these are recalled in the poem 'Reminiscences of a Dancing Man' (*TL*).

The remark of Knight on novel-writing (*PBE*. xvii), 'It requires a judicious omission of your real thoughts to make a novel popular', must have been written with the recent history of *The Poor Man and the Lady* in mind. It has a proleptic significance when we consider the career of the author of 'Candour in English Fiction' with particular reference to the publication of *Tess of the d'Urbervilles* and *Jude the Obscure*.

One criticism of *The Poor Man and the Lady* had important consequences. In view of its episodic construction, George Meredith, reader for Chapman & Hall, advised Hardy to write a novel with a more complicated plot. The result was *Desperate Remedies*.

DESPERATE REMEDIES

Hardy went much further than Meredith had intended, and decided to write a sensational novel with a highly complicated mystery plot in the style of Wilkie Collins. *The Moonstone*, which was published in 1868, was an exemplar, but *The Woman in White* (1860) probably had a greater influence on the story (see J. W. Beach, *The Technique of Thomas Hardy*). This venture in a kind of fiction Hardy 'had never contemplated writing' was attended with deep misgiving, as the passage which he marked in his copy of *Hamlet* on 15 December 1870 indicates: 'Thou wouldst not think how ill all's here about my heart: but it is no matter!' (*Life*, 83). He had worked on *Desperate Remedies* at Weymouth when he was not engaged on Crickmay's church-restoration projects. Early in February 1870 he returned to Higher Bockhampton to concentrate on the novel, and he had almost completed the first draft when he made his first visit to Cornwall. Ultimately, the novel was accepted by Tinsley Brothers, the publishers of *The Moonstone*. It was published anonymously in March 1871. After two not unfavourable reviews, it suffered a slashing attack in *The Spectator*. Hardy's disappointment was keen; he wished he had never been born. His major offence lay in 'daring to suppose it possible that an unmarried woman owning an estate could have an illegitimate child'. The novel was described as 'a desperate remedy for an emaciated purse'.

Years later, when his reputation as a novelist and his future were not at stake, Hardy could dismiss *Desperate Remedies* as a crude melodrama after 'the Miss Braddon school' and 'quite below the level of *The Poor Man and the Lady*'. He could afford to indulge in such self-depreciation, but it does not square with his bitterness at the harsh treatment the novel received in 1871. Although the plot depends on events that occasionally suggest cheap sensationalism and improbability, it is carefully articulated and presents tensions and mounting mystery with no mean skill; its tightly constructed plot is enriched with a laudable variety of effects, from the poetic and tragic to the vernacular and humorous. The writing is amazingly disciplined and rarely dull. Today the interest is enhanced by revelations of the power which Hardy developed in later novels, in poetic overtones, tragic insights, and humorous dialogue.

The extent of transfer from *The Poor Man and the Lady* cannot be estimated. Large-scale transcriptions are not suspected. The Knapwater setting is the Tollamore setting of 'An Indiscretion in the Life of an Heiress', and it is most likely that a number of passages were adapted for inclusion in some of the London and rural scenes. Sentences and quotations which occur in 'An Indiscretion' are found again in this novel, and at least one passage, which contains one of these sentences (towards the end of iii 2), bears sharply on the handicaps confronting the poor man of genius in a class-ridden society.

Certain tragic scenes are of special interest because they contain ideas and impressions which were adopted or developed in much later novels. In the concluding paragraphs of xii 6 will be found two passages which were transferred almost verbatim to *The Return of the Native* (iii v); garden symbolism, which, divested of its Gothic associations, is the forerunner of a scene at Talbothays farm in *Tess of the d'Urbervilles*; and the presentation of the tragic heroine overborne by circumstance 'as one in a boat without oars, drifting with closed eyes down a river – she knew not whither'. Though incidental, the image is impressive, doubly so because it recurs more tragically in *Tess*. It is the summation of a whole scene in George Eliot's *Romola*.

There are further links with *Tess of the d'Urbervilles*. The heroine in each novel sacrifices herself in marriage, solemnized or *de facto*, for the sake of her family. *Desperate Remedies* anticipates *Tess* in one other respect. John Morley advised Alexander Macmillan not to 'touch' the story because it originated in the violation of a young lady. His letter of advice (Charles Morgan, *The House of Macmillan*, 93–4) suggests that the most objectionable scene was subsequently removed, and that Hardy took steps to make the *point de départ* of the story as unobtrusive as possible. Morley also objected to the scene 'between Miss Aldclyffe and her new maid in bed'. Lesbianism was probably totally alien to Hardy's intuitive conception of a situation in which the passionate feelings of a woman denied the husband she had loved are transferred to his daughter, whom she regards pitifully as her own. Hardy regarded the abnormality of the scene as the natural outcome of the situation; it was not an attempt at the sensational, and certainly not intended as an affront to Victorian susceptibilities.

18

In a few scenes, particularly xiii 4, Hardy's first experiments in counterpoint or the fusion of emotion and situation with external surroundings may be noted. Gothic elements are present, but the technique gives a foretaste of ampler harmonies and poetic overtones in *The Return of the Native* and *Tess of the d'Urbervilles*, where parallelism of natural background accentuates the human drama and underlines the indifference of Nature to human suffering.

In the early novels from *Desperate Remedies* to *Far from the Madding Crowd* the influence of George Eliot may be suspected. Comic rustics in the same tradition as those who meet in 'The Rainbow' in *Silas Marner* comment on leading characters and events. Of the first of these, Mr Crickett is the most noteworthy. They were to become more Shakespearian.

Literary quotations and references to painters show that Hardy assumed from the start that a writer was expected to be cultured. Sometimes they are an encumbrance, and suggest that the writer is diverted from natural expression by the desire to impress. In general, they are integral to conceptions rather than decorative or associative.

The characteristics of *Desperate Remedies* are mixed. The true Hardy elements are combined with sensationalism and Gothic effects. One thing is certain: complications in plot were never likely to present unmanageable problems to the author of this book. In this respect, *Desperate Remedies* marks an important step in Hardy's apprenticeship as a novelist.

Weymouth and Hardy's experiences as a poet provided material for some of the earlier scenes; Kingston Maurward House, the old decaying manor-house nearby, and the not far distant railway line to London presented ready possibilities for a contemporary murder-mystery story (the main action lasts from 1863 to 1867); and a traditional Wessex tale – of which Hardy had already written a humorous version in dialect in 'The Bride-Night Fire' (*WP*) – may have sparked off the crucial episode of the story, the fire at the Three Tranters. (The melodramatic possibilities of a fire at an inn could have been suggested by *Lady Audley's Secret*, the first novel from the prolific pen of Miss Braddon; it appeared in 1862, and made a fortune for her and her publishers.) In other respects the Wessex background, like that of 'An Indiscretion', is sketchy and general rather than topographical. The Wessex place-names were altered in the 1896 edition in order to bring *Desperate Remedies* in line with Hardy's subsequent fiction.

UNDER THE GREENWOOD TREE

Hardy responded barometrically to criticism of his first published novel. He had not forgotten John Morley's approval of 'the opening pictures of the Christmas Eve in the tranter's house' in *The Poor Man and the Lady*, or the following passage in the *Spectator* review of *Desperate Remedies:* 'there is an *unusual* and *very* happy facility in catching and fixing phases of peasant life – in producing for us, not the manners and language only but the tone of thought . . . and simple humour of consequential village worthies, and gaping village rustics. So that we are irresistibly reminded of the paintings of Wilkie and still more perhaps of those of Teniers, etc. The scenes allotted to these humble actors are few and slight but they indicate powers that might, and ought to be extended largely in this direction.' He concluded that he must avoid complications of plot and any hint of moral obliquity in his next novel. A light 'pastoral story', which allowed scope for 'rustic characters and scenery', seemed 'the safest venture'. Among the Christmas Eve 'pictures' at the tranter's which he decided to adapt, there was one in particular which could be transferred to the new novel with very few modifications. Around this he created and reconstructed a series of scenes which provided 'a good background' to the love-story. With the later, pastoral scenes, they formed, as it were, 'A Rural Painting of the Dutch School'. The choir story and background were so important that Hardy wished the novel to be known as *The Mellstock Quire*; it was because 'titles from poetry were in fashion' that he was persuaded to call it *Under the Greenwood Tree* (Charles Morgan, *The House of Macmillan*, 87–8, 94–6; *Life*, 86).

The subject was one Hardy had been intimate with from childhood (*Life*, 8–12, 248), and to which he returned several times in his novels, short stories, and poems (cf. Mellstock, pp. 410–12). No doubt he had heard many stories of the old choir from his parents and grandmother, for the Hardy family had been the mainstay of the Stinsford string choir for almost the first forty years of the nineteenth century. Hardy had studied the family music notebooks, and though, as he tells us, 'there was, in fact, no family portrait in the tale', the tranter's house is recognizably the Hardys' at Higher Bockhampton, and old William Dewy, Reuben

Dewy, Dick Dewy, and Michael Mail occupied the same seats and played the same instruments as Thomas Hardy senior, Thomas Hardy junior, James Hardy, and James Dart in 'Mellstock' church gallery (*Life*, 93, 11). It was Hardy's cousin Teresa, the daughter of James Hardy, who played the harmonium at Stinsford after the revolution in parochial church music which provided the background accompaniment to the early love-story of Dick Dewy and Fancy Day. Hardy's interest in rural church affairs had been revived when his sister Mary became a church organist; 'Tell me about the organ and how the Sundays go off – I am uncommonly interested,' he wrote to her from London in 1863.

The detective of autobiography in fiction may trace a resemblance to Tryphena Sparks, another of Hardy's cousins, in the description of Fancy Day (I vii), and perhaps also in the waywardness of her affections.

One might surmise from Hardy's 1896 preface that the period of the story is about 1840. This seems to be borne out in 'The Fiddler of the Reels' (*LLI*), in which the strange course of events in the lives of Caroline Aspent and Mop Ollamoor begins not later than 1847. Here we read that Ollamoor's 'date was a little later than that of the old Mellstock quire-band which comprised the Dewys, Mail, and the rest'. A remark in the novel (I iv) seems to indicate that the story could not have begun before 1845; one cannot be certain, therefore, whether Hardy was aware that there were no Queen's Scholars before 1846 (cf. IV ii).

Recent critics have hastened to discover the foreshadowing of tragic overtones in this humorous idyll. There are no deeply ominous notes. The disturbance caused by an owl as it kills a bird in the adjoining wood is the prelude to Geoffrey Day's refusal to accept Dick Dewy as his daughter's suitor, just as her consequent distress is reflected in rain and mist and the writhing of trees in the wind; but no one attaches serious-ness even to this incidental reminder of Nature's cruelty in a scene where Shiner and Dick vie risibly for favour, and the hero's overtures are made over the rail of a piggery. Clouds quickly pass, and the tone of the novel brooks no heartaches. Dick's jealousies are amusing, and Fancy Day's 'temptation' jars only momentarily. In its context, it is one of life's little ironies, and they are not always presented tragically in Hardy's fiction. It is never allowed to disturb the hero's happiness. The scene between Dick and his father at Mellstock Cross discloses the lover in his most serious mood; the tranter's comments reflect what 'the common world says', and 'the world's a very sensible feller on things in jineral'. Its views are not disconsolate or tragic. Appropriately, this comic romance ends on a delicious equipoise of comic irony. Serious conjectures about the matrimonial future of the lovers (unlike those relating to Grace Melbury and Fitzpiers in *The Woodlanders*) would be alien to the spirit of *Under the Greenwood Tree* (see p. 132 and p. 163). The reader's sympathies are most likely to be linked with the passing of the old choir, but even such sentiments are adventitious. Hardy's detached view was that the 'realities . . . were material for another kind of story for this little group of church musicians than is found in the chapters here penned so lightly, even so farcically and flippantly at times'. The tug-of-war between the choir and Mr Maybold is amusing and somewhat Dickensian.

In a story which skilfully combines light romance with the declining fortunes of the choir, it is obvious that the role of the latter is not a subordinate one. The members of the Mellstock choir are not presented equally, but among them are lesser, static, perennial figures, which are undoubtedly the forerunners of the comic rustics in the chorus of commentators and gossips to be found in *Far from the Madding Crowd* or *The Return of the Native*. They owe something to the observation of a countryman who could regard local characters with keen humorous detachment after a period of absence in London, but much more to creative genius inspired by Shakespearian and Dickensian influences. Their quaint angularity is Hardy's most idiosyncratic achievement in *Under the Greenwood Tree*. In saying that 'the attempt has been to draw the characters humorously, without caricature', Hardy implied a sympathetic treatment.

Hardy's observations of nature as well as of character show an original distinctiveness and precision; his pervasive humour and detachment combine with a widespread use of choice dialogue and reminiscence in dialect to give this minor work a high and special place among the Wessex novels.

John Morley thought the opening scenes lacked 'sufficient sparkle and humour' for 'such minute and prolonged description' (Morgan, 97), and their reduction was recommended. Hardy was discouraged, asked for the return of his manuscript, and decided to give up novel-writing. But for the encouragement of Emma Lavinia Gifford, and a chance encounter with Mr Tinsley, who asked him for another story (*Life*, 88), Hardy would have made architecture his career. He had completed *Under the Greenwood Tree* in the summer of 1871; it was published by Tinsley

Brothers in May 1872. Hardy had not revised it. Subsequently he gave it more topographical definition, and changed the place-names to conform to the 'Wessex' plan which he had adopted for the series of novels he projected when he wrote *Far from the Madding Crowd*.

A PAIR OF BLUE EYES

Though most of the story was fictitiously contrived to fit a general design which Hardy had 'thought of and written down long before he knew' Emma Lavinia Gifford, its background owes much to his visits to Cornwall. Autobiographical elements can be easily exaggerated. On actual sources, Hardy was more than usually explicit, and deserves close study (*Life*, 73–4). His note, for example, that there is more of himself in Knight than in Smith should be taken seriously. No single character is a faithful portrait from life. Elfride has 'points in common with those of Mrs Hardy in quite young womanhood', but is drawn too unflatteringly to be the heroine of Hardy's personal Cornish romance.

In October 1871, on his fourth visit to St Juliot, Hardy made further notes on 'the opening chapters and general outline' of his novel (*Life*, 90; letter to William Tinsley, 20 October: Purdy, 331). It was not until the end of the following July, when *Under the Greenwood Tree* had been favourably reviewed, that Hardy was persuaded to return to novel-writing and agreed on terms for the serial publication of *A Pair of Blue Eyes* in *Tinsleys' Magazine*. He found it difficult to keep pace with the time-schedule for instalments (cf. Purdy, 333), and in September retired to the seclusion of Bockhampton, having given up his architectural commitments in London, to concentrate on writing. The final chapters were sent off in March 1873 (*Life*, 89–92).

When Hardy began the novel, 'he had shaped nothing of what the later chapters were to be like'. The first five were composed 'in an incredibly quick time', and appeared on 15 August. Eight days earlier he had left London by boat for Cornwall, and his impressions of the voyage were noted for a later chapter. The class-prejudice theme may have been part of the original design; scenes were drafted from *The Poor Man and the Lady* for adaptation to the Smith *ménage* (x) and the introduction of Knight in London (xiv). The latter scene had been commended by Alexander

Macmillan, and it is significant that Chevron Square is the Swancourts' Kensington address and that of the Allenvilles in 'An Indiscretion'.

There may have been other reasons for the revival of 'the poor man and the lady' motif. Hardy's 'wooing in the "Delectable Duchy" ' of Cornwall did not proceed without a hitch: his introduction to Emma's father at Bodmin in August 1872 led to the painful discovery that he was not considered the social equal of a retired solicitor's daughter. Whether Miss Gifford proposed a runaway marriage, or whether the *contretemps* suggested the resolution of Elfride and Stephen Smith and the critical part it was to play in the heroine's fortunes, is conjectural. Hardy's 'discarded' preface (Weber, *Hardy of Wessex*, 1965, p. 86) is irrelevant here, since it proves to be Collins' first preface to *The Moonstone*. One wonders, too, whether Knight's jealousies were a projection of Hardy's on discovering that Emma had another admirer (cf. *MV*. 'The Young Churchwarden' and the MS. note 'Evening service, August 14, 1870': Purdy, 196).

Of greater general importance is a note in the same preface that the novel attempted to show 'the influence of character on circumstances'. It is a timely reminder that chance is not the sole determining factor in the course of Hardy's stories, and that character is an important element in the evolution of destiny. The indecisiveness of Elfride is her undoing; confronted by Knight's Victorian perfectionism and rigidity, her timid disingenuousness and silence foreshadow the deeper tragedy of Tess's submission to Angel Clare's intractability. This, it would seem, is the allusion in Hardy's cryptic statement that the action of the novel 'exhibits the romantic stage of an idea which was further developed in a later book'.

The emphasis is, however, on plot. Favourable views on *Desperate Remedies* by 'critic-friends' had caused Hardy to set aside *Under the Greenwood Tree* to make notes on the new novel; its 'essence', he wrote, was 'plot, *without* crime'. The plot of *A Pair of Blue Eyes* is unusual and startling rather than ingenious and complicated. One peculiarity of this two-phase courtship story is the parallelism of design which takes Elfride and Knight to the same places as Elfride and Smith, to further the action and enliven it with ironic implications. Dramatic irony is achieved through *synchronized* coincidence when Elfride's admirers draw together or meet. Smith gazes at the Cliff without a Name, totally unaware that the imminent drama of life and death which is to be played upon it spells the extinction of his hopes; the irony reaches its climax in the Luxellian vault. Nothing is more bold and bizarre than the tragical ironies of the triple coincidence in the final dénouement, which by slow relentless degrees turns the comedy of jealous lovers into solemn tragedy.

Retrospectively, the weakness and follies of Elfride and Knight sink before the final tragic realization, just as all that is jejune and laboured in the execution of the novel is subordinated to the imaginative appeal of scenes artistically linked by the recurrent theme of death. The first note which strikes deep is the bell tolling the death of the first Lady Luxellian (it is anticipated at the opening of the story in the 'sad apostrophe' of the Shelley song sung by Elfride). Two succeeding scenes in the Luxellian vault point by gradations of tone towards a tragic ending: the humour of the first flickers reminiscently round the coffined dead (recalling incidentally the story of Lady Susan at Stinsford) in a style which loses little by comparison with the gravediggers' scene in *Hamlet*; the dramatic irony of the second, as Knight loftily declaims on death, in ignorance of 'the severed hearts at his side', is overcast with premonition, notably through adroit quotation from Psalm 102.

The theme is presented in other aspects. As Knight clings for life above the cliff, he is confronted by the eyes of an imbedded fossil, and time closes up like a fan. This dramatic glimpse of the ephemerality of human life in the context of geological ages discloses one aspect of the intellectual background to Hardy's conception of life.

The third presentation is Gothic. Its central shadowy figure is Mrs Jethway, appropriately associated by Elfride with the mother in Coleridge's 'The Three Graves'. Aware of Elfride's elopement, and awaiting the opportunity to avenge her dead son, she is the embodiment of Elfride's guilt spectre that 'waxed taller with every attempt to conceal it', like the spirit in Scott's romantic ballad 'Glenfilas'. She haunts the graveyard almost ghoulishly, and is killed when the tower is brought down by the church-restorers. While she lies buried beneath the heap of stones, Knight and Elfride sit by the altar steps, their shadows silhouetted against the rich colours cast by the moonlight from the eastern window behind them. Presently a cloud passes over, and the iridescence vanishes. The re-emerging moon lights up the white tomb of Felix Jethway; Knight's probing of the past is resumed, and at the end of it the 'glory' and the 'dream' are fading. Soon afterwards Mrs Jethway is avenged.

The poetic symbolism in the Gothic extravaganza is incidental. It is more effective than the coincidental association of the falling tower and Elfride's pathetic trust in Knight, but it suggests incidental inspiration, as do many other items in this novel of mixed elements. The dialogue of the rustics is a relief from discussions on serious themes, especially those which turn on prying jealousy, Victorian proprieties, and feminine caprice; but on the whole it is not as time-encrusted and memorable as in *Under the Greenwood Tree*. The three principal characters are interesting rather than impressive.

A Pair of Blue Eyes was the first of Hardy's novels to bear its author's name on the title-page. It was praised for its artistic construction, and became a favourite with many famous writers, including Tennyson, who may have been gratified to find in it more quotations from *In Memoriam* than from any other single work.

FAR FROM THE MADDING CROWD

Under the Greenwood Tree pleased Leslie Stephen so much that he invited Hardy to contribute a serial to *The Cornhill Magazine*. Hardy was busy with *A Pair of Blue Eyes*, but he replied that he had in mind a pastoral tale entitled *Far from the Madding Crowd*, and that the chief characters would probably be a young woman-farmer, a shepherd, and a sergeant of cavalry. (Boldwood seems to have been an afterthought; he may have been introduced primarily to dispose of Sergeant Troy and promote the happy ending.) The early chapters were submitted in June 1873, before Hardy took a short holiday. He returned to Bockhampton at the beginning of July, and finished the novel within a year. It appeared anonymously in *The Cornhill* throughout 1874. Chap. xvi was inserted at the proof stage, and the novel was published in November of the same year.

Leslie Stephen had recommended for his serial-readers a story with more incident than he found in *Under the Greenwood Tree*. Hardy – who was always looking for a change of subject and structure in his next novel – did not wish to be too constricted by plot, and had in mind a rather leisurely narrative with a swift conclusion, which would give scope for a succession of pastoral scenes, visually presented for readers who were unfamiliar with Dorset rustics, customs, and features. Stephen became anxious that the Fanny Robin story should be handled 'gingerly', and thought the sheep-shearing scene too long for periodical purposes. His views on the melodramatic conclusion are not known; it was written 'at a gallop', and lacks the richness of texture which is typical of earlier scenes.

Hardy rarely, if ever, allowed himself the amplitude which he took for rural scenes and occupations in *Far from the Madding Crowd*. They are not presented so much for their own sake as they are, for example, in George Eliot's *Adam Bede*. The interest in narrative and character never flags. The situation between Oak, Bathsheba, and Boldwood is more vividly expressed through Gabriel's accidental snipping of a sheep than would be possible through the spoken word; a song at the shearing-supper enlists conjecture about the next turn of events; and the conversation of rustics never roams far from the main lines of interest.

Hardy was not content with mere scenic description. He uses imagery on a greater scale than ever before to reflect feeling and situation. Such impressionist overtones may be seen in miniature when Oak surveys the pit where he has lost his sheep and independence, or at greater length during the storm, which not only gives excitement to the action of the narrative but conveys a growing sense of crisis in Bathsheba, and, by the revelations of lightning flashes, a ghastly realization of her error in marrying Troy. Pictorial presentations in which the actual takes on the significance of metaphor or symbolism are numerous. They include the scene outside the barracks, Boldwood's *bouleversement* as he contemplates the valentine in the weird light of moon and snow, Bathsheba's first encounter with Troy, the spell-binding of Bathsheba by dazzling sword-play, Yalbury Great Wood as Poorgrass rides to Weatherbury with the coffin containing Fanny Robin and her child, the woodland swamp by which Bathsheba finds herself after Troy's perfidy has been revealed, and the scene outside Weatherbury church where the gargoyle pours its 'vengeance' on Fanny's grave and Troy is stripped of all his self-centred illusions. These scenes show a striking range in tone and colour, but all contain features which are imaginatively selected to impart extra-sensory effects: states of feeling, the relation of situation to past or future, or the author's attitude to events and character. The 'poetry' which Stephen admired in the prose is more intensive here than in direct description, though, as the auditory and visual imagery of the scene on Norcombe Hill reminds us at the beginning, this reaches unusual levels of perception.

The novel marks a distinct advance in characterization. In later novels, Hardy created greater single characters, but in none did he create as many leading characters who are imaginatively realized as in *Far from the Madding Crowd*. In Bathsheba, Gabriel Oak, Boldwood, and Troy, we have a remarkable diversity. Of these the solitary Boldwood is the least convincing, but his powerful feelings when unleashed have a dramatic appeal. When the narrative 'gallops', the impressiveness of the characters is diminished, but for the greater part of the story their hold on the reader is such that the idiosyncrasies of the rustics tend to be overlooked.

The contrast between the sensational events of the story and the uneventful lives of the rustics – not all of whom meet at Warren's Malthouse, or form part of the 'chorus' – provides the general irony of the novel and its title. Modern changes (the valentine episode indicates that the period was 1869–73) have not affected their lives; the shearers 're-clined against each other as at suppers in the early ages of the world'. For them, the news that Dicky Hill's wooden cider-house has been pulled down, and Tompkin's old cider-apple tree has been rooted up, is indicative of 'stirring times'.

In this novel Hardy used 'Wessex' for the first time to signify the general topographical background. Thenceforward he adhered to a scheme of pseudonyms for places which were only 'partly real'. Often they are composite. Bathsheba's farm and Boldwood's, for example, are much closer to the church and malthouse than their originals.

THE HAND OF ETHELBERTA

Far from the Madding Crowd was concluded 'at a gallop' in time for Hardy's marriage and a short tour in France. Novel-writing as a career had now become a serious matter; Hardy 'had to consider popularity'. He did not know where his forte lay; it was too early to gauge the success of *Far from the Madding Crowd*, and he always felt that it might be necessary to write about the society in which most readers were in-terested. Even when he was a successful novelist, he kept records of observations for such a contingency (*Life*, 291). At this stage, he was impelled to test public response, and show that he was not restricted to the rural groove, and that 'he did not intend to imitate anybody'. Perhaps

28

the recollection that the early instalments of his last novel had been thought the work of George Eliot was mainly responsible for Hardy's immediate *volte-face*. Certainly *The Hand of Ethelberta* came as a surprise and disappointment to the publishers of *The Cornhill*, in which it appeared from July 1875 to May 1876.

The quotation from Lucretius on the title page may have had a special meaning for Hardy, since Ethelberta's London enterprise for her family was suggested by a 'rather adventurous scheme' on the part of his mother. (The details were intended for the *Life*, but were omitted by Florence Hardy.) Thomas Hardy's maternal grandmother was left a widow with seven children; his mother, before she was married, formed the idea of being a club-house cook, and applied to the Earl of Ilchester to assist her. He sent her to his brother's, where she became a skilful cook, accompanying the family to London.

The plot was conceived according to a set of formulae very much the reverse of several that Hardy had adopted for fiction. The characters were to be members of society and family servants; the principal scenes were to be in London; and the comic presentation was to depend to some extent on views of 'the drawing-room' from 'the servants' hall'. In lieu of 'The Poor Man and the Lady', the principal theme concerned 'The Poor Lady and the Lord'. The tragic theme of the heroine's self-sacrifice in marriage for the sake of her family gave way to the calculating careerism of a lady who deliberately rejected her true love to marry an old aristocratic profligate for the security of her parents and their numerous progeny. As an ironical climax to a series of comic and satirical situations, members of the poor family were desperately anxious to save the heroine from such a disgraceful union: 'The times have taken a strange turn when the angry parent of the comedy, who goes post-haste to prevent the undutiful daughter's rash marriage, is a gentleman from below stairs, and the unworthy lover a peer of the realm!'

For such artificial comedy, which may have been more appropriate for the stage, neither the time nor Hardy was ripe. In their different ways, Oscar Wilde and Shaw could have handled it. Hardy's knowledge of the upper class was too restricted and superficial, and his novel too contrived and sketchy, to be equal to the design. The comedy presents some amusing situations, but the dialogue has little life or sparkle, and the *bons mots* are somewhat leaden; the more farcical situations tend to be of the 'hee-hee-hee, ho-ho-ho' variety. Some of the satire may have been transferred from *The Poor Man and the Lady* (e.g. occasional passages in ix, xi). The nightmarish horror of the Farnfield visit is a 'heart-of-darkness' or Inferno vision of man's inhumanity to animals, which makes one realise that Hardy possessed satirical gifts in no slight measure when they were directed to issues which affected him deeply.

The direction of *The Hand of Ethelberta* depends on a reversal of Hardy's attitudes to society and careerism. 'He constitutionally shrank from the business of social advancement, caring for life as an emotion rather than for life as a science of climbing . . .' (*Life*, 53). Ethelberta is sometimes depressed, but she plays her hand coolly, and succeeds at a price Hardy was not prepared to pay. Her virtual separation from her family, and the collusion with which they conceal her origin, provide in retrospect an amusing and more subtle commentary on a class-ridden age than any direct satire.

The background of the story is makeshift rather than inevitable; and continual changes of scene, in London, to Rouen, and in parts of Wessex, were necessary to maintain or heighten interest. Hardy relied on observation rather than on creative imagination: he and his wife had recently visited Rouen; they lived in London in the early part of 1875 'on account of Ethelberta'; and they moved to Swanage the following July. The London scenes, except for minor pictorial touches, are sketchy; the narrative moves too slowly to elicit interest in them, and only when the plot quickens, at Cripplegate Church, is the scene dramatically fused with situation. Background scenes continue, enlivened with farce, across the Channel and at Rouen, at Corvsgate Castle and Melchester, and in the environs of Knollsea, as the more exciting complications of the finale are reached. In this, some of the more crucial scenes are reminiscent of minor Restoration drama.

Characters are presented on various planes. Many are mere types, from minors such as Yore and Breeve to principals such as Ladywell and Neigh; members of the Chickerel family are more human – Joey almost Dickensian; there are the mildly romantic Julian and Picotee; and, above all, the calculating Ethelberta, who reads Mill on 'utilitarianism', and commands respect and occasional impulses of sympathy, but hardly admiration. The most engaging figure is Lord Mountclere, and he belongs to the world of farce.

Whatever Hardy's justifications, in his *Life* (108) and prefaces to the novel, for this 'somewhat frivolous' comedy of society, his private and perhaps undefined dissatisfaction with *The Hand of Ethelberta* seems to be implicit in his next novel, *The Return of the Native*, and the startling change from a series of background scenes to one which provides a dominant impression so integral and unifying that the fortunes of the characters are inseparable from it. The natural scene which survives longest from *The Hand of Ethelberta* is brief and prelusive: it links the heroine with the wild duck that evades the hawk at prey, and symbolizes Ethelberta's ability ultimately to fend for herself. The ambivalence of the title is not disclosed until the end of the story.

THE RETURN OF THE NATIVE

Hardy was probably exhausted at the end of a long period of writing to keep pace with the demands of serialization. In the spring of 1876 he and his wife toured Holland and the Rhine valley. Subsequently he spent two of the happiest years of his life at Sturminster Newton. It was largely a recreative period. He found time for the planning of some tragic poems, for outings and reading. *The Return of the Native* was begun early in 1877 (*TLS*, 21 August 1970); it shows a wider range of scholarship than any of his previous works. More obviously, it bears ample testimony to a resurgence of imaginative power. Hardy had chosen a subject more congenial to his 'idiosyncratic mode of regard' than *The Hand of Ethelberta*, and a setting which was steeped in early memories.

The opening words of IV v, in conjunction with a hint in the 1895 preface, indicate that the period of the story was 1842–3 or 1847–8. The scene was the heath on the edge of which Hardy had lived. His grandmother's recollections of heath-croppers (cf. 'Domicilium', *Life*, 4) and of the Napoleonic invasion scare (the subject of his next novel), tales of the reddleman-bogy, his grandfather's almost legendary feats on the fiddle, his own boyhood fears when crossing the heath at dusk, stories of witchcraft and superstitious practices (still lingering in Wessex when the novel was written), memories of the mummers' play, knowledge of quaint local rustics, all contributed in some measure to the enrichment of the story. Clym's sacrifice of a city career, and his mother's disappointment, owed something, no doubt, to Hardy's abandonment of architecture.

Flaubert's *Madame Bovary* may have had its influence on the creation of Eustacia Vye; if not directly, then through the medium of Miss Braddon's *The Doctor's Wife* (C. Heywood, *Nineteenth-Century Fiction*, June 1963). Miss Braddon was the editor of the monthly magazine *Belgravia*, in which *The Return of the Native* appeared during 1878. Leslie Stephen, strictly bound as editor of *The Cornhill* to enforce the commandment 'Thou shalt not shock a young lady' (or was it the young lady's mamma?), had objected to the use of the word 'amorous' and 'the very close embrace in the London churchyard' in *The Hand of Ethelberta*, and feared that the relations between Eustacia, Wildeve, and Thomasin in the original opening of the novel might develop into something 'dangerous'. He refused to publish *The Return of the Native* until he had seen the whole work. Hardy took note of the objections, and turned to Miss Braddon.

Originally, he had intended that Thomasin was to be deceived by Wildeve through a false marriage ceremony, as Tess was to be in the serial version of her story. The opening of the novel in its present form suggests that Thomasin was cast for a more important tragic role than she eventually played. Eustacia's reputation as a witch seems to have been more strongly stressed than it is in the present novel.

Hardy's recasting of the story (after several chapters had been written), with Eustacia as the romantic tragic heroine, resulted in a plot of remarkable unity. This derives partly from the limitation of the action to one place (in marked contrast to that of *The Hand of Ethelberta*) and to the cyclical time-scheme of a year; partly from a nexus of circumstance which soon involves all the leading characters in its tragic sequence (in no other Hardy novel are so many characters simultaneously involved in tensions and conflict); largely from the fact that Egdon Heath broods over all, plays a part in the turn of events, and universalizes Hardy's tragic conception of life; more subtly, from a pattern of imagery that links character and action. The fires, for example, that light up the heath are emblematic of the Promethean rebelliousness of Eustacia against her fate; for her, Egdon Heath is Hades. The extent to which this interrelationship of images contributes to the artistic unity of the novel is admirably presented in John Paterson's *The Making of 'The Return of the Native'*.

The plot is neither over-swift nor over-complicated. It turns, however, on strands of possibility so tenuous that they nearly snap. Mrs Yeobright is not a voluble woman, but her failure to see that Eustacia would be offended when asked if she had received money from Wildeve seems almost implausible. The murmuring of 'Mother' by Clym in his sleep is a coincidence which few novelists would risk. Such a possibility is more questionable in fiction than in life, particularly when it leads to a tragic climax.

The opening chapters are richly diversified. The first provides a microcosmic setting in time, mood and philosophical outlook, in the context of which the story takes on its larger thematic significance. The second builds up interest with slow impressiveness until it reaches its climax with the mysterious figure of the woman on Rainbarrow, who dominates the darkening scene premonitorily. The third provides contrast in fire and revelry. It is difficult to determine whether the rustic chorus excels that at Warren's Malthouse in *Far from the Madding Crowd*, but it is more functional, and awakens interest in developing events, past, present, and to come. Even more artistic is the acoustic introduction to Eustacia, as her 'lengthened sighing' merges with the sounds of the wind on the heath.

The chapter 'Queen of Night' is an interpolation which seems less defensible than the opening chapter. The influence of Pater's famous passage on La Gioconda may be suspected. But Hardy's portrait is overdone, a composite piece of work which endows Eustacia, despite her Greek origins, with attributes out of all proportion to the young woman of the novel. Had these qualities been more related to her actions – and they are often such that this seems impossible – or to Clym's impressions of her, she might have been more the goddess Hardy imagined her. In his presentation of Tess, he avoided such a dissociation, and the heroine gains immeasurably.

Weather and the heath's seasonal changes accord with mood and situation in passages of poetic overtones, from the large scale to the small, from the most vividly colourful to the funereal. Hardy thought it worth while to transcribe two such passages almost word for word from *Desperate Remedies* (cf. the end of III v with *DR*. xii 6). Such harmony of the outer scene with the thought and feelings of the beholder are paralleled in 'the chaos of the world without' and the chaos of Eustacia's mind when she stood for the last time on Rainbarrow. A new type of symbolism enters the novel in dramatic scenes when Eustacia and Clym talk by the pool at Mistover Knap, after the recovery of the bucket from the well, and again when they meet at Rainbarrow during the moon's eclipse.

Clym's partial blindness may be related to his mistakes *vis-à-vis* Eustacia and his mother, and to the premature idealism which convinces him that he can bring light to a people still walking in darkness.

The ending is not altogether satisfactory. Clym's preaching earns respect rather than admiration. The development of the happy ending is too facile and lengthy to harmonize with the novel as a whole. It was not part of the original plot, but a sop to the magazine public. The reddleman was intended to disappear mysteriously from the Heath, and Thomasin to remain a widow. Some will assert that Hardy did not make it clear whether Eustacia met her death intentionally or not. If Clym's words, 'It is I who ought to have drowned myself', are unambiguous, it should be remembered that he did not spare himself in self-condemnation for the deaths of his mother and his wife. Eustacia had been tempted to think of suicide, but she had recovered. When she fell into Shadwater pool, she was intent on escape to Paris, the city of her dreams. Egdon Heath had been her 'cross', and, like Mrs Yeobright, she was its victim.

The Return of the Native is a remarkable novel by any standards. As a tragedy it is memorable, not so much by its drama – the climax of which is over-wrought, theatrical, and imitative of Webster – as by the implications or overtones of its descriptive scenes. In Eustacia, Mrs Yeobright, and Clym we have three markedly different characters of tragic stature. The new scientific perspectives of nature or the universe as symbolized in the Heath, particularly with reference to time ('A Face on which Time makes Little Impression'), reduce their tensions and catastrophes to relative insignificance. It is the character of the Heath which gives imaginative expression to the larger dimensions of Hardy's tragic vision.

THE TRUMPET-MAJOR

At Sturminster Newton, before *The Return of the Native* was begun, and in London, after its completion, Hardy extended his reading and researches on the Napoleonic wars, a boyhood interest which was to grow until *The Dynasts* was written. *The Trumpet-Major* may be regarded as a by-product of his research. In February 1879 Hardy visited Dorset to add local investigations to the notes he had compiled at the British Museum, and to sketch and gather topographical impressions for his story. He was there again in August, staying at Weymouth to make further investigations for 'the popular Royal watering-place' scenes in the latter part of the novel. By the middle of September half of it was ready for serial publication in *Good Words*, where it appeared throughout 1880.

Local history was to provide the background to the fictional plot. The period was 1804–5, from the time when preparations were made against the landing of the French near Weymouth until the threat of invasion vanished with the naval victory of Trafalgar. Leslie Stephen regretted that Hardy did not give him the opportunity to publish the novel. He liked stories with 'old George the Third round the corner', though he thought the heroine married the wrong man. Hardy commented that they usually did. 'Not in magazines,' answered the editor of *The Cornhill*.

The plot is well-proportioned and neatly contrived, though it presents a series of events rather than a great action. It gives the impression that Hardy was too busy with research and other plans and activities to give it much serious forethought. Compared with *The Return of the Native*, it is a rather plain narrative, combining a not very exciting love-story with local historical events and conventional comedy. Squire Derriman belongs to the same archaic world of stage convention as Lord Mountclere, and Festus is the *miles gloriosus* of ancient tradition in a new setting. Though unpleasant, he can never be taken seriously. Names such as those of German soldiers in the York Hussars, the dentist Rootle, and Timothy Titus Philemon, Bishop of Bristol, are reminiscent of *The Hand of Ethelberta*. Anne Garland's vacillations are tedious in the long run, and the modesty and self-denying ordinances of the trumpet-major make him a rather dull figure. His brother is more lively though less admirable. Miss Matilda Johnson imparts life to the story for a short while. Anthony Cripplestraw is the most vital character in the comic scenes; and Captain Hardy, though he appears briefly, seems to engage more of Hardy and become more alive than any other character. Though a little sentimental, the scene on Portland Bill, where Anne watches the departure of the *Victory*, and a later one, where she meets the King, are the most moving in the book. The heroic ending produces a climax, and also a suggestion of the factitious.

The weather-vane at Overcombe Mill (ii) may be regarded as an apt emblem of the story. The sergeant's song (v) had been written in 1878. One chapter (xxiii) is remarkable for transcriptions. The opening paragraph suggests recourse to the writer's notebook, for it is very close to the first paragraph of *Desperate Remedies*, xii 1; the 'Address to all Ranks and Descriptions of Englishmen' was copied at the Dorset Museum, and the drilling scene, from Gifford's *History of the Wars of the French Revolution*. It had an interesting sequel. Hardy was charged over and over again with plagiarism, and ultimately discovered that the passage he had copied from Gifford was a piece of American satire which John Lambert had quoted in his *Travels through the United States*, as Gifford had acknowledged. Hardy's oversight created a storm in a tea-cup, and his allusion to it in the preface shows a true sense of proportion (cf. Weber, *Hardy of Wessex*, 119–22). The false alarm (xxvi) had long been a subject of interest in the Hardy family; his grandfather's dilemma when it was raised is the subject of 'The Alarm' (*WP*).

The work is characterized by competence rather than genius, and, had it appeared anonymously and without Wessex place-names, few would have suspected that it was written by the author of *The Return of the Native*.

A LAODICEAN

The greater part of this novel was composed in untoward circumstances. When Hardy fell seriously ill in October 1880, only thirteen chapters had been written. The remainder was dictated, the first draft being completed on 1 May 1881. Serial publication in *Harper's Magazine* lasted from December 1880 to December 1881. Hardy insisted that the venture be completed in fairness to his publishers 'and also in the interests of his wife, for whom as yet he had made a poor provision in the event of his own decease' (*Life*, 145–6). In these circumstances, Hardy's achievement was considerable.

The plot is articulated with an ingenuity which recalls that of *Desperate Remedies*. It is more exciting than that of *The Trumpet-Major*, yet, for a long phase, it is less controlled. There can be little doubt that Hardy's illness was responsible for a weakening of critical judgment. The story 'turned out to be one-third longer than the guaranteed length', and the publishers, to Hardy's surprise and pleasure, paid 'the proportionate third above the price agreed on' (Edmund Blunden, *Thomas Hardy*, 48). If Hardy had had the time and health which he needed for critical revision, a general tautening of the narrative would have resulted, and the many chapters dealing with the Rhine valley tour, which further the plot hardly at all, would have been much reduced. It is here that the novel loses all proportion. Parts IV, V, and VI may originally have been conceived as two phases in the conclusion of the story, the design of which follows a conventional pattern: plot, counterplot, complications, reversal of fortune, and dénouement. There is no weakening in the first three books; thereafter, until the conclusion, it is clear that Hardy was so enervated that he turned to memory and travel notes to maintain production. Some indication of his indebtedness to his notebook may be obtained from comparing the succinct notes on his European tours in the *Life* (110, 120, 138, 139) with the more detailed impressions in the novel (v vii–x; VI i–iii), especially of the Rhine valley, Scheveningen, and Amiens Cathedral. The argument on paedobaptism and the garden party at Stancy Castle were also recollections (*Life*, 29–30, 128), but these must be regarded as items in the original narrative rather than expletory material.

Hardy's continual changes of subject and treatment from novel to novel are greater than is generally assumed. In *A Laodicean* we are in another era from that of *The Trumpet-Major*. It is 'A Story of To-day', an age of railway engineering, telegraphy, and the romance of scientific achievement, of tourism, photography, and revolvers, an era of conflict between Arnold's Dissidence of Dissent and the new Hellenism. The attachment of the new industrial magnates of England to feudal architecture and aristocratic trappings provides the background for a story of romance and sensational intrigue, devised according to the Gothic pattern, in settings which are alternately medieval and modern. At the centre of this curious *mélange* of new and old is Paula Power, daughter of the wealthy railway contractor who bought Stancy Castle. She is modern and Grecian in her gymnastic cult, but the conflict of tradition and the new outlook makes her vacillate. Dissenting loyalties compel, only to be abjured at the immersion ceremony. She gives orders for an extension of the castle in Grecian style only to cancel them. She cannot make up her mind to marry a modern architect when she is courted by a de Stancy. At the end she is determined to show a modern spirit, but wishes that her castle had not been burnt down.

It is typical of the romantic story that it quickens near a modern triumph of engineering, a railway tunnel, and concludes happily at a modern resort. The counterplot is Gothic in modern dress, and reaches its climax in the confrontation of the ex-revolutionary Abner Power and the cosmopolite Monte Carlo gambler Will Dare over the vestry table in the medieval church of Markton. Substitute swords for revolvers, and we have a typical scene in a popular romantic historical novel of the Harrison Ainsworth school.

The name of the hero was suggested by the county in which the prototype of Stancy Castle is to be found. There is no evidence that Hardy ever visited Dunster. The 1912 postscript to his preface indicates that his castle is largely imaginary; the extracts from its 'history' (I xiii) may have been written by Hardy. When he said that *A Laodicean* 'contained more of the facts of his own life than anything else he had ever written' (Blunden, 48–9), he was thinking mainly of his architectural experience and European tours (see p. 475, however).

The erotic titillation with which Hardy ventured to generate the counter-plot seems to have created little Victorian comment, probably because it was the work of the villain, who was initially more the Devil himself than a mere daredevil. His Satanic or Mephistophelian associations were never developed. The unknown identity and the un-English appearance of Dare and Abner Power were calculated to arouse suspicions and prepare the way for counterplot and sub-counterplot.

For the short passage (I v) which Hardy copied and then revised, after being charged with plagiarism, see Weber, *Hardy of Wessex*, 126–8.

A Laodicean is bold in its originality and ingenuity. Had it been more critically controlled, and the comic irony of its plot been presented in sharper relief, Hardy's intentions would have won greater recognition. Perhaps its greatest failing is that it does not contain a single character of great imaginative appeal. The 'modern fever and fret' which the single wire connecting Stancy Castle with the cosmopolitan world is intended to convey, and which is reflected in the unrest and tourism of the principal characters, might have been expressed more dramatically had not Paula been cast for a Laodicean role.

TWO ON A TOWER

The *Return of the Native* presented human tragedy against a localized background which expressed the timelessness and indifference of the universe. In the tragedy, or tragi-comedy, of *Two on a Tower*, the background emphasis is on space, the 'ghast heights' or the 'ghastly gulfs' of sky against which Hardy meditated the significance of the mortal lot. It was the subject of 'In vision I roamed' (written in 1866) and 'At a Lunar Eclipse' (written about the same time). The second poem is near in conception to the more comprehensive scheme of *The Dynasts*; the first, to *Two on a Tower*. It is not identical, for the irony of the novel lies in the fact that the hero has to learn that human tragedy is not an ephemeral triviality in relation to 'astronomical stupendousness'. The story 'was the outcome of a wish to set the emotional history of two infinitesimal lives against the stupendous background of the stellar universe, and to impart to readers the sentiment that of these contrasting magnitudes the smaller might be the greater to them as men'.

Hardy did not do justice to his theme; he told Edmund Gosse that he aimed to make science 'not the mere padding of a romance' but its 'actual vehicle'. The conception, however, is intermittent and does not permeate the whole in the way that Egdon Heath with all its tragic and philosophical implication remains central to *The Return of the Native*. Hardy wished he had found time to rewrite the novel. Its composition was 'lamentably hurried' (Purdy, 44), and bears witness in its late stages to the exigencies of serial publication. The first nine chapters were sent in March, and the remaining in September 1882, to Boston, where it appeared in *The Atlantic Monthly* from May to December 1882.

The scene was largely imaginary and composite; it was suggested by 'two real spots' near Wimborne Minster, where Hardy lived when the novel was written. The sight of the new comet from the conservatory of their new home (*Life*, 149) may have suggested the fictional possibilities of the theme which occurred to Hardy in 1866. Possibly a brief passage in George Eliot's *The Mill on the Floss* was the germ of the story: 'I suppose it's all astronomers: because, you know, they live up in high towers, and if the women came there, they might talk and hinder them from looking at the stars.' As J. I. M. Stewart has pointed out, Hardy's reading of *Love's Labour's Lost* for its introduction as a dramatic spectacle in *A Laodicean* may have suggested the rival attractions of study and love. The 'heavenly rhetoric' of the eyes is implicit in Swithin's admission that in thinking of the heaven above he had not perceived the better heaven beneath, and his declaration that Lady Viviette's eyes are to be his stars for the future. The title-page quotation from Crashaw's 'Love's Horoscope' was recommended by Edmund Gosse.

In the early chapters, the style is compact and disciplined, and the story charged with great emotive power. Unfortunately it declines. The rustic humour of the opening scenes returns more rarely and perfunctorily; poetic overtones are limited and facile; and the love-story and its tragic implications degenerate into plot-manipulation and the farcical comedy which results in the fooling of the Bishop of Melchester. If this was part of a larger plan to present the follies of sublunary lovers as a metaphysical comedy, it failed. The final sentence, 'The Bishop was avenged', seems insignificant in the poignancy of the last meeting of Viviette and Swithin, where the revenges brought by Time are felicitously fused with the stellar theme: 'the masses of hair that were once darkness visible had become touched here and there by a faint grey haze, like the Via Lactea in a midnight sky.'

THE MAYOR OF CASTERBRIDGE

It is hardly surprising that when Hardy went to live in Dorchester he should think of the place as a setting for his next novel. The town was a small agricultural centre, richly invested with historical associations and personal memories. With a few shifts in chronology and the location of buildings, the background for a dramatization of fictional events presented little difficulty. *The Mayor of Casterbridge* is unique among Hardy's novels in its town setting, the long-drawn conflict between two men, the subordination of the love element, and its presentation of a hero of dynamic and explosive personality. In many ways it forms an obvious contrast to *The Return of the Native*, not least in its frequent iteration of sensational event, surprise, dramatic suspense, irony of circumstance, and reversal of fortune.

These characteristics were determined by weekly serialization. *The Mayor of Casterbridge* was written 'off and on' from the early part of 1884 to April 1885, and appeared from 2 January to 15 May 1886, on both sides of the Atlantic, in *The Graphic* and *Harper's Weekly*. Hardy afterwards thought that, though the plot was organic or possible, it strained probability at times (*Life*, 176, 179). The fight in the loft and the bull scene indicate the aim and the risk. Nevertheless, the economy demanded by weekly serialization helped to produce a compact and highly charged novel, though descriptive effects were reduced to meagre proportions at times. Hardy took comfort in the thought that probability of character was more important than probability of incident. Here he did not fail; Henchard holds our interest more powerfully than any other of his heroes.

In revising for volume publication, Hardy made various changes. He introduced more Wessex and actual place-names and more literary parallels and allusions; and he removed red herrings which he had used to excite the sensational expectations of serial-readers. The return of Henchard with his wedding-present was omitted from the first edition, but restored 'at the instance of some good judges across the Atlantic' (see p. 430).

The influences which coalesced in the creation of Henchard were probably more literary than actual. Hardy may have been influenced by the account of the character and misfortunes of Anthony Trollope's father in the novelist's *Autobiography*, which appeared in 1883 (Weber, *Hardy of Wessex*, 148–9). The romantic suggestion that Henchard is the heroic representative of a dying community, with an ancestry in Scott's Waverley novels, should be studied, however, with critical circumspection (see Douglas Brown, *Thomas Hardy: The Mayor of Casterbridge*, Edward Arnold, 1962, 43–6). In rash impulsiveness, tragic blunders, suffering, and self-redemption, he recalls *King Lear* at frequent points; his initial folly and his volcanic temperament are in some ways more closely paralleled in *The Winter's Tale*. The greatest influence was that of Saul and his jealous clash with the young rival David whom he loved. On a minor level, the clash of the irascible, unforgiving, bankrupt Tulliver and Lawyer Wakem in *The Mill on the Floss* should not be ignored. Hardy noted George Eliot's comments in the same novel on one of the 'questionable' aphorisms of Novalis that 'character is destiny'. He quotes it with approval (xvii). Henchard's undoing is mainly the result of his past follies and blindness. He is the victim of nemesis rather than of chance. A high-tragedy queen like Eustacia, 'instead of blaming herself', may arraign 'some indistinct, colossal Prince of the World, who had framed her situation and ruled her lot'; but that, Hardy insists, is merely avoiding the issue. A superstitious man like Henchard, when he has blundered, may wonder if someone has been 'roasting a waxen image' of him, or 'stirring an unholy brew to confound' him (the latter image links his initial folly in selling his wife with the nemesis that is to overtake him), but Hardy's comment is precise: 'the momentum of his character knew no patience' (xxvii). The question is one of emphasis, for character in Hardy's philosophy is one of the elements of chance that combine with circumstance to determine fate. In *The Mayor of Casterbridge* the main emphasis is clear; it is 'A Story of a Man of Character'. On the other hand, if ever a character was the victim of circumstance for a long period, it is Elizabeth-Jane. Again, though nemesis plays a hand in the death of Lucetta, and pride contributes to her fall, she is really caught in a network of circumstance that seems unpredictable and inescapable.

Parallels between Henchard and Saul are frequent, and confirmed by the pointed resemblance between Farfrae and David which Hardy introduced in the 1912 revision of the novel (vi). Overtones of *King Lear* are also of interest, especially when the 'fool' Whittle is the only one to befriend Henchard on the heath. A Cain–Abel link at the end is also suggestive. Some parallels may be seen with Sophocles' play *King Oedipus* (the plague at Thebes, Oedipus's jealousy of Creon, and the concluding reflections on life).

The trading in life with which the novel opens (one of the events based on actual occurrence) is related in Hardy's criticism of life to the dismal lot of the labourer, whether glimpsed in Henchard's, and Farfrae's, treatment of employees, or in the market-place. The skimmington-ride was certainly suggested by local contemporary events; accounts of at least three skimmington-rides occurred in Dorset newspapers in 1884. An observation which Hardy made on 4 December 1884 (*Life*, 169), when he was living almost next to the original of High-Place Hall, appears in modified form in the novel (xxvii).

The style varies from the laboured and Latinized to the most moving simplicity. Hardy's study of the Bible is reflected in the style even more than in the allusions and parallels (cf. *Life*, 170–1). The most moving passages are in the unlettered vernacular of Mother Cuxsom and Abel Whittle, the tragic ending as narrated by the latter being perhaps the most successful Hardy achieved. Henchard's will has the grandeur of Hebrew poetry. Occasionally expressions seem a little clumsy or inadequate, but the need to pack events into the story precludes the larger amplitudes of description which are to be found in Hardy's next two novels and are characteristic of *Far from the Madding Crowd* and *The Return of the Native*.

It is impossible to date the story with absolute precision, so many

liberties has Hardy taken not only with the location of buildings in
Dorchester but also with dates of actual events. When the Royal visitor
passed through Casterbridge the railway had not reached the town. The
line to Dorchester was opened in 1847, and Prince Albert passed through
in 1849. The archway leading to North Square was demolished in 1848.
The museum was not moved into 'a back street' until 1851. The year of
the Candlemas Fair (xxii) cannot be calculated, for fairs by statute were
not held on holy days. The uncertain harvests are no more fixed to the
era of the Corn Laws than Prince Albert's visit in 1849. They were
merely one of the three actual events which Hardy used for the purpose
of his story. The trade in grain from North America did not revolutionize
and stabilize prices until much nearer the time *The Mayor of Casterbridge*
was written. Outside this area of imprecision and inconsistency for artistic
ends, two things can be safely assumed: Hardy wrote about the Dorchester
he knew when he was a boy; and he did not err significantly when he
spoke in 1910 of the liberties he took with Dorchester sixty years
previously (*Life*, 351). The main story, therefore, begins about 1850; and
the whole action lasts twenty-five years, from 1831 to 1856.

THE WOODLANDERS

Written mainly in 1886, and finished in February 1887, *The Woodlanders*
appeared in *Macmillan's Magazine* and, in America, in *Harper's Bazaar*
from May 1886 to April 1887. Several slight bowdlerizations were made
in the English serial version, the most important being concerned with
Suke Damson and Fitzpiers; Hardy was requested to 'let the human
frailty be construed mild'.

The note (*Life*, 176) in which Hardy tells us that he was working on
the final details of the story before he began writing in November 1885
makes it clear that, after considering modifications, he had decided to
keep to the main outline of the 'woodland story' he had put aside in 1874
to write *The Hand of Ethelberta*.

To some extent, as the title-page quotation indicates, the novel is a
tragic counterpart to *Under the Greenwood Tree*. It revives, rather faintly,
the theme of *The Poor Man and the Lady*, and its pastoral tragic ending
is not dissimilar from the concluding scenes of 'An Indiscretion in the

Life of an Heiress'. The mysterious stranger from South Carolina suggests the less mature plot-inventor; his role is minimal, but though his appearance on Midsummer Eve adds an odd dimension to our impressions of rural superstitions, it is hardly necessary. The new divorce law of 1878 and Hardy's reference in 1926 to the period of the novel ('fifty years ago': *Life*, 432) leave no doubt that the story extends from 1876 to 1879.

The contrast between the setting of *The Woodlanders* and that of *The Mayor of Casterbridge* could not be greater. Sherton Abbas is the town to which the inhabitants of Little Hintock resort, but the main scene is 'one of those sequestered spots . . . where, from time to time, dramas of a grandeur and unity truly Sophoclean are enacted in the real, by virtue of the concentrated passions and closely-knit interdependence of the lives therein'. There is irony in the title as in that of *Far from the Madding Crowd*; the Unfulfilled Intention which is found on closer inspection in the woods is to be seen in the lives of all the principal characters in the story.

Released from the fetters of weekly serialization with its insistent demand for events, Hardy could write more freely; this sense of release may be felt in the colourful description of landscapes, and the rich evocation of autumn in association with Giles Winterborne and cider-making. In comparison, *The Mayor of Casterbridge* is grey and sombre. Nature is beautiful and bountiful, never more so, ironically, than when it is the background to Fitzpiers's infidelity and baseness; elsewhere the more unpleasant aspects of the Unfulfilled Intention (which in *Jude the Obscure* is presented as marring the whole Creation) are artistically linked with human suffering and turpitude in a manner which may be traced back through *The Return of the Native* and *Far from the Madding Crowd* to *Desperate Remedies*.

Yet one aspect of the main theme resides in the antithesis between nature and civilization. On the one hand we have Marty South and Giles Winterborne; on the other, Mrs Charmond and Fitzpiers. In between, subject to the 'pressure of events' and her own weaknesses, is Grace Melbury. At times 'the veneer of artificiality which she had acquired at the fashionable schools' is thrown off, but it is Marty South alone who approximates to Winterborne's 'level of intelligent intercourse with Nature', and who remains loyal to him after his death. Hintock produced Suke Damson as well as Marty South, but there can be no doubt that Hardy entertained Rousseauistic sympathies, as his next novel was to show more openly. In *Jude the Obscure* his attacks on the social order were to be more clamant and persistent.

The quarrel with society, which is adumbrated in the divorce issue, marks a new phase in Hardy's fiction. It does not, however, eliminate the force of chance. Giles is largely the victim of circumstance, and the death of John South affects the future of Grace, Winterborne, Fitzpiers, and Mrs Charmond as well. Behind all is the 'intangible Cause' which is 'too elusive to be discerned and cornered' by humanity at all times. Hardy takes pains to show that Giles might have avoided his eviction, but the ramifications of this event could not have been predicted or forestalled. One of them is the death of Mrs Charmond.

Reprehensible as he is, Fitzpiers shares some of Hardy's intellectual tendencies: he believes that marriage is a civil contract, and he is a scientific determinist. His Shelleyan idealism provides the unpleasant obverse of the theme which Hardy presented light-heartedly in *The Well-Beloved*.

The Woodlanders contains some of Hardy's best writing; its main weakness is structural. It presents a theme rather than a closely integrated dramatic action such as we find in *The Return of the Native*. The tragedy is one of unfulfilment: Marty South never speaks her love for Giles until he is dead; Giles loves Grace, but she marries Fitzpiers and does not discover her mistake until it is too late; and Fitzpiers deserts Grace for Mrs Charmond. The central conflict is rarely dramatized. Giles and Marty South endure. There is no dominant character as in *The Mayor of Casterbridge* or *Tess of the d'Urbervilles*, and the conflict is most evident in Grace and her father when both indulge in pathetic hopes that the new divorce law will enable the latter to make amends for his unfulfilled intentions. Integrity, devotion, and endurance (or 'charity', the crescendo motif of *Tess of the d'Urbervilles* and *Jude the Obscure*) go unrewarded; 'life offers, to deny'.

Winterborne's self-sacrifice exerts a strain on the reader's credulity; there is nothing to suggest that, like Henchard, he had renounced the will to live; only delicacy and circumstance can explain his death. Less probable, and more amusing, is the scene where Suke Damson and Mrs Charmond hurry distressfully to Grace's chamber to see how seriously the absent Fitzpiers had been injured through falling from his horse. The main problem for Hardy came at the end, when two of the principals were removed by death. Grace Melbury was not of the stuff which makes tragic heroines, but to reconcile her to Fitzpiers was not easy. The man-trap device was ingenious, but it hardly creates that 'willing suspension of disbelief' which constitutes poetic or imaginative conviction. No happy ending was intended (cf. *Life*, 220).

TESS OF THE D'URBERVILLES

Originally, the last chapter began with a statement which would never have been penned but for the objections which had hampered the serial publication of the novel for nearly two years. It was written to shield 'those who have yet to be born' from misfortunes like those of Tess. The key to Hardy's main motive for writing the story is to be found in the sub-title, however.

Plans for the novel were begun in the autumn of 1888. Hardy's notes from August to December (*Life*, 213–15) relate very largely to *Tess of the d'Urbervilles*. They include some of the topographical background, the decline of Wessex families, reflections on 'the determination to enjoy' and on farce and tragedy, and animadversions on the Prime Cause. About half the novel was accepted by the newspaper syndicate of Tillotson & Son for the publication of the novel under the title of *Too Late Beloved* (or *Too Late, Beloved*), and it was not until the first sixteen chapters were read at the proof stage in September 1889 that objections were raised and the agreement cancelled at Hardy's request (Purdy, 71–2). The story was later declined by the editors of *Murray's Magazine* and *Macmillan's Magazine*. By this time, Hardy knew the 'fearful price' he had to pay 'for the privilege of writing in the English language' (see 'Candour in English Fiction', pp. 150–1). He decided to excise or alter passages which had proved to be unacceptable; by the 'latter part' of 1890 the novel was adapted for serial publication in *The Graphic* and *Harper's Bazaar* from July to December 1891. Not until March 1891, however, was Hardy able to put the 'finishing touches' to *Tess of the d'Urbervilles*.

The most important serial omissions were the baptism scene, which was published in *The Fortnightly Review* in May 1891 under the bold title of 'The Midnight Baptism: A Study in Christianity', and chaps. x and xi, which were published in *The National Observer* the following

*'r Penny's workshop' and Bockhampton Lane (see Mellstock). From a
nting by Emma Hardy, 1883, after H. Moule*

'r Shiner's house' (facing), *and the bridge, Lower Bockhampton*

The church-hatch,
Stinsford (Mellstock)

The keeper's cottage, and –
beyond – 'the greenwood tree',
Yellowham Wood (Yalbury)

November under the title of 'Saturday Night in Arcady' – both as the 'episodic adventures of anonymous personages'. Among the changes for the serial, two are of special interest: Tess was tricked into a bogus marriage with Alec d'Urberville; and Angel used a wheelbarrow to carry the three dairymaids in turn over the flooded road (one of the modifications Hardy carried out with 'cynical amusement'). Subsequently, the visit to the d'Urberville Aisle at Kingsbere, which Tess originally made on her way to Talbothays, was postponed for artistic reasons to a point where the irony of circumstances is heavily charged with tragedy.

Hardy's regret that he added the sub-title did not amount to a recantation, only an admission of futility. He retained it because it defined his purpose and conviction. Tess's fate is partly due to a Durbeyfield tendency to accept or drift, a willingness to endure which cannot be dissociated from indecisiveness, and a certain d'Urberville strain that shows itself in occasional heedlessness and impulsive outbreaks. She is much more the victim of circumstances than Henchard. She never surrenders to Alec except during a brief period when flattery overcomes her self-esteem to the extent of accepting presents (Hardy's 'That was all' is frequently overlooked), and again when, despairing of Angel's return, she consents to live with him as his mistress for the sake of her family. (Without infringing the proprieties, Hardy had depicted such self-sacrifice of the heroine in *Desperate Remedies*.) In the sight of the world, she stood condemned; she was a fallen woman, a kept mistress, and finally a murderess. Yet for Hardy she was pure of heart, with all the gifts of 'charity' which he thought the greatest of the virtues. Bird imagery recurs in association with Tess's misfortunes, and Tess could not have been absent from Hardy's thoughts when he wrote 'The Blinded Bird' (*MV*). After *her* 'wrong', she rallies and endures with hope long after her desertion by Angel. The ending of the poem, 'Who is divine? This bird', is an echo of the challenging subtitle of *Tess of the d'Urbervilles* (cf. p. 164).

It is Tess's misfortune to attract Alec d'Urberville and fall in love with Angel Clare. Both are responsible for the breaking of her spirit. If Alec is the Tempter (cf. p. 158), Angel is no Adam to the fallen Eve until experience and suffering have softened the 'hard logical deposit, like a vein of metal in a soft loam, which turned the edge of everything that attempted to traverse it', and taught him humanity too late (cf. the ending of the novel and the close of *Paradise Lost*). The reformed Alec is not without loving-kindness, and is far from being a mere melo-dramatic villain and libertine.

Hardy's reliance on symbolism, or the expression of a wider significance within an image or nexus of imagery, is more noticeable in *Tess of the d'Urbervilles* and *Jude the Obscure* than in any of his other novels. Alec's blind mother is more strange than real (see p. 164), and the garden scene at Talbothays has associations with *Hamlet* (pp. 165–6). It externalizes the blight of Tess's world, and in its context reveals the inner conflict of hope and fear, love and despair, which constitutes the tragic current of Tess's life after her recovery from her first disaster. The sleep-walking scene was obviously suggested by *Macbeth*; its significance is not allusive, how-ever, but implicit: it expresses Tess's acquiescence and the death of Angel's idealized love. The threshing scene has infernal or Plutonic associations; it ends in slaughter. Its central figure is Tess, 'Once victim, always victim'. The machine is presented as an automaton, which works regardless of suffering like the First Cause or the Will of *The Dynasts*.

More general and successful is the consonance between scenes and seasons and Tess's experiences. On a large scale, it is seen in the lushness of the Froom valley meadows in spring and summer, and the flinty uplands of Flintcomb-Ash farm in winter. On a small scale, it may be seen in the presentation of the river Froom. When Tess first sees it, in the rallying spring-time of life, it is as 'clear as the pure River of Life shown to the Evangelist'; when she returns to Talbothays after her disastrous marriage, 'The gold of the summer picture was now gray, the colours mean, the rich soil mud, and the river cold.' The projection of feeling into the outer scene occasionally suggests the relevance of Hardy's note of 9 January 1889 (*Life*, 216) on the water-colours of Turner: 'each is a landscape *plus* a man's soul. . . . What he paints chiefly is *light as modified by objects.*' This may be seen in the radiance which invests the meadowlands when Tess is in love with Clare, or, ironically, in the 'irradiation' which accompanies the Saturday night revellers on their return from Chaseborough.

Parallelism is related predominantly to natural and rural settings, but similar effects may be found in the concluding scene at Stonehenge or in the interior scenes which mark the extinction of Angel's love at Well-bridge Manor. For ironical juxtaposition, no scene in Hardy is more poignant than that beneath the traceried d'Urberville window at Kings-bere.

Amid the scenic overtones which enrich this novel are proleptic or thematic images, none more striking than the recurrent crimson and blood in association with Alec d'Urberville, 'the blood-red ray in the spectrum' of Tess's 'young life'.

Hardy's 'casual thought' of July 1889 (*Life*, 221) has a direct relevance to the murder of Alec. The Sandbourne scenes accentuate the unnaturalness of Tess's life with Alec; the gigantic ace of hearts which the bloodstain assumes on the ceiling seems fanciful, as if an attempt at symbolism had misfired. (Does it represent the spilling of Tess's life-blood, and is it related to Angel's impression of the Tess 'who had ceased to recognize the body before him as hers – allowing it to drift like a corpse upon the current, in a direction dissociated from its living will'?)

Hardy's authorial intrusions present shifting viewpoints or 'impressions'. Sometimes Nature is idealized; elsewhere it is presented as cruel. Sometimes the Primal Cause is blamed; more often, the social law. A note of 5 May 1889, 'That which socially is a great tragedy may be in Nature no alarming circumstance', may be compared with the endings of xiii and xli. In arguing, however, Hardy tends to lose sight of the whole. Tess's initial misfortunes do not spring from 'a cloud of moral hobgoblins'. Her revulsion from Alec was natural or instinctive; his outrage, an ill-chance which caused Hardy to impugn Providence. Yet he can argue that 'but for the world's opinion' it would have been the beginning of 'a liberal education' for Tess. The desert-island Tess who would not have been greatly wretched at what had happened to her is certainly not the Tess of the novel. Such inconsistency is reflected in the fling at 'the President of the Immortals'. This Grecian conception is found in Tennyson's 'The Lotos-Eaters', but it is quite foreign to Hardy's general presentation of a First Cause which is unconscious of human suffering.

THE WELL-BELOVED

When Tillotson & Son asked Hardy for another serial after the rejection of *Too Late Beloved*, Hardy promised 'something light' and later sent notes on *The Pursuit of the Well-Beloved* (Purdy, 94–5), in which he stated that it was morally innocuous, and that its interest ranged from peers and peeresses to peasants. The main theme had been set down on

19 February 1889 (*Life*, 217). Combined with this was another, which had occurred to him in March 1884: the idea of *Time against Two* 'in which the antagonism of the parents of a Romeo and Juliet *does* succeed in separating the couple and stamping out their love'.

The story was serialized in *The Illustrated London News* and *Harper's Bazaar* from October to December 1892. Despite his intentions, Hardy allowed his feelings on marriage to get the better of him. The hero cannot act as Phillotson does when Sue returns to him at the conclusion of *Jude the Obscure*; for him 'natural instinct' is the true law in marriage, 'not an Act of Parliament', and he sheers off. The dénouement of the story is summary, and suggests almost a contemptuous attitude towards the serial public. After the publication of *Jude the Obscure*, Hardy did not recast the novel as he had hoped to do, but he revised it, removed all reflections on the marriage laws, and provided a new solution of the plot with skilful regard to the artistic unity of the whole.

In view of Miss Lois Deacon's interpretation, it should be stressed, as Hardy took occasion to stress when the revised version of the novel was published in March 1897, that the hero was 'an innocent and moral man throughout' (letter published in *The Academy*, 27 March; cf. *Life*, 286). Situations in the serial make this even more obvious.

The sketches of London society are not the least interesting part of the book. They are a reminder that Hardy kept notes in readiness for the time when he might 'be driven' to write society novels (*Life*, 291). Observations on Ellen Terry (January 1891; *Life*, 232) will be found at the end of II ii.

The Platonic Idea which provides the main current of this 'fantastic tale' was not taken too seriously by the author (cf. note, 28 October 1891: *Life*, 239), but its reality, 'the truth that all men are pursuing a shadow, the Unattainable', led Hardy to hope that his 'tragi-comedy' would be redeemed from 'the charge of frivolity'. Hardy's interest in the Idea or embodiment of perfection derives from Shelley, and may be seen in *The Woodlanders* (xviii, xx, xxviii). In *The Well-Beloved* he chose for his central figure an artist who pursues the perfect form in woman and sculpture. The idea that beauty is a subjective experience, a creation of the fancy, is a commonplace. Hardy playfully adopts a metaphysic, and offers it as an interpretation of the amusing behaviour of people who imagine they are continually in and out of love with this person and that, but who are just as continually haunted by the image of their first love and all the illusory radiance which absence, time, and imaginative sensibility can create. The *reductio ad absurdum* of this kind of temperament comes when the image is pursued through three generations, and the third Avice asks Pierston whether he was in love with her great-grandmother as well. The first Avice is simple; the second indifferent to him, just as liable to transfer her affections as he is (the quasi-parody here is an ironical comment on the lure of the Idea), and a washerwoman; the third is the most elegant and educated of all, but naturally unenthusiastic about the attentions of an old man.

The comedy ends on a poignant note. The processes that have carved the Isle of Slingers out of a single stone (preface) have been at work on Marcia, who, like Jocelyn, has been subject to 'the raspings, chisellings, scourgings, bakings, freezings of forty invidious years'. The chisel of 'never-napping Time' which Hardy noted in 1890 (*WP*. 'In a Eweleaze near Weatherbury'; cf. *TL*. 'The Revisitation') is overheard in the 'tink-tink' of the quarries. Its long-term effects are disclosed with startling emphasis in the grim tragi-comic realism with which the story concludes. The motif had been presented tragically in *Two on a Tower*, and is to be found in 'Amabel', a poem of 1865. One might have expected that the Idea would persist despite physical decay, but the light goes out, and Jocelyn finds no beauty in art or life. The Alastor or 'curse' which had been his inspiration as a sculptor, and led him in pursuit of many a 'Jill-o'-the-wisp', is removed. Here we have the deepest note of pessimism in a story which is not without its fascination if it is read light-heartedly in the spirit in which it was written. For Hardy it was largely a *divertissement* between two serious major works of fiction.

JUDE THE OBSCURE

In some ways this novel is antithetical and complementary to *Tess of the d'Urbervilles*. It clearly demonstrates, as Hardy stated in his contribution to 'The Tree of Knowledge' in *The New Review* of June 1894, that boys need sex education as much as girls, for 'it has never struck me that the spider is invariably male and the fly invariably female'. The disasters of Tess and Jude spring largely from early sexual misfortunes, and both are tragically fated to fall in love with intellectuals who are 'ethereal'. The comparison must not be pushed too far. Arabella is not exactly the counterpart of Alec; Sue is more subtilized and irrational than Angel, and far more a central figure in the main tragedy; and *Jude the Obscure* is too complex a novel to be regarded as a mere companion-piece to *Tess of the d'Urbervilles*.

In April 1888 Hardy had made notes for a short story on the suicide of a young man who failed in his efforts to 'go to Oxford'. The deep feelings implicit in the unusually immodest claim which follows – 'There is something [in this] the world ought to be shown, and I am the one to show it to them' – may have arisen from recollections of the academic frustrations of his friend Horace Moule (pp. 419–20). A later note that this projected story was probably 'the germ of *Jude the Obscure*' is only partially exact, for Jude's academic struggles were eventually to form a secondary theme in the novel. Examination of the early part of the manuscript shows that, however much Hardy changed course, the love story was an important element from the first. The divorce question had been a serious issue in The Woodlanders, and it was widely discussed in 1890 in relation to the famous Parnell case (*Life*, 230). Hardy could not have kept to the outline of 1892–3, for he assured the American publishers of his serial that 'the tale could not offend the most fastidious maiden'. How far Hardy's recollections of his cousin Tryphena Sparks entered the novel is discussed elsewhere (see p. 438). In his preface to the first edition, Hardy says that 'some of the circumstances' were 'suggested by the death of a woman' in 1890 (cf. *Life*, 224; the poem 'Thoughts of Phena' was written in March 1890). One thing is fairly certain: the epicene in Sue – 'a type of woman' which had always had an 'attraction' for Hardy (*Life*, 272) – is not drawn from Tryphena. The second Mrs Hardy said that Sue was drawn from Mrs Henniker, an authoress with whom Hardy was friendly when the novel was being written (Purdy, 345).

In preparation for the novel, Hardy visited two teacher-training colleges in London in 1891 (*Life*, 235–7), and Fawley and Oxford (the Marygreen and Christminster of the novel) in 1892 and 1893 (*Life*, 250–1, 257). The narrative 'was written in outline in 1892 and the spring of 1893, and at full length, as it now appears, from August 1893 onwards into the next year' (1895 preface). The manuscript, however, indicates that Hardy – for reasons given below – did not finish working on his script until March 1895.

In the meantime he had encountered the same difficulties he met in the serial publication of *Tess of the d'Urbervilles*, and had taken similar counter-measures. The story appeared in *Harper's New Monthly Magazine* from December 1894 to November 1895, the first instalment under the title of *The Simpletons*, (a bitterly ironic comment on the age, but also a reflection on the two leading characters), the remainder under the original title of *Hearts Insurgent*. The novel did not assume its present title until it appeared in book form.

In order not to offend the magazine-readers, Hardy omitted Jude's seduction (Jude was enticed into marriage by Arabella's talk of another young man who wished to marry her), allowed no intimacy between Sue and Jude (she took charge of Father Time and had an adopted child), and did not present the scene of Sue's expiation with Phillotson at the end. The task of mutilating and restoring the novel was so wearisome that Hardy was not able to revise and improve the original as he wished to do (*Life*, 269). He had in fact written to Harper's in April 1894 requesting that the agreement to supply the story be cancelled.

Hardy's statements that 'no book he had ever written contained less of his own life' and that 'there is not a scrap of personal detail in it' (*Life*, 274, 392) need some elucidation. *Jude the Obscure* certainly contains far more of Hardy's views and feelings than *A Laodicean*, which he described as factually the most autobiographical of his novels. Jude's classical and theological studies were very much the same as Hardy's, nowhere more remarkably so than in the *Iliad* (the list of readings in I vi coincides with those noted in Hardy's copy: Rutland, *Thomas Hardy*, 21–2); and the photograph of Sue as a girl recalls that of Hardy's cousin Tryphena Sparks (see p. 15 of Lois Deacon's *Tryphena and Thomas Hardy*, J. Stevens Cox, 1962). It is noteworthy that in *Jude the Obscure* Hardy did not become involved in authorial comments as he did in *Tess of the d'Urbervilles*; he used scenes of inner and outer conflict for incidental self-expression. After the marriage of Sue and Phillotson, Jude 'projected his mind into the future, and saw her with children more or less in her own likeness around her'. If, at her estrangement or death, he could see her in her child . . . Then he realized that Nature scorned 'man's finer emotions' (cf. *WP*. 'To a Motherless Child', which was written after the death of Tryphena; see also p. 438). 'Sue in her days when her intellect scintillated like a star' expressed many of Hardy's convictions on the Church and academic institutions; her view that 'the First Cause worked automatically like a somnambulist, and not reflectively like a sage' is found in Hardy's poems, in *The Dynasts*, and in his *Life* (cf. 218, 7 April 1889). What Hardy meant by saying that *Jude the Obscure* was not autobiographical was that none of the events of the story was taken from his life. In this sense, his asseverations need not be questioned. On the other hand, there can be little doubt that many of the thoughts and feelings which entered into certain scenes of the novel had their ultimate origin in the deep-seated unhappiness of Hardy's marital life.

The story, Hardy wrote (*Life*, 271), was intended for 'those into whose souls the iron has entered'. It had entered into his own. The narrative is disciplined to its predestined end. 'How cruel you are!' wrote Swinburne, and he wished for 'another admission into an English paradise "under the greenwood tree" ' (*Life*, 270). Hardy was too much involved with his quarrel against society to disengage himself critically and consider the novel in all its aspects. He may have been impelled somewhat by the plays of Ibsen which he had witnessed, and the 'attitude of the English press towards these tragic productions – the culminating evidence of our blinkered insular taste being afforded by the nickname of the "Ibscene drama" which they received' (*Life*, 256). He had already lost patience with English readers and critics, and was probably prepared at this stage to relinquish novel-writing for poetry. Whatever the reason, he seems to have decided that he had nothing to lose by expressing himself to the full. *Jude the Obscure* is in many ways a great tragic novel, but it is too depressing and too contrived to command common assent. In this contrivance, Sue is the critical factor; she is so exceptional that Hardy did not dare to be as explicit as he might have been (cf. *Life*, 272).

Many readers question the probability of the plot. It is misleading, however, to judge by realistic standards. Nowhere is this more so than in the horrible scene which discloses the hanging of Sue's children and the suicide of Father Time. All this is part of a theme which is centred in Christminster, and relates to Jerusalem and the Crucifixion. In the end both Jude and Sue choose to be 'crucified' (they first meet near the Martyrs' Cross), but the hanging-scene is a ghastly epitome of suffering in a city of uncharity, darkness, and bigotry. Its conclusion alludes to the world and the flesh, ('the rashness of those parents' recalls *Paradise Lost*) and the Atonement: 'For the rashness of those parents he had groaned, for their ill-assortment he had quaked, and for the misfortunes of these he had died.' Biblical parallelism is confirmed at innumerable points.

Among the later ones, it may be noticed that leaving Kennetbridge for Christminster is, to Sue, like 'coming from Caiaphas to Pilate'. She and Jude return to Christminster on Remembrance Day (the Feast of the Passover). When, after the loss of her children, she decides that the flesh, the curse of Adam, should be mortified, and that she must leave Jude, he declares: 'let the veil of our temple be rent in two from this hour.' For Jude the whole 'Creation groans' with pain; 'charity' or compassion is snuffed out by society and the Church. Established conventions reassert themselves. Sue submits to her expiation; 'I will drink my cup to the dregs,' she insists. Jude wishes he had never been born, and welcomes death, but there will be no peace in this world for Sue, however much she abases herself before 'the holy cross'.

Hardy intended the book to be 'all contrasts': 'Sue and her heathen gods set against Jude's reading the Greek Testament; Christminster academical, Christminster in the slums: Jude the saint, Jude the sinner; Sue the Pagan, Sue the saint; marriage, no marriage; &c, &c' (*Life*, 272–3). Among these the obvious Sue–Arabella antithesis is implicit, but the emphasis is rightly on Sue and Jude and Christminster. Paradigmatically, their story forms a cross. When Sue and Jude are observing the model of Jerusalem at Christminster (the presence of the schoolchildren emphasizes the light of inexperience in which observations are made), it is the Hellenic Sue who fancies that it is unreal and Jude who is absorbed. At the end, crushed by misfortune, Sue gives up her intellectual faith and returns to the Church 'creed-drunk', and it is Jude who has turned against it.

The story tends insistently towards uprootedness (physical and spiritual), separation, and isolation. In this larger context, Jude and Sue are the Janus aspects of the central protagonist, the one 'a chaos of principles', the other 'tossed about with aberrant passions'. The shuttle-like action which is characteristic of many scenes before and after the short-lived happiness of Jude and Sue is a reflection of the unrest and torment, 'the strange disease of modern life', the 'heads o'ertax'd' and 'palsied hearts' which Arnold had foreseen. Symbolism and parabolic patterns help to knit together these scenes. The rabbit caught in the gin is the nodal point of the novel, symbolizing the plight of both Jude and Sue. The pig-imagery is recurrent with reference to Jude, but it is the Christminster imagery which is most significant. The city of light (i iii) proves to be a place of dubious illumination and lonely alleys, where Jude begins to sense his isolation, and finds comfort only in the shadows of the past (ⅠⅠ i). Just before the catastrophe which spells final dissolution, Sue finds herself a room into which 'the outer walls of Sarcophagus College – silent, black and windowless – threw their four centuries of gloom, bigotry, and decay . . . shutting out the moonlight by night and the sun by day'. The fog through which the lost souls of Sue and Jude proceed 'like Acherontic shades' in the final tragic scenes is Arnold's 'darkling plain', but love or charity is barred by ill-chance and the despotism of 'social formulas'.

From this dilemma, there is no facile or romantic escape. Nature is no longer held up as an ideal. From his boyhood at Marygreen, Jude discovers the cruelty of Nature's law and the harsh necessity of compromise. The conflict between flesh and spirit is externalized in Jude's relations with Arabella and Sue; they represent the lower and higher aspects of his nature, the dichotomy which Shelley found in Venus Pandemos and Venus Urania. The pig-symbolism links Jude's abhorrence of the sensuality into which he falls and his abhorrence of the natural world in which one species, mankind in particular, preys on another to live. Jude's periodic falls from grace in bouts of liquor and sex are not just a representation of *l'homme moyen sensuel* or 'an ordinary sinner', but part of the allegorical pattern or symbolism which is enlisted to give greater unity and unversality to the novel. The marriage of themes and realism occasionally suggests, however, an incompatibility similar to that of the three human marriages. It may be questioned, for example, whether Phillotson, who had displayed magnanimity in releasing Sue from marriage (and suffered inhumanly in consequence), would have behaved as he is made to do when she returns to him. Jude, it seems, is sacrificed as a heroic tragic figure in order to fulfil the requirements of the larger design. Again, if the marriage-question is centred in 'the tragic issues of two bad marriages, owing in the main to a doom or curse of hereditary temperament peculiar to the family of the parties' (*Life*, 271), it is a pathetic illusion of Jude that his 'marriage' to the epicene Sue is 'Nature's own marriage'. It is certainly not borne out circumstantially in the narrative (though Sue's views that love is likely to perish when it submits to the law are those which Hardy held – cf. *TL*. 'The Christening'). Sue's life with Jude is an unnatural compromise, and Jude knows when she leaves him that he will turn to his 'wallowing in the mire'. If he is the Jude of the New Testament epistle, he is a fallen Jude. He has 'all the vices of his virtues, and some to spare' (ⅤⅠ vi).

Jude the Obscure is a disturbing rather than moving novel, though one or two of its scenes reach the highest pitch of dramatic expression in Hardy. One feels that the polemicist often got the better of the artist in directing the course of the action, and that Hardy's explanation in the 1895 preface – the work 'is simply an endeavour to give shape and coherence to a series of seemings, or personal impressions, the question of their consistency or their discordance . . . being regarded as not of the first moment' – admits as much. Its tragic effect is weakened because situations or the turn of events often suggest contrivance rather than probability. Hardy spoke of Jude as his 'poor puppet' (*Life*, 272), and there is sufficient truth in the expression to explain why the novel does not create a powerful sense of tragic inevitability comparable to that of *The Mayor of Casterbridge*. The tragedy of 'unfulfilled aims' and rejection is extensively developed, but it might have been more impressive had Hardy been more exclusive. He was attempting a new kind of novel, moving towards the drama of inner conflict, and deliberately economizing in scenic effects. Background features show an increasing tendency towards the symbolical. Artistic patterns, realism, and personal 'impressions' do not cohere at all points, however; and *Jude the Obscure* is too elaborately conceived and too inclusive to be wholly satisfying as a work of art.

The story contains the material for two or three novels. The Christminster theme sufficed for one; Sue Bridehead was the subject for another. A more normal marriage relationship than was possible with Sue was necessary, however, to make Jude's love the basis for a convincing protest against the letter of the marriage law. For, however much they are drawn together as companions, their marriage is forced and unnatural. Nature is part of the gin of circumstance or chance in which each is caught. No liberalizing of the marriage code could have rescued Jude from his dilemma. The main 'villain of the piece' is 'blind Chance' (*Life*, 433). Sue's 'abnormalism' is ultimately responsible for her disasters, her sense of sin, and her final self-abasement. It is not without irony that Jude, who has learned from 'the grind of stern reality' to shed many of his illusions, can persist, and even sacrifice his life, in the belief that his marriage with Sue was sanctified by Nature.

THE SHORT STORIES

An Indiscretion in the Life of an Heiress

This slight romance was drawn from scenes in Hardy's first novel, *The Poor Man and the Lady*. Many modifications were undoubtedly made (for example, the hero of the novel was an architect), but the original style, which Hardy later dismissed as 'the affected simplicity of Defoe's', is preserved, and the closing scene achieves a distinctiveness and pathos which indicate a remarkable combination of discipline and poetic feeling. The period of the story is 1848–53. It was published in *The New Quarterly Magazine* and *Harper's Weekly* in July 1878. Hardy did not include it in his collected works, and the place-names were therefore not changed to conform to the Wessex nomenclature which he adopted in the writing and revision of his novels from 1873. The topography is too general to appear localized, but Tollamore and Melport are easily identifiable.

Egbert Mayne, the young schoolmaster at Tollamore, fell in love with Squire Allenville's daughter, after saving her life. She had gone to see a threshing-machine, 'had inadvertently stepped backwards, and had drawn so near to the band which ran from the engine to the drum of the thresher that in another moment her dress must have been caught, and she would have been whirled round the wheel as a mangled carcase'. She visited the school to thank him. His grandfather, Farmer Broadford, with whom he lived, was worried because, in the manner of liviers' property, his house and farm had lapsed to the squire, who needed the land for extensions to his park. Egbert asked Geraldine to speak to her father on the question. They met frequently, and Egbert was relieved to hear that the scheme of enlargement had been postponed indefinitely. She revisited the school, and, after the children had been dismissed, he kissed her. A week later it was announced that the park was to be extended. Soon afterwards Farmer Broadford fell from a corn-stack and died, but not before Egbert had told him that he was in love with Geraldine. While Egbert was alone in the house of the dead, Geraldine arrived, anxious to know that she was not to blame. They were reconciled. Geraldine was 'on the verge of committing the most horrible social sin – that of loving beneath her, and owning that she so loved'. Eventually Egbert decided he would go to London 'to rise to her level by years of sheer exertion'.

Five years later he was becoming famous as an author. Geraldine had gone abroad with her father, but one day Egbert caught sight of her in a carriage in Piccadilly. Later he had reason to believe she would attend a performance of the *Messiah*, and booked a seat as near as possible to the seats reserved for the Allenvilles. At the concert, the opportunity came to hold hands and arrange to meet at her front door at midnight. As the hour struck, a letter was slipped under the door; it was from Geraldine, who wrote that circumstances had changed and that they must forget each other. Next morning he saw the announcement of her engagement to Lord Bretton. A letter from Geraldine indicated that the announcement was premature. Egbert's ambition left him, and he retired to a cottage at Fairland, the village adjoining Tollamore.

The wedding, he learned, was to take place shortly. He decided to face the 'sacrifice', and visited the church to see the preparations for the ceremony. Here he met Geraldine, and learned that she was not in love with Lord Bretton. In the early hours of the morning she came to Egbert's, and they decided to marry at once. He borrowed a horse, and rode off to procure a licence. They were married the same day, and set off for London via Melport, where they stayed three days. It was agreed that her father should be seen before they left. They reached Tollamore House in the evening. Geraldine was ill with anxiety before she entered. Half an hour later, Egbert saw a man gallop off from the stables. A carriage arrived, and ten minutes later Egbert was summoned. Geraldine was very ill: on meeting her father she had fainted, and a blood-vessel had been ruptured. It had happened before, and her life was in danger. Egbert remained, but on the third day Geraldine had another attack and died peacefully.

Destiny and a Blue Cloak

The story was published in the *New York Times* in 1874. It is of special interest as Hardy's first short story, and also in its retention of actual place-names, with the exception of Cloton, the scene of the main action.

Frances Lovill was the beauty of Cloton village, where Agatha Pollin lived at the mill with her uncle. The two girls travelled together one morning to Maiden-Newton, Agatha proceeding thence by train to Weymouth. She wore a blue autumn wrap like Frances Lovill's, and, while walking on the Esplanade, was mistaken for her by Oswald Winwood. As she had already lost her heart to him, she did not disillusion the young man, who changed his plans in order to spend the afternoon with her on Portland. He accompanied her home in the evening. The second stage of the journey, from Maiden-Newton to Beaminster, was by the carrier-van, which they caught just in·time. Agatha perceived that Oswald was in love with her, and confessed her deception. He kissed her, said he liked her more than anybody else in the world, but admitted that he had been looking for Miss Lovill that morning. At Beaminster, a person whom they had not noticed in the darkness of the van stepped out; they learned from the driver that it was Miss Lovill.

Oswald was soon to take a competitive examination – thanks to Macaulay, who had swept away all 'bureaucratic jobbery' – for a post in India. Like one of Hardy's Dorchester friends (cf. *Life*, 32, 161–2), Winwood headed the examination lists when the results were announced in *The Times*. He left for India almost at once, corresponded with Agatha, and told her that he had hopes of becoming a judge. Then it was announced that Humphrey the miller, Agatha's uncle, was to marry Frances Lovill.

A merry old bachelor named Lovill, who was distantly related to Frances, fell in love with Agatha, and the miller, who owed him a large sum of money and wished to emigrate with his family to Australia after his marriage, urged his niece to accept him. She refused, and explained her position. Eventually she signed a contract, on the advice of the parson Mr Davids, to accept Lovill if Oswald did not return to marry her by November. She wrote to him at once, was assured that he would return, and was happy.

By the evening of her wedding-day Oswald had not returned, however, and she had come to an understanding with a young worker at the mill named John. Early next morning she concealed herself in a cart loaded with sacks of flour for local delivery. It moved; she concluded all was well, and went to sleep. Suddenly she realized that the cart was returning. She then discovered that the driver was not John, but old Lovill disguised in a miller's smock-frock. He was highly amused at the joke. She was defeated, and married him the next morning.

In the evening, her uncle's wife, the former Frances Lovill, came to her room wearing the blue cloak which had meant so much in Agatha's destiny. She revealed that Mr Davids was an old admirer of hers, and that she had persuaded him to advise Agatha as he had done. She had heard Agatha making her plans with John the previous evening, told Mr Lovill, and 'helped him to his joke' to avenge her deprivation and marriage to a man she did not love. She informed Agatha that Winwood had arrived that morning, after being delayed by illness; she had told him that Agatha had gone out for a drive with the man she was to marry. Agatha did not flinch 'in face of her adversary', but said that the information was 'interesting' and that she was her husband's darling and would not make him jealous for the world.

Hardy's use of a similar ruse towards the end of *The Hand of Ethelberta* may be the main reason why he did not attempt to collect this story for publication in England (Weber, *Hardy of Wessex*, 98).

The Duchess of Hamptonshire

The story first appeared as 'The Impulsive Lady' in a British weekly called *Light* (April 1878) and in *Harper's Weekly*, New York (May 1878). The unfortunate heroine is Lady Saxelbye of Croome Castle; in the story which appeared as 'Emmeline, or Passion vs. Principle' in *The Independent*, New York (February 1884), she is Lady Emmeline of Stroome Castle; in the version which appeared in *A Group of Noble Dames* (1891), she is the Duchess of Hamptonshire, or Emmeline of Batton Castle. All three stories are essentially unchanged; the first is the shortest, the second the longest.

An attachment had grown between Emmeline, the vicar's daughter, and the curate, Alwyn Hill, but the Duke of Hamptonshire fell in love with her when she was seventeen, and she was married to him. He was jealous of Alwyn, and she was so terrified by his ill-treatment of her that, when she heard that the curate was sailing to America, she asked him to take her with him. The young man's principles were such that he refused. He became a Professor of Rhetoric at Boston. Years later, after reading about the death of the Duke, he returned to England to find that the Duchess was still alive. When he saw her, he discovered she was not Emmeline. Emmeline had eloped with a young curate to America, he learned.

Investigations led him to Plymouth, where he discovered that she had sailed on the same ship as he to Boston, but had died on the voyage and been buried at sea; he himself had officiated at the service. Alwyn left England with no intention of returning.

The Distracted Preacher

Richard Stockdale, a temporary Methodist preacher at Nether-Moynton, fell in love with the attractive widow, Lizzy Newberry, with whom he lodged. He soon discovered that she had access to contraband liquor, and was mystified by her late rising, her disappearance for whole days, and the sight of a muddied greatcoat, with hat and breeches. One night, as he was groping upstairs for a light, he caught a glimpse of someone wearing them. Lizzy had left the house, and he overheard her telling one of his devout parishioners that there was danger and that she must warn the lugger off. He followed her to Ringsworth, where she lit a branch of furze as a warning to a lugger from Cherbourg.

At home, Lizzy admitted that she and her cousin Owlett the miller were engaged in smuggling. The next night the lugger would make for Lulwind Cove. Stockdale accompanied Lizzy, who followed all the chosen local men to meet Owlett at Lulwind. The contraband was brought to Nether-Moynton and hidden under loose floor-boards in the church tower and in Owlett's orchard. The next day the Custom-house or Preventive officers arrived. The tubs in the church tower were soon discovered; later, the smugglers concealed in the church tower watched the officers working round an apple tree in the orchard. The tree was lifted, and found to be growing in a shallow box. When this was removed, a square hole was revealed containing tubs of smuggled spirits. After various set-backs, the officers took the tubs away in requisitioned carts. They were set upon by the disguised smugglers at a crossroads, and bound to trees. When released by Mr Stockdale, the officers decided that they could take no further action. But the villagers were marked men, and were later caught in an affray in which Owlett was badly wounded. Lizzy had refused to give up the business when Mr Stockdale asked her to marry him. He left, returned two years later, and proposed successfully.

Hardy would have preferred to end the story in close conformity with the facts (see the note he added in 1912), but thought the happy ending most suitable for *The New Quarterly Magazine* and *Harper's Weekly*, in which the story appeared in the spring of 1879. During the winter of 1875–6 he had heard stories of smuggling exploits in the area from the captain with whom he lodged at Swanage (*Life*, 107–8), but he had been interested in smuggling from his early years. His grandfather had hidden spirits at Higher Bockhampton, a lonely place by the heath. The apple-tree device for concealment was described by an ex-carrier who worked for Hardy's father for over thirty years.

Fellow-Townsmen

The story was first published in the spring of 1880, in *The New Quarterly Magazine* and *Harper's Weekly*. It shows the behaviour of 'the whimsical god' known as 'blind Circumstance'. The first part and the opening of the second were revised for its inclusion in *Wessex Tales*.

Mr Barnet had given up Lucy Savile owing to a misunderstanding, and married a society lady, who proved to be incompatible. For this reason he envied the young lawyer Mr Downe and his happy life with his wife and children. Mr Downe was sympathetic, and arranged for his wife to meet Mrs Barnet in the hope that she could smooth out his friend's domestic troubles. Mr Barnet had seen Lucy and acknowledged his mistake. Mrs Barnet and Mrs Downe drove down from Port-Bredy to the shore, and were tempted to sail. The boat capsized; Mrs Barnet was recovered and survived, but Mrs Downe was drowned. When Lucy told Mr Barnet that she intended to move and teach elsewhere, he was prompted to advise Mr Downe to secure her as governess to his children. Lucy accepted the post, and the children took pleasure in exploring the house which had been designed to please Mrs Barnet, and which was now nearing completion. Mrs Barnet had left her husband and settled in London. When she died, Mr Barnet was relieved to think the way was now clear to marry Lucy, as he had long wished. He had hardly read the letter announcing his wife's death when a note was delivered informing him that Mr Downe had been accepted by Lucy, and they were to be married that morning. Mr Barnet recovered from the shock, and was in time to see the wedding to which he had been invited. He immediately sold all his property and business in Port-Bredy, and set out on a world tour. He lived in many countries, and did not return for more than twenty-one years. He discovered that many of his friends were dead, including Mr Downe, who had bought the new residence which had been intended for Mrs Barnet. As soon as he discovered that Mrs Downe was living there, he called and proposed marriage. Lucy refused. On reconsideration, she changed her mind, but found that Mr Barnet had left Port-Bredy. He never returned.

The Honourable Laura

This story, with the title 'Benighted Travellers', was sold to the Tillotson & Son fiction agency, and was published first in the *Bolton Weekly Journal* and *Harper's Weekly* in December 1881.

A young lady eloped with Signor Smittozzi, an opera singer, one Christmas Eve. They stopped for the night at the Prospect Hotel on the wild north coast of Lower Wessex. Shortly afterwards her father, Lord Quantock, and his nephew arrived in pursuit. The nephew, Captain Northbrook, adopted a peremptory tone towards Laura, and, when his uncle expressed surprise at his manner, claimed the right of a husband; they had married secretly three months earlier. Lord Quantock left, and the captain challenged Signor Smittozzi to a duel with pistols. They left Laura at the hotel, and reached a point on the cliff near a waterfall. Obeying a sudden impulse, the opera singer pushed the young man over the edge. He then returned and told Laura her husband had relinquished her. They left the hotel to catch a train to Downstable. By the turnpike, they overheard a conversation about a man who had been pushed over the edge of a chasm. Further on, near Cliff-Martin, Smittozzi was uncertain of the route, and Laura suggested that he should walk ahead to reconnoitre. As soon as he had left, she hurried back to the hotel. Smittozzi did not return, but her husband was brought in on a stretcher, and she nursed him back to health. He would not forgive her, and went abroad at the time of her father's death. She was lonely, and eventually lost all hope of her husband's return. The twelfth Christmas after his mishap was near when suddenly he returned, and they were happily reunited.

The most interesting modification in the story when it was revised for inclusion in *A Group of Noble Dames* is the change in the heroine's name. Originally it was Lucetta; in the meantime *The Mayor of Casterbridge* had become well-known.

What the Shepherd Saw

This story of events on four moonlight nights at Christmastide appeared in the 1881 Christmas number of *The Illustrated London News*.

Most of the incidents of the first three nights were witnessed by Bill Mills, the shepherd-boy who had been left to watch the sheep at lambing-time on Marlbury Down. On the first night, the Duchess of Shakeforest Towers met her cousin, who wished to save her from her unkind husband. She agreed to meet him at the same place the following night or the next. When they left, a figure appeared from behind the Druidic trilithon near the shepherd's hut. On the next night the Duke arrived, slew the cousin, and hid his body near the trilithon. The Duchess did not appear, but the shepherd-boy, who had followed the Duke at a safe distance, saw the Duchess come out to meet him at Shakeforest Towers, and heard her tell him about her cousin's strange behaviour and suggest that they should meet him the following night. They appeared; as they were moving off, the boy left the hut and was seen. The Duke asked if he watched the sheep every night. Later he appeared again, and made the boy swear that he would never tell anyone what he had seen, or disclose that he had ever kept sheep on Marlbury Down. He took the boy with him and sent him to a boarding-school.

Twenty-two years later, Mills, now a steward at Shakeforest Towers, informed the Duke that an old shepherd, his former master, had made a confession to the vicar just before his death: he had witnessed the murder. The Duke said he would stop the vicar's tongue. That night the steward walked up to the trilithon, and saw a white figure approach in the moonlight. It was the Duke sleep-walking, in his nightshirt. The next morning the Duke was discovered dead; he had been wandering, and had fallen down the stairs.

Shepherds say that flitting shapes may be seen around the trilithon during the nights of Christmastide, 'with the gleam of a weapon, and the shadow of a man dragging a burden into the hollow'.

A Tradition of Eighteen Hundred and Four

The story tells very simply how a shepherd-boy was accompanied by his uncle to watch the sheep at lambing-time one night above the Cove (Lulworth). They were roused from sleep by voices, and two Frenchmen were seen discussing a map by the light of a lantern. Uncle Job, sergeant in the Sixty-first foot, recognized one of them as Bonaparte, and wished he had brought his new-flinted firelock with him.

The story was published in *Harper's Christmas*, 1882. Hardy was astonished later to find that his invention had become a tradition (*Life*, 391–2).

It was included in *Life's Little Ironies* (1894), but transferred to *Wessex Tales* in 1912.

The Three Strangers

A lively christening-party was taking place one stormy evening in a remote upland shepherd's cottage, when a stranger arrived, who immediately made himself at home. Then another came, dressed in grey uniform; he helped himself liberally to the mead, and sang a song which gradually revealed that he was the hangman for the execution of a sheep-stealer who was in gaol at Casterbridge. A third stranger arrived, took one look round the room, and fled. Then the distant sound of a gun was heard, announcing the escape of a prisoner from the gaol. The men set off in pursuit of the third stranger. The first returned and helped himself to more food. He was joined by the hangman. Long after they had departed in different directions, the captured man was brought in. Two officers from Casterbridge Gaol had arrived in the meantime, and saw at a glance that a mistake had been made. A description was given, and it was obvious that the man they were after was the first stranger. The prisoner then said that he was his brother, and that he had been on his way from Shottsford to visit him at the gaol. The courage of the escaped sheep-stealer excited the admiration of local inhabitants, and he was never recaptured.

The story appeared in *Longman's Magazine* and *Harper's Weekly* (March 1883), and was dramatized under the title of 'The Three Wayfarers' in 1893.

The Romantic Adventures of a Milkmaid

This strange mixture of realism and the supernaturally romantic suggests a fairy-tale for adults. It is over-elaborated. The dairymaid Margery

Tucker is a kind of Cinderella whose wish to attend a magnificent ball is granted by a supernatural Baron as a reward for saving him from depression and suicide. If he is one of Hardy's 'Mephistophelian visitants', his conduct is exemplary, although he is tempted to abscond with her in his yacht. It is as if the Prince of Darkness *had* become a gentleman, and was proof against his own temptations. His horses are black and daemonic; his influence over Margery is mesmeric – 'he was like a magician to me. . . . He could move me as a loadstone moves a speck of steel.' Was he pale, depressed, and ill because he fought against his inclinations? Does he present the lure of worldliness to a simple country girl? Is his renunciation of his hold over her a built-in proof that this is a 'fairy tale'?

Margery's wish was to attend a Yeomanry Ball. She met the Baron at the appointed place in a wood, where she changed into her ballroom dress in a hollow tree. The dress was of gossamer and so festooned with flounces that it was impossible to get out of the tree by the rift through which she entered. 'Who would have thought that fine clothes could do so much!' he exclaimed as he released her. They drove to a far-away mansion, and when they arrived the hot breath from the horses' nostrils 'jetted forth like smoke out of volcanoes'. After the ball, they returned to the tree, where Margery changed into her rustic dress. Despite her protests, the Baron burnt the ballroom costume, and told her that he might need her again to deliver him from 'that darkness as of Death' which sometimes encompassed him.

A lime-burner named Jim, in dress and complexion very much a contrast to the Baron, wished to marry Margery, but when she thought of the intoxicating polka and the splendour of the ball she said, 'Jim, you don't know the world, and what a woman's wants can be'. 'Anybody would think the devil had showed you all the kingdoms of the world since I saw you last!' he replied. 'Perhaps he has!' she murmured. When the Baron heard from Jim how Margery had changed, he sent him a waggon-load of the most splendid furniture, with articles of silver and gold; but when he heard that Jim's wedding prospects were improving he grew meditative. In retrospect Margery seemed more 'a heavenly messenger than a milkmaid'. He wandered to the hollow tree, murmured her name, and she was there behind him as if by magic; he was about to turn away, but when he saw her unhappiness he kissed her. A few weeks later he wrote asking her to see him again, to disperse the 'plaguy glooms' from which he suffered. She came, and he offered her a locket of pearls as a wedding present. She had, in fact, responded to the call just when her wedding was due. When the Baron heard this, he rushed her home in his coach, making her promise that if he sent for her again she would not respond – 'your salvation may depend on it'. They were too late, and her father was furious.

The Baron was ill when he sent for her again, telling her to prepare for a solemn ceremony. She imagined she was to be the Baroness; but it was Jim who was there for the ceremony. Though she consented to marry him, she refused to live with him. Jim, after encountering her father's displeasure, joined the Yeomanry. In the meantime the Baron was carried down to the shore and laid in a yacht, which was soon 'a small shapeless phantom out at sea'.

Handsome in his red uniform, Jim had attracted the attention of a young widow named Mrs Peach. The jealousy kindled in Margery is expressed in a phantasmagoric scene, which 'wore the aspect of some unholy assignation in Pandaemonium' and was witnessed by the occupant of a carriage drawn by a pair of dark horses. Margery left in the carriage. The Baron had intended to take her home to wait for Jim, but was tempted to ask her to sail with him 'all the world over'. She could not come to a decision, but the Baron overcame his temptation and took her home, where she was soon reconciled to Jim. Report had it that the Baron died. Margery admitted that, were he to come and call her, she would have to obey. He was like a magician. 'Yet no,' she added, hearing her infant cry, 'he would not move me now. It would be so unfair to baby.'

This feminine equivocation recalls that at the conclusion of *A Laodicean*. The story was written hastily at Wimborne in the winter of 1882–3, and appeared in *The Graphic* and *Harper's Weekly* in the summer of 1883. When revising it for inclusion in *A Changed Man* (1913), Hardy transferred the setting from the Stickleford–Casterbridge area to a remoter part of Wessex to avoid incongruous associations with *The Return of the Native* and *Tess of the d'Urbervilles*. The milkmaid of Talbothays, it should be added, has little in common with Margery Tucker.

Interlopers at The Knap

The story was first published in *The English Illustrated Magazine* in May 1884. The affluence and 'commercial subtlety' of Darton's father form an interesting link with Hardy's essay on the Dorset agricultural

labourer (pp. 138–40) and his presentation of the agricultural world in
The Mayor of Casterbridge.

Accompanied by his friend Japheth Johns, Charles Darton, a
wealthy farmer, rode northward in the gloom of a wintry evening
to The Knap, in the Hintocks, to marry Sally Hall. They lost their
way. When they arrived, they met the family of Philip Hall, Sally's
brother, in the barn, and Darton recognized in the mother the girl
Helena who had refused his hand in marriage years previously.
She had gone out to Australia to marry Philip Hall, and they had
just returned in great poverty. Philip was very ill. Darton was
detained by rain and was sitting alone by the hearth late at night
when Helena came in to boil some water for her husband. Darton
heard her story and offered to take care of her children, adding that,
as she belonged to another, he could not take care of her. 'Yes, you
can!' said Sally, who had heard all, and had come to announce that
her brother was dead.

Darton took charge of Helena's eldest child, a son, and sent him to
a school in Casterbridge. Later, much to the disgust of Japheth
Johns, he married Helena. Helena was frail and plaintive, and died
after childbirth. Darton, thinking that Sally would brighten up his
home, rode to The Knap to make a second proposal, almost five years
after his previous visit. Sally refused him; Darton met Japheth just
as he was leaving and learned that he too had come to propose.
When he learned that Japheth had not been successful, he proposed
again, by letter. Again he was refused. Circumstances led him to
believe that Sally would change her mind, and, 'anniversaries
having been unpropitious', he waited until a bright day in May to
ride once more to The Knap. Sally still refused, and made him
promise never to propose to her again. She had several offers of
marriage, but preferred to remain single.

A Tryst at an Ancient Earthwork

The story was first published in the *Detroit Post* in March 1885, and then,
with several changes in the text, some slight additions, and four photographs, in *The English Illustrated Magazine* of December 1893. It may
be regarded as a by-product of Hardy's investigations into ancient
monuments and history in the Dorchester area when he was working

on *The Mayor of Casterbridge*. He was a member of the Dorset Natural History and Antiquarian Field Club.

The story is very slight, and the main part may be regarded as an essayist's impression of the great prehistoric fortress of Mai-Dun on a stormy night. In an imaginary encounter, the writer met an archaeologist who wished to prove his theory that the earthworks contained proof of Roman as well as Celtic occupation. He dug and came across a mosaic pavement and various objects, which he returned when he was satisfied. The writer, however, did not see him restore a gilt statuette of Mercury, and fancied he had seen him slip it into his pocket. Years later, when the archaeologist died, it was found among his effects, and presented to the Casterbridge Museum.

A Mere Interlude

This story was sent to Tillotson & Son, and first appeared in the *Bolton Weekly Journal* in October 1885. It presents a grim situation, with a comical ending, and is the only fiction by Hardy to be based in the Isles of Lyonesse (the Scilly Isles).

Baptista Trewthen was induced to marry, not because she was in love but because she disliked teaching. She set off on her journey to one of the Isles to marry a rich but elderly general merchant who lived near her parents. Unfortunately she missed the boat at Pen-zephyr, and had to wait three days for the next. While waiting, she met a former sweetheart, who was so persistent that she was induced to marry him. Their plan was to catch the next boat, inform her parents, and return to the mainland. He went for a swim in the sea and was drowned. Baptista did not dare to tell her parents what had happened, and was married to Mr Heddegan. Their first stopping-place on their honeymoon was Pen-zephyr. A room was taken at an inn facing the sea; that evening, Baptista discovered that it had been occupied by the corpse of her first husband, which had been removed to the next room. She lay that night between her two husbands, the living and the dead. Heddegan suspected nothing, but the situation became serious a few weeks afterwards, when a glazier, who had consented to witness her first marriage, recognized her. The threat of being continually held up to ransom made her confess to her husband. He was pleased; he also had a confession to make. He was a widower with four children, and had married

Baptista so that she could educate them. In time she grew to like them so much that they formed the link of 'a sterling friendship at least between a pair in whose existence there had threatened to be neither friendship nor love'.

Alicia's Diary

This was written, after the Hardys' visit to Italy, for publication in provincial papers through Tillotson & Son. The most detailed scenes are in Venice (cf. *Life*, 192–5).

Alicia remained at Wherryborne rectory with her father while her mother and sister Caroline stayed with friends at Versailles. Here Caroline became engaged to the painter Charles de la Feste. Her mother died, and Caroline stayed in England after the funeral. When Charles came to England he fell in love with Alicia, and she with him. Disappointment at hope deferred made Caroline ill, and the two lovers agreed that only a form of marriage might save her life. The mock marriage took place, and Caroline recovered. Charles left immediately for Venice, and after a while Caroline left, without warning, to find him. Alicia and her father followed. Caroline was informed that her marriage was a false one which was undertaken for her recovery, but she was so indignant that Alicia refused to marry Charles and insisted that he should offer to marry Caroline. He agreed for the sake of honour, and told Alicia she must accept the consequences. Caroline and Charles were married in England, and Charles immediately drowned himself.

The Withered Arm

The story was published in *Blackwood's Edinburgh Magazine* in January 1888.

It belongs to a period in the early part of the nineteenth century when Wessex rustics commonly believed in supernatural agencies. Rhoda Brook was thought to be a sorceress; her dislike of the young bride Gertrude who had displaced her in Farmer Lodge's affections occupied her mind so much that one night she dreamt that Gertrude appeared as an old hag, flashing the wedding-ring on her left hand, and almost suffocating her. Rhoda seized the arm and threw the spectre to the floor. Later she discovered that Gertrude Lodge had been seized with pain in her left arm at precisely the same time. Subsequently it withered. Rhoda accompanied Gertrude on her visit to Conjuror Trendle on Egdon Heath to discover the cause of the malady. Gertrude did not disclose what she had learned, and Rhoda and her illegitimate son disappeared from the neighbourhood. Six years later, Gertrude rode to Casterbridge across the heath and made arrangements for making her blood turn – her only hope of a cure, the 'white wizard' Trendle had told her – by placing her arm against the neck of a man who had just been hanged. She did so, and her shriek was echoed by a second: Rhoda Brook stood near with Farmer Lodge. It was their son who had been executed for being present when a rick was fired by trouble-makers. Gertrude collapsed, and died in three days.

The Waiting Supper

Christine Everard, a squire's daughter, and Nicholas Long, a young local farmer, were in love; they would have married by licence had not the clergyman insisted on the squire's consent. Rumours that they were married reached the squire, who expressed his views in such a way that Nicholas felt he must go abroad to improve his fortune. Meanwhile, the nephew of a neighbouring squire had won Squire Everard's favour, and Christine was married to him. He was a traveller; the marriage was not a happy one, and he soon went abroad again. Years later, it was reported that he had been murdered. After fifteen years' absence, Nicholas returned; he was rich. Christine was the last of her family who remained; her brother had sold the manor-house, but she still had rooms there. She and Nicholas decided to marry, and had a paragraph inserted in the Wessex papers to that effect. The wife of the farmer who lived in the rest of the house prepared a supper which was to take the place of the wedding-breakfast next day. After striking seven, the clock fell full length upon the floor. Soon afterwards someone called with the portmanteau of Christine's husband, and announced that he would arrive later. When Nicholas arrived, he was told the news, and soon departed. Christine sat on in oppressive silence and suspense until she was disturbed by the farmer's wife. . . . Years passed; nothing was heard of the husband; and the lovers met regularly. Then, in the seventeenth year of their 'parallel march towards the common bourne', a skeleton was found jammed in the piles of the weir, near which they had sat so often listening to the 'sarcastic hiss' of the water 'whose rush was a material rendering of Time's ceaseless scour over themselves, wearing them away without uniting them'. A gold watch which was found with the skeleton was identified as Christine's husband's. Long deferment of hope had weakened passion and resolve. 'Is it worth while, after so many years?' Christine asked. Nicholas accepted her views, and his fervour declined.

The story clearly shows the influence of Browning's 'The Statue and the Bust', which is quoted. The theme occurs in Hardy's 'Long Plighted' (*PPP*), which begins: 'Is it worth while, dear . . .?' When revising 'The Waiting Supper' for its inclusion in *A Changed Man* (1913), Hardy heightened the suspense by substituting the arrival of the portmanteau for the husband's reappearance (Purdy, 152). It is strange that the anachronism of quoting from Browning's *Men and Women* (1855) in connection with events that took place 'fifty years ago'* escaped Hardy's notice. The story was published in two parts in *Harper's Weekly* (31 December 1887 and 7 January 1888) and *Murray's Magazine* (January and February 1888).

Wessex Tales appeared in 1888. It included the five stories: 'The Three Strangers', 'The Withered Arm', 'Fellow-Townsmen', 'Interlopers at The Knap', and 'The Distracted Preacher'.
'An Imaginative Woman' (pp. 94–6) was added to the 1896 edition.
In the 1912 edition it made way for 'A Tradition of Eighteen Hundred and Four' and 'The Melancholy Hussar' (pp. 74–5).

A Tragedy of Two Ambitions

This story was sent to H. Quilter, by request, in August 1888, for publication in his magazine (*Life*, 213). It appeared in *The Universal Review* the following December.

The two Halborough brothers had been denied the university education their mother had expected her legacy to give them; their father had become a wastrel and drunkard. They studied at home, went to a training-college for teachers, and sent their sister to a

---

* The phrase is found in the first published version of the story.

boarding-school at Sandbourne. Joshua proceeded to a theological college, and his brother Cornelius became a teacher. Joshua was the main driving-force, and he had borrowed money for the education of Rosa, who was now at a school in Brussels. Their father was an embarrassment, especially when he appeared at the theological college with a 'step-mother'. The couple were persuaded to go to Canada. Joshua was a great success in his first parish, Narrobourne, where he deliberately set out to impress the squire, Mr Fellmer, and his mother. Rosa impressed Mr Fellmer (a widower) even more, and it occurred to Joshua that 'the physical gifts of nature to her might do more for them both than nature's intellectual gifts to himself'. The marriage of Rosa and the squire was announced, but Halborough had returned from Canada and insisted on coming to the wedding. He reached Narrobourne the worse for drink, and the two brothers were afraid he would wreck their ambitious schemes. As he proceeded on his way, they saw him fall into a stream. Joshua resisted his brother's impulse to rush to his rescue. When they arrived it was too late: their father had been carried under a culvert and did not emerge. The wedding took place; Joshua was presented to a living in a small town; and Cornelius replaced him at Narrobourne. Soon afterwards their father's body was found, and Joshua took the funeral service for the 'Person Unknown'; Cornelius was unequal to the occasion. Both were present for the christening of Rosa's son, and both were disenchanted with the Church and life. They walked to the weir, where their father had slipped, and Joshua suddenly realized that his father's walking-stick, which he had stuck in the mud among the sedge after the body's disappearance, had grown into a silver-poplar sapling. (This detail did not appear in the magazine story.) Each thought it might be a happy release to end life at this place.

The Melancholy Hussar of the German Legion

It does not seem likely that Hardy interrupted the writing of *A Group of Noble Dames* – the six stories which follow – to prepare a tale on a subject which he had in mind years earlier. It may have been written in 1887 (when Hardy was the same age as the narrator). Evidence for the shooting of the deserters is contained in the research notes he compiled at the British Museum for *The Trumpet-Major*; it came from the *Morning Chronicle*, 4 July 1801 (cf. *Life*, 116). The story was sent to

Tillotson & Son in October 1889, and made its first appearance in the *Bristol Mirror and Times* the following January.

Phyllis Grove lived with her father, a retired doctor, at a village in the downs, five miles from Budmouth. The York Hussars, one of the regiments of the German Legion, were encamped on the downs, and Phyllis fell in love with one of them, Matthäus Tina, a sad-looking corporal from Saarbrück, who, like many of the Germans, wished to be at home. Phyllis was engaged to Humphrey Gould, but his protracted stay at Bath led her to think she was free. Matthäus divulged a plan for escape by boat, and she consented to accompany him. While waiting near the highway for this flight, she saw Humphrey alight from a stage-coach, and overheard a conversation which suggested that he was still true to her. She therefore refused to accompany the hussar, only to learn that Humphrey was married. Several mornings later she saw the regiments lined up on the down, two empty coffins before them. Two soldiers were shot. Phyllis recognized one of them, and fainted. Matthäus and his friend Christoph Bless had landed on Jersey, assuming the island was the French mainland. They had been brought back to England, and made an example to the remainder of the Legion. The two bodies were buried behind the church, and Phyllis tended the graves until her death.

The First Countess of Wessex

The story was woven round the life of Elizabeth Horner, the wife of the first Earl of Ilchester (and the mother of Lady Susan of Stinsford House; see p. 485). It first appeared in *Harper's New Monthly Magazine* in December 1889.

Squire Dornell and his wife Susan quarrelled over the marriage of their daughter Betty, who, when she was a mere girl, had been taken by her mother, during her father's absence, and married to Stephen Reynard in London. Squire Dornell favoured Charles Phelipson, with whom Betty fell in love. When Stephen returned to England about six years later to claim his wife, Betty deliberately contracted smallpox to avoid him. In doing so she unwittingly put her lovers to the supreme test; it was Stephen Reynard, not Charles Phelipson, who proved equal to it. On hearing of Stephen's return, the squire had risen from his sick-bed and ridden to Bristol to persuade him to waive his rights, but the mission had failed, and the squire's exertions hastened his death. In deference to her late husband's wishes, Betty's mother urged her to postpone her union with Stephen, only to discover that they had been meeting at several places, and that it was necessary for him to join her publicly as soon as possible. They were very happy. Stephen became an earl, and Betty, the first Countess of Wessex.

The Lady Penelope

The story relates to Lady Penelope Darcy of Wolfeton House near Dorchester. It was published in *Longman's Magazine* in January 1890.

This beautiful and vivacious lady had three ardent suitors, and said jokingly that she would marry all three if they would be patient and not quarrel. She married Sir George Drenghard, who soon died of 'convivialities'; she had hoped to marry Sir William Hervy next but he was abroad, and at length she accepted Sir John Gale. She was very unhappy, and when he died, after a visit by Sir William, gossip had it that she had poisoned him. Sir William did not hear of this rumour until after he had married Lady Penelope. He decided to go abroad again. Later, his wife heard the rumour, and the thought that this was the reason for her husband's long absence caused her to grieve and pine away. He returned. She protested her innocence, but died within a few weeks. Sir William consulted his physician, who told him that, at the request of a relative of Sir John's, he had made a private examination and found that Sir John died of natural causes. Sir William was stung with remorse, and left the country, never to return.

Barbara of the House of Grebe

This story was founded on the life of Barbara Webb, wife of the fifth Earl of Shaftesbury. It was published with the next five stories as *A Group of Noble Dames* in *The Graphic* (December 1890) and *Harper's Weekly* (November–December 1890). They were written at intervals when Hardy disengaged himself from the problems involved in adapting *Tess of the d'Urbervilles* for serialization. For comments on the story, see p. 542.

A young earl, Lord Uplandtowers, was bent on marrying Barbara Grebe, but she eloped with Edmond Willowes. Such was her father's love, and so pleased was her mother with Edmond's attractiveness, that they were soon reconciled to the marriage, and decided to send Edmond abroad with a tutor to complete his education. He was shockingly disfigured in a fire at a Venetian theatre, while rescuing people from the flames; when he returned, Barbara was so horrified at his appearance that he could not think of staying with her, but decided to go abroad for a further year before testing her feelings again. He died six months later and Lord Uplandtowers married Barbara.

He was irritated at her lack of warmth, and discovered that her love for Edmond had revived with the arrival of a beautiful statue of him, which Edmond had commissioned for her while he was at Pisa. Lord Uplandtowers discovered from Edmond's tutor exactly what form his disfigurement had taken, and had the statue hacked to simulate the 'human remnant', the 'écorché', which had confronted Barbara when Edmond had at length dared to remove his mask. With heartless and relentless insistence, he made Barbara face this image night after night until she broke down in terror and revulsion, and promised the Earl that she would love him for ever. She became utterly dependent on him and submissive to his will, and bore him eleven children in nine years. At length, she was taken abroad by her husband 'to try the effect of a more genial climate on her wasted frame'. She died at Florence, a few months after her arrival in Italy.

The Marchioness of Stonehenge

Lady Caroline, courted and flattered by many young noblemen and gentlemen, fell in love, by reaction, with the son of the parish-clerk, and married him secretly. She soon discovered they had little in common, and, anxious about her position, grew critical. He was a sensitive youth with a weak heart, and her sharp words provoked a spasm from which he died. It was past midnight; she conveyed the body downstairs from her room and finally to his door, where she laid him, placing the door-key in his hand. Soon afterwards she met Milly, the girl he had admired, told her what had happened, and persuaded her to pretend that she and the young man had been secretly married, and that she had carried him home to prevent discovery by her parents. Milly agreed, appeared in widow's weeds, and took delight in tending his grave. The posthumous romance became a living reality to her, and Lady Caroline grew jealous. Finding herself pregnant, she felt that the truth must be told. Milly would not give up her 'husband', however. Lady Caroline confided in her mother, and they left for London, Milly leaving soon afterwards, ostensibly for the north of England; she went to London, and came back with an infant.

Two or three years later, Lady Caroline married the Marquis of Stonehenge, 'who had wooed her long and phlegmatically'. Milly was most devoted to her 'son', who became a soldier and attained the rank of quartermaster when he was still young. Lady Caroline was left a childless solitary widow, and wished to claim her son. Milly objected, but said he must decide. The young man was not altogether surprised at the Marchioness's disclosures; he rejected her overtures. She had neglected him, while Milly had been a mother to him. Bitter disappointment at what appeared to be unrequited love 'was the beginning of death to the unfortunate Marchioness of Stonehenge'. She died of a broken heart.

Lady Mottisfont

Sir Ashley Mottisfont proposed to Philippa Okehall, asking her at the same time if she would show interest in a little village girl he had 'found in a patch of wild oats'. Philippa willingly agreed, and they were married in Wintoncester Cathedral. The young wife visited the girl, and grew so fond of her that she persuaded her husband to have Dorothy live with them at Deansleigh Park. A contessa came to live at the next manor – the same person, it proved, who had made indirect overtures to acquire Dorothy. Sir Ashley thought she should have the girl, and an incident which occurred while they were at Bath brought mother and child together (Philippa had already perceived the relationship). When the child said she preferred to live with the contessa, she was allowed to go. When the contessa wished to marry again, however, Sir Ashley was anxious that Philippa should take charge of Dorothy. Philippa steadfastly refused; by this time she was expecting a child. Formerly 'doubly-desired' and now 'doubly-rejected', poor Dorothy was returned to the kind cottage-woman who had brought her up as a baby; she became inured to the hardships of poverty, and married a road-contractor.

The Lady Icenway

Maria Heymere, who lived with her uncle in the west of England during the reign of George III, married a Dutchman named Ander-

The County Gaol entrance, Dorchester (on the site of the old archway, and rather similar in design. See Casterbridge, the County Gaol)

George III statue,
Weymouth (Budmouth)

Lanhydrock House (near Bodmin, Cornwall), which suggested Endelstow House

Waterston House, from which Bathsheba Everdene's 'bower' at Weatherbury was drawn

ling. On their way to Guiana, where his business lay, they passed through London, and there (as he confessed when they were crossing the Atlantic) he discovered that his first wife, from whom he had separated on discovering her scandalous reputation, was still alive. On hearing this, Maria insisted that she return to England and announce his death. He agreed. She returned home, donned a widow's garb, and gave birth to a son. She then married Lord Icenway, who lived on the other side of Wintoncester. Later Anderling arrived with the news of his wife's death. He left the country at Lady Icenway's request, but, after losing his wealth in reckless gambling, returned to see his son. Lady Icenway learned that Anderling had been engaged as Lord Icenway's under-gardener. He behaved with the utmost propriety, and two years passed. Lord Icenway's reproaches that he had no heir made Maria think of Anderling. It was too late: he was critically ill, she discovered, and dead within a few days. Lord Icenway grew crustier and crustier, and complained that she could bear her former husband a son, and not produce an heir for him. 'Ah! if only I had thought of it sooner!' she murmured.

Squire Petrick's Lady

During the eighteenth century Timothy Petrick by his legal astuteness gained possession of many estates, including Stapleford where he lived. When he was over eighty, his son was dead, but he had two grandsons, Timothy and Edward. Timothy's wife Annetta gave birth to a son whom she called Rupert; shortly afterwards she died, having confessed that the boy was the son of the Marquis of Christminster. Timothy persuaded his grandfather to ensure that 'the intruder' did not inherit his estates. Grandfather Petrick died, and Timothy resolved that he would not marry again. He envied his brother's marriage to a viscount's daughter, but began to love Rupert and take pride in his aristocratic blood. He wished he had not had his grandfather's will altered, and post-dated the earlier will to make it effective. It was not disputed. Years later, Timothy met the physician who had been adviser to his wife's family and learned that Annetta had been subject to a form of hallucination which made her believe her dreams to be realities. On further inquiry, he found that the Marquis had been abroad during the whole period of Annetta's marriage. As the boy grew up there could be no doubt about his paternity: he had the Petrick nose. Timothy wished his son had more aristocratic lineaments, and treated him more and more coldly.

Anna, Lady Baxby

During the Civil War, Lady Baxby found herself besieged in Sherton Castle by a Parliamentarian army under her brother. Her husband was absent raising forces. Anna's brother urged her to flee before he attacked. She rode out to him and told him she would be found buried in the castle if he levelled it to the ground as he threatened. He delayed his attack, and had to retreat when General Lord Baxby's troops arrived. Lady Anna reproached her husband for supporting a king whom he had once agreed with her brother in criticizing. They quarrelled; Lord Baxby went to bed; and Lady Baxby decided to go over that night to her brother. She took the precaution of putting on her husband's cloak and hat, and was just leaving the castle when she was accosted by a Sherton girl who was waiting by appointment for her husband. Lady Baxby returned and ensured that her husband did not leave the castle that night. He had, in fact, forgotten his engagement. They did not quarrel again, it is said, and Lady Baxby remained with him through the vicissitudes which culminated in a long exile. Lady Baxby had been removed from the castle by the time it was besieged and taken by Fairfax.

A Group of Noble Dames. The last six stories were set in a sketchy, almost skeletal, framework of the traditional *Decameron* kind to produce the 'short novel' which was commissioned by *The Graphic* as early as April 1889. A tincture of dramatic *vraisemblance* or appropriateness may occasionally be found between narrator and story (compare the sentimental member's story with the after-dinner tale told by the 'thoroughly primed' churchwarden). Two points about the setting should be noted: the pervasive irony of stories which associate deceit, hypocrisy and cruelty with noble bearing in 'dear, delightful Wessex', where 'the honest squires, tradesmen, parsons, clerks, and people still praise the Lord with one voice for His best of all possible worlds'; and the relative insignificance of lords and ladies as they assume their final place in geological time with the ichthyosaurus and varnished skulls of Vespasian's soldiery.

Hardy used an author's licence in the invention of these stories, but as most of them were based on the genealogical histories of living families, he took great risks. What local repercussions there were have been largely dissipated by time, and until records are found must remain conjectural. 'The Doctor's Legend' (pp. 81–3) may have been excluded for fear of giving offence. Five stories are based on Hardy's detective work in Hutchins's *History and Antiquities of the County of Dorset*: 'The First Countess of Wessex'; 'Barbara of the House of Grebe'; 'Squire Petrick's Lady'; 'Anna, Lady Baxby'; and 'The Lady Penelope'. For a sixth, see pp. 93–4).

In order to meet the wishes of the editor of *The Graphic*, several of the stories had to be 'chastened' (cf. *Life*, 227). The problem was a trivial one compared with that which confronted Hardy in preparing *Tess of the d'Urbervilles* for two levels of the reading public. The stories were journey-work undertaken as relief from a major and intricate preoccupation, and, to judge by the syntactical errors which remain, he does not appear to have attached great importance to them.

A Group of Noble Dames was enlarged for volume publication in 1891 to include ten stories: 'The First Countess of Wessex'; 'Barbara of the House of Grebe'; 'The Marchioness of Stonehenge'; 'Lady Mottisfont'; 'Squire Petrick's Lady'; 'The Lady Icenway'; 'Anna, Lady Baxby'; 'The Lady Penelope'; 'The Duchess of Hamptonshire'; and 'The Honourable Laura'. Miss Rebekah Owen noted that they were all 'true' except the second, and added that Hardy's information came from old people who knew 'old family servants of the great families' concerned (Weber, *Hardy and the Lady from Madison Square*, Colby College Press 1952, 238).

The Doctor's Legend

The conclusion of the story suggests that it was written for *A Group of Noble Dames*. Two reasons may be advanced for its exclusion: the first is that the Lady Cicely of the story is a minor figure; the second is that Hardy was afraid of offending a local family. The story was published in America only, in *The Independent* (26 March 1891). See pp. 415 and 209.

A young man of the last century owned a small estate 'not more than half a dozen miles from the Wessex coast'. He kept a jealous eye on his property, and was much annoyed because a little girl, the daughter of a neighbouring widow, would trespass on his lawn in search of flowers. One day he pursued her with a cane, and so terrified her, as she escaped his clutches, that she fell to the ground in an apoplectic fit. She was carried home by the gardener who had observed the scene. It seemed that fright had deprived her of her reason. Her hair came off, her teeth fell out, and she was called 'Death's Head'.

The young squire married Lady Cicely, the daughter of an ancient and noble family. One evening she was returning home by the light of the harvest moon when the widow and her child were in the churchyard. As the lady was passing, the mother hurried her child to the churchyard wall, pulled off her hood, and told her to grin. Lady Cicely shrieked with terror and fell to the ground. Great anxiety arose, as she was expecting a child in the spring, but no evil consequences seemed to result.

On the death of his uncle, the squire inherited a large fortune, and bought an abbey and its estates. A year later he was made a peer. His son, who was 'exceedingly timid and impressionable', grew up and married a beautiful woman who was a sculptress of great skill. The widowed mother seemed to have been 'blasted out of existence by the success of her long-time enemy. She declined and died, her death having, happily, been preceded by that of her child.'

The abbey was too small for the wealthy lord, and the village was close to his very doors. He had it removed to make way for extensions, and built a new village with 'convenient' cottages and a small 'barn-like' church a mile or more away; but the villagers still intruded upon his privacy. They loved to ring the abbey bells. He sold them.

Soon afterwards his wife died. The renovation of the peer's residence continued, and the abbey was pulled down wing by wing. The cloisters and the tombs of the abbots were removed, and it seemed there never would be an end to the removal and reburial of bones. The lord told the workmen to throw the 'wormy rubbish' into any ditch they could find. His son's wife asked if she could have a skull to copy in designing a marble tomb for a church in London. The son was much depressed by what he saw.

One evening he returned to his home in London much the worse for liquor. He entered the studio to look for his wife, and, by the light of a candle which he held unsteadily above his head, caught sight of a sheeted figure with a death's head above it – the draped dummy which his wife had set up to copy. Next morning it was discovered that he had shot himself at a tavern.

People said that his death was a retribution for his father's wickedness; few could know how his mother had been terrified almost to death by the sight of 'Death's Head'. Some said the lord, like Herod, died of 'the characteristics which he had imputed to the inoffensive human remains'. A fearless dissenter preached a sermon on the Sunday after the funeral, taking as his text Isaiah xiv. 10–23.

Whether as a Christian moralist he was justified in doing so, the doctor left others to judge. His listeners continued gazing thoughtfully at the fire at the conclusion of the story.

Old Mrs Chundle

The last of the stories for *A Group of Noble Dames* was completed not later than the beginning of May 1890. 'Old Mrs Chundle' may have been written earlier; the MS. indicates 'about 1888–1890'. It was first published in the *Ladies' Home Journal* (Philadelphia) in 1929 by arrangement with Mrs Hardy, and with a note to the effect that it was the only short story by Hardy which had not been published. A limited edition (Crosby Gaige, New York) followed almost immediately. Sydney Cockerell, one of Hardy's executors, resisted its publication. He objected to its humour, but overlooked the transforming, if not shattering, power of its pent-up irony. The reverential note on which the story ends is Wordsworthian, but the technique whereby it is achieved is startling. It has the effect on the reader which was felt by the curate, and is said to have been felt by the wedding-guest when he heard the story of the Ancient Mariner:

> He went like one that hath been stunned,
>   And is of sense forlorn:
> A sadder and a wiser man,
>   He rose . . .

Purdy (268) writes that the story is 'a true one', which 'Hardy had from Henry Moule'. This must be Henry J. Moule, Horace's eldest brother. He was a landscape artist, who became Curator of the Dorset County Museum (cf. Orel, *Thomas Hardy's Personal Writings*, 66–73); and his avocation and association with the story undoubtedly suggested the sketching curate.

The new curate at Kingscreech had been painting a distant view of Corvsgate Castle ruins; he discovered it was lunch-time and, feeling hungry, called at a nearby cottage for a meal. An old woman prepared him one cheaply. She told him she had never visited Enckworth; the only two places she visited were Anglebury once a fortnight for marketing, and the parish church at Kingscreech once a week.

When discussing the old woman with the rector, the curate discovered that she was Mrs Chundle, and had never been seen in the church. The new curate visited her to reproach her for her falsehood and persuade her to attend services. She said she had attended years ago, but was too deaf to hear anything. The zealous curate said he would obtain an ear-trumpet for her. She attended but was unable to hear a word; the curate might just as well have been 'mouthing' at her 'from the top o' Creech Barrow'. He promised that if she would try again he would have a speaking-tube fitted to the pulpit at his own expense, with the lower mouth opposite where she sat.

The next Sunday morning everything was in readiness, and Mrs Chundle sat immediately under the pulpit. It was a fine frosty morning, and the curate noticed soon after beginning his sermon that vapour arose from the bell-mouth of the speaking-tube immediately below him. This was obviously caused by Mrs Chundle's breathing, and he soon detected a suggestion of onion-stew. When he could endure it no longer, he dropped his handkerchief into the bell-mouth. Then he heard a hoarse whisper, 'The pipe's chokt!' This was repeated more loudly and hoarsely. Suddenly there was a puff of warm air, and his handkerchief floated to the pulpit floor. Mrs Chundle had cleared the tube by blowing with all her might. Some little boys in the gallery laughed, thinking that a miracle had happened. The curate dared not stop the orifice again for fear of greater disturbance; the odour, he decided, was not onions, but peppermint, and cider, and pickled cabbage. For five minutes he continued his address till he could bear it no longer; he thrust his thumb into the bell-mouth and brought his sermon to a premature close.

He did not visit Mrs Chundle during the next week, but saw her at another cottage he was visiting. She said she could hear beautifully, except when he forgot what he was doing and put his handkerchief on top of the speaking-tube. She would attend church every Sunday now. The next Sunday the ordeal was repeated. The curate did not know what to do; at length he had the speaking-tube removed. A day or two later, he received a message asking him to see her. He found the curtains of her cottage drawn, and learned that Mrs Chundle was dead. The previous Sunday she had been late setting off to church, and run up the hill, not to be late. She had overstrained her heart and been ill, and sent for him, knowing that he was anxious for her spiritual welfare. She refused to send a second message, thinking he might be visiting others in need. She had died in the assurance that she had found a friend at last, and left him all she possessed.

The curate went out 'like Peter at the cock-crow'. When he reached a lonely spot on the road, he knelt down, rested his elbow in one hand, and covered his face with the other. So he remained for a few minutes, 'a black shape on the hot white of the sunned trackway'. Then he rose, brushed the knee of his trousers, and walked on.

A Few Crusted Characters

The device for telling these brief local stories is an interesting variant of that employed for *The Canterbury Tales*. John Lackland returned after thirty-five years as an emigrant, and was travelling by carrier-van to his native village, thinking he might settle there. The other occupants of the van took a natural interest in him as a stranger, and he was soon asking about people he had known in his boyhood. One reminiscential story led to another by association and curiosity until Longpuddle was reached. Here John Lackland soon discovered that, instead of being at home, he was among strangers. He left after a few days to start life afresh elsewhere. His name suggests his plight. 'A Few Crusted Characters' appeared as 'Wessex Folk' in *Harper's New Monthly Magazine* (American and European editions) from March to June 1891.

(*a*) 'Tony Kytes, the Arch-Deceiver' (told by the carrier, Mr Burthen).

Tony Kytes was engaged to Milly Richards. He gave a lift in his waggon to Unity Sallet, another of his girl friends, on his way from Casterbridge to Longpuddle, but when he saw Milly waiting for him he asked Unity to hide under a tarpaulin. Further on he saw Hannah Jolliver looking out of a window; she was the first girl he had proposed to, and, afraid that she would be angry at his recent engagement, he asked Milly to hide under some empty sacks at the front of the waggon. Hannah joined the waggon party, and soon Tony was making advances. When he saw his father beckon to him from a field, he left the horse and waggon in Hannah's charge. His father pointed out his folly and advised him to stick to Milly. In the meantime the horse had moved on; Milly had discovered the presence of Unity, and Hannah was too staggered by the appearance of both to know what she was doing. They quarrelled; she loosed her hold on the reins, and the horse ran on down the hill, turned the corner too soon, and caused the waggon to tilt so much that all three rolled into the road. Tony came along and announced that Hannah was his choice, but her father was on the scene, and his presence ensured Tony's rejection. As his father's recommendation had made Tony averse to Milly, he proposed next to Unity. She scorned to be second choice, and there was nothing for it but to propose to Milly, who gladly accepted him.

(b) 'The History of the Hardcomes' (begun by the parish clerk, Mr Flaxton, and completed by the curate).

As a result of the prolonged dancing at Tony Kytes's wedding celebrations, two engaged couples changed their minds and their partners for life. Stephen Hardcome married Emily Darth; his cousin James, who had been engaged to Emily, married Olive Pawle. After a year or two they all began to wonder whether they had erred. They went on an outing to Budmouth, where Stephen and Olive decided to row in the bay. They rowed until they were out of sight. The next day it was heard that their bodies had been cast ashore in Lullwind Bay. A year and a half later, James and Emily married, and their marriage proved to be a happy one.

(c) 'The Superstitious Man's Story' (told by the seedsman's father, the registrar).

One Sunday the sexton noticed that the church-bell sounded dull and heavy, and concluded it meant a death in the parish. The next week Mrs Privett heard her husband William go out late in the evening, but was astonished to find him asleep in bed. The following day she met Nancy Weedle, who told her that she had been with others at the church porch the previous evening – Old Midsummer Eve – and that they had been frightened at what they had seen. Mrs Privett guessed they had seen her husband, and that he had entered the church and not re-emerged – a sure sign of his imminent death. Three days later, when William was mowing in James Hardcome's meadow, he fell asleep after his meal, and his companion saw a miller-moth fly out of his mouth. He was soon found to be dead. Later it was reported by Philip Hookhorn that William had appeared near the spring where his son had been drowned, and at the identical time of his death. (Cf. *HS*. 'Premonitions'.)

(*d*) 'Andrey Satchel and the Parson and Clerk' (told by the master-thatcher, Christopher Twink).

It was urgent that Andrey Satchel should marry Jane Vallens, and the marriage was arranged to take place at Scrimpton Church. Andrey had been up all night celebrating the christening of his neighbour's child, and was so tipsy when he appeared for the wedding that Parson Toogood refused to perform the marriage service. Jane was afraid that she might never succeed in bringing Andrey back for the marriage, and she therefore requested that they should be locked in the church until he was sober. For fear that they might be seen through the windows, she persuaded the clerk to lock them in the tower. Unfortunately, both the parson and clerk went hunting and did not return until late at night. The next morning the clerk remembered that the pair had been locked in the church tower, and was alarmed lest Jane had died in childbirth. All was well, however, and after the wedding-service the hungry couple were given a good breakfast by the parson.

(*e*) 'Old Andrey's Experience as a Musician' (told by the schoolmaster, Mr Profitt).

Andrey's father once joined the choir to partake of the supper at the manor-house after the carol-singing. He was too old to pass as a chorister, but borrowed a fiddle and was admitted with the rest. Then it was noticed he was not playing. He said he had broken his bow. The squire's mother found one for him. He pretended to play, and then it was noticed that he held his fiddle upside down. He was turned out as an impostor by the squire's mother, but when the choir went to the servant's hall for supper he was there. He had been allowed to enter by the squire's wife.

(*f*) 'Absent-Mindedness in a Parish Choir' (told by the master-thatcher).

On the Sunday morning after Christmas, when the choir at Long-puddle was tired out with playing at dances night after night, it was so cold that the leader decided they would have a warming drink for the afternoon service. They brought a gallon of hot brandy and beer, and partook of it at intervals during the service. Before the long sermon was over, they were all asleep. The Evening Hymn was announced, but the tune was not played. Then a boy who sat in the gallery with the choir nudged the leader and told him to begin. By this time the church was almost dark, and the leader thought he was still at the previous night's party. He immediately struck up the popular jig, 'The Devil among the Tailors', and the rest followed suit. The squire never forgave them. It was the last time they played in the church, and a barrel-organ was installed.

(*g*) 'The Winters and the Palmleys' (told by the aged groceress). The central character in this story is Jack Winter; see pp. 511–12.

(*h*) 'Incident in the Life of Mr George Crookhill' (told by the registrar).

George Crookhill overtook a young farmer on the way from Melchester fair, and, when it began to rain, suggested that they should share a room for the night at Trantridge. Early in the morning when the farmer was asleep, Crookhill dressed in the farmer's clothes and rode off on his horse; a transaction at the fair made him feel that the disguise was expedient. The farmer was pleased to find that his money was not stolen, and did not seem to mind the substitution of poorer clothes and an inferior horse for his own. Two miles on, he saw Crookhill struggling with two constables. He would have turned away had he not been called upon for assistance. Crookhill was arrested as a deserter, who had robbed a farmer of his clothes and money and left him with his military uniform. He protested that the young 'farmer' was the man they were looking for, but he was handcuffed and marched away. The chief constable soon saw that he was not the man. The deserter, helped by 'his double shift of clothing', escaped, and Crookhill was given a light sentence for stealing.

(*i*) 'Netty Sargent's Copyhold' (told by 'the world-ignored local landscape-painter', Mr Day).

Netty Sargent lived with her uncle, and was courted by Jasper Cliff. He was more interested in her uncle's house, which was copyhold and held 'upon lives' in the traditional way. When Netty's uncle died it would become the squire's property unless the ownership was renewed. Jasper supplied the money for this, but Mr Sargent kept deferring the renewal. When at last, upon Netty's insistence, all was in readiness for the new agreement, old Mr Sargent died. Netty decided to act immediately. Her uncle's body still sat in his wheel-chair. She pushed it to the table near the window, and opened his eyes to make it appear he was reading the Bible which she had placed open upon the table. Then she sent for the squire's steward, and persuaded him to witness the signature from the garden, explaining that her uncle's hand was a little paralysed and would need her assistance. As she took his hand, she stepped between him and the window. The agreement was signed and accepted. Jasper married Netty, and did not treat her kindly. When she complained to the neighbours, she confessed what she had done to please him. After the squire's death, his son heard the story; at the time she was a 'pretty young woman' and he a 'pretty young man'; he raised no objections.

For Conscience' Sake

This story was published in *The Fortnightly Review* in March 1891.

Mr Millborne, a bachelor of means, was able to retire early from banking in London, and felt that he ought to marry a woman he had deserted twenty years earlier. She was beneath him socially, and it had been inexpedient for him to marry her. He still had no wish to be married; nevertheless, for conscience' sake and against the friendly advice of a doctor whom he consulted on the subject, he travelled to Exonbury, where she and her daughter Frances taught music, and proposed to her. Mrs Frankland (who posed as a widow) declined; finally it was agreed that the marriage would elevate her daughter's social status and increase the prospects of her marriage to a young curate at Ivell.

After their marriage, Mr and Mrs Millborne settled in London. They spent a holiday in the Isle of Wight, and were joined by the curate, the Reverend Percival Cope. While they sailed in a yacht, the sea was so rough that all were ill except Mr Cope. He noticed the changing complexions of his companions, and was struck by the physiognomical resemblance between Mr Millborne and Frances. His inquiries led Frances to probe further, and her mother admitted that Mr Millborne was her father. The engagement was at a standstill, and mother and daughter were much embittered against Mr Millborne. They accepted his suggestion that he should rent a manorhouse for them near Ivell; he saw them off at the station, and then went abroad. At Brussels he was delighted to read that his daughter and the Reverend Percival Cope were married. Having done everything possible to make amends, he felt that he had earned 'the reward of dishonourable laxity', and had to be helped home occasionally by his servant through having imbibed a little too much.

To Please His Wife

This was first published in *Black and White* in June 1891.

After several years' absence, the sailor Shadrach Jolliffe returned to Havenpool and paid his addresses to two girls, Emily Hanning and Joanna Phippard. When Joanna saw that Emily was in love with him she was so jealous that she could not give him up. Shortly after their marriage, Joanna's mother died, and it was decided that Shadrach could not go to sea again. The young couple took a grocer's shop, but Shadrach was not a successful businessman. Two boys were born. Meanwhile Emily had married Mr Lester, a thriving merchant, and lived almost opposite the grocery shop. She also had two boys. Joanna had to serve in the shop, and it galled her to see Emily enjoying affluence and genteel society, with a governess to take care of her children. Ultimately she persuaded Shadrach to go to sea again to make money for the children's education. He returned with what he thought a fortune, three hundred guineas; but it was not enough to keep up with the Lesters. Shadrach said that he could make more if he took his sons with him. They sailed in the *Joanna*. Months after the brig's return was overdue, Joanna was so destitute that she accepted asylum at the Lesters'. Eventually she came to think that Emily's plan was to keep her away from her lost ones when they returned. One dark night she thought she heard steps and the voices of Shadrach and her sons in the street. She hurried out – nobody was visible; she knocked up the occupant of her old house to see if anyone had come. The young man answered her kindly, for he knew 'how her baseless expectations moved her': 'No; nobody has come.' (Cf. *LLE*. 'The Sailor's Mother'.)

On the Western Circuit

The story is dated 'Autumn 1891'. It was published, somewhat bowdlerized in *Harper's Weekly* and *The English Illustrated Magazine* at the end of 1891.

At Melchester, a young barrister, Mr Raye, on his western circuit from Wintoncester to Casterbridge and beyond, fell in love with a beautiful country girl named Anna. He saw her several times, and won her 'body and soul'. In due time he returned to London, and wrote to her. He received a most charming letter in return. Anna could neither read nor write; she had been brought up on the Great Mid-Wessex Plain too far from a school to be educated, and lived at Melchester with Mrs Harnham, who had written to Mr Raye for her. The correspondence continued, and soon Mrs Harnham's feelings were so involved that she wrote for Anna independently. She was a lonely woman, who had married an elderly wine-merchant at an early age. Anna found that she was with child, and Mrs Harnham wrote so tenderly and intelligently that Mr Raye was completely won over and felt that his career would not suffer if he married Anna. Despite Mrs Harnham's entreaties, Anna had to leave Melchester, and in her absence Mrs Harnham continued the correspondence with 'a flow of passionateness as was never exceeded'. She wished she were in Anna's position. She accompanied Anna to London, and the marriage took place. Mr Raye discovered that Anna could not write, and that 'in soul and spirit' he had married Mrs Harnham, whose thoughts turned to him as she joined her husband at Melchester. At the same time Mr and Mrs Raye were travelling by train to Knollsea for their honeymoon. His only relief came from re-reading all those sweet letters signed by 'Anna'.

The Son's Veto

This highly charged story, smouldering with indignation against the inhumanity engendered by class superiority, was published in *The Illustrated London News* in December 1891. A printer's error has led readers to think that Hardy was inconsistent and careless; for 'black' hair, read 'back'. Hardy told Rebekah Owen (p. 430) that he thought this his best short story.

Mr Twycott, the vicar of Gaymead, was a widower. During an illness, he was tended by his parlourmaid Sophy, who slipped as she was walking downstairs with a tray, and was never able to walk again. She decided she must leave, but the vicar could not part with her and married her. Having 'committed social suicide', he left the country and took a living in London, where he died. Sophy was left with a boy, for whose education she spared no expense. Already he had lost his childhood sympathy; he was painfully conscious of his mother's social inferiority and her grammatical lapses. In the early hours of the morning she would watch from her window the country waggons passing loaded with vegetables for Covent Garden. Her love of the country returned. She was watching one morning when she saw Sam Hobson walking beside one of them and gazing at the house-fronts as he passed. She had fallen in love with him when he was the gardener at Gaymead; hearing of Mr Twycott's death, he had taken on the managership of a market-gardener's business near London in the hope of meeting Sophy again. She called to him as he passed on the return journey, and their acquaintance was renewed. He wished to have a greengrocer's business at Aldbrickham and marry her. She wanted nothing more, but felt that her son's education must have first consideration. She found that her son's opposition to the marriage was inexorable. He proceeded from a public school to Oxford. During an Easter vacation he made her swear before the cross and altar in his bedroom that she would never marry Sam Hobson. 'His education had completely ousted his humanity.' She pined away, grieving that she could not marry Sam, and was buried at Aldbrickham. A middle-aged man stood mourning by the largest fruiterer's shop in the town as the vehicles passed by, while, from the mourning-coach, 'a young smooth-shaven priest in a high waistcoat looked black as a cloud at the shopkeeper standing there'.

The Fiddler of the Reels

The story was posted to Messrs Scribner, New York, on 13 January 1893 (*Life*, 252), and its close link with the Great Exhibition of 1851 in Hyde Park suggests that it was written specially for the 'Exhibition Number' of *Scribner's Magazine* which was published in May 1893 to mark the Chicago World Fair.

The fiddling of Wat Ollamoor – nicknamed 'Mop' from his abundance of hair – had a peculiar fascination. Caroline Aspent had to dance to his music as he stood fiddling on his doorstep at Lower Mellstock; and thereafter, when she learned that he was playing at a dance, she had to be present. She lived at Stickleford, and Mop frequently passed through on his way to Moreford, where a woman he spoke of as his Intended lived. Caroline was jealous; she met Ollamoor secretly several times, and rejected her wooer Ned Hipcroft, who went to work in London.

Four years passed, and the Great Exhibition was opened. Ned

received a letter from Caroline saying that she wished to marry him. He at length wrote to say that, should she come to him and apologize, he would marry her. She arrived by excursion-train, with a girl of three or so. Ollamoor's, he guessed; Caroline did not deny it. He was sorry for them (for they had been exposed to wind and rain on the journey), took them home, made tea for them, and soon found that he liked the child and had forgiven her mother. After their wedding, he took Caroline to the Exhibition. Here she thought she caught sight of Wat Ollamoor.

One autumn, when Ned had found it difficult to obtain work, he decided they would return to Stickleford. They travelled by train to Casterbridge, where Ned stayed to inquire about employment. Caroline and her girl walked on towards Stickleford in the evening dusk, and rested at the Quiet Woman Inn. Many people were present after a local auction, and there was Mop, preparing to fiddle. Once again Caroline fell under the spell and had to dance. She was very tired and about to go when he started 'My Fancy-Lad', a tune she could not resist. One by one people dropped out of the reel until she was dancing alone; finally she collapsed.

At this juncture Ned arrived. Caroline was in convulsions, weeping violently. Suddenly it was discovered that her girl and Ollamoor had disappeared. A search was made on the heath opposite, in vain. Days and weeks passed; then it was heard that a man answering his description had been seen in London playing a violin, with a girl dancing on stilts. Hipcroft was upset at the loss of little Carry, and went to live in London again. For hours in the evenings he searched in the streets for her. It was generally assumed that Ollamoor had emigrated with her to America, where he may be performing now, an old scamp of nearly seventy, and Carry a woman of forty-four.

Master John Horseleigh, Knight

In the Havenpool marriage-register, we read that John Horseleigh, Knight, married Edith, the wife of the late John Stocker, on 14 December 1539. There is no record of the marriage in the long and elaborate pedigree of the Horseleigh family, where we read that Sir John married the daughter of Richard Phelipson of Montislope. Perhaps a local tradition explains the mystery.

One evening a young sailor named Roger landed at Havenpool, learned that his sister's husband Stocker had died, and that Edith had married again about a year previously. She was last heard of at

Oozewood in Upper Wessex. Roger found her there, at the house of a timber-merchant named Wall, with a baby. Edith explained that her husband John was a gentleman who lived in the next county and visited her secretly. Roger was very suspicious, and followed John from Oozewood one Saturday night to a mansion near Ivell. In the morning, he saw him escorting a portly dame to chapel, with two girls and a boy beside them. He learned that he was Sir John Horseleigh, Knight, and that his wife was the daughter of Richard Phelipson of Montislope. Then he went to Casterbridge, where he drank heavily before returning to Havenpool. The next day he went to Oozewood and told Edith what he had seen and heard. She would not believe him, and pushed him out as steps were heard outside. It was Sir John. Roger rushed in, and a tussle ensued in which the Knight was stabbed. Before he died, he explained that Dame Horseleigh, who had borne him three children, was legally the wife of another man who had been a rebel, but had been discovered to be alive overseas; his wife had thought he was dead. The King had advised Sir John to wed Edith, and she was his only lawful wife. Edith retired to Havenpool, and Roger was never seen again in England.

The story appears to have been planned for *A Group of Noble Dames*. This is borne out by the introduction ('said the thin-faced gentleman'); the historical basis was found in Hutchins. The appended date suggests that the story was revised or completed in the spring of 1893. It was published in *The Illustrated London News* and in *McClure's Magazine* (New York) in the summer.

An Imaginative Woman

It is not known when this less mature story – based on a contemporary psychological fantasy, which is inconsistent with the story of 'Squire Petrick's Lady' – was written, but a note for December 1893 (*Life*, 260) should not be overlooked: 'Found and touched up a short story called "An Imaginative Woman".' It may owe something to the poetical 'Bovaryism' of the heroine in Miss Braddon's *The Doctor's Wife* (1864). See (ed. Evelyn Hardy and F. B. Pinion) *One Rare Fair Woman* (1972).

For their holiday at Solentsea, the Marchmill family took rooms at Coburg House; to accommodate them, the landlady, Mrs Hooper, had to let them have apartments belonging to a poet, Mr Robert Trewe, who was away 'on the island opposite'. Ella Marchmill wrote poems under the pseudonym of John Ivy. Mr Marchmill was a gunmaker and had little in common with his wife; he went yachting without his wife, who was a poor sailor. She bathed, walked, read Trewe's poems until she knew his last volume by heart, and tried in vain to emulate them. It was not the intellectual but the personal element in the poems which fascinated her. One day she put on his macintosh, hoping that it would inspire her. She declined to go yachting with her husband, as Mr Trewe was expected to call for some of his books. He did not call. The landlady told her where she could find his portrait, and Mrs Marchmill thought that the poet with his large dark eyes (showing 'an unlimited capacity for misery') was nearer to her than her husband, though she had never seen him. She placed the portrait by her bedside and rapturously read his poems again. When she heard her husband's footsteps, she pushed the picture under his pillow. There it remained until her husband discovered it the next morning. She was looking at it yesterday, and 'it must have dropped in then', she explained. Hearing that the poet was calling in a week's time, she wished to prolong the holiday. Her husband agreed to stay for the rest of the week, but the poet did not come.

When she returned home she began a correspondence with him, which lasted for two months. She then heard that the brother of her husband's friend was with him in Wales, and she invited them to call. The friend, a landscape-painter, arrived alone, explaining that Trewe was too depressed to see anybody. His last poems had been unfavourably reviewed. In answer to her question, the caller informed her that the poet had received letters from John Ivy; he was not aware that Mr Trewe was interested in Ivy or his poems. A day or two later she read in a newspaper that Robert Trewe had committed suicide at Solentsea; his last volume of verse was entitled 'Lyrics to a Woman Unknown'; a letter which was read at the inquest indicated that he had never known a tender, devoted woman, and that the imaginary quest for such an unattainable creature had inspired his last volume. 'If only he had known of me!' cried Mrs Marchmill. She wrote to Mrs Hooper for a lock of his hair and his photograph, and these she received. She went to Solentsea to attend the poet's funeral. Marchmill guessed her intentions rightly, and found her beside his grave, Months later, she died in childbirth, after attempting to tell him what happened at Solentsea, 'how she wanted a fuller appreciator, perhaps, rather than another lover . . .'.

Nothing further was said. Two years later, in turning over papers he wished to destroy before his second wife entered the house, Marchmill came across the lock of hair and photograph, and found that the child, 'by a known and inexplicable trick of Nature', bore strong resemblance to Trewe. She *had* been false; the dates confirmed it: 'the second week in August . . . the third week in May. Yes . . . yes. . . . Get away, you poor little brat! You are nothing to me!'

Life's Little Ironies was published in 1894. It contained nine stories: 'The Son's Veto', 'For Conscience' Sake', 'A Tragedy of Two Ambitions', 'On the Western Circuit', 'To Please His Wife', 'The Melancholy Hussar of the German Legion', 'The Fiddler of the Reels', 'A Tradition of Eighteen Hundred and Four', and 'A Few Crusted Characters'.

'An Imaginative Woman' (which was added to the 1896 edition of *Wessex Tales*) replaced 'The Melancholy Hussar' and 'A Tradition of Eighteen Hundred and Four' in the 1912 edition of *Life's Little Ironies*, 'as being more nearly in its place, turning as it does upon a trick of Nature, so to speak'.

A Committee-Man of 'The Terror'

Some of the few stories published after the appearance of *Jude the Obscure* may have been written earlier; some were written in fulfilment of commitments (*Life*, 286). None of them is outstanding. 'A Committee-Man of "The Terror" ' is slight; it was published in *The Illustrated London News* in November 1896.

It tells of the arrival of a Frenchman at Budmouth during the cessation of hostilities in 1802–3, and the growth of his acquaintance with Mademoiselle V—, an *émigrée* whose family he had sentenced to the guillotine when he was a member of the Committee of Public Safety. He was not a Bonapartist, but she could not forgive him. As she realized his poverty, she grew to like him. When George III arrived, security measures made it advisable for him to leave. He proposed marriage, and she suddenly realized she loved him. The wedding-day was fixed, but when she received a letter from a friend whose fiancé had also been executed by the Committee of Public Safety her animosity revived. She decided to flee, and booked the only seat available on the London coach. As her feelings had subsided by the time she reached Melchester, she returned to Budmouth. Here she found a letter from her lover stating that, in deference to her scruples, he had released her and was taking the evening coach to London. Then she remembered seeing someone like him among the outside passengers of the coach on which she had travelled. She remained a governess in Weymouth, and died in complete ignorance of what had happened to 'her family's foe and her once affianced husband'.

The Duke's Reappearance

The story is a traditional one, which was handed down in the Swetman family from which Hardy was descended on his mother's side. It was published in *The Saturday Review* and *The Chap-Book* (Chicago) in December 1896.

One July morning just before dawn, Christopher Swetman at his home on the outskirts of King's Hintock heard a man approaching. When Swetman called to him, he said he needed shelter. He was a tall dark cavalry man, who urgently requested a suit of yeoman's clothes in exchange for his own and his sword. The exchange was made, and the stranger given lodging. The next morning was Sunday. Stragglers who had gone to the support of the Duke of Monmouth returned with news that a battle further north had been fought at midnight; the Duke's forces had been defeated, and he had fled. In the afternoon, Swetman found the stranger attempting to kiss his daughter, and dismissed him at once. The stranger apologized for his abuse of hospitality, requested permission to retain his yeoman's clothes, and departed after supper. He left foreign money, an Andrea Ferara sword which he stated to have belonged to his grandfather, the plume of the Prince of Wales, and portraits of King Charles and his Queen. Some days later it was reported that the Duke had been captured disguised as a countryman. One night Swetman was disturbed; he saw a man with large haggard eyes – who seemed to be the stranger – remove the precious articles from their hiding-place and withdraw. He found that the articles had disappeared. Rumour spread that it was not the Duke but one of his officers who had been executed. Swetman always believed that it was the Duke who had visited him, and that he had escaped from the country. (Cf. *HS*. 'At Shag's Heath'.)

A Hardy Companion

The Grave by the Handpost

This was published as a Christmas story in *St James's Budget* and *Harper's Weekly* in 1897.

William Dewy, Michael Mail, and others of the Mellstock choir used to tell how the Chalk-Newton choir arrived at the intersection of Sidlinch Lane and Long Ash Lane one Christmas Eve just in time to witness the last of the burial of old Sergeant Holway, who had committed suicide on hearing that his son, whom he had persuaded to join the army, was unhappy in India under General Wellesley, and resented not being allowed to stay at home as he had wished. The choir played a carol over the grave in sympathy, and were moving off when who should arrive but Luke Holway, the sergeant's son, himself. He was completely upset at what his rash words had done, but made arrangements for the choir to bury his father in the graveyard at Chalk-Newton if the rector would agree. As was expected, he was not antagonistic like the young parson at Sidlinch, and arrangements were made for the sergeant's reburial. Luke had a tombstone inscribed before he left to fight in Spain. When it was discovered that his father had been buried with a stake through his body, nothing was done. After serving with honour in Spain and at Waterloo, Luke returned and discovered that his father's dishonour had not been removed. He lived alone at Chalk-Newton. On Christmas Eve the choir made its rounds as usual, and the next morning Luke was found shot through the head at the crossroads where his father lay buried. He had left a note asking to be buried with him, but it was not discovered until he had been buried in the churchyard at Chalk-Newton.

A Changed Man

The story is an indirect tribute to the work of Horace Moule's father, the vicar of Fordington, during the cholera outbreaks of 1849 and 1854 (cf. *Life*, 391). It was published in *The Sphere* and *The Cosmopolitan* (America) in the spring of 1900.

The —th Hussars reached Casterbridge with their splendid band. Soon it was noised abroad that they were always followed by a ghost. The curate of the chapel-at-ease which was attended by the troops objected to the playing of the band on Sunday afternoons, as it reduced his congregations; and Captain Maumbry was so impressed by him that the band-playing ceased, much to the disappointment of Laura, a Casterbridge lady whom he had just married. The curate's influence went further: Captain Maumbry, again to his wife's disappointment, announced that he intended to enter the Church. He became a curate at Durnover, where cholera broke out. His wife took lodgings at Creston near Budmouth, and became acquainted with an infantry lieutenant. When his regiment was due to move to Bristol, she agreed to go with him. On their way, they skirted Casterbridge and came to Durnover. Here Laura found her husband so worn out with burning the clothes of the infected that she had to stay to assist him. The lieutenant went his way. Mr Maumbry had caught cholera, however, and died within two days. Six weeks later, the lieutenant returned and asked Laura to marry him. There was no material obstacle to the union, only the 'thin figure' of 'that unconscious one . . . moving to and fro in front of the ghastly furnace in the gloom of Durnover Moor'. What happened to the lieutenant is not known; Mrs Maumbry lived and died a widow.

Enter a Dragoon

This was published in *Harper's Monthly Magazine* in December 1900.

Selina Paddock and John Clark would have married had not her father objected that John was leaving the country on military service in a day or two. It was learned that he was killed at the battle of Alma. Two or three years later when Selina was about to marry Bartholomew Miller, she received a letter to say that her former lover was coming to see her. She realized her mistake in assuming that John had been killed when she read 'James Clark' in the list of killed and wounded. As she had a son out of wedlock, she was naturally anxious to marry John. He arrived when Bartholomew was present making final preparations for the wedding. A party was arranged. After a meal, dancing began; and Selina and Sergeant-Major Clark danced together. He continually regretted that he had not come earlier, and finally suggested that they should emigrate to New Zealand. John learned incidentally that she had intended to marry Mr Miller, and as the dance proceeded looked ill but insisted on finishing it. He had to sit down, and died soon afterwards. He had had a heart-attack. He was buried with military honours at Durnover. Bartholomew still wished to marry Selina, but grew tired of waiting. She insisted that she was Mrs Clark, 'John's widow in the eyes of Heaven'. Bartholomew married someone else. One day Selina went to the churchyard, as was her custom, to tend John's grave, and found another widow there with a small boy. The widow told her that John had married her on returning from the Crimea, but had left her after a few months, threatening to emigrate to New Zealand.

A Changed Man. Of Hardy's published but uncollected stories, two had been written for young people:

'The Thieves Who Couldn't Help Sneezing', published by *The Illustrated London News* in *Father Christmas: Our Little Ones' Budget* in 1877, and

'Our Exploits at West Poley', a story for boys, first published in *The Household* (Boston) in six instalments, 1892–3, but written as early as 1883. It was rediscovered by Professor R. L. Purdy and published by the Oxford University Press in 1952.

Omitting these, and the semi-fictional 'How I Built Myself a House', published in *Chambers's Journal* in 1865, there were fourteen published but uncollected stories when Hardy made his last revisions of the novels and short stories for the 1912 Wessex edition. Two remained uncollected: 'Destiny and a Blue Cloak' and 'The Doctor's Legend' ('Old Mrs Chundle' was published posthumously). The other twelve were added to the series in 1913 under the title of *A Changed Man*. They are:

'A Changed Man'; 'The Waiting Supper'; 'Alicia's Diary'; 'The Grave by the Handpost'; 'Enter a Dragoon'; 'A Tryst an at Ancient Earthwork'; 'What the Shepherd Saw'; 'A Committee-Man of "The Terror"'; 'Master John Horseleigh, Knight'; 'The Duke's Reappearance'; 'A Mere Interlude'; and 'The Romantic Adventures of a Milkmaid'.

DRAMA

THE DYNASTS

Interest in the French Revolution and the Napoleonic Wars was kindled in Hardy when he was very young (cf. *TM*. preface). From his grandmother he heard stories of the Revolution and of the threatened invasion of England (cf. pp. 356–7). At this time Hardy's grandfather was a volunteer (cf. *WP*. 'The Alarm'); after the war he bought a highly illustrated periodical containing Gifford's *History of the Wars*. Hardy was fascinated by it: 'The torn pages of these contemporary numbers with their melodramatic prints of serried ranks, crossed bayonets, huge knapsacks, and dead bodies, were the first to set him on the train of ideas that led to *The Trumpet-Major* and *The Dynasts*.'

He was too busy to give the subject a great deal of thought until he had completed his first novel, *The Poor Man and the Lady*. A few months later, in June 1868, he recorded a full outline of a narrative poem, the subject of which was the Battle of the Nile. It was never completed. Hardy had to think of a career, and it was not until he set to work preparing *The Trumpet-Major* that he was able to pursue his Napoleonic researches on a considerable scale. In the meantime the subject had not been forgotten. In 1874 he made an entry in his notebook: 'Let Europe be the stage and have scenes continually shifting.' Later, he was surprised to find that he had contemplated a drama on Napoleon as early as this; 'Can this refer to any conception of *The Dynasts*?' he added (Evelyn Hardy, *Thomas Hardy's Notebooks*, 45). The following year he talked to Chelsea Pensioners who had fought at Waterloo (*Life*, 106). In 1876 he visited the Waterloo battlefield and

101

spent some time trying to find the scene of the Duchess of Richmond's ball (*Life*, 110). On returning to England he visited Chelsea to discuss the battle once again 'over glasses of grog' (*Life*, 111). In June 1877 he was contemplating a 'grand drama', based on the wars with Napoleon, or a single campaign. His interest in Josephine is noteworthy: the play might be called *Napoleon* or *Josephine* or by some other person's name (*Life*, 114). He wrote to Admiral Sir Thomas Hardy's daughter to gain information about his life (117). In October 1878 he was at Chelsea Hospital again, and talked to a pensioner who had served under Sir John Moore in the Peninsula and fought at Waterloo (123). The following year he carried out many researches in Dorset and at the British Museum, particularly for the background of *The Trumpet-Major*. He reverted to the idea of a 'Great Modern Drama' on the Napoleonic Wars in 1880 (*Life*, 146). By March 1881 he was thinking of a Napoleon whose actions were 'automatic . . . Not the result of what is called *motive*'. Here, he noted later, was the germ of 'a philosophic scheme or framework as the larger feature of *The Dynasts*' (148). In 1886 his growing sense of mankind as a whole made a significant contribution to his plans: 'The human race to be shown as one great network or tissue which quivers in every part when one point is shaken. . . . Abstract realisms to be in the form of Spirits, Spectral figures, etc.' These 'Realities . . . hitherto called abstractions' were to be 'the true realities of life', and 'the old material realities' only 'shadowy accessories' (*Life*, 177). This may not seem to be the principle followed in *The Dynasts*; the human scenes are not shadowy, but they are subordinated to the Spirits, and the Spirits – of compassion, or love of destruction, for example – are clearly the crucial elements in the progress of civilization; the note on Altruism (*Life*, 224) is relevant. Nearly all his spare time in London in 1886 was spent in the British Museum Library and elsewhere, considering the question of *The Dynasts* (*Life*, 183). Further entries in Hardy's *Life* (cf. 195–6, 221, 225, 247) show that he was continually thinking of his project in terms of growing magnitude. In 1891 he had in mind 'A Bird's-Eye View of Europe. . . . It may be called "A Drama of the Times of the First Napoleon" ' (*Life*, 234). When he gave up writing fiction, there can be no doubt that Hardy looked forward to the completion of a work which had been his major interest for many years. He lost very little time. In October 1896 he was studying the field of Waterloo a second time, and planning a drama provisionally called *Europe in Throes*. It was to be in three parts, each of five acts. His researches continued; he had scores of volumes on the subject by French and English historians in his library at Max Gate; and he was fastidious to the last degree and to the very end. When he could not find time to visit the British Museum, and he needed information or verification which he could not find at home, Miss Florence Dugdale worked willingly for him at the British Museum. *The Dynasts* was published in three parts, in 1904, 1906, and 1908.

The evolution of Hardy's plans shows that four of its main characteristics had been accepted long before the work was begun.

The first, with special reference to Napoleon, was that the action should be 'mostly automatic. . . . Not the result of what is called *motive*, though always ostensibly so, even to the actors' own consciousness' (27 March 1881: *Life*, 148). Here, it seems, however much we may rationalize in defence of Hardy's viewpoint, lies the source of one of the common objections to the philosophy of *The Dynasts*.

The second that of the human race as one organism: 'The human race to be shown as one great network or tissue which quivers in every part when one point is shaken, like a spider's web if touched' (4 March 1886: *Life*, 177). It is doubtful whether this conception is related to the submergence of individuality in the crowd (noted at the end of *DR.* xvi), which, in London, appeared as 'an organic whole', a creature or monster, its movements being like that of a wheel (*Life*, 131, 137, 171). This suggests automatic behaviour; cf. *D.* (2) VI v (the 'Wheel'), and *Life*, 140, 184. Rather it is, in anticipation, the existing basis for Hardy's hope that all men will ultimately realize that 'No man is an island'; that Altruism will spread 'by the pain we see in others reacting on ourselves, as if we and they were a part of one body. Mankind, in fact, may be and possibly will be viewed as members of one corporeal frame' (*Life*, 224). The centre of altruism must move 'from humanity to the whole conscious world collectively', since, as evolution shows, 'all organic creatures are of one family' (*Life*, 346). It is for this reason that Hardy showed animals and butterflies suffering in the carnage of Waterloo, as well as peoples in their various cities and nationalities 'writhing, crawling, heaving, and vibrating'. In an age of dynastic struggles, such altruism had not evolved; but it is the only hope for humanity. Not until such a consciousness informs the General or Immanent Will, will It 'fashion all things fair'. That such was Hardy's belief is clear not only from *The Dynasts* but also from the Apology to *Late Lyrics and Earlier*, written after the First World War. The collective organism exists for such a development, as the Fore Scene to *The Dynasts* shows:

> A new and penetrating light descends on the spectacle, enduing men and things with a seeming transparency, and exhibiting as one organism the anatomy of life and movement in all humanity and vitalized matter. . . .

(Cf. *MV*. 'The wind blew words', and pp. 179–80.)

The third idea – which was to determine the structure of *The Dynasts* – occurred to Hardy in conjunction with the second. 'Abstract realisms to be in the form of Spirits, Spectral figures, etc. The Realities to be the true realities of life, hitherto called abstractions. The old material realities to be placed behind the former, as shadowy accessories.' This implies the subordination of historical figures and events to the higher realities which are to be found in the supernatural framework of *The Dynasts*, pre-eminently the Spirit of the Years and the Spirit of the Pities. They are higher because they are more potent to affect the destiny of humanity. They are real because the Spirit of the Years is 'By truth made free' and has no illusions about the present or future (cf. *WW*. 'He Resolves to Say No More'); and because the Spirit of the Pities expresses the suffering and inextinguishable hope of mankind. Once again, confirmation is found in the Apology to *Late Lyrics and Earlier*: there is no hope unless pain to all upon the globe, 'tongued or dumb', is 'kept down to a minimum by loving-kindness [the Spirit of the Pities], operating through scientific knowledge [the Spirit of the Years]'.

Lastly, we notice that when Hardy was completing *Tess of the d'Urbervilles* he was thinking of 'A Bird's-Eye View of Europe. . . . It may be called "A Drama of the Times of the First Napoleon".' The technique he envisaged was not altogether new; he had used it on a minor scale in some of the panoramic backgrounds of his novels and short stories (compare, for example, the anticipation of *D*. (1) ɪɪ iii in *TM*. xxvi). Its importance in relation to the 'realities' and philosophical perspectives of *The Dynasts* was crucial.

Two further developments in Hardy's thought were integral to his design. They relate to the First Cause and the Unfulfilled Intention, and are to be found incidentally in his novels, and more emphatically in certain poems. The First Cause or Immanent Will is unconscious of humanity and its suffering; if Its intentions had been fulfilled, It would have eliminated, after making a human race sensitive to pain, all the evils and defects of nature: 'The emotions have no place in a world of defect, and it is a cruel injustice that they should have developed in it' (9 May 1881: *Life*, 149). This complaint is echoed by the Spirit of the Pities:

> But O, the intolerable antilogy
> Of making figments feel!

The second development has been anticipated. It was the hope that sentience would in time inform the Will until the Intention was fulfilled and all things fashioned fair. Hardy's hope for this rested on mankind. It is not clear, however, how the altruism of man could affect Nature's inclemencies, which are a significant part of the 'universal' harshness in *Tess of the d'Urbervilles* (cf. the Arctic birds, xliii).

The view that 'The will of man is by his reason sway'd' was introduced as a comic irony by Shakespeare, and was one to which Hardy could not subscribe: 'The will of a man is ... neither wholly free nor wholly unfree. When swayed by the Universal Will (which he mostly must be as a subservient part of it) he is not individually free; but whenever it happens that all the rest of the Great Will is in equilibrium the minute portion called one person's will is free ...' (*Life*, 335; cf. *LLE.* Apology, and *Life*, 368). Men are continually actuated by forces of good and evil (*D.* (2) II iii). During a dynastic struggle, when national or imperial passions are overriding, man cannot be considered free; cf. (2) I iii (the Chorus of Pities on 'the soul of a nation distrest'). Events may turn popular passions from hatred to hero-worship; cf. (3) IV vi and V iii. Man is subject not only to 'the rest of the General Will' but to defects and taints of character (cf. *HS.* 'On the Portrait of A Woman about to be Hanged'). It is in this sense that 'character is fate' (*D.* (2) VI vi; *MC.* xvii). At the outset of *The Dynasts*, the Spirit of the Pities observes that 'the large potencies' instilled into Napoleon's 'idiosyncracy' are 'taking taint'; and it is significant not only that his first act is to crown himself King of Italy as God's Elect but that Hardy endows the scene with 'the preternatural transparency' which reveals 'the volitions of a Universal Will, of whose tissues the personages of the action form portion'. In such issues, Hardy seems to be saying, men are swayed by forces which usurp human judgment (cf. the note of 20 October 1884: *Life*, 168). After his final defeat, Napoleon admits his folly:

> Yes, 'tis true. I have ever known
> That such a Will I passively obeyed . . .
> To shoulder Christ from out the topmost niche
> In human fame, as once I fondly felt,
> Was not for me.

In a crisis, a cool leader like Wellington is shaken in the web of the Immanent Will, and is seen 'acting while discovering his intention to act' ((3) VII vii).

Before rejecting or impugning this view, it should be noted that Napoleon does not say that he always obeyed the Will passively; there were times when he was not swayed by irrational forces. Less debatable is Hardy's contention that the decisions of men like Napoleon sway the lives of nations. So we proceed from cause to effect; but where does cause begin? The whole complex of causes throughout the universe constitutes the Immanent Will. In this network, character is a contributory cause. Modern scientific theory supports Hardy's view: 'The whole antecedent world conspires to produce an occasion' (A. N. Whitehead, *Nature and Life*, Cambridge U.P., 1934). Thinking only of human forces, in the rage of battle, Hardy, through the Spirit of the Years, speaks of

> A Will that wills above the will of each,
> Yet but the will of all conjunctively.

Scientific thought affected Hardy's outlook so completely in his early years that one must approach the question of his indebtedness to some philosophers very guardedly. Assuming certain premises – the idea of Crass Casualty, for example, which Hardy had reached not later than 1866 – his philosophy is simple and logical. He was capable of observing and thinking for himself to an unusual degree, and the fact that his views find support in Schopenhauer and Hartmann may often be coincidental. 'My pages show harmony of view with Darwin, Huxley, Spencer, Hume, Mill, and others, all of whom I used to read more than Schopenhauer', he wrote, when Helen Garwood sent him a copy of her doctoral dissertation, 'Thomas Hardy, an Illustration of the Philosophy of Schopenhauer' (1911). He may, nevertheless, have been indebted to Schopenhauer and Hartmann for the formulation of his impressions. The idea of the Will rather than the First Cause can be attributed to Schopenhauer; and J. O. Bailey provides evidence of close parallelism in further refinements of thought between Hardy and Hartmann in his *Thomas Hardy and the Cosmic Mind*. Yet Hardy always insisted that the idea of the development of consciousness in the unconscious Will was his own (*Life*, 335, 454: 'At any rate I have never met with it anywhere'). It may have occurred to him notionally when reading John Stuart Mill's *Three Essays on Religion* (1874), without having been adopted as a possibility until much later when he had forgotten its origin. His disagreement with the un-redeemed pessimism or determinism of Schopenhauer was stated about 1890 (*TD*. xxv), and he does not appear to have derived much hopeful philosophy from Hartmann (*LLE*. Apology).

Of the literary influences which had a bearing on the shaping of the supernatural framework in *The Dynasts*, only one or two are of special interest. With the commentary of the Greek Chorus on dramatic action, Hardy was, of course, familiar; he may have owed something to 'the semi-dramatic, contrasted, philosophical reflections' at the end of Goethe's *Faust* (Weber, *Hardy of Wessex*, 243). It is not likely that he missed Robert Buchanan's *The Drama of Kings* (1871), the first part of which is centred in Napoleon Bonaparte. The fact that in 1888 he thought 'A Drama of Kings' a suitable title for his projected work does not imply familiarity with Buchanan's work; rather the reverse. Yet, at some time or other, Buchanan's 'strange Intelligences' acting as Celestial Spectators may have given him the clue he wanted. On the other hand, Hardy did not need to look outside his favourite poet Shelley to find the form and spirit which he wished to express in the contemplation of war and wrong. The aerial spirits and song of *Prometheus Unbound*, and the chorus and semi-choruses of *Hellas*; pity for human suffering expressed by the spirits in the former; the uncertain optimism with which the latter concludes – all have their counterpart in *The Dynasts*. The Shade of the suffering Earth may also have been suggested by *Prometheus Unbound*. More significantly, Shelley's spirits 'come from the mind Of Human kind', and, like Hardy's Chorus of the Years (cf. *Life*, 321), are 'the flower of Man's Intelligence' (*Prometheus Unbound*, iv 93–122; *D*. (1) VI viii). An even more Shelleyan note enters the Chorus of Pities in the Fore Scene:

> We would establish those of kindlier build
> In fair Compassions skilled . . .
> Those, too, who love the true, the excellent,
> And make their daily moves a melody.

In Shelley's lyrics and *Prometheus Unbound,* music and musical imagery are associated with happiness and the ideal.

The Spirit of the Years represents the modern intellectual outlook unswayed by emotion. His growing scientific knowledge reveals man's turmoils as a relative insignificance in the universe of space and time ((1) I vi; (3) VII ix; After Scene). There was a time when he believed in a merciful God, as does the Spirit of the Pities, but time has proved his faith a dream. The 'bounded prophecy' with which he is endowed is a dramatic device, without philosophical significance; cf. (1) V v, (2) VI vii, (3) IV ii. Hardy does not pretend that the truth is known; we must face it as it is seen by 'the passionless Insight of the Ages'. The Absolute may always be concealed from man (conclusion of the Fore Scene; cf. *Life,* 410).

The Spirit of the Pities represents the heart of man, his awareness of 'Creation's groan' and human suffering in particular. He approximates to ' "the Universal Sympathy of human nature – the spectator idealized" of the Greek Chorus'. A 'mere juvenile' ((1) I vi, V iv, VI iii – cf. *JO.* VI iii), he is 'impressionable and inconsistent . . . as wrought on by events' (preface). When, like Hardy, he criticizes the Will for having made men sensitive to pain, the more experienced and philosophical Spirit of the Years urges patience, and suggests that judgment is not possible until evolution has run its course ((1) V iv). It is on the existence and growth of the Spirit of the Pities that hope for humanity depends, however.

Hardy accepted Horace Walpole's view of life (p. 209). When he began *Tess of the d'Urbervilles,* he wrote: 'If you look beneath the surface of any farce you see a tragedy; and, on the contrary, if you blind yourself to the deeper issues of a tragedy you see a farce.' He illustrated the first half of the observation in the novel (xxi, xxix), and the second in *The Dynasts* through the Spirit Ironic (and elsewhere; see (3) IV iii). Less neutral than the Spirit of the Years, the Spirit Ironic observes the discrepancy between illusions and reality with a sly detachment and humour; cf. (2) VI iii. Sometimes his comments are set in a Gilbertian key, e.g. (1) VI v, (2) V vi, VI vi. He finds irony in the logic of the Spirit of the Years and the illogicality of the Spirit of the Pities ((1) I vi); yet 'the intolerable antilogy' felt by the Spirit of the Pities seems logical to him, and his observation that war is conducted

> by frenzied folks who profit nought
> For those who profit all

is one that in the course of time could make war an irrelevance. Such is the hope of the Spirit of the Pities ((1) IV v, (3) VII viii, (3) IV iv).

The Spirit Sinister and the Spirit of Rumour are subordinate. Though his views are sometimes almost those of the Spirit Ironic, the Spirit Sinister takes pleasure in destruction and evil; cf. (1) II v. His spirit exists in the human race, though he is the 'Iago of the Incorporeal World' ((1) I vi) and repugnant to the Spirit of the Years and the Spirit of the Pities. It is significant that his role is slight and diminishing, while that of the Pities assumes a growing importance as *The Dynasts* proceeds.

The Spirit of the Years, the Spirit of the Pities, the Spirit Ironic, and the Spirit Sinister all present ways of looking at the human spectacle; they are human realities, and therefore subject to the Will ((1) II ii, VI viii). Their second function is to present historical links, which are not sufficiently important for descriptive scenes or dramatic action; sometimes they prepare the reader for coming events. This may be done individually and dramatically, as when the Spirit of Rumour talks to a Parisian prostitute and tells her the latest news of Napoleon just before his approach ((1) VI vii). Less convincingly, in the tradition of classical gods and their messengers, they impart intimations and premonitions to mortals; cf. (1) II i, II ii, V vi, (3) I i, VI ii. The guise is new, but the convention hackneyed, like that (honoured by Shakespeare in *Richard III*) when, the night before the battle of Waterloo, a vision of skeletons and corpses from various battlefields, with the Duke of Enghien as showman, passes before Napoleon.

Hardy's greatest innovation in *The Dynasts*, and the key to its general design, was his cinematic technique. From the Overworld with its cosmonaut view of Europe, we move by swift or graduated transitions from 'bird's-eye' or panoramic spectacles on land or sea to close-ups in battle, from scenes in cities or open country to interiors which range from palaces or a cathedral to a cellar in Spain. Sound-effects are not forgotten; we hear, for example, the din and shrieks of battle, and, 'endowed with enlarged powers of audition as of vision', we detect the clink of icicles hanging from the hair of stragglers in their disorganized retreat from Russia. (We leave the battlefield of Waterloo with the stench of gunpowder in our nostrils.)

Aerial views have more than a visual function; by the reduction of armies to caterpillars and insects, for instance, they create a sense of individual insignificance, and promote the vision of the Spirit of the Years, who sees the upheaval caused by Napoleon's 'flings' as the gyration of animalcula in tepid pools (Fore Scene), and the whole Napoleonic struggle as 'but one flimsy riband' in the 'web Enorm' of causation in space and time (After Scene).

A kind of X-ray device discloses the 'anatomy' of the Immanent Will, and its volitions twitching the puppet-like Napoleon. These visual aids are a crude simplification, and one feels that the commentary of the Spirit of the Years would be better without them. Hardy's 'knowings of the Unknowable' – see (3) VII viii – and his attempts to represent Its operations, whether in terms of jack-o'-clocks or puppetry, are self-defeating, and constitute the main weakness of *The Dynasts*. The mechanism creaks repeatedly.

Scenes are presented dramatically or by spectacle; sometimes in the commentary of the Spirits themselves. The action lasts from 1805 to 1815:

Part I: England is threatened by a French invasion. Napoleon, after crowning himself as King of Italy, finds .that his navy has not engaged the English fleet, and, lacking protection for his transports across the Channel, turns to defeat the Austrian and Russian allies. The Austrians capitulate at Ulm. Pitt has failed to persuade Prussia to join the Alliance. The French navy is defeated by Nelson at Trafalgar. The Russians and Austrians are defeated at Austerlitz. The death of Pitt. Throughout, Napoleon regards England as the enemy and schemer, and the allies as its hirelings.

Part II: Prussia enters the war, and is defeated at Jena. Napoleon reaches an agreement with Russia at Tilsit. Having secured peace in the rest of Europe, he turns to Spain. The escape of Godoy, the Queen's favourite, from the Spanish mob. English forces sent to the aid of the Spanish patriots. The French fail to defeat them at Vimiero. The English retreat to Coruña, where the French are repulsed and Sir John Moore is killed. The Austrians take up arms and are defeated at Wagram. The French fail in Spain in the battle of Talavera. An abortive English expedition to the island of Walcheren. Napoleon casts round to rid himself of Josephine and secure an heir; he marries Maria Louisa of Austria. The battle of Albuera in Spain. Scenes representing the aged and failing George III, the Prince Regent, and rumours of a split between France and Russia.

eatherbury Upper Farm': the sheep-washing pool, a 'glistening Cyclops' eye' to ...ds on the wing; part of the great barn — from the tithe-barn at Cerne Abbas ...bot's Cernel)

Puddletown (Weatherbury) Church

The Devil's Den (the Devil's Door) near Marlborough

Part III: Two campaigns which are to result in the defeat of the
French begin with the French crossing the Niemen in Russia, and
the English crossing a ford at Salamanca in Spain, where the French
are decisively beaten. The Old Guard marches past a picture of
Napoleon's son, the young King of Rome, while Russian soldiers
kneel before their icon and other religious insignia borne by priests
at Borodino, where the Russian campaign begins bloodily. The
French enter Moscow to find it deserted. The burning of Moscow,
and the French retreat. The onset of winter, and the crossing of the
Beresina river; winter and the Russians reduce the French army to a
remnant. In Spain, the French are routed at Vitoria. Austria and
Prussia join Russia, and defeat the French at Leipzig. Meanwhile,
Wellington has neared the south border of France. The allies enter
Paris, and Napoleon abdicates. The death of Josephine.

Napoleon's escape from Elba breaks up the Allied Conference in
Vienna. The plight of Marie Louise. After a scene in the House of
Commons (faithfully dull) and a comic Wessex scene, we turn to the
campaign which ends with Napoleon's defeat at Waterloo. More than
any other campaign, it reveals Hardy's persistence in ascertaining
factual detail for the historical part of his work.

A work on this scale demands continual variation to sustain interest.
For this reason, most of the one hundred and thirty scenes are short.
The most effective transitions are those which arise from cinematic
techniques. In dramatic scenes, we move from political debate and dynastic
intrigue to battles on sea and land; from the views of citizens in London
and Paris to deserters in Spain and rustics in Wessex; from carnage to
comedy; and from verse to prose. Some scenes, it may be thought, assume
undue proportions; perhaps Hardy attributed too much importance, for
example, to the higher drama of the Josephine scenes and Napoleon's
preoccupations with heirship; the Godoy scenes are vividly presented but
insufficiently related to the dynastic struggle to forward the action. The
question of such proportions is arguable but not highly pertinent. More
important is the question of Hardy's verse. The scenes of major significance in the historical action are in blank verse; its general uniformity
is mediocre. Hardy's preoccupation not to lose the *vraisemblance* of speech
suggests that he would often have been more successful with prose. His
fidelity to historical records,* which is noticeable almost at the outset in

* This fidelity is general rather than absolute. For a detailed account of
Hardy's indebtedness to historical sources and the licence he took for artistic

the House of Commons debate, shackled his creativity. In battle scenes
and campaigns, he is much more effective; dramatic scenes of his own
invention are more vigorous and true to life, whether with Wessex
rustics, deserters in Spain, or, at a higher social level, at the Marchioness
of Salisbury's. Even the humdrum blank verse assumes a livelier hue
when, for a brief imaginative moment, he recalls through Captain
Hardy, just before Nelson's death, the village of Portisham which he
knew so well. Hardy was too cribbed by the massiveness of his material
for imaginative flights in the speech of his main characters. The metaphor
in

> His last conscription besomed into it
> Thousands of merest boys

is no more than a disguised cliché. A venturesome conceit suggests a
poeticizing variation of Milton's 'So, when the sun in bed . . .':

> Enjoy this sun, that rests its chubby jowl
> Upon the plain, and thrusts its bristling beard
> Across the lowlands' fleecy counterpane.

Hardy's variation of verse-forms for his aerial spirits is noteworthy;
but even here, where he was less hampered by historical considerations,
the verse is rarely equal to the theme. It is more stylized and elevated,
'concentrating the "ornaments of diction" in particular places' (*Life*, 203)
but generally stiff in texture, rough with idiosyncratic words quarried
and hacked from many a source, and studded with rhetorical rather than
functional alliteration. Incidental words and phrases are telling, but
rarely does the verse rise to poetry. The more successful 'poems' in this
strand of *The Dynasts* are those voiced by the Pities at Walcheren
((2) IV viii) and at Albuera ((2) VI iv); and that of the Pities and the Years
at Waterloo, where Hardy, for once, freeing himself from historical
action and the wearisome repetition of cosmic views, writes imaginatively
on a subject which stirred his feelings. One would hesitate to place even
this, however, among his greatest poems; certainly one would not classify
The Dynasts as a poetic drama. Its poetry is rare and incidental; more
frequently, in word and phrase, it is rather accidental. The best of *The*

or other reasons, see Walter F. Wright, *The Shaping of* The Dynasts,
University of Nebraska Press, 1967. This work includes a summary of
successive textual revisions which is of great literary interest.

Dynasts is to be found in the prose, and the verse in general must be rated as one of its drawbacks.

The play was intended 'simply for mental performance and not for the stage'. Hardy's remarks on 'a monotonic delivery of speeches' (which refer, not to *The Dynasts*, but to a way of presenting Greek and Eliza-bethan drama) have suggested that he deliberately reduced distinguishing features of character in conformity with the notion that human beings are little more than puppets twitched by the First Cause. This ignores his view that character is part of the determining complex of causes. It should be clear that Napoleon's overriding ambition contributes to his downfall, and that, though the disposition of *The Dynasts* in continually changing scenes does not allow much development of character, Napoleon is of very different stuff from the more phlegmatic Wellington, and that Nelson and Villeneuve form an obvious contrast. Hardy's dramatic genius, however, was rarely notable (outside the restricted world of his Wessex rustics); and it is this deficiency which accounts for the stylistic limitations of most of the higher drama in *The Dynasts*.

The best of *The Dynasts* is to be found in the descriptive backgrounds of dramatic scenes. Here we find some of Hardy's finest prose:

> What has floated down from the sky upon the Army is a flake of snow. Then come another and another, till natural features, hitherto varied with the tints of autumn, are confounded, and all is phantasmal grey and white.
>
> The caterpillar shape still creeps laboriously nearer, but instead of increasing in size by the rules of perspective, it gets more attenuated, and there are left upon the ground behind it minute parts of itself, which are speedily flaked over, and remain as white pimples by the wayside.
>
> Pines rise mournfully on each side of the nearing object; ravens in flocks advance with it overhead, waiting to pick out the eyes of strays who fall. The snowstorm increases, descending in tufts which can hardly be shaken off. The sky seems to join itself to the land. The marching figures drop rapidly, and almost immediately become white grave-mounds.
>
> Endowed with enlarged powers of audition as of vision, we are struck by the mournful taciturnity that prevails. Nature is mute. Save for the incessant flogging of the wind-broken and lacerated horses there are no sounds.
>
> With growing nearness more is revealed. In the glades of the

113

forest, parallel to the French columns, columns of Russians are seen to be moving. And when the French presently reach Krasnoye they are surrounded by packs of cloaked Cossacks, bearing lances like huge needles a dozen feet long. The fore-part of the French army gets through the town; the rear is assaulted by infantry and artillery.

Scenes like this are an imaginative distillation of extensive historical reading. In their clarity and succinctness, they suggest that Hardy's most enduring imaginative re-creations were predominantly visual. A higher proportion of such scenes combined with dramatic sketches of soldiers and army-followers like those of the cellar-scene in Spain would have been welcome, but would have run counter to Hardy's design of presenting the whole dynastic struggle in perspective. As it stands, it needs great actions, like those ending at Trafalgar, or with the defeat of Napoleon's plans in Russia, or in the battle of Waterloo, to sustain or quicken interest.

The question of whether *The Dynasts* has a hero is complex. Of the leading figures, Napoleon is the most central and important; others like Nelson and Wellington are the heroes of episodes. Any parallel drawn between Satan and Napoleon is rather too general to be important. Both suffer from pride at the beginning of the action; the physical deterioration of Napoleon in his last campaigns is merely a matter of history, and no reflection of design on the part of the author as with Milton's Satan; he is the prime mover in the dynastic struggle, and fitly therefore, in Hardy's vision, most conscious of being subject to the Will. Hardy was aware of the persistence of England's role in his defeat, but one cannot assume that, like Shakespeare, he presented England with conscious patriotic pride. His subject was not the heroic part played by a nation; it was rather the international suffering of humanity caused by a few. The central and most consistent role in this complex is played by the higher realities; it is in their conflict, the antinomy of the Spirit of the Years and the Spirit of the Pities, facing the reality of causation and yearning for a better world, that the tragedy of the human spirit is played. The historical spectacle is larger, but minor, and it is with the Spirits, or through them, that we contemplate life and suffering in the whole cosmic perspective of space and time as far as it is revealed. In this conflict, our sympathies are with the Spirit of the Pities, and it is significant that this Spirit, the only one that 'approximates to "the Universal Sympathy of human nature" ', grows more impressive as the dynastic conflict is waged, and gains the sympathy of the Spirit of the Years at Waterloo. This 'juvenile' learns from events, and represents the growing consciousness of the human race, which was Hardy's only hope for the future. In a new kind of drama, for 'mental performance', this is the leading part in the play. What had 'hitherto' been regarded as an abstraction is the growing and true reality, to which the 'material realities' of the Napoleonic era, large though they may be in the aggregate, are no more than 'accessories' (cf. *Life*, 177).

Some doubt about the ending may remain. It is bound up with the question whether the final chorus is that of the Spirit of the Pities. When Hardy intends a chorus of all the Spirits he writes 'General Chorus' (Fore Scene). The sequence 'Semichorus I . . . Semichorus II . . . Chorus' indicates elsewhere that the Chorus comprises no more than the preceding Semichoruses; cf. (2) vi iv, (3) i x, iii iii. It should be noted, too, that the Spirit of the Years has not changed its views; it still sees the 'All-mover'

> Moulding numbly
> As in dream,
> Apprehending not how fare the sentient subjects of Its scheme.

The conclusion of *The Dynasts* expresses therefore not a conviction but simply a cry from the heart of the human race which lives in hope. Hardy could see little cause for such hope when he wrote *The Dynasts*, and still less a few years afterwards at the outbreak of the First World War.

Hardy's reading and research before he could begin the writing of innumerable scenes in *The Dynasts* was enormous, and enough to daunt most writers. Few have attempted or achieved as much in a single work. Whatever criticisms are levelled against *The Dynasts*, they should not blind us to its greatness. It contains some of Hardy's most vividly pictorial and dramatic scenes, any one of which bears the stamp of distinction. It is not merely a massive work; in its *ordonnance*, vision, and technical presentation, it shows the artistry, integrity, and originality of a major achievement.

THE FAMOUS TRAGEDY OF THE
QUEEN OF CORNWALL

This is a minor work. Although a first draft was begun in 1916, after Hardy had revisited Tintagel with his second wife, it was not resumed until 1923. It was completed in August and published in November. It is dedicated to the four persons associated with Hardy's visits to Tintagel: Emma Lavinia Hardy, the Reverend Caddell Holder, Mrs Helen Catherine Holder (Emma's sister), and Florence Emily Hardy (see *Life*, 78, 373). The 1916 visit revived memories of his first wife: 'I visited the place 44 years ago with an Iseult of my own, and of course she was mixed in the vision of the other' (Sydney Cockerell, *Friends of a Lifetime*, Cape, 1940, 284).

For the second edition of 1924, slight alterations were made in the text after Hardy had attended rehearsals of the play by the local Hardy Players; second verses were added to Iseult's song (vii) and Tristram's song (xix); and scene xiii was expanded into three scenes.

Hardy considered the addition of songs for Rutland Boughton's setting of the play to music (*Life*, 424–6). At the end, he suggested that the dirge by the Chanters 'may be wordless, and they then may break into singing the poem called "A Spot" (or part of it) . . .' (Lois Deacon and Terry Coleman, *Providence and Mr Hardy*, Hutchinson, 1966, 139). The poem (*PPP*) is strikingly apt.

The Chanters perform the role of the Greek Chorus, and the prologue and epilogue are spoken by Merlin. The main story is conveyed in an action which coincides approximately with the time of performance and takes place in the great Hall of Tintagel Castle (as early as 1891, Hardy thought that 'the rule for staging . . . should be to have no scene which would not be physically possible in the time of acting': *Life*, 234.) The style shows measured economy and strength, but is never excitingly dramatic or highly lyrical. Some indication of its quality may be gathered from Hardy's statement that he 'tried to avoid turning the rude personages of, say, the fifth century into respectable Victorians, as was done by Tennyson, Swinburne, Arnold, etc.' (For his remarks on the play generally, see *Life*, 422–3.)

The past is recalled by Merlin and the Chanters: King Mark of Tintagel in Lyonnesse had sent Tristram to fetch his bride, the dark

Iseult, from Ireland. On the homeward voyage, they had by chance drunk a love-potion. Iseult married Mark, though she was in love with Tristram, who roved abroad and married the fair Iseult of Brittany. Subsequently, he fell a prisoner to Mark, but escaped with Queen Iseult and lodged with her at Gard Castle 'in matchless joy'. She returned to Mark, and Tristram to Iseult of Brittany. Then, when Mark had gone hunting, the Queen sent letters asking Tristram to come with his wife to Cornwall.

The action begins with the return of Mark. When he discovers that Iseult has been on a voyage, he is suspicious. On his departure, the Queen reveals that she had sailed to Brittany, but had learned that Tristram was dead. News arrives that Iseult of Brittany had led Tristram, who was ill, to believe that Queen Iseult had not come at his request. When he discovered her deception, he decided to sail for Cornwall at once. He arrives disguised as a harper, and Iseult of Brittany follows him. Tristram thinks that she should return, but Queen Iseult allows her to stay in her room. King Mark observes the lovers, creeps up behind Tristram, and stabs him. Tristram dies; Queen Iseult stabs Mark to death, and rushes off to leap over the cliff to her death. Iseult the Whitehanded returns, mourns her loss, and departs for Brittany.

The play was arranged for mummers. Hardy's use of 'monotonic' in the preface to *The Dynasts* alludes to their manner of intoning speeches, and implies the subduing rather than the suppression of dramatic accent and gesture. He believed that the 'curiously hypnotizing' effect of this kind of presentation would lend distance to the spectacle, and assist in conveying the impression that it was a dream conjured up from the remote past by the magician Merlin.

THE POEMS

Hardy was famous before any of his poems were published, and many readers besides Leslie Stephen have recognized 'the poetry which was diffused through the prose' in much of his fiction. Some, despite the trend of modern criticism, might argue that his best writing is to be found in his prose. No valid comparison is possible, however. The prime of his life was devoted primarily to prose, and most of his poetry belongs to his later years. As a writer of fiction, Hardy had to compromise with his reading public; as a poet, he pleased himself, and could express 'ideas and emotions which run counter to the inert crystallized opinion' with comparative immunity (*Life*, 284–5). Even so, some of the novels present an operative, though intermittent, poetic vision on an ampler scale than was possible in the poems, not one of which is extended in subject.

After failing to secure the publication of any of his early poems, Hardy destroyed the poorest (*Life*, 49). It is significant that he subsequently regretted having destroyed too many, and in later years seems to have preserved and published nearly all he wrote; only six unpublished poems have been discovered. Over nine hundred poems survive, and, with the exception of a few small groups, they appear to follow no regular pattern. The Hardy student would probably find a majority of the poems of interest or consequence; the seeker after poetry would continually find his freshness dulled by pedestrian or contrived verse. If the miscellaneous disposition of the bulk of the poems provides variety, it hampers continuity of interest. Hardy's poetry would have gained had he been more critical and exclusive, and had he taken pains to arrange his poems more artistically. From the first task he took refuge in the thought that posterity was the only sound arbiter of poetic merit; in anticipation of the second criticism, he voiced his regret that 'the less alert' should be 'thrown out of gear by a consecutive piping of vocal reeds in jarring

118

tonics', explained that 'irrelation was almost unavoidable with efforts so diverse', and placed his trust for 'right note-catching' in 'those finely-touched spirits who can divine without half a whisper' and 'whose intuitiveness is proof against all the accidents of inconsequence' (*LLE.* Apology). A problem which was intractable to Hardy must be even more formidable to the reader.

Certain groups emerge. They include the early poems; dramatic or 'impersonative' stories and lyrics; ballads of various kinds; 'satires of circumstance' (sketches and narrative); poems related to the novels and short stories; philosophical poems; travel and occasional poems; town and country vignettes; more personal poems (autobiographical and reflective); poems on friends and relatives; and, most personal and poignant of all, a large number which sprang from the event which stirred him more profoundly than anything else in his later years, the death of his first wife. There can be little doubt that poems closely associated in subject or experience are better read in juxtaposition than at intervals. So many of Hardy's are autobiographical and allusive (cf. *Life,* 392) that such a collocation is more than usually advantageous. The difficulty of distinguishing the autobiographical from the 'impersonative' should not be overlooked; even in single poems the personal may be interwoven with the fictitious.

The problem of reaching a reliable critical judgment of Hardy's poetry is confirmed by most selections. What is most evident about them is not the degree of concurrence but their wide range of variation and some astonishing omissions. One of the prerequisites for sounder critical evaluation is a liberal rather than slender selection from all the types of poetry in which Hardy's genius flourished. It does not seem too much to claim that nearly a quarter of his poems will repay close reading, and that of these there must be at least forty or fifty, any one of which serious readers of poetry would not willingly forgo. The verdict of Ezra Pound on reading the *Collected Poems* ('Now *there* is clarity. There *is* the harvest of having written 20 novels first') is hardly an approximation to the restrictive view of F. R. Leavis that any real claim Hardy 'may have to major status rests upon half-a-dozen poems alone'.

Hardy's first literary aspirations had been poetic (*Life,* 384–5). The poems of 1865–7 are remarkable in their relentless confrontation of the truth, however chilling. Love deceives; beauty is subject to the ravages of time; and chance and indifference rule the universe. Hardy was so

119

impressed by the wisdom of Ecclesiastes that he attempted to turn it into Spenserian stanzas (*Life*, 47). These searing convictions were not the sophistications of a disappointed young man or of a versifier bent on shocking the bourgeois. They were the product of the new scientific reading of the universe and Hardy's own observations, and they were to remain fundamentally unshaken for the rest of his life. The poet of the final poems of *Winter Words*, 'by truth made free', is the same in spirit as the poet of 'Discouragement' (1863–7). Like another sonneteer, Robert Trewe, he was intent on facing resolutely 'the worst contingencies' in nature and life; unlike the fictitious poet's (*LLI.* 1), his disillusionment was matched by a complete abnegation of poetic luxuriance. For a writer who at an impressionable age had been so drawn to English poetry that for about two years he had read little else (*Life*, 49), and whose novels (cf. *DR.* iii 2) show creatively and by quotation how much he had fallen under the spell of poetic phrases, this determination to forge his own poetic style is an index of rare critical judgment, which is far more laudable than the immediate results. It is evident that Leslie Stephen's observations on the poetic folly of mimicking the notes of one's predecessors merely confirmed Hardy's earlier convictions.

From this time Hardy wrote poems intermittently until 'the middle period of his novel-writing', when he produced few or none. Thereafter they were 'added to with great rapidity, though at first with some consternation he had found an awkwardness in getting back to an easy expression in numbers after abandoning it for so many years; but that soon wore off' (*Life*, 292). His first published collection (*Wessex Poems*, 1898) is a strange assortment, which may well have disconcerted his admirers. It consists principally of early poems, poems relating to *The Trumpet-Major* and anticipating *The Dynasts*, poems arising from the death of his cousin Tryphena Sparks, a few preliminary skirmishes with the Church, and narrative poems, sometimes dramatic in form. The Wessex element, particularly Casterbridge, is more prominent in this volume of poetry than in any other, and 'My Cicely' is encrusted with place-names recalling the historic past *pari passu* with the hero's journey to Exonbury. This fictive fancy has an air of unreality and gesticulation not far removed from the pseudo-heroics of 'Her Death and After' and 'Her Immortality':

> I'll use this night my ball or blade,
> And join thee ere the day.

A more genuine and lyrical note is struck in 'Thoughts of Phena', but the gap between this and the factitious in 'My Cicely' and 'Her Immortality' is so great that no one could have suspected that the three poems were written about the same person. The most remarkable poem is 'Neutral Tones', which was written as early as 1867; rarely did Hardy convey feeling more completely and organically through imagery, and never more intensely.

In 'Her Immortality' we have the incongruity of modern thought in an antique mode. Yet the Shade is more real than the living figures in the Gothic fantasy of 'The Supplanter' (*PPP*), with the phantom beckoning in despair from the Field of Tombs to the 'sad wight' who is seduced. The poem must rank as a Hardyesque curiosity, an egregious amalgam of the ballad-derivative and the inventive. In 'The Revisitation' (*TL*), two Hardy themes – 'Love is lame at fifty years' (cf. 'The Waiting Supper') and 'Time's transforming chisel' (cf. *The Well-Beloved*) – combine to give poignancy to the strange, almost ghostly, coincidence of the lovers' meeting by the Sarsen stone.

The last two poems suggest that Hardy had certain narrative fancies in mind, or in draft, before he finally turned from prose to poetry. The appeal of the story remained strong, and numerous ballads and 'life's little ironies' in verse were to follow. 'We cannot write living poetry on the ancient model,' Hardy wrote in 1901, copying Leslie Stephen once again with approval, a few months before he sent the manuscript of his second volume of poetry to the publishers. Yet in some of the ballads in this volume the influence of Wordsworth is clear (*PPP*. 'The Well-Beloved', 'The Widow Betrothed'). His interest in the style of *Lyrical Ballads* is illustrated in his *Life* (306); he realized that the most moving language was the least artificial and, in its diction, not remote from common speech. The earliest of his extant poems, 'Domicilium', may be his most Wordsworthian. In trying to formulate cosmic certitudes with reference to man, Hardy belongs to the nineteenth-century tradition from Wordsworth to Browning; he owes more to the style of these two poets than to any others. His is the poetry of protest born of scientific belief which allows no evasion and accepts no comfortable doctrines. Yet he turned to both of these poets because, though far apart in their poetic styles, they had, in the poetry which appealed to him most, avoided the literary and traditional manner, and expressed themselves in language close to that of life. From Browning he caught, in his earlier poetry, the trick of unfolding a story or situation to end with a moral question (cf.

WP. 'The Burghers', 'Her Death and After'; *LLE.* 'The Contretemps'; *HS.* 'A Poor Man and a Lady'). More pervasive and important is the use of speech idiom; it is less exaggerated and dramatic than Browning's, but the value of it in Browning's lyrics could not escape notice, though it passes unacknowledged. 'Between us now' (*PPP*) might pass as a Browning lyric, and a few lines in 'Under the Waterfall' (*SC*) almost echo Browning. Hardy noticed a similar characteristic in William Barnes; but for his loyalty to dialect, Barnes might have 'brought upon his muse the disaster that has befallen so many earnest versifiers of recent time, have become a slave to the passion for form, and have wasted all his substance in whittling at its shape'. By 'a felicitous instinct' he broke into 'sudden irregularities in the midst of his subtle rhythms and measures, as if feeling rebelled against further drill'. Thereby 'naturalness' was saved (preface to *Select Poems of William Barnes*, Oxford U.P., 1908). It was a principle Hardy had practised for most of his poetic career, 'the art of concealing art' (*Life*, 105) or 'the principle of spontaneity', which he had noticed in architecture, and which results in emphasis on stress rather than syllable and on 'poetic texture rather than poetic veneer' (*Life*, 301). The appeal of Hardy's best poetry resides as much in the 'naturalness' or sincerity of expression as in the integrity of feeling and outlook which it transmits.

The influence of the ballads themselves is noticeable in the repetition which marks some of his most sensational tales (*TL*. 'A Trampwoman's Tragedy', 'A Sunday Morning Tragedy', and *SC*. 'The Sacrilege'). Hardy's unpretentiousness may be gauged from the fact that he thought the first of these to be 'upon the whole, his most successful poem'. Two ballads relating to the Mellstock choir (*TL*. 'The Dead Quire' and *HS*. 'The Paphian Ball') have a legendary charm and uniqueness of vision which makes them more distinctive, and characteristic of the Hardy who, 'particularly when writing verse', believed in 'spectres, mysterious voices . . . omens . . . haunted places, etc., etc.' (*Life*, 370). Intellectually a modern, Hardy lived imaginatively in the Wessex of the past; he was fascinated by the supernatural and local superstitions; the *revenant* haunts many a poem, and omens and premonitions are a subject to which he continually returns. It would be wrong to say that he believed in them; they were part of his world and imagining, and could no more be dismissed than the intellectual probings which caused him to mourn a vanished faith (cf. *MV*. 'The Oxen').

Yet, though Hardy's choice of style was influenced by certain kinds of poetry, no poet was less imitative from first to last. Variations in diction as well as rhythm reflect subject and treatment (cf. *SC*. 'The Convergence of the Twain' and 'Regret Not Me'), but in general, as may be expected in a writer most of whose poetry was written in his later years, there is little significant development in style. Hardy's sturdy independence carried him beyond the 'natural', however, and nowhere with more bizarre effects than in the homespun diction of some of his earliest poems. He believed that language to be kept alive needed constant renewal, but his innovations are bold rather than felicitous or justifiable. He drew from various sources – dialect and archaic, foreign, and technical. His neologisms include the changing of parts of speech (*upped, inkled, smalled, colding*), the curtailing of words (*vill* for 'village', *says* for 'sayings'), hybridizations (*cohue*), and derivatives (*Byss*). The charitable reader will hold that this quirkishness reflects the author's meaning; sometimes it is almost a private language. It may become a labour-saving device, and is often ungainly. Only an admixture of obstinacy can explain the retention of such a rhyme as

> The purl of a runlet that never ceases
> In stir of kingdoms, in wars, in peaces.

'Cohue' seems to have been invented to meet the demands of rhyme. At the other extreme

> A globe that rolled
> Around a sun it warmed it at

as a rhyming conclusion to a verse in a drinking-song might be excused as a humorous improvisation. In a poem which is almost technically perfect, and which reveals an intellectual compass in cosmic philosophy far exceeding that of any other poem by Hardy, it is astonishingly inept and incongruous. Hardy's honesty could lead him into pedestrianisms and banalities which match or even out-Wordsworth Wordsworth at his prosiest. 'Her laugh was not in the middle of her face quite' inauspiciously opens a poem, much of which is uncertainly poised little above conversational idiom, and suggests interest rather than a directing and shaping force. Technically it is more interesting than many of Hardy's poems, but it suggests a rapid sketch or first essay none the less (*SC*. 'Under the Waterfall', *TL*. 'The Conformers', *WW*. 'Drinking Song', 'A Countenance').

Hardy's experiments with 'innumerable original measures, some of which he adopted from time to time' (*Life*, 301), did not lead to a style as idiosyncratic or remarkable as that of Gerard Manley Hopkins. The first poem in *Wessex Poems* is in sapphics; 'Sine Prole' (*HS*) is in a 'medieval Latin sequence-metre'. He believed that English might be enriched by adopting some of the verse-forms of Latin hymns (*Life*, 306). The simpler forms of English hymnology had a greater influence on more of his poems, however. His verses are never over-elaborate, but they display an immense variety of stanzaic forms. Few poets have used as many; in *The Dynasts* alone, the range is remarkable.

Hardy had the faculty for 'burying an emotion . . . for forty years, and exhuming it . . . as fresh as when interred' (*Life*, 378):

> But Time, to make me grieve,
> Part steals, lets part abide;
> And shakes this fragile frame at eve
> With throbbings of noontide.

In 'So Various' (*WW*) he notes his contrarieties: the zest of youth and the coldness of old age; love and fickleness; dullness and vision; melancholy and gaiety. . . . They are all to be found in his poetry. If the zest and gaiety do not preponderate, it is due partly to his philosophy of life, partly to his misfortunes, and largely to the fact that most of his poems were composed in his later years (half of them, perhaps, after he had turned seventy), when he was haunted by the 'ghosts' of the past, and unfading recollections of happiness were tinged with sadness. In youth, joy could charm 'life's lourings' (*LLE*. 'A Young Man's Exhortation'); and in poems such as 'Great Things' (*MV*) and 'Weathers' (*LLE*) he showed that he could still 'enjoy the earth no less', though

> the all-enacting Might
> That fashioned forth its loveliness
> Had other aims than my delight.

He had a rustic humour which could be turned to poetry, as in 'The Homecoming' (*TL*); and in an exquisite dramatic lyric, 'Autumn in King's Hintock Park' (*TL*), he showed that he could emerge from shadowy self-communings and contemplate serenely the revolution of growth and decay. Not for long, however, could he forget the immutable 'Frost's decree' which ran through life; nor his own disappointments:

124

Within the common lamp-lit room
Prison my eyes and thought;
Let dingy details crudely loom,
Mechanic speech be wrought:
Too fragrant was Life's early bloom,
Too tart the fruit it brought!

Looking back on life, he said that fortunately he had never expected much; but, it may be argued, he had expected too much and had never learned, like Carlyle, to accept the universe. He had found indifference instead of Providence, chance instead of plan, and a cruel illogicality in making human beings sentient and suffering. The positive faith in which he had been brought up had proved to be negative.

The novels, particularly *The Woodlanders* and *Tess of the d'Urbervilles*, had shown that Hardy could enjoy and communicate the 'loveliness' of nature, but intellectualism had destroyed the possibility of that 'intelligent intercourse' with Nature which he found in Marty South and Giles Winterborne, and fostered 'visions ghast and grim'. To one aware of 'the defects of natural laws' and the Unfulfilled Intention, 'Nature was played out as a Beauty'. Hardy rarely describes scenery for its own sake in his novels and poems. Rather it reflects or comments ironically on 'the human condition'. In the poems it is most effectively presented in quick graphic strokes as both background and expression of 'the tragical mysteries of life', as in the sequence from *MV*: 'The Five Students', 'The Wind's Prophecy', 'During Wind and Rain'. With Crabbe-like insistence, Hardy attributes beauty to the imagination (cf. *PPP*. 'On a Fine Morning' and 'The King's Experiment'; *Life*, 50 – note for 23 August 1865 – and 310, on the 'Idealism of Fancy'). His tragic outlook was more attuned to the grey landscape at Scheveningen (p. 467); the sombre, lonely face of Egdon Heath, 'slighted and enduring' (p. 314); the forlorn upland by Cross-in-Hand ('so far removed from the charm which is sought in landscape by artists and view-lovers as to reach a new kind of beauty, a negative beauty of tragic tone'); Waddon Vale at its most lugubrious (*PPP*. 'The Lacking Sense'); or the wintry scene in 'The Darkling Thrush' (*PPP*). In rhythm and imagery, in terms of felt experience, no other poem of Hardy's succeeds to the same extent in expressing his sense of alienation and deprivation. In 'The Impercipient' (*WP*) he had regretted such deprivation; here the joyful song of the thrush makes him ponder the wisdom of modern percipience:

125

So little cause for carolings
Of such ecstatic sound
Was written on terrestrial things
Afar or nigh around,
That I could think there trembled through
His happy good-night air
Some blessed Hope, whereof he knew
And I was unaware.

However much the younger Hardy had luxuriated in fine phrases in *The Golden Treasury* or in Tennyson or Swinburne, and however rich the scenes in some of his novels, where he aimed at a different reading class, it was typical of a poet resolutely opposed to illusions not to indulge in 'fulth of numbers' or in 'the jewelled line', which he regarded as effeminate. He claimed an affinity with Donne; this lay in a rejection of sensuousness and traditional imagery, in a modern scientific outlook, and a style close to speech idiom and uncompromisingly controlled. He sympathized with Swinburne's spirit of passionate revolt, and the questioning of Tennyson in *In Memoriam* and *Maud.* In the latter (as well as in Shelley's *The Revolt of Islam*, VIII v) he may have found confirmation of impressions he had drawn from scientific reading and life:

For nature is one with rapine . . .
We are puppets, Man in his pride, and Beauty fair in her flower.

But the 'bower' which had been 'shrined' to the more orthodox Tennyson was 'roof-wrecked':

He who breathes All's Well to these
Breathes no All's Well to me,

and the Wordsworthian link with the infinite had been severed (cf. 'the inland company' and 'the glorious distant sea' of *WP*. 'The Impercipient', and *MV*. 'Midnight on the Great Western').

'My opinion is that a poet should express the emotion of all the ages and the thought of his own' (*Life*, 386). In promulgating *avant-garde* convictions about man's place in a neutral rather than providential universe, Hardy often ran counter to another of his theories about poetry: 'I hold that the mission of poetry is to record impressions, not convictions . . . *Absit omen!*' (*Life*, 377–8). The wish is confessional, and the modestly defensive use of 'impressions' somewhat sophistical for the author of 'Discouragement' and *The Dynasts*. The Spirit of the Years in Hardy insisted on exegetical reiteration, and was most didactically vocal in *Poems of the Past and the Present* (when Hardy was preoccupied with *The Dynasts*). Only in terms of immediate experience were its 'impressions' conducive to poetry (compare *TL*. 'New Year's Eve', and *LLE*. 'A Drizzling Easter Morning'). Where direct expression fails, 'A Darkling Thrush' succeeds; thought and sensibility are fused in an imaginative re-creation of experience; and the poem communicates a sense of artistic and personal integrity.

Hardy's contemplation of life in *The Dynasts* is presented in three major aspects: intellectual, tragic, and ironic. Whatever their value as poetry, the poems which may be ascribed to the Spirit of the Years are indispensable for an understanding of Hardy's outlook and his plea for loving-kindness or charity. In the latter, he is at one with Matthew Arnold (compare the endings of *SC*. 'A Plaint to Man' and 'Dover Beach'); but his general attitude is less resigned and stoical, more aggressively critical and dogmatic. The Spirit of the Pities is swayed by events, and felt more deeply in the slower unfolding of a novel such as *Tess of the d'Urbervilles* than in short poems (e.g. *TL*. 'Bereft', *SC*. 'Beyond the Last Lamp'). In certain poems the tragedy is conveyed by the Spirit Ironic (cf. *WP*. 'The Slow Nature', *TL*. 'John and Jane'). Frequently it gives way to an overriding sense of 'life's little ironies'. The lure of satires of circumstance was irresistible; often the story takes precedence over the feelings, and gives the impression of contrivance. 'The Workbox' (*SC*) presents an ironical situation dramatically, but the tragic story is left unrealized in the inadequate simplicities of

> . . . poor John Wayward's coffin, who
> Died of they knew not what

and

> Yet still her lips were limp and wan,
> Her face still held aside,
> As if she had known not only John,
> But known of what he died.

'In the Days of the Crinoline' (*SC*) is no more than a competent versification of a parish joke. 'The Curate's Kindness' (*TL*), though dramatic, is little above the farcical. The mood varies from the tragic to the humorous,

127

from the satirical (cf. *PPP*. 'The Ruined Maid') to the philosophical. Often the ironical perception appears to be no more than habitual, and the sole *raison d'être* for another 'poem'. Where the situation is inherently tragic, it may have been understood too readily to be actualized, and the result gives the impression of cynical humour and superficiality, or a lack of sensibility which does not reflect the whole of Hardy's nature. The range of his responses to momentous and prosaic ironies may be judged from 'The Convergence of the Twain' (*MV*) and 'The Children and Sir Nameless' (*LLE*). Not surprisingly, some of the ironic stories have little pretence to poetry, and decline to the banal, e.g. *HS*. 'The Turnip-Hoer':

> 'What is it, Ike?' inquired his wife;
> 'You are not so nice now as you used to be . . .'

'The Whaler's Wife' (*WW*) has more to commend it as a story; but there can be little doubt that Hardy could have presented it more effectively in prose.

Hardy's creative imagination worked intermittently in his later years. The charm of recollected youth and the increasing bleakness of his philosophical outlook were expendable sources of poetry, yet he continued writing poetry until a few days before his death. A new regenerative experience was required to stir Hardy to his depths. It came, not so much with the horror of the First World War as with the sudden death of his first wife. All personal restraints and inhibitions were loosened by regrets; the past was revived with all its changing emotions, its magic lights and shades. Rarely before had Hardy been so profoundly moved by vivid recollection of his own experience and feelings. The result was a long succession of lyrical poems which form the most genuine elegy in the English language. Among them will be found some of his greatest poems (e.g. *SC*. 'The Going', 'The Voice', 'After a Journey', 'At Castle Boterel'); without them, it is doubtful whether critics would have been nearly as insistent on Hardy's claims to be a major poet.

These successes may divert attention from lyrical and dramatic poems in various other moods, e.g. *PPP*. 'The Colonel's Soliloquy', To Lizbie Browne'; *TL*. 'Autumn in King's Hintock Park', 'The Homecoming', 'She Hears the Storm'; *SC*. 'Regret Not Me'; *LLE*. 'Last Words to a Dumb Friend'; *HS*. 'Queen Caroline to her Guests'. So diversified are Hardy's poems that it is impossible to select any which are wholly typical;

and this arises inevitably with a writer who held that 'the road to a true philosophy of life seems to lie in humbly recording diverse readings of its phenomena as they are forced upon us by chance and change' over a long period. What poet has recorded so many, particularly after the age of seventy?

Wessex in Transition

Much of what follows relates to Dorset and neighbouring regions to the north and east. As Hardy went further afield for the settings of some of his stories and novels, notably *A Pair of Blue Eyes*, *A Laodicean*, and *Jude the Obscure*, Wessex assumed large cartographic dimensions, and the area (mainly Dorset) which Hardy knew best became 'South Wessex'. Yet, in terms of Hardy's work, the importance of this area is almost inversely proportional to its size in the context of greater Wessex. All that is most Wessex in character – its people, language, customs, traditions, architecture, landscape, and far-reaching history – derived from certain regions of Dorset, Hardy's knowledge of which was unrivalled in his time. His interest in the past and the passing was as great as in the present; and his sense of time and change, of the temporal linked with the universal, imparted depth to his vision of life.

The main source for Hardy's antiquarian and historical knowledge of Dorset was undoubtedly the four volumes of the third edition (1861–73) of John Hutchins, *The History and Antiquities of the County of Dorset* (first published in 1773). If his presentation of the Roman road-system is not always in accordance with modern views, it is because Hardy took Hutchins as his authority. His topographical quotations from Domesday Book, from Leland, and from Drayton's *Polyolbion* are also from that source. It was in the genealogical tables of county families that he found the background and clues for several of the largely imaginary stories in *A Group of Noble Dames*, and for many others in both prose and verse, e.g. 'The Doctor's Legend', 'Master John Horseleigh, Knight', 'The Inscription' (*LLE*), and 'Squire Hooper' (*WW*). From Hutchins too came much of his historical knowledge of places such as Mai-Dun, Casterbridge, and Shaston (Maiden Castle, Dorchester, and Shaftesbury).

For the more recent history of events at the time of the expected

French invasion (1803–5), he relied on his own researches in the British Museum, at Weymouth, and in neighbouring villages (see *TM*. preface), to give life and detail to traditions with which he had been familiar from boyhood.

His interest in age-old customs and superstitions began, no doubt, with the stories told by his mother and grandmother; his *Life* shows that this interest never waned. In answer to a correspondent, Hardy wrote: 'To your question, – if the legendary matter and folk-lore of my books is traditionary and not invented, – I can answer yes, I think, in every case, this being a point on which I was careful not to falsify local beliefs and customs' (J. S. Udal, *Dorsetshire Folk-Lore*, 176).

Witchcraft was still believed in (cf. *HS*. 'Night-time in Mid-Fall'). Even one of Hardy's cousins, like Elizabeth Endorfield, was regarded as a witch (Hermann Lea). It need occasion no surprise, therefore, that Eustacia Vye first played a rather 'demonic' role and that in the final version of the story she was regarded as a witch by many of the inhabitants of Egdon Heath. Susan Nunsuch stabbed her in the arm in church, in the hope that by drawing blood she could put an end to the spell she believed Eustacia had cast over her ailing son Johnny (cases of this kind were reported as late as 1883 and 1884). On the night of Eustacia's death, she recited the Lord's Prayer backwards as she melted the wax effigy of Eustacia which she had made and stuck through and through with pins (cf. Evelyn Hardy, *Thomas Hardy's Notebooks*, 37; *Life*, 202–3, 249). The crooked sixpence which Eustacia gave Johnny Nunsuch as a charm against witchcraft, the hour-glass which she carried (associated with Satan, *W*. xxi), the suggestion of a Witches' Sabbath as the revellers danced on Rainbarrow, the eclipse of the moon, Eustacia's living with Clym near 'the Devil's Bellows', and her dancing by moonlight at East Egdon – all these may be residual features from the original theme, though they have lost their connotations of witchcraft in the final form of the novel. When Susan Nunsuch heard her son Johnny tell Clym Yeobright what he had seen when Mrs Yeobright knocked at the door at Alderworth, and Eustacia looked out of the side-window at her, she must have thought that Mrs Yeobright was the victim of Eustacia's evil spell (*RN*. v ii. For a strange story of 'the evil eye', see *Life*, 204–5).

When Henchard was threatened with financial ruin, he wondered if someone had roasted a waxen image of him. He visited Conjuror Fall, and, before disclosing the purpose of his visit, asked him if he could cure 'the evil' (*MC*. xxvi, xxvii). The remedy was to wear the toad-bag (a limb from a toad in a small linen bag, which was worn round the neck). The cure came from the twitching of the limb, which gave the blood a 'turn' (cf. *Life*, 112).

Such a 'turn' could be effected in a more gruesome way, as when Gertrude Lodge tried the only method which Conjuror Trendle could advise to cure her withered arm – by placing it on the warm neck of a man who had just been hanged. The arm had shrivelled as if some witch, or the devil himself, had seized it. Trendle had divined from the yolk of an egg that Rhoda Brook, who was reputed to be a sorceress, had been – despite herself – the cause of the 'evil' (*WT*. 4. For this method of divination, compare the fortune-telling – in Plymouth – which disclosed that Emma Lavinia Gifford would marry a writer: Emma Hardy, *Some Recollections*, 40–1).

When Darling was found exhausted in Melbury's stable after Fitzpiers's nocturnal visit to Middleton Abbey, the stable-man insisted that the horse was 'hag-rid'. A whole series of tales about equestrian witches and demons followed (*W*. xxviii).

Witches were associated with woods. The bark-rippers told stories of white witches and black witches which had been handed down for generations. When Tess was making her return home by night along the roads of Blackmoor Vale, 'it seemed to assert something of its old character', and 'an impish multitude' of creatures presented themselves from trees and tall hedges to her fearful imagination, among them 'witches that had been pricked and ducked' (*W*. xix; *TD*. 1).

When people were ill, or anxious about the future, they consulted 'white witches' or 'conjurors' like Trendle, who claimed, or were thought to have, magical curative powers. Dairyman Crick threatened to visit one if the butter did not 'come'. Henchard went to consult Conjuror Fall about the weather, and we learn that weather-prophets calculated not only by sun, moon, stars, and clouds, but also by trees and grass, candle-flame and swallows, the smell of herbs, cats' eyes, ravens, leeches, spiders, and dung-mixen (*UGT*. IV iii–iv; *MC*. xxvi; *TD*. xxi; *WW*. 'The Catching Ballet of the Wedding Clothes').

Many common superstitions are to be found in Hardy's prose and poetry. Being married on Friday (*DR*. xii 9) was considered unlucky, but when bees belonging to one of the wedding couple swarmed on their wedding-day it was a good omen (*UGT*. v i). Presenting a lock of hair to a lover was unpropitious. The chapter which introduces this superstition (*PBE*. xxx) seems to provide 'the special verse in the *Book of Ruth*' which was used in the time-honoured ritual for divining one's luck in marriage by Bible and key (*FMC*. xiii).

The breaking of a key boded misfortune (*FMC*. xxxiii). There was a common saying, 'No moon, no man', but Christian Cantle's ill-luck was offset by his being born with a caul, which safeguarded him from drowning (*RN*. I iii, III vii). The immediacy of a letter was indicated by a burning candle-wick (*TM*. xii). In the Hintocks, it was 'the universal custom' to 'wake the bees by tapping at their hives whenever a death occurred in the household, under the belief that if this were not done the bees themselves would pine away and perish during the ensuing year' (*WT*. 6). If the eyes of a corpse were not closed, it was assumed that another death would shortly follow (cf. *MC*. xviii). A falling clock portended a death in the family (*CM*. 2). Bad luck accrued if a fortune-telling book was kept in the house at night; and being pricked by a rose was an ill-omen, like the crowing of a cock in the afternoon (*TD*. iii, vi, xxxiii, xxxiv).

A howling dog, a limp corpse, flies with 'crape scarves', the sound of deer, the screech-owl, the raven, the inexplicable striking of a clock, and a candle-shroud, all boded death (*DR*. vi 2; *MV*. 'Signs and Tokens'; *HS*. 'Premonitions', *WW*. 'Standing by the Mantelpiece'). Imagining the bell toll also portended death, but whether of the hearer (as in *HS*. 'She Saw Him, She Said') is not clear: Joseph Poorgrass, during a night of 'horrors', heard the 'news-bell' ringing in his left ear enough to indicate a murder. He had, moreover, 'seen a magpie all alone' (*FMC*. viii).

Breaking a mirror, thirteen at dinner, shivering, and the tolling of a bell as lovers parted, were all ominous (*MV*. 'Honeymoon Time at an Inn'; *HS*. 'At a Fashionable Dinner', 'The Shiver', 'A Poor Man and a Lady'). A sundial was hazardous; the person on whom it cast its shadow was fated to die very soon (*MV*. 'In the Garden'). After these dismal portents, it is a relief to recall the tradition of the oxen kneeling on Christmas Eve (*MV*. 'The Oxen').

'The Superstitious Man's Story' (*LLI*) combines three superstitions. If a church bell seemed heavy to ring, a death in the parish was imminent (cf. *HS*. 'Premonitions', to which the story is related); on Old Midsummer Night the faint forms of those who were to die during the year could be seen entering the church but not returning; and the soul of a dying person might be seen issuing from the mouth in the form of a large white moth (cf. *MV*. 'Something Tapped'). This was the 'miller-moth', sometimes called the 'miller-soul'.

Girls who sat up till midnight on Midsummer Eve (Old Style) would see their future husbands (cf. Mrs Penny: *UGT*. I viii). In the outdoor ritual (*W*. xx), the 'black art' was 'connected with the sowing of hemp-seed, a handful of which was carried by each girl'. (The hempseed was thrown over the left shoulder as the girl recited a verse to the effect that the husband would appear who was to mow what had been sown.) In the same chapter, Hardy mentions hole-digging on Midsummer Day to discover the trades of future husbands. (Listen at the hole at noon, and his occupation will be known by the noises heard: *Thomas Hardy's Notebooks*, 37.) Jude sat up after the wedding of Sue and Phillotson, and towards midnight carried out the Old Midsummer Eve practices ('I put the bread-and-cheese and beer quite ready, as the witch's book ordered, and I opened the door, and I waited till the clock struck twelve . . .', Mrs Penny related): 'His supper still remained spread; and going to the front door, and softly setting it open, he returned to the room and sat as watchers sit on Old-Midsummer eves, expecting the phantom of the Beloved. But she did not come.' Jude belongs to the modern era. (See *MV*. 'On a Midsummer Eve').

Rain on St Swithin's Day was regarded as the 'christening' of the apples (*TM*. xvii; *CM*, 12. viii).

Fat from another adder was considered a charm against adder-bite (*RN*. IV vii). In 'The Romantic Adventures of a Milkmaid' (xv), a curious practice to prevent forgetfulness of one's deceased lover is described: 'I've pulled grass from my husband's grave to cure it – wove the blades into true lover's knots; took off my shoes upon the sod. . . . To feel the damp earth he's in, and make the sense of it enter my soul.'

Most of the above superstitions and practices had lasted for countless generations. In the first half of the nineteenth century they were dying out rapidly. For Hardy they held the attraction of the unusual. He used them in stories to capture or sustain interest; in his later poems, one sometimes feels that he deliberately recorded them in the hope that they might not be forgotten.

Pagan rites were still popular. The fires lit on 5 November, such as that on Rainbarrow, are 'rather the lineal descendants from jumbled Druidical rites and Saxon ceremonies than the invention of popular feeling about Gunpowder Plot'. May Day celebrations seemed to be losing their gaiety, if we can judge by stories set nearly forty years apart (*RN.* I iii, VI i; *TD.* ii).

There were stranger practices. Wife-selling occurred in the early part of the nineteenth century, and skimmington-rides were reported in local newspapers when Hardy was working on *The Mayor of Casterbridge* (see p. 42. The custom was centuries old, and is described in Butler's *Hudibras*). On Portland, pre-marital engagements had long been accepted as trial periods to ensure that marriages would be procreative, but the 'Island Custom' was dying out (*MC.* i; *WP.* 'The Bride-Night Fire' (1867); *RN.* I v; *MC.* xxxvi, xxxix; *WB.* I ii, iv).

Mechanization in agriculture about the middle of the nineteenth century was regarded with mixed feelings (*MC.* xxiv), and with suspicion and resentment by workers. Popular prejudice against the threshing-machine may be ascribed to its presentation in 'An Indiscretion in the Life of an Heiress' (I 1) and *Tess of the d'Urbervilles* (xlvii). Hardy was a realist, however; the first presentation is merely a fictional device, and the second has a symbolical as much as a literal significance.

Agricultural labourers lived in a state of chronic hardship and poverty. Unemployment was common; and the system of supporting the destitute (often in work-houses) out of parish-rates encouraged farmers to pay low wages. In order to keep down rates, 'old Twills' employed the maltster in his younger days only eleven months a year, thus disqualifying him for parish relief if he were disabled (*FMC.* viii). The indignation of the working class led to sporadic outbreaks of rick-burning, Ludditism (the smashing of machines which reduced employment), and house-breaking. Penalties were severe, sometimes hanging, sometimes transportation. A youth who was a mere spectator when a rick was fired was hanged (see Rhoda Brook, p. 250). Poaching was common, sometimes as a livelihood, sometimes to eke out starvation wages (cf. *MC.* xxxvi; *Life*, 213). Keepers like Geoffrey Day were employed permanently by owners of wooded country to preserve game; and, in an earlier period, man-traps were set against marauders. Grandfather James recalled the non-appearance of a bridegroom at a wedding because he had been caught in Oaker's Wood; three months passed before he recovered from his injuries, and the banns were re-published (*UGT.* v i). Varieties of these horrible mechanisms are described in *The Woodlanders*. The one which Timothy

Tangs set for Fitzpiers had a cruel history: 'Tim Tangs's great-uncle had endured a night of six hours in this very trap, which lamed him for life. Once a keeper of Hintock woods set it on the track of a poacher, and afterwards, coming back that way forgetful of what he had done, walked into it himself. The wound brought on lockjaw, of which he died. This event occurred in the thirties, and by the year 1840 the use of such implements was well nigh discontinued in the neighbourhood' (*W.* xlvii).

Emigration provided opportunities for the more enterprising, and escape for others. Many emigrated to North America. Joseph Chinney was on his way when he fell overboard and was drowned (*DR.* xviii 2). Troy worked his way to the United States, and Gabriel Oak thought of emigrating to Canada (*FMC.* l, lvi). Wildeve, who had relatives in Wisconsin, suggested that he and Eustacia should settle in America (*RN.* i ix). Jim Owlett, the smuggler, settled in Wisconsin, after being pardoned at the Assizes (*WT.* 7). Captain de Stancy thought that he and his illegitimate son Dare might 'go off to America or New Zealand, where we are not known, and there lead a quiet, pastoral life, defying social rules and observances'; Abner Power suggested that Dare go to Peru or, alternatively, to Australia or California: 'As long as you choose to remain in either of those wealth-producing places, so long will Cunningham Haze go uninformed' (*L.* ii v, v xi). Nicholas Long, in the hope of returning to marry a squire's daughter, emigrated to America, and made a fortune in one of the gold-fields. The list could be continued.

Angel Clare emigrated to Brazil, 'the Brazil movement among the English agriculturalists having by chance coincided with his desire to escape from his past existence' (*TD.* xlix). Carl Weber has an interesting note on this movement, and the fevers and hardships likely to be encountered, in *Hardy of Wessex*, 223 (cf. *Life*, 229).

Australia and New Zealand attracted others. The miller, Agatha Pollin's uncle, intended to go to Australia when his business was declining (*DBC*). Mrs Hall's son went, and came back destitute and on the brink of death. The decline in their pig-jobbing business impelled the Donns to Australia, and they were accompanied by Arabella, whose marriage with Jude had broken down; they had 'rather a hard struggle over there', and returned (*JO.* i xi, v iii). Suke Damson wanted to emigrate when she married Tim Tangs, probably to avoid Fitzpiers and lead a new life; when Tim's suspicions were aroused, he comforted himself with the thought that they would soon be in New Zealand, but took steps to make it physically impossible for Fitzpiers to visit his wife before their departure. Had it not been for 'Suke's reputation and his own dignity', he would gladly have stayed at Little Hintock (*W*. xlv, xlvi). Sergeant-Major Clark, another person with matrimonial troubles, proposed emigration to New Zealand (*CM*. 5).

One class of families was peculiarly vulnerable. They were the 'liviers' or lifeholders, people whose cottages and gardens were leased by the lord of the manor for three lives or generations. The lease was renewable by agreement, but, for one reason or another, was often not extended. If such a cottage was not required for farm-workers, it was generally demolished (*TD*. li). The sudden death of the third lifeholder frequently led to the eviction of a family; Tess's final catastrophe was undoubtedly caused in this way. The families of many liviers who had lost their homes in the surrounding villages found refuge in Mixen Lane, Durnover, 'unless they chose to lie under a hedge by the wayside' (*MC*. xxxvi). If the lifeholder held several cottages, his sudden death could mean the eviction of several families; Giles Winterborne had to live in a woodland hut as a result of the death of Marty South's father (*W*. xii, xiii, xiv). There was nothing new in this deplorable disruption of family and village life; it is the subject of 'The Homestead a-vell into Hand', a moving lyric by William Barnes. Hardy saw it happening at Higher Bockhampton: 'But the lifeholds fell into hand, and the quaint residences . . . have now perished one by one . . .' (*Life*, 3). The Hardys themselves were lifeholders, and it is probably for this reason that Hardy was alive to the problem from his early years (cf. *ILH*. 13; *DR*. x 6), and associated it with disaster and tragedy in two of his major novels. Netty Sargent was fortunate (*LLI*. 8*i*).

The plight of the agricultural labourer belongs to the background of the Wessex tales, and is often incidental. In *Two on a Tower*, Nat Chapman says that the Lord concerns himself only with gentlemen, and that it is not to be supposed that 'a strange fiery lantern' like the comet 'would be lighted up for folks with ten or a dozen shillings a week and their gristing, and a load o' thorn faggots when we can get 'em' (xiii). The agricultural wage in Dorset was the lowest in the country, often not more than seven shillings a week. An unambitious farmer like Charles Darton, 'without commercial subtlety', had a 'turnover' of probably £30,000 a year (*WT*. 6).

Hardy's growing interest in agricultural conditions is reflected in 'The

Dorsetshire Labourer', which was published in *Longman's Magazine* in July 1883. Some of its views and much of its descriptive detail were repeated in *The Mayor of Casterbridge* and *Tess of the d'Urbervilles*. A summary follows:

The conventional image of Hodge is false and little better than a generic caricature. Live with these country labourers, and you will find they are individuals of great variety. It is thought that they live in squalor, but this impression arises from the dingy colours used in decorating their homes. They are assumed to be wretched and miserable, but 'it is among such communities that happiness will find her last refuge on earth, since it is among them that a perfect insight into the conditions of existence will be longest postponed'.

In times of stress the 'Complaint of Piers the Plowman' is still echoed in the heart of the agricultural labourer, but he is less despondent than the drudge in the city. 'A pure atmosphere and a pastoral environment are a very appreciable portion of the sustenance which tends to produce the sound mind and body.' Melancholy arises over security of tenure; 'Like Burns's field-mouse', workers are 'over-awed and timorous lest those who can wrong them should be inclined to use their power' (cf. Elizabeth-Jane's 'field-mouse fear of the coulter of destiny': *MC*. xiv). To see the Dorsetshire labourer at his saddest, you should view him at a wet hiring-fair at Candlemas, when he is in search of a new master. Then follows a picture of an old shepherd, being valued by farmers in the background (cf. *MC*. xxiii).

Today the crowd at a hiring-fair is as dark as a London crowd. Twenty or thirty years ago, the general colour was 'whity-brown flecked with white'. The labourers appeared in smock-frocks and gaiters, the shepherds with crooks, and the thatchers with straws tucked in the brim of their hats. The women too are less interesting pictorially; the wing bonnet, 'like the tilt of a waggon', and the cotton gown no longer appear (cf. *MC*. xxiii).

Removals take place on Lady Day (Old Style), 6 April. The hiring farmer is the remover. His carter rises 'when Charles's Wain is over the new chimney', and reaches the house for loading to begin at six o'clock. The dresser is placed at the front of the waggon like 'some Ark of the Covenant', and on top of the furniture a circular nest is made of the bed and bedding for the wife and the children, who sit there during the journey. If there is no infant, she holds the clock; the next object of solicitude is the mirror (cf. *TD*. lii).

Migrations are on the increase, and the labourers are becoming more shrewd through variety of experience. The 'humorous simplicity' of the men and the 'unsophisticated modesty' of the women are disappearing. They are becoming more like townsfolk. Their brains are less frequently 'as dry as the remainder biscuit after a voyage', but their observations are less original. 'They are losing their individuality, but they are widening the range of their ideas, and gaining in freedom.' Children's education suffers considerably as a result of frequent removals. Of the seventy-five scholars in the village school, thirty-three left last Lady Day, and this may be regarded as a typical instance. Some weeks elapse before the new arrivals attend, and a longer period before they 'take root' in school.

The labourer is becoming more independent. At one time, he was sometimes treated with a contempt which 'could not have been greatly exceeded in the days when the thralls of Cedric wore their collars of brass'. The efforts of Mr Arch have done much to improve the lot of the working-class in Dorset. He came from Shakespeare's county, and, 'like his renowned fellow-dalesman Corin', he might have described himself as a 'natural philosopher' who had discovered that 'he that wants money, means, and content, is without three good friends'. He was a social evolutionist, what M. Émile de Laveleye would call a 'Possibilist'. The result has been an addition of three shillings a week to the eight or nine shillings the labourer used to receive. Such an increase in times of agricultural depression shows that he 'must have been greatly wronged' in more prosperous times. He receives extras, at harvest time, for example, and, in addition, a cottage and garden, with, not infrequently, wood faggots for fuel. If he has a family of girls, he will suffer hardships; if he has several boys, who earn more than girls, he is well off. Women work on farms, weeding crops, hay-making, harvesting, and 'turnip-hacking'. At threshing their work is arduous and distasteful, especially feeding the threshing-machine and keeping up with the 'steam tyrant' (cf. *TD*. xliii, xlvii).

In some parts depopulation is taking place at an alarming rate. Many life-holders had built their cottages at their own expense. As 'the lives dropped, and the property fell in', they would have been glad to stay on as tenants. Most property-owners disapprove of tenants who are not employed on their estates, and demolish the cottages as they 'fall in', leaving only sufficient for those working on the land. Well might these evicted families protest in the words addressed to Henry IV by his fallen subject:

Our house, my sovereign liege, little deserves
The scourge of greatness to be used on it;
And that same greatness, too, which our own hands
Have holp to make so portly.

It is not surprising that such people, drifting into towns, with over-crowding and lack of regular employment, join the ranks of the discontented.

We have seen that many of them went to Mixen Lane, on the out-skirts of Casterbridge; they help to swell the murmur of discontent which forms, as it were, the undertow in *The Mayor of Casterbridge*. Rain and bad harvests meant poor bread and soaring prices. One of Henchard's men told him that all he was aware of was that he earned eight shillings a week. When Abel Whittle was taken on by Farfrae, he received a shilling a week less than he did under Henchard. It is not surprising that Christopher Coney saw no reason why death should rob life of fourpence, or that stealing, poaching, and vice were common. Farmers 'with extensive stomachs' were to be seen in the market-place; 'many carried ruffled cheque-books in their pockets which regulated at the bank hard by a balance of never less than four figures. In fact, what these gibbous human shapes specially represented was ready money – money insistently ready – not ready next year like a nobleman's – often not merely ready at the bank like a professional man's, but ready in their large plump hands.' (iv, viii, xviii, xxii, xxiii, xxvii, xxxi, xxxvi.)

Hardy's views on Hodge were repeated, sometimes verbatim, in *Tess of the d'Urbervilles* (xviii, xxii). The hardships endured by women on farms are seen at Flintcomb-Ash. There were tyrannical farmers like Groby, as is plain from an unpublished verse which Hardy pencilled in one of his books (to be seen at the Dorset County Museum). It is entitled 'Epitaph by Labourers on Jas.—':

All day he cursed and called us brutes:
Then Time said 'James, 'tis night!'
Fear floor'd him: Shame pulled off his boots,
And Death put out his light.

Hardy's interest in such rural occupations as sheep-farming (*FMC*), dairy-farming (*TD*), and the timber-industry (*W*) is clear. On cider-making he wrote from first-hand experience. During the autumn of 1873 he assisted his father at cider-making, 'a proceeding he had always enjoyed from childhood – the apples being from huge old trees that have now long perished. It was the last time he ever took part in a work whose sweet smells and oozings in the crisp autumn air can never be forgotten by those who have had a hand in it.' That Hardy never forgot can be seen in *The Woodlanders*, where Giles Winterborne is seen super-intending the process of cider-making in the yard of the Earl of Wessex hotel at Sherton Abbas, 'on the margin of Pomona's plain', the country which produced 'the best cider and cider-wine in all Wessex' (*WT.* 6). Later he is seen on his way back from cider-making at Middleton Abbey; 'he looked and smelt like Autumn's very brother' (*W.* xxv, xxviii). Hardy's experience had provided the background to one of the most amusing scenes in his first published novel (*DR.* viii 3). Like Reuben Dewy, he knew the taste of ciders, and the blend of apples from which they were made (*UGT.* i ii; *TM.* xvi).

One virtue of 'the custom of granting leaseholds for three lives' was that it did 'at least serve the purpose of keeping the native population at home' (*Life*, 314). 'The Dorsetshire Labourer' drew attention to the harmful effects of frequent migrations, and Hardy referred to them in 1888 (*Life*, 205), 1895 (*FMC.* preface), and 1902 (*Life*, 312–14). They were fatal to local traditions and cottage horticulture, to 'the preservation of legend, folk-lore, close inter-social relations, and eccentric individu-alities'. Time was when 'ballads appertained to such and such a locality, ghost tales were attached to particular sites . . . .'.

The railway played a part in this process. Reapers looked up at a passing train, in the middle of the nineteenth century, 'as something foreign' and 'but dimly understood' (*FMC.* xvii). One unforeseen result of speedier transport was that 'the orally transmitted ditties of centuries', such as the ballads Hardy heard sung in the barn at Kingston Maurward, were 'slain at a stroke by the London comic songs that were introduced' (*Life*, 20). Visiting Portland at this time, Jocelyn Pierston noticed that the aim seemed to be to make Avice Caro 'an exact copy of tens of thousands of other people . . . to teach her to forget all the experience of her ancestors', and 'to drown the local ballads by songs purchased at the fashionable music-sellers' ' (*WB.* i ii).

Villages which could maintain church bands were fortunate, but the hazards were great. Often, in the early part of the century, the barrel-organ, with its limited repertoire of tunes, was preferred; later, the 'cabinet-organ' or harmonium (*UGT.* i iv, *LLI.* 8f, *UGT.* ii iv).

The widespread 'restoration' of churches in the nineteenth century led to changes which Hardy found 'tragic and deplorable', so much so that he thought they would have been richer architecturally if they had been spared 'the expenditure of millions in a nominal preservation' and been left to the dilapidations of time. His recollections of church-restoration are drawn upon slightly in *Desperate Remedies* and more significantly in *A Pair of Blue Eyes*, but for an adumbration of the views which he expressed in 1906 ('Memories of Church Restoration') we have to turn to one of the short stories (*GND*. 2), where the eighteenth and nineteenth centuries are ironically contrasted: 'for such was the luke-warm state of religion in those days, that not an aisle, steeple, porch, east window, Ten-Commandment board, lion-and-unicorn, or brass candlestick, was required anywhere at all in the neighbourhood as a votive offering from a distracted soul – the last century contrasting greatly in this respect with the happy times in which we live, when urgent appeals for contributions to such objects pour in by every morning's post, and nearly all churches have been made to look like new pennies'.

Improved travelling facilities led to the development of seaside resorts such as Budmouth, Knollsea, Sandbourne, and Solentsea (Weymouth, Swanage, Bournemouth, and Southsea). It was at Swanage that Hardy's interest in smuggling stories was renewed (*Life*, 107–8); his home at Higher Bockhampton had proved to be an excellent hiding-place for smuggled spirits in his grandfather's time, because of its remoteness (*WT*. 7; Evelyn Hardy, *Thomas Hardy's Notebooks*, 35; *D*. (1) II v). The new pretentiousness of Knollsea is the subject of fitting comment in *The Hand of Ethelberta* (xxxvii); Sandbourne is a 'glittering novelty' on the verge of 'that tawny piece of antiquity', Egdon Heath (*TD*. lv).

An agricultural revolution is foreseen in *The Mayor of Casterbridge*, and Henchard is ruined in trying to match rule-of-thumb procedures against the acumen and up-to-date business methods of Farfrae. The transition to modernity, with its engineering feats, improved communications, and new ways of living for the wealthy, forms a significant aspect of the dilemma at the heart of *A Laodicean*, but the changes are superficial compared with those which are inchoate in *Jude the Obscure*, a novel of anguished frustration and protest in the conflict between ancient bigotries and new ideas which dimly foreshadows the future. 'Our ideas were fifty years too soon,' Jude laments when he is dying.

The first of Hardy's collected poems is 'The Temporary the All'; it begins with 'Change and chancefulness'. The temporary is not 'the all' in Hardy's literature, but it provides one of its most distinctive facets.

ove: *Corfe (Corvsgate) Castle*   Below: *Lulworth (Lulwind) Cove*

Firs above 'Alderworth'

Above 'Shadwater Weir'

Views on Art, Tragedy, and Fiction

Art and Tragedy

Hardy's observations on art are scattered, but progressively they form a picture which reflects his philosophy of life.

For Hardy, art was no mere copying of life. He dismissed 'photographic' writing as an 'inartistic species of literary produce' (cf. *Life*, 351, and 'The Science of Fiction'). Hence, too, his abhorrence of the thought that one day he might have to write novels of 'modern artificial life and manners'. Turner's water-colours appealed to him because 'each is a landscape *plus* a man's soul'. One might say that art is informed by a vision of life (or the Arnoldian 'criticism of life'). 'As, in looking at a carpet, by following one colour a certain pattern is suggested, by following another colour, another; so in life the seer should watch the pattern among general things which his idiosyncrasy moves him to observe, and describe that alone. . . . Art consists in so depicting the common events of life as to bring out the features which illustrate the author's idiosyncratic mode of regard; making old incidents and things seem as new.' Or, again, 'Art is a changing of the actual proportions and order of things, so as to bring out more forcibly than might otherwise be done that feature in them which appeals most strongly to the idiosyncrasy of the artist. The changing, or distortion, may be of two kinds: (1) The kind which increases the sense of *vraisemblance*: (2) That which diminishes it. (1) is high art: (2) is low art.' In short, imaginative art does not evade life, but intensifies it in an individual way. 'My art', Hardy wrote, 'is to intensify the expression of things, as is done by Crivelli, Bellini, etc., so that the heart and inner meaning is made vividly visible' (*Life*, 153, 225, 228, 177).

Hardy saw life as basically the same through the ages, though subject to changes of outlook. 'My opinion', he wrote in 1918 (*Life*, 386), 'is that a poet should express the emotion of all the ages and the thought of his own.'

Contemporary scientific thought led Hardy to believe in the insignificance of humanity in the stellar universe, and the cruelty of Nature, which everywhere evinced the struggle for existence and the Unfulfilled Intention. The problem was to find beauty in a world of natural defect or 'ugliness' (*Life*, 121, 213). When 'false romance' or illusions had been removed, Hardy found enough 'poetry' in what was left 'to make a sweet pattern' (*Life*, 114). In the love, enjoyment, suffering, endurance (cf. *RN.* III i), and hope of ordinary people, he found the poetry and tragedy of life. The world might be bleak, but he saw 'the determination to enjoy . . . in all nature, from the leaf on the tree to the titled lady at the ball' (*Life*, 213). The current of his sympathies ran with 'the intense interests, passions, and strategy that throb through the commonest lives', however (*Life*, 153).

Though radically removed in his view of life from Wordsworth, he shared his sympathy with common humanity. With Keats, he felt that human nature was finer than nature: 'An object or mark raised or made by man on a scene is worth ten times any such formed by unconscious Nature. Hence clouds, mists, and mountains are unimportant beside the wear on a threshold, or the print of a hand' (*Life*, 116). Hence the attraction of Hobbema's paintings and the view that 'the beauty of association is entirely superior to the beauty of aspect' (*Life*, 120). It was this association which led him to believe that 'Nature was played out as a Beauty, but not as a Mystery', and that 'the deeper reality' was related to 'the tragical mysteries of life' (*Life*, 185). The plight of man with nobler aspirations than were reflected in the rest of nature was best expressed for 'the more thinking of mankind' in Egdon Heath, or the sand-dunes of Scheveningen (see p. 467). The 'new kind of beauty, a negative beauty of tragic tone', was to be found in the forlornness of the spot called 'Cross-in-hand' (*TD.* xlv). Tess's 'appetite for joy' (xv, xvi, xxx), and all the beauty of her character, which exemplified the highest virtues for Hardy, were of no avail against circumstance.

Circumstance implies not only the network of environment (cf. *Life*, 274), but also the character of the person centrally involved. The first of Hardy's definitions of tragedy (*Life*, 120, 176, 251) makes clear that circumstance or 'situation' includes 'ordinary human passions, prejudices, and ambitions' (cf. the remarks on Jude: *Life*, 433). Its weakness lies in the phrase 'taking no trouble to ward off the disastrous events . . .'. This suggests passivity, and the charge of passivity or drift has, with some justification, been levelled against Tess. Many other factors combine, however, to make her tragedy inevitable, and the most crucial is altruistic. The definition applies to Elfride and Knight, and to most people in life; they live in hope, and the simple reason why they do not take measures to ward off disastrous events is that they are unforeseen. Human nature deceives itself, and it is in the element of the unforeseeable that the tragic irony is implicit.

'High art may choose to depict evil as well as good, without losing its quality. Its choice of evil, however, must be limited by the sense of worthiness' (*Life*, 228–9). This accords with Hardy's last definition of tragedy: 'The best tragedy – highest tragedy in short – is that of the WORTHY encompassed by the INEVITABLE. The tragedies of immoral and worthless people are not of the best.' An example of the worthy, until crime and power have thoroughly corrupted him, is Macbeth; another – and his worthiness, like Lear's, increases with experience and suffering – is Michael Henchard.

Fiction and the Victorian Reading Public

With the exception of 'The Romantic Adventures of a Milkmaid' and *The Well-Beloved*, two widely different excursions into fantasy, and 'An Imaginative Woman', a story on a physical possibility which was substantiated by 'medical practitioners and other observers of such manifestations', the probability of Hardy's stories according to artistic standards is not seriously questioned. Although, in general, far removed from 'realism', they are founded to a considerable degree on history, tradition, personal impressions of people and scenes, and local events, customs, and superstitions. Their imaginative re-creation and development proceeded, Hardy felt, in accordance with principles found in the great writers of the past.

He consistently held that a story must present the unusual; it must be exciting or 'worth the telling' (*Life*, 362). To make the unusual credible, the characters must be probable (*Life*, 150). When *The Mayor of Caster-*

bridge was making its first serial appearance, he was apprehensive about its reception: 'I fear it will not be so good as I meant, but after all, it is not improbabilities of incident but improbabilities of character that matter' (*Life*, 176). In 1891 he wrote: 'Howells and those of his school forget that a story *must* be striking enough to be worth telling. Therein lies the problem – to reconcile the average with that uncommonness which alone makes it natural that a tale or experience would dwell in the memory and induce repetition.' Almost at the end of his career as a writer of prose fiction, he returned to the subject: 'A story must be exceptional enough to justify its telling. We tale-tellers are all Ancient Mariners, and none of us is warranted in stopping Wedding Guests (in other words, the hurrying public) unless he has something more unusual to relate than the ordinary experience of every average man and woman. The whole secret of fiction and the drama – in the constructional part – lies in the adjustment of things unusual to thing eternal and universal. The writer who knows how exceptional, and how non-exceptional, his events should be made, possesses the key to the art' (*Life*, 239, 252).

As his exemplars, he had 'the old masters of imaginative creation from Aeschylus to Shakespeare' in mind, and he found confirmation of his views in the artistry of Old Testament stories. 'Is not the fact of their being so convincing an argument, not for their actuality, but for the actuality of a consummate artist who was no more content with what Nature offered than Sophocles and Pheidias were content?' he asked.

Great stories appeal to 'the emotional reason rather than to the logical reason', he wrote. Perhaps it would be more true to say that this kind of fiction is addressed to 'the imaginative reason' (cf. *Life*, 147).

Had Hardy found the time to write fiction merely to please himself, he might have experimented. One idea which he had for novel-writing resulted in the supernatural framework of *The Dynasts* (*Life*, 177). Elsewhere (*Life*, 204) he discusses the 'psychical' novel and anticipates the modern 'stream of consciousness'; notes on 28 March and 8 July 1888 (*Life*, 206, 210–11) seem to illustrate the tendency of his thinking. Perhaps he was influenced by Browning; 'Incidents in the development of a soul! little else is worth study', he quoted, on hearing that Browning had died (*Life*, 223).

Hardy wrote, by invitation, two general essays on fiction. The first of these, 'The Profitable Reading of Fiction', appeared in *The Forum* (New

York) in March 1888, and contains Hardy's most important reflections on the novel:

First he deals sympathetically but not very seriously with the reader who comes to the novel for nothing but relief. Such a reader needs a complete change of environment, and is most likely to find it if he allows the narrative to absorb him, however improbable it may be.

Those who seek intellectual or moral profit may find it in some less successful novels, or, better still, in essays.

The mental enlargement we look for in a novel depends on 'intuitive conviction, and not upon logical reasoning. . . . Our true object is a lesson in life, mental enlargement from elements essential to the narrative themselves and from the reflections they engender.' In great fiction there is nothing intrinsically new. 'Good fiction may be defined as that kind of imaginative writing which lies nearest to the epic, dramatic, or narrative masterpieces of the past.' Techniques may change, but greatness will reside in the finer manifestations of human nature. 'The higher manifestations must ever rank above the inferior – intellectual tendencies above animal, and moral above intellectual', as in 'the old masters of imaginative creation from Aeschylus to Shakespeare'. The appeal will be to 'the emotional reason rather than to the logical reason'.

The art of writing novels is 'in its youth, if not in its infancy'. For this reason the reader must be content with excellence in parts. He will 'go with the professed critic so far as to inquire whether the story forms a regular structure of incident, accompanied by an equally regular development of character – a composition based on faithful imagination, less the transcript than the similitude of material fact'. He will 'catch the vision which the writer has in his eye'. The writer's specialty may not be his popular attribute; it may lurk 'like a violet in the shade of the more obvious'.

Despite the claims of 'realism', the best fiction is more true than history or nature can be. 'No dozen persons who were capable of being animated by the profound reasons and truths thrown broadcast over *Hamlet* or *Othello*, of feeling the pulse of life so accurately, ever met together in one place in this world to shape an end. . . . What is called the idealization of characters is, in truth, the making of them too real to be possible.'

Didactic novels do not impress as much as those with 'inevitableness of character and environment in working out destiny, whether that destiny be just or unjust, enviable or cruel'.

Novelists may lose sight of life by excessive attention to 'social minutiae' or the 'garniture' of life. This attention has its virtues if it does not involve 'blindness to higher things'. The treatment matters more than the subject.

Artistically constructed stories can develop the aesthetic sense as much as masterpieces in other forms of art. So far little attention has been given to this aspect of fiction. A story should be an 'organism'. Many remarkable novels are deficient in their structural quality as narratives. 'No person who has a due perception of the constructive art shown in Greek tragic drama can be blind to the constructive art' in Richardson's *Clarissa Harlowe*, whatever its deficiency in other respects. This point has been stressed 'not because I consider it to rank in quality beside truth of feeling and action', but because few non-professional readers are aware that such an attribute can be claimed by fiction.

Style is generally assumed to be 'literary finish', whereas it can only be treatment, which depends on the mental attitude of an author, and therefore enters into 'the very substance of the narrative'.

As education has so far done little to modify 'the waves of human impulse on which deeds and words depend' – so that in emotional and dramatic scenes ('the highest province of fiction') 'the peer and the peasant stand on much the same level' – the question of the social class from which characters are drawn has little bearing on the value of a novel. In unemotional scenes, social refinement is often 'prejudicial to vigorous portraiture, by making the exteriors of men their screen rather than their index, as with untutored mankind'.

The above considerations may help the discriminating to derive more profit from fiction, but there is no outside power which will 'help a reader to gain good from such reading unless he has a natural eye for the finer qualities in the best productions of this class'.

'The Science of Fiction' was the third and last of a series to which Paul Bourget and Walter Besant made the first contributions. It was published in *The New Review* in April 1891.

Hardy found himself in a dilemma: for him the 'science' of fiction did not really exist, and the 'art' of novel-writing was outside his commission. The essay is very brief. He crosses swords with the realists, and takes the view that the science of fiction means 'that comprehensive and accurate knowledge of realities which must be sought for, or intuitively possessed, to some extent, before anything deserving the name of an artistic performance in narrative can be produced'.

As soon as he selects or omits, 'with an eye to being more truthful than truth', an author shows artistry. Creativeness is ceasing to attract in a world which no longer believes in the abnormal, and is giving way to realism, 'an artificiality distilled from the fruits of closest observation'. Unfortunately, 'realism' is an ambiguous term, sometimes implying 'copyism', sometimes pruriency.

'A sight for the finer qualities of existence, an ear for the "still sad music of humanity", are not to be acquired by the outer senses alone, close as their powers in photography may be. What cannot be discerned by eye and ear, what may be apprehended only by the mental tactility that comes from a sympathetic appreciativeness of life in all its manifestations, this is the gift which renders its possessor a more accurate delineator of human nature than many another with twice his powers and means of external observation, but without that sympathy.'

Thus an attempt to set forth the science of fiction is futile; 'it is to write a whole library of human philosophy, with instructions how to feel.' The true means towards the science of fiction is 'a power of observation informed by a living heart'. This reflection leads one to think that 'true novelists, like poets, are born, not made'.

By 1886 Hardy was quite resigned to 'novel-writing as a trade, which he had never wanted to carry on as such'. This implies that he was tired of accommodating himself to the requirements of magazine-readers. He recognized with Gissing the 'misery' of writing for 'English people': 'reticences and superficialities have so often to fill places where one is willing to put in honest work' (*Life*, 182–3). He had already noted Ruskin's reason for 'the want of imagination in works of the present age': 'Men dare not open their hearts to us if we are to broil them on a thorn fire' (172). This 'flippant sarcasm of the time' was to prove Hardy's plague with *Tess of the d'Urbervilles* and *Jude the Obscure*. The work of excising and patching them up for serial-readers, and their reception when published in their original form, made him resolve to write no more novels. It was a relief to know that he was spared the tedium of writing 'society novels'.

'He had mostly aimed at keeping his narratives close to natural life and as near to poetry in their subject as the conditions would allow, and had often regretted that those conditions would not let him keep them nearer still.' An epigrammatic statement which he wrote on completing *The Mayor of Casterbridge* expresses his aim: 'The business of the poet and novelist is to show the sorriness underlying the grandest things, and the grandeur underlying the sorriest things' (*Life*, 291, 171).

Soon after beginning *Tess of the d'Urbervilles*, he wrote: 'The besetting sin of modern literature is its insincerity. Half its utterances are qualified, even contradicted, by an aside, and this particularly in morals and religion' (*Life*, 215). He expressed himself more fully in 'Candour in English Fiction'. This essay was the third and last of a symposium in *The New Review* in January 1890. Hardy's case is simply but firmly reasoned, and quite clearly proceeds from the problems he was encountering in trying to tailor *Tess of the d'Urbervilles* for the magazine public. One feels that, though he argues his case dispassionately, he was nearing the end of his patience with compromise before *Jude the Obscure* was begun.

His view is that, by and large, the amount of latent genius and imagination does not vary greatly from age to age, but that some ages are more inimical to their expression than others. He then proceeds to discuss why 'the great bulk of English fiction of the present day is characterised by its lack of sincerity'.

Hardy's view of a serious novel is significant: it is 'impassive in its tone and tragic in its developments'. Writers are conscious that 'high tragedy' needs an original treatment which seeks to show 'Nature's unconsciousness not of essential laws, but of those laws framed merely as social expedients by humanity, without a basis in the heart of things'.

In the Periclean and Elizabethan ages, drama 'reflected life, revealed life, criticised life. Life being a physiological fact, its honest portrayal must be largely concerned with, for one thing, the relations of the sexes.' The difficulty is that the popular vehicles for the introduction of the novel are the magazine and the circulating library; even 'adults who desire true views for their own reading insist, for a plausible but questionable reason, upon false views for the reading of their young people . . . the crash of broken commandments shall not be heard; or, if at all, but gently, like the roaring of Bottom – gently as any sucking dove, or as 'twere any nightingale, lest we should fright the ladies out of their wits.'

Hardy then raises in general terms the special problem with which he was beset: 'The opening scenes of the would-be great story may, in a

rash moment, have been printed in some popular magazine before
the remainder is written; as it advances month by month the
situations develop, and the writer asks himself, what will his characters do next? . . . What he often does, indeed can scarcely help
doing in such a strait, is, belie his literary conscience, do despite to his
best imaginative instincts by arranging a *dénouement* which he knows
to be indescribably unreal and meretricious, but dear to the Grundy-
ist and subscriber. If the true artist ever weeps it probably is then,
when he first discovers the fearful price that he has to pay for the
privilege of writing in the English language. . . . Fancy a brazen
young Shakespeare of our time – *Othello, Hamlet,* or *Antony and
Cleopatra* never having yet appeared – sending up one of those
creations in narrative form to the editor of a London magazine. . . .'

If the objection were to 'a prurient treatment of the relations of
the sexes, or to any view of vice calculated to undermine the essential
principles of social order, all honest lovers of literature would be in
accord with them. All really true literature directly or indirectly
sounds as its refrain the words in the *Agamemnon*: "Chant Ælinon,
Ælinon! but may the good prevail." '

If the magazine is indispensable, there might be 'magazines for
adults; exclusively for adults, if necessary. . . . *La dignité de la
pensée,* in the words of Pascal, might then grow to be recognised in
the treatment of fiction as in other things . . . the position of man and
woman in nature, and the position of belief in the minds of man and
woman – things which everybody is thinking but nobody is saying –
might be taken up and treated frankly.'

Aspects of the Unusual
and Irrational

Hardy's Fiction and the Ballad

Hardy's interest in ballads, local and literary, is discussed elsewhere (p. 205). Their influence on his plots is sometimes highly overstressed. Reduced to its essential minimum, the story of Tess or Fanny Robin recalls many a ballad theme. Parallels with Scott's ballad-like shorter poems are presented in some of the epigraphs to *A Pair of Blue Eyes*. Yet the plot is too elaborate and too sophisticated an artifact to suggest that it originated in balladry. Some of the shorter stories such as 'The Three Strangers' and 'The Fiddler of the Reels' would, it is true, make excellent ballads, but the argument *post hoc propter hoc* is rather ingenuous. In a different vein, 'The Romantic Adventures of a Milkmaid' would make a ballad sequence. Transfer the story of Eustacia's attempt to escape with her lover to a medieval setting, and we have an excellent subject for a ballad. Endow her with witchcraft, make Susan Nunsuch the central figure, and the subject is medieval. One could continue with 'The Winters and the Palmleys' and 'Master John Horseleigh, Knight'; or, on a larger scale, 'What the Shepherd Saw'. As a final confirmation, the ballad style and subject of several of Hardy's poems might be adduced.

It must be remembered that the Wessex of Hardy's youth had changed very little from medieval and Elizabethan times. People were ignorant and superstitious; the belief in witchcraft still existed; executions took place; and country people heard the same kind of stories about unusual events that were related in earlier centuries and provided the source material for ballads. People like Susan Nunsuch and Rhoda Brook lived in Dorset in the early part of the nineteenth century; and the seduction and desertion of a local girl by a soldier at the barracks was far from being an improbable event.

152

Hardy did not believe that a story of ordinary life was worth the telling. It had to contain unusual incidents. It is for this reason preponderantly that his stories are reminiscent of ballads. Most of the incidents around which they grew were suggested by events in Hardy's own age, and by local history and tradition, rather than by literature. (This does not apply to Hardy's two fantasies, 'The Romantic Adventures of a Milkmaid' and *The Well-Beloved*, which derive respectively, to some extent, from such writers as Goethe and Shelley; nor, as has been seen, were other novels and stories by Hardy unaffected by other writers.)

The Gothic Influence

From its hey-day at the end of the eighteenth century, Gothic literature assumed many forms; its influence survived in many popular Victorian novels. To what extent Hardy was familiar with this literature is largely conjectural, but he was particularly fascinated in his youth by the romances of Harrison Ainsworth, and one does not have to look much further to trace the Gothic influence in his work. (It will be found in some of his narrative poems.)

As Cytherea Graye approached the old manor house on her way home, 'livid grey shades . . . made a mystery of the remote and dark parts of the vista, and seemed to insist upon a suspension of the breath. Before she was half-way across the park the thunder rumbled distinctly.' She falls under the spell of Manston (the murderer and villain of the piece) to loud organ music and peals of thunder. He is 'an extremely handsome man' with full, red, 'luscious' lips, and gives the impression of 'one who took upon himself to resist fate with the vindictive determination of a Theomachist'. (In this last respect, his ancestry may be found in the melodramatic literature of the Romantic period.)

Manston persisted in his suit, and as Cytherea's resistance weakened she could almost fancy she heard the shrieks of the mandrakes in the overgrown hedge by which they stood. (The mandrake flourishes in one of Harrison Ainsworth's novels.) On the night before their marriage, the icicle-laden trees rattled in the wind 'like a man playing castanets or shaking dice'; she dreamt 'she was being whipped by dry bones suspended on strings, which rattled at every blow like those of a malefactor on a gibbet. . . . She could not see the face of the executioner for his mask, but his form was like Manston's' (*DR*. viii 4; xii 6; xiii 1).

In *A Pair of Blue Eyes* there are two moonlight scenes where the lovers Stephen Smith and Elfride, and then Elfride and Knight, meet by the tomb of Mrs Jethway's son. His mother thought he had died from unrequited love of Elfride. A 'crazed, forlorn' widow, she is an avenging spirit, and her dark form haunts the gloom of the evening scene, as Stephen sees the illuminated figures of Elfride and Knight through the wooden bars of the Belvedere, 'which crossed their forms like the ribs of a skeleton'. Knight found the dead body of Mrs Jethway beneath the stones of the fallen church-tower. Scenes, varying from humorous to grave, in the Luxellian vault make an unforgettable impression, and prepare the way for the tragic conclusion (viii, xxv, xxvi–xxvii, xxxii–xxxiii).

Professor Weber found a striking resemblance between the storm in Harrison Ainsworth's *Rookwood* and that in *Far from the Madding Crowd* (xxxvi–xxxvii). The 'sinister aspect' of the night, the 'lurid metallic look' of the moon, the breeze which seems 'as if breathed from the parted lips of some dragon about to swallow the globe', the 'forms of skeletons' which appeared in the air, and with which were intertwined 'undulating snakes of green' in the lightning's 'perfect dance of death', the sulphurous smell which ensued, and the silence 'black as a cave in Hinnom' when lightning and thunder ceased, are not all evoked by phrase or suggestion in Ainsworth, but they indicate how vividly Hardy's youthful imagination was impressed by such scenes as that in *Rookwood*. It is interesting to note that the hero of that novel is impersonated by Troy at Greenhill Fair.

Two incidental descriptions of Egdon Heath suggest the same Gothic provenance. When Eustacia left Mistover Knap for the last time, the night was funereally dark; the 'spiky points of the fir trees behind the house rose into the sky like the turrets and pinnacles of an abbey' (*RN.* v vii). As Angel Clare and Tess drove with the milk to Wellbridge, the notched tips of the fir trees could be seen on the summit of Egdon Heath 'like battlemented towers crowning black-fronted castles of enchantment' (*TD.* xxx).

Hardy's Christmas stories make strange reading. The principal events in 'What the Shepherd Saw' seem more appropriate to Gothic fiction than to their Wessex setting. 'The Honourable Laura' transposes a typically Gothic story and romantic setting to the era of the railway and tourist photography. More original, and more significantly related to railway and photography, is the adaptation of the Gothic story at the most exciting crisis in *A Laodicean* (see pp. 37–8).

One of the more startling manifestations of the complex Gothic tradition in literature recurs in *The Woodlanders*. Late at night Felice Charmond's attention was arrested by a tapping at the window. She pulled back the shutter. 'What she saw outside might have struck terror into a heart stouter than a helpless woman's at midnight. In the centre of the lowest pane of the window, close to the glass, was a human face, which she barely recognized as the face of Fitzpiers. It was surrounded with the darkness of the night without, corpse-like in its pallor, and covered with blood. As disclosed in the square area of the pane, it met her frightened eyes like a replica of the Sudarium of St. Veronica' (xxxvi).

The Gothic influence is more apparent, however, in the earlier novels. One of the scenes which it inspired is that in the church after Cytherea Graye's marriage to Manston. Through the open-work of the chantry screen, the candlelight illuminated the effigies of cross-legged knights and a classic monument 'sculptured in cadaverous marble'. Here Cytherea caught sight of Edward Springrove, 'or his spirit'. 'His eyes were wild, their orbits leaden. His face was of a sickly paleness, his hair dry and disordered, his lips parted as if he could get no breath. His figure was spectre-thin . . .' (*DR*. xiii 3). *Desperate Remedies* does not end without a ghostly visitation. About four o'clock one morning, Cytherea was awakened and transfixed by the sight of Miss Aldclyffe at the foot of her bed, 'wan and distinct' but 'in flesh and blood', just before her death, it transpired, several miles away at Knapwater House (xxi 3).

Phantom figures were to appear in many of Hardy's poems. Some are fancies, the expression of haunting memories of his first wife, for example (cf. *MV*. 'Something Tapped'); but the *revenant* occurs in wholly imaginary scenes and stories, e.g. *PPP*. 'The Supplanter', *SC*. 'The Re-enactment', *LLE*. 'The Second Night'. In setting and atmosphere, each poem has its own identity. The first is weirdly Gothic; the last is a ballad, in which the ghost of the woman who had leapt to her death that morning meets her lover the following evening, and the supernatural is dramatized by a shooting star which is reflected in her eyes before she vanishes.

Hardy's obsession with ghostly visitants is perplexing. Intellectually, he did not believe in them; imaginatively, they were inescapable, partly from the lure of Gothic romances in novel and ballad form, partly, one suspects, because he was not convinced that psychic phenomena were wholly amenable to rationalistic interpretation (see pp. 122 and 158–9).

The Mephistophelian or Satanic Element

The subject was brought to the fore in J. O. Bailey's 'Hardy's "Mephistophelian Visitants" ' (*Publications of the Modern Languages Association,* lxi, December 1946). His survey is illuminating and remarkably thorough, but it seems odd, for example, that Newson and Farfrae should be included, and Alec d'Urberville excluded, from this category.

A story told by his wife's brother-in-law, the rector of St Juliot, Cornwall, may provide a clue to the fascination exerted upon Hardy by the Mephistophelian myth. 'It was what had been related to him by some of his aged parishioners concerning an incumbent of that or an adjacent living many years before. This worthy ecclesiastic was a bachelor addicted to drinking habits, and one night when riding up Boscastle Hill fell off his horse. He lay a few minutes in the road, when he said "Help me up, Jolly!" and a local man who was returning home behind him saw a dark figure with a cloven foot emerge from the fence, and toss him upon his horse in a jiffy. The end of him was that on one night of terrific lightning and thunder he was missed, and was found to have entirely disappeared.' Stories of this kind were rife in the Middle Ages, and culminated in the legend of Faust. In the Mephistopheles of Goethe's *Faust* may be recognized the Satan of the book of Job, whose main business seems to have been 'going to and fro in the earth' and 'walking up and down it' to tempt mankind.

The phrase 'Mephistophelian visitants' occurs with reference to Diggory Venn. If, as J. O. Bailey suggested, the name Diggory derives from 'to work like diggory' (i.e. to work like the devil) and Venn suggests 'fen', the reddleman's name is strikingly appropriate without any Satanic connotation. With his shotgun, he may have been the devil to Wildeve, but from the reader's viewpoint he is the protector of Thomasin Yeobright's interests; in this self-sacrificial role he is assiduous, and his 'vermilion figure' has an uncanny habit of turning up in the nick of time and disappearing from the heath like a will-o'-the-wisp. 'He was to have retained his isolated and weird character to the last, and to have disappeared from the heath, nobody knowing whither – Thomasin remaining a widow' (*RN.* vi iii, footnote). Serial publication, however, demanded a different ending to the story. It would be hard to imagine anyone less Satanic than the reddleman, and a study of the opening of I ix can lead to only one conclusion: the colour of reddlemen recalled Mephistopheles' cloak, and made them forbidding figures, and at one time terrifying 'bogeys' to young children. 'A child's first sight of a reddleman was an epoch in his life. That blood-coloured figure was a sublimation of all the horrid dreams which had afflicted the juvenile spirit since imagination began. "The reddleman is coming for you!" had been the formulated threat of Wessex mothers for many generations.'

In *A Laodicean* there can be no doubt that William Dare belongs to the Devil's party. The name, A. J. Guerard suggested, means 'daredevil'. When Captain de Stancy asks him where he comes from, he replies: 'From going to and fro in the earth, and walking up and down it, as Satan said to his Maker.' Later in the same scene (II v), the Captain observes that he is 'quite a Mephistopheles'. He is certainly a cosmopolite, quite unprincipled, and full of devilish ingenuity in the pursuit of his own ends and the damnation of others. He presents the image of a beautiful woman (in a pink flannel costume) to inflame de Stancy's passions, as Mephistopheles does with Faust, and he disappears mysteriously at the end, after setting fire to Stancy Castle. His machinations in architecture, and through photography, his fortune-seeking, and casino habits are too worldly to invest him with the Mephistophelian and supernatural attributes which are hinted at in his first appearances and his final departure.

The Baron von Xanten of 'The Romantic Adventures of a Milkmaid' is more mysterious and Mephistophelian. He is endowed with magical powers, and magnetically attractive to Margery Tucker. Yet he is a dying man, and though tempted, at one point, to abscond with the milkmaid, he holds fast to his determination to do good and secure a happy marriage between her and her lover. It is as if, to quote *King Lear*, 'The prince of darkness is a gentleman'. He is 'a fine dark gentleman with black mustachios, and a very pale prince-like face'; his coach is drawn by 'two coal-black horses', which appeared 'daemonic against the slanting fires of the western sun'. He 'schooled impassioned sentiments into fair conduct', however, and nobody knew what happened to him in the end. Perhaps, as on a former occasion, and in a manner reminiscent of the passing of Tennyson's Arthur, the model of Victorian goodness, he took

157

to his yacht, which 'spread her woven wings to the air', and was soon 'a small shapeless phantom' out at sea. If the mysterious baron was Mephistopheles, he was tired of his earthly role.

Suggestions of evil in *The Mayor of Casterbridge* are more Shakespearian. The 'haggish' furmity-woman with the 'three-legged crock' recalls the witches of *Macbeth*. When Henchard sold Susan, a 'lurid colour' seemed to fill the tent. When misfortune overtook him, he thought somebody might have been 'stirring an unholy brew to confound' him (i, xxvii).

In *Tess of the d'Urbervilles* the associations are Miltonic.* Alec d'Urberville leaps over the wall into the garden at The Slopes much as Satan entered Eden. In the garden at Marlott, after disguising himself in a smockfrock, he works on the same plot as Tess in the gathering gloom of evening. The glow from the burning rubbish illuminates the prongs of his fork. As she approaches the fire, it flares up and reveals the face of d'Urberville. He says that she will think he is the Devil in disguise, come to tempt her, and quotes Milton on the fall of Eve (ix, l). This conjunction of ancient superstition – the Devil, his pitchfork, and the 'everlasting bonfire' – and literary reference marks the last variation of the Satanic element (and the most serious) in all Hardy's works. Dare is little more than the agent of intrigue in a plot which 'may perhaps help to while an idle afternoon of the comfortable ones whose lines have fallen to them in pleasant places'. The most evocative and fascinating of Hardy's Mephistophelian visitants is Baron von Xanten, though he is metamorphosed in spirit as well as in form.

Psychic Phenomena

The general impression from Hardy's life and works is that he was unusually interested in psychic phenomena, but that his attitude towards their less credible manifestations was sceptical rather than rationalistic. On this question, a passage in a letter written in 1915 (*Life*, 369–70) is revealing, though not altogether perspicuous: 'You must not think me a hard-headed rationalist for all this. Half my time – particularly when writing verse – I "believe" (in the modern sense of the word) not only in the things Bergson believes in, but in spectres, mysterious voices, intui-

* The influence of Richardson's *Clarissa* should not be discounted. See Dorothy Van Ghent, *The English Novel*, Rinehart & Co., New York, 1953.

tions, omens, dreams, haunted places, etc., etc. But I do not believe in them in the old sense of the word any more for that. . . .' In 1901 he had written: 'My own interest lies largely in non-rationalistic subjects, since non-rationality seems, so far as one can perceive, to be the principle of the Universe' (*Life*, 309).

‾ Hardy told William Archer that he would have given ten years of his life to see a ghost. Late in life, he did see one, that of a man in eighteenth-century dress in Stinsford churchyard. It said 'A green Christmas', and passed into the church. Hardy followed and found no one (Sydney Cockerell, *Friends of a Lifetime*, 305). For another late-life apparition which Hardy recalled (or saw again?) a few years later, see *Life*, 441.

The spectres or phantoms in Hardy's poetry seem to be literary devices rather than 'psychic phenomena'. They express memories, like the phantoms seen by Jude in Christminster (cf. *PPP*. 'The Supplanter'; *SC*. 'Spectres that Grieve'). Many are associated with his first wife (e.g. *SC*. 'The Haunter', 'The Voice').

Some of the stories are of peculiar psychical interest. 'The Withered Arm' belongs to an era of superstition when the psychosomatic effects of 'the evil eye', for example, were commonly accepted. The incubus thrown to the floor by Rhoda Brook (with, it was believed, harmful effects on her supplanter's arm) did not appear at night, Hardy was informed by 'an aged friend' who knew her, but while she was lying down on a hot afternoon (*WT*. preface).

A curious hallucination occurs to Lady Constantine before she realizes her pregnancy. She was returning from the column on Rings-Hill 'when suddenly in a dusky vista among the fir-trunks she saw, or thought she saw, a golden-haired, toddling child. The child moved a step or two, and vanished behind a tree. Lady Constantine, fearing it had lost its way, went quickly to the spot, searched, and called aloud. But no child could she perceive or hear anywhere around. She returned to where she had stood when first beholding it, and looked in the same direction, but nothing reappeared. The only object at all resembling a little boy or girl was the upper tuft of a bunch of fern, which had prematurely yellowed to about the colour of a fair child's hair, and waved occasionally in the breeze' (*TT*. xxxvii). More curious still, though 'a trick of Nature' which was well-known by 'medical practitioners and other observers of such manifestations', is the physical resemblance of a child to the man whose image possessed the mother at the time of its conception, but whom she had never met (*LLI.* 1); the phenomenon recurs in 'San Sebastian' (*WP*).

Hardy's psychological interest in the effect of shock on an unborn child is seen in 'The Doctor's Legend' (pp. 81–3).

Certain occurrences which have been described as 'psychokinetic' seem to be no more than traditional portents. There appears to be no reason why the falling of the portrait of Marie Antoinette when Maria Louisa agrees to marry Napoleon should not be accepted at the unsophisticated level of superstition, like the falling clock in 'The Waiting Supper' (see pp. 72–3). It is an obvious device for linking events by presentiment, like the stumbling of Napoleon's horse at the beginning of the Russian campaign,* and part of the stage-management of the play for mental performance. The Spirit of the Years comments ironically on the second incident; his dissociation of the former from the Will reduces the Earth's reaction to the realm of fancy (*CM.* 2; *D.* (2) v iii; cf. (3) i i).

Premonitions are experienced by Nelson, Villeneuve, and Brunswick (*D.* (1) ii i, ii ii, (3) vi ii; the last recalls Byron's *Childe Harold*, iii xxii–xxiii). Here we seem to be in a debatable territory, with natural fears, surmise, and the superstitious lore of tradition against the claims of precognition. The prelude to death, or 'Death's prophetic ear' (Byron), which Brunswick's lineage knew, is vague compared with the d'Urberville tradition that the sight or sound of a coach was a sign of ill-omen to a member of the family (*TD.* xxxiii, li).

A 'curious instance of sympathetic telepathy' was noted by Hardy (*Life*, 224). He wrote the first lines of 'Thoughts of Phena' (*WP*; see p. 438) while on a train to London. 'The woman I was thinking of – a cousin – was dying at the time, and I quite in ignorance of it. She died six days later.' J. O. Bailey finds evidence of telepathy and clairvoyance in *The Dynasts*. The Spirit of Rumour brings a 'new surprise' before 'material transit' can (*D.* (1) i v; cf. (1) vi vii). Perhaps this should be assessed technically rather than psychologically. The Spirits have many functions, but one (which is acceptable from supernatural agency) is to prepare the reader for coming or intervening events. When Berthier voices rumours of a retreat in Spain ((2) vi iii), these may be founded on knowledge of strategic provisions planned long previously to meet various contingencies. Clairvoyance does not seem to be implied.

* An actual occurrence. See A. Brett-James, *1812*, Macmillan, 1966, pp. 38–9.

The question is involved, and depends largely on the extent of Hardy's indebtedness to the philosophy of von Hartmann. Hardy believed that the mind of man was part of 'the General Will' (*MV*. 'He Wonders about Himself'), and that evolution to higher things would come with the spread of Altruism or the sympathetic consciousness into the General Will, 'till It fashion all things fair'. At present the Will is unconscious, and 'thinking and educated humanity' in advance of it (*JO*. vi iii; *D*. (1) v iv). If the Will is von Hartmann's Unconscious, its 'clairvoyance' includes past, present, and future, and makes itself felt in presentiments which are 'dark, incomprehensive, and symbolical, because they are obliged to take a sensible form in the brain' (J. O. Bailey, *Thomas Hardy and the Cosmic Mind*, 133). Hardy told Archer in 1901 that Hartmann's *Philosophy of the Unconscious* suggested 'a consciousness, infinitely far off, at the other end of the chain of phenomena, always striving to express itself, and always baffled and blundering . . .' (William Archer, *Real Conversations*, Heinemann, 1904).

Towards Symbolism

Bird Imagery

The most persistent symbolism in Hardy is connected with birds. Its
significance varies, but its main theme is human happiness and suffering.
The happy notes are sometimes ironical, like those heard by Bathsheba
when she found herself by a pestilential swamp the morning after discovering Troy's perfidy (*FMC*. xliv).

In 1885, reflecting on the roar and artificial life of London, Hardy
wrote: 'The people in this tragedy laugh, sing, smoke, toss off wines,
etc., make love to girls in drawing-rooms and areas; and yet are playing
their parts in the tragedy just the same. Some wear jewels and feathers,
some wear rags. All are caged birds; the only difference lies in the size
of the cage. This too is part of the tragedy' (*Life*, 171).

At one point in the novels, bird symbolism suggests the cruelty of
Nature. When Clym Yeobright, full of a sense of Eustacia's inhumanity
to his mother and infidelity to him, returned home to confront her, the
only life visible at the front of the house was 'a solitary thrush cracking a
small snail upon the door-stone for his breakfast' (*RN*. v iii).

Whether the 'croud' of the night-hawk in 'The Romantic Adventures
of a Milkmaid' sounds a warning note is not clear, but there is no
mistaking its jar in *The Return of the Native* and *The Woodlanders*.
It is sarcastic, and rather like the Spirit Sinister in *The Dynasts*. Soon
after Clym set out from Alderworth, 'a night-hawk revealed his presence'
in almost every isolated and stunted thorn 'by whirring like the clack of a
mill'. Three miles further on he heard the moan of his dying mother.
While Fitzpiers and Suke Damson 'remained silent on the hay' in the
moonlight, 'the coarse whirr of the eternal night-hawk burst sarcastically
from the top of a tree at the nearest corner of the wood'. The season for

the nightingale was over (*RN.* IV vii, *W.* xx; cf. *HS.* 'A Hurried Meeting'). The bird which is free and delights in song is the symbol of human happiness for Hardy. The nightingale sings with happy overtones at the end of *Under the Greenwood Tree.*

The experienced wild duck which eludes the hawk at the opening of *The Hand of Ethelberta* symbolizes the heroine. The escape of the swallow from the furmity-seller's tent is a prelude to Susan's release from Henchard; and the winging heron, like burnished silver in the sunbeams, expresses Mrs Yeobright's wish to be released from life (*RN.* IV vi).

When Cytherea Graye feels doomed to marry Manston against her will, she suggests the image of a 'poor little bird . . . terrified, driven into a corner, panting and fluttering about for some loophole of escape' (*DR.* xii 5). A bird image may have suggested Fanny Robin's name.

On his way to Alderworth to make preparations for married life with Eustacia, Clym Yeobright, full of a sense of the rift between her and his mother, passed a plantation where, at every onset of the gale,' convulsive sounds' came from the branches 'as if pain were felt'. A finch was trying to sing, but the wind made him give up (*RN.* III vi); 'no bird sang' in the previous scene.

The 'weak bird singing a trite old evening song' reinforces the suggestion that 'the atmosphere of stale familiarity' which the Henchard 'trio carried with them like a nimbus as they moved down the road' towards Weydon-Priors – a very ordinary road – was no more than a commonplace in time. The selfsame song might have been heard 'at any sunset of that season for centuries untold'.

The caged goldfinch which Henchard carried from Shottsford to present to Elizabeth-Jane on her wedding-day, in the hope that it would help to create a reconciliation with her after his deceit, recalls King Lear's hope of reconciliation and happiness when he is restored to Cordelia:

We two alone will sing like birds i' the cage.

Henchard is not forgiven, however, and the cage is left undiscovered in the garden until the bird has been starved to death (*MC.* i, xliv, xlv).

Tess's early tragedy had taught her that 'the serpent hisses where the sweet birds sing', but Nature's indifference to her suffering is reflected in the song of the birds. When she rallies and sets off for Talbothays, her zest for life is heard in every bird's note. Happy bird-song is rarely heard, however. Birds are not heard again at Marlott until Tess and her family have left. At Talbothays, when she is reminded of the past, 'a solitary cracked reed-sparrow greeted her from the bushes by the river, in a sad, machine-made tone, resembling that of a past friend whose friendship she had outworn'.

The birds principally associated with Tess indicate suffering of an intensity unparalleled elsewhere in Hardy. Their agony is the result of the cruelty and indifference of both man and nature, and emphasizes a 'harshness' which is 'universal', and of which Tess is the victim. Tess, who 'could never hurt a fly or a worm', and whom 'the sight of a bird in a cage' often made cry, is caught in 'her days of immaturity like a bird in a springe'; later, she is drawn to Angel 'like a fascinated bird'; and eventually she is caught like a bird 'in a clap-net' (*TD*. xi, xii, xiv, xvi, xxi, xxxi, xli, xliii, xix, lviii).

Symbolism, as well as irony, may be suspected in the blind, sleeping mother of Alec. She cares inordinately for her birds, including bull-finches, but she is unaware of Tess's danger (ix). She may be associated with the blind Mother of 'The Lacking Sense', and the sleeping Mother of 'The Sleep-Worker' and 'The Bullfinches' (*PPP*):

> Busy in her handsome house
> Known as Space, she falls a-drowse; . . .
> While beneath her groping hands
> Fiends make havoc in her bands.

'The Blinded Bird' (*MV*) has the Pauline virtues ascribed to, and exemplified by, Tess. The last line, 'Who is divine? This bird' echoes the challenging sub-title of the novel: 'A Pure Woman'.

'The Caged Goldfinch' (*MV*) suggests a general rather than a literal interpretation. Its symbolism links it with one of Hardy's latest poems, 'We are getting to the end':

> We know that even as larks in cages sing
> Unthoughtful of deliverance from the curse
> That holds them lifelong in a latticed hearse,
> We ply spasmodically our pleasuring.

Though the poem expresses a greater (and a Shelleyan) disillusionment, the thought approximates to that of the London note of 1885.

One does not associate moonlight and the nightingale's song with Hardy. If the thrush sings in winter, it is for some natural reason which is beyond his comprehension. For Hardy, the music of humanity was harsh and grating. The birds most significant of his 'idiosyncratic mode of regard' were earth-bound, caged or snared, blinded or bleeding; they had to endure 'the Frost's decree' (*PPP*. 'The Darkling Thrush'; *WP*. 'The Impercipient'; *MV*. 'The Caged Goldfinch', 'The Blinded Bird'; *TD*. xli; *PPP*. 'The Caged Thrush Freed and Home Again'; *TL*. 'The Reminder', *TD*. xliii). Life's 'decree' was indelibly associated with the image of the starved, half-frozen bird which had haunted his imagination since childhood (*Life*, 444).

Things Rank and Gross in Nature

Darwinian thought filled Hardy with a sense of Nature's 'passioned plans for bloom and beauty marred' (*HS*. 'Discouragement', 1863-7), and it was for this reason that the imagery of Hamlet's world, as 'an unweeded garden' possessed by 'things rank and gross in nature', and that of Shelley's 'A Sensitive Plant' acquired a special and lasting significance.

Shelley's poem is full of the imagery of corruption. As Winter approached, 'All loathliest things began to grow' in the garden of ideal Love and Beauty:

> And agarics, and fungi, with mildew and mould
> Started like mist from the wet ground cold . . .
>
> When Winter had gone and Spring came back
> The Sensitive Plant was a leafless wrack;
> But the mandrakes, and toadstools, and docks, and darnels,
> Rose like the dead from their ruined charnels.

In 'The Mother Mourns' (*PPP*), we have these lines:

> 'Let me grow, then, but mildews and mandrakes,
>   And slimy distortions,
> Let nevermore things good and lovely
>   To me appertain;
>
> 'For Reason is rank in my temples,
>   And Vision unruly . . .'

The garden, or the fungi, and the distortions, appear in the novels at times of distress or tragic crisis:

DR.   The 'wet old garden', rank broad leaves, marshy ground, and the hedge overgrown and choked with mandrakes (xii 6).

FMC. The red and yellow leaves fleeing like ghosts (suggested by 'The Sensitive Plant' as well as 'Ode to the West Wind'), the swamp dotted with fungi, which grew from rotting leaves and tree-stumps. Some of the fungi were marked with 'great splotches, red as arterial blood . . .'. The general aspect of the swamp was 'malignant'; the hollow was a 'nursery of pestilences' (xliv). Note also the clouds and scrolls of mist, 'atmospheric fungi which had their roots in the neighbouring sea', and gradually enveloped Yalbury Great Wood as the coffin containing Fanny Robin and her child was being taken to Weatherbury (xliv).

RN. The 'twisted furze-roots, tufts of rushes, or oozing lumps of fungi, which at this season lay scattered about the heath like the rotten liver and lungs of some colossal animal' (v vii).

W A black slug, dead boughs like ichthyosauri in a museum, perishing woodbine stems like old ropes, yellow fungi like lemons and apricots, branches of trees disfigured with wounds, rotting stumps rising from their mossy setting like black teeth from green gums (xlii).

TD. The uncultivated garden at Talbothays, damp and rank with grass and flowering weeds, through which Tess is drawn 'like a fascinated bird' by Angel's music; the snails; the cuckoo-spittle, slug-slime, and sticky blights which she gathers as she makes her way through 'this profusion of growth', and which stain her hands and arms – all combine to emphasize the world in which Tess finds it a 'hobble' to be alive because of her 'corporeal blight' (xix).

(For other hints of symbolism in Hardy's novels, see, in particular, pp. 27, 48–9, 55–6, and 500.)

Christianity, Scientific Philosophy, and Politics

The Church

Although a Christian at heart and a lover of church services all his life, Hardy found much that was unacceptable in the Christian Church. 'Whispered at the Church-Opening' (*WW*) suggests that something more worldly than Christianity is required for promotion:

> 'Oh, he'd no touches of tactic skill:
> His mind ran on charity and good will:
> He's but as he was, a vicar still.'

Joshua Halborough was ambitious and realized that his own advancement in the Church might be secured more by his sister's 'physical gifts of nature' and marriage to a person of influence than by his own ability. He wrote to his brother: 'To succeed in the Church, people must believe in you, first of all, as a gentleman, secondly as a man of means, thirdly as a scholar, fourthly as a preacher, fifthly, perhaps, as a Christian, – but always first as a gentleman, with all their heart and soul and strength' (*LLI.* 4). (According to an unconfirmed oral tradition, Hardy was refused admission to the Church because he was not of genteel origin.)

In *Tess of the d'Urbervilles*, the question of the double damnation of the unbaptized and illegitimate child is raised in a poignant way. It was the terror of hell-fire and other 'curious details of torment sometimes taught the young in this Christian country' which made Tess baptize her child herself lest it should die during the night. The question extends to the burial of the unbaptized in unhallowed ground. Sorrow was buried 'in that shabby corner of God's allotment where He lets the nettles grow, and where all unbaptized infants, notorious drunkards, suicides, and others of the conjecturally damned are laid' (xiv).

Angel Clare's brothers had made the Church their career. They were conventionally correct, all Church or College, but quite aloof from the general public, who were to be tolerated rather than reckoned with and respected. They disapproved of Angel's marriage to Tess on social grounds, and refused to attend the wedding. One married Mercy Chant, whose view of life was such 'that events which produced heartache in others wrought beatific smiles upon her – an enviable result, although, in the opinion of Angel, it was obtained by a curiously unnatural sacrifice of humanity to mysticism' (xxv, xxxiii, xl).

The Reverend Percival Cope would probably have allowed his engagement to Frances Frankland to lapse, if Mr Millborne had not given her and her mother social status by renting a manor-house near Ivell for them (*LLI.* 3).

The indictment in 'The Son's Veto' is much stronger. A public-school and university education 'ousted' Randolph Twycott's humanity. He refused to allow his mother to marry a greengrocer, though she pined away for love. At the funeral, he is 'a young smooth-shaven priest in a high waistcoat', and he looks 'black as a cloud' at the prosperous shopkeeper who stands watching the procession with moist eyes and hat in hand (*LLI.* 2).

Cumulatively, Hardy's criticisms are most powerful in *Jude the Obscure*. They are linked with the marriage laws, and reach their peak when Sue, assuming that the loss of her children is retribution for sin, or 'insolence' to God, returns to Phillotson, though she does not love him. A bitter, almost Aristophanic, commentary is implicit in Jude's remarriage to Arabella; 'It's true religion,' he says. Sue, 'creed-drunk', and Jude, 'gin-drunk', sacrifice themselves in remarriages which are wholly unsatisfactory but conventionally sanctified. 'The letter killeth' (*JO.* vi iii–xi).

God

Christian theology, chiefly the idea of Providence, Redemption, and Life after death, was overthrown for Hardy when, in his early twenties, he was introduced to contemporary scientific thought. He did not abandon his belief in the higher moral values proclaimed in the Bible and by the Church. Sometimes he regretted the passing of the old faith, but intellectually he believed in

the sure, unhasting, steady stress
Of Reason's movement . . .
(*HS.* 'A Cathedral Façade at Midnight'; cf. *MV.* 'The Oxen').

Perhaps the fullest statement of Hardy's religious views is that written in 1907, after the composition of 'New Year's Eve', a poem which sums up his most consistent impression of the First Cause or the Will (*Life*, 332–3). Other statements will be found in his *Life*, 375–6, and, most important of all, though brief, in the Apology to *Late Lyrics and Earlier*.

For Hardy, the universe was not wielded by God's Love as it was for Dante and Shelley; it was neutral or indifferent. It seemed that the Creator or First Cause could not have intended any form of life to reach the pitch of emotional and intellectual percipience of defect, cruelty, and suffering which had been reached by man. Perhaps the higher impulses of man would in the course of time lead to the world's amendment (*PPP.* 'A Commonplace Day'; cf. the end of *The Dynasts*).

For his rejection of Christian theology, with occasional misgivings, see: *WP.* 'A Sign-Seeker', 'The Impercipient'; *PPP.* 'The Darkling Thrush', 'The Church-Builder'; *D.* (1) I vi ('A local cult . . .'), and the comment of the Spirit of the Years on the Magnificat of the Pities, *D.* (3) After Scene; *SC.* 'A Plaint to Man', 'God's Funeral' (cf. *Life*, 354; Hardy's alternative title seems less appropriate), 'Aquae Sulis'; *MV.* 'In a Whispering Gallery'; *LLE.* 'A Drizzling Easter Morning'; *HS.* 'The Graveyard of Dead Creeds'; *WW.* 'Yuletide in a Younger World'.

Immortality

Hardy's view was that a person lived after death only in the memories and thoughts of other people. In this rationalization he was certainly influenced by Pater's *Marius the Epicurean*. See: *WP.* 'A Sign-Seeker', 'Her Immortality'; *PPP.* 'His Immortality', 'The To-be-Forgotten' (cf. 'The Souls of the Slain'). For a change in Hardy's view, see *MV.* 'He Prefers Her Earthly', and *HS.* 'Paradox'.

The idea that the progress of the world depends on the survival of the ideas of the great ('The To-be-Forgotten', vii) can be traced in Shelley's *A Defence of Poetry*.

The Insignificance of the Individual in Time and Space

In the vast scheme of the universe, even dynasts, and cults like Christianity, are local and ephemeral: *D.* (1) I vi; (3) After Scene. Men like Napoleon, who make an epoch,

> Are in the elemental ages' chart
> Like meanest insects on obscurest leaves.

That Hardy's views had not changed for more than forty years when he wrote this may be seen in *PPP*. 'At a Lunar Eclipse', which the MS. shows to have been written in 186–.

Hardy's reflections on individual insignificance are noticeable in his first published novel. 'There is in us an unquenchable expectation, which at the gloomiest time persists in inferring that because we are *ourselves*, there must be a special future in store for us, though our nature and antecedents to the remotest particular have been common to thousands.' The heroine's feeling of 'a sense of bare equality with, and no superiority to, a single entity under the sky' recurs, almost word for word, in *The Return of the Native*, and suggests an observation in the author's notebook (*DR.* i 5, xii 6).

Individual insignificance against the background of geological time is graphically presented when Knight is in imminent danger of falling to his death (*PBE.* xxii).

Egdon Heath has a complex significance. It is a microcosm. Preeminently it represents the vast span of time. It is 'a face on which time makes but little impression'. The Celtic barrow and the Roman highway had been 'almost crystallized to natural products by long continuance'; its trifling irregularities remained 'as the very finger-touches of the last geological change'. When Eustacia and Wildeve leave Rainbarrow at night, their dark figures sink and disappear 'from against the sky'; it was as if the heath had drawn in two horns 'like a mollusc'. When Clym is faced with the prospect of no reconciliation between his mother and Eustacia, he is invaded by 'a sense of bare equality with, and no superiority to, a single living thing under the sun'. He is no more than one of the lizards, grasshoppers, and ants in the ferny vegetation which seems to belong to 'the ancient world of the carboniferous period'. As a furzecutter, he seems 'to be of no more account in life than an insect'. A colony of ants suggests a city. In a crisis of frenzy, Clym is faced by 'the imperturbable countenance of the heath, which, having defied the cataclysmal onsets of centuries, reduced to insignificance by its seamed and antique features the wildest turmoil of a single man' (*RN*. I i, ix; III v; IV v, vi; V ii).

The insignificance of man's emotional life against stellar space is part of the theme of *Two on a Tower*. Conversely, Hardy's aim was to show that the smaller of 'these contrasting magnitudes' might be the greater. The insignificance is re-emphasized in terms of time when Swithin is preparing for his marriage: 'Embedded under his feet were possibly even now rude trinkets that had been worn at bridal ceremonies of the early inhabitants. Little signified those ceremonies to-day, or the happiness or otherwise of the contracting parties. That his own rite, nevertheless, signified much, was the inconsequent reasoning of Swithin, as it is of many another bridegroom besides; and he, like the rest, went on with his preparations in that mood which sees in his stale repetition the wondrous possibilities of an untried move' (*TT*. iv, xviii, xli).

The 'lonely courses' of Marty South and Giles Winterborne 'formed no detached design at all, but were part of the pattern in the great web of human doings then weaving in both hemispheres from the White Sea to Cape Horn' (*W*. iii).

Lords and ladies take their infinitesimal place in time while their stories are told in close proximity to the varnished skulls of Vespasian's soldiery and the fossilized ichthyosaurus and iguanodon (*GND*).

In *Tess of the d'Urbervilles* the heroine is seen against a landscape of 'verdant flatness' like 'a fly on a billiard table of indefinite length, and of no more consequence to the surroundings than that fly'. Similarly, between the desolate drabness of Flintcomb-Ash and the 'white vacuity' of the sky, there was nothing but the two girls (Tess and Marian) 'crawling over the surface of the former like flies'. Tess had sensed early that her life was like that of thousands and thousands before her, and of thousands and thousands to come. The transitory insignificance of human happiness is glanced at when Tess, wishing it would always be summer and autumn, delayed her marriage-promise: 'Gnats, knowing nothing of their brief glorification, wandered across the shimmer of this pathway, irradiated as if they bore fire within them, then passed out of its line, and were quite extinct' (*TD*. xvi, xix, xxxii, xliii).

In another perspective, the long succession of time is indicated by reference to paganism and May Day rites, the primeval yews and oaks of

171

the Chase, Tess's mailed ancestors, and primitive sacrifice at Stonehenge. Classical comparisons have the same effect. A ballad by Jacob Smallbury might be as long 'as that with which the worthy toper old Silenus amused on a similar occasion the swains Chromis and Mnasylus, and other jolly dogs of his day'. At Talbothays the sun threw the shadows of humble milkers 'with as much care over each contour as if it had been the profile of a Court beauty on a palace wall; copied them as diligently as it had copied Olympian shapes on marble *façades* long ago, or the outline of Alexander, Caesar, and the Pharaohs' (*TD*. ii, xi, lviii; *FMC*. xxiii; *TD*. xvi).

The technique of aerial presentation in *The Dynasts* reflects Hardy's philosophy of man's insignificance in the immensity of space and time. The vast Austrian army creeps 'like molluscs on a leaf'. At Torres Vedras the movement of the English columns 'seems peristaltic and vermicular like that of three caterpillars'. The English at Waterloo 'hurry to and fro like ants in an ant-hill' (*D*. (1) iii ii, (2) vi i, (3) vii i).

In a light-hearted mood, 'Drinking Song' (*WW*) traces changes in philosophical thought by which man's significance in the universe has been steadily diminished from the era of Thales to that of Einstein.

Nature

The significance of this subject is complex: its emphases fall on the universe; natural life, as opposed to human life and civilization; and (a debatable ground) on inalienable human rights and values which conflict with the laws and conventions of society.

'The Poor Man and the Lady' theme is the first which Hardy raised in fiction. Sincerity and intrinsic worth are opposed to affectation, privilege, and snobbery. Social prejudices which oppose the course of true love or natural affection may be seen in a number of stories (e.g. *ILH*; *PBE*; *GND*. 2, 6; and *W*). The 'ousting' of humanity by education and ambition is the subject of *LLI*. 2, 4. In his view that 'social refinement' is a 'screen' rather than an 'index, as with untutored mankind' (*PRF*), Hardy is quite Wordsworthian. Perhaps this is best illustrated in *The Woodlanders*. Giles Winterborne and Fitzpiers, Marty South and Felice Charmond are antithetical. At the centre is Grace Melbury. Too late she learned to prize real worth: 'Her heart rose from its late sadness like a released bough; her senses revelled in the sudden lapse back to Nature unadorned. The consciousness of having to be genteel because of her husband's profession, the veneer of artificiality which she had acquired at the fashionable schools, were thrown off, and she became the crude country girl of her latent early instincts' (xxviii).

Hardy's view of rural life was not idyllic. He knew that it contained feckless poverty (as in the Durbeyfield household), and squalor and crime (as in Mixen Lane, the 'Adullam of all the surrounding villages'). If such impressions do not seem to loom as large as rural virtues in his novels, it is because the principal characters 'express mainly the author, his largeness of heart . . . his culture, his insight . . .' (*PRF*). Hardy's sympathies ran with 'whatsoever things are true, whatsoever things are honest, whatsoever things are just, whatsoever things are pure, what-soever things are lovely, whatsoever things are of good report'. He found these more undisguised in country people than in society and the life of the 'caged birds' of the city. For. him the 'social conventions and contrivances – the artificial forms of living' – were not the cardinal facts of life (cf. *Life*, 213; *TD*. xx).

The danger of looking at Nature through rose-tinted spectacles was not always avoided by Hardy. He averts it after Henchard's sale of his wife: the difference between 'the peacefulness of inferior nature' ('horses rubbing each other caressingly') and 'the wilful hostilities of mankind' was such that one might 'abjure man as the blot on an other-wise kindly universe; till it was remembered that all terrestrial con-ditions were intermittent, and that mankind might some night be innocently sleeping when these quiet objects [valleys and woods and sky] were raging loud' (*MC*. i). In *The Woodlanders* we watch, with Grace, 'small members of the animal community that lived unmolested' and 'know neither law nor sin' (xli). Yet the internecine cruelty of such creatures is presented with some particularity earlier (iv). In *Jude the Obscure*, the horror of the struggle for existence is presented over and over again, with special emphasis on man as the preying species. Before this, in *Tess of the d'Urbervilles*, Hardy's argumentative intrusions had placed him in an illogical position. On the one hand Nature is cruel (cf. the Arctic birds, xliii); on the other, the 'Innocence' of the natural world is made the basis for attacking the moral code. Tess 'had been made to break an accepted social law, but no law known to the environment in which she fancied herself such an anomaly' (xiii; cf. xiv, xli). No argu-ment with reference to natural law could defend Alec d'Urberville's

conduct: 'Doubtless some of Tess d'Urberville's mailed ancestors rollick-
ing home from a fray had dealt the same measure even more ruthlessly
towards peasant girls of their time. But though to visit the sins of the
fathers upon the children may be a morality good enough for divinities,
it is scorned by average human nature . . .' (xi). The whole course of
Hardy's thought, as seen in his poetry, indicates that progress for
civilization depended upon the development in man of a higher consciousness and morality than is found in Nature as a whole.

In *Jude the Obscure*, 'the whole creation groaneth and travaileth in
pain', and conditions imposed by both nature and civilization are harsh.
Hardy's contention with the conventional attitude towards marriage is
weakened and bedevilled, however, by Sue's 'epicene' nature. Intellectually and spiritually Jude's right companion, she is averse to marriage;
in her, as well as in Arabella, Jude was tricked by Nature.

Personal disappointments on the score of heredity lead to strange
authorial observations in two of the novels. The fact that Elizabeth-Jane
is the daughter of an illegal marriage, and also a 'flower of Nature',
suggests 'Nature's jaunty readiness to support unorthodox social principles'. This is a strange conclusion, adduced as one of Nature's 'con-
trarious inconsistencies', which strengthened Henchard's 'wish to wash
his hands of life' (*MC*. xliv). The truth is simpler, and is brought out
clearly in the story: Henchard was friendless; he would have wished to
continue living with Elizabeth-Jane, despite his disappointment that she
was not his daughter, and despite his deception of her and Newson, had
not the latter returned to claim her. The 'scorn of Nature for man's finer
emotions' is felt by Jude after Sue's marriage to Phillotson; he 'saw her
with children more or less in her own likeness around her. But the
consolation of regarding them as a continuation of her identity was
denied to him, as to all such dreamers, by the wilfulness of Nature in
not allowing issue from one parent alone' (III viii). That this irrationaliza-
tion of Nature is Hardy's own is clear from 'To a Motherless Child' (*WP*;
see p. 438) and from 'At a Bridal' (*WP*), a poem written as early as 1866.

Whatever their cogency, behind these complaints lies the greater and
more logical one of Nature's indifference to the lot of man. Natural laws
are 'purblind Doomsters', and 'Crass Casualty obstructs the sun and rain'
(*WP*. 'Hap', 1866). On the blindness, sleep, or witlessness of the unconscious 'Mother', see *PPP*. 'The Lacking Sense', 'Doom and She'
(where the possibility is ventured that Nature may be aware of creation's

oxwell Manor (Oxwell Hall)

he home of Admiral Hardy (Captain Hardy of The Trumpet-Major) *at ortisham (Po'sham)*

The White Horse on the downs above Sutton Poyntz and Osmington

Faringdon Ruin

sentience and groan, which are quite meaningless to her lord, the First Cause), 'The Sleep-Worker', 'The Bull-Finches', and 'The Last Chrysanthemum'. (Cytherea Graye fondly hopes that the wintry weather will prevent her wedding; perhaps it is 'a scheme of the great Mother to hinder a union of which she does not approve': *DR*. xiii 1.)

Nature's imperfections, as seen in the universe, man – 'A soul's direction [dependent] on a body's whim' – and society – 'A whole life's circumstance [dependent] on hap of birth' – are the subject of the early poem, 'Discouragement', 1863–7. Its 'lawless caprice' (*PBE*. xxii), the defects and the cruelty of its laws (*RN*. III i; *TT*. xli), the 'vocalized sorrows of the trees' (*W*. iii; cf. *RN*. III vi), and the Unfulfilled Intention (*W*. vii; cf. *WP*. 'In a Wood') may be observed incidentally in the novels. For less casual, and more mythological, treatment, see *PPP*. 'The Mother Mourns', 'The Lacking Sense', 'Doom and She', 'The Subalterns', 'The Sleep-Worker'; and *HS*. 'Genitrix Laesa'.

A letter (*Life*, 315) makes Hardy's indictment clear. It is concerned with the existence of pain, and refutes the idea that Nature 'may practise a scheme of morality unknown to us, in which she is just'. To show that the difficulty 'recognized by thinkers like Schopenhauer, Hartmann, Haeckel, etc., and by most of the persons called pessimists, remains unsurmounted', he continues:

> Pain has been, and pain is: no new sort of morals in Nature can remove pain from the past and make it pleasure for those who are its infallible estimators, the bearers thereof. And no injustice, however slight, can be atoned for by her future generosity, however ample, so long as we consider Nature to be, or to stand for, unlimited power. The exoneration of an omnipotent Mother by her retrospective justice becomes an absurdity when we ask, what made the foregone injustice necessary to her Omnipotence?
>
> So you cannot, I fear, save her good name except by assuming one of two things: that she is blind and not a judge of her actions, or that she is an automaton, and unable to control them: in either of which assumptions, though you have the chivalrous satisfaction of screening one of her sex, you only throw responsibility a stage further back.

Finally, he states that 'to model our conduct on Nature's apparent conduct, as Nietzsche would have taught, can only bring disaster to humanity'.

This was in 1902. For many years he had held that the development of emotional sentience and intellectual percipience in man was a tragic incongruity. Only the lesser creatures, such as those sporting in the water-butt (*DR.* xii 3), the 'worlds of ephemerons', and the maggoty shapes in shallow ponds on the heath (*RN.* IV v), enjoyed unalleviated happiness. The Unfulfilled Intention is explained in a note of 1881 (*Life*, 149): Nature's imperfection is either that it produced in man a creature beyond its intentions ('on the emotional side') or that it did not proceed further by eliminating evil; see also *Life*, 163, 218 (cf. *TL.* 'Let Me Enjoy', i); *JO.* VI iii; *PPP.* 'The Mother Mourns'; *D.* (1) I vi (Shade of the Earth), IV v:

> But O, the intolerable antilogy
> Of making figments feel!

and v iv:

> The cognizance ye mourn, Life's doom to feel,
> If I report it meetly, came unmeant,
> Emerging with blind gropes from impercipience
> By listless sequence – luckless, tragic Chance,
> In your more human tongue.

Among the later poems, see *TL.* 'Before Life and After', 'New Year's Eve'; *HS.* 'The Aërolite'.

The First Cause or Immanent Will

In one of his happiest poems (*WP.* 'Ditty', 1870), thinking of the fortuitous circumstances which had led to his first meeting with Emma Lavinia Gifford, Hardy expresses his reflections on his apparent good fortune, not in the providential terms of convention, but in a striking affirmation which derives from earlier speculations on life and scientific thought:

> What bond-servants of Chance
> We are all.

'Hap' (1866) concludes with the thought:

> These purblind Doomsters had as readily strown
> Blisses about my pilgrimage as pain.

In 1870 it seemed they had; years later he was to look back upon the event as 'a stupid blunder of God Almighty' (p. 372).

Hardy censures Eustacia for attributing misfortunes she could have avoided to 'some indistinct, colossal Prince of the World, who had framed her situation and ruled her lot' (*RN.* iv viii), but he clearly felt that she was the victim of circumstances also: 'The gloomy corner into which accident as much as indiscretion had brought this woman might have led even a moderate partisan to feel that she had cogent reasons for asking the Supreme Power by what right a being of such exquisite finish had been placed in circumstances calculated to make of her charms a curse rather than a blessing' (iv iii). On Clym's misfortunes he took a sterner view than the sufferer, and had no hesitation in affirming that the First Cause was on a lower level morally than the best of mankind (*RN.* vi i).

Milder outbreaks occur elsewhere. We have 'the ingenious machinery contrived by the Gods for reducing human possibilities of amelioration to a minimum' (*MC.* xliv); the 'Intangible Cause which has shaped the situation no less for the offenders than the offended, but is too elusive to be discerned and cornered by poor humanity in irritated mood' (*W.* xi); a cryptic passage noted on 10 December 1888, which may have a personal reference: 'He, she, had blundered; but not as the Prime Cause had blundered . . .' (*Life*, 215); and the 'unsympathetic First Cause', the universal harshness, and the President of the Immortals in *Tess of the d'Urbervilles* (xxv, xlix, lix) – the last an unfortunate afterthought, since it is incongruous with Hardy's conception of the unconscious Will.

After *Jude the Obscure*, Hardy decided it would be safer to express his views in poetry. 'To cry out in a passionate poem that (for instance) the Supreme Mover or Movers, the Prime Force or Forces, must be either limited in power, unknowing, or cruel – which is obvious enough, and has been for centuries – will cause' readers whose opinion is 'inert' or 'crystallized . . . merely a shake of the head' (*Life*, 284–5).

In 'Discouragement' (*HS.* 1863–7) he had presented Nature as 'racked and wrung' by her unfaithful lord. In 'Nature's Questioning' (*WP*), four alternative theories are raised:

1. Has some Vast Imbecility, mighty to build, but impotent to tend, created us in jest, and left us to chance?
2. Is the First Cause an unconscious Automaton?
3. Or is Godhead dying, 'brain and eye now gone'?
4. Or is there a plan, beyond our comprehension, of Evil stormed by Good, humanity being 'the Forlorn Hope over which Achievement strides'?

That Hardy did not believe in the first is clear from a letter he wrote to Alfred Noyes (*Life*, 409); the idea of the Prime Mover as malignant seemed 'irresistibly comic' to him. The third does not reappear, and Hardy's further thought on the subject is limited to the second and last. There is no question of Achievement 'striding' *through* mankind. In his later years, after *The Dynasts*, Hardy thought that hope of amelioration through man was very forlorn indeed (cf. *WW*. 'We are getting to the end').

The First Cause is like Shelley's Power in *The Revolt of Islam* (VIII v). It has no moral sense, and is unaware of humanity's pain on this 'tainted ball'. *Not to mend* means *not to know*. We have to think not so much of the Unknown God as of the 'Unknowing God' (*PPP*. 'Doom and She', 'God-Forgotten', 'The Bedridden Peasant'). In 'By the Earth's Corpse', a God is imagined who, after the extinction of the human race, becomes aware of its suffering; He is sorry that it was created.

More hopeful is 'To the Unknown God', the last poem in *Poems of the Past and the Present*. When this was written, Hardy was about to begin *The Dynasts*, a work which may appear to end optimistically (see p. 115). His optimistic evolutionary view was that the consciousness of man, being part of the Immanent or General Will, will gradually influence It for the better (*MV*. 'He Wonders about Himself').

Other poems on the Will are: *TL*. 'A Dream Question', 'Before Life and After', 'New Year's Eve'; *SC*. 'The Convergence of the Twain'; *MV*. 'To the Moon', 'The Blow', 'Fragment', 'The Masked Face'; *LLE*. 'According to the Mighty Working' (cf. *Life*, 388); *HS*. 'Xenophanes, the Monist of Colophon'; *WW*. 'A Philosophical Phantasy'.

Pessimism and Meliorism

On this question, Hardy's views are best reflected in a conversation he held with William Archer in 1904: '. . . I believe, indeed, that a good deal of the robustious, swaggering optimism of recent literature is at bottom cowardly and insincere . . . my pessimism, if pessimism it be, does not involve the assumption that the world is going to the dogs. . . . On the contrary, my practical philosophy is distinctly meliorist. What are my books but one long plea against "man's inhumanity to man" – to woman – and to the lower animals? Whatever may be the inherent good or evil of life, it is certain that men make it much worse that it need be.'

Equally significant is the quotation from Galsworthy which Hardy kept on the framed photograph of its author (Vere H. Collins, *Talks with Thomas Hardy at Max Gate 1920–22*, Duckworth, 1928): 'The optimist appears to be one who cannot bear the world as it is, and is forced by his nature to picture it as it ought to be; and the pessimist one who can not only bear the world as it is, but loves it well enough to draw it faithfully'. It matches Hardy's self-description in 'In Tenebris' (ii) as one

> Who holds that if way to the Better there be, it exacts a full look
>   at the Worst.

Hardy's pessimism arose from the contemporary scientific outlook, which left no place for Providence or the Christian idea of a God of Love. The universe spelt indifference to man, and reduced him to a level of significance little higher than that of other species. Cruelty, disease, and suffering were the consequence of the general struggle for survival. Careerism, and the social unrest which it created, class distinctions, nationalism, and war reflected competitiveness and the struggle for survival in man. Against this Hardy proposed the Christian doctrine of 'charity' or 'loving-kindness', and an alliance between this humanitarian religion and 'complete rationality'. Otherwise, he felt, the world would perish (*LLE*. Apology). His views had been expressed earlier in 'A Plaint to Man' (*SC*):

> The truth should be told, and the fact be faced
> That had best been faced in earlier years:
>
> The fact of life with dependence placed
> On the human heart's resource alone,
> In brotherhood bonded close and graced
>
> With loving-kindness fully blown,
> And visioned help unsought, unknown.

This 'Altruism, or The Golden Rule, or whatever "Love your Neighbour as Yourself" may be called, will ultimately be brought about I think by the pain we see in others reacting on ourselves, as if we and they were a part of one body. Mankind, in fact, may be and possibly will be viewed as members of one corporeal frame' (*Life*, 224). Most people, contrary to what was said, were 'waiting to give and receive sympathy' (*Life*, 253).

The Immanent Will was not percipient, but percipience was to be found in humanity; and Hardy trusted that it would spread and gradually inform the General Will 'till It fashion all things fair' (*PPP*. 'A Commonplace Day'; *MV*. 'He Wonders about Himself').

For this reason he regarded himself as a 'meliorist' and not a pessimist. It is genuine idealists who think profoundly, and to whom, in the words of Keats,

the miseries of the world
Are misery, and will not let them rest.

Hence Hardy's sense of kinship with Shelley, and his disapproval of Browning's philosophy. For him the optimist deceived himself (see *Life*, 383). Hardy's 'optimism' was dampened by man's irrationality (*WW*. 'Thoughts at Midnight') and by events such as the First World War. 'He said he would probably not have ended *The Dynasts* as he did end it if he could have foreseen what was going to happen within a few years' (*Life*, 368; cf. *MV*. 'The wind blew words'; *WW*. 'We are getting to the end').

Political Views

During his stay in London of 1862–7, Hardy developed Radical sympathies. The offices of the Reform League were on the floor below those of Blomfield, for whom he worked; he was interested in their activities and in favour of their general aims. He attended one of John Stuart Mill's electioneering meetings in 1865, and probably became acquainted with Professor Beesly, one of the Reform leaders, at this time (*Life*, 37–8, 168, 330).

The Poor Man and the Lady was too Radical for publication, Alexander Macmillan thought. Hardy *meant mischief*. The hero addressed a working-class crowd in Trafalgar Square, and was rejected by the heroine's family for his Radicalism (Edmond Gosse, *The Sunday Times*, 22 January 1928). Satire of the upper classes is most notable in *A Pair of Blue Eyes*, *The Hand of Ethelberta*, and *The Well-Beloved*.

By 1881, Hardy's views could be summarized as follows: 'To conserve the existing good, to supplant the existing bad by good, is to act on a true political principle, which is neither Conservative nor Radical' (*Life*, 148).

Hardy regarded himself later as an Intrinsicalist: a person should be judged by his intrinsic worth, not by class or conventions. (This attitude lies at the root of much of Hardy's writing, particularly his fiction, and most remarkably in *Tess of the d'Urbervilles* and *Jude the Obscure*, or a short story like 'The Son's Veto'; it is one of the reasons for his popularity.) *The Dynasts* illustrates the exploitation of the masses for political power. Hardy was no longer biased by party politics; he stood for equality of opportunity for all, and foresaw the dangers of proletarianism (*Life*, 204, 236).

As might be expected of the author of *The Dynasts*, he was in 'hearty agreement' with a League of Peace after the First World War. The sentiment of 'patriotism' should be 'freed from the narrow meaning attaching to it in the past . . . and be extended to the whole globe'; that of 'foreignness' should 'attach only to other planets and their inhabitants, if any' (*Life*, 374–5).

War

General reflections: Life, 322 (Tolstoy), 365–6 (the quotation, 'Quicquid delirant reges, plectuntur Achivi', was entered in Hardy's notebook forty-four years earlier with reference to the Franco-Prussian War; see *Life*, 78); *PPP*. 'Departure', 'A Christmas Ghost-Story', 'The Sick Battle-God'; *TL*. 'The Man he Killed'; *SC*. 'Channel Firing'; *MV*. 'His Country', 'The Pity of It', 'In Time of "the Breaking of Nations" ', 'Often when warring', 'I met a man'; *HS*. 'A Night of Questionings'; *WW*. 'Christmas: 1924', (?) 'He Resolves to Say No More' (fears of the Second World War?). For *The Dynasts*, see pp. 105–6.

The Boer War: PPP. 'Embarcation', 'Departure', 'The Colonel's Soliloquy', 'The Going of the Battery', 'At the War Office', 'A Christmas Ghost-Story', 'Drummer Hodge', 'A Wife in London', 'The Souls of the Slain', 'Song of the Soldiers' Wives and Sweethearts', 'The Sick Battle-God'.

The First World War, 1914–18: MV. 'The Blow', 'Men who March Away', 'His Country', 'England to Germany in 1914', 'On the Belgian Expatriation', 'An Appeal to America on Behalf of the Belgian Destitute', 'The Pity of It', 'In Times of Wars and Tumults', 'In Time of "the Breaking of Nations" ' (cf. *Life*, 78–9, 378), 'Cry of the Homeless', 'Before Marching and After' (in memory of Frank William George, the son of Hardy's second cousin, who was killed at Gallipoli: *Life*, 371),

'Often when warring', 'Then and Now', 'A Call to National Service' (written, like many of the above poems, in response to a special appeal to authors; see *Life*, 366–7), 'The Dead and the Living One' (described by Hardy as 'a war ballad of some weirdness', *Life*, 372), 'A New Year's Eve in War Time' (Hardy's actual experience at Max Gate), 'I met a man', 'I looked up from my writing'; *LLE*. 'Jezreel', 'And there was a Great Calm', 'The Wood Fire' (in this Crucifixion story, Hardy was venting a wry comment on the removal of the wooden crosses from the burial-grounds on the Western Front. This poem 'brought down on Hardy the allegation of blasphemy, which he very keenly resented': Edmund Blunden, *Thomas Hardy*, 167), 'By Henstridge Cross at the Year's End' (see Henstridge Cross, p. 365), 'Outside the Casement'; *HS*. 'The Peace Peal'.

Cruelty to Animals

For Hardy, this subject was inseparable from war (in the usual sense) and from 'meliorism', since (as the law of evolution shows) 'all organic creatures are of one family'. With Shelley (see *Adonais*), he believed that 'the web of being' included all living things. For human progress, the centre of Altruism (see p. 179) should be shifted 'from humanity to the whole conscious world collectively' (*Life*, 346, 349). It is for this reason that Hardy introduces the sufferings of animals in *The Dynasts*. His most striking presentation of organic Nature is to be found in the poem 'The wind blew words' (*MV*). Hardy's views were perhaps too emotional for him to face the issue realistically (Nature is too prolific for general survival), but he was averse to cruelty for pleasure, and anxious to promote humane slaughter as far as it was necessary. He did not overlook Nature's cruelty; the horror of it was brought home to him in childhood and remained with him all his life (cf. *Life*, 444, and the Arctic birds, *TD*. xliii); it was thoughtless, he maintained, to say 'What a lovely frosty day!' when one remembered the suffering caused by wintry weather to birds and animals (Collins, *Talks with Thomas Hardy at Max Gate 1920–22*, 37). His books were 'one continued plea against man's inhumanity to man – to woman – and the lower animals' (Clive Holland; cf. Hardy's conversation with William Archer, above). On the treatment of horses, blood-sports, vivisection, and humane slaughter, see *Life*, 211, 303, 321–2, 346–7, 434. See also: *HE*. xxv; *TD*. xli; *JO*. I ii, x, IV ii, v vi; *PPP*. 'The

Puzzled Game-Birds' (cf. 'Sportsman Time but rears his brood to kill' in *WP.* 'She, to Him', i); *D.* (2) VI v (a simile recalling Hardy's *Life*, 444), (3) I v (horses at Borodino), VI viii (Chorus of the Years); *MV.* 'The Blinded Bird' (see p. 164), 'Afterwards'; *LLE.* Apology; *HS.* 'Compassion, an Ode' (in celebration of the centenary of the R.S.P.C.A.), 'The Bird-Catcher's Boy'; *WW.* 'The Lady in the Furs'.

Influence and Recollections of Architecture, Music, Painting, and Literature

Architecture

The recurrence of the architect as hero in Hardy's early novels suggests that, with varying degrees of mutation, his own experience contributed to some extent to their background. Only in *A Laodicean*, however, does architecture form an important part of the story. Hardy's observations when he was an architect in London, at Weymouth, and on his first visit to Cornwall provided the background for scenes in *The Poor Man and the Lady*, *Desperate Remedies*, and *A Pair of Blue Eyes*, the heroes of which were all architects. In the first of these novels, one scene (which was transferred to 'An Indiscretion in the Life of an Heiress') related to an experience of Arthur Blomfield which Hardy witnessed at New Windsor, when the Crown Princess of Germany laid the memorial-stone of a church (*Life*, 48). Hardy's familiarity with the work involved in free-stone cutting and carving for building and restoration is apparent in *Jude the Obscure*.

It is rather fanciful to assume, as some critics have done, that Hardy's architectural training is reflected in the design of his novels. J. W. Beach's statement that *The Woodlanders* is 'a bungled narrative' is far too sweeping, but it has its validity with reference to the chapter or so which kindled his consternation. Hardy often wrote hurriedly and with an eye to pleasing his magazine-readers. No doubt, like Shakespeare, he could lament that Fortune

> did not better for my life provide
> Than public means which public manners breed.

He presents his dilemma in 'Candour in English Fiction'. The conclusions of *The Return of the Native* and *The Woodlanders* were a sacrifice of artistic integrity to meet a public demand. As an example of what he was prepared to do and what he could do, given the time, the endings of the serial version and the final novel form of *The Well-Beloved* should be compared. When he refused to compromise, his first resource, in *Tess of the d'Urbervilles*, was argument, which did anything but strengthen his case, and was artistically indefensible. His next was to transfer views which could not be embodied in the action of the story to the principal characters – not in accordance with any blue-print, however. The growth of *Jude the Obscure*, like that of *The Return of the Native*, shows a change of emphasis and direction, and even more, one suspects, a continual admission of the new. 'The rectangular lines of the story were not pre-meditated, but came by chance' (*Life*, 273). He had no idea what the later chapters of *A Pair of Blue Eyes* would be like when he started the novel (*Life*, 91).

The influence of architecture on Hardy's writing is to be seen more assuredly elsewhere. It enabled him to see the general and distinctive characteristics of buildings, and, whether remembered or imagined, to delineate them with deft attention to their salient details. Knapwater House (*DR.* v) and Endelstow House (*PBE.* v) are presented in single paragraphs of masterly compression and clarity. In this respect, and in the evocation of 'atmosphere', the great barn in *Far from the Madding Crowd* is an outstanding example. Buildings, especially of Ham-hill stone, are a characteristic feature of the Wessex landscape.

Occasionally, Hardy's predilections are expressed. Melchester (Salisbury) Cathedral is 'the most graceful architectural pile in England' (*JO.* III i); 'the mullioned and transomed Elizabethan' is the 'never-to-be-surpassed style for the English country residence'. One sentence shows us Hardy regarding a scene with an architectural eye: the lines of the buildings (on Chief Street, Christminster) were 'as distinct in the morning air as in an architectural drawing' (*JO.* III ix).

In general, Hardy's descriptions are designed for the common reader. A tendency towards specialization appears in the presentation of High-Place Hall: 'It was Palladian, and like most architecture erected since the Gothic age, was a compilation rather than a design.' The danger of over-specialization is evident in the description of Mount Lodge; it was 'of the Italian elevation made familiar by Inigo Jones and his school' (*MC.* xxi; *CM.* 12).

The opening chapter of *A Laodicean* has a special importance, since it appears to recapitulate Hardy's thoughts on fashions in architectural style. In the novel, technicalities are not unduly obtrusive. They provide a greater barrier in a few of the poems, e.g. *PPP*. 'Rome: Building a New Street in the Ancient Quarter' and 'The Church-Builder'. 'The Abbey Mason' (*SC*) is dedicated to John Hicks, to whom Hardy was apprenticed in Dorchester, and its subject is the origin of the English Gothic style. Rare architectural terms are used elsewhere, as in the poem on the refusal of the Dean of Westminster to allow a tablet in Poets' Corner to the memory of Byron:

> 'Twill next be expected
> That I get erected
> To Shelley a tablet
> In some niche or gablet.

More significant is the figurative use of architectural terms in Hardy's prose and verse:

> Viewed sideways, the closing-line of [Eustacia's] lips formed, with almost geometric precision, the curve so well known in the arts of design as the cima-recta, or ogee. *RN*. I vii
>
> [Lucetta] flung herself on the couch in the cyma-recta curve which so became her . . . *MC*. xxii
>
> The smoke of the kindled wood rose from the chimney without like a lotus-headed column. *TD*. xxxvi
>
> And count as framework to the stagery
> Yon architraves of sunbeam-smitten cloud.
> *D*. Fore Scene
>
> Nay, nay, nay;
> Your hasty judgments stay,
> Until the topmost cyme
> Have crowned the last entablature of Time. *D*. (1) v iv

Familiarity with building operations is evident in the description of firelocks 'heavy as putlogs' (*D*. (2) II vii); and who but Hardy would have thought of the 'cusps' of the moon at 'demilune' (*HS*. 'Once at Swanage')?

An interesting note shows how architectural observations influenced his poetry:

> Years earlier he had decided that too regular a beat was bad art. He had fortified himself in his opinion by thinking of the analogy of

architecture. . . . He knew that in architecture cunning irregularity is of enormous worth, and it is obvious that he carried on into his verse . . . the Gothic art-principle in which he had been trained – the principle of spontaneity, found in mouldings, tracery, and such like – resulting in the 'unforeseen' (as it has been called) character of his metres and stanzas, that of stress rather than of syllable, poetic texture rather than poetic veneer. . . .   *Life*, 300–1

Music

For years Hardy's grandfather and father had been the mainstay of the Stinsford string choir, and had played at local weddings and dances. He himself by the age of four (when he was given an accordion) was 'extraordinarily sensitive to music' and familiar with 'endless jigs, hornpipes, reels, waltzes, and country-dances' which his father played in the evenings, and to which he danced rapturously 'a *pas seul* in the middle of the room'. In later years, he recalled 'Enrico', 'The Fairy Dance' (the enchantment of which he turned to good account in 'The Fiddler of the Reels'), 'Miss Macleod of Ayr' (to which Farfrae danced with Elizabeth-Jane), and 'My Fancy-Lad'. So deeply moved was he by some of these that he danced on to conceal his weeping (*Life*, 15).

Under his father's instruction, he was soon able at an early age 'to tweedle from notation some hundreds of jigs and country-dances that he found in his father's and grandfather's old books'. In 1852 he began to accompany his father at local festivities, often at small farmsteads like that of 'The Three Strangers'; he recalled being stopped by his hostess on one occasion, after he had played a favourite country-dance, 'The New-Rigged Ship', for three-quarters of an hour; she was afraid he might 'burst a blood-vessel' (*Life*, 22, 23).

Equally marked was his love of church music. Its appeal had been strong from his earliest years (*Life*, 414). The staple tunes of the old choir were well-known to him: the 'Old Hundredth', 'New Sabbath', 'Devizes', 'Wilton', 'Lydia', and 'Cambridge New', which they played to Tate and Brady's metrical psalms; and 'Barthélémon' and 'Tallis', to which Bishop Ken's Morning and Evening Hymns ('Awake, my soul, and with the sun' and 'Glory to Thee, my God, this night') were sung each Sunday (*Life*, 10). Whether he attended a choir-practice like that at the opening of *Two on a Tower* is conjectural, but his interest in the musical settings to metrical psalms and hymns remained with him all his life (cf. *MV*. 'Apostrophe to an Old Psalm Tune'). When Hardy was President-elect, he sent 'the following old-fashioned psalm tunes associated with Dorsetshire to the Society of Dorset Men in London': Frome, Wareham, Blandford, New Poole, Bridport, Lulworth, Rockborne, Mercy, Bride-head, Charmouth (*Life*, 337). In 1862 he thought it worth while to inform his sister Mary that they sang 'most of the tunes in the Salisbury hymn book' at the church he attended at Kilburn. She became a church organist. He himself, when nearly eighty, after listening to 'the beautiful anthem "God is gone up" (Croft)' at Exeter Cathedral, felt that he would like to be a cathedral organist more than anything else in the world (*Life*, 404).

Hardy's predilections were not radically altered by the new hymnology. A visit to his father's grave in 1919 set him reflecting on the superiority of Tate and Brady's Psalm 90 to Dr Watt's version (*Life*, 393; cf. 275). It was formerly sung at the graveside to the tune of St Stephen (cf. 'The Rash Bride'). Hardy's visit to Tintagel church with his wife Florence in 1916 was unfortunate, but he derived some compensation from hearing 'the beautiful 34th Psalm to Smart's fine tune "Wiltshire" ' (*Life*, 373–4). After attending an evening service at Stinsford in 1921, he wrote: 'A beautiful evening. Evening Hymn Tallis' (*Life*, 414).

The poem 'The Vatican: Sala delle Muse' (*PPP*) records Hardy's love of 'Story, and Dance, and Hymn'. In *The Poor Man and the Lady* he drew 'largely' on dances he had attended at famous ballrooms in London; they are the subject of 'Reminiscences of a Dancing Man' (*TL*), which recalls the Drum-polka at 'The Argyle' and Jullien's 'grand quadrilles' at Cremorne (*Life*, 42–3, 123). Country-dances took place at the tranter's Christmas party and the wedding of Dick Dewy and Fancy Day, but only 'The Triumph',* or 'Follow my Lover', and 'Haste to the Wedding'* are named; Hardy said that the dance which began with six-hands-round must have been 'The College Hornpipe' (*UGT*. I vii, viii; v ii). Gabriel Oak's favourite appears to be 'Jockey to the Fair',* and the highlight of the harvest-supper dance is the 'immortal tune' of 'The Soldier's Joy',* which, 'at the end of three-quarters of an hour of thunderous foot-ing, still possesses more stimulative properties for the heel and toe than

* Included in the Hardy music notebooks (Elna Sherman, 'Thomas Hardy: Lyricist, Symphonist', *Music and Letters*, xxi, April 1940).

the majority of other dances at their first opening' (*FMC*. vi, viii, xxxvi). Among the Christmas Eve dances at Mrs Yeobright's were 'Nancy's Fancy' and 'The Devil's Dream' ('The Devil among the Tailors').

Margery Tucker could dance reels and jigs and country-dances like The New-Rigged Ship',* 'Follow-my-Lover', 'Haste-to-the-Wedding', 'The College Hornpipe', 'The Favourite Quickstep', and 'Captain White's Dance', but she needed the Baron's tuition to dance the polka at the Yeomanry Ball; it is described as 'a new dance at Almack's, and everywhere else, over which the world has gone crazy' (*CM*. 12).

'Miss McLeod of Ayr',* an air which Hardy thought Burns might have danced to, is described as 'a tune of a busy, vaulting, leaping sort – some low notes on the silver string of each fiddle, then a skipping on the small, like running up and down ladders'. It was 'an old country thing', the only one Elizabeth-Jane knew (*MC*. xvi). Earlier in the century, at Athelhall, the Mellstock fiddlers played 'Speed the Plough'* and that 'delightful last-century measure', 'The Honeymoon' (*CM*. 2). The Longpuddle players blazed away with 'The Dashing White Sergeant' at the Tinker's Arms, and confounded their audience by striking up 'The Devil among the Tailors' in church (*LLI*. 8*f*). 'The Jilt's Hornpipe' is described as a sound old melody which had been 'taken and doctored, and twisted about, and brought out as a new popular ditty' (*WB*. II ii). Mop Ollamoor played 'My Fancy Lad' for a five-handed reel; it was 'the strain of all seductive strains' which Caroline Hipcroft found irresistible. When only three dancers were left, he modulated into 'The Fairy Dance'* (*LLI*. 7). Sergeant-Major Clark suffered a fatal heart-attack while dancing to the lively strains of 'Off she goes' (*CM*. 5).

At the Phoenix ball in Casterbridge (*WP*. 'The Dance at the Phoenix'), the King's Own Cavalry played 'Soldier's Joy', 'Fancy-Lad', 'Maiden Coy', 'Speed the Plough', 'The Triumph', 'Sylph',* 'The Row-dow-dow',* 'Major Malley's Reel' (cf. *FMC*. l), 'The Duke of York's',* 'The Fairy Dance', 'The Bridge of Lodi' (a French tune; cf. *Life*, 195–6), and 'The Fall of Paris' (cf. *LLE*. 'A Duettist to her Pianoforte').

Among the quadrilles in the early part of the nineteenth century were Weippert's 'First Set' (*LLE*. 'A Gentleman's Epitaph on Himself and a Lady, who were Buried Together'). Some of the most popular dances of the period are recalled in *The Dynasts*: 'The Regency Hornpipe',* 'Speed the Plough', 'The Copenhagen Waltz',* 'La Belle Caterina',*

189

'Down with the French', 'The Plains of Vitoria', 'Voulez-vous danser',*
'Enrico', 'Lord Wellington's Hornpipe', 'The White Cockade',* 'The
Hungarian Waltz',* 'The Hanoverian Waltz',* and 'The Prime of Life'
(*D* (2) vi vii; (3) ii iv, v vi, vi ii).

Hardy's grandmother used to tell how they formed for country-
dances such as 'The Triumph' and 'The New-Rigged Ship' (*TL.* 'One
We Knew'). A dream recalled his own early fiddling, and the jigging of
fieldfolk to 'Haste to the Wedding' (*LLE.* 'In the Small Hours'). 'The
Dashing White Sergeant' forms the background to a scene in a story of
cuckoldry (*HS.* 'At a Pause in a Country Dance').

Psalm 102 is quoted by Knight and Elfride (*PBE.* xxvii), and again
('a pelican in the wilderness'; *FMC.* ix). 'Lead, kindly light', one of
Hardy's favourite hymns (*Life*, 274–5) is aptly introduced (*FMC.* lvi).
He recalled one of the hymns of his Sunday School days, 'Here we suffer
grief and pain', to deepen a tragic scene (*TD.* li); its title was 'Joyful' and
it was set to the tune 'Rejoicing'; its theme was the joys of Heaven.
Psalm 119 and Psalm 73 are also ironically introduced (*JO.* ii iii, vi
ii).

In 'Apostrophe to an Old Psalm Tune' (*MV*), Hardy recalls his choir-
boy days. Psalm and hymn tunes are introduced in the novels and poems:
'Lydia' (Psalm 133), *RN.* i v; 'New Sabbath', *L.* i i, *TL.* 'A Church
Romance', *LLE.* 'The Chapel-Organist'; 'Devizes', *TT.* ii; 'Wiltshire'
(Psalm 109), *MC.* xxxiii; 'Langdon' (Psalm 25), *TD.* xiii; Mount
Ephraim', *TL.* 'A Church Romance'; 'St Stephen', *TL.* 'The Rash
Bride', *LLE.* 'The Chapel-Organist'; the 'Old Hundred-and-Thirteenth',
SC. 'Places'; 'Cambridge New', *MV.* 'Afternoon Service at Mellstock';
'Eden New', *MV.* 'Jubilate'; 'Ravenscroft', *LLE.* 'On the Tune Called
the Hundred-and-Fourth' ('Remember Adam's Fall' (*UGT.* i iv) may
have been sung to it by the Mellstock choir; cf. Elna Sherman, p. 188 n.);
'Barthélémon', *LLE.* 'Barthélémon at Vauxhall' (it was sung to Bishop
Ken's Morning Hymn and described by Hardy as 'probably the most
popular hymn-tune ever written'; for the occasion which gave rise to the
poem, see *Life*, 414); 'The Old Hundredth', 'Mount Zion', 'Miles-Lane',
Holy Rest', 'Arabia', 'Eaton', 'Tallis', *LLE.* 'The Chapel-Organist'.
'Tallis' was sung to the Evening Hymn of Bishop Ken, 'a gentle-voiced
prelate' (*JO.* ii i).

Christmas hymns and carols which Hardy knew well from his choir-
boy days or from the family music books are recalled in stories of the

three choirs: Mellstock (*UGT*. I iv, v; *TL*. 'The Rash Bride', 'The Dead Quire'; *HS*. 'The Paphian Ball'), Longpuddle (*LLI*. 8*e*), Chalk-Newton (*CM*. 4). The old carol which is heard at the beginning and end of the last story is 'Hark, the glad sound, the Saviour comes'.

He always loved an old song (cf. *IIS*. 'Any little old song'). Some of his poems were composed to old tunes, and several folk-songs enter his stories, e.g. 'With the rose and the lily' (lines from a sheep-shearing song, *UGT*. I i), 'Dame Durden', 'The Seeds of Love' (*FMC*. viii, xxiii), 'Down in Cupid's Gardens' (*RN*. VI iv; *TD*. xlix), 'The Barley Mow' (*RN*. VI iv), 'The Spotted Cow' (*W*. xlviii; *TD*. iii), 'I have parks, I have hounds', 'The break o' day' (*TD*. xlix). Tess discovered that Angel Clare seemed to like the last two, but not 'The Tailor's Breeches' and 'Such a beauty I did grow'. The former was to the taste of Tony Kytes (*LLI*. 8*a*), who no doubt would have approved of the song sung by Suke Damson (*W*. xx) and prized by the septuagenarian singer Grandfer Cantle (*RN*. VI iv). Farfrae sang popular Scottish songs (*MC*. viii); an Irish one, 'Take me, Paddy, will you now?' provided the theme for 'Sitting on the Bridge' (*MV*). Several Irish songs are recalled in 'Donaghadee' (*HS*). For popular ballads which were sung, see p. 205.

A Pair of Blue Eyes (iii) recalls Hardy's first visit to Cornwall, and his memory of the songs by Emma Lavinia Gifford and her sister (*Life*, 75). They are the subject of 'A Duettist to her Pianoforte' (*LLE*). Among the songs sung by Elfride was 'Should he upbraid', 'the most marvellous old song in English music in its power of touching an audience', Hardy wrote after hearing it sung at Sturminster Newton. His exquisite description of the singing expresses a sensitive appreciation (*Life*, 118; *LLE*. 'The Maid of Keinton Mandeville'). There is a tantalizing note in his *Life* (243) on a plan Hardy never fulfilled: 'Title: — "Songs of Five-and-Twenty Years". Arrangement of the songs: Lyric Ecstasy inspired by music to have precedence.'

At an early age 'he was puzzled by what seemed to him a resemblance between two marches of totally opposite sentiments – "See the conquering hero comes" and "The Dead March in *Saul*". Some dozen years were to pass before he discovered that they were by the same composer' (*Life*, 16). Military music was a feature of public life in Dorchester. It revived in 1851 with the arrival of the Scots Greys; they gave public concerts in the Town Hall, and their playing of 'The Dead March in *Saul*' at the funeral of a comrade created an unforgettable impression. Its recollection in the last story Hardy wrote suggests that he may have been present (see p. 266).

A marching-tune of a different cast was 'The Girl I Left Behind Me', which was played by the Eleventh Dragoon-Guards as they 'pranced down the street' on leaving Casterbridge; with them went Sergeant Troy, forsaking Fanny Robin (*FMC*. x). It recurs in the moving context of 'The Colonel's Soliloquy' (*PPP*). The march in *Athalie* is associated with the moods of Eustacia Vye (*RN*. I vii). 'When War's Alarms' (*D*. (3) v vi) was found by Hardy among the musical entries in his grandfather's notebook. Regiments passing through Brussels before the battle of Waterloo play 'Brighton Camp, or the Girl I've left behind me', 'Hieland Laddie', and 'The British Grenadiers' (*D*. (3) vi iv).

Some of Hardy's numerous 'songs' may have been written to favourite airs; at least three poems (*MV*. 'Timing Her'; *LLE*. 'Meditations on a Holiday', 'O I won't lead a homely life') were composed to folk-tunes, and one to music from Mozart (*MV*. 'Lines to a Movement in Mozart's E-Flat Symphony').

While he was in London from 1862 to 1867, Hardy not only attended dances; he bought an old fiddle to practise pieces from the romantic Italian operas he had enjoyed at Covent Garden and Her Majesty's (*Life*, 43). The *Messiah* concert of 'An Indiscretion in the Life of an Heiress' (undoubtedly from Hardy's first novel) seems to be based on actual experience. In 1879 he dashed out of his London lodgings to find out the name of a tune played by an organ-grinder; he had not heard it for over twenty years, yet he had never forgotten its fascination (*Life*, 123). Years later, he and Mrs Hardy attended concerts given by famous European orchestras at the Imperial Institute (*Life*, 281, 292, 298). He 'followed up' Tchaikovsky at the Queen's Hall concerts, and discussed Wagner with Grieg (*Life*, 324, 329–30). 'Haunting Fingers' (*LLE*) subtly expresses Hardy's love of various forms of music – orchestral, harpsichord, military, dance, religious, and theatrical. When the composer Holst visited Max Gate in 1927, he found that Hardy was familiar with his work, 'The Planets', and was impressed by 'his comprehensive knowledge of music no less than with his remarkably keen ear' (Elna Sherman).

Hardy's interest in music may be observed in his incidental imagery: the eyebrows of two of his heroines are like slurs in music; Thomasin 'seemed to belong rightly to a madrigal', and, as they 'shocked' their sheaves, the harvesters at Marlott drew together 'like dancers in a quadrille'. His aural discrimination may be noticed more frequently in onomatopoeic effects, which are more remarkable when they form a dramatic accompaniment; typical examples are the ironic gurgle of the whirlpools outside the barracks when Fanny Robin reminds Troy of his forgotten pledge, and the 'never-ending sarcastic hiss' of the waterfall by which the frustrated lovers sit in 'The Waiting Supper'. Musical denotation is used in 'the baritone buzz of the holly tree', and the 'stopt-diapason' which Tess's voice acquired when 'her heart was in her speech'; still more in the description of the waters overheard in the stillness of a dark night on the moor outside Casterbridge (*MC.* xli):

> The wanderer in this direction, who should stand still for a few moments on a quiet night, might hear singular symphonies from these waters, as from a lampless orchestra, all playing in their sundry tones, from near and far parts of the moor. At a hole in a rotten weir they excuted a recitative; where a tributary brook fell over a stone breastwork they trilled cheerily; under an arch they performed a metallic cymballing; and at Durnover Hole they hissed. The spot at which their instrumentation rose loudest was a place called Ten Hatches, whence during high springs there proceeded a very fugue of sounds.

The 'acoustic pictures' at the opening of *Under the Greenwood Tree* and on Norcombe Hill (*FMC.* ii) are well known. More subtle and artistic is the orchestration of the varying sounds of the wind on the heath and their modulation into the lengthened sighing which introduces Eustacia (*RN.* i vi).

Painting

Hardy's study of paintings began in the National Gallery (cf. *Life*, 52), and was extended here and elsewhere in England and on the Continent. His note of 9 January 1889 (*Life*, 216–7) suggests that he was in the habit of recording his impressions. In his earliest novels, his references are sometimes accretive rather than creative; they indicate a clear visual memory, but may seem little better than a pedantic hindrance to a reader unfamiliar with the paintings. An instance occurs at the opening of *A Pair of Blue Eyes*:

193

Elfride had as her own the thoughtfulness which appears in the face of the Madonna della Sedia, without its rapture: the warmth and spirit of the type of woman's feature most common to the beauties – mortal and immortal – of Rubens, without their insistent fleshiness. The characteristic expression of the female face of Correggio – that of the yearning human thoughts that lie too deep for tears – was hers sometimes, but seldom under ordinary conditions.

The description is too analytical and qualified, too composite and negative, to present a clear picture. Simpler and more imaginative collocations are generally to be found. The majority of the references occur in the earlier works, and the emphasis – unlike that of the above passage – is on external technicalities of colour and feature; in the later works, it is on the deeper emotions or inner realities of experience (see the Crivelli references below, and Hardy's comments on Turner: *Life*, 185).

One suspects that recollections of paintings sometimes contributed to Hardy's imaginative creation of landscape and human scenes, the latter especially. Three candlelight scenes, for example, illustrate a cultivated aptitude for presenting pictures; the second of these is avowedly Impressionistic (see *PBE*. iii; *W*. ii; *TD*. xiv).

The notes which follow give, first of all, some of Hardy's more general impressions of painters and schools of painting, and secondly, his references to particular artists:

Unlike Hardy, who went from 'sheer liking', Egbert Mayne entered picture galleries in order to further his ambition, and impress other people by cultural pretentiousness. 'He examined Correggio to criticize his flesh shades . . . Benozzi Gozzoli was better worth study than Raffaelle, since the former's name was a learned sound to utter, and all knowledge got up about him would tell.'   *ILH*. ii 1

'Livid grey shades, like those of the modern French painters, made a mystery of the remote and dark parts of the vista. . . .'   *DR*. viii 4

'A Rural Painting of the Dutch School' *UGT*. title-page.

'They sat stiffly side by side at the darkening table, like some Tuscan painting of the two disciples supping at Emmaus. Lucetta, forming the third and haloed figure, was opposite them. . . .'   *MC*. xxv

'Angles were taking the place of curves, and reticulations of surfaces –

a change constituting a sudden lapse from the ornate to the primitive on Nature's canvas, and comparable to a retrogressive step from the art of an advanced school of painting to that of the Pacific islander.'

'. . . those long eyes so common to the angelic legions of early Italian art'

'. . . a snowy cloth . . . reticulated with folds as in Flemish Last-Suppers' *W.* vii, viii, x

'The impressionist school is strong. It is even more suggestive in the direction of literature than in that of art. . . . their principle is, as I understand it, that what you carry away with you from a scene is the true feature to grasp; or in other words, *what appeals to your own individual eye and heart in particular* amid much that does not so appeal, and which you therefore omit to record.' *Life*, 184

'. . . a broad tarnished moon that had risen from the ground to the eastwards, its face resembling the outworn gold-leaf halo of some worm-eaten Tuscan saint'
'The pensive character which the curtained hood lent to their bent heads would have reminded the observer of some early Italian conception of the two Marys.' *TD.* xiv, xliii

Jude's interest at Wardour Castle was in 'the devotional pictures by Del Sarto, Guido Reni, Spagnoletto, Sassoferrato, Carlo Dolci, and others'; Sue waited for him before a Lely or Reynolds. *JO.* iii ii

Angelico (Italian, 1387–1455)
    '. . . the pink faces of his saints' *ILH.* ii 1

Correggio (Italian, 1494–1534)
    See above (*ILH* and *PBE*).
    '. . . the greenish shades of Correggio's nudes' *DR.* xii 3

'. . . a tender affectionateness which might almost be called yearning; such as is often seen in the women of Correggio when they are painted in profile' *L.* i iii

'. . . her eyes beaming with a long lingering light, as if Nature had been advised by Correggio in their creation' *MC.* xvi

Crivelli (Italian, 1435–93)

'. . . a narrow bony hand that would have been an unmitigated delight to the pencil of Carlo Crivelli' *DR*. ix 4

The skinny legs of storks at Strassburg, 'like the limbs of dead martyrs in Crivelli's emaciated imaginings' *L*. v i

'You could see the skeleton behind the man, and almost the ghost behind the skeleton. He matched Crivelli's dead *Christus*.' *TD*. liii

'My art is to intensify the expression of things, as is done by Crivelli, Bellini, etc., so that the heart and inner meaning is made visible.'
Life, 177

Dahl (Swedish, 1656–1743)
'A woman with a double chin and thick neck, like the Queen Anne portrait by Dahl' *PBE*. v

Danby (Irish, 1793–1861)
'. . . the angry crimson of a Danby sunset' *FMC*. xx

Douw (Dow or Dou, Dutch, 1613–75)
See passage quoted under *Terburg*. *FMC*. ix

Dürer (German, 1471–1528)
'The brilliant lights and sooty shades which struggled upon the skin and clothes of the persons standing round [the bonfire] caused their lineaments and general contours to be drawn with Dureresque vigour and dash.' *RN*. i iii

El Greco (Spanish, *c*. 1545–1614)
Do I know these, slack-shaped and wan,
Whose substance, one time fresh and furrowless,
Is now a rag drawn over a skeleton,
As in El Greco's canvases . . .?
HS. 'In a Former Resort after Many Years'

Gérôme (Professor of Painting in the School of Fine Arts, 1824–1904)
'. . . religious enthusiasts of all sorts. They talk the old faiths with such new fervours and original aspects that such faiths seem again arresting. They open fresh views of Christianity by turning it in reverse positions, as Gérôme the painter did by painting the *shadow* of the Crucifixion instead of the Crucifixion itself as former painters had done'. *Life*, 76, 206

Giotto (Italian, 1267–1337)
   'They moved on hand in hand, and never spoke a word, the drooping of their heads being that of Giotto's "Two Apostles".'   *TD.* lix

Greuze (French, 1725–1805)
   'Those who remember Greuze's "Head of a Girl" have an idea of Cytherea's look askance at the turning.'   *DR.* iv 2
   Elfride, 'her head thrown sideways in the Greuze attitude'   *PBE.* ix

Guido (Guido Reni, Italian, 1575–1642)
   '. . . the conscience-stricken look of Guido's Magdalen'   *PBE.* xxvii

Hobbema (Dutch, 1638–1709)
   See quotation under *Ruysdael.*   *FMC.* xlvi

   The approach to Rook's Gate, the home of Margery Tucker's grandmother, was along 'a straight open road, bordered by thin lank trees, all sloping away from the south-west wind-quarter, and the scene bore a resemblance to certain bits of Dutch landscape which have been imprinted on the world's eye by Hobbema and his school'   *CM.* 12

   His method (and Boldini's): 'that of infusing emotion into the baldest external objects either by the presence of a human figure among them, or by mark of some human connection with them'.   *Life,* 120

Holbein (German, 1497–1543)
   '. . . the dinted nose of the de Stancys outlined with Holbein shadowlessness'   *L.* I iii

Lely (English, 1618–80)
   See quotation under *Reynolds.*   *HE.* xxxviii

Moroni (Italian, *c.* 1525–78)
   Mr Penny, 'like a framed portrait of a shoemaker by some modern Moroni'   *UGT.* II ii

Murillo (Spanish, 1618–82)
   '. . . a certain silliness in the look of his old men'   *ILH.* II 1

Piombo (Italian, 1485–1547)
   See *Sebastiano* (below), and *RN.* v ix.
                   And Lazarus with cadaverous glare
                   (As done in oils by Piombo's care)
   PPP. 'The Respectable Burgher on "The Higher Criticism" '

A Hardy Companion

Poussin (French, 1594–1665)

'. . . the mellow hue of an old sketch in oils – notably some of Nicholas Poussin's' *FMC.* xxii

Prout (English, 1783–1852)

See quotation under *Vandyck.* *W.* v

Raffaelle (or Raphael, Italian, 1483–1520)

'. . . the added softness and finish of a Raffaelle after Perugino, which, while faithfully reproducing the original subject, entirely distances the original art' *RN.* ii iv

Lucy Savile's face: 'the Raffaelesque oval of its contour was remarkable for an English countenance' *WT.* 5

'Raffaelesque resignation' *L.* i ii

'. . . a complexion as that with which Raffaelle enriches the countenance of the youthful son of Zacharias' *TT.* i

Rembrandt (Dutch, 1606–69)

'an area of two feet in Rembrandt's intensest manner . . . though his whole figure was visible, the observer's eye was only aware of his face' *RN.* ii vi

'. . . he saw a face in the square of darkness formed by one of the open windows, the effect being that of a high-light portrait by Vandyck or Rembrandt' *L.* i xv

Reynolds (English, 1723–92)

'. . . Ethelberta, in a dress sloped about as high over the shoulder as would have drawn approval from Reynolds, and expostulation from Lely' *HE.* xxxviii

Mrs Barnet, thought to be still alive by her husband after her immersion at sea: 'Her complexion was that seen in the numerous faded portraits by Sir Joshua Reynolds; it was pallid in comparison with life, but there was visible on a close inspection the remnant of what had once been a flush.' *WT.* 5

Rubens (Flemish, 1577–1640)

See passage quoted above from *A Pair of Blue Eyes.* *PBE.* i

198

The profile of the second Avice: 'It was not unlike that of one of the three goddesses in Rubens's "Judgment of Paris".... '   *WB.* ii vii

Ruysdael (Dutch, *c.* 1628–82)

'... leaves, now sparkling and varnished by the raindrops to the brightness of similar effects in the landscapes of Ruysdael and Hobbema'

FMC. xlvi

Sallaert (Belgian, 1590–1648?)

'... the throngs which cover the canvases of Sallaert, Van Alsloot, and others of that school – vast masses of beings, jostling, zigzagging, and processioning in definite directions, but whose features are indistinguishable by the very comprehensiveness of the view'   *RN.* iii iii

'The green lea was speckled as thickly with them [cows] as a canvas by Van Alsloot or Sallaert with burghers.'   *TD.* xvi

Sebastiano (S. del Piombo, above)

Jude's great-aunt had risen from her sick-bed, and sat wrapped in blankets; as Jude entered with Mrs Edlin, she turned 'upon them a countenance like that of Sebastiano's Lazarus'   *JO.* iii ix

Terburg (Ter Borch, Dutch, 1617–81)

'... perfection of hue ... the softened ruddiness on a surface of high rotundity that we meet in a Terburg or a Gerard Douw; and, like the presentations of those great colourists, it was a face which kept well back from the boundary between comeliness and the ideal'   *FMC.* ix

Titian (Italian, *c.* 1477–1576)

'Miss Templeman deposited herself on the sofa in her former flexuous position – somewhat in the pose of a well-known conception of Titian's....'   *MC.* xxii

Turner (English, 1775–1851)

'the wild colouring of Turner's later pictures'   *PBE.* xiii

'as if the blue component of the grey had faded, like the indigo from the same kind of colour in Turner's pictures'   *FMC.* v

'I feel that Nature is played out as a Beauty, but not as a Mystery. . . . The "simply natural" is interesting no longer. The much decried, mad, late-Turner rendering is now necessary to create my interest. . . .'

'Turner's water-colours: each is a landscape *plus* a man's soul. . . . What he paints chiefly is *light as modified by objects.*'   *Life,* 185, 216

Van Alsloot (Belgian, 15—?–1626)
See quotations under *Sallaert*.　　　　　　　*RN.* III iii; *TD.* xvi

Van Beers (Belgian, 1852–1927)
'Nevertheless humanity stood before him no longer in the pensive sweetness of Italian art, but in the staring and ghastly attitudes of a Wiertz Museum, and with the leer of a study by Van Beers.' [The Musée Wiertz is in Brussels.]　　　　　　　*TD.* xxxix

Vandyck (Flemish, 1599–1641)
See quotation under *Rembrandt*.　　　　　　　*L.* I xv

'. . . well-formed eyebrows which, had her portrait been painted, would probably have been done in Prouts's [*sic*] or Vandyke brown'　*W.* v

Hardy wrote that his father had 'dark Vandyke-brown hair'.　*Life*, 13

Wouvermans (Wouwerman, Dutch, 1619–68)
The white pony Darling against a deep violet sky: 'a mere speck now – a Wouvermans eccentricity reduced to microscopic proportions' (cf. p. 212, and Wouverman's 'eternal white horses': Miss Braddon, *Lady Audley's Secret*, 1862).　　　　　　　*W.* xxviii

Zurbarán (Spanish, 1598–1662)
'At this time [1904–5] he was much interested in the paintings of Zurbarán, which he preferred to all others of the old Spanish school. . . .'
　　　　　　　　　　　　　　　　　　　　Life, 323

Comparisons drawn from other visual arts such as ceramic decoration (*UGT.* I i) and sculpture (Nollekens and Flaxman, for instance: *PBE.* iv, *FMC.* xxxviii) are rarer. The Hardy who looked outward at life responded to colour and tone. His memory was vivid. Not only were paintings recalled by association; their influence may be felt in the direct presentation of a scene, or in its imaginative re-creation to convey a character's mood or outlook (see the conclusions of *FMC.* v and *TD.* xxviii). At a deeper level, below 'optical effects' (*Life*, 185), some acquired an intense significance for Hardy in their expression of the 'deeper reality' and 'tragical mysteries' of life.

Literature

Hardy's reading was extensive; it includes *inter alia* romance novels in his youth, poetry, Shakespeare, French authors, contemporary fiction, contemporary scientific thought, literary theory and criticism, philosophy, and numerous histories of the Napoleonic era. It was often intensive, as his references to *In Memoriam*, Shakespeare, Shelley, Browning, and the Bible show. For samples of his periodic reading, see *Life*, 59, 203–4, 230. The notes which follow are limited to more particular references and quotations in Hardy's principal works. They could be extended considerably from his incidental writings. Scientific and philosophical works which influenced his general thought, and historical reading for *The Dynasts**, have been excluded. Similarly, works which appear to have no precise or significant bearing on Hardy's writings have been omitted. Many quotations have not been traced, and more, undoubtedly, have been overlooked. Hardy's quotations would form a valuable anthology, and the omission of many of them from dictionaries of quotations is regrettable. His familiarity with an author (e.g. Fielding or Crabbe) is not always to be gauged by the number of quotations or references; Gray is recalled more frequently, but the quotations are restricted to a few poems in the *Golden Treasury*.

For convenience, authors are presented alphabetically. The first group comprises those whose work is slight, and those with whom Hardy's acquaintance seems limited or general rather than close (this list is representative rather than exhaustive); the second, those he knew more intimately. These are followed by authors he knew unusually well; lastly, by Shakespeare and the Bible.

I

Addison (1672–1719)   See *Life*, 105.

The Spectator, 267, 321, 26	*PRF*; *Life*, 203; *JO*. II i
Aristotle (384–322 B.C.) cathartic . . . qualities	*JO*. 1912 preface
Ascham (1515–68) *The Scholemaster*	*TD*. xv

Aurelius, Marcus (121–180) . .
'. . . Be not perturbed . . .'   *L*. IV i; *Life*, 176; *TD*. xxxix
Burke (1729–97)   See *Life*, 105.

A Philosophical Inquiry into the Origin of our Ideas of the Sublime and Beautiful (ease after torment is delight)   *FMC*. xxi

---

* See W. R. Rutland, *Thomas Hardy, a Study of his Writings and their Background* and, for a more detailed account, Walter F. Wright, *The Shaping of* The Dynasts, University of Nebraska Press, 1967.

A Hardy Companion

Burns (1759–96)
  'My love is like a red red rose' *PBE*. vi *ep.*
  'Auld Lang Syne' *PBE*. xxiii *ep.*
  'Bonnie Peg' *MC*. viii
  'To a Mouse' *DLa*; *MC*. xiv
  'On the Late Captain Grose's Peregrinations . . .' *JO*. vi iii
Butler, Samuel (1835–1902) See p. 169).
Byron (1788–1824)
  'When we two parted' *PBE*. xxviii *ep.*
  Childe Harold: ('the banks that bear the vine') *Life*, 110, *L.* v viii;
  Life, 131, ('Tasso's echoes . . . songless gondolier') 194, 207; *JO*.
  ii vi. See Purdy, 297. *Manfred*: *Life*, 292.
Campbell (1777–1844)
  'How delicious is the winning' *UGT*. v i, title; *JO*. v iii
Campion (1567–1620)
  'Cherry-Ripe' (the old Elizabethan simile) *Life*, 220; *TD*. xxiv
Chatterton (1752–70)
  Ælla ('When the fair apples . . .') *W*. xxv
Chaucer (c. 1345–1400) *GND*. 3; *Life*, 413
Cicero (106–43 B.C.) ('Cui bono?') *DR*. xiv 3; *L.* i v; *TT*. vii
Collins (1721–59) 'The Passions' (Music) *DR*. xii 1
Congreve (1670–1729) *The Way of the World* *W*. xxix
Cowper (1731–1800)
  'John Gilpin' *FMC*. xxxiii; *MC*. xxx
  'On the Loss of the Royal George' *HS*. 'The Sea Fight'
Crabbe (1754–1832)
  Hardy honoured him as an apostle of realism (*Life*, 327). The basic
  resemblance between Crabbe's 'The Lover's Journey' and 'The
  King's Experiment' (*PPP*) suggests more than a coincidence. An
  entry in Hardy's notebook on 23 August 1862 (*Life*, 50) may be a
  transposition of Crabbe's

      It is the soul that sees; the outward eyes
      Present the object, but the mind descries.

  Compare the scene in *DR*. xii 6 and *RN* iii v, *HS*. 'Alike and Unlike',
  and p. 125.
Crashaw (1612–49)
  'Wishes to his (Supposed) Mistress' *DR*. x 4; *WB*. i *ep.* (cf. *MV*. 'I
  said and sang her excellence')

202

'Love's Horoscope' *TT.* title-page.
De Quincey (1785–1859) *DR.* xii 5
Dryden (1631–1700) *HE.* xxiv
  For his translation of Virgil, see p. 209.
  Absalom and Achitophel (Zimri) *L.* I vi; *WW.* 'So Various'
  'Alexander's Feast' (Music) *TT.* viii
Dyer (1540-1607) 'My mind to me a kingdom is' *RN.* III i, title
Ford (1586–1639?) *Life,* 15
France, Anatole (1844–1924) *Life,* 363
Gosse, Edmund (1849–1928)
  'Two Points of View' Verses quoted *W.* xxv
Gray (1716–71)
  'Elegy . . .' *PBE.* iv *ep.*; *FMC.* xliii; *DLa*; *TD.* xviii
  'Ode on the Spring' *PBE.* xiv *ep.*
  'Ode on a Distant Prospect of Eton College'
              (a fearful joy) *FMC.* xxiii; *RN.* II vi
  'Ode on the Pleasure arising from Vicissitude' *Life,* 149
Hawthorne (1804–64)
  The House of the Seven Gables (Hepzibah Pyncheon) *HE.* xl
Herbert (1593–1633) 'Vanity' (from *The Church*) *W.* xliii
Herrick (1591–1674)
  'To Dianeme' and 'Delight in Disorder' *PRF*; *Life,* 105
Howells, W. D. (1837–1920) *Life,* 239
Johnson (1709–84) *Rasselas* *Life,* 16; *RN.* IV ii; *PRF*
Menander (342–291 B.C.)
  'A perplexing and ticklish possession is a daughter' *W.* xii
Meredith (1828–1909) See p. 414.
  Modern Love (i) (lay a sword) *HS.* 'To a Sea-Cliff'
Ovid (43 B.C.–A.D. 17) *FMC.* xxvi; *MC.* xxx; *JP,* II *ep.*
Pascal (1623–62) *CEF*; *TD.* xviii
Rochefoucauld (1613–80) *MC.* xv
Rossetti, D. G. (1828–82) 'The Blessed Damozel' *DR.* v 2
St Augustine (354–430) *TD.* xv, *Life,* 31
St Jerome (c. 340–420) *TD.* 1891 preface
Sappho (born c. 650 B.C.)
  (and Phaon) *HE.* ii; (Aphrodite, 'the Weaver of Wiles') *W.B. passim*;
  JO. III *ep.*; *PPP.* 'Sapphic Fragment'; cf. 'the Lesbian . . . the music-
  mother' (*SC.* 'A Singer Asleep'), and *Life,* 287.

Schiller (1759–1805)   *GND*. 1; *TD*. 1892 preface; *PPP*. 'After Schiller'
Shelley, Mary (1797–1851)   *Frankenstein*   *L*. III ii
Sheridan (1751–1816)
 The Critic   *PBE*. xiv; *D*. (2) II iii
 The School for Scandal   *PBE*. xvii
Spencer (1820–1903)   General Preface to the Novels and Poems
South, Robert (1634–1716)   *GND*. 3; *TD*. xiii
Sully-Prudhomme (1839–1907)   *TD*. xxxvi
Swift (1667–1745)   See *Life*, 134.
 (Lilliputian)   *PBE*. xx; (Yahoo) *MC*. xxix
Taylor, Jeremy (1613–67)   *TD*. xv
Terence (c. 190–159 B.C.)
 Eunuchus ('Ingenium mulierum . . . ultro', 'plenus rimarum')
              DR. ix 1, xiv 3
Thackeray (1811–63)
 Hardy read him in his twenties. (*Life*. 40, 57, 59).
 The Book of Snobs   *ILH*. I 7 *ep.*
 Vanity Fair   *PRF*
Thomson (1700–48)
 The Castle of Indolence   *RN*. II i
 The Seasons ('Summer')   *Life*, 200
Trollope (1815–82)
 Barchester Towers recommended (*Life*, 51). Did the 'Barsetshire'
novels suggest the Wessex background to Hardy? For Trollope's
Autobiography, see p. 41.
Voltaire (1694–1778)   See 'The Respectable Burgher' (*PPP*).
 Candide (best of all possible worlds, and the Lisbon earthquake)
     GND. 1 (conclusion); *D*. (1) I i; *LLE*.Apology
Walton (1593–1683)
 The Compleat Angler (to torture and to love simultaneously)   *GND*. 6
Webster (c. 1580–c. 1625)
 The White Devil (influence of IV ii)   *RN*. v iii
Whitman (1819–92)   *DR*. viii 3; *TD*. xxv
Wotton (1568–1639)
 'On his Mistress, the Queen of Bohemia'   *MC*. xxv
Wyatt (1503–42)   *PBE*. xxxv *ep.*; *HE*. ii; *WB*. II *ep.*

II

Aeschylus (b. 525 B.C.)   *RN.* III i
  Agamemnon: reference to Clytaemnestra, bearing on Tess, *Life*, 221;
  CEF; *JO.* VI ii; allusion to the question raised by one of the Chorus
  whether the news of the fall of Troy is true or some deception of the
  gods. *D.* After Scene.
  Prometheus Bound (169)   *TD.* lix
Ainsworth, Harrison (1805–82)
  With Dumas *père*, James Grant, and G. P. R. James (*PBE.* xv), he
  was one of Hardy's favourite authors in his youth. For his influence,
  see pp. 153–5.
  Old St Paul's (the heroine's name recalled?)   *WP.* 'Amabel'
  Windsor Castle (Herne the Hunter and 'Cardinal College')
                                                    Life, 25; *JO.* I iii, II iii, etc.
Arnold, Matthew (1822–88)
  For criticisms of, see *Life*, 134, 146–7: quoted, *Life*, 135; a 'finished'
  writer, his phrase 'the imaginative reason' quoted, *L.* VI v (cf. *Life*,
  147); the arts, 'a criticism of life', *PRF*; 'home of lost causes', 'Beauti-
  ful city . . .', *JO.* II i; influence of 'Isolation', *WP.* 'At an Inn', and of
  'Dover Beach', *SC.* 'A Plaint to Man'; 'the application of ideas to life',
  LLE. Apology.
Ballads See *Life*, 321, 19–20, and *HS.* 'The Harvest-Supper'.
  Ballads included traditional songs with little but vestigial narrative;
  an excellent example is 'The Banks of Allan Water' (*FMC.* xxiii); one
  of its lines supplied the title Hardy had in mind for *A Pair of Blue Eyes*
  ('A Winning Tongue Had He'). Shiner sang a popular ballad-derivative
  folk-song about King Arthur's three sons (*UGT.* IV ii), and Tess's
  companions at Marlott mischievously sang verses from the ballad about
  the maid who went to the green wood (*TD.* xiv). Hardy was interested
  in Percy's *Reliques of Ancient English Poetry* and Scott's *Minstrelsy of
  the Scottish Border*. In the former he found 'Queen Eleanor's Confession', a version of which was a favourite with Grandfer Cantle
  (*RN.* I iii), and 'The Boy and the Mantle', the 'ballad of the mystic
  robe' which Tess recalled hearing her mother sing (*TD.* xxxii). Scott's
  collection contains 'Glenfinlas', which clearly made a deep impression
  on Hardy (*PBE.* xxvii, *TT.* xx). A quotation from 'Jamie Douglas'
  probably came from the excerpt, 'O waly waly up the bank', in *The*

Golden Treasury (*PBE.* xxxii *ep.*). 'Alonzo the Brave', a ballad by 'Monk' Lewis (1775–1818), is alluded to (*FMC.* lii).

Barnes, William (1800–86)   See p. 235.

Hardy edited a selection of his poems in 1908, and the humour of some of them may have suggested certain scenes in *Under the Greenwood Tree.* Quotations occur in *FMC.* lvi and *JO.* IV iv.

Bunyan (1628–88)

The Pilgrim's Progress: L. v xi; (slough of despond, Giant Despair) *DLa*; (Hill Difficulty) *CM.* 6; (Interpreter's parlour) *W.* xxiii; (Valley of Humiliation) *W.* xxxvii, *TD.* xix; (Apollyon) *Life*, 441–2, *JO.* I iii; (Vanity Fair) *LLE.* 'A Gentleman's Epitaph on Himself and a Lady, who were Buried Together'.

Carlyle (1795–1881)   Hardy's 1867 notebook includes several quotations from Carlyle. See *Life*, 137, 233, 438; Purdy, 297.

'Goethe's Helena' (description of Faust and Bellerophon)   *MC.* xvii
The French Revolution ('the eye sees . . . seeing')   *PRF*

Coleridge (1772–1834)

'The Ancient Mariner', *DR.* iii 1, *Life*, 252; 'precipitance of soul', *DR.* ix 1; 'The Three Graves', *PBE.* xix; 'Christabel', *HE.* xviii; 'that willing suspension of disbelief . . . which constitutes poetic faith', *D.* preface (cf. *Life*, 152); a long poem neither can be nor ought to be all poetry, *LLE.* Apology (cf. *Life*, 203).

Dante (1265–1321)

The Divine Comedy (Cary's translation) *DR.* viii 5; *RN.* I iii; *LLI.* 5, 7

Defoe (*c.* 1660–1731)

Hardy was long attracted to the 'affected simplicity' of his style, and imitated it in his first novel (cf. *ILH*). He returned to Defoe 'in a study of style' in 1875 (*Life*, 61, 105). *Robinson Crusoe* was one of his favourite books (cf. *Life*, 203). Ethelberta thought Defoe's style more suitable for telling than writing stories (*HE.* xiii). For the critic's comment that 'he had the most amazing talent on record for telling lies' (*HE.* xvi), cf. Hardy's *Life*, 391. References to *Robinson Crusoe* are frequent: *DR* v I; *PBE.* xii; *L.* II i (Man Friday), II iv; *TT.* ix; *W.* xix; *WB.* III viii; *JO.* II vi.

Eliot, George (1819–80)

Hardy admired her as a thinker, but did not regard her as a 'born storyteller' (*Life*, 98 146). How much he was influenced by her novels is conjectural; for *Silas Marner, The Mill on the Floss,* and

The White Horse Inn, Maiden Newton (Chalk-Newton), which was removed in 1900. From a painting by Emma Hardy, 1888

Original of the Sallows 'waterfall' below Stafford (Froom-Everard) House

The memorial on Weatherbury (or Weatherby) Castle (see Rings-Hill Speer and Welland) which suggested the setting for Two on a Tower

The avenue along the 'Port Bredy' road outside 'Casterbridge' in 1875

Romola, see pp. 18, 19, 39 and 41. Her fiction may have impressed on him the potentialities of rustic humour (though he did not think her country-folk were true rustics, and he had a greater exemplar in Shakespeare), and of the harmonization between scene and situation (especially in *Middlemarch*). The disinclination of the heroine of *Daniel Deronda* to save her drowning husband may have suggested the catastrophe in 'A Tragedy of Two Ambitions'. The suggestion of the approach of the sinister in the distant figure of Alec d'Urberville (*TD*. xlvi) has its parallel in *Middlemarch* (ch. 53).

Fielding (1707–54)   See *Life*, 98, 273, 298.

Joseph Andrews, Tom Jones   **PRF**

Gibbon (1737–94) See Lausanne, p. 388.

An author 'read again' for style, *Life*, 105   *JO*. II i; *W*. 1895 preface

Goethe (1749–1832)   See pp. 107, 153, 156, 157.

Heine (1797–1856)

His whimsical description of Amiens Cathedral, *L*. V x; quoted (in translation), *TT*. xi, *JO*. II vi; thoughts of Heine and his grave, *Life*, 229; *PPP*. 'Song from Heine'; *LLE*. Apology.

Homer

Jude's reading in the *Iliad* (*JO*. I vi) corresponds to the items noted in Hardy's copy, and dated 1858 (Rutland). Ulysses before Melanthus (*Odyssey* xvii), *ILH*. I 4; *FMC*. xxiii; Bellerophon (*Iliad* vi), *MC*. xvii; Achillean moodiness, *W*. xxvii.

Horace (65–8 B.C.)

Odes quoted in translation (IV xiii) *DR*. xii. 1, (I xxii) *TD*. xxxiv (see also Lalage, p. 386); *Epodes* (xvii), *PBE*. vii; *De Arte Poetica* quoted or referred to, *PRF*, *D*. (1) I iii, *Life*, 49; 'Carmen Saeculare', *JO*. I v; *Epistles* (I ii, 'Quicquid delirant reges, plectuntur Achivi'), *Life*, 78, 365, (I xii, 'concordia discors'), *D*. After Scene, *HS*. 'Genitrix Laesa'; *Satires* (I ix, scene remembered), *Life*, 190, (II iii, 'Par nobile fratrum'), *D*. (2) I vii; Horatian sentiments, *WW*. 'A Private Man on Public Men'

James, Henry (1843–1916)

The 'Polonius' of novelists, etc.   *Life*, 181, 211, 246, 370

Mill, J. S. (1806–73)

Ethelberta found solace in the 'distorted Benthamism' of Mill's *Utilitarianism*, *HE*. xxxvi. Hardy remembered seeing Mill in 1865 speaking on the hustings in Covent Garden during his 'candidature for Westminster'; at that time he knew the treatise *On Liberty* almost by heart; he included it in the list of his 'cures for despair' (*Life*, 330, 58). Sue Bridehead quotes from it, *JO*. IV iii. Hardy's first novel shows that he was in sympathy with Mill's Radicalism; *On Liberty* undoubtedly encouraged him to think independently; and *Three Essays on Religion* (1874) may have influenced his views on Nature and the First Cause (see p. 107).

Richardson (1689–1761) *Clarissa*. See p. 158n.   PRF

Sophocles (*c*. 496–*c*. 405 B.C.) (dramas . . . truly Sophoclean)   *W*. i
    Oedipus Tyrannus: influence on *The Mayor of Casterbridge*, p. 42; quoted (autobiographically?), *Life*, 220. *Antigone: LLI*. 3, *JO*. VI ix. *Trachiniae: D*. (1) V iv (see *Life*, 285, 383). *Oedipus Coloneus:* 'Thoughts from Sophocles', an unpublished poem on 'the good of knowing no birth at all' (cf. William Archer, *Real Conversations*).

Sterne (1713–68) See *Life*, 22, 105.
    Letters, DR. xi. 1; *Tristram Shandy* (trenches . . . Uncle Toby), *L*. III iv, *PRF*; *A Sentimental Journey, W*. viii, ix.

Swinburne (1837–1909) See p. 486.
    Atlanta in Calydon (the Mother of the Months, and 'Behold when thy face is made bare')   *W*. xxxiv; *TD*. xxxv.
    'Fragoletta' ('The maiden's mouth . . .')   *TD*. xlii
    'Faustine'   Cf. *Life*, 212, and *TD*. liii
    Prelude to *Songs Before Sunrise*   *JO*. II ep. (cf. *Life*, 56, 345)
    'Hymn to Proserpine': ('Thou hast conquered . . .' and 'O ghastly glories . . .') *JO*. II iii, III iv.
    See *Life*, 287 (*WB*). For other quotations, see *Life*, 344–5.

Tennyson (1809–92)
    Hardy's early interest in Tennyson's poetry is clear from his *Life* (75, 78) and *A Pair of Blue Eyes*.
    In Memoriam: (lxiv, lxv, lxxviii) *PBE*. xx ep., xxviii ep., ('O last regret . . .') xxxv; (xxxiii) *TD*. xxvii; (lxiii, xcv) *Life*, 220, 259; (cxxvi, cxxvii: 'all is well') *WP*. 'The Impercipient', *PPP*. 'In Tenebris' (ii); (lxxvii) *LLE*. Apology.
    'Break, break, break'   *Life*, 75; *PBE*. xxi ep.
    'The Two Voices'   *PBE*. xxvi ep.
    'Oenone'   (many-rilled Ida) *PBE*. xi; *TT*. xxxvii
    The Princess   *MC*. xx; *TL* (title)
    'Morte d'Arthur'   *TD*. lii

'A Dream of Fair Women'   *D.* title-page
Maud: Hardy sympathized with philosophical and socio-political views
in this poem.   (O that 'twere possible!) *LLE.* Apology.
Virgil (70–19 B.C.)
Hardy's mother gave him a copy of Dryden's translation before he
was ten. He quotes from it: *ILH.* II. 1 *ep., DR.* xii 5, xx 2.
Aeneid ('of which he never wearied') is quoted or referred to: *DR.*
xvi 4, xix 1; (feats of Euryalus) *PBE.* ix, (like Helen's robe) xii, xiv;
(Acheron) *FMC.* xxxiv; *RN.* II vi, IV vii; (Libyan bay) *WT.* 5;
('mollia tempora fandi') *TT.* xxxviii; *Life,* 188; *WB.* III vii; (Acherontic shades) *JO.* VI, iv; ('Veteris vestigia flammae') *SC.* 'Poems of
1912–13' *ep. Eclogues:* (Silenus) *FMC.* xxiii. *Georgics:* ('dapes
inemptae') *TD.* xxv.
Walpole, Horace (1717–97)
Hardy's *Life* (9, 163–4, 376) and *The Hand of Ethelberta* (xxxviii,
Sequel) show his familiarity with Walpole's letters. He read the six
volumes of letters to Sir Horace Mann in 1868 (*Life,* 59), but the
quotation relating to Lady Susan, daughter of the first Earl of Ilchester
(the Stephen Reynard of *GND.* 1; see pp. 75–6 and 485) indicates that
his knowledge of Walpole's correspondence was not limited to these
volumes. From them he learned much about another Dorset family,
'the tragic Damers of the last century, who owned Abbey property'
(*Life,* 237). The conversion of this property, John Damer's marriage
to Horace Walpole's cousin, Anne Seymour Conway (who became a
sculptress of distinction), and his suicide provided the material on
which Hardy's imagination worked rather gruesomely in 'The
Doctor's Legend' (see pp. 81–3 and 415). In relating Damer's death to
another of his correspondents, Walpole repeated a sentence he had
written to Mann more than four years previously: 'I have often said,
this world is a comedy to those that think, a tragedy to those that feel.'
The thought was often in Hardy's mind (cf. *TD.* xxi, xxix), resulting
in the Spirit Ironic as well as the Chorus of Pities in *The Dynasts.* No
one can read Walpole's letters to Mann during the War of American
Independence without a sense of the vanity and, occasionally, the irony
of human affairs, of the ephemerality of reputations and dynasties, and
of the direction of events by Chance rather than Wisdom. The apparently irrational behaviour of the people of London during this period
occasioned the remark that there is 'nothing so unnatural as the

feelings of a million of persons that live together in one city'. It was, one feels, the mature and disillusioned philosophizings of this racy writer on political affairs and society gossip which made the most permanent impression on Hardy, and played a part in confirming and promoting the vision of life which found its most complete expression in *The Dynasts*.

III

Browning, Robert (1812–89)

'Instans Tyrannus'   *ILH.* I 5 *ep.*

'The Statue and the Bust' (cf. *Life*, 192, 199)   *ILH.* I 8 *ep.; DR.* iii 2, xiii 4; *W.* xlvi; quoted in, and the whole story inspired by, *CM.* 2; ('The soldier-saints . . .') *JO.* IV v, VI iv.

Sordello (darkness . . . 'quieted by hope')   *DLa*

Dedication ('Incidents in the development of a soul . . .')

Life, 223, 378–9

'Old Pictures in Florence' ('wronged great soul . . . master') *Life*, 190

The Ring and the Book   *Life*, 190

'By the Fire-side'   *TD.* xxxv; *JO.* II i, ('the shadowy third') IV v

'Too Late'   *JO.* III iv, VI *ep.*; *Life*, 246

'A Toccata of Galuppi's'   *Life*, 195; preface to *Select Poems* of

William Barnes

Prologue to *Asolando* ('His own soul's iris-bow'): *WP.* 'To Outer Nature'; *PPP.* 'On a Fine Morning'; *MV.* 'Looking at a Picture on an Anniversary;' *LLE.* 'Her Apotheosis'; *HS.* 'The Absolute Explains'.

Epilogue to *Asolando*   *Life*, 383.

'The Last Ride Together'

General Preface to the Novels and Poems, 1912

'Abt Vogler'   (14 May 1920) *Life*, 404

'Rabbi Ben Ezra'   *Life*, 445–6

Browning's philosophy: *Pippa Passes* ('God's in his heaven . . .') amended, *TD.* xxxvii; character not only in achievement but among things willed, *TD.* xlix, *Life*, 310, 334; *Life*, 383; 'the last of the optimists', *JO.* II i; *LLE.* 'The Child and the Sage'

For Browning's influence on Hardy's poetry, see pp. 121–2.

Keats (1795–1821)

At Rome, Hardy visited the house where Keats died, and his grave (*Life*, 188–9; *PPP.* 'At the Pyramid of Cestius'). He studied his life and poetry closely (cf. his emendation, 'tiar' for 'jar', in Keats's 'On

Leaving Some Friends at an Early Hour', and *LLE.* 'At Lulworth Cove a Century Back'); he had the highest regard for Severn, who accompanied Keats to Rome (*Life*, 442); and he joined the National Committee in 1920 for acquiring Wentworth Place as a Keats memorial (*Life*, 404; *LLE.* 'At a House in Hampstead').

'Ode to a Nightingale' *DR.* iii 2, x 4; *PBE.* ii; *FMC.* xxiii; *L.* ɪ ii, ɪɪ vii; *Life*, 230; *JO.* 1895 preface

'Ode to Autumn' *DR.* xii 6; *RN.* ɪɪɪ v; *L.* ɪ i; *TD.* xiv

'La Belle Dame Sans Merci' *PBE.* vii; (withering fast) *FMC.* xliv; (no bird sang) *RN.* ɪɪɪ v

'Eve of St Agnes' *FMC.* lvii

'Ode to Sorrow' (*Endymion*) *RN.* title-page

'On First Looking into Chapman's Homer' *TT.* xiv

'When I have fears . . .' (high-piled granary) *PRF*

'Ode on a Grecian Urn' (garlands . . . heifer . . . sacrifice) *JO.* v iv

Milton (1608–74)

'Lycidas' *DR.* ii 4, iii 2; *FMC.* xxi; *WB.* ɪɪ iii

'Il Penseroso' *DR.* iii 2; *Life*, 141

'L'Allegro' *PBE.* v *ep.*; *GND.* title-page, preface, and 4; preface to *Select Poems of William Barnes*

Paradise Lost: *PBE.* xxxi; *FMC.* ii, liii (*gutta serena*; cf. 'drop serene', *PL.* iii); *HE.* ii, (Mammon) xxvii; (Ithuriel's spear) *RN.* ɪɪ vii; (darkness visible) *TT.* xli; *Life*, 210; (Satan–Alec parallel, entering garden) *TD.* ix, l, (closing lines of the two works) lix; *WB.* ɪ v; (rashness of those parents; cf. ix 780) *JO.* vɪ ii.

Comus *MC.* xxxix

'On the Late Massacre in Piedmont' (stocks and stones) *GND.* 4

The Doctrine and Discipline of Divorce: *JO.* ɪv *ep*; paraphrased, *PPP.*

'Lausanne: In Gibbon's Old Garden' (cf. *Life*, 294n.).

Areopagitica *Life* (Freedom of Dorchester speech), 352

Scott (1771–1832)

In his twenties, Hardy thought *Marmion* the most Homeric poem in the English language. *Life*, 49

Scott on the writing of romances: *DR.* title-page

'A weary lot is thine, fair maid' *PBE.* vii *ep.*

Rokeby *PBE.* viii *ep.*

Marmion *PBE.* ix *ep.*; *FMC.* lv; (on deceit) *CM.* 3; (its romance) *Life*, 239

Ivanhoe (unreal portions of) *PBE*. xv; (Cedric) *DLa*; (Gurth) *MC*.	
	xxix
'The Maid of Neidpath'	*PBE*. xvii *ep.*; *L.* v v
'Ah! County Guy, the hour is nigh'	*PBE*. xxiv *ep.*
'Glenfinlas'	*PBE*. xxvii; *TT*. xx
'Proud Maisie is in the wood'	*PBE*. xl *ep.*
The Lay of the Last Minstrel (Cranstoun's Goblin Page)	*MC*. ix

The Bride of Lammermoor (Ashton . . . Ravenswood)

MC. xxxvi; *PRF*

Kenilworth   *PRF*; (Amy Dudley) *W*. xxxi

'The Eve of St John': 'a ballad which was among the verse which [Hardy] liked better than any of Scott's prose' (*Life*, 239). Yet he had fallen under the spell of Scott's novels:

> Throbbing romance has waned and wanned;
> No wizard wields the witching pen
> Of Bulwer, Scott, Dumas, and Sand,
>   Gentlemen.

LLE. 'An Ancient to Ancients'

The fact that Scott and Hardy have much in common as writers of fiction does not necessarily argue a direct influence, but it seems likely that Hardy was encouraged in certain directions by Scott's example, possibly in the choice of Gothic plots and settings, exciting and romantic incidents, and landscape artistry; more probably in the introduction of superstitious elements, snatches of ballad and song, and literary references and quotations. Among the latter must be reckoned those from Latin writers and, even more, from the Bible. Hardy's references to pictures and painters far exceed Scott's, and are generally more specific, but he may have noticed how Scott's pictures are sometimes imaginatively presented in terms of painters' (e.g. Rembrandt's: *The Antiquary*, xxxii, and *The Heart of Midlothian*, xii). It is in detailed references that one suspects the most direct influence. Proof is out of the question; one can only ask, for example, whether *Redgauntlet* drew Hardy's attention to such significant Biblical situations and thoughts as the cave of Adullam (*MC*. xxxvi. Scott quotes the original passage in full) and the 'return of the washed sow to wallowing in the mire' (cf. *JO*. vi iii); recalled, or stimulated interest in, Wouverman's pictures (cf. *W*. xxviii); and elicited thoughts on the advantages of 'a marriage of reason' over 'a union of romantic attachment' (cf. *FMC*. lvi). Again, what part, if any, in the development of Hardy's bird imagery was played by the artistic association of the wounded bird and the tragic heroine in *The Bride of Lammermoor*?

In the last two novels, Scott's presentation of 'doom' is predominantly romantic, with more than hints of the supernatural; Hardy's is basically analytical and philosophical, implying the predominance of 'chance' or the interrelationship of circumstance and character.

Shelley (1792–1822)

The poet whom, above all others, Hardy would have liked to meet (May O'Rourke, *Thomas Hardy*, Toucan Press, 1965); 'our most marvellous lyrist' (*Life*, 17). The kinship which Hardy felt with Shelley's essentially Christian spirit may be seen in the Chorus of the Pities, which owes more to Shelley than to any other source outside Hardy. For his close knowledge of Shelley, see *Life*, 188, 192–3, the 'pencillings . . . ideas in the rough, like Shelley's scraps' (*LLI*. 1) and the reference to his paper-boats (*LLE*. Apology).

The Revolt of Islam: (IX xxxi, calumny) *ILH* I 7; (VIII vi, 'shade from his own soul') *MC*. xliv, (I liv, 'gestures beamed with mind') xlv, *WB*. II i; (II xxiii, 'She moved upon this earth . . .') *W*. xvi; (I xxvii) *WB*. title page; (Laon and Cyntha) *JO*. IV iv, (III xxiii, 'Shapes hideously multiplied') v iv.

Epipsychidion: ILH. II 2 *ep.*; (Time, 'in his own grey style') *MC*. xlii; *W*. xxviii (cf. the Idea, xviii, xx); 'Too Late, Beloved', the first title of *Tess of the d'Urbervilles* (cf. *TD*. lv); (the Idea) *WB, LLI*. 1; (ethereal . . . spirit . . . trembling . . . limbs) *JO*. III ix, IV v.

'When the lamp is shattered'   *ILH*. II 3 *ep.*; *DR*.
                                        vi 1; *PBE*. iii; (cold reason . . . mock) *TD*. xiii
'One word is too often profaned'   *DR*. ii 4
'Stanzas written in Dejection, near Naples'
            ('many a voice . . . ') *DR*. iii 2; ('like a tired child') *HE*. xxvii
'Ode to the West Wind'   *DR*. x 3; *FMC*. xliv

Adonais: HE. xvii; (Death . . . Life . . . borrow) *W*. xxvii; (Venus Urania as opposed to Venus Pandemos, Sue to Arabella; cf. Shelleyan love, *TD*. xxxi) *JO*. III vi; ('Far in the Unapparent') *D*. preface; ('a slope of green access') *Life*, 353; (Shelley's 'eclipsing curse') *WW*. 'We are getting to the end'.

Prometheus Unbound: (Æolian modulations) *MC*. xi; ('Forms more real . . . on a poet's lips') *LLI.* 1; *D.* Fore Scene (cf. p. 107): the Chorus of Pities would establish

> Those, too, who love the true, the excellent,
> And make their daily moves a melody.

Alastor (avenging spirit)   *MC.* xxvi
'Lines written among the Euganean Hills'   *Life*, 192–3
'The Sensitive Plant'   See p. 165.
Hellas: See p. 107.

   D. preface ('Riddles of Death Thebes never knew'); *Life*, 383
'A Lament' ('O World! O Life! O Time!') was selected by Hardy as one of the finest passages in all poetry; see Purdy, 297.

   See also the poems: *PPP.* 'Shelley's Skylark', 'At the Pyramid of Cestius near the Graves of Shelley and Keats'; *HS.* 'A Refusal'.
Wordsworth (1770–1850).

'It is a beauteous evening, calm and free'   *DR.* viii 2
'To the Cuckoo'   *DR.* xii 3; *PBE.* xv *ep.*
'Intimations of Immortality' *PBE.* i, xx, xxxii; *TD.* li; *SF; JO.* ii i;
   WP. 'The Impercipient'; *MV.* 'Midnight on the Great Western'
   (see p. 126); *LLE.* Apology
'Ode to Duty'   *PBE.* xx
'The Small Celandine'   *PBE.* xxii; *W.* iii
'She was a Phantom of Delight'   *FMC.* xlix
'London, 1802'   *HE.* xxvii
'Elegiac Stanzas'   *Life*, 114
'Written in London, September 1802'
                                   RN. iii ii; *TD.* xxv; *LLE.* Apology
'Inside of King's College Chapel, Cambridge' quoted three times, *Life*, 141; 'Memories of Church Restoration' (1906).
'Resolution and Independence' (cure for despair, *Life*, 58)   *W.* xxv
'She dwelt among the untrodden ways' (a violet in the shade)   *PRF*
'Lines Written in Early Spring'   *TD.* iii
'Lines Composed . . . above Tintern Abbey' (cf. *Life*, 93)
                                                                   SF; D. preface
'A slumber did my spirit seal'   *MV.* 'While Drawing in a Churchyard'
   Three quotations from Wordsworth's preface to *Lyrical Ballads* occur in the Apology to *Late Lyrics and Earlier.*
   The influence of Wordsworth on Hardy's poetry may be seen in 'Domicilium' (1860–1), the 'lyrical ballad' style of narratives such as

'The Well-Beloved' (*PPP*), and the patriotic sonnet, 'A Call to National Service' (*MV*). For considerations of Wordsworth on style, see *Life*, 147, 306.

Shakespeare

Few writers can have had a closer knowledge of Shakespeare than Hardy. In London he saw Phelps's production of a series of the plays, and followed from the text (*Life*, 53). 'To an Impersonator of Rosalind' (*TL*) marked the performance of Mrs Siddons's great-granddaughter in April 1867. In later life Hardy thought Shakespeare's theatrical value was 'infinitesimal beside his distinction as a poet, man of letters, and seer of life' (*Life*, 341; cf. *MV*. 'To Shakespeare'). For his critical comment on *King Lear*, see *Life*, 282. The quotations and references which follow are a first skimming:

ILH. *M for M:* I 1 *ep.*; *Sonnet* 111: I 4 *ep.*; *M of V:* II 5 *ep.*; *R and J:* II 6 *ep.*

DR. *M of V:* iv 1 (good deed in a naughty world); *Cymb:* ix 3 (Imogen); *Sonnet* 116: xi 4.

UGT. *AYL:* title and close ('Come hither'); I vi, *MND:* III iii, IV v (course of love); *Ham:* III iii (stale, flat, and unprofitable)

PBE. *Ham:* title-page, ix ('Let a beast . . . '), xiii (sicklied o'er . . . pale cast), xxvii; *MND:* I *ep.*; *TN:* xi *ep.*, xxxi *ep.*; *HS:* xi (so far will I trust thee, gentle . . .); *V and A:* (told the steps); *R2:* xviii; *A and C:* xxxv.

FMC. *Mac:* iv; *TGV:* xviii:

> O! how this spring of love resembleth
> The uncertain glory of an April day.

Ham: xxii (Guildenstern), xxix (steep and thorny . . . rede'); *Tem:* xlvii (Gonzalo).

HE. *TN:* vii ('What great ones do . . .'); *R and J:* xviii; *1.H4:* xxiv (the continuation of this passage is echoed in 'not regarded', ii), xxvii (common as blackberries); *Sonnet* 87: xxiv; *Ham:* xxiv (ministering angel), xxxiv; *Mac:* xxxi.

RN. *Ham:* II vi (thought is a disease of flesh, the coil of things); *TN* (and elsewhere): IV vi (Can there be beautiful bodies without hearts inside?); *Lear:* IV vi (I would not have done it against a neighbour's cat) and v i (like an animal kicked out).

TM.	*1H4:* xvi; *Ham:* xvii, xxxvi (stale and unprofitable); *JC:* xxxvi (take the current . . . served); *M of V:* xxxvi (world. . . stage . . . sad one); *MND:* xxxvii (smooth course of love); *C of E:* xxxix (Dromios).
WT. 5.	*Oth:* iii (poppy . . . mandragora).
L.	*TN:* I ii (dying falls); *M of V:* I ii ('Still quiring . . . cherubim'), II i (purse and person); *2.H4:* II i (seems to refer to the hostess of the Tabard rather than the hostess of the Garter in *MWW*); *MND:* III vi (Hermia and Helena); *LLL:* III vi–viii (with a few lines from *R and J* interpolated); *1.H4:* III ix (a little more . . . much too much); *A and C:* IV ii; *Mac:* V xiii (Thick-coming fancies); *AYL:* VI iv (cat will after kind).
GND. 10.	*Oth:* (words of Brabantio).
TT.	*M for M:* vi (Lord Angelo); *Ham:* xvi ('nothing either good or bad . . .'); *M of V:* xxiv ('skip . . . hare . . . counsel'); *R2:* xxvii; *MND:* xxxix (Puck-like . . .); *TN:* xli (whirligig of time, Time . . . revenges).
WT. 1.	*Tim:* (enough to isolate a Timon); *Lear:* (Prince of Darkness); *Mac:* (raze . . . written troubles . . . brain, sere and yellow leaf).
CM. 12.	*AYL:* viii (Jacques); *Tem:* viii (Prospero . . . Ariel); *2.H4:* x ('cankered . . . gold').
DLa.	*Mac:* (dusty death); *1.H4:* ('Charles's Wain . . . chimney', 'Our house, my sovereign liege . . .'); *AYL:* ('dry as the remainder biscuit after a voyage', Corin's remarks); *T and C:* (touch of nature).
MC.	*2.H4:* xxviii (Shallow and Silence); *AYL:* xxxiii (Rosalind's exclamation); *TN:* xxxiv (worm i' the bud); *JC:* xxxvii (Calphurnia); *Oth:* xlv (his nature to extenuate nothing).
CM. 11	*Ham:* iii (enterprise of such pith).
W.	*Ham:* iv (sea of troubles), xxx (cf. lines quoted in *Life*, 248, on Hardy's father), xlv ('nature is fine in love . . .'); *Oth:* xxxvi (poppy . . . mandragora), xxxix (as Desdemona said); *Cymb:* xlv; *M for M:* xlv.
PRF.	*Oth:* 'moving accidents . . . field'
CM. 2.	*Ham:* iii (staleness . . .), viii (common bourne); *M of V:* viii.
WT. 3.	*Oth:* Like Desdemona, she pitied him

GND. 1.   *AYL:* (Rosalind).

CEF.   *MND:* (the roaring of Bottom).

GND. 3.   *Lear:* (sharper than a serpent's tooth) to have a thankless child.

TD.   *TGV:* title-page; *Mac:* ii (uncribbed, uncabined), xviii (the road to dusty death), liv (tale told by an idiot); *TN:* (*Impatience on a monument*); *M for M:* ix ('Take, O take those lips away'); *Ham:* xix (unweeded garden; cf. Hamlet's soliloquy, I ii), xxvi, xxviii ('sigh gratis'), xxxv (passion's slave), xxxvi (endure the ills we have than fly to others), 1892 preface (galls somebody's kibe); *AYL:* xxiii (sermons in stones); *R and J:* xxxiii (Friar Laurence); *Lear:* xxxv (more sinned against than sinning), 1892 preface; *Sonnet 116:* liii (love, 'which alters . . .').

SF.   *Tem:* ('We are such stuff/As dreams . . . sleep.')

WB.   *R and J:* I v (Montagues and Capulets), vi, viii ('Too rash . . .'); *A and C:* I ix (green in judgment); *Sonnet 73:* III *ep.*; *TN:* III vii (Time's revenges).

LLI. 7.   *TN:* (foods of love . . . manufactured by his bow).

JO.   *Sonnet 111:* III i (a man's hands subdued to what he works in); *Oth:* IV vi (my occupation's gone); *Ham:* VI xi (pale to a sickly cast).

PPP.   'Sapphic Fragment': *HS*, ('Tombless, with no remembrance').

General Preface to the Novels and Poems: *1.H4* ('Thought's the slave of life').

LLE.   Apology: *Lear* (madness lies that way); *Tem* (such stuff as dreams are made on).

The Bible

Hardy's knowledge of the Bible is remarkable. It was due to his love of Church services from boyhood, a period of study in preparation for ordination (like Jude, he studied Griesbach's edition of the New Testament; cf. *Life*, 29, 376), the fascination of its style (*Life*, 170–1), and the wealth of its reflections on life. In 1862 he began a letter to his sister: ' "After the fire a still small voice" – I have just come from the evening service at St. Mary's Kilburn and this verse, which I always notice, was in the 1st Lesson' (*Life*, 38). Three years later, he 'began turning the Book of Ecclesiastes into Spenserian stanzas, but finding the original

217

unmatchable abandoned the task' (*Life*, 47). Hardy's habit of quoting the Scriptures may have been encouraged by Scott's example (cf. p. 212).

Although the new scientific thought led to his uncompromising dissent from the theology of the Church, he held fast to Christian values, and looked forward – with an optimism so qualified by contemporary conditions and events that it was dubbed 'pessimism' – to a new religious outlook, combining 'scientific knowledge' with 'loving-kindness' to all (*LLE*. Apology). Hardy found the highest human virtues expressed in the New Testament; they are summed up in Paul's conception of 'charity'.

No other book, not even the works of Shakespeare, informed the thought and character of Hardy as much as the Bible; and no other work was so continually in his mind.

ILH	II 4 *ep*. (Eccl. ii 15); II 5, 'Better ... not vow ... pay' (Eccl. v 5).
DR.	v 1, baker ... Pharaoh; ix 2; x 5, Cushi, David; xi 3; xii 1; xii 4, cloud ... man's hand; xii 6, tithe-paying ... cummin; xiii 2, Bel and Nebo (Isa. xlvi 1); xiv 3, Abigail ... Michal, 'a land of darkness ...'; xiv 4, tents of Kedar; xx 2, Naboth.
UGT.	I vii, Cain; II iv, Laodicean, vi, Noah (and v i); IV v, a verse quoted' (Ps. xliv 17–18); v i, stalled ox (Prov. xv 17), Jeremiah (ii 32).
PBE.	xi, Jael; xiii *ep*.; xviii, Shadow of Death; xxv *ep*. (Ps. lv, *Book of Common Prayer* version); xxx, Naomi, Pool of Bethesda; xxxi, 'a strong tower ...' (Ps. lxi, *Common Prayer*); xxxiii *ep*. (Ps. cxxxvii, *Common Prayer* version); xxxiv *ep*. (ibid.); xxxviii *ep*. (Song Sol. viii 6).
FMC.	i, Laodicean; ii, Noah's Ark on Ararat; iv, Ecclesiastes; vi, Siddim; viii, Elymas; ix, pelican in the wilderness (Ps. cii 6), Philistines; xiii, Daniel; xx, Moses . . . Pharaoh; xxii, '. . . the woman whose heart is snares . . .' (Eccl. vii 26); xxiv, ninth plague of Egypt; xxvi, ewe-lamb (see *RN*. below); xxviii, Moses in Horeb; xxxiii, the prophet Matthew, Shimei (2 Sam. xvi 5); xxxvii, Hinnom; xxxviii, Jonah and the gourd; xlii, Noah; xliii, Esther . . . Vashti, Mosaic law, the 'It is finished' of her union with Troy; xlix, mustard seed, Jacob . . . Rachael; lii, Shadrach . . . Abednego; lv, weigh . . . balances . . . found wanting (Dan. v 27); lvii, Hosea quoted.

HE. iii, Egyptian plague of darkness; vi, dove ... serpent; x, Naomi, Ruth; xxiii (1 Cor. xv 19); xxiv, Satan ... to and fro ... earth (Job i 7), put my hand ... plough (Luke ix 62), Hezekiah, Sennacherib; xxv (Joel ii 28, Gen. xlii 9); xxvii, Bartimeus; xxxi, moved ... mountains (1 Cor. xiii 2), vanity and vexation (Eccl. i 14), wonders of the deep (Ps. clvii 24); xxxv, Hosea quoted; xlv, Abishag; Sequel, little finger ... loins (1 Kings xii 10).

RN. I i, Ishmaelitish; iii, the Philistine (Goliath), Nebo (Deut. xxxiv 1); vi, Belshazzar, witch of Endor; vii, love ... told the towers thereof ... (Ps. xlviii 12–13); ix, ewe-lamb (2 Sam. xii 3). II iii, Nebuchadnezzar; iv, Balaam; vi, Jared, Mahalaleel (Gen. v); vii (Israel in Zin). III ii, John the Baptist, creation groaning and travailing (cf. *JO*), Pontius Pilate; vii, 'a time to laugh' (Eccl. iii 4). IV v, Ahimaaz. V i, title (Job iii 20) ii, Famine and Sword (Isa. li 17–20); vii, last plague of Egypt, Sennacherib, Gethsemane; ix, Lazarus. VI i, weep by the waters of Babylon; iii, words of Job; iv, 'And the king ...' (1 Kings ii 19–20).

WT. 7 i, Abigail; iv, vii, 'Render unto Caesar'.

TM. x, land of Lot; xvii, Pharaoh's baker; xxvi, 'eating ... Noe' (Matt. xxiv 37–8); xxvii, Ark ... Philistines; xxxiv, Ps. cvii quoted; xxxv, Valley of the Shadow of Death; xxxvi, '... ewe-lamb'.

WT. 5. iii, Tophet; v, '... was dead ... alive again' (Luke xv 24).

L. Title (Rev. iii 14–18); I i, Nazarite ... razor (Num. vi 1–5); ii (as for title); xv, everything ... season (Eccl. iii 1). II i, Didymus; v, going to and fro ... as Satan said (cf. *HE* above), Samson. IV. i, things lawful which are not expedient (1 Cor. vi 12); iii, Athenians ... unknown God (Acts xvii 23), star ... Magi. V i, '... kin ... defiled' (Lev. xxi 1–2); iv, sun ... Gibeon; vii, Jacob's Ladder. VI ii, Nebuchadnezzar's furnace.

TT. ii, stoning of Stephen, woman in Deuteronomy ,'His wife ... vine ... bring' (Ps. cxxviii 3, metrical version); iii, St Paul and Ecclesiastes quoted; xiv, Absalom; xvi, Sodom and Gomorrah; xxvii, Moses; xxx, Samson; xxxix, Tobit (Apocr.); xli, Israel (Gen. xlvi 30), Joseph (Exod. i 8), charity which 'seeketh not her own'.

WT. 1.	Nebuchadnezzar, thorns . . . crackled . . . fool' (Eccl. vii 6), Belshazzar's Feast.
DLa.	accursed swine, thought . . . morrow, Ark of the Covenant.
MC.	vi, ruddy and of a fair countenance; cf. David, 1 Sam. xvi 12; xii, Job; xiv, Solomon's temple; xv, Baruch (Apocr.); xvii, Jacob; xix, brethren . . . Joseph; xxii, Apostle (Peter) at the accusation; xxiv, the Preacher, i.e. Ecclesiastes (quotation, xi 4); xxvi, Emmaus, Saul . . . Samuel (1 Sam. ix 24). Henchard's visit is paralleled in Saul's to the witch of Endor (1 Sam. xxviii); xxviii, clouds drop fatness; xxix, breeding . . . Abrahamic success; xxx, Nathan; xxxii, the Prophet's chamber (2 Kings. iv 10); xxxvi, Adullam (1 Sam. xxii 1–2); xxxvii, Pharaoh's chariots; xl, repentant sinner . . . joy in heaven, Job; xliii, Cain; xliv, Samson; xlv, Capharnaum (Matt. iv. 16).
W.	ix, Moses . . . Mount: xiv, Gideon; xvi, '. . . gathered the wind . . . garment' (Prov. xxx 4); xvii, Jehovah . . . mercy . . . sacrifice; xxv, handwriting on the wall; xxix, Absalont, i.e. Absalom; xxxi, Vashti, Cain; xxxiv, without charity . . . tinkling simples (cf. 1 Cor. xiii I); xxxv, horse . . . Death in the Revelation, Psalm of Asaph (Ps. lxxiii. 14); xxxvi, veil . . . temple is rent in twain; xxxvii, Stephen; xxxix, Cain; xliii, hairs . . . sorrow . . . grave (Gen. xliv 29); xliv, Elijah.
PRF.	Joseph and the chief butler, jot or tittle, gather grapes . . . thistles.
CM. 2.	vii, the four Evangelists, a sorely tried man in the land of Uz (Job).
LLI. 4.	iii, cloud no bigger than a man's hand.
WT. 3.	Assyrians . . . Destroying Angel.
GND. 1.	(conclusion) valley of Ezekiel's vision . . . dry bones.
DL.	like Herod (Acts xii 23), quotation from Isa. xiv 10–23.
OMC.	like Peter at the cock-crow.
TD.	ii, years drawing nigh . . . no pleasure in them' (Eccl. xii 1); xi, ironical Tishbite . . . awaked (1 Kings xviii 27), visit the sins . . . children; xiv, Aholah and Aholibah (Ezek. xxiii), reference to Gen. xxxv 18, where 'Benoni' means 'son of my sorrow'; xv, Babylon; xvi, River of Life; xviii, Heb. xii 27 quoted; xix, the man of Uz (Job) quoted, Abraham . . .

ring-straked, Queen of Sheba, sun . . . just . . . unjust; xx,
Resurrection . . . Magdalen; xxiii, 'A time to embrace . . .'
(Eccl. iii 5), Leah . . . Rachel; xxxi, true . . . lovely, and of
good report (Phil. iv 8); xxxiii, meekness . . . endurance
(Col. iii 12 and 1 Cor. xiii 4–7), Angel . . . St. John (Rev. xix
17); xxxiv, words of Paul (1 Tim. iv 12), Last Day (Rev. vi);
xxxvi, sought not her own . . . Apostolic Charity (1 Cor. xiii
5); xxxvii, Samson; xxxix, said the Nazarene (John xiv 27),
good thing . . . Nazareth (John i 46), virtuous woman (Prov.
xxxi); xl, prophet . . . Peor (Num. xxiii 28—xxiv 10); xli,
'All is vanity' (cf. *Life*, 112); xliv, Gal. iii 1; xlv, fleshly
tabernacle (2 Cor. v 1–4); xlvi, 'The unbelieving husband . . .' (1 Cor. vii 14), Sermon on the Mount, like the
devils . . . tremble (James ii 19), mountains . . . groves
(associated with worship of the true God and Baal), 'servants
of corruption . . .' (2 Pet. ii 19–20), Eve . . . witch of Babylon;
xlvii, Tophet, the seven thunders (Rev. x 3–4), Hymenaeus
and Alexander (1 Tim. i 19–20), bachelor-apostle (St Paul),
let go the plough (Luke ix 62), Hos. ii 7; xlix, Abraham . . .
Isaac, grapes of Ephraim . . . (Judg. viii 2); l, 'pillar of a
cloud' (Exod. xiii 21); li, Egypt . . . Land of Promise; lii,
Ark of the Covenant (cf. *DLa*), little finger (1 Kings xii 10),
Canaan – the Egypt (cf. li); liii, woman taken (John viii 1–11),
wife of Uriah; liv, How are the Mighty Fallen; lv, the
prophet's gourd (Jonah iv); lviii, Like a greater than himself
(John xix 9). 1892 preface: servant, ox, ass . . . neighbour's
wife. 1895 preface: 'gone down into silence' (Ps. cxv 17).

LLI. 8.   Introduction, race . . . swift, . . . battle . . . strong (Eccl. ix
11); (*b*) 'in their death they were not divided'; (*d*) To everything there's a season; (*f*) Sodom and Gomorrah; (*g*) 'only
son . . . widow' (Luke vii 12).

WB.   I ii, fleshly tabernacle (cf. *TD.* xlv); v, Children of Israel
(crossing the Red Sea); ix, dies daily, like the Apostle's
corporeal self (1 Cor. xv 31). II ix, Demetrius of Ephesus.
III vi, sea . . . boil like a pot (Job xli 31), viii, image and
superscription, 'Instead of sweet smell . . . burning instead of beauty' (Isa. iii 24), who knew not Joseph (Exod.
i 8).

LLI. 1.   mentally walked round it (cf. *RN.* I vii), mantle of Elijah, 'Behold . . . lattice' (Song Sol. ii 9).

JO.   Title-page (2 Cor. iii 6); I *ep.* (Apocr.); I ii, as Job said; iii, the new Jerusalem, Nebuchadnezzar's furnace, Tower of Babel; iv, Israel in Egypt. II ii, 'For wisdom is a defence . . .' (Eccl. vii 12); iii, Ps. cxix, dew of Hermon (Ps. cxxxiii); iv, tempted unto seventy times seven (Matt. xviii 22); vi, Job quoted; vii, well . . . poor Christ (John iv). III ii, Ishmaelite; iv, Sue on the chronological order of the New Testament, and on the Song of Solomon. IV i, Joseph the dreamer, St Stephen; iii, whited sepulchre; v, neither length nor breadth . . . (Rom. viii 38–39). v iii, 'Let the day perish . . .' (cf. VI xi); iv, 'For what man is he . . .' (Deut. xx 7), the house of Jeroboam; vi, 'we have wronged no man . . .' (2 Cor. vii 2); viii. 'Then shall the man . . .' (Num. v 31). VI *ep.* (Apocr.); VI i, Lycaonians (Acts xiv 6–19), 'For who knoweth . . . sun?' (Eccl. vi 12), from Caiaphas to Pilate; ii, Ps. lxxiii, all creation groaning (Rom. viii 22); iii, 'We are made a spectacle . . .' (1 Cor. iv 9), pig . . . washed . . . wallowing in the mire (2 Pet. ii 22), veil . . . temple be rent; iv, 'Charity seeketh not her own . . .' (1 Cor. xiii. *'Its verses will stand fast when all the rest that you call religion has passed away'*); v, 'saved as by fire' (1 Cor. iii 15); vi, 'Though I give my body . . . and have not charity . . .'; vii, shorn Samson, Capharnaum (cf. *MC.* xlv), 'W— of Babylon'; viii, Creation's groan, 'the letter killeth'; ix, drink my cup to the dregs (Luke xxii 42); xi, Jude's request for water (cf. the Crucifixion, John xix 28), verses from Job iii.

The novel was written for those into whose souls the iron had entered (*Life*, 271). The expression is repeated in the 1896 preface to *A Laodicean*, a story for 'the comfortable ones whose lines have fallen to them in pleasant places' (Ps. xvi 6) rather than those 'into whose souls the iron has entered, and whose years have less pleasure in them than heretofore' (Ps. cv 18, *Book of Common Prayer* version, and Eccl. xii 1).

CM. 4   'worthy to be called thy son' (Luke xv 21).

WP.   'San Sebastian', Cain; 'The Burghers', the furnace in Daniel

PPP. 'The Souls of the Slain', lovely and true, Pentecost; 'Zer-matt: To the Matterhorn', Joshua x 12, and the Crucifixion; 'The To-be-Forgotten', Things true, things lovely, things of good report; 'The Respectable Burgher', various references; 'In Tenebris', Latin quotations from Ps. cii, cxlii, cxx (English version). The last poem is 'To the Unknown God' (Acts xvii 23).

D. (1) II v, 'round world' (Ps. xcviii 8. *Book of Common Prayer*), horn of salvation (Ps. xviii 2), seven thunders (cf *TD*. xlvii), enemy ... tares (Matt. xiii 25); v ii, like David (1 Sam. xvii 28); VI vii, the woman of Samaria.

(2) III ii, prophets ... Judah; III iii, His hollowed hand (Isa. xl 12); v i, like Aaron's serpent-rod; VI v, 'The good that I would do ...' (Rom. vii 19); VI vii, Saul, Belshazzar's Feast.

(3) I ix, The host ... Israel-like ... is made to wander; III i, Last Supper; VII v, Amalekites, Goliath the Philistine; VII viii, Esdraelon (Apocr., Judith).

TL. 'The Flirt's Tragedy', Tophet, Cain; 'A Dream Question', Micah iii 6, Moses; 'New Year's Eve' (tabernacle, groan; see above, *TD* and *JO*); 'Aberdeen', Isa. xxxiii 6.

General Preface to the Novels and Poems: 'the night cometh' (John ix 4).

SC. 'The Face at the Casement', cf. *PBE* xxxviii *ep.* above; 'Wessex Heights', Charity who 'suffereth long and is kind'; 'God's Funeral', wept in Babylon; 'In the Servants' Quarters'.

MV. 'Apostrophe to an Old Psalm Tune', Saul and the witch of Endor; 'Quid Hic Agis?' (1 Kings xix); 'The Blinded Bird' (Charity; cf. p.164); 'In the seventies', Job quoted (Latin); 'The Interloper', Fourth Figure the Furnace showed (Dan. iii 25); 'The Something that Saved Him' (Ps. lxix 1); 'The Clock of the Years', Job iv 15 quoted; 'In Time of "the Breaking of Nations" ', Jer. li 20 quoted in title; 'Then and Now', Rama and Herod; 'I met a man', Moses' face after Sinai, 'mistake ... I made with Saul' (cf. 1 Sam. xv and xxviii).

LLE. Apology: Levitical passing-by (Luke x 32), Athenian inquirers on Mars Hill (Acts xvii 22 ff.), belief in witches of Endor is displacing the Darwinian theory and 'the truth that

223

shall make you free' (John viii 32), 'removing those things that are shaken' (cf. *TD*. xviii above); 'Jezreel' (Elijah, Jehu, and Jezebel; cf. *Life*, 208); 'And there was a Great Calm' (Matt. viii 26); 'The Collector Cleans his Picture', Ezekiel quoted (Latin); 'The Wood Fire'; 'She who Saw Not', shine like the face of Moses; 'Her Apotheosis', 'Secretum . . .' (Isa. xxiv 16, marginal reading); 'The Chosen' (Gal. iv 24 – 'Which things are an allegory' – quoted from Greek text); 'After Reading Psalms xxxix, xl, etc.'; 'Surview', Ps. cxix 59 quoted (Latin; in *Common Prayer* version, *Life*, 405): the theme is Charity (cf. *JO*. vi iv above).

HS.   'Waiting Both' (Job. xiv 14; cf. *Life*, 390–1); 'There seemed a strangeness', Men have not heard, men have not seen (1 Cor. ii 9), glass . . . face (1 Cor. xiii 12); 'A Night of Questionings', Go down to the sea in ships; 'Freed the fret of thinking', Creation's groan; 'An Inquiry', Ps. xviii. 4; 'On the Portrait of a Woman about to be Hanged', Sowed a tare; 'The Sheep-Boy', moving pillar of cloud; 'Compassion', 'Blessed are the merciful'; 'The Bird-Catcher's Boy', captivity in Babylon.

WW.   'The Clasped Skeletons', David and Bathsheba, Jael and Sisera, Aholah; 'An Evening in Galilee' – cf. *TL*. 'Panthera' for 'one other'; 'The Tarrying Bridegroom' (Matt. xxv 5); 'He Resolves to Say No More', Pale Horse (Rev. vi 8), By truth made free (cf. *LLE*. Apology above).

Hardy's poems, it should be noted, were arranged with little regard for the chronology of their composition.

DICTIONARY
OF PEOPLE AND PLACES
IN HARDY'S WORKS

Notes which are based directly on Hardy's text are in ordinary type; *italics* are used throughout (except in footnotes) for explanations, comments, and indications of actual people and places, where they are not well known or are presented under fictitious names.

ABBOT'S CERNEL. *Cerne Abbas, seven miles north of Dorchester. On Giant's Hill, just outside this ancient town, there is an enormous figure of a giant, of unknown origin, cut into the chalk, with a club 120 feet long. Of the Benedictine Abbey all that remains is the gatehouse, with a beautiful two-storeyed oriel window. The tithe-barn is in an excellent state of preservation; one half of it now forms a large farmhouse. See plates facing pp.* 110, 335.

The architectural features of the tithe-barn were transferred to the great barn at Weatherbury.

Mrs Dollery's carrier-van business extended from Sherton Abbas (*Sherborne*) to Abbot's Cernel.

Alec d'Urberville was on his way from Evershead to preach at Abbot's-Cernel when he overtook Tess and made her swear on the pillar Cross-in-Hand never to tempt him again.

FMC. xxii; *W.* i, xxiv; *TD.* xlv; *LLI.* 8b; *MV.* 'Old Excursions'

The evening light 'in the direction of the Giant's Hill by Abbot's-Cernel dissolved away' before the threshing finished at Flintcomb-Ash. There are two references to the Giant. Old Andrey Satchel 'knew no more of music than the Giant o' Cernel'. At the time of the expected French invasion of Wessex, it was rumoured that 'Boney' (Napoleon Bonaparte) lived on human flesh, and ate 'rashers o' baby' for breakfast, 'for all the world like the Cernel Giant in old ancient times'.

TD. xlviii; *LLI.* 8e; *D.* (1) II v

Betty Dornell met Stephen Reynard 'by accident' in the 'ruined chamber' of the Abbey Gatehouse, and elsewhere. The natural consequences demanded that her marriage to Stephen be made public without delay.

The priest of the miraculous legend associated with Cross-in-Hand, or Christ-in-Hand, came from Cernel's Abbey.

GND. 1; *PPP.* 'The Lost Pyx'

ABBOTSEA. *Abbotsbury, near the coast, eight miles to the north-west of Weymouth.*

Mistaking a light on Abbotsea Beach for a signal that the French had landed, the keepers on the hill near Overcombe lit their beacon, and raised the alarm, with the result that local defence forces moved in towards Budmouth, and many civilians – and Festus Derriman – moved out, intending to reach King's-Bere.

In *The Dynasts* it was rumoured that Napoleon had landed near Abbot's Beach. This was in August 1805. (A third presentation of 'the alarm', based on a tradition in the Hardy family, is to be found in *WP*. 'The Alarm'.) *TM*. xxvi; *D*. (1) ɪɪ v

AGNES. *Mrs (afterwards Lady) Grove, the daughter of General and Mrs Pitt-Rivers of Rushmore, near Tollard Royal, in the heart of the Chase country south-east of Shaftesbury. The Hardys were guests at Rushmore in September 1895, partly to witness the games and country-dancing. The 'house-party' dancing was led off by 'the beautiful Mrs Grove' (Life, 269). It is traditionally held that King John's huntsmen used to meet by the Larmer Tree.*

Hardy met her again one evening in London (Life, 281), at the Imperial Institute, where the Hardys 'would sit and listen to the famous bands of Europe that were engaged'. The Blue Danube waltz being started, Hardy and Mrs Grove danced two or three turns to it among the promenaders, 'who eyed them with a mild surmise as to whether they had been drinking or not'. Lady Grove died in 1926. WW. 'Concerning Agnes'

AGNETTE. Recalling – as did her old lover at Casterbridge Barracks – the meetings which had been broken off by a quarrel twenty years earlier, she walked late one summer night from her father's farm (*in the Piddle valley*) to the Sarsen stone, and found him there. In the early morning light, he noted the effect of 'Time's transforming chisel' on her countenance and form. She sensed his disappointment and left him. They never met again: 'Love is lame at fifty years.'

TL. 'The Revisitation'

ALDBRICKHAM. *Reading, Berks.*

When interviewed by Miss Aldclyffe, Cytherea Graye said that Mr Thorn, a solicitor at Aldbrickham, would be her referee.

Mr Ladywell's family owned 'a good bit of land somewhere out Aldbrickham way' according to the butler Mr Chickerel, Ethelberta's father.

Sam Hobson took over a prosperous greengrocery business here, in the hope that the widow Sophy Twycott would marry him.

Arabella Donn was a barmaid at Aldbrickham before her marriage to Jude. She and Jude stayed at *the George Hotel* after her return from Australia. She stayed at the Prince Inn when Jude and Sue, who had left Mr Phillotson, were living almost in the country, in Spring Street. Arabella was about to remarry Mr Cartlett, but she left undisclosed the purpose of her visit, which was to persuade Jude to take charge of his son, born in Australia. She wrote on the subject later, and 'Father Time' reached Spring Street. He had been sent unaccompanied by train from London. Sue deferred her marriage to Jude at Aldbrickham; it seemed to her that legal bondage was inimical to love. Their dubious relationship, and the advent of the boy, created gossip and suspicion. Jude lost his work in consequence, and they left Aldbrickham.

DR. ɪ v, iv 2; *HE.* vii; *LLI.* 2; *JO.* ɪ ix, ɪɪɪ viii, ɪᴠ v, ᴠ i–iv, vi
ALDCLYFFE, CYTHEREA. She fell in love with the architect Ambrose Graye, but was unable to marry him because of an affair with her cousin, a 'wild officer', and the birth of an illegitimate child. She had inherited much property from her great-uncle, and assumed his name (cf. GRAYE, AMBROSE). When Ambrose Graye died, his daughter Cytherea had to seek employment, and, by chance, became engaged as lady's maid to Miss Aldclyffe, who soon discovered that she was the daughter of the man she had vainly loved, and became jealously in love with her. Her fatal scheme was to plan the marriage of her own son Manston to Cytherea. With this in mind, she ill-advisedly appointed him to manage her estate, little knowing that he had made an unfortunate marriage (cf. MANSTON, AENEAS, and SPRINGROVE, EDWARD). DR
ALDERWORTH. *On Affpuddle Heath, near crossroads south of Bryants Puddle. The firs on the knoll above the house still mark the spot; see plate facing* p. 143.

The home of Clym Yeobright and Eustacia, six miles from Blooms-End, and two beyond East Egdon. When Eustacia realized that her dreams of life in Paris were not to be fulfilled, she turned to Wildeve again. Until he was deterred by Diggory Venn's 'rough coercion', it became his habit after dark to walk to Alderworth in the hope of seeing her. On one occasion he succeeded by the time-honoured device of securing a moth and releasing it at the window-chink, whence it flew to the candle on Eustacia's table, 'hovered round it two or three times, and flew into the flame'. Scared by Venn's shot-gun, he decided to venture by day, and entered the house while Clym was sleeping after furze-cutting in the 'torrid' heat, just before Mrs Yeobright, on her mission of reconciliation, knocked at the door. Her dying disclosures to Johnny Nunsuch, on the return journey after her fruitless mission, led, after Clym's illness, to inquiries and jealous suspicions which precipitated a quarrel and Eustacia's return to her grandfather at Mistover Knap. After their separation, Clym returned to Blooms-End. *RN.* ɪɪɪ vi, ɪᴠ i–viii, ᴠ i–iii; *SC.* 'The Moth-Signal'

ALDRITCH, MR. The surgeon summoned from Casterbridge when Troy was shot by Boldwood at Little Weatherbury.   *FMC.* liv

ALFREDSTON. *Wantage, Berkshire, the birthplace of King Alfred in 849. His statue stands in the market place. The Bear (Hotel) is mentioned* (*JO.* VI v).

Jude served as a stone-mason's apprentice here and learned the rudiments of freestone-working and church-restoration. After Arabella left him, he lived in Alfredston before moving to Christminster. Arabella lived here a while after the death of Mr Cartlett. No scenes of any importance take place at Alfredston. It is frequently mentioned with reference to journeys to and from Marygreen.   *JO.* I iv, v, vii, viii, ix, xi; II vii; III viii, ix; IV ii, iii; V vii, viii; VI iii, iv, v, vi, viii

ALICIA. The daughter of the rector of Wherryborne, who fell in love with her sister Caroline's fiancé, and ultimately insisted that he should offer to marry her for honour's sake.   *CM.* 3

ALL SAINTS' and ALL SOULS'. These two churches were situated in 'a certain town . . . many miles north of Weatherbury', where Sergeant Troy agreed to marry Fanny Robin. By mistake, she attended All Souls' and kept Troy waiting too long at All Saints' for the wedding to take place. *The chapter describing this 'satire of circumstance' was an afterthought, which Hardy wrote on the proofsheets of the novel (Purdy). Too often it is wrongly assumed that these churches were in 'Casterbridge'.* *FMC.* xvi

ALLENVILLE, GERALDINE. The daughter of Squire Allenville, who lived at Tollamore House. She fell in love with Egbert Mayne.   *ILH*

AMABEL. *The name seems to indicate 'à ma belle'. It may have been suggested by the name of the heroine in Harrison Ainsworth's* Old St Paul's *(Weber, Hardy of Wessex, 40). The illustration in the first edition shows an hour-glass with two moths. Time (and death, possibly; cf. p. 134) as the tyrant and devourer of Beauty is the subject of the poem. The thought may have arisen from meeting 'the manor-lady' (Julia Augusta Martin of Kingston Maurward House) in London in 1862. When the door was opened to him, Hardy noticed that the butler 'looked little altered. But the lady of his dreams – alas!' (cf. Life, 18–20, 41, 102). The poem is an early one, but the thought provides the climax of two novels,* Two on a Tower *and* The Well-Beloved.   *WP.* 'Amabel'

AMIENS. After touring in the Rhine valley, Holland and Belgium, Paula Power and her party came to Amiens. She and Captain de Stancy visited the cathedral during a church festival. Two dramatic events took place in this city. Paula's uncle left suddenly with a warning that she must not accept de Stancy until he had been to England and inquired into matters he had heard of. Yet – perhaps the most surprising example of feminine caprice in all Hardy's novels – the cool, self-disciplined ('Laodicean') Paula, perhaps tired out through watching all night by the bedside of the feverish Charlotte, and possibly tempted now that de Stancy had become Sir William through the death of his father, promised shortly afterwards to become his wife.

In the novel Hardy comments on the cathedral as follows: 'an edifice doomed to labour under the melancholy misfortune of seeming only half as vast as it really is, and as truly as whimsically described by Heine as a monument built with the strength of Titans, and decorated with the patience of dwarfs.' (*Hardy's notes on his impressions in 1880 are more succintly but less picturesquely expressed in his* Life, *138*.)   L. v x

ANDERLING. A Dutchman who owned plantations in Guiana. He was of 'amorous temperament', and, wrongly thinking his first wife was dead, married Maria Heymere without disclosing his former marriage. He confessed on discovering his error, and followed Maria back to England from Guiana when he learned that his first wife was dead. When he found that Maria had married Lord Icenway, he recklessly gambled away his fortune on the Continent. The desire to see his son drove him back to England, where he was engaged as under-gardener to Lord Icenway for more than two years before his early death.   *GND. 5*

ANDRET, SIR. Sir Tristram's attendant.   *QC*

ANGLEBURY. *Wareham on the River Frome near Poole Harbour. It was an important port in Saxon times; hence its 'Wessex' name. 'Wareham' may derive from the ancient name of the river (the 'Var' of TD). No scene of major importance in Hardy's novels takes place here.*

The centres of principal interest are the railway station (on the line from London to Casterbridge), *and the Red Lion Hotel.* There are amusing scenes between the milkman and the ostler of the Red Lion, a hotel which had 'become the fashion among tourists, because of the absence from its precincts of all that was fashionable and new'; Ethelberta stayed there with her mother-in-law. Sol and the brother of Lord Mountclere, followed by Christopher Julian, called there on their fruitless mission to prevent Ethelberta's marriage at Knollsea.

Wildeve and Thomasin intended to be married at Anglebury, but found that the licence was valid only in Budmouth. The Quiet Woman

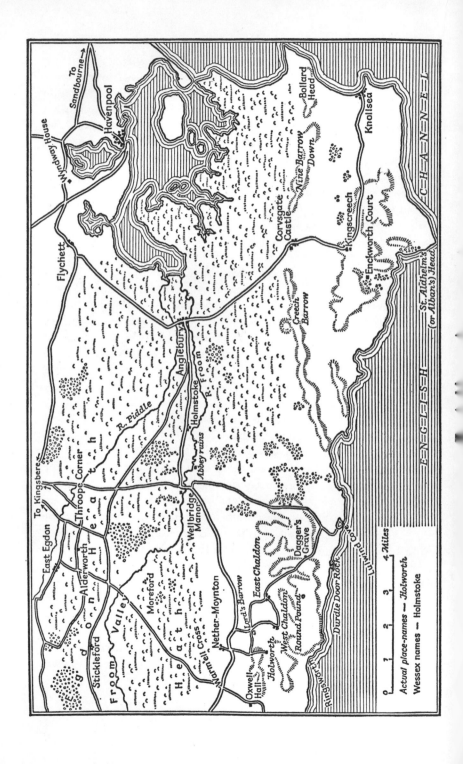

To Sandbourne

Wyndway House

Havenpool

Flychett

Corvsgate Castle

Bollard Head

Nine Barrow Down

Knollsea

Kingscreech

Enckworth Court

St. Aldhelm's (or Alban's) Head

E—N—G—L—I—S—H   C—H—A—N—N—E—L

Anglebury

Holmstoke

R. Froom

R. Piddle

Abbey ruins

Creech Barrow

Throope Corner

To Kingsbere

East Egdon

Alderworth

E g d o n   H e a t h

Stickleford

Froom Valley

Moreford

Wellbridge Manor

Narmell Cross

Nether-Moynton

Lord's Barrow

East Chaldon

Dagger's Grave

West Chaldom Round Pound

Oxwell Hall

Holworth

Ringsworth

Durdle Door Rocks

Lulwind Cove

H e a t h

0 1 2 3 4 Miles

Actual place-names — *Holworth*
Wessex names — Holmstoke

Inn was very busy when people were on their way to Anglebury Great Fair. A specialist was called from the town when Clym's eyesight was threatened.

Henchard died in a deserted old cottage on the heath a few miles north of Anglebury.

Farmer Lodge was frequently seen in the market-place, but only once after the execution of his illegitimate son and the death of his wife Gertrude. Old Mrs Chundle visited the market every fortnight.

When it was announced that Tess and Angel were to marry, the question which arose in the dairy at Talbothays was: 'Who would make the ornamental butter-pats for the Anglebury and Sandbourne ladies?' *DR.* ii 4, xvii 1; *HE.* i, xxxix, xliv, xlvi, xlvii, Sequel; *RN.* I ii, v; III vii; IV ii; *MC.* xlv; *WT.* 4; *OMC*; *TD.* xxxii

ANNA. She had been brought up by her aunt on the Great Mid-Wessex Plain (*Salisbury Plain*), too far from any school to be educated. She went to Melchester to be trained as a servant by Mrs Harnham, who, before her marriage, had lived near Anna's home. Anna was a beautiful girl. A young barrister on the western circuit fell in love with her while he was on duty in Melchester, and won her 'body and soul'. As a result of the letters written for her by Mrs Harnham, his love grew, and he thought her a girl of such rare sensibility that he did not hesitate to marry her when he found that his unrestrained passion at Melchester made marriage his duty. After the wedding, he discovered that Anna could not yet read or write with ease, though she had made progress in these arts under Mrs Harnham's tuition. Spiritually he was in love with Mrs Harnham, who had written the letters signed 'Anna'. Anna and her husband proceeded to Knollsea for their honeymoon. His prospects were ruined, and he re-read the letters with a sigh. *LLI.* 5

ANNY. Arabella Donn's friend. She and her friend Sarah were surprised that Arabella did not know how to secure Jude Fawley as husband. It was Anny who told her. *JO.* I vi, vii, ix, x; V v, vii, viii; VI vi

ARISTODEMUS. In order to save Messenia from the Spartans, he was about to sacrifice his daughter. Her lover suggested she could save herself by pretending she was no longer a virgin, but Aristodemus killed her to prove she was a maid. The story is presented dramatically in hendeca-syllabics. *WW.* 'Aristodemus the Messenian'

ARROWTHORNE LODGE. The gatehouse of Arrowthorne House, a new half-timbered Gothic mansion which stood in a large park by a turnpike road somewhere about midway between Melchester and Sandbourne, in the New Forest region. Christopher Julian, on his way there to see Ethelberta, expected to find an imposing country house, but was directed to a cottage in a shrubbery. Here he met Picotee, Ethelberta's sister, who was home on holiday, and Ethelberta telling one of her sensational tales to some of her brothers and sisters, in preparation for a London season of public appearances as 'Professed Story-Teller'. Her father was in London, acting as a butler. Her mother, Mrs Chickerel, was bedridden at Arrowthorne Lodge; 'Emmeline attends to the household, except when Picotee is at home, and Joey attends to the gate.' There were ten children, including Dan and Sol, Georgina and Myrtle, and Gwendoline and Cornelia (who were in employment elsewhere). *HE*. xi–xiii, xv, xxv

ARTNELL, THOMAS. He, William Rogers, Stephen Sprake, and Samuel Shane were farmers at Nether-Moynton. When the Customs officers discovered the contraband spirits, the villagers employed by Jim Owlett and Lizzy Newberry took the linch-pins out of the cart-wheels and the screws from the waggons on the farms, to prevent the transport of the liquor to Budmouth Custom-house. *WT*. 7

ASPENT, CAROLINE. Daughter of the parish clerk at Stickleford; 'a pretty, invocating, weak-mouthed girl' of hysterical tendencies, who could not resist Mop Ollamoor's music or his other attractions. See OLLA-MOOR. *LLI*. 7

ASPENT, JULIA. Caroline's sister. *LLI*. 7

ATHELHALL. *Athelhampton Hall (mainly Tudor), east of Puddletown. This ancient seat of the Martin family is said to occupy the site of King Athelstan's palace. The Martins are buried in the Athelhampton Chapel on the south side of Puddletown Church.*

The origin of the elopement story has not been traced. The story Hardy invented about 'Sir Nameless' was dated a hundred years back to remove doubt about the ruff (Sydney Cockerell, Friends of a Lifetime).

Christine Everard and her lover Nicholas Long attended a party here. Bellston, the nephew of the Squire of Athelhall, was present. Christine married him to please her father, when Nicholas had gone abroad to improve his fortunes. *CM*. 2; *PPP*. 'The Dame of Athelhall'; *LLE*. 'The Children and Sir Nameless'

BADBURY RINGS. *A prominent hill near the Wimborne Minster – Blandford Road. Its prehistoric ramparts take the form of concentric rings.*

It is believed that King Arthur defeated the West Saxons here in the sixth century.

A beacon was built here at the time of the expected French invasion.

TM. xii

BADEN. See STRASSBURG (and the RHINE VALLEY).

Dr Fitzpiers, after leaving Grace, joined Mrs Charmond on the Continent. They were seen together in Baden.   *L*. v ii–iii; *W*. xxvi, xxxvii

BADGER'S CLUMP. One of the hiding-places for smuggled spirits at or near Nether-Moynton.   *WT*. 7

BAKER, MR. A farmer and friend of John Springrove. The two stood in Casterbridge and saw Manston's coffin being taken into the County Gaol.

DR. xxi 1

BALL, ABEL. A youth who was under-shepherd to Oak at Bathsheba's farm. He was known as Cain from his mother's mistake at his christening. His account of his visits to Bath, and the wonderful things he saw there, including the sight of Troy arm-in-arm with Bathsheba, provides a humorous chapter.   *FMC*. x, xv, xix, xx, xxii, xxxiii, l, lv

BARBREE. See SWEATLEY.   *WP*. 'The Bride-Night Fire'

BARKER, MR. He was a Budmouth doctor, who, while walking on the cliffs above Lulwind Cove, saw Troy carried out to sea. He wrote a letter to the editor of the local paper, and this with other evidence led to the conclusion that Troy had been drowned.   *FMC*. xlviii

BARNES, WILLIAM. *Schoolmaster, philologist, and poet (1800–1886). After a long period at Mere, just north of Blackmoor Vale, he came to Dorchester. His school was next door to John Hicks's offices, where Hardy worked as a pupil-architect. He was an expert in many languages, and a dialect poet of great lyrical appeal. Hardy edited a selection of his poems in 1908. In 1847 Barnes was ordained. He was a curate at Whitcombe, three miles from Dorchester, and from 1862 until his death rector of Winterborne Came not far from Max Gate. Hardy's obituary notice of William Barnes presents an unforgettable description of him, walking along South Street to the Bow, Dorchester. It is included in Harold Orel's Thomas Hardy's Personal Writings. See Life, 28, 161, 175–6, 183.*

MV. 'The Last Signal'; *LLE*. 'The Collector Cleans His Picture', 'The Old Neighbour and the New' (*Barnes died in October*)

BARNET, GEORGE. The son of a flax-merchant at Port-Bredy, and 'a well-educated, liberal-minded' man. He was a town councillor and a trustee of the Town Savings-Bank. He had been in love with Lucy Savile but they parted owing to a misunderstanding, and he married a society lady some years older than himself. The marriage proved to be a failure as he revealed to his fellow-townsman and friend, the young and happily married lawyer, Mr Downe, as well as to Lucy, whom he visited one evening after returning home to find his wife had an engagement with her dressmaker. Mrs Barnet and Mrs Downe were tempted to go for a sail when they drove together to the harbour. The boat capsized. Mrs Downe was carried out to sea and drowned; Mrs Barnet was recovered from the waves and carried home. The surgeon Charlson certified that she was dead, thinking that the freeing of Mr Barnet to marry Lucy Savile would recompense Mr Barnet for the £50 he owed him. Mr Barnet, however, just when he was thinking of marriage with Lucy, thought he detected signs of life in his wife. He gave her a stimulant and sent for another surgeon. With his help, she was restored. Soon afterwards she left home and settled near London. In the meantime the fine mansion that her husband had had built to please her (and which she insisted on calling Château Ringdale) was completed. News came of Mrs Barnet's death, and once again his thoughts turned to Lucy. Immediately afterwards a letter was brought to him from Mr Downe, announcing that he was to be married that morning to Lucy Savile. Mr Barnet was shocked, but managed to put on a brave face and attend the conclusion of the wedding service. He then sold all his property and left Port Bredy. Château Ringdale was bought by Mr Downe. Mr Barnet travelled extensively and lived in America, Australia, India, at the Cape, 'and so on', until over twenty-one years had passed. On returning to Port-Bredy, he discovered that Mr Downe was dead, but that his wife was still living at Château Ringdale. He visited her and proposed marriage. This she declined. Soon she regretted her decision, but when she inquired a few days later, she found Mr Barnet had left Port-Bredy a second time. He never returned. *WT.* 5

BARTHÉLÉMON, FRANÇOIS HIPPOLITE. *First fiddler at the Vauxhall Gardens, and composer of the tune to which Bishop Ken's Morning Hymn, 'Awake, my soul', was sung each Sunday at Stinsford. Hardy wrote three drafts of a story in which he imagined how the melody came to Barthélémon as he was returning home tired and dejected early one morning. In two of these, as in the poem, the composer watches the sunrise from Westminster Bridge. The poem was published in* The Times *on 23 July 1921, to mark the anniversary of Barthélémon's death in 1808. For the visit to St Peter's, Dorchester, which probably inspired the poem, see Life, 414.*

LLE. 'Barthélémon at Vauxhall,'

BARWITH STRAND. *Trebarwith Strand, Cornwall; cf.* Life, *71, 295.*

PBE. xx

BATES. The oldest of the Duchess of Hamptonshire's tenant-farmers. He was seventy-eight. It was expected that the Duchess would 'lead off the dance' at the tenantry ball with 'neighbour Bates'. GND. 9

BATH. *A spa which became famous as a resort in the eighteenth century. Its history dates from pre-Roman times.*

After hearing Boldwood's threats, Bathsheba impulsively drove to Bath to warn Troy. Instead of breaking off her engagement to Sergeant Troy as she intended, she allowed jealousy and the fear of scandal to master her judgment, and consented to marry him. The wedding took place at St Ambrose's Church, Bath. A humorous account of the sights of Bath, including that of Bathsheba arm-in-arm with Sergeant Troy, is given by Cain Ball when he returns to tell his tale to the harvesters at Weatherbury Upper Farm.

Lady Constantine and the young astronomer Swithin St Cleeve were secretly married at Bath.

Lucetta 'arrived at Casterbridge as a Bath lady'; 'there were obvious reasons why Jersey should drop out of her life'.

Humphrey Gould told his fiancée Phyllis Grove that he had to stay in Bath to look after his invalid uncle; he had in fact secretly married 'a dear young belle'.

Lady Caroline and the son of the local parish-clerk travelled from a point not very far from Melchester (*possibly Wilton House*) to be married secretly at Bath.

Lawyer Gayton of Bath, acting on behalf of the Contessa, wrote to Sir Ashley Mottisfont, informing him that he had found a home for his natural daughter Dorothy. When Sir Ashley and Lady Mottisfont visited 'The Bath' during 'the season', they found everybody 'of any note' there, including the Earl and Countess of Wessex (*GND.* 1), Sir John Grebe (*GND.* 2), the Drenkhards (*GND.* 8), and the old Duke of Hamptonshire (*GND.* 9). Here, for a while, the Contessa gained possession of her daughter, much to Lady Mottisfont's alarm.

'*Aquae Sulis*' *was probably written after Hardy's visit to Bath in 1911. The Romans called the place Aquae Sulis because they found there a temple* to the British goddess Sul. *They built their own temple to her, identifying her with Minerva, in the north-west corner of the Thermae. The Abbey is adjacent to the Baths.*

Another poem recalls Hardy's visit to Bath in June 1873, to see Emma Lavinia Gifford, who was staying there. From the heights of Beechen Cliff, a fine view of the city is obtained.

FMC. xxxi–xxxiv, xxxvii; TT. xvi–xix; MC. xxii, xxiii, xxvi; WT. 3; GND. 3; GND. 4; TL. 'Geographical Knowledge'; SC. 'Aquae Sulis'; HS. 'Midnight on Beechen'

BATH, DR. A Casterbridge doctor and councillor. He had recently married, and his wife, a newcomer to the town, sat near Lucetta when the Royal Personage passed through Casterbridge.   MC. xxxvii

BATTON. *Originally Croome, then Stroome (see p. 61). If the story is true (see p. 81), the question remains whether Hardy's location of Batton in the vicinity of Tottenham House, south-east of Marlborough (earlier pocket edition of the novels and short stories, Macmillan) was a feint or a genuine clue.*

The Duke of Hamptonshire lived at Batton Castle.   GND. 9

BAXBY. *A Lord Digby of Sherborne Castle.*

Among the guests invited to King's Hintock Court by Squire Dornell, when he found that his wife and daughter had gone to London, was Baxby of Sherton Castle. His news that Betty had been married in London caused the squire to fall in an apoplectic fit.   GND. 1

BAXBY, GENERAL LORD. Lady Anna's husband (see below).   GND. 7

BAXBY, LADY ANNA. In the absence of her husband, who had gone to raise troops for the King, Lady Anna found herself besieged in Sherton Castle by Parliamentarian forces under her brother. She refused to escape, as he urged her to do. Her sympathies were with her brother, however; when her husband returned, she reminded him that he had been critical of the King and would be wiser to join the Parliamentarian cause. They quarrelled; he went to bed; and Lady Anna would have joined her brother had she not discovered that her husband had made an assignation with a Sherton girl that night. Lady Baxby immediately returned to her lord's chamber, and ensured that he did not move without waking her. She remained with him despite his occasional eccentricities, even in exile.   GND. 7

BAXBY, LORD and LADY. Guests one Christmas at the manor house near Longpuddle (*possibly Athelhampton Hall*).   LLI. 8e

Dorchester (Casterbridge): the King's Arms, and the house in Trinity Street which was the Museum from 1851 to 1871

The Three Mariners Inn.

Dorchester.

Drawn by Thomas Hardy

Beeny Cliff (Aug.22.'70)

The Figure in the Scene.

"....'I scooed back that I might pencil it
With her amid the scene;
Till it gloomed & rained.'"

BEACH, ESTHER. See COMFORT.

BEALAND, MR. The rector at Froom-Everard who refused to marry Christine Everard and Nicholas Long without her father's consent.

CM. 2

BEAUCOCK, FRED. Formerly a very able lawyer's clerk and dandy at Sherton Abbas. He had become dissipated, and had lost his post in consequence. He gave legal advice for astonishingly low fees, and told Melbury about the new divorce law. The two spent some time in London in the hope that Grace Melbury could be divorced from Fitzpiers, only to discover that Fitzpiers had not done her '*enough* harm'. *Beaucock refers to the previous divorce act (1857), whether from 'dupery' or 'ignorance' of the new law (1878) 'was never ascertained'.* *W.*xxxvii–xxxix

BEDE'S INN. *In 1870 Hardy assisted the London architect Mr Raphael Brandon for a few weeks. Brandon's offices were in 'the old-world out-of the-way corner of Clement's Inn', one of the old Inns of Court, and Knight's chambers were drawn from them* (Life, 77).

The sycamore tree described in chap. xiii of the novel, with the 'thick coat of soot upon its branches', is the tree of Hardy's poem.

PBE. xiii, xxxv; *WW.* 'To a Tree in London'

BEECH, PATTY.   *TL.* 'At Casterbridge Fair' (v)

BEENY. *High cliffs on the Cornish coast which are associated with Hardy's courtship of Emma Lavinia Gifford. Two rocks offshore are known as the Beeny Sisters. See plate facing p. 239.*

Beeny Cliff and High Cliff to the north-east suggested 'the Cliff without a Name', where Elfride Swancourt saved Henry Knight from imminent death.

PBE. xxi–xxii; *SC.* 'In Front of the Landscape' (stanza vii), 'The Place on the Map', 'The Going', 'A Dream or No', 'A Death-Day Recalled', 'Beeny Cliff'; *MV.* 'The Figure in the Scene', 'Why did I sketch?', 'It never looks like summer'; *QC.* v:

the tidings every troubled billow
Wails to the Beeny-Sisters from Pen-Tyre.

BELL, MISS BARBARA. An actress at the Regent's Theatre, London, whom Miss Power engaged to play her part in the second performance of *Love's Labour's Lost* at Stancy Castle, after de Stancy's unexpected appearance in the part of the King of Navarre in the first performance.

L. III x

P.H.C.

BELLSTON, JAMES. He was the nephew of the squire of Athelhall, and an explorer, who married Christine Everard in the absence of Nicholas Long. He was irascible, and a scar on Christine's forehead recorded his temper. He left Christine, and it was falsely reported in England that he had been murdered in Asia. He was in Ireland when he heard that Christine and Nicholas Long, who had returned after an absence of fifteen years, were to be married. He arrived at Casterbridge station, and sent his portmanteau to Froom-Everard Hall, just before Christine and Nicholas were to sit down to supper on the wedding-eve. Nicholas left immediately after hearing the unwelcome news, but Bellston did not arrive. Seventeen years later his skeleton and watch were discovered among the piles supporting the edge of the waterfall by which he used to cross. The plank which he had had placed there had been removed during his long absence. *CM.* 2

BELMAINE, MR and MRS. Friends of the Doncastles and Ethelberta.

HE. ix, xxii, xxvii

BELVEDERE, THE. A pavilion in the grounds of The Crags, Elfride Swancourt's home after the marriage of her father and Mrs Troyton. It commanded a view of the (*Valency*) valley to Castle Boterel. Here, in the twilight, Stephen Smith caught sight – 'through the horizontal bars of wood-work, which crossed their forms like the ribs of a skeleton' – of Henry Knight with his arm around Elfride's waist. They were observed by Mrs Jethway, 'a shadowy outline'. Soon afterwards the bell tolling the death of the first Lady Luxellian was heard. *PBE.* xxv

BELVEDERE HOTEL. Here, at Budmouth, Miss Aldclyffe interviewed Cytherea Graye. *DR.* iv

BENCOMB, MARCIA. The daughter of Mr Bencomb, the owner of the Best-Bed Stone Company on the Isle of Slingers, and an inveterate business rival of Jocelyn Pierston's father. Jocelyn met her when, after his engagement to Avice Caro, he was on his way to Budmouth. They travelled to London together and would have married, but such was the enmity between the two families that Mr Bencomb refused permission. Marcia travelled with her father round the world. He lost most of his fortune in large speculations, and she married a Jersey gentleman, a widower with a stepson (Henri Leverre). Forty years after their first meeting, Jocelyn met Marcia unexpectedly at East Quarriers; the stepson had eloped with Avice Pierston (granddaughter of Avice Caro), whom Jocelyn was on the point of marrying. Marcia helped to nurse

Jocelyn during his illness in London. Time had brought ravages to the face he had once kissed, but he still admired her. The Vision which he had pursued had vanished. Both settled on the Isle of Slingers, where they were married.   *WB.* I iv–ix; II i, ii; III i, vi–viii

BENVILL LANE. *The upper part of the road leading from Evershot to Toller Down; the road beyond leads down to Beaminster.*
TD. xliv, liv; *TL.* 'The Homecoming'

BILES, HEZEKIAH. See FRY.

BILES AND WILLIS. A firm of building contractors at Aldbrickham who employed Jude to re-letter the Ten Commandments at a church they were restoring two miles off.   *JO.* V vi

BINCOMBE. *A village in the downs five miles by road from Weymouth.*

Two deserters from the German regiment of the York Hussars were shot on Bincombe Down in 1801, and buried behind the church below the house of Phyllis Grove.   *WT.* 3

BINDON, DR. The friend and medical adviser to whom Mr Millborne imparted what was on his conscience.   *LLI.* 3

BINEGAR. *In the Mendip Hills, not far from Wells.*

Joshua Halborough's father called to see him at Fountall Theological College, escorted by a gipsy-like woman whom he introduced as Joshua's new 'step-mother'. 'Why, we're called to ask ye to come round and take pot-luck with us at the Cock-and-Bottle, where we've put up for the day, on our way to see mis'ess's friends at Binegar Fair, where they'll be lying under canvas for a night or two.'   *LLI.* 4

BIRCH, MRS MILLY. Paula Power's maid. She accompanied Mrs Power on her European tours.   *L.* II vi; III v; V x, xiv; VI i, iii

BLACK DIAMOND, THE. A press-gang ship which came into Budmouth with marines to seize men for naval service against the French.
TM. xxx–xxxi

BLACKMOOR (BLACKMORE) VALE. *In Hardy this is more extensive than in actuality, and covers all the undulating pastoral and wooded country running north from the chalk hills which include Bubb Down, High Stoy, Nettlecombe-Tout, and Bulbarrow. The vale proper is mainly to the north of Sturminster Newton, where Hardy lived for two years, and is watered by the upper part of the Stour and its tributaries.*

Pursuing, as they thought, a horse-thief, Gabriel Oak and Jan Coggan rode north one night from Bathsheba's farm (*up the Piddle valley*) and over the hills into Blackmore Vale. At Sherton Pike on the main Casterbridge – Sherton road, they found they had been pursuing Bathsheba, who was on her way to Bath.

The first clash between Henchard and Farfrae arose over the unfortunate Abel Whittle, who had a habit of oversleeping. Henchard was so outraged at his repeated failure to arrive punctually for work that he went to his home and hauled him out of bed, without allowing him to put on his breeches. But for Farfrae's interposition, poor Abel Whittle would have gone to Blackmoor Vale with the corn-merchant's waggons, so terrified was he of his master: 'Yes – I'll go to Blackmoor Vale half naked as I be, since he do command; but I shall kill myself afterwards; I can't outlive the disgrace; for the women-folk will be looking out of their winders at my mortification all the way along. . . .'

The Hintocks are to the west of Blackmoor Vale, which is presented in *The Woodlanders* from High Stoy and its neighbourhood.

Marlott, where the Durbeyfields lived, is in the Vale, which was known at one time as White Hart Forest for reasons given in *TD*. ii, *the third and fourth paragraphs of which are taken from Hardy's anonymous review of Barnes's poems in 1879 (see Orel*, Thomas Hardy's Personal Writings, 94–5).

It is the country of many of William Barnes's best poems, quotations from which, with glimpses of the Vale from Shaston (*Shaftesbury*), are found in *Jude the Obscure.*

> *FMC*. xxxii; *MC*. xv; *W*. i, xix, xxiii, xxviii; *TD*. i, ii, v, xvi, xxxvii, xxxviii, xliv, l, liv; *CM*. 9; *JO*. IV i, iii, iv, vi; *PPP*. 'The Bullfinches', 'The Lost Pyx'; *TL*. 'A Trampwoman's Tragedy', 'Geographical Knowledge'

BLACK'ON. *Black Down, or Blackdon, or Blagdon, north-east of Portisham. It is 777 feet high and commands extensive views. On top is the memorial to Admiral Hardy.*

It was one of the beacon-points at the time of the expected French invasion in 1805. The beacon was built of large faggots thatched with straw, 'on the spot where the monument now raises its head'.

The beacon was seen burning on the west horizon by the beacon-keepers at Rainbarrows, and the alarm – a false one – was spread.

> *TM*. xii; *D*. (1) II v, V iv; *TL*. 'At Casterbridge Fair' (iii)

BLANDSBURY, SIR CYRIL and LADY. Two members of the Imperial Archaeological Association who visited Corvsgate Castle with Lord Mountclere, and were his guests at Enckworth Court; 'a lively pair of persons, entertaining as actors, and friendly as dogs'. 'Not a single clergyman was there. A tendency to talk Walpolean scandal about foreign courts was particularly manifest.' *HE.* xxxi, xxxviii

BLESS, CHRISTOPH. His home was in Alsace. See TINA. *WT.* 3

BLOMFIELD, SIR ARTHUR. *The son of Dr Blomfield, Bishop of London. He was 'a Rugbeian, a graduate of Trinity College, Cambridge, where he had been a great boating man, and a well-known church-designer and restorer'. When Hardy joined his London office in 1862, he was President of the Architectural Association, though only thirty-two years of age. Hardy and Blomfield kept up their friendship until Sir Arthur's death in 1899. Before he left Blomfield's offices on the first floor of 8 Adelphi Terrace, Hardy wrote a poem which he dedicated to his friend. See pp.* 4–5, CHRISTMINSTER, TOLLAMORE HOUSE and Life, *36–7, 44–7, 48, 249, 305.* *WP.* 'Heiress and Architect'

BLOOMS-END (BLOOM'S END). *A green valley running south from Rushy-Pond to Heedless William's Pond on the western side of one of the most impressive aspects of 'Egdon Heath'. Further east, along the present Stinsford – Tincleton road, which runs along the southern lower slopes of the heath, stood the Travellers' Rest, the Quiet Woman Inn of* The Return of the Native.

Hardy's map of Egdon Heath – specially prepared for The Return of the Native *– shows clearly that he did not adhere exactly to local topography in this novel. The valley running down to 'Blooms' End', for example, is parallel to the Tincleton road, and 'Bloom's End' much further from it than it could actually have been. In 'The Fiddler of the Reels' – written for an American audience – there is no disguise. See map, p. 313.*

It is north-east of Lower Mellstock. Mr Penny was walking in that direction when the body of a drowned man (which he had no difficulty in identifying, from the foot) was recovered from Parkmaze Pool.

Mrs Yeobright lived at Blooms-End. Here the mummers' play in which Eustacia contrived to play a part was given shortly after Clym's return from Paris. Nearby stood the cottages of Fairway, Sam, Humphrey, and the Cantles.

On their return from London, Caroline and her little girl passed 'Heedless-William's Pond, the familiar landmark by Bloom's End', before they came to the Quiet Woman, and met Mop Ollamoor again.

UGT. I iii; *RN.* II i–ii, v–vi, viii; III ii, iii, iv, v, vii; IV ii, iv, v, vii; V ii, v, vi, viii; VI i–iv; *LLI.* 7; *D.* (1) II v; *WW.* 'In Weatherbury Stocks'

BLORE, SAMMY. See FRY.

BLOSSOM, RALPH. A Budmouth fornicator of the seventeenth century.

TL. 'One Ralph Blossom Soliloquizes'

BLOWBODY, MR. A Casterbridge magistrate. His wife sat next to Lucetta for the Royal visit. *MC.* xxxvii, xxxix

BOLDWOOD, WILLIAM. He was the tenant-farmer of Little Weatherbury Farm, next to Bathsheba's. It was his apparent indifference to her at Casterbridge Corn Exchange which prompted her to send him a valentine. So far he had been preoccupied with farming, but he was very concerned for Fanny Robin and distrustful of Sergeant Troy. The valentine changed him. When Sergeant Troy returned to Weatherbury and attracted Bathsheba, he expressed his feelings so strongly that Bathsheba was alarmed for Troy's safety. After Troy's supposed death, he renewed his suit, and ultimately Bathsheba promised to marry him. Bathsheba had become his obsession; he had neglected his farming; and her marriage to Troy had made him 'like an unhappy Shade in the Mournful Fields by Acheron'. His farming problems were solved when Bathsheba allowed Oak to act as overseer of both farms. Thwarted love, however, had mentally unsettled this dignified farmer, 'with his bronzed Roman face and fine frame'. When Troy made his sudden irruption at the party he was holding in Bathsheba's honour, and seized Bathsheba – just after her promise to marry him – it was too much for Boldwood; he seized a gun and shot Troy dead. He walked straight to the County Gaol at Casterbridge and delivered himself up to justice. It is no surprise to find that his death sentence is commuted to imprisonment for life.

There is a glimpse of him about twenty years earlier in *The Mayor of Casterbridge*, where he appears as 'a silent, reserved young man'.

FMC. ix ff.; *MC.* xxxi

BOLLARD HEAD. *Ballard Point, on the coast north of Swanage.*

WW. 'The Brother'

BOLLEN, FARMER. His daughter had married a workman named Stephen, who was conscious of his social inferiority. Stephen's pride had been hurt more than once, and the culmination came one Christmas Eve when, arriving home from his week's work, he found the house empty and cold with nothing prepared for his meal. His wife had taken the children to her father's. He left, never to return.

HS. 'One who Married above Him'

BOLLENS, MR. A farmer at Nether Mynton who married Adelaide
Hinton.   *DR.* xiii 2

BOMBAY. Stephen Smith, after his rejection as Elfride's suitor by Mr
Swancourt, went to Bombay to earn more money in the hope that
affluence would change the rector's mind. Here he became famous as an
architect.   *PBE.* xiii, xiv, xix, xxxvi; *TL.* 'Geographical Knowledge'

BONAPARTE, NAPOLEON. The persistence of Hardy's interest in the
Napoleonic era is shown in his writings. It may be illustrated first from
incidental comparisons: 'much as Wellington antecedently surveyed the
field of Waterloo' (*ILH.* I 5), 'dark and motionless as Napoleon at St.
Helena' (*FMC.* v), 'Napoleon refusing terms to the beautiful Queen of
Prussia', and 'the Château of Hougomont' (*RN.* I x, IV v), 'a face as im-
passable as Talleyrand's' (*TM.* xviii), 'he was quite a Talleyrand' (*CM.*
12), the dinner at the King's Arms 'had been Henchard's Austerlitz'
(*MC.* xx), and waggons 'bulging and curving at the base and ends like
Trafalgar line-of-battle ships' (*W.* iii).

The *Return of the Native* supplies further evidence that Hardy was
already thinking of the historical background for the *Trumpet-Major*
in 1877–8. For a while Napoleon supplanted the reddleman-bogy as a
threat from Wessex mothers with difficult children. Captain Vye recalled
his days in the Royal Navy when he was in charge of the *Triumph*; he
was seven years below the water-line, and saw 'men brought down to the
cockpit with their legs and arms blown to Jericho' in actions against the
French. Grandfer Cantle recalled being a soldier in the Bang-up Locals
in 1804, and running out of Budmouth when it was thought that
Napoleon had landed.

Besides *The Trumpet-Major*, Hardy wrote two short stories relating
to the defence of the Wessex coast against the French invasion: 'A
Tradition of Eighteen Hundred and Four', and 'The Melancholy Hussar
of the German Legion'.

'The Sergeant's Song' (*TM.* v) was written in 1878, and the first
draft of 'Valenciennes' belongs to the same year. These appeared in
Wessex Poems with four other poems on the war with France: 'San
Sebastian', 'Leipzig', 'The Peasant's Confession', and 'The Alarm' (see
p. 357). Some of these may have been written in accordance with the
plan which Hardy set down in June 1875, soon after his visit to Chelsea
Hospital on the sixtieth anniversary of Waterloo: 'Mem: A Ballad of the
Hundred Days. Then another of Moscow. Others of earlier campaigns –

forming altogether an Iliad of Europe from 1789 to 1815.' Another such poem, 'The Bridge of Lodi', was written in 1887 (cf. *Life*, 195–6).

Hardy's major work, *The Dynasts*, presents the Napoleonic Wars from 1805 to 1815. It is discussed on pp. 101–15. A note in his *Life* (162) is of interest with reference to the scene at Rainbarrows Beacon (where, incidentally, Private Cantle and his wife discuss *sotto voce* the rumour that the ogre Napoleon lived on human flesh, and ate baby-rashers every morning at breakfast).

Bos. *Bossiney Haven, a cove on the rocky coast of north Cornwall between Tintagel Head and Boscastle.*　　　　*SC.* 'Self-Unconscious', 'A Dream or No', 'A Death-Day Recalled'

'Bower o' Bliss. *The name was suggested by Spenser's* The Faerie Queene, II xii.

She and 'Freckles' were two 'ladies who sported moral characters of various depths of shade, according to their company' at Christminster. They were members of the tavern audience which heard Jude, after drowning in drink his disappointment at being rejected by Biblioll College, recite the Creed in Latin. Drunk again, he suggested that they should be invited to his second wedding to Arabella. Arabella 'took him at his word as far as the men went, but drew the line at the ladies'.　　*JO.* II vii; VI vii

Bowles, Knowles and Cockton. George Somerset's architectural assistants.　　　　*L.* II ii, iv; III x; VI ii

Bowman, Joseph. A member of the Mellstock choir.

UGT. I i–v, II ii, v; *TL.* 'The Dead Quire'

Bowring. *Benjamin Bowring, who died in 1837 and was buried at Stinsford.*　　*LLE.* 'Voices from Things Growing in a Churchyard'

Bradleigh, Captain. A retired naval officer and father of Cytherea, with whom Ambrose Graye fell in love when he visited the family, who were then living in Dukery Street, Bloomsbury, London. The Bradleighs inherited a great deal of property, including Knapwater, on condition that they assumed the name of Aldclyffe.　　*DR.* i 1, v 3, vi 2–4

Bramshurst Court. *Moyles Court, three miles north-north-east of Ringwood.*

An old unoccupied brick mansion in the New Forest, where Angel Clare and Tess stayed for a while after Tess had murdered Alec d'Urberville at Sandbourne.　　*TD.* lvii, lviii

Brangwain, Dame. The attendant of Queen Iseult of Cornwall.　*QC*

Brazil. After his desertion of Tess, Angel Clare 'in a fit of desperation' emigrated to Brazil with other English agriculturists. He was ill with fever for a long time at Curitiba, and returned to England a changed man, physically and mentally, determined to right the wrong he had done Tess.   *TD.* xxxix, xl, xli, xlix, liii

BREDY KNAP. See PORT-BREDY.

BRETT, SERGEANT. He and Trumpeter BUCK, Farrier-extraordinary Johnson, Saddler-sergeant Jones, and Sergeant-major Wills, were comrades of Trumpet-major John Loveday in the —th Dragoons, who were stationed near Overcombe and at Budmouth when the French invasion was expected in 1804 and 1805. They left for Spain to fight under Sir Arthur Wellesley (afterwards Duke of Wellington). *TM.* iii, xli

BRETTON, LORD. A marriage was arranged between him and Geraldine Allenville to ensure that she did not marry one of low degree.

ILH. II 3–5

BRIDEHEAD, SUSANNA. *The name may be an amalgam. 'Susanna' recalls 'The History of Susanna' in The Apocrypha; it was at one time the name for Tess. 'Bridehead', by analogy with 'maidenhead', suggests Sue's marital squeamishness. 'Head' was at first Jude Fawley's surname, and derives from Hardy's grandmother, who lived at Fawley or 'Marygreen' (see p. 356). Whatever the reasons for Hardy's choice, the name was familiar, being that of a psalm-tune associated with Dorset (Life, 337). Bridehead is at Little Bredy (see p. 445). Hardy's letters show that her Shelleyan qualities derived from Mrs Henniker (p. 364. See also p. 438).*

She was Jude's cousin. Her father had been an ecclesiastical metal-worker at Christminster. Her mother had left him and lived with Sue in London. He had left Christminster when Jude arrived there, but Sue worked in Miss Fontover's ecclesiastical warehouse. She had been very friendly with a Christminster undergraduate, who lent her many books. She had read widely and had most advanced views. To Jude, her outlook was quite Voltairean. When her friend left Christminster, she lived with him in London, sharing a sitting-room for fifteen months, but refused to love him. He died broken-hearted. But for the complications arising from his marriage to Arabella, this was very much the pattern that Jude was to follow with Sue. She was a creature of 'epicene' sweetness and aversion to sex, with an astonishing freedom of intellect. When Miss Fontover smashed Sue's Greek statuettes, they quarrelled, and Sue decided to leave. It was Jude who found her a position as pupil-teacher with Phillotson at Lumsdon. She was an apt pupil, and became a Queen's

Scholar at Melchester Training College for teachers. She and Jude missed their train back to Melchester late one evening, after an excursion to Wardour Castle, and as a result Sue was condemned to solitary confinement for a week. She escaped and took refuge at Jude's. Though she loved him, she decided to fulfil her engagement to marry Phillotson, then schoolmaster at Shaston, when she heard that Jude was married. Jude acted as best man at her request. The marriage was a failure from the start, and Sue was finally released. She was a woman 'tossed about, all alone, with aberrant passions, and unaccountable antipathies'. She delighted in Jude's company and returned to him, but her delight was of a supremely delicate kind which she did not wish to endanger by sexual passion or the 'iron contract' of marriage. Even when she and Jude had been freed by divorce, she could not contemplate matrimony for reasons which Hardy set out succinctly in a letter to Edmund Gosse (*Life*, 272): 'one of her reasons for fearing the marriage ceremony is that she fears it would be breaking faith with Jude to withhold herself at pleasure, or altogether, after it; though while uncontracted she feels at liberty to yield herself as seldom as she chooses'. Only when she felt certain that Jude might leave her for Arabella did she yield. The coming of Father Time, whom Sue took to her heart immediately, the fact that their marriage had been deferred, and Jude's failure to defend himself in both divorce cases, created so much scandal at Aldbrickham that both he and Sue found it increasingly difficult to obtain work. Two children were born, and a third was expected. It was at Christminster that Father Time, feeling that he was an intruder, and the children were the cause of their parents' afflictions, hanged them and himself. Sue never recovered from the shock. Earlier, her intellect had 'scintillated like a star', and 'played like lightning over conventions and formalities' which Jude had respected. Like Hardy, she had believed that the First Cause worked automatically like a somnambulist and had never contemplated the development of emotional perceptiveness in the human race. But now affliction made opposing forces anthropomorphic. She could not oppose God. She must expiate her 'insolence of action' and accept the only marriage which was right in the sight of Heaven. So, although she loved Jude still, she returned to Phillotson and assumed a relationship which was right in the eyes of the world but 'adultery' to her former self. Circumstance and the 'letter' of the law had killed her spirit.   *JO.* I ii, v, xi, II i ff.; *SC.* 'Wessex Heights' (v. *The 'tall-spired town'* is

Melchester; *see footnote, p.* 309), 'The Recalcitrants'
BRIDLE, MR. The farmer at Durnover whose barton supplied the straw
for Napoleon's effigy. *D.* (3) v vi

BRIGHTON. The Prince of Wales ('Prinny') announced the English
victory at Talavera in Spain at his birthday party in the Royal Pavilion,
and later at the County Ball which was held in the neighbouring
Assembly Rooms in his honour. *D.* (2) IV vi, vii

BRIGHTWALTON, THE HON. MRS. An old lady of seventy who asked
Pierston, as he was leaving the Countess of Channelcliffe's assembly, to
dinner the next day but one, 'stating in the honest way he knew so well
that she had heard he was out of town, or she would have asked him two
or three weeks ago'. There, he met Mrs Pine-Avon again. *WB.* II ii

BRINE, WILLIAM. *HS.* 'Inscriptions for a Peal of Eight Bells'.

BRISTOL. Knight returned from Ireland, and Stephen Smith from his
first stay in India, to St Juliot via Bristol and Castle Boterel.

When Farfrae arrived in Casterbridge he was on his way to Bristol and
North America. Lucetta went to Bristol to see her only relative, her rich
Aunt Templeman, and intended returning to Jersey via Casterbridge
and Budmouth.

Stephen Reynard returned to England via Bristol to claim Betty
Dornell, whom he had married when she was a girl. Squire Dornell, who
was seriously ill, rode from Falls-Park to Bristol in a vain effort to dissuade
him, and returned the same night, anxious to know from Tupcombe if
they had passed Three-Man-Gibbet, as he could hardly hold on to his
horse.

The smugglers at Nether-Moynton were eventually caught and
committed to the Assizes, but were let off. Their leader, Jim Owlett,
gave up his mill, 'and at last went to Bristol, and took a passage to
America, where he settled' in Wisconsin.

Among the deserters along the route towards Coruña were soldiers
from Bristol. One wished he were home again (where there was 'old-
fashioned tipple' instead of wine), leaning against old Bristol Bridge,
'and the winter sun slanting friendly over Baldwin Street as 'a used to
do'. 'Ay, to-night we should be a-setting in the tap of the "Adam and
Eve" – lifting up the tune of "The Light of the Moon".' *PBE.* xii, xx,
xxi, xxv; *MC.* vii, viii, xviii; *GND.* 1; *WT.* 7; *D.* (2) III i

BRITISH MUSEUM, THE. *For Hardy's reading at the British Museum,
see pp.* 8, 103, *and the index to his* Life.

Among the visitors to the British Museum were Henry Knight, and Christopher Julian's sister Faith, to whom it was a 'temple'. Her attempt to interest Christopher in the figure of Sennacherib on his throne was fruitless after he had just lost hope of winning Ethelberta. Miss Paula Power's interest in Greek pottery took her to the Museum; she fancied she would like statues like those she saw there at Stancy Castle.

It was here that Simon Stoke looked over 'the pages of works devoted to extinct, half-extinct, obscured, and ruined families appertaining to the quarter of England in which he proposed to settle', came across the name *d'Urberville*, and decided that it 'sounded as well as any of them'.

Two poems relate to the Elgin Room. Here, it was said,* was the base of a pillar which came from the Areopagus or Hill of Mars, where Paul had preached (Acts xvii).

PBE. xxxviii; *HE.* xxiv; *L.* i iv, x; *TD.* v; *SC.* 'In the British Museum'; *WW.* 'Christmas in the Elgin Room'

BROAD SIDLINCH. *Sydling St Nicholas, near Maiden Newton and seven miles north-north-west of Dorchester. The old mill is now demolished.*

When Sergeant Holway committed suicide, the parson would not allow him to be buried in the churchyard at Broad Sidlinch. He was buried at crossroads with a stake through his body.

CM. 4; *MV.* 'Old Excursions'

BROADFORD, RICHARD. The maternal grandfather of Egbert Mayne. Egbert lived with him in the farmhouse at Hawksgate until his grandfather died. *ILH.* i 3–6

BROOK, RHODA. She was a milkmaid who had been deserted by Farmer Lodge, and naturally took an aversion to the young and pretty Gertrude whom he married (see p. 390). After their visit to Conjuror Trendle, Rhoda Brook disappeared with her son from Holmstoke. She was not seen again until six years later, when Gertrude, in the hope of curing her withered arm, applied it to the neck of a young man who had been hanged at Casterbridge gaol. Rhoda Brook and Farmer Lodge were present. It was their son who had been hanged; his guilt was no more than being present when a rick was fired (*cf. the story told to Hardy by his father: E. Hardy*, Thomas Hardy, 42). Farmer Lodge left Holmstoke, but Rhoda returned and continued her milking. She refused to accept the

* There is no evidence that a stone from the Areopagus ever found its way to the British Museum (J. O. Bailey). Whether it is the 'labouring man' or Hardy who was mistaken remains conjectural.

annuity which he had arranged to be paid her.   *WT*. 4

BROOKS, MRS. The landlady of The Herons, a boarding-house at Sandbourne, where Tess murdered Alec d'Urberville.   *TD*. lvi

BROWN, NATHAN. One of the old labourers at the farm of Egbert Mayne's grandfather. He prepared Egbert's breakfast when the hero of the romance was setting off for London.   *ILH*. I 8

BROWN HOUSE. *Red Barn, 'a weather-beaten old barn of reddish-gray brick and tile', which stood where the Ridge Way crosses the main road to Wantage.*

Jude climbed to the top of the barn to catch sight of Christminster, only to find its reflections soon veiled in mist, or its light subdued by fog. It was by the Brown House that he and Arabella caught sight of a fire in the same direction. Their marriage ended Jude's hopes of studying at Christminster, and they took a cottage near a few unhealthy fir trees, where the field path from Marygreen joined the highway, south of the Brown House. North of it, where the Fensworth road leaves the highway, Jude's parents had finally parted, near the site of the gibbet on which one of the ancestors of Jude and Sue had been hanged as a result of marital dissension.   *JO*. I iii, v, vii, ix, xi; III ix; IV ii; V iv; VI viii

BROWNE, ELIZABETH. *Elizabeth B—, the pretty daughter of a gamekeeper, with whom Hardy imagined he was in love in 1853 or 1854. He admired 'her beautiful bay-red hair. But she despised him, as being two or three years her junior, and married early'* (Life, 25–6, 206).
    PPP. 'To Lizbie Browne'

BROWNJOHN. See STUBB.

BROWNJOHN, MRS. Daughter of Mrs Penny. She was expecting another child – 'And how many will that make in all, four or five?' 'Five; they've buried three. Yes, five; and she not much more than a maid yet.' *UGT*. I ii

BRUSSELS. After their tour of the Rhine country, Paula and her party went on to The Hague and Scheveningen, and then to Brussels. While she and her uncle talked on 'the situation of affairs between herself and her admirer', de Stancy, the captain, had 'gone up the Rue Royale with his sister and Mrs Goodman, either to show them the house in which the ball took place on the eve of Quatre-Bras or some other site of interest'. ('*Here Hardy – maybe with his mind on* The Dynasts *– explored the field of Waterloo, and a day or two later spent some time in investigating the problem of the actual scene of the Duchess of Richmond's ball, with no result that satisfied him.' This was in 1876; cf.* Life, 110).

Joshua Halborough borrowed money to send his sister Rosa to school for two years in Brussels after she had been to a 'high-class school' in Sandbourne. It was a profitable investment.

When Mr Millborne had done everything possible to repair the wrongs he had done two people, he retired to Brussels. He now thought he was entitled to 'dishonourable laxity', and was occasionally seen being helped home by his servant after drinking to excess.   *L.* v ix; *LLI.* 4, 3;
WP. 'The Peasant's Confession'; *D.* (3) vi ii, vii

BUBB DOWN. *A chalk hill – near Melbury Bubb and east of Melbury Park – which forms part of the range of hills south of Blackmoor Vale.*
TD. ii; *PPP.* 'The Lost Pyx'

BUCK, TRUMPETER. The 'trusty lieutenant' of the trumpet-major, John Loveday.   *TM.* iii, xxxvii, xli

BUCK'S HEAD, THE. *An inn at Troy Town, about a mile from Puddletown on the road to Dorchester. It was important in stage-coach days, but was pulled down at the beginning of this century.*

When Fanny Robin stole away from Bathsheba Everdene's, she asked the newcomer Gabriel Oak 'how late they keep open the Buck's Head Inn'. She was on her way to Casterbridge, hoping to meet Sergeant Troy. Here Joseph Poorgrass stopped with the waggon carrying the coffin which enclosed Fanny Robin and child, on his way from Casterbridge Union to Weatherbury.

Nicholas Long stayed at the inn, to find out what had happened to Christine Everard, after his long absence from England. 'Before he left home it had been a lively old tavern at which High-flyers, and Heralds, and Tally-hoes [stage-coaches] had changed horses on their stages up and down the country; but now the house was rather cavernous and chilly, the stable-roofs were hollow-backed, the landlord was asthmatic, and the traffic gone.'   *FMC.* vii. viii, x, xlii; *CM.* 2

BUDMOUTH. *Weymouth. It was once two boroughs, Melcombe Regis north of the harbour, and Weymouth to the south. They were incorporated in the reign of Elizabeth I. The northern part of the town became a fashionable resort when George III chose it for his summer residence; it has a mile-long esplanade. To the east of the old town, the Nothe ('nose') projects into the sea between Weymouth Bay and Portland Harbour.*

Hardy worked for the architect Crickmay at Weymouth from the summer of 1869 until May 1870; in his spare time he wrote some poems (cf. p. 507) and began Desperate Remedies. *Some of his impressions and*

experiences enter the early part of the novel. Years later, he stayed at Weymouth for a short period when he was working on The Trumpet-Major.

In 'An Indiscretion in the Life of an Heiress', Weymouth is called Melport. In 'Destiny and a Blue Cloak', another story which remained outside the Wessex edition of Hardy's fiction, the name 'Weymouth' is retained; it appears again in one of Hardy's best-known poems, 'Great Things' (*MV*).

Dick Dewy saw Fancy Day at Budmouth Regis, at the corner of Mary Street near the King's statue (*see plate facing p. 78*), and drove her 'past the two semi-circular bays of the Old Royal Hotel, where his Majesty King George the Third had many a time attended the balls of the burgesses', back to Mellstock (*cf. Life, 229*).

Soon after his marriage to Bathsheba, Troy lost heavily at races outside Budmouth. He met Fanny Robin again near Grey's Bridge, and when she failed to keep her engagement a second time (she was dead) set off in a reckless mood to Budmouth races. But 'Fanny's image . . . returned to his mind, backed up by Bathsheba's reproaches. He vowed he would not bet, and he kept his vow.'

Budmouth was a magnet to Eustacia Vye, who hated Egdon Heath. Her father had been a Budmouth bandmaster, and she remembered its gaiety at a time when ' "Budmouth" still retained sufficient afterglow from its Georgian gaiety and prestige to lend it an absorbing attractiveness to the romantic and imaginative soul of a lonely dweller inland'. After leaving Clym, it was Eustacia's intention to sail from Budmouth on her way to Paris.

Officials at Budmouth Custom-house were kept busy trying to put an end to the smuggling of spirits from France. Thirteen, under the direction of William Latimer, were engaged in an encounter of varying fortunes with the smugglers of Nether-Moynton and the neighbourhood.

Among the places and events at Budmouth which form a background to the story of *The Trumpet-Major* are the barracks, the Bay, the arrival of George III to stay at Gloucester Lodge (*The Gloucester Hotel*), his visit to the theatre to see one of Colman's plays with Bannister in the leading part (Elliston the manager?, cf. xvi), the band playing 'God Save the King' as he emerged from his first dip in the sea, 'dinners at Stacie's Hotel, and the King below with his staff' (xxvi), recruiting and press-ganging – the 'Old Rooms' of Cove Row being regarded as a place for a good haul.

In his palmy days, Sir William de Stancy had owned many racehorses, 'twelve hunters at his box t'other side of London' and 'four chargers at Budmouth'. When George Somerset was on his way from Toneborough to Normandy, he intended to cross the Channel by steamboat from Budmouth. Paula and Mrs Goodman followed by the same route.

On finding his sister Lady Constantine away from home, Louis Glanville went to Budmouth for two or three weeks.

Lucetta left England for Jersey, after her visit to Bristol, and later came to Casterbridge, via Budmouth. When she was critically ill after the skimmington-ride, a second doctor was called in from Budmouth. A string band from Budmouth was present at the marriage celebrations of Elizabeth-Jane and Farfrae. Soon after his daughter's wedding, Newson left Casterbridge to live near the sea at Budmouth.

Dr Fitzpiers would have bought a practice at Budmouth to escape the dullness of Little Hintock but for the fascination of Mrs Charmond. After her death on the Continent, he returned to Little Hintock via Budmouth.

Caroline suddenly left Wherryborne to find the man she assumed she had married, Charles de la Feste, in Venice, and travelled via Budmouth Regis.

The melancholy hussar planned to escape back to Germany with Phyllis Grove in the summer of 1801, when George III was at Gloucester Lodge. His friend was to row the boat in which they were to cross the Channel round to the southern side of the Nothe, or Look-out Hill as it was then called. He and Phyllis would walk across the harbour-bridge and climb over Look-out Hill to meet him at the appointed time.

Only after discussing his deceased wife's hallucinations with the Budmouth physician who advised her family did Timothy Petrick realize that Rupert was his son and not of aristocratic descent.

Stephen Hardcome went for a row in the bay at Budmouth with his cousin's wife (formerly his fiancée, Olive Pawle). They were both drowned.

Jocelyn Pierston sometimes stayed there. His friend Alfred Somers was seen there on the Esplanade, with his wife and 'a row of daughters tailing off to infancy'.

A telegram came to Ella Marchmill from her husband to say that he had gone yachting down the Channel as far as Budmouth, and would not be able to return to Solentsea until the next day.

Monsieur B—, previously a member of the Committee of Public Safety, came to Budmouth in 1802, and hired a cheap bedroom at the Old Rooms Inn in Cove Row. He and Mademoiselle V— attended a performance of Sheridan's *The Rivals*, in which Mr S. Kemble played the part of Captain Absolute. The arrival of the King on his customary summer visit made it expedient for him to leave Budmouth, although he was no supporter of Bonaparte. (*St Thomas Street is mentioned.*)

Lt Vannicock was stationed at Budmouth infantry barracks with his regiment, the —st Foot. He and Mrs Maumbry took leading parts in a play at Budmouth which was performed to raise funds for the people who suffered as a result of the cholera epidemic in her husband's parish at Durnover.

In *The Dynasts* we see Pitt in consultation with the King at Gloucester Lodge; boatmen in the Old Rooms Inn celebrating Trafalgar – their song refers to the Back-sea (of the harbour), Dead-man's Bay (west of Portland), and the Nothe; and soldiers at Vitoria recalling the summer of 1805 at Budmouth. Sergeant Young, whose girl had married a tallow-chandler's dipper in Little Nicholas Lane 'afore we struck camp', sings the song 'Budmouth Dears'.

> *ILH.* 18; *DR.* i 5, ii–v, xx 1; *UGT.* III i; *FMC.* xxxix, xlv; *RN.* I v, vii, x; III iv, v; V v, vii; *WT.* 7; *TM.* i, v, ix, xi, xiii, xxvi, xxix, xxx, xxxiii, xxxiv, xli; *L.* I v; V xii; VI i; *TT.* xx; *WT.* 2; *MC.* xviii, xx, xl, xliv, xlv; *W.* xxiii, xxv, xxvii, xxx, xxxvi, xl; *CM.* 3; *WT.* 3; *GND.* 6; *LLI.* 8*b*; *WB.* I ii, iii, v, vii; II ix, x; III i, iv, vi, viii; *LLI.* 1; *CM.* 8; *WP.* 'The Alarm'; *CM.* 1; *D.* (1) II iv; IV i; V vii, (3) II 1; *TL.* 'At Casterbridge Fair' (ii), 'One Ralph Blossom Soliloquizes'; *SC.* 'At a Watering-Place'; *HS.* 'A Watering-Place Lady Inventoried' (?); *WW.* 'The Ballad of Love's Skeleton'. For the Weymouth' poems, see p. 507

BULBARROW. *A high hill – south of Sturminster Newton – in the chalk range which forms the southern boundary of the Vale of Blackmoor.*

> *TM.* xii; *TD.* ii, iv, xlii, l; *SC.* 'Wessex Heights'

BURDEN, SIMON. A 'poor old' soldier. He was now a pensioner and, with Corporal Tullidge, beacon-keeper near Overcombe. *TM.* i, iv, xxvi

BURTHEN, MR. The carrier from Casterbridge to Longpuddle. Among

his passengers were the narrators of the stories in *A Few Crusted Characters*. He himself told the story of 'Tony Kytes, the Arch-Deceiver'.
LLI. 8

BUTTERMEAD, LADY MABELLA. A guest at the Countess of Channelcliffe's assembly. She appeared in 'a cloud of muslin', and was a warm-hearted girl. *WB.* II i

BUZZFORD. A Casterbridge general dealer, who was often to be found at the Three Mariners in the company of Christopher Coney and Solomon Longways. *MC.* vi, viii, xiii, xxxvii, xliii

BYRT, SIR WILLIAM. The curate who married the widow Edith Stocker and Sir John Horseleigh at Havenpool in 1539. *CM.* 9

CALLCOME, NAT. The best man at Dic Dewy's wedding. He was supported by Ted Waywood. *UGT.* V i, ii

CAMELOT. *The hill-fort known as Cadbury Castle, south of Castle Cary in Somerset. It is associated traditionally with the legendary King Arthur.*
SC. 'Channel Firing'

CAMELTON. *Camelford, Cornwall.* *PBE.* xx, xxi, xxxix, xl

CAMPERTON, MRS. A 'dapper little lady', the wife of Major Camperton of Captain de Stancy's battery. She was a friend of George Somerset's father, whom she asked to design costumes for *Love's Labour's Lost*, the presentation of which at Stancy Castle she helped to organize in support of County Hospital funds. *L.* III v–viii

CANNISTER, MARTIN. The sexton at Endelstow. He married Unity, the cook at Mr Swancourt's, and became landlord of the Welcome Inn.
PBE. ix, xxiii, xxv–xxvi, xl

CANTLE, CHRISTIAN. The youngest son of Grandfer Cantle, aged thirty-one, and a nervous simpleton: 'mother told me I was born some time afore I was christened'. He was born with a caul, and, on the one occasion when he ventured to gamble, plucked up courage with the thought that perhaps he could be no more ruined than drowned. There was no moon when he was born, and the common saying was 'No moon, no man'. No woman would marry him; the last he asked turned on him with 'Get out of my sight, you slack-twisted, slim-looking maphrotight fool,' which was not encouraging, as Timothy Fairway remarked. He was 'a faltering man, with reedy hair, no shoulders, and a great quantity of wrist and ankle beyond his clothes'. He was continually starting with fright, and was afraid of ghosts and evil spirits. He believed that Eustacia Vye was a witch, and that perhaps the old serpent or Satan still lived in adders and snakes. Grandfer Cantle regretted that all his soldiering and smartness seemed to count for nothing in his son.

He was employed by Mrs Yeobright and commissioned to carry two bags of guineas to Clym and Thomasin, but, after winning a raffle at the Quiet Woman, he was tempted to gamble further with Wildeve, and lost all the money with which he had been entrusted. He was promptly dismissed. Subsequently he did odd jobs for Clym at Blooms-End.

RN. I iii, v; II vi; III ii, vii, viii; IV i, vii; V ii; VI iv

CANTLE, GRANDFER. The most ancient of the Egdon rustics, a 'wrinkled reveller', much given to song, jigging, and drink. He continually recalled the great days of 1804, when he was a soldier in the Bang-up Locals, who were called up in preparation for the expected landing of Bonaparte: 'there wasn't a finer figure in the whole South Wessex than I, as I looked when dashing past the shop-winders with the rest of our company on the day we ran out o' Budmouth because it was thoughted that Boney had landed round the point'. Eustacia might have been a witch, but he would have married her if she had been willing, and taken the risk of 'her wild dark eyes ill-wishing' him.

As Private Cantle, home on a night's leave, he had walked up from Bloom's-End to Rainbarrow with his wife Keziar, who was anxious to know if the beacon-keepers had any news about the expected invasion. 'Boney's expected every day, the Lord be praised!' said Cantle. He was told to mind that he didn't take to his heels when the next alarm came as he did 'at last year's' (i.e. in 1804). He was present at the burning of Boney's effigy on Durnover Green.

RN. I iii, v; II v, vi; IV vii; VI i, iv; *D.* (1) II v, (3) V vi

CAPE OBSERVATORY, THE. Swithin St Cleeve spent the greater part of his time abroad working at the Royal Observatory at the Cape, before returning to England in the expectation of making his former marriage to Lady Constantine legal. *TT.* xxxvi–xxxviii, xl–xli

CARLSRUHE. See STRASSBURG (and the RHINE VALLEY)

CARO, ANN AVICE (MRS ISAAC PIERSTON). *Caro is an imitation of a Portland name, and was adopted from its resemblance to the Italian for 'dear'. For the origin of 'Avice', see* Life, 6.

Avice the Second was a washer-woman, who was always falling in and out of love; the ordinary counterpart to the artistic Jocelyn Pierston. He met her just after her mother's death, and for a short time she was his servant in London, where he proposed to her only to discover that she was secretly married. When he returned to Portland the third time, forty years after he thought he was in love with her mother, Ann Avice was ill and anxious that he should marry her daughter Avice.

WB. II iv–xiii, III i–viii

CARO, AVICE. The first of the three Avices with whom Pierston thought he was in love. She was a girl of seventeen or eighteen with brown hair and bright hazel eyes, and had promised to walk with Pierston as far as Henry the Eighth's Castle when he was returning to London. She thought this indiscreet. Pierston met Marcia Bencomb, and she became his ideal. Avice married her cousin Jim Caro, a quarryman.

WB. I i–iv, v, vii, viii; II ii, iii, vii

CARO, MRS. She lived on the Isle of Slingers at East Quarriers with her daughter Avice. She did not oppose 'Island Custom' as her daughter did. *This alludes to the old Portland practice of trial courtship: marriages were not made officially until 'wives' proved to be capable of bearing children. See plate facing p. 399.* *WB*. I i, iii, iv

CAROLINE. (1) Jim Cornick visited Overcombe Mill after the battle of Trafalgar to bring news of Robert Loveday, whose family had expected a letter from him; Jim explained that Bob had been busy courting Caroline, 'a very nice young master-baker's daughter'. This could have been the end of Bob for Anne, had he not written later to tell his loyal brother John that he had given up Caroline and his heart had come back to 'its old anchorage'. *TM*. xxxv, xxxvii

(2) Sister of Alicia. *CM*. 3

(3) *Caroline Fox Hanbury, of Kingston Maurward House, Stinsford. Hardy was godparent at her christening in September 1921* (Life, *414*).

HS. 'To C. F. H.'

CAROLINE, LADY. *The 'classical mansion' where she lived before marrying the Marquis of Stonehenge is probably Wilton House, west of Salisbury. The river Avon flows near, through Amesbury and Salisbury. Originally she was the Marchioness of Athelney* (Purdy, 65).

She was the daughter of the Earl of Avon. Surfeited with attentions from numerous noblemen and gentlemen, she secretly married an assistant of her father's land-steward. His sudden death and her pregnancy led her to persuade Milly, an earlier sweetheart of his, to act the part of widow and mother. Two or three years later she married the Marquis of Stonehenge, and after his death was so lonely that she wished to claim her son. Her neglect of him, and Milly's love, however, made him unwilling to humour her. The Marchioness never recovered from this unexpected set-back, and died of a broken heart. **GND. 3**

CAROLINE, QUEEN. *Caroline of Brunswick, the Princess of Wales in* The Dynasts, *where 'her ungracious fate' is sympathetically dramatized:* (2) VI *vi, vii,* (3) II *iv,* IV *viii. On the accession of George IV to the throne in 1820, she returned from the Continent, where she had lived indiscreetly. Popular feeling caused the withdrawal of the bill to deprive her of the title of queen and dissolve her marriage. She was refused admission to the Coronation, however, and committed suicide within three weeks.*

HS. 'Queen Caroline to her Guests'

CARRIFORD. *Mainly an imaginary village, situated near the railway from Dorchester to London. The name was suggested by West Stafford, though, like Lower Bockhampton, the village is near Kingston Maurward House, the 'Knapwater House' of the novel.*

Cytherea Graye travelled by train from Budmouth to Carriford Road Station when she went to Knapwater House; and the train from London bringing Eunice, the ill-fated wife of Manston, stopped here. The railway porter, Joseph Chinney, confessed after the wedding of Manston and Cytherea that he had seen Manston's first wife return to the station after the fire at the Three Tranters in which she was thought to have been burnt. Edward Springrove's father lived at the Three Tranters Inn.

DR. v, viii 2, 3, ix 1, 2, 4, x, xi 2, 5, xii 6, 7, 8, xiii 3, 5, xiv, xvi 1, 3, xviii 1, 2, xix 1, Sequel

CARTLETT, MR. A hotel-keeper at Sydney, to whom Arabella was bigamously married. He came to England, and, wanting her to assist him in a thriving business at the Three Horns, Lambeth, remarried her, after her divorce from Jude, at St John's Church, Waterloo Road. He was a 'rather bloated man, with a globular stomach and small legs, resembling a top on two pegs'. The two visited the Great Wessex Agricultural Show at Stoke-Barehills. He died about two and a half years later. JO. III ix, V ii, iii, v, vii

CASTERBRIDGE. *Dorchester. Its name derives from the British 'Dwrinwyr' (the settlement by the Dwyr, or dark river) and 'castra' (a Roman camp). The Walks along the levelled remains of the old Roman walls were planted with avenues of trees from 1700 to 1712; see plate facing p. 207.*

It is 'the county-town' of *Desperate Remedies*, though of little importance in this novel except in relation to the arrest and death of Manston.

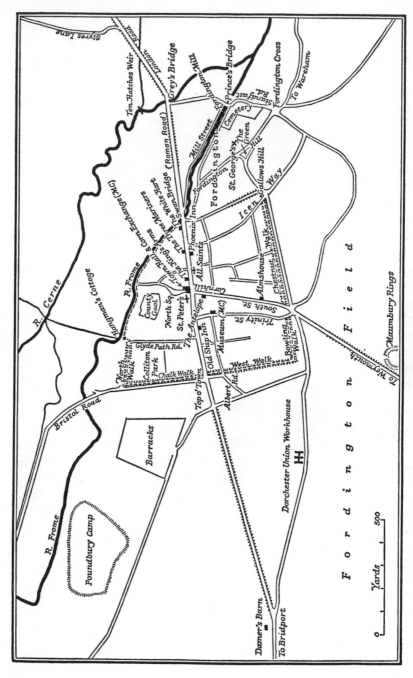

Dorchester

Styres Lane
Ten Hatches Weir
London Road
Grey's Bridge
Durngton Mill
Prince's Bridge
Fordington Cross
To Wareham
R. Cerne
Hangman's Cottage
R. Frome
Durnover & Corn Exchange (CMC)
Barclays Three Mariners
The King's Arms
The White Hart
The Swan Bridge (Roman Road)
Hill Street
Phoenix Inn
Fordington
Cemetery
Standfast Rd.
St. George's
The Green
Fordington Hill
St. George's Hill
Gallows Hill
Icen Way
Almshouse Walk
Chestnut Walk
All Saints
Cornhill
County Gaol
North Sq.
St. Peter's
The Antelope
Museum (CMC)
Old Ship Inn
South St.
Trinity St.
Bowling Walk
Glyde Path Rd.
Chalk Walk
Colliton Park
North Walk
West Walk
Albert Rd.
Top o' Town
To Weymouth
Maumbury Rings
Fordington Field
Bristol Road
Barracks
Dorchester Union Workhouse
R. Frome
Poundbury Camp
Damer's Barn
To Bridport

Yards
0   500

Casterbridge

In *Under the Greenwood Tree*, some interesting vignettes of the town are presented anecdotally. See HAYLOCK, MAIL, NINEMAN, and SAUNDERS.

For *Far from the Madding Crowd*, see the BARRACKS, the CORN EXCHANGE, the COUNTY GAOL, the UNION, and the WHITE HART (pp. 267–70).

Though the main scene and action of *The Return of the Native* are near Casterbridge, the town receives only one mention. Just before his death, Wildeve, who had inherited a fortune from his uncle, told Thomasin that they would be leaving the Quiet Woman Inn to live in Casterbridge.

Festus Derriman suggested that Anne should join him and his local friends at their yeomanry sprees in Casterbridge or Shottsford-Forum.

The trumpet-major thought St Peter's had the finest tenor bell in the district.

His brother Bob went to meet his 'intended', Miss Matilda Johnson, who was due to arrive in Casterbridge one Sunday from Melchester. He stabled at the Old Greyhound (*in South Street*) and walked on to the Bow (*'The old name for the curved corner by the cross-streets in the middle of Casterbridge.' The name, in fact, has been revived and marks the corner at the east end of St. Peter's Church*), saw the mail-coach rise above the arch of Grey's Bridge, but found she was not among the passengers who alighted at the King's Arms. He waited not far from All Saints' Church, where he could hear the afternoon service 'as distinctly as if he had been one of the congregation', until the road-waggon arrived with Matilda, who had spent so much 'in the adornment of her person' that she could not afford to travel by mail-coach.

Against the French invasion, Casterbridge had a body of militia known as the Consideration Company, ninety strong under Captain Strickland.

Charles Darton came to the help of Helena Hall when she lost her husband, and entered her son at a popular school in Casterbridge. Darton's 'nice long speeches on mangold-wurzel, and such like topics, at the Casterbridge Farmers' Club' were read with interest by Sally Hall.

The Mayor of Casterbridge gives a large-scale impression of Casterbridge in the mid-nineteenth century (cf. *Life*, 351). From the east, by which Susan Henchard and Elizabeth-Jane approached it, the town appeared to be enclosed in a square wall of trees. 'County and town met at a mathematical line.' Avenues of trees marked the western approach from Port-Bredy, the southern from Budmouth, and the eastern from London, Melchester, and Shottsford via Weatherbury. The 'square wall' of trees consisted of avenues along the walks which had been constructed on the remains of the Roman walls. The north-east side was contained by the river; on the south-east lay Durnover. Apart from this, the town was immediately surrounded by country. The occupations of the people were predominantly rural. Walking down the High Street (i.e. from west to east), one passed St Peter's Church (iv, ix, xxvii, xxix), the arched entrance to the market-place (xxvii, xxxviii), the Corn Market (ix, xvii, xxvii, xlii), and the Town Hall above it (xvii, xxvii, xxviii, xxxvii), the King's Arms Hotel (v–vi, ix, xxi, xxxi, xxxvii, xli), and the Three Mariners (vi–viii, xxxiii, xliii), all on the left. Almost opposite the Three Mariners stood the church (All Saints'), the choir of which sang the comminatory verses for Henchard (xxxiii). At the bottom of the High Street was the brick bridge (*Swan Bridge*), and further on, where the London highway crossed the Frome valley meadowland, or Durnover Moor, the stone bridge or Grey's Bridge (xix, xxxii, xxxviii, xli), from which a path by the river led to the Ten Hatches. From the brick bridge Mixen Lane on the right led to the lowest quarters of Durnover. The path to the left by the river took one past the Franciscan priory ruins and mill (xix, xxxi, xxxii), with the County Gaol above a cliff, its main entrance providing 'a pedestal' for executions (all on the left). Further, on the right, was the hangman's cottage (xix). The route round Casterbridge continued along the tree-lined Walks: first, the North Walk; then, on the west side, Chalk Walk (ix, xiii, xxxii) to the High Street entrance, with West Walk (xvi, xvii) below; on the south side, Bowling Walk (xvii) and Chestnut Walk or South Walk (xxvi, xxix, xxxiv) to the corner known as Gallows Hill (viii) from the executions which took place after the Monmouth Rebellion; then north. The Budmouth road reaches Casterbridge between Bowling Walk and Chestnut Walk, continuing along South Street and Corn Street to the centre. Set back a little on the right of South Street was Henchard's house (later Farfrae's, *now Barclay's Bank*). On the left of Corn Street stands the Antelope Hotel (xviii); behind it (in Trinity Street) stood the Museum (xxii). Across the High Street and immediately below St Peter's was the arched thoroughfare leading to the market square (*North Square*) or Bull Stake. The Town Hall, including the Court House (ix, xxviii), extended over the archway. *The market place actually extended from Corn Street or Cornhill across into the High Street and North Square. In the centre of the crossroads by St Peter's and the Town Hall stood the town pump* (xvii, xviii). *See plate facing p. 270.* On the left of Cornhill, overlooking St Peter's and the town pump was High-Place Hall (xxxvi). Beyond North Square was the entrance to the County Gaol.

(*The original of High-Place Hall is Colliton House in Glyde Path Road, not far to the west of North Square. The arched entrance to the 'square' was demolished in 1848. The Museum was not transferred to Trinity Street until 1851. For chronological liberties, see p. 43.*)

Outside the town the main points of interest, in addition to Grey's Bridge and Ten Hatches Weir, were the Bristol Road which turned off below the north-west corner (ix), the barn (*Damer's Barn*) on the Port-Bredy road, where Lucetta was saved from the bull by Henchard (xxix), the Ring (*Maumbury Rings*) or Roman amphitheatre on the Budmouth road just outside the town (x, xi, xxviii, xxxv, xlii; cf. *HS.* 'The Mock Wife'), and two prehistoric camps – the first, Pummery or Poundbury, where Henchard planned holiday entertainments at his own expense (xvi); the second, Mai-Dun (xliii).

In 'The Waiting Supper', the market town nearest Froom-Everard (*West Stafford*) is Casterbridge. The High Street and Casterbridge station are mentioned. Nicholas Long occupied a large house in the town on his return from America.

The widow Susan Dornell learned that her daughter had met Stephen Reynard in Casterbridge while she was away in London.

It was here that Angel Clare struck Farmer Groby and unwittingly aggravated Tess's lot at Flintcomb-Ash.

Some four years or so before the opening of the Great Exhibition of 1851, the railway to South Wessex was 'in process of construction'. (*The line to Dorchester was opened in July 1847.*) Excursions were laid on for the Exhibition, and it was on such a train that Caroline Aspent and her three-year old daughter travelled without any protection from the wind and rain. Ned Hipcroft met them at Waterloo Station. When they returned more than a year later, the train did not stop at 'the petty roadside station that lay nearest to Stickleford, and the trio went on to Casterbridge'.

After his long and arduous journey by night from Oozewood to Clyfton Horseleigh near Ivell, to discover – as he thought – that his sister Edith had been basely deceived by Sir John Horseleigh, Roger, the sailor (who returned to Havenpool in 1540 or 1541), followed the highway to Casterbridge, where he drank heavily all the afternoon and evening, and stayed for the next two or three days before proceeding to Havenpool.

An interesting view from 'Top o' Town' (*the upper end of High West Street*) is presented at the beginning of 'A Changed Man'. To the west could be seen the end of the Town Avenue (West Walk), the Port-Bredy road, and, turning off to the right, the road which led to the cavalry barracks. Eastwards, the road passes down through the town and merges in the highway across Durnover Moor. 'The white riband of road disappeared over Grey's Bridge a quarter of a mile off' (*in fact, it is approximately half a mile off*). Later Laura watches the —th Hussars 'smalling' towards Mellstock Ridge, and wishes she and her husband, the former Captain of the regiment, were with them.

Selina Paddock misread the casualty lists posted up on the Town Hall door, and was convinced that her intended husband, John Clark, had been killed at the battle of Alma. He came to see her (in the hope that she would agree to emigrate) and brought with him a nine-gallon cask of beer from the Phoenix (*High East Street*). His sudden death created so much sympathy that he was given full military honours by the Scots Greys. The procession marched down the High Street to the tune of *Saul*. After the burial at Durnover, Selina turned over Swan bridge homeward to Mellstock, while the band and military contingent diminished up the High Street.

The wronged husband in 'The Burghers' (*WP*) lived by 'Glyd'path Rise'. *The 'pleasaunce' he crossed was Colliton Park. Glyde Path Road, sometimes called Shirehall Road, used to run from High West Street by Colliton Park into Glyde Path Hill.* Mention is made of the Froom river (*running around the town on the north and east*), Grey's Bridge (*east*) Dammer's Crest (*a hill on the west, approaching Damer's Barn*), Pummery-Tout (*to the north-west*), and the Gibbet (*on Gallows Hill, at the south-west corner of the town*).

The Old Ship Inn, where the story of 'Leipzig' (*WP*) is told, *is in High West Street.*

The Field of Tombs of 'Her Death and After' is the cemetery (*on the Weymouth road*) by the 'earthworks' (*the Roman amphitheatre or Maumbury Rings*). The Western Wall is *West Walk, where the Roman wall ran.*

The Phoenix Inn, where 'The Dance at the Phoenix' (*WP*) took place, *is in High East Street.* St Peter's Church, Bullstake Square (*North Square*), Pummery Ridge, Maembury Ring, and Standfast Bridge (*Prince's Bridge by Fordington Mill, at the end of Standfast Road*) – *the last three north-west, south-west, and south-east of Casterbridge respectively* – are mentioned.

Three Casterbridge captains served in the Indian wars. *Two were killed in the Khyber Pass; they were John Bascombe Lock and J. Logan. The third was Henry G. Besant. A monument to the first is to be found in St Peter's Church; the panel with the carved names of Hardy's illustration indicates that the church of the poem is All Saints' (Purdy, 101).*

The noble Elizabethan 'pile' of 'A Man' (*PPP*) *must have stood in High Street. 'It smiled the long street down for near a mile', i.e. in the Stinsford direction. It may have been 'the fine mansion of the Trenchards at the corner of Shirehall Lane', the loss of which Hardy regretted in the speech he made when he was presented with the freedom of Dorchester in 1910* (Life, 352). *The identity of 'H. of M.' remains conjectural.*

> DR. xvi 2, xix 2, 6, xxi 1; *UGT* (references above); *FMC* (references above); *RN.* v v; *TM.* v, xi, xv, xvi, xxvii; *WT.* 6; *MC* (references above); *CM.* 2; *GND.* 1; *TD.* iv, xvi, xxi, xxxiii, xlvi; *LLI.* 7; *CM.* 9; *CM.* 1; *CM.* 5; *WP.* 'The Burghers', 'Leipzig', 'Her Death and After', 'The Dance at the Phoenix', 'The Casterbridge Captains'; *PPP.* 'A Man', 'The Supplanter'; *TL.* 'The Curate's Kindness', 'The Rejected Member's Wife', 'At Casterbridge Fair' (*the Cross is the intersection of streets in the centre of the town by the Bow*; *Cornmarket-place is North Square*), 'One We Knew' ('the neighbouring town'); *SC.* 'At the Altar-Rail' (*the Street of the Quarter Circle is Albert Road, by the Park, 'where the Fountain leaps'*); *MV.* 'The Chimes' (*autobiographical, with reference to Hardy's first wife and St Peter's chimes*); *LLE.* 'The Chapel-Organist' (*the chapel was in Casterbridge; the deacon was the chemist in High Street*); *HS.* 'The Mock Wife' (*relating to the execution of Mary Channing for the murder of her husband in 1705; cf.* MC. *xi*), 'The Peace Peal' (*the ringing of bells at St Peter's at the end of the First World War, after four years' silence*); *WW.* 'The Third Kissing-Gate' ('the town').

THE BARRACKS. At Corporal Nineman's funeral Mr Penny heard the 'Dead March' for the first time (see below).

William Smallbury visited the barracks in search of Fanny Robin, only to discover that she had returned to Weatherbury *en route* for Melchester, in pursuit of Sergeant Troy, who had left with the Eleventh Dragoon-Guards.

It is important to notice that Casterbridge Barracks are nowhere presented in Far from the Madding Crowd. *The scene outside the barracks* (*xi*) *recalls the north-eastern side of Dorchester, but is outside 'a certain town many miles north of Weatherbury'. Again, it is in this unnamed town – not Casterbridge – that Fanny's fatal mistake over All Souls' and All Saints' churches occurs* (*xvi*).

As soon as his regiment reached Casterbridge Barracks from India, Luke Holway heard the news that his father had just committed suicide.

The —th Dragoons, in which John Clark served, were stationed at Casterbridge Barracks when Selina Paddock made his acquaintance. When he died at Mellstock, the barracks were occupied by the Scots Greys. The services of the fine reed and brass band were offered that he might have a funeral marked by due military honours. His body was conveyed to the barracks, and the funeral procession moved slowly and dramatically through the town to the tune of *Saul*, on its way to Durnover churchyard.

Here Hardy is drawing on actual recollections. When the Scots Greys arrived in the summer of 1851, they inaugurated a new phase in the musical life of Dorchester. They had a splendid band, and gave concerts in the Town Hall on Thursday afternoons. Their playing of the 'Dead March' at the funeral of a 'comrade' created 'a profound sensation' and was the subject of a fine article in the local Chronicle (*from Charles Keats*, The Writings and Recollections of a Durnovarian, *Dorchester, 1894*). *Hardy alludes to this occasion in* Under the Greenwood Tree (*above*).

There was much sadness when the King's Own Cavalry left Casterbridge and 'vanished over Mellstock Ridge'.

Hardy saw the Battery (*the 73rd, R.F.A.*) *march in rain and darkness to the station on 2 November 1899, on its way to the Boer War.*

The soldier from the barracks walked, as midnight approached, down High Street, and along the Lane of Slyre (q.v.) in the hope that he might meet Agnette, from whom he had parted twenty years earlier, by the Sarsen stone where they had often met when they were lovers.

> *UGT.* I viii; *FMC.* x; *CM.* 4; *CM.* 5; *WP.* 'The Dance at the Phoenix'; *PPP.* 'The Going of the Battery'; *TL.* 'The Revisitation'. *MV.* 'Sitting on the Bridge'

THE CORN EXCHANGE. After seeking work unsuccessfully at Casterbridge hiring-fair, Gabriel Oak earned some money by playing his flute
near 'the corn-exchange'.

On market days, Bathsheba Everdene attracted the attention of
farmers inside the 'low though extensive hall' which was 'latterly'
dignified by the name of 'Corn Exchange'.

She was moving through a crowd nearby when she heard that her
husband, Troy, had been drowned.

FMC. vi, xii, xvii, xlviii; *MC*. ix, xvii, xxvii, xlii

THE COUNTY GAOL. Here Manston hanged himself, and his coffin
was seen being taken across the gravelled square towards the 'grim and
heavy archway' of the entrance. 'The small rectangular wicket, which
was constructed in one of the two iron-studded doors, was opened from
the inside' and 'the coffin dragged its melancholy length through the
aperture'.

Boldwood, after shooting Troy, walked to the gaol to give himself up:
'he halted before an archway of heavy stonework, which was closed by
an iron studded pair of doors.' At last the small wicket was opened, and
he was admitted. The scaffold, as was customary, was erected over the
archway, so that hangings could be seen by the public. Boldwood was
reprieved.

The sound of a distant gun announces a prisoner's escape from Casterbridge Gaol in 'The Three Strangers'.

The top of the entrance is seen from below, by the river-path between
the town and the meadows, as a square mass cutting into the night sky
like 'a pedestal lacking its statue. The missing feature . . . was, in truth,
the corpse of a man. . . . The lugubrious harmony of the spot with his
domestic situation' was not lost on Henchard.

It is the setting for the grim tragic climax in the story of Gertrude
Lodge, who came to the gaol after making private arrangements with
the executioner at the hangman's cottage *(see plate facing p. 271)* to
cure her withered arm by touching the neck of a person just hanged. *For
the hangman's information that executions were fixed at noon 'or as soon as
the London mail-coach gets in. We always wait for that, in case of a
reprieve'*, compare *Life, 125 (where the time is given as one o'clock).*

Jack Winter had to be hanged in the heaviest fetters that could be
found to ensure that his neck would be broken.

A rustic from Stourcastle thought that Napoleon Bonaparte had been caught on his way from Elba, and imprisoned in Casterbridge Gaol. *See plate facing p. 78. DR.* xxi 1; *FMC.* liv, lv; *WT.* 1; *MC.* xix; *WT.* 4; *LLI.* 8*g*; *D.* (3) v vi

THE COUNTY MUSEUM. The writer met an archaeologist one stormy night at Mai-Dun. The 'well-known antiquary with capital letters at the tail of his name' proceeded to dig without permission, because he knew it would not be given, and discovered objects which proved to his satisfaction that the stronghold was occupied by the Romans as well as the Celts. All were carefully restored, though the writer fancied he saw the excavator slip something into his coat pocket. Years later, when he died, the gilt statuette which he had exhumed was found among his effects, labelled 'Debased Roman'. The figure was bequeathed to the Casterbridge Museum. (*The story is fictitious.*)

The Museum undoubtedly suggested the setting for the narration of the stories in *A Group of Noble Dames. It was opened in 1884.*

The stone-mason Jude Fawley helped to build it.

CM. 6; *GND* (conclusions of 1 and 10); *JO.* v vii

THE KING'S ARMS. *A hotel in High Street, Dorchester, below St Peter's Church; see plate facing p. 238.*

Bathsheba heard that her husband Troy had been drowned at Lulwind Cove when she was making her way through 'the crowd of rural businessmen' in front of the market-house or Corn Exchange. She fainted, and was carried into the King's Arms Inn by Boldwood.

Bob Loveday went one Sunday to meet the mail-coach at the King's Arms, expecting Matilda Johnson to arrive. He was disappointed.

Through the bow-window which projected into the street over the main portico, Susan Henchard saw the husband who had sold her nineteen years previously. He was now the Mayor of Casterbridge, attending 'a great public dinner'.

When Henchard told Newson that his daughter was dead, he watched Newson depart by coach outside the King's Arms.

(We learn incidentally that George III had stopped there to change horses one night.)

When Fitzpiers returned to England from the Continent, he hired a carriage at the King's Arms Hotel to travel to Hintock.

The postilion of the coach in which Tess and Angel Clare drove to their wedding had 'a permanent running wound on the outside of his right leg, originated by the constant bruising of aristocratic carriage-poles during the many years that he had been in regular employ at the King's Arms, Casterbridge' (cf. the second postilion, *D.* (3) IV vi).

UGT. I ii; *FMC.* xlviii; *TM.* xv, xvi; *MC.* v, vi, xx, xxi,

xxxi, xxxvii, xli; *W.* xl; *TD.* xxxiii

SOUTH STREET ALMSHOUSE. *Napier's Mite.* The clock (*which was the subject of Hardy's 'first effusion . . . to see the light of print'* ; *see* Life, *33, and Purdy, 291–2*) pointed to five minutes to three as the waggon bearing the coffined Fanny Robin and her child passed the end of the street.   *FMC.* xlii

THE THREE MARINERS. *This inn was the King of Prussia, the name Hardy first used for it. It stood in High Street, below the King's Arms. The old building described in* The Mayor of Casterbridge *has been replaced. See plate facing p. 239.*

Michael Mail ate his meal in the kitchen to the tune a brass band struck up.

Susan Henchard stayed at the inn with Elizabeth-Jane when they arrived in Casterbridge. Farfrae also stayed here, and Henchard came to persuade him to act as his manager. It was at this inn, after Sunday morning service, that Henchard made the choir (*from All Saints'*) sing the comminatory verses from Psalm 109 against Farfrae.   *UGT.* I viii;

MC. vi–viii, x, xiii, xiv, xviii, xx, xxx, xxxiii, xxxvii, xliii

THE UNION. *After 1834, parishes combined under 'Guardians of the Poor' to provide for the needs of paupers. For this reason the name was changed from the 'Workhouse' (where able-bodied but unemployed paupers were given work) to the 'Union'. The Casterbridge Union building stands on Damer's Road, to the south-west of the old town.*

To reach it, Fanny Robin, after following the main road across Durnover Moor, turned left on arriving at 'the bottom of the town' (*the eastern end of High Street*) into 'the dense shade of a deserted avenue of chestnuts', continuing her route along the walk on the southern side of the town, and so directly to the Union.

An MS. note to 'To an Unborn Pauper Child' runs ' "She must go to the Union-House to have her baby." Casterbridge Petty Sessions' (Purdy, 112).

FMC. xl–xlii; *PPP.* 'To an Unborn Pauper Child'; *TL.*

'The Curate's Kindness'; *WW.* 'Christmastide', 'A Night-

mare, and the Next Thing' (*Christmas Day*)

THE WHITE HART. *An inn of the same name occupies the site of the old tavern at the eastern end of High Street.*

269

Troy stayed here, before going to Boldwood's Christmas party to claim his wife Bathsheba after his long absence.

When she came to Casterbridge, to cure her withered arm by touching the neck of a man just hanged, Gertrude Lodge stayed at the White Hart.

The carrier's van belonging to Mr Burthen stood in the forecourt of the White Hart, before starting its journey to Longpuddle with its passengers, some of whom told the stories in *A Few Crusted Characters*.

The Reverend John Maumbry's merits as a preacher were discussed in the bar-parlour. *FMC.* lii;

WT. 4; *LLI.* 8; *CM.* 1; *TL.* 'At Casterbridge Fair' (vii)

CASTLE BOTEREL. *Boscastle, two miles from St Juliot.*

Stephen Smith landed at Castle Boterel from Bristol, after his first stay in India, while Knight was being rescued from imminent death on the 'cliff without a name'.

PBE. ii, xi, xvii, xviii, xxi–xxiii, xxiv, xxv, xxxiii, xxxiv, xxxix, xl; *SC.* 'At Castle Boterel', 'Places' (*Despite the footnote, the poem seems to have been composed at Boscastle*).

CASTLE ROYAL. *Windsor Castle. See p. 392.*

CATKNOLL. *Chetnole, formerly Chateknolle, a village near Melbury Osmond, where Hardy's maternal ancestors used to live. In the register of baptisms at Melbury Osmond, which Hardy would consult to trace his ancestry, there is an entry for 30 June 1817 on the private baptism of a boy whose mother was the wife of 'a soldier who has been out of England more than two years'. I have generalized the record, for which I am indebted to J. O. Bailey. The rest of the story may be regarded as imaginary.* *WW.* 'The War-Wife of Catknoll'

CATTSTOCK, EZRA. The 'cello player in the Chalk-Newton choir, and sexton of the parish. *CM.* 4

CAWTREE, FARMER. A dairyman farmer who kept a cider-house at Little Hintock. He was a friend of the hollow-turner, with whom he was in the habit of playing langterloo. *W.* iv, ix, x, xxiv, xxv, xlviii

CECIL, MR. Lady Constentine's solicitor. He came from Warborne to see her when it was learned that her husband Sir Blount had died much more recently than had been announced. *TT.* xxxii–xxxiii

CHALDON. *East Chaldon or Chaldon Herring, north-west of Lulworth Cove.*

Jim Owlett had gone to meet the French lugger carrying contraband

rchester Fair, 1835, showing the Bow by St Peter's, the Town Hall, and the rance to North Square. From the painting by Frederick Barry, engraved by wton Fielding

'Blackwater' (the Froom) below the County Gaol, and (below) the hangman's cottage, Dorchester (Casterbridge)

spirits to Lulwind Cove; and Lizzy Newberry (whose business it was to give the alarm) – accompanied on this occasion by Richard Stockdale, the temporary Wesleyan minister at Nether-Moynton – walked by night over Lord's Barrow to Chaldon Down. In a ravine they were joined by the carriers she and Jim employed; Lizzy paid them their wages and told them the rendezvous was Dagger's Grave (*Dagger's Gate*), where they would meet Jim. They proceeded over Chaldon Down, leaving East Chaldon to the left until they reached the crest of a hill not far from the ancient earth-work called Round Pound. They were soon at Dagger's Grave, not many hundred yards from the landing-point.   *WT. 7*

CHALK-NEWTON. *Maiden Newton, eight miles north-west of Dorchester. For the White Horse Inn, see plate facing p. 206.*

Maiden Newton (its name unchanged) is an important point in Hardy's first short story, 'Destiny and a Blue Cloak'.

Here, at the White Horse Inn (*the site now occupied by a modern one in red brick – Hardy's note, 1912*), Helena Hall handed over her son to Charles Darton's bailiff. The boy was entered at a popular school at Casterbridge.

Tess walked from 'west of the River Brit' in the Port-Bredy area to seek work at Flintcomb-Ash. Her route lay through Chalk-Newton. On the way, meeting the 'well-to-do boor' whom Angel had knocked down at Casterbridge, she took to her heels, and slept that night in a plantation, breakfasting at an inn in Chalk-Newton. Here young men were 'troublesomely complimentary' about her good looks. As soon as she left the inn, therefore, she entered a thicket, put on an old field-gown, and cut off her eyebrows, to keep off 'casual lovers'.

Hardy had heard much of the three local instrumental choirs: at Stinsford, where members of his own family had been principal players for approximately forty years, at Puddletown, and at Maiden Newton. Under the Greenwood Tree *had been written about the first, and 'Absent-Mindedness in a Parish Choir' (LLI. 8f), about the second; 'The Grave by the Handpost' was devoted to the third; cf.* Life, *10.*

One evening at Christmas time, the Chalk-Newton choir met near the White Horse Inn, and decided to play first outside some outlying cottages in Sidlinch Lane, where the people had no clocks and would not know that the choir had arrived before the usual time. They saw a light beyond the houses, and, coming to the handpost at the crossroads where Long Ash Lane cuts across the road to Broad Sidlinch, found that four Sidlinch men had just finished burying Sergeant Holway, who had committed suicide as a result of despondency caused by his son's letter from India. The choir sang a carol over the grave, and were about to return to Chalk-Newton, where they reckoned they would be able to sing outside the parson's at 12.30, when who should arrive but Holway's son Luke himself! (See p. 371 for the conclusion of the story.)

After the sudden death of Sergeant-Major Clark, her 'intended husband', Selina Paddock left Mellstock with her son Johnny and opened a small fruit and vegetable shop at Chalk-Newton. She called herself Mrs John Clark, and painted the name on her signboard.

DBC; *UGT*. ɪ iv (Joseph Ryme and the choir); *WT*. 6; *TD*. xli, xlii, liii; *CM*. 4; *CM*. 5

CHALKFIELD, DR. He succeeded Henchard as mayor of Casterbridge, died after less than a year in office, and was succeeded by Farfrae.

MC. xxviii, xxxiv

CHALLOW, MR. Jude's pig had been starved a day or two preparatory to killing; as Challow, the pig-killer, did not arrive and Jude was sorry for the pig, he killed it himself in an inexpert way. Challow arrived shortly afterwards. *JO*. ɪ x

CHAMPREAU. The carrier and valet engaged by Abner Power for the tour in northern France which followed the tour in the Rhine valley. He sat with Milly Birch in the cathedral at Amiens, behind Paula Power and de Stancy. *L*. v x

CHANCERLY, MR. Lady Petherwin's lawyer, whom she visited to change her will, after Ethelberta had refused to withdraw her published poems. *HE*. x

CHANGLEY, JACK. After celebrating Guy Fawkes' Night on Rainbarrow, the Egdon rustics discussed the marriage which they assumed had at last taken place between Thomasin Yeobright and Wildeve. Timothy Fairway recalled his own marriage: 'all the time I was hot as dog-days, what with the marrying, and what with the woman a-hanging to me, and what with Jack Changley and a lot more chaps grinning at me through church window'. *RN*. ɪ iii

CHANNELCLIFFE, THE COUNTESS OF. It was at one of her assemblies that Pierston, the sculptor, met Mrs Pine-Avon; 'hers was one of the neutral or non-political houses at which party politics are more freely agitated than at the professedly party gatherings'. *WB*. ɪɪ i

CHANNELCLIFFE, LORD. Just when Pierston caught a second view of the lady who had attracted him, he had to converse with his host, who discovered that she was Mrs Pine-Avon, the granddaughter of his father's old friend, Lord Hengistbury. *WB.* II i

CHANNING, JOHN. *Thomas Channing. See 'Maumbury Ring' (Harold Orel, Thomas Hardy's Personal Writings, 228–30).*

This grocer lay dying in High Street (*Dorchester*) in 1705, not knowing that his wife had been arrested for poisoning him. Just before his death, he said he would like to kiss his wife for the last time. . . . *Mary Channing was strangled and burnt before thousands of spectators at Maumbury Rings*; *cf.* MC. *xi.* *HS.* 'The Mock Wife'

CHANT, MERCY. Angel Clare's parents hoped he would marry her. She was the daughter of their neighbour and friend at Emminster, the earnest-minded Dr Chant. She gloried in her church work, and was ladylike but rather prim. She was 'great at Antinomianism and Bible-classes', but 'such was her view of life that events which produced heartache in others wrought beatific smiles upon her'. No doubt she did well to marry Angel's brother Cuthbert. *TD.* xxiii, xxv, xxvi, xl, xliv, lvii

CHAPMAN, NATHANIEL. See FRY.

CHARD. *A town in south Somerset, west of Crewkerne.*
LLE. 'Growth in May'

CHARL. A poacher on friendly terms with his old enemy Joe, who had formerly been a keeper at Yalbury Wood but had lost his post. The two frequented Peter's Finger, an inn in Durnover, and undoubtedly played an important part in organizing the skimmington-ride and ensuring that the participants were not arrested. *MC.* xxvi, xxxix

CHARLEY. A youthful admirer of Eustacia who played the part of the Turkish Knight in the mummers' play of St George and allowed her to take his part when it was produced at Blooms-End. Eustacia's plan was to gain her first sight of Clym, the man on whom she pinned her hopes of an exciting life in Paris. After her separation from Clym at Alderworth, she returned to her grandfather's at Mistover Knap. Charley caught her eyeing a pair of pistols, and locked them away lest she took her life.
RN. II iv, v; III vi, viii; V iv, v, ix; VI iv

CHARLSON, MR. A surgeon of Port-Bredy, who was able but did not prosper. He owed Mr Barnet £50 which he was always going to pay in 'three weeks' but never intended to pay. As compensation, he was quite ready to certify that Mrs Barnet was a drowned woman. Mr Barnet, though he longed to be free to marry Lucy Savile, suspected that she was not dead, gave her a stimulant, and called in another surgeon. She revived. *WT.* 5

CHARMLEY. *Probably Charminster, north of Dorchester.*

Dick Dewy had to attend the funeral of his friend John Dunford, as bearer, on the Sunday when Fancy Day inaugurated the organ services at Mellstock church. *UGT.* IV v–vii

CHARMOND, FELICE. *The name suggests a seductive worldly woman, and may derive from* 'le monde' *and from the Charmian of Shakespeare's* Antony and Cleopatra.

A young widow who owned the Hintock estate and lived at Hintock House, when she was not travelling. She had been an actress. She found life at Little Hintock very boring, and her main preoccupation was to preserve her womanly attractiveness. For this purpose she engaged Mr Percomb to buy Marty South's chestnut hair, and failed to engage Grace Melbury as her companion from fear that her presence would make her look older. She fell in love with Dr Fitzpiers after his marriage to Grace Melbury. They had met when she was a girl and he a student at Heidelberg, and she was soon in love with him again. When the scandal of their liaison could no longer be concealed, they went off to Baden. Her false hair contributed to her death. Marty had written to Fitzpiers on the subject for the sake of Grace; he teased Felice; they quarrelled, and he left. She travelled to Homburg in search of him, and met a former suitor, an Italianate American from South Carolina, who had followed her from England. An altercation ensued, and he shot her. *W*

CHASE, THE. *Woodland, originally part of the extensive forested area of Cranborne Chase, in the region of Pentridge.*

It was here that Tess fell a victim to Alec d'Urberville.

GND. 2; *TD.* iv, v, xi, xiv

CHASEBOROUGH. *Cranborne, a small market town south of the Blandford – Salisbury road.*

The Saturday-night venue for many people in the remote village of Trantbridge, including young wives, whose companionship Tess sought on her way home each week from marketing. One Saturday evening in September, when the fair at Chaseborough had been the occasion for 'double delights' at the inns, Tess parted company with her companions to avoid a quarrel instigated by the Queen of Diamonds, and accepted the protection of Alec d'Urberville. Alec deliberately lost her in the Chase, and Tess was undone for life, so 'immeasurable' was the 'social chasm' which divided 'our heroine's personality thereafter from that previous self of hers'. *TD.* v, vi, x, xi

CHÂTEAU RINGDALE. Mr Barnet of Port-Bredy had a large new residence built on the road to the coast to please his difficult wife. She insisted on having it called by this pretentious name, because she once had a fancy for Lord Ringdale. She did not stay to live in it; when Mr Downe married Lucy Savile, Mr Barnet left Port-Bredy, and Mr Downe bought the house as a family residence. *WT.* 5

CHENE MANOR. *Canford Manor, near Wimborne. Part of the old manor containing what is called 'John of Gaunt's Kitchen' still exists.*

The home of Sir John Grebe, the father of Barbara Grebe. *GND.* 2

CHESIL BANK. *A ridge of shingle which almost joins Portland to the mainland, and sweeps north-west for eleven miles to Abbotsbury. Behind it is a narrow creek known as the Fleet. Chesil means 'pebble'; the pebbles decrease in size from Portland to Abbotsbury. The bank was formed by the action of south-western gales; in November 1824 a sloop was blown over the bank into the Fleet. This gale is mentioned in* The Woodlanders. *In* The Well-Beloved, *the bank is called Pebble-bank.*

PBE. xxix; *W.* xxvi; *WB. passim*

CHESTMAN, DR. He was consulted before Owen Graye underwent an operation for his lameness. *DR.* xii 4

CHETTLEWOOD. Manston had an engagement here at Lord Claydonfield's the day his wife Eunice travelled by train from London to join him at Knapwater. Manston misread the railway time-table, and failed to meet her at the station. *DR.* x 1, 4

CHEVRON SQUARE. *In Kensington, London.*

Near this stood the town-house of the Allenvilles. The Swancourts' town-house was at 24 Chevron Square. *ILH.* II 2–3; *PBE.* xiv–xv

CHICKEREL, EMMELINE. A younger sister of Ethelberta, who kept house at Arrowthorne Lodge for her bed-ridden mother, in the absence of Picotee. In London, she taught the youngest Chickerel children 'the rudiments of education'. Picotee thought she was too young to have control over them. When Ethelberta settled at Enckworth and began writing an epic poem, she employed Emmeline as her 'reader'.

HE. xiii, xvii, xxv, Sequel

CHICKEREL, ETHELBERTA. See ETHELBERTA.

CHICKEREL, GWENDOLINE and CORNELIA. Sisters of Ethelberta and Picotee Chickerel, and out in service when Ethelberta visited her family at Arrowthorne Lodge. They gave up their posts when they learned that Ethelberta needed them as cook and housemaid for the family when it moved to her house at Exonbury Crescent, London. Gwendoline grew tired of preparing meals in the 'underground cellar' for French lodgers who did not appreciate her culinary art. Ethelberta took Cornelia as her maid when she visited her aunt Charlotte in Rouen. Gwendoline and Cornelia married two brothers, who were farmers, and emigrated to Queensland. *HE.* xv, xvii, xviii, xxiii, xxxi, xxxiii–xxxv, Sequel

CHICKEREL, JOEY. One of the younger members of the Chickerel family, brother of Ethelberta, and gatekeeper for Arrowthorne House. When the Chickerels moved to London, they occupied Ethelberta's house at Exonbury Crescent, and Joey's principal duty was to act as doorkeeper or page. He had a suit of green, 'thickly populated with little buttons'. He fell in love with flighty Louisa Menlove. He had the face 'of a Graeco-Roman satyr to the furthest degree of completeness' until love made him melancholy. Louisa had no difficulty in discovering Ethelberta's secret from Joey. The last we hear of him is that he is being educated to be a parson. He knows some Latin and Greek; and 'if you could hear how beautiful the boy tells about little Cupid . . . and the rows between . . . Jupiter and his wife because of another woman, and the handsome young gods who kissed Venus, you'd say he deserved to be made a bishop at once!'

HE. xiii, xv, xvii, xviii, xxii, xxviii, xxxiii, xxxiv, Sequel

CHICKEREL, MRS. She had been a nurse in a nobleman's family. She had ten children, including Gwendoline and Cornelia, Sol and Dan, Ethelberta and Picotee, Emmeline, Georgina and Myrtle. They lived at Arrowthorne Lodge, but, after the death of Lady Petherwin, Ethelberta soon contrived to lodge them in her house at Exonbury Crescent, where they were near to Mr Chickerel, the butler at the Doncastles'. Mrs Chickerel was bed-ridden. When Ethelberta had reached her goal of marrying someone with sufficient affluence to provide for her family, she set them up in Firtop Villa, a new house on the outskirts of Sandbourne. Here Mrs Chickerel lived with the retired butler, and her health had so far improved that she could recline on a couch.

HE. xiii, xv, xvii, xviii, xxiii, xxiv, xxxiii–xxxvi, Sequel

CHICKEREL, PICOTEE. See PICOTEE.

CHICKEREL, R. Ethelberta's father, a discreet and dignified butler at the Doncastles' in West London. His relationship to Ethelberta, a friend of the Doncastles as Lady Petherwin's daughter-in-law, was unknown outside his family. He was not happy at leaving his family in the country near Melchester, and had accepted his present position in the hope that a home for them could soon be found in London. This was soon arranged by Ethelberta, to whom he had tactfully recommended Ladywell as a suitor. His alarm at hearing of her engagement to Lord Mountclere vented itself in a powerful expression of spontaneous feeling, which led to the immediate disclosure that he was Ethelberta's father. His efforts to save Ethelberta from marrying an old profligate were in vain, but he was rewarded by his managing daughter with the gift of a house, Firtop Villa, on the outskirts of Sandbourne, where he could live with his family.

HE. vii, xv, xxviii–xxix, xxxiii, xxxvi, xlii, xliv–xlv, Sequel

CHICKEREL, SOL and DAN. Two of Ethelberta's brothers. Sol was a carpenter and joiner, Dan a house-painter. At Ethelberta's house in London, they were responsible for the new decoration and improvements. They lodged in Marylebone. Ethelberta thought it a good idea that they should see Paris and the kinds of joinery and decoration practised in France. They came to Rouen when she was there with her suitors in close attendance, and stayed discreetly at the same hotel, the Hôtel Beau Séjour (to them the 'Bold Soldier'), kept by their aunt Charlotte. They returned to London after their visit to Paris, and Lord Mountclere's brother enlisted the help of Sol in trying to prevent Ethelberta's marriage. Sol was concerned about his sister's reputation, Edgar Mountclere about the inheritance. After her marriage, Ethelberta set them up as builders in London. *HE.* xiii–xiv, xvii, xviii, xxv, xxvi, xxxv, xli, xliii–xlvii, Sequel

CHILES, JOHN. He mowed with William Privett in James Hardcome's meadow. Both took a nap after lunching under a tree. When Chiles awoke he saw a large white 'miller's soul' issuing from William Privett's mouth, and found that he was dead. *LLI.* 8c

CHILLINGTON WOOD. *The story was originally set in the 'Swenn' (Frome) valley near 'Stickleford' (Tincleton), and 'Chillington' was suggested by Pallington, to the east.*

Baron von Xanten met Margery Tucker at Three-Walks-End in this wood, and there, in a hollow tree, she changed for the ball they were attending at Lord Toneborough's. She appeared there again, as if by magic, in response it might seem to his wish rather than by chance.

CM. 12

CHIMLEN, BILLY. One of the Mellstock 'singing-boys'. Before the choir set off to sing carols around the parish, he was warned by William Dewy not to sing 'quite so raving mad' as he would like. *UGT.* I iv

CHINNEY, JOSEPH. A railway-porter at Carriford Road Station. He was so worried by having conspired to make the illegal marriage of Manston and Cytherea Graye possible – through keeping secret the fact that Mrs Eunice Manston had spoken to him *after* the fire at the Three Tranters – that, after making his confession, he left Carriford and embarked from Liverpool for America. He fell overboard on the way, and was drowned.

DR. x 1-2, 5, xi 2, xiii 5, xiv 1, xviii 2

CHIPPENHAM. Stephen Smith and Knight were travelling separately by train, each with renewed hopes of marrying Elfride. At Chippenham station (*Wiltshire*) they discovered they were on the same train. It was St Valentine's Day. Shortly afterwards the carriage containing the coffined Elfride was re-attached to the train. *PBE.* xxxix

CHRISTMINSTER. *Oxford. The Wessex name originated at the time when Hardy was preparing* Jude the Obscure; *for its special significance in the novel, see pp. 54–5. The reference to Christminster in* Desperate Remedies *did not appear before the 1896 edition.*

Timothy Petrick fondly imagined that his wife's son Rupert was the offspring of the Marquis of Christminster, and 'began to read up chronicles of the illustrious house ennobled as the Dukes of South-westerland'.

In Jude the Obscure, *many places are readily identifiable, but some, especially colleges, are mere names (one, Sarcophagus, so satirical that Hardy took precautions to baulk identification. Hardy knew Oxford well enough to do this; he had worked there when he was architectural assistant to Arthur Blomfield; and he visited Oxford again when he was at work on the novel). Hardy's notes on the subject – to be found in Clive Holland,* Thomas Hardy – *are deliberately evasive, except for the more obvious. St Silas Church is St Barnabas in the region of Oxford known as 'Jericho'; it was designed by Arthur Blomfield.*

Specific references: Crozier Hotel (*suggested by the Mitre*) I iii; Beersheba ('*Jericho*') II i, III viii, VI iii, iv – Jude's lodging was near the church of St Silas, II iii, iv, VI iii; the Meadows (*Christ Church Meadow*) II ii, VI ix; the Cathedral (*Christ Church*) II ii, iii; Cardinal College (*Christ Church College – the name is from Harrison Ainsworth's* Windsor Castle) II iii, III viii; VI ix, xi; Crozier College, in Old-time Street (*Oriel College in*

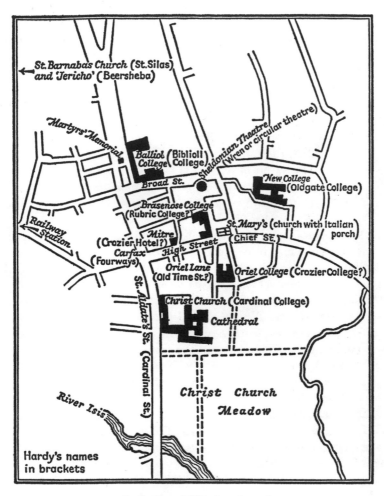

St. Barnabas Church (St. Silas) and 'Jericho' (Beersheba)

Martyrs' Memorial

Balliol College (Biblioll College)

Sheldonian Theatre (Wren or circular theatre)

Broad St.

New College (Oldgate College)

Brasenose College (Rubric College?)

Railway Station

Mitre (Crozier Hotel?)

Carfax (Fourways)

St. Mary's (church with Italian porch)

Chief St.

High Street

Oriel Lane (Old Time St.?)

Oriel College (Crozier College?)

St. Aldate's St. (Cardinal St.)

Christ Church (Cardinal College)

Cathedral

River Isis

Christ Church Meadow

Hardy's names in brackets

Oxford and 'Christminster'

279

Oriel Lane? – Hardy's note) II ii, VI ix; the Martyrs' Cross (*inlaid in Broad Street*) II iv, VI vi; the circular theatre *(the Sheldonian)* II vi, VI i, xi; Biblioll College (*Balliol*) II vi; the Fourways (*Carfax*) II vi, III viii, ix, VI i; the Lamb and Flag Inn, II vii, III viii, VI vi; Chief Street (*High Street*) III ix, VI i, xi; the church with the Italian porch and helical columns (*St Mary's*) VI i; Mildew Lane, VI i; Sarcophagus College, VI ii, ix; Rubric College (*Brasenose? – Hardy's note*) VI ii, ix; Tudor College, VI ix; Oldgate College (*New College*) VI xi; Cardinal Street (*St Aldate's Street*) VI xi. *See plates facing p. 462.*

For OXFORD references, see p. 430.

> *DR.* i 1; *GND.* 6; *JO* (general references): I i, iii, vi, vii, viii, xi; II; III iv, viii–x; V v, viii; VI; *LLE.* 'Evelyn G. of Christminster' (*The poem was written on the death of Evelyn Gifford at Arlington House, Oxford, in September 1920. See p.* 339.)

CHUNDLE, MRS. An old woman, who lived in a cottage on the outskirts of the parish of Kingscreech, two miles from Corvsgate Castle and three miles from Enckworth. For her story, see pp. 83–5.   OMC

CICELY. *Though set in the eighteenth century, it is very doubtful whether 'My Cicely' is in any way historical, or founded on any actual experience, except the imaginary. Nevertheless, despite its dramatized heroics and romantic exaggerations, it may have been suggested (like 'Her Immortality', the poem that follows it and also suffers from pseudo-heroic flourishes) by thoughts of Tryphena Sparks (see p. 435–40), Hardy's 'lost prize', who had died in 1890. Her husband had kept a hotel and a beer-house at Topsham near Exeter.*

The route followed is from the city (London) to Exonbury (Exeter), and follows the Icen Way at intervals. *The landmarks are the House of Long Sieging (Basing House near Basingstoke, which was reduced to ruins in the Civil War), the thin steeple of Poore's olden episcopal see (Salisbury Cathedral), the Stour-bordered Forum (Blandford Forum),* Weatherbury or Weatherby Castle (*see* RINGS-HILL SPEER), Casterbridge, Maidon Castle, Pummerie, Eggardon earthworks (*north of the Bridport road*), the Nine-Pillared Cromlech (*the Nine Stones by the roadside just west of Winterborne Abbas*), the Bride-streams (*the Brit and its tributary, the Mangerton River, at Bridport; for the Bride, see p. 445*), and the Axe, Otter, and Exe rivers. *The Three Lions (which Hermann Lea stated was ten miles outside Exeter, on the Taunton road) must be on the Honiton –*

Exeter road, whether it was real or imaginary. Hardy had Topsham in mind, however. WP. 'My Cicely'

CICELY, LADY. *Caroline, daughter of the Duke of Dorset. She married Joseph Damer.*

See 'The Doctor's Legend', p. 82, and MIDDLETON ABBEY.

CLARE, ANGEL. *Hardy said that Angel Clare was drawn partly from Charles Moule, a younger brother of Horace who became President of Corpus Christi College, Cambridge. The name Angel was recalled from the mural monument of the Grey family in Stinsford church. Hardy sat beneath it when he was a boy; it is described in the opening chapter of 'An Indiscretion in the Life of an Heiress'. For a comment on Angel Clare – which may be found more briefly at the end of TD. xxxix – see Hardy's note of 28 October 1891* (Life, 239).

The youngest son of the Reverend James Clare of Emminster. His studies led him to reject the 'redemptive theolatry' of the Church, and his father failed to see how a university education could benefit him unless he were ordained. He spent years in desultory study, and began to despise 'material distinctions of rank and wealth'. In London he was 'nearly entrapped by a woman much older than himself, though luckily he escaped not greatly the worse for the experience'. Eventually he decided on farming as a career, in the Colonies, America, or at home. At the age of twenty-six, when Tess arrived, he was at Talbothays Dairy for six months' practical training, after working at other types of farms. All the young dairymaids fell in love with him, but it was not long before he showed a preference for Tess. Tess was drawn to him, but indulged in no rash hopes, so aware was she of her 'corporeal blight'. His love for her was so pure and noble that she worshipped him. She swerved to 'excess of honour' for Angel Clare, in reaction to the indignation against the male sex which her former experience had engendered. His love was 'rather bright than hot', and so ideal that it would not admit any flaws. *If the harp music which he played and which fascinated Tess as she listened in the unweeded rank-smelling garden (cf. p. 166) has overtones of meaning, it is to be noted that 'both instrument and execution were poor' (xix).* She tried first to discourage him; then, as he became more ardent, she tried to tell him about her past, only to be baulked by him or by circumstances. Eventually she consented to marry him, but, having heard of marital discord through concealment of the truth, decided to tell all. Angel had his past to confess, and was forgiven; but, though he sinned and she was

281

sinned against, he could not accept her. Tess was no longer the ideal image he had created. Deeply entrenched in him, despite his intellectual independence, was a conventional moral sense which he could not overcome. 'Within the remote depths of his constitution . . . there lay hidden a hard logical deposit, like a vein of metal in a soft loam, which turned the edge of everything that attempted to traverse it.' He was full of grief that the Tess of his imagination was dead (xxxviii), but too intellectual and inexperienced to feel or judge rightly. Later, he felt that, had he known Tess's past earlier, love would have prevailed.

In the circumstances, a temporary separation at least was inevitable. Angel was persuaded to try his agricultural fortunes in Brazil. Before leaving, he invited Izz Huett to accompany him, but, on hearing that nobody could love him more than Tess, thought better of it. In Brazil he was struck down by fever, and had time to reflect more maturely. The more he did so, the more he realized he had been harsh. He returned home too late.

After Tess had murdered Alec d'Urberville, his hope was that he and Tess could escape from England. Their best chance lay in the north. After staying in Bramshurst Court, which they found unoccupied, they made their way through Melchester at night, but Tess was arrested at Stonehenge in the early morning, after a rest. She had asked Angel to marry her sister 'Liza-Lu. The two visited Wintoncester gaol just before Tess was executed. (*The ending is immeasurably sad but not without hope. The final sentence recalls the close of* Paradise Lost. *It is suggestive rather than conclusive. Did Angel marry* 'Liza-Lu?)   *TD.* ii,
          xvii ff.; (?) *MV.* 'The Head above the Fog' (see p. 309)
CLARE, CUTHBERT and FELIX. Angel's elder brothers. Cuthbert was a classical scholar, and Fellow and Dean of his college at Cambridge. Felix was a curate at a town in the neighbouring county. Both were short-sighted, physically and mentally. The one was 'all College', the other 'all Church'; each recognized that there were 'a few unimportant millions of outsiders in civilized society'. In their own limited circles they were correct and unimpeachable; in cultural tastes they were borne on by the tide of fashion. They were dutiful sons but disapproved of Angel's heterodox views, and were singularly lacking in true Christian charity. It is hardly surprising that they did not attend the marriage of Angel and Tess. Cuthbert married Mercy Chant.

                    TD. ii, xxv, xxvi, xxxiii, xliv, lvii

CLARE, REV. JAMES. The vicar of Emminster. His first wife had died and left him a daughter. He married again late in life and had three sons, Cuthbert, Felix, and Angel. He saw no reason why Angel should have a university education if he did not intend to take Orders. He was a sincere and devout Christian, who had made up his mind on the deeper problems of existence very early, and admitted no further reasoning on them. 'The New Testament was less a Christiad than a Pauliad to his intelligence.' He was a man of Apostolic simplicity in life and thought, a Calvinist, 'an Evangelical of the Evangelicals', and a Conversionist. Among the many whom he had converted by his fervour was Alec d'Urberville. Unlike their sons Cuthbert and Felix, the Clares were people of true Christian charity, and, had Tess stayed to see them when she made her fateful visit to Emminster, she would undoubtedly have won their sympathies. *Based partly on the Rev. Henry Moule.*

TD. xii, xvii, xviii, xxv, xxvi, xxxiii, xxxix, xliv, xlv, xlix, liii

CLARE, MRS. The second wife of the Reverend James Clare. She was simple and frugal in her habits but had a genuine affection for her sons, especially her youngest, Angel. Her only complaint was that he had not been sent to a university like his brothers. She was too ladylike to approve of black puddings and mead, or of Angel's marriage to Tess. Her letter to Angel when she forwarded the wedding-present which she had held in trust from Mrs Pitney lacks warmth, but there is no doubt that she was very interested in Tess after the marriage, and very hopeful, if only for her son's sake. Tess's goodness and misfortunes would have won her affection and her husband's forgiveness. Her deep feelings are shown when Angel returned from Brazil.

TD. xviii, xxv, xxvi, xxxiv, xxxix, xliv, xlix, liii, lvii

CLARK, JOHN. A corporal who was on the point of marrying Selina Paddock when he had to leave for service in the Crimea. Selina, reading the casualty lists carelessly after the battle of Alma, had assumed that he was killed. When he returned to England, he married a woman in the north, quarrelled with her, and left her. He arrived at Mellstock when preparations were in their final stage for the marriage of Selina and Mr Miller. As Selina had borne 'her first intended husband' a son, she was anxious to marry John Clark, but he died of a heart-attack on the evening of his arrival, after urging her to emigrate with him to New Zealand.

*CM.*5

CLARK, MARK. One of Bathsheba Everdene's farm-labourers at Weather-

bury. Like Jan Coggan, he had a 'most appreciative throat'; he was 'a
genial and pleasant gentleman, whom to meet anywhere in your travels
was to know, to know was to drink with, and to drink with was, unfortunately, to pay for. . . . He secreted mirth on all occasions for special
discharge at popular parties.'   *FMC.* vi, viii, xv, xxv, xxxvi, xlii, lvii
CLARK, SAMUEL. An officer's servant who was at Waterloo. *It is likely
that Hardy talked to him about the battle. He died in 1857, and was buried
at West Stafford.*   *D.* (3) VII v
CLARKE, JIM. He and Matt Grey are the only two of the villagers
employed in smuggling by Jim Owlett and Lizzy Newberry of Nether-
Moynton to be named.   *WT.* 7
CLAVEL, CARREY. She loved Charley, and turned her back on another
admirer.   *TL.* 'To Carrey Clavel'
CLEMENTINE. Paula Power's elderly French maid. She accompanied
her mistress to Normandy.   *L.* V xiv, VI i–iii
CLIFF, JASPER. See SARGENT.
CLIFF-MARTIN. *Combe Martin, on the north coast of Devon. See p. 64.*
     GND. 10
CLOTON. *The mill suggests Netherbury, south of Beaminster.*   *DBC*
CLYFFE-HILL-CLUMP. *A fir-crowned hill near Clyffe House, east of
Tincleton.*   *TL.* 'Yell'ham-Wood's Story'; *HS.* 'The Paphian Ball'
CLYFTON HORSELEIGH. *A fifteenth-century manor-house at Clifton
Maybank, near Yeovil. Of this building, little remains; its description is
drawn from Hutchins (iv 426). Some of its fine ornamental stone work was
transferred to Montacute House, the 'Montislope' of the story. The manor
belonged to the Horsey family.* See HORSELEIGH.   *CM.* 9
COGGAN, BOB. Jan Coggan's son, employed at Bathsheba's farm.
     FMC. xxii, xxiii
COGGAN, JAN. A 'crimson man with a spacious countenance, and private
glimmer in his eye', who had frequently acted as best man or witness in
countless marriages at Weatherbury and neighbouring parishes. He
courted his first wife Charlotte, a dairymaid, at Farmer Everdene's
(before Bathsheba succeeded to the farm at Weatherbury), and was able
to drink as much ale as he wished there – 'Such lovely drunks as I used
to have at that house!' His first wife never allowed swearing or 'taking in
vain'; 'I wonder if she had the good fortune to get into Heaven when 'a
died! But 'a was never much in luck's way, and perhaps 'a went down-
wards after all, poor soul.' His second wife was 'a wholesome-looking

lady', who could 'toss a pancake or twirl a mop with the accuracy of pure mathematics', and was employed at Bathsheba Everdene's. Gabriel Oak lodged with the Coggans for a while. Coggan was Bathsheba's master-shearer. *FMC.* vi, viii, ix, xix, xxii, xxiii, xxxii, xxxiii, xxxv, xxxvi, xlii, l, lv, lvii

COGGS, ISAAC. Old Mrs Chundle had given up going to church because she had found that she was so deaf that she could not hear anything 'when Isaac Coggs used to cry the Amens out loud beyond anything that's done nowadays, and they had the barrel-organ for the tunes – years and years agone, when I was stronger in my narves than now'. *OMC*

COKER RILL. A stream running through the Coker villages south-west of Yeovil. *HS.* 'The Pat of Butter'

COMFORT, JAMES. One of the Volunteers at Overcombe when the French invasion was feared; 'a soldier by courtesy, but a blacksmith by rights'. The Comforts lived near Miller Loveday, and Mrs Comfort was one of the neighbours who stood by his doorway as he read aloud the letter from his son Bob, announcing his forthcoming marriage at his father's house. Other interested neighbours were Job Mitchell and Esther Beach. *TM.* iv, v, xiv, xv, xix

CONEY, CHRISTOPHER. An associate of Solomon Longways, particularly at the Three Mariners. Such was his lot, and that of many more of 'his tribe', that he had no more love for his country than he had for Botany Bay. When he heard that the pennies which had been used for closing the eyes of the dead Susan Henchard had been buried in the garden, he dug them up and spent them at the Three Mariners. 'Faith,' he said, 'why should death rob life o' fourpence?' (*cf.* '*coney-catcher*', *a cheat or swindler*). *MC.* v, viii, xiii, xviii, xxxii, xxxvii, xliii

CONSTANTINE, SIR BLOUNT. Sir Blount Constantine's marriage to Viviette had clearly been one of social and probably of economic convenience. He was eccentric and jealous. There is no doubt that he ill-treated his wife, and that she was afraid of him. He had a mania for lion-hunting, and soon left her to go, as he maintained, on geographic exploration in Africa. The report came to England that he had died of illness out there, and the lawyers found that Lady Constantine had been left an impoverished widow. It was later discovered that he had married a native princess, drunk heavily, and shot himself in a fit of depression, some time after Lady Constantine's secret marriage to Swithin St Cleeve. *TT.* i–v, vii, xi, xii, xvi, xxi, xxii, xxxii–xxxiv, xxxvii–xxxix

CONSTANTINE, LADY VIVIETTE. She had been unhappily married to Sir Blount Constantine, who had deserted her and gone lion-hunting in Africa. Her soft dark eyes were 'the natural indices of a warm and affectionate, perhaps slightly voluptuous temperament, languishing for want of something to do, cherish, or suffer for'. Her hair was 'black as midnight'. Though twenty-eight or twenty-nine, she could not resist her love for the handsome young Swithin St Cleeve, whom she found pursuing his astronomical studies at the top of the tower on Rings-Hill. News came to her of the death of her husband in Africa, and her lawyer soon discovered how straitened her circumstances had become through his improvidence. So genuine was her love for Swithin, for whom she had bought the expensive apparatus he needed, that she did not regret her impoverishment. When he realized his love for her, Swithin insisted on marriage, and she gave way, on the condition that it be kept secret until he had made a name for himself. She was religious, and insisted on his confirmation. The Bishop of Melchester, who came to Welland for the service, was fascinated by her, and proposed marriage. She remained indifferent. When her brother Louis Glanville told her that Swithin was in love with Tabitha Lark, she showed some natural jealousy. News came that Sir Blount had died much later than had been reported; in fact, after her marriage to Swithin. At the very point when the two lovers had decided on legalizing their marriage publicly, Lady Constantine discovered that Swithin would forfeit a regular income from his great-uncle's legacy if he married before the age of twenty-five. She insisted on his fulfilling his earlier plans of travelling and studying astronomy abroad in the meantime. So great was her solicitude that she made him promise not to write to her until the conditions of the will were carried out. When she realized that she was pregnant, she rushed to Southampton in the hope of marrying him. She was too late. In her despair, she was momentarily tempted to leap from the tower. She succumbed to her brother's machinations, and married the Bishop of Melchester. Her second marriage proved to be unhappy. When the Bishop died, she returned with her boy to Welland House. She had aged considerably. Swithin was shocked when he saw her. 'Her cheeks had lost for ever that firm contour which had been drawn by the vigorous hand of youth, and the masses of hair that were once darkness visible had become touched here and there by a faint grey haze, like the Via Lactea in a midnight sky.' When, however, Swithin told her that he

Constantine, Lady Viviette – Corvsgate Castle

had come home to marry her, her emotion was too great, and she died in his arms. 'Sudden joy after despair had touched an over-strained heart too smartly.'   TT

CONTESSA, THE. See Life, *194–5.*

After the death of her Italian husband, she came to Fernell Hall in the hope of recovering her daughter. This was Dorothy, the girl whom Sir Ashley Mottisfont (her father) had encouraged his young wife Philippa to adopt. The Contessa was beautiful and wealthy; her vivacity and 'finished Continental manners' were engaging; and it was obvious that she would soon be sought in marriage again. See p. 78.   GND. 4

COOMB-FIRTREES. *On an eminence near Coomb ewelease, between Puddletown and Puddletown Heath.*   TL. 'Yell'ham-Wood's Story'

COPE, REV. PERCIVAL. He had been a curate at Exonbury, where he became engaged to Frances Frankland before proceeding to a curacy at Ivell. After the marriage of Mrs Frankland and Mr Millborne, he joined the family for a holiday in the Isle of Wight. While they were sailing on a yacht, he observed the changes of physiognomy induced by a choppy sea, and discerned a startling resemblance between Frances and Mr Millborne. He communicated his suspicions to Frances, and the engagement remained at a standstill. When Mr Millborne found his wife and daughter a manor-house near Ivell, and made financial provision for them, his objections were removed, and soon afterwards he married Miss Frankland.   LLI. 3

CORNICK, JIM. The son of old James Cornick, with whom Anne Garland watched the *Victory* passing Portland Bill on its way to Plymouth. On board were Jim Cornick and Bob Loveday. 'Old James' took Anne back from Hope Cove to Budmouth in his boat. Jim Cornick visited Overcombe to tell the Lovedays that Bob was alive and well after the battle of Trafalgar, but detained and courting in Portsmouth. *TM.* xxxiv–xxxvi

CORTON-HILL. *Corton Beacon, 645 feet high, five miles north of Sherborne.*   MV. 'Molly Gone'

CORVSGATE CASTLE. *Corfe Castle, between Wareham and Swanage.*

Edward Springrove passed the castle, and soon afterwards met Owen Graye walking in that direction from Lulwind Cove. Owen was limping, but Springrove advised him to go on and take a train back to Budmouth from Anglebury. (*For Corfe Castle see plate facing p. 142.*)

The Imperial Archaeological Association held a meeting there, and a talk was given on the history of the castle by Dr Yore. Ethelberta arrived

287

on a donkey, and was taken aback to see 'a file of shining carriages' out of which stepped a crowd of lords and ladies who soon gathered in a ring round 'her faithful beast', which they regarded with amusement. She recognized the laughter of Lord Mountclere.

The new curate at Kingscreech had been making a water-colour sketch of the Corvsgate ruin two miles off when he discovered it was lunch-time, and called at Mrs Chundle's cottage for something to eat.

DR. ii 4; *HE.* xxx–xxxi, xliv, xlv, xlvi; *OMC*

COX, MRS. The wife of a retired farmer at Little Hintock. When Dr Fitzpiers arrived in search of a home, they 'accommodated him by receding from their front rooms into the kitchen quarter, whence they administered to his wants, and emerged at regular intervals to receive from him a not unwelcome addition to their income'. *W.* xvi, xviii, xxv

CRAGS, THE. See TROYTON and BELVEDERE.

PBE. xiv, xvi, xvii, xxiii, xxv, xxviii, xxxiv

CREEDLE, ROBERT. An old man who worked for Giles Winterborne indoors and out. He had worked for Giles's father when Giles was a boy; now he did everything that required doing, from making Giles's bed to catching moles in his field and manuring his garden. He accompanied Giles on his cider-pressing expeditions; and Marty South, when Giles was dead, expected she would travel with his apple-mill and press, and continue the business with the assistance of Creedle. His cooking was not over-refined; at Giles's Christmas party he served Grace Melbury with cabbage, which he afterwards found had contained a slug. As far as he was concerned, green slugs didn't matter very much: 'they've lived on cabbage, so they must be made of cabbage'. But 'God forbid that a *live* slug should be seed on any plate of victuals that's served by Robert Creedle.' *W.* iv, vii, ix, x, xii, xv, xix, xxv, xxviii, xliii, xliv, xlviii

CREMYLL. See PLYMOUTH.

CRESSCOMBE. *Letcombe Bassett, a village by a stream thick with water-cress, on the northern side of the hills between Fawley and Wantage, Berkshire.*

Arabella Donn lived with her parents in a roadside cottage at Cresscombe, and here Jude's seduction took place.

JO. I i, vi, vii, viii; V viii; VI vi

CRESTON. *Preston, north of Weymouth Bay.*

When Edward Springrove and Cytherea Graye were boating, they decided to steer towards Creston Shore, but forgot their intentions as they talked. Further east, opposite the cliffs of Ringsworth Shore, Springrove declared his love.

While at Creston, to which she had been sent from Durnover by her husband to avoid the cholera epidemic, Mrs Maumbry fell in love with Lt. Vannicock of the —st Foot, which was stationed at Budmouth infantry barracks. *DR.* iii 2; *CM.* 1

CREWKERNE. *A small town just within Somerset and little more than three miles from Wynyard's Gap.* *HS.* 'At Wynyard's Gap'

CRICK, RICHARD. The master-dairyman at Talbothays, where he lived with his wife Christiana, who was in charge of domestic arrangements for the resident milkmaids and Angel Clare. Altogether, the household was a happy one. Mr Crick was sturdy, middle-aged, and equable in temperament; he inspired a local rhyme:

Dairyman Dick
All the week: –
On Sundays Mister Richard Crick.

TD. xvii, xviii, xx–xxii, xxv, xxix, xxxi–xxxiii, xxxvii

CRICKETT, RICHARD. Parish clerk at Carriford, and Hardy's first great comic character. Third husband of Mrs Crickett, a 'scandal-loving' woman, employed as charwoman by Manston.

DR. viii 3, ix 4, xiii 2, Sequel

CRIMMERCROCK LANE. *Originally 'Cromlech Crock Lane', part of the road from Maiden Newton, leading up to Toller Down on its way to Crewkerne.*

When the Clares at Emminster were eagerly awaiting Clare's return from Brazil, the Vicar assured his wife that there was 'plenty of time yet'. From Chalk-Newton, where he was not due by train until six o'clock, Angel has 'ten miles of country-road, five of them in Crimmercrock Lane', and they 'are not jogged over in a hurry by our old horse'.

TD. liii; *TL.* 'The Dark-Eyed Gentleman', 'The Home-coming'

CRIPPLEGATE CHURCH. *St Giles's, Cripplegate, London.*

Visited, at Ethelberta's suggestion, to see Milton's tomb. The party included the Belmaines, Mrs Doncastle, and Ethelberta, and they were joined by the rival admirers of Ethelberta, Neigh and Ladywell. *Superficially the scene is typically comic, but it is enhanced by greater visual impressiveness than is to be found in most of the London scenes and by the theme of Mammon-worship, which stems from Milton, and Wordsworth on Milton, and is obviously related to Ethelberta's ambition. The 'Harle-*

quin-rose incident at Cripplegate' led to a great coolness between Ladywell and Neigh. *HE*. xxvii, xxxv

CRIPPLESTRAW, ANTHONY. He lived at Overcombe, and was a member of the Locals, who were trained in preparation for the French invasion. He was employed by old Mr Derriman at Oxwell Hall to do odd jobs in the yard and garden, 'and like his employer had no great pretensions to manly beauty, owing to a limpness of backbone and speciality of mouth, which opened on one side only, giving him a triangular smile'. He took great delight in tormenting the cowardly Festus by harping on the glory which he would win when he was mown down in the front line by the invading French, just as he loved to hear Corporal Tullidge crunching the bones in the arm that had been smashed at Valenciennes. When the invasion alarm was sounded erroneously, he humoured Festus in a scene of high comedy, satirically agreeing that it was best for him to hoard his valour 'for a higher class of war – the defence of yer adorable lady'.

TM. iv–vi, ix, x, xxiii, xxiv, xxvi, xxx, xxxvi

CROOKHILL, GEORGE. One of the 'shady sort' in Longpuddle. *LLI*. 8*h*

CROSS-IN-HAND. *A stone pillar on the road which runs south of High Stoy over Batcombe Hill to Holywell, Evershot, Toller Down, and Beaminster. It may have been an ecclesiastical boundary stone; it may 'mark the site of a miracle or murder, or both'. See plate facing p. 367.*

Here Alec d'Urberville, after his conversion by the Reverend James Clare of Emminster, overtook Tess on his way from Evershead (*Evershot*) to Abbot's-Cernel, and, in order to resist temptation, insisted that she place her hand on the stone and swear never to tempt him again. Alec assumed that the pillar was all that remained of a Holy Cross, and that the figure of a hand carved on it was still to be seen on the stump.

The miracle associated with the stone is the subject of 'The Lost Pyx'. For the 'Christ-in-Hand' of Hardy's footnote, cf. *LLE*. 'The Chosen'.

TD. xliv, xlv, liv; *PPP*. 'The Lost Pyx'

CRUMPLER, MR and MRS SIMON. Guests at the Dewys' Christmas party. He sat talking and nodding with grandfather James by the chimney-corner. In the dance, Mrs Crumpler moved so smoothly that she appeared to roll on castors. *UGT*. I vii, viii

CUCKOO LANE. *The road which runs north from Bockhampton Cross, past the lane to Higher Bockhampton, to the Dorchester – Puddletown (or London) road opposite the entrance to Grey's Wood.* *UGT*. IV i; *MC*. xl

CULLIFORD. *Culliford Tree is a barrow on the downs almost due south from Max Gate* (Life, *173*). *Culliford Hill and Wood are east of Came Plantation, where the road from Broadmayne reaches the top of the downs.*   WW. 'The Ballad of Love's Skeleton'

CUXSOM, MOTHER. A fat widow of the lower-class community of Casterbridge (whose 'smiling countenance' was 'a circular disc reticulated with creases'). She did not regret the death of her husband. He used to beat her: 'Ah, yes, Cuxsom's gone, and so shall leather breeches!' It is she who described 'the incidents of Mrs Henchard's death, as she had learnt them from the nurse' to a few of the old inhabitants who had met around the town-pump.   MC. viii, xiii, xviii, xxxii, xxxvi

DALBIAC, MRS SUSANNA. 'A Wessex woman, blithe, and somewhat fair', the wife of Colonel Dalbiac. One of the generals at the battle of Salamanca asked Wellington if he had heard that she rode in the charge behind her husband.   D. (3) i ii, iii

DAMER'S WOOD. *Came Wood, two miles south of Dorchester. The Damer family lived at Came House; one of them, who later became the first Earl of Dorchester, bought Milton Abbey in 1752; see* MIDDLETON ABBEY, *and* Life, *175, 237.*   TM. ii

DAMON, MRS. When the 'Joker' Kit Twink brought her the news that her husband had been gored to death by an escaped bull, he was 'depressed by his neighbour's doom' and amazed that Mrs Damon was more concerned about the untidiness of the chamber which was to receive the corpse and what her neighbours might say than about her loss. Soon she could take no food and pined away, while Kit became his gay self again.

WP. 'The Slow Nature'

DAMSON, SUKE. A 'hoydenish' girl of Little Hintock, with whom young Timothy Tangs was in love. *Her affair with Dr Fitzpiers had to be bowdlerized in the English serial version of the story.* She married Tim Tangs, with whom she emigrated to New Zealand, after he had set a man-trap to injure Fitzpiers in retribution for his intimacy with Suke.

W. xvi, xx, xxiv, xxix, xxxiv, xxxv, xlv–xlviii

DARCH, CAR. A 'dark virago', called Queen of Spades, who lived at Pentridge. She was a woman of easy virtue, and had been Alec d'Urberville's mistress. Hence, perhaps, her readiness to quarrel with Tess. Her sister Nancy was nicknamed the Queen of Diamonds. Tess met the two 'Amazonian sisters' at Flintcomb-Ash, but they did not appear to recognize her, and probably had no recollection of her, for they were intoxicated when they had tried to fight her, and did not stay long anywhere. They preferred men's work such as well-sinking, hedging, and ditching; and they were expert reed-drawers.   *TD.* x, xliii

DARE, WILLIAM. *Dare was conceived as a Satanic character; his name is associated with 'devil', as in 'daredevil'. See p. 157.*

The 'invisible stranger' of the inn at Sleeping-Green introduced himself at Stancy Castle as an amateur photographer who had lived mostly in India, Malta, Australia and Canada, and wished to take views of the castle. George Somerset engaged him as an assistant in preparing his architectural plans for additions to the castle, but found him unsatisfactory and dismissed him. He was the illegitimate son of Captain de Stancy. Will's great aim was to see his father married to an affluent wife, and ensure thereby that he was never short of money himself. Paula Power had the wealth; his father, though fallen, was of aristocratic lineage; and everything pointed to this as the most desirable marriage to promote Dare's ends. One obstacle in the way was George Somerset. Dare witnessed 'the tender episode' between him and Paula in Markton church. To remove him from the neighbourhood it was necessary that Havill's plans for the castle extensions should be accepted by the R.I.B.A. He took Havill one night to Stancy Castle to study George Somerset's plans. Although the result of the competition was a tie, events fell out as Dare had hoped, for Paula Power was persuaded to give the work to Havill when it was known that he was on the verge of bankruptcy. Dare had found it more difficult to persuade his father to think of marriage, but he soon found the way to inflame his passions. The advent of Abner Power promoted his schemes. Dare studied Moivre's *Doctrine of Chances*, and his behaviour at Monte Carlo showed that gambling had become an obsession with him. Somerset met him there and refused to lend him money. In return Dare sent Paula a telegram which injured Somerset in her eyes, and almost succeeded in estranging the lovers permanently. His further discrediting of Somerset by means of the faked photograph may have happened fortuitously, but Dare was prepared as always, and would have played this hand had occasion demanded. How Abner Power discovered the relationship between de Stancy and Dare and the aims they were pursuing is not known, but when Abner confronted him Dare was more than his match; Abner left for Peru, and, but for Charlotte de Stancy, Dare's plans would have succeeded. What happened to him after he set fire to Stancy Castle is not known.   *L.* I v,
vi, xii–xv; II i–vii; III ii–v; IV iv, v; V iii–v, xi–xiv; VI iv, v

DARLING. The light-grey mare which Giles Winterborne bought for Grace Melbury, and on which, ironically, her husband Fitzpiers rode on his nocturnal visits to Mrs Charmond at Middleton Abbas.

W. xi, xv, xxviii, xxix, xxxiv–xxxv

DARTH, EMILY. See HARDCOME.

DARTON, FARMER CHARLES. A rich farmer who lived three or four miles from Casterbridge. He went to The Knap near King's-Hintock to marry Sally Hall; the first person he met on his late arrival was her sister-in-law Helena, who had just returned from Australia with her impoverished family and dying husband. He married Helena, but she soon died. Charles sought out Sally Hall again to propose to her, but she declined. She was pleased to read his speeches 'on mangold-wurzel, and such like' at the Casterbridge Farmers' Club. Unlike his father, he was unambitious and 'unstrategic'; he lacked his commercial subtlety. Financially he had all he desired – a 'turnover' of thirty thousand a year. (On farmers and working class poverty, see *MC*, xxii. The Darton of this novel is probably Charles's father.)   *WT.* 6; *MC.* xvii

DAVID. An old man, and 'indoor factotum' at Miller Loveday's. His sight was bad; he was very good at making beds and oiling the legs of chairs and other furniture, but 'a dunder-headed feller for getting up a feast'. Even so, he could please Bob Loveday, for whom he made an omelet and a seed-cake, 'the latter so richly compounded that it opened to the knife like a freckled buttercup'. He gave up domestic work for military activities when it was thought the French had landed; his only achievement of note was to pull the spigots out of Miller Loveday's barrels before he went to secure his pike from the church, to ensure that the French should not drink what the Lovedays were to be deprived of.

TM. ii, xii–xiii, xv–xvii, xix, xx, xxii, xxiii, xxvi, xxviii, xxxii, xxxviii, xxxix

DAVIDS, MR. The parson at Beaminster who advised Agatha Pollin according to Frances Lovill's wishes.   *DBC*

DAVIES. *Hardy told Rebekah Owen (p. 430) that this was his real name, and that he had been a friend of the Hardy family.* The hangman at Casterbridge gaol in 1825 who arranged for Gertrude Lodge to lay her withered arm on the neck of a youth who had just been hanged.   *WT.* 4

DAY, FANCY. The heroine of *Under the Greenwood Tree.* Her mother, Geoffrey Day's first wife, had been a teacher 'in a landed family's nursery'. Fancy was first among the Queen's Scholars of her year. She lived at Mellstock school-house (*Lower Bockhampton*). Her father, keeper of Yalbury Great Wood, had ambitious marriage plans for her, and therefore disapproved of Dick Dewy as her suitor.

UGT. I iii, v–ix; II i–viii; III i–iv; IV i–vii; V i, ii

DAY, GEOFFREY. Fancy Day's father, and keeper of Yalbury (*Yellowham*) Great Wood. He had married a second time, and had great ambitions for his daughter in marriage. He lived in a miserly way so 'that if any gentleman, who sees her to be his equal in polish, should want to marry her, and she want to marry him, he shan't be superior to her in pocket'. He was a taciturn man – 'That man's dumbness is wonderful to listen to.'

Joseph Poorgrass said that he would not have answered the owl when he was lost in Yalbury Wood, had he not been drinking Keeper Day's mead. *UGT.* II v–vii; III iv; IV ii, iv; V i, ii; *FMC.* viii

DAY, JANE. Geoffrey Day's second wife. 'It was her doom to be nobody's wife at all in the wide universe. But she made up her mind that she would, and did it twice over.' She was very house-proud. Her husband thought her queer. *UGT.* II vi; III ii; V i, ii

DAY, JOHN. Gardener at Knapwater House. *DR.* xiii 2

DAY, MR. The narrator of 'Netty Sargent's Copyhold'. He was 'the world-ignored local landscape-painter', an elderly man who had never sold a picture outside his native place, where every home exhibited three or four of his admired productions. *LLI.* 8, introduction and (*i*).

DEANSLEIGH PARK. *Broadlands, south of Romsey, Hampshire.* The home of Sir Ashley Mottisfont. *GND.* 4

DE LA FESTE, M. CHARLES. The landscape and marine painter with whom Caroline fell in love while she was staying with her mother at the Marlets' in Versailles. When he came to England, he fell in love with Caroline's sister, accepted a form of marriage with Caroline for the sake of her health, and later, on Alicia's insistence, married her for honour's sake. After the marriage he disappeared. His body was later recovered from the river near Wherryborne. The disappointed lover had drowned himself. *CM.* 3

DERRIMAN, BENJAMIN. Squire Derriman had inherited a great deal of wealth and property from his deceased wife, and lived at Oxwell Hall. The place was shockingly neglected; it was crumbling and damp, and the interior of its quadrangle 'a bed of mud and manure', inhabited by pigs, calves and poultry. He was so light that he could move with incredible rapidity, and was in the habit of making sudden appearances when least expected. His coat and breeches were of the same colour as his farmyard; and he was so wizened that 'the edge of the skull round his eye-sockets was visible through the skin'. Since King George's arrival, he had found prices ruinously high in Budmouth. He liked Anne Garland, who came to read the newspaper to him occasionally, but he was terrified by the bullying manner of his nephew Festus. He was afraid that his money and legal documents would be lost if the French invaded the country, and took them to be hidden at Overcombe Mill. Anxiety got the better of him, and he decided to bury them under a flagstone in one of his cellars, in the presence of Anne, to whom he committed a paper on which were written notes on their location. In escaping from Festus on the way home, Anne lost the paper, which was found by Matilda Johnson and given to Festus. When 'old Benjy' realized that his nephew had some clue to the whereabouts of his treasure, he dug it up and took it late one evening to Anne, with Festus and Matilda after him. He died of a heart attack on the way home, and was found little more than a 'husk, dry and fleshless as that of a dead heron found on a moor in January'. The treasure box which he was so anxious to keep out of Festus's hands was found to contain his will; by this Anne inherited nearly all his property, including Oxwell Hall.

TM. vi, viii, ix, xiv, xviii, : ᵤv, xxvi, xxviii, xl

DERRIMAN, FESTUS. A cowardly braggadocio and traditional comedy type, the nephew of Squire Derriman of Oxwell Hall. He was proud to flaunt in the uniform of the yeomanry cavalry, and loved to boast of the deeds he would do against the French. This 'florid son of Mars' was red-haired, a 'bouncing Rufus . . . about the size and weight of the Farnese Hercules'. He was a bully by nature, and the terror of his uncle, whose property and wealth he hoped to inherit and spend. 'He was early in love, and had at the time of the story suffered from the ravages of that passion [he was twenty-three] thirteen distinct times. He could not love lightly and gaily; his love was earnest, cross-tempered, and even savage. It was a positive agony to him to be ridiculed by the object of his affections, and such conduct drove him into a frenzy if persisted in.' All this Anne Garland was to discover. He wanted her to accompany him on yeomanry sprees in South Wessex, and was relentless in his pursuit of her, especially when the invasion alarm was raised, and he thought it his honourable duty to escort her safely from the expected battle area to Kingsbere.

Anthony Cripplestraw, who had derived great satirical entertainment
from harping on the heroic role Festus would play when he was in the
front line against the French, and doomed to be among the first of the
valiant to be mown down, did not lose the opportunity of supporting his
arguments for displaying his valour in a more chivalrous role than that
of facing the French. Anne's rejection of his assistance, and her loneliness, revealed the worst in Festus. The trumpet-major came to her
rescue as she was fleeing, overtook Festus at an inn in the gloom of the
evening, and administered a monitory beating. Festus mistook him for
Bob, and had no hesitation in accepting Matilda Johnson's suggestion that
the press-gang should be set on him. In this way, each thought to wipe
out old scores, Festus principally to remove his rival. Festus and Matilda
had designs on the squire's hidden money, but he was too clever for them.
When he died it was found that he had left nearly all his property to
Anne; Festus married Matilda.   *TM*. v–x, xiii, xiv,
          xx, xxi, xxiii, xxv–xxviii, xxx, xxxii, xxxiv, xxxvi, xl, xli

DE STANCY, CAPTAIN. He was the son of Sir William de Stancy, and a
captain (who lacked advancement, according to his illegitimate son Will
Dare) in the Royal Artillery. Soon after George Somerset had fallen in
love with Paula Power of Stancy Castle, his battery was stationed at
Toneborough Barracks, and this gave Dare the opportunity he had been
waiting for to promote the marriage of his father to a wealthy woman,
so that his own financial future would be secure. 'Captain de Stancy was
a personage who would have been called interesting by women well out
of their teens. . . . He was sufficiently old and experienced to suggest a
goodly accumulation of touching amourettes in the chambers of his
memory, and not too old for the possibility of increasing the store.' He
was striking in appearance; his hair and moustache were raven black;
and his eyes, large, dark, and soft in expression. He had occasioned
Dare's mother much sorrow, and for that reason forsworn 'the society,
and if possible the sight', of young and attractive women. Owing to
Dare's machinations, he soon became passionately enamoured of Paula
Power, and hoped that their marriage would result in the return of
Stancy Castle to his family. He accompanied her on the Continental tour which Abner Power arranged in order to disengage her
affections from George Somerset; but despite Will Dare's success in
damning Somerset, his suit never prospered until, suddenly, near the end
of their long tour, when he heard that his father was dead and he would

become Sir William de Stancy, she agreed to become engaged. They were on the point of being married, when his sister Charlotte met Somerset by chance. Her discoveries led to the immediate breaking-off of the engagement, and the wrecking of all Dare's plans for his own advancement through that of his father.

L. II iii–vii; III i–xi; IV iv–v; V i–x, xiii, xiv; VI iv

DE STANCY, CHARLOTTE. Daughter of Sir William de Stancy and sister of Captain de Stancy. She lived at Stancy Castle and was very fond of Paula Power. Her health was delicate, and she was ill on the European tour with Paula. Secretly she was in love with George Somerset. They met by chance after he and Paula had become estranged; and the result of this encounter was that she discovered Dare's perfidy. Principles gained over self-interest; she might lose George and destroy her brother's chances of marrying Paula, but she had to disclose what she had learned. She retired to live with an Anglican Sisterhood, much to Paula's regret. 'She was genuine, if anybody ever was; and simple as she was true,' said George Somerset.

L. I iii–vi,

viii, x, xiv; II iv, vii; III i–viii, xi; V i–vii, x; VI i, v

DE STANCY, SIR WILLIAM. Father of Charlotte and Captain de Stancy, and formerly owner of Stancy Castle. He had lived above his means and had to sell the castle. In his old age, he affected to have little use for the medieval ('why should we preserve the shadow of the form?'), and was a utilitarian. He lived in a comfortable, cheerful cottage, a typical example of 'mushroom modernism', called Myrtle Villa, near Marktown. His hair and beard had once been raven black, but all save a few dashes of their original shade had vanished with age. His eye-sockets were large cavernous arches, 'reminding the beholder of the vaults in the castle he once had owned. His hands were long and fleshless, each knuckle showing like a bamboo-joint from beneath his coat-sleeves.' His 'clever childishness' (*reminiscent of Polonius and Micawber*) expressed itself in the advice he continually gave the younger generation. 'If a man knows how to spend less than his income, however small that may be, why – he has the philosopher's stone.' He recommended foreign travel.

L. I v; III i; IV iii; V x, xi

DEVERELL, MISS. The only lady – apart from the hostess – who was designated by name at Paula Power's garden-party at Stancy Castle. George Somerset would have given 'a year of his life' to dance once with Paula. She suggested that he dance with Miss Deverell, who had not been asked once during the evening. Somerset looked at her, and said he had thought of going home. She was 'a sallow lady with black twinkling eyes, yellow costume, and gay laugh'.   *L.* I xv

DEVIL'S DOOR, THE. *A dolmen or 'Druidical trilithon' in the upper part of Clatford Bottom, two miles west of Marlborough. Its real name is the Devil's Den; see plate facing p. 111.*

A landmark from Lambing Corner. Nearby the Duke of Shakeforest Towers hid the body of Fred Ogbourne, whom he had murdered.   *CM.* 7

DEWY, ANN. Wife of Reuben Dewy, the tranter, and mother of Dick Dewy. Her other children, Susan, Jim, Bessy and Charley, graduated 'uniformly . . . from the age of sixteen to that of four years'.

UGT. I ii, iii, vi–viii; v i, ii

DEWY, DICK. Son of the tranter Reuben, and treble-player in the old Mellstock choir. He married Fancy Day.   *UGT*

DEWY, REUBEN. The tranter of Upper Mellstock. He played the tenor violin in the choir. Exertion made him very hot: 'Reuben always was such a hot man,' his wife remarked.

The Dewys' house is the Hardy house at Higher Bockhampton, though not one of the Dewys was drawn from the Hardy family. 'He had been the many years' neighbour of the Hardys, and did the haulage of building materials for Hardy's father'; cf. Life, 92, 97. See plates facing p. 14.

UGT. I i–viii; II ii–v, viii; v i, ii; *WP.* 'Friends Beyond';
TL. 'The Dead Quire'; *LLE.* 'The Country Wedding'
(*at Puddletown*); *HS.* 'Winter Night in Woodland'

DEWY, THEOPHILUS. Reuben's younger brother. He used to say there was no 'plumness' – no bowing, no solidity – in Mop Ollamoor's fiddling.   *LLI.* 7

DEWY, WILLIAM. Grandfather of Dick Dewy. He played the bass viol in the Mellstock choir.

Coming home from a wedding on a moonlight night, he took a short cut across a field in the Froom valley and was pursued by a bull. He began to play his fiddle, and the bull paused while he backed. Finally, remembering how he had seen cattle kneel on Christmas Eve, he played a Nativity hymn. The bull knelt down and he escaped (cf. *MV.* 'The Oxen').

The story was told by Mr Crick, the dairyman at Talbothays. He added: 'and I can tell you to a foot where he's a-lying in Mellstock Churchyard at this very moment – just between the second yew-tree and the north aisle'. (*See p. 357.*)

William used to tell the story of the Chalk-Newton choir ('The Grave by the Handpost', p. 98).

For the Dewys and the Mellstock choir, see pp. 410–12.
UGT. I i–vii; II ii–v; IV iv, v; V i, ii; *TD.* xvii; *WP.*
'Friends Beyond'; *TL.* 'The Dead Quire'; *HS.* 'Winter
Night in Woodland'

DICKSON, MR. Manston had arranged for Anne Seaway to masquerade as his wife, whom he had killed. To prepare the way for her arrival, he read a bogus letter from his wife Eunice to his bachelor friend Dickson from Casterbridge, knowing that he was 'a chatterer' who 'boasted of an endless string of acquaintances'. *DR.* xiv 3

DOGBURY. *A hill near High Stoy on the chalk escarpment overlooking Blackmoor Vale. The Sherborne road running north from Cerne Abbas crosses the wooded ridge at Dogbury Gate.*

Grace accompanied her husband Dr Fitzpiers as far as the base of High-Stoy and Dogbury Hill when, unknown to her, he was on his first visit to Mrs Charmond at Middleton Abbey.

Tess's upland walk from Flintcomb-Ash to see Angel's parents at Emminster took her across the high road from Sherton Abbas to Caster-bridge (*as opposed to the lower road via Minterne Magna and Cerne Abbas*) and immediately south of Dogbury Hill and High-Stoy and the intervening dell called 'The Devil's Kitchen'. *TM.* xii; *W.* xxviii;
TD. ii, xliv; *HS.* 'Life and Death at Sunrise' (*1867*)

DOLLERY, MRS. The carrier between Sherton Abbas and Abbot's Cernel. The Sherton hairdresser Mr Percomb travelled on her van to visit Marty South at Little Hintock. *W.* i, xxiv, xxxiii

DOLLOP, JACK. When the butter 'would not come', Dairyman Crick told the story of Jack Dollop, who courted a young woman at Mellstock and deceived her as he deceived many before. He was a milkman at Talbothays, and her mother came armed with an umbrella to deal with him. When Jack saw her he took refuge in the milk-churn. She found out where he was hiding, and set to turning the churn with such vigour that he readily agreed to marry her daughter. These reminiscences touched a sorrowful chord in Tess; she felt faint and went out of doors.

Later Crick told how Dollop had been deceived in marrying a widow in the expectation of her income. They had led a cat-and-dog life. Crick's other listeners thought she should have told him the truth before marrying; Tess decided she must refuse Angel Clare. *TD.* xxi, xxix

DONAGHADEE. *A port in County Down, Northern Ireland. There is ample evidence that Hardy received a letter from a stranger in Donaghadee; her maiden name was Hardy, and she wished to know if they were related. The name of the town suggested this 'impromptu', as Hardy described it in a letter to St John Ervine, 25 August 1924. (For this note, I am indebted to J. O. Bailey.)* HS. 'Donaghadee'

DONCASTLE, MR and MRS. They lived in 'a moderately fashionable square' in West London. Ethelberta's father, Mr Chickerel, was their butler. Mrs Doncastle was a great friend of Ethelberta, whom she thought to be the orphan child of a clergyman (others said a bishop). It was at the Doncastles' that Ethelberta first met Lord Mountclere. When it was revealed that Chickerel was her father, Mrs Doncastle said that her blunder was worse than if she had 'honoured unawares the daughter of the vilest Antipodean miscreant and murderer'.

HE. vii, ix, xv, xxvii, xxviii, xxix, xlii

DONN, ARABELLA. *See the note of 1 March 1888* (Life, *206*).

The daughter of a pig-jobber at Cresscombe. She had been a barmaid at Alfredston before she met Jude. She was 'a fine dark-eyed girl, not exactly handsome, but capable of passing as such at a little distance'. Her bosom was round and prominent, her lips full, her teeth perfect, and her complexion a rich brown. 'She was a complete and substantial female animal – no more, no less.' The pig's pizzle which she threw at Jude makes Hardy's intentions clear. When he was seduced and tricked into marriage by Arabella, Jude's dreams of Christminster ended, until they quarrelled and she left him. She emigrated to Australia with her parents and married Mr Cartlett, a 'hotel-keeper' at Sydney. She remarried him in England, after her divorce from Jude, and helped him to run the Three Horns tavern in a gin-drinking district at Lambeth. As soon as he reached England from Australia, where he had lived with the Donns, she sent her son 'Father Time' to Jude. After Cartlett's death, she sought consolation in religion; Sue's remarriage to Phillotson provided her opportunity, and she took advantage of Jude's drunkenness to marry him at Christminster. Jude was ill and indifferent to life, and it was the amorous Vilbert she had in mind as his successor. Jude had scarcely died when she left with friends for the regatta, where she was seen with Vilbert's arm round her waist. *She is the Venus Pandemos to the Venus Urania in Sue Bridehead; cf. pp. 55–6.* JO. I vi–xi;

III viii, ix; IV ii, v; V ii, iii, v, vii, viii; VI iii, iv, vi–xi

DONN, MR. Arabella's father and a pig-jobber. He was an energetic, black-whiskered man. He emigrated with his family to Australia, and Jude's son, who was born in Australia, stayed with them when Arabella married Mr Cartlett. Mrs Donn died of dysentery, and Mr Donn re-returned to the Cresscombe district near Alfredston. He then opened a pork-shop in a poor outlying part of Christminster. Arabella ensured that Jude was 'gin-drunk' when she married him for his father's house. The celebration party made the 'miserable little pork and sausage shop' better known, and the Donns acquired a 'real notoriety' among people of a lower social level in Christminster. *JO.* I vii, viii, xi; VI iii, vi, vii, xi

DORA. *This seems to be, as Purdy suggested, Dora Sigerson, wife of Clement Shorter (who as editor of various magazines printed several of Hardy's stories and poems; cf. Purdy, 349–50). She died in 1918 and was taken to Dublin for burial.* WW. 'How She Went to Ireland'

DORNELL, BETTY. *Elizabeth Horner (1723–92). She was the mother of* LADY SUSAN, *who lived at Stinsford House. See* Life, *9, 163–4, 250.*

The daughter of Squire Dornell. Without his knowledge or permission, she was married at the age of twelve or thirteen to Stephen Reynard. The ceremony meant little to her, and, much to her father's delight, she fell in love with her father's favourite, Charles Phelipson. When Stephen returned to England and insisted on claiming Betty as his wife, she deliberately contracted smallpox to keep him away, and decided to elope with Charles, only to find that his love was not proof against that. It was Stephen who stood up to the test. Their marriage was a very happy one, and Betty became the first Countess of Wessex. *GND.* 1

DORNELL, SUSAN. *Susannah Strangways of Melbury House. Stinsford House was one of the Strangways' possessions.*

She was the wife of Squire Dornell, and had inherited King's Hintock Court. They could not agree about Betty's marriage, and the result was that Susan took her to London and had her married to Stephen Reynard at the age of twelve or thirteen. After the death of her husband, Susan's devotion to him revived; she rebuilt the church at King's Hintock, and established many charities in the villages to the east, including Little Hintock, in his memory. Out of respect to his wishes, she insisted that Stephen should not reside with Betty until she was nineteen, but Betty saw no reason to wait, and soon her mother advised her to make their marriage public – to avoid a scandal. *GND.* 1

DORNELL, SQUIRE THOMAS. *Thomas Horner of Mells Park, Somerset.*

He opposed his wife's choice of a husband for his daughter Betty, and, when defeated by her strategy, returned in dudgeon to his estate at Falls-Park, leaving his wife at her ancestral home, King's Hintock Court. He had become 'what was called a three-bottle man, and, in his wife's estimation, less and less presentable to her polite friends from town'. When Betty, who was too young to realize what her marriage ceremony meant, fell in love with his favourite Charles Phelipson, he was highly pleased. He rose from his sick-bed and travelled to Bristol in a fruitless effort to dissuade Stephen Reynard from residing with Betty when he returned after an absence of several years. His exertions undoubtedly hastened his death. *GND.* 1

DOWDEN, OLLY. She lived on Egdon Heath, and made 'heath brooms or besoms'. 'Her nature was to be civil to enemies as well as to friends, and grateful to all the world for letting her remain alive.' When the bonfire died down on Rainbarrow, and Timothy Fairway began whirling round in a dance with Susan Nunsuch, Olly Dowden was seized by Sam, the turf-cutter, who, 'somewhat more gently, poussetted with her likewise'. Soon 'all that could be seen on Rainbarrow was a whirling of dark shapes amid a boiling confusion of sparks'. 'The chief noises were women's shrill cries, men's laughter, Susan's stays and pattens, Olly Dowden's "heu-heu-heu!" and the strumming of the wind upon the furze-bushes....' Olly accompanied Mrs Yeobright down Rainbarrow, and, assuming that Wildeve and Thomasin were married, asked her to remind Wildeve to send the bottle of wine he had promised her sick husband when the wedding took place. *RN.* I iii, iv, v; IV vii; V ix

DOWLE, MR. A curate who lived in a 'small blind' street off East Commercial Road, London. *HS.* 'An East-End Curate'

DOWNE, CHARLES. He was a young lawyer with a moderate income and three young children. Unlike his friend Mr Barnet, he was happily married. His wife Emily was affectionate. Mr Downe suggested that his wife with her winning ways might be able to help Mr Barnet if she met his wife. They drove together down to the beach and were tempted to sail out beyond one of the cliffs. The boat was capsized, and Mrs Downe was drowned. Mr Downe was very upset, and his house soon became neglected. On Mr Barnet's advice, he invited Lucy Savile to take charge of his family. See BARNET, GEORGE. *WT.* 5

DOWNSTABLE. *Barnstaple, north Devon.*

After he had pushed her husband, Captain Northbrook, over a chasm,

rey's Bridge

n Hatches Weir

Turnworth House, and Hermitage Church (see the Hintocks)

Dornell, Squire Thomas – Dunford, John

Dornell, Squire Thomas – Dunford, John

Signor Smittozzi planned to take the Honourable Laura via Cliff-Martin to Downstable, whence they were to proceed in their elopement by train.

GND. 10

—TH DRAGOONS. This horse regiment, together with the German cavalry of the York Hussars, and several battalions of foot soldiers, was stationed near Overcombe in preparation for the expected French invasion in 1804. After a period at Exonbury, they were stationed at Budmouth barracks the following summer. The —th Dragoons contained many local young men, including Trumpet-major John Loveday and Sergeant Brett. Subsequently the regiment joined Sir Arthur Wellesley in the Spanish Peninsula.   *TM.* i–iii, x, xii, xxi, xxviii, xxxv, xli

DRENGHARD, SIR GEORGE. *Sir George, one of the Trenchards, 'now extinct in the male line'. He lived at Wolfeton House, near Charminster and one mile north of Dorchester, in the reign of James I (Hutchins, iii 326, 329).*

He was the first husband of Lady Penelope and one of 'the ancient and knightly family of the Drenghards, or Drenkhards . . . whose name, according to the local chronicles, was interpreted to mean *Strenuus Miles, vel Potator'.*

One of the Drenkhards told Lord Uplandtowers that he would never succeed in winning Barbara Grebe, on whom his heart was set.

The Drenkhards were among the Wessex families, including the Hardys, for whom Angel Clare professed anything but respect because they had declined through the centuries (cf. *GND.* 4).

For the house of the Trenchards in Dorchester, see p. 265.

GND. 8; GND. 2; TD. xix

DUKE OF YORK, THE. The inn at Overcombe.   *TM.* i, xl

DUNCLIFFE HILL. *The 'traveller's mark', two miles west of Shaftesbury.*

Phillotson left Duncliffe Hill on the left as he walked one evening to consult his friend Gillingham at Leddenton about his marriage with Sue.

JO. IV iv

DUNDAGEL. *Tintagel Castle, on the north coast of Cornwall; cf. PBE. xxi, where Knight from the top of Beeny Cliff looks to right and left 'over the waste of waters between Cam Beak and "grim Dundagel throned along the sea" '. The headland is 'famed' through the associations of its ruined castle with King Arthur and Tristram and Iseult. See* TINTAGEL.

PBE. xxi; SC. 'I found her out there'

DUNFORD, JOHN. On the Sunday when Fancy Day inaugurated organ

303

L   303   P.H.C.

services at Mellstock church, Dick Dewy was unable to attend. He had to go to Charmley to act as a bearer, in fulfilment of a long-standing engagement, at the burial of John Dunford, 'a young acquaintance' who had died of consumption. *UGT.* IV v–vii

DUNMAN, FARMER. He was buried, according to his wish, on a Sunday so that poor folk could attend his funeral and be entertained afterwards.

HS. 'Farmer Dunman's Funeral'

D'URBERVILLE, ALEC. A libertine, with Satanic associations (ix, 1), but not without redeeming features. He was the son of Mr Simon Stoke, who had retired from business and adopted the name of d'Urberville to acquire county status. His father had lately died, and he lived with his blind mother at The Slopes near Trantridge. He was sensual and cruel by nature (cf. viii), and other girls besides Car Darch had fallen victims to his enticements. After an appraisal of Tess's physical luxuriance, he soon managed to find employment for her at The Slopes. His aim was accomplished when he rescued her from physical violence at the hands of the 'Amazonian sisters' and their friends, and tricked her into thinking he was taking her home. That Tess was a victim is a note which is repeated significantly in the narrative. Alec's ruthlessness is stressed first and last: 'Doubtless some of Tess d'Urberville's mailed ancestors . . . had dealt the same measure even more ruthlessly. . . . ' (xi), and 'you have . . . made me be what I prayed you in pity not to make me be again!' (lvi). It was because she feared his enticements and despised herself for having accepted presents from him that she returned home. The thought of marrying him was anathema (xiii).

Alec's reputation was known, and reached the ear of the Evangelical parson Mr Clare, who made him realize his unworthiness to such effect that Alec became a conversionist preacher himself. After seeking the help of Mr and Mrs Clare to reconcile Angel and herself, Tess had the misfortune to be seen by him when he was preaching at Evershead. His old passions revived – despite himself and his dramatic gesture when he made her swear at Cross-in-Hand that *she* would never tempt *him* again. It was not until this meeting that he knew about Tess's child, and it was not until he had offered her marriage in reparation that he discovered she had married and had been deserted. Ironically, it was Angel Clare's heterodox arguments as communicated by Tess which made him lose his newly acquired faith and give up preaching. He was genuinely sorry to see her toiling like a slave for the tyrant Groby at Flintcomb-Ash, and ultimately intervened to some effect. He would have done anything to help Tess and her family in their need. His remarks on Angel Clare were obviously not disinterested, and his persistent attentions took on the hue of persecution to Tess. 'Once victim, always victim – that's the law!' she cried, as she smote him across the mouth with her glove. When she returned to Marlott, he pursued her there. Her father's death and the eviction of the Durbeyfield family were Tess's undoing. Out of desperation, for the sake of her family, she sacrificed herself to one she did not love, and went to Sandbourne to live with Alec as his wife: 'He was very kind to me, and to mother, and to all of us after father's death.' When Angel returned and Tess found herself tricked by fate, she stabbed Alec d'Urberville to death in her frenzy. It was the one way she saw of 'killing the situation' (cf. Hardy's note, *Life*, 221).   *TD*. v–xiv, xxvi, xxvii, xxx, xxxiv, xli, xliv–xlviii, l–lii, liv–lvi

D'URBERVILLE, MRS. The mother of Alec. She was not a genuine d'Urberville. Her husband was Mr Simon Stoke, a merchant from the north of England, who decided to retire to the south as a county man. 'Conning for an hour in the British Museum the pages of works devoted to extinct, half-extinct, obscured, and ruined families appertaining to the quarter of England in which he proposed to settle, he considered that *d'Urberville* looked and sounded as well as any of them.' At first, they called themselves Stoke d'Urbervilles, then simply d'Urbervilles. Their new, spick-and-span property, near the Chase and Trantridge, was called The Slopes. The owner had died not long before Tess arrived. Mrs d'Urberville was blind, and her main interest was in her pet fowls (the keeping of which was fashionable at the time; cf. Emma Hardy's *Some Recollections*, 6) and bullfinches. (*For the oblique symbolism, see* p. 164.)   *TD*. v, vi, ix

DURBEYFIELD, ABRAHAM. Tess's brother. He accompanied her on the night-journey when the horse Prince was killed. Earlier he had asked many questions about the stars; he wished to know whether we live on a 'splendid' or a 'blighted' one. At this time he was nine years old.

TD. iii, iv, vi, xiv, li, lii

DURBEYFIELD, ELIZA LOUISA ('LIZA-LU). Tess's younger sister. She walked to Flintcomb-Ash from Marlott to tell Tess that their mother was ill. Before her arrest, Tess asked Angel to marry 'Liza-Lu; and they visited Tess together just before her execution at Wintoncester. She was 'a tall budding creature – half girl, half woman – a spiritualized image of Tess, slighter than she, but with the same beautiful eyes'.

TD. iii, iv, vii, xiv, xlix–lii, lviii, lix

DURBEYFIELD, HOPE and MODESTY. Younger sisters of 'Liza-Lu.
(The babes of the family were two boys.)   *TD*. iii, iv, vii, xiv, li, lii

DURBEYFIELD, JOAN. Before marrying John Durbeyfield, she had been
a dairymaid. She believed in ancient superstitions and folk-lore, and loved
to sing traditional songs and ballads, which she acquired by ear with
remarkable facility. When she and her eldest daughter were together,
'the Jacobean and Victorian ages were juxtaposed'. She had seven children
and was an affectionate mother despite all her difficulties. Visits to the
local alehouse afforded relief from the drabness and toil of home life.
She retained much of her early beauty, and Tess's good looks derived
from her. In promoting Tess's association with the 'd'Urbervilles' near
Trantridge, she had hopes that her daughter would marry advan-
tageously; Tess 'ought to make her way' with Alec, she said, 'if she
plays her trump card aright. And if he don't marry her afore he will
after. For that he's all afire wi' love for her any eye can see.' When Tess
wrote to her about her forthcoming marriage to Angel Clare, she warned
her not to 'say a word of your Bygone Trouble to him. I did not tell
everything to your Father, he being so proud on account of his Respecta-
bility'. Tess did tell, with catastrophic results. Her mother thought her a
fool. She had learned, however, to accept set-backs stoically: 'what's
done can't be undone!'

TD. iii–vii, xii-xiii, xvi, xxxi, xxxii, xxxviii, xli, xlix–liv

DURBEYFIELD, JOHN. Tess's father was a 'haggler' or local carrier.
He was rather a shiftless character, and preferred to work when it suited
him. Physically he was far from fit; he seemed to have convinced himself, and his wife, that he needed liquor to restore his strength. His lack
of will-power was shown in the way he 'celebrated' the news that he
belonged to a great historic family a few hours before he was due to set
off on business that night. As he was incapable of doing so, Tess took his
place, and the horse Prince was killed. This disaster and the news of his
aristocratic connections set in train the tragic course of events which
ruined Tess's life. He was the last of the 'liviers' to possess the home at
Marlott, and on his death his family was evicted. John Durbeyfield was
debilitated in body and mind; before his death, he had thought of in-
viting all the antiquarians in the area to support him; 'living remains'
with historic and romantic associations were more interesting than 'old

ruins', he said. 'How are the Mighty Fallen' was inscribed on his head-
stone.   *TD.* i–vii, xiv, xvi, xxxi, xxxviii, xlix–li, liv

DURBEYFIELD, TERESA ('TESS'). *The name was suggested by that of
Hardy's cousin, Teresa Hardy, who lived at Higher Bockhampton. When
the novel was published she told Hermann Lea that 'the main episodes
happened to a relative of theirs'. Another of Hardy's cousins (who lived at
Puddletown) stated that 'Tess's life and adventures and final death are
practically what happened to a relative of ours'. (Hermann Lea,* Thomas
Hardy through the Camera's Eye, *Toucan Press, 1964, 38, 43, 48*.)

She was the eldest of the Durbeyfield family, Between her mother
and Tess, with her National School education, lay 'a gap of two hundred
years', that between the Jacobean and the Victorian ages. Her sensitive
perceptiveness made her 'quite a Malthusian towards her mother for
thoughtlessly giving her so many little sisters and brothers, when it was
such a trouble to nurse and provide for them'. In order to help her
family, she went to work, as soon as she left school, on nearby farms,
hay-making, harvesting, and, preferably, milking and butter-making, as
she had learned to do at home when her father owned cows. A guilty
sense of responsibility for the death of her father's horse Prince impelled
her to accept employment at The Slopes, which she had visited when
her parents fondly thought they were related to the 'd'Urbervilles'
there, and had hopes that the link might work to Tess's advantage. Tess
overcame her reluctance to go, after forming an unfavourable impression
of Alec d'Urberville. She was a handsome girl, of a physical maturity
which belied her years. Alec had had one aim when he contrived to find
work for her, and his opportunity came when Tess accepted his protection to escape physical violence from the two 'Amazonian' Darch
sisters, as they were returning from their Saturday-night revels at
Chaseborough. 'Out of the frying-pan into the fire!' laughed dark Car's
mother. Lost in the Chase, Tess was at Alec's mercy, and he was ruthless:
'Doubtless some of Tess d'Urberville's mailed ancestors . . . had dealt
the same measure even more ruthlessly. . . .' Afterwards she forgot her
principles to the extent of accepting presents from him, but she soon
realized her folly, despised him, and left for home. Marriage to such a
man was out of the question, whatever her mother thought.

After the death of her child, Tess rallied and accepted work as a dairymaid at Talbothays. Here, from spring to autumn, she spent her happiest
days, though they were clouded at times by recollections of the past, and

increasingly when Angel Clare wanted to marry her. She felt she was not worthy of him, and tried to tell him about the past, but was baulked and deferred the task. She did not wish to stand in the way of the other dairymaids who were in love with Angel. But the time came when she could no longer refuse an answer to his proposals. She was in love with him, but wished that 'it would always be summer and autumn, and you always courting me, and always thinking as much of me as you have done through the past summer-time'. Despite her mother's advice, Tess had to tell the truth. She wrote to Angel, but the letter she slipped under his door was thrust under the carpet, and he did not see it. On the evening of the wedding-day, Angel confessed to dissipation with a woman in London. Tess readily forgave, and told her story. But, despite his intellectual freedom, Angel's love was so ideal and his Victorianism so engrained that he could not compromise; his idealized Tess was 'dead', and separation followed almost inevitably. Where a woman of the world might have prevailed, Tess accepted his decision 'as her deserts'. She 'sought not her own; was not provoked; thought no evil of his treatment of her.'

When Angel left for Brazil, she maintained herself by working on farms as far from Talbothays and her home as possible. Most of the money Angel left her she gave to her impecunious parents. She did not persist in her attempt to see Angel's parents at Emminster; the result was that she met Alec d'Urberville again, and his passions revived. The hardships she endured at Flintcomb-Ash made her conclude that there was no escaping the law: 'Once victim, always victim'. Hearing of her mother's illness, she left the farm at once, though it meant walking many miles in the dark. Her father's death and the eviction of the family from Marlott meant great distress, and the thought of it haunted her. Despairing of Angel's return, she gave way to Alec's importunities for the sake of her family, and went to live with him at Sandbourne. 'He was very kind to me, and to mother, and to all of us after father's death.' She had become a victim of circumstance. On his return, Angel saw 'that his original Tess had spiritually ceased to recognize the body before him as hers – allowing it to drift, like a corpse upon the current, in a direction dissociated from its living will'. Fate had tricked her, but to her agonized and overwrought mind it was Alec, who had always said Angel would never return, who had played her false; and she stabbed him to death (cf. *Life*, 221). Before her arrest, she enjoyed short-lived happiness with

Angel. When it came, she was glad. The end had to come, and she was ready for it.

Tess was a woman of high principles, with certain characteristics such as a careless and unselfish acceptance of her lot which at critical points contributed to the tragedy of her life after her early downfall. But chance, or fate, played a great part in directing her life along tragic courses. The most significant feature of Tess is that she expressly shows what to Hardy were the greatest virtues as enunciated by St Paul. (Cf. the references to xxxiii and xxxvi, p. 221, and the poem 'The Blinded Bird' (MV), the conclusion of which challenges comparison with the subtitle of Tess of the d'Urbervilles: 'A Pure Woman'. It seems impossible that Hardy could not have thought of Tess when he wrote this poem.)

TD. ii ff.; PPP. 'Tess's Lament'; SC. (?) 'Wessex Heights' (v, vi; cf. MV. 'The Head above the Fog');* WW. 'We Field-Women' (i, ii)

DURDLE-DOOR. *A rock which projects into the sea, forming a natural archway, west of Lulworth Cove.* HS. 'The Bird-Catcher's Boy'

DURNOVER. *Fordington, on the south-eastern side of Dorchester. Hardy was very familiar with it through friendship with Horace Moule, the son of the Rev. Henry Moule of Fordington. The name derives from 'Durnovaria', the Roman name (according to Hutchins) for their camp at Dorchester; it is a modification of the British name 'Dwrinwyr', which meant 'the settlement by the dark river'. This river, the Frome (the Blackwater of* The Mayor of Casterbridge*), flows through Fordington.*

After leaving Mr Maybold at Grey's Bridge, Dick Dewy turned left to collect a horse-collar at Durnover Mill (*i.e. by the corn-mill*).

Durnover Moor is a flat marshy meadowland through which the Frome and Cerne flow immediately east of Dorchester and Fordington. After collapsing by Grey's Bridge, Fanny Robin surveyed the road across the Moor into Casterbridge. It was along this road that Boldwood walked, after shooting Troy, to deliver himself up at the County Gaol. The Moor is referred to in *The Mayor of Casterbridge* (v, xxxvi, xl, xli).

It was at one of the farms on Durnover Hill that Susan Henchard

* Florence Hardy stated in a letter to Lady Alda Hoare that 'the four people mentioned [in 'Wessex Heights'] are actual women. One was dead and three living when it was written – now [6 December 1914] only one is living.' It is not clear precisely where the four are alluded to; nor can one be certain that Hardy had all of them in mind in his fiction.

arranged for Farfrae and Elizabeth-Jane to meet, hoping they would fall in love and marry. When Farfrae was dismissed by the jealous Henchard, he was induced to set up a corn business on Durnover Hill. Here were the farmyards of farmers who cultivated the open land south of Caster-bridge; 'wheat ricks overhung the old Roman street, and thrust their eaves against the church tower', and great barns 'were so numerous as to alternate with every half-dozen houses along the way'. The church with its great tower (*St. George's*) had been built on the old Roman-British burial-ground, where Susan Henchard was buried, and where Elizabeth-Jane met Lucetta. The 'less picturesque side' of Durnover was to be found lower down by the river, and especially along Mixen Lane (*Mill Street*), the 'Adullam' of all the surrounding villages. 'It was the hiding-place of those who were in distress, and in debt, and trouble of every kind.' The skimmington-ride against Henchard and Lucetta was planned at Peter's Finger inn, 'the church of Mixen Lane'.

Soon after the Reverend John Maumbry became curate at Durnover, cholera broke out. It was worst in Mixen Lane. His wife had been sent to Creston to avoid the plague. There, disappointed with her husband for not remaining in the army, she fell in love with a lieutenant. She decided to elope with him to Bristol. In the evening gloom they approached Casterbridge and turned to the right by the Roman amphitheatre, bearing round to Durnover Cross (*at the junction of Fordington Hill road and Standfast Road*). Further on, by Standfast Corner, they saw bonfires in Mixen Lane, where infested clothing was being burnt, and a vast copper where linen was being washed and disinfected. Here was her husband working industriously. He lived in a humble house at Durnover Cross. Laura decided she must stay to help him. Mr Maumbry caught cholera and died. The lieutenant returned and tried to persuade her to marry him. But she could not: between them moved the thin figure of her husband, 'moving to and fro in front of the ghastly furnace in the gloom of Durnover Moor'. (*The story is based upon the magnificent work done by the Reverend H. Moule to fight the cholera outbreaks at Fordington in 1849 and 1854.*)

Sergeant-Major John Clark of the —th Dragoons was buried in the churchyard at Durnover with full military honours. It was here that Selina, who claimed to be his widow 'in the eyes of Heaven', met his actual wife, whom he had married in the north of England soon after his return from the Crimea. See pp. 99–100.

Durnover – East Quarriers

The manor of Fordington belongs to the Duchy of Cornwall; its landed property to the south and west of Dorchester is extensive, and includes Fordington Field, north of the prehistoric camp of Mai-Dun (or Maiden Castle) – the 'Durnover Great Field and Fort' of 'The Alarm', though they are south-westerly from the point where the bird was released.

The effigy of 'Boney' (Napoleon Bonaparte) was burnt on the green, opposite the church on Durnover Hill.

The MS. of 'On Martock Moor' has a note, 'On Durnover Moor', which suggests that Hardy changed the location because the story was true. 'Weir-water' is by Ten Hatches (p. 262), the weir of 'Before My Friend Arrived', which commemorates the burial of Horace Moule in the churchyard of St George's, Fordington – 'the towered church on the rise'.

> UGT. iv vii; FMC. viii, xl, liv; MC. xiv, xv, xvii, xx, xxi, xxvi, xxvii, xxxii, xxxvi, xxxvii, xxxix; CM. 1; CM. 5; WP. 'The Alarm'; PPP. 'Winter in Durnover Field'; D. (3) v vi; TL. 'Bereft'; HS. 'The Fight on Durnover Moor', 'On Martock Moor' (cf. p. 402), 'Before My Friend Arrived' (see p. 420); WW. 'No Bell-Ringing'

EAST EGDON, *Affpuddle, three miles east of Puddletown.*

Eustacia and Clym Yeobright were married in the church at this small village near Alderworth. After a few weeks of happiness, Eustacia grew tired of life with a furze-cutter and no prospects of living in Paris, and decided to attend the 'gipsying' or afternoon picnic at East Egdon. Not meeting the cattle-dealer's wife who had suggested that she should come, she went on to a cottage for tea and returned to watch more dancing before returning home in the evening. She met Wildeve, and they joined in the dancing. 'To clasp as his for five minutes what was another man's through all the rest of the year was a kind of thing he of all men could appreciate.' The dance came 'like an irresistible attack upon whatever sense of social order there was in their minds, to drive them back into old paths which were now doubly irregular.' On their way to Throope Corner, Eustacia decided she would keep what company she chose, 'for all that may be said by the miserable inhabitants of Egdon'.

> RN. iii vi, vii, iv iii

EAST QUARRIERS. *Easton, Portland. See plate facing p. 399.*

Jocelyn Pierston had lived here in his youth. Here, too, not far from Sylvania Castle and Red-King Castle, lived the three generations of Avices, with whom he fell in love.　WB. i i–iii; ii iv, viii; iii i, v–vii

311

EDLIN, MRS. A kindly Marygreen widow who went to live with old Miss Drusilla Fawley (when Drusilla was bed-ridden). She attended for the wedding which failed to take place between Jude and Sue, and assisted when Sue was expecting her third child, and when she was remarried to Phillotson at Marygreen. She visited Christminster to see Jude when he was ill, and again for his funeral. 'Weddings be funerals 'a b'lieve nowadays. Fifty-five years ago, come Fall, since my man and I married! Times have changed since then!'

JO. II vi; III viii, ix; IV ii, vi; V iv, vii, viii; VI v, vi, ix, x, xi

EDWARD VII. *From the Athenaeum, Hardy watched the procession for the removal of the King's body to Westminster, and the procession of the funeral from Westminster three days later. These events suggested the poem* (Life, *350*). *SC.* 'A King's Soliloquy'

EGDON HEATH. *The heath extends eastward for about fourteen miles from Higher and Lower Bockhampton to the area north of Wareham and Poole Harbour* (cf. *the 1895 preface to* The Return of the Native). *The westerly portion provides the setting for this novel, and is the area usually designated by* 'Egdon'; *some of the eastern tracts constitute the background for scenes in* The Hand of Ethelberta. *For topographical detail see* ALDERWORTH, BLOOMS-END, EAST EGDON, MISTOVER, *the* QUIET WOMAN, RAINBARROWS, *the* ROMAN ROAD, RUSHY-POND, *and* SHADWATER WEIR.

The Heath behind the Hardy house at Higher Bockhampton is briefly described in 'Domicilium' (*Life*, 4). It is referred to in *Under the Greenwood Tree* as 'He'th'.

In *The Return of the Native*, Egdon Heath is more than a background (cf. pp. 32, 34). In the restricted terms of narrative time and place, it changes according to the season, weather, and hour of the day. The opening and closing scenes, which contribute most to the dominant impression and theme, are set in November and the gloom of evening or the storm of blackest night. Egdon, however, is seen in a variety of moods, according to season and temperament. Clym and Thomasin Yeobright are in sympathy with the heath, though for different reasons; Mrs Yeobright is not at home there, and it contributes to her death. Wildeve, 'the Rousseau of Egdon', is not there by choice, and abhors it. But it is Eustacia who suffers most: "Tis my cross, my shame, and will be my death'. She dominates the novel, and it is in consonance with her moods that Egdon assumes a preponderance of tragic gloom.

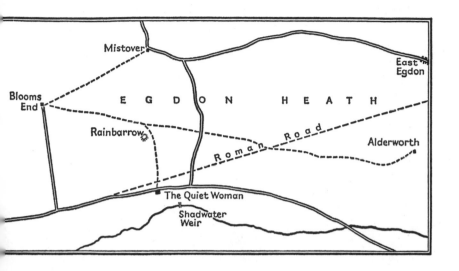

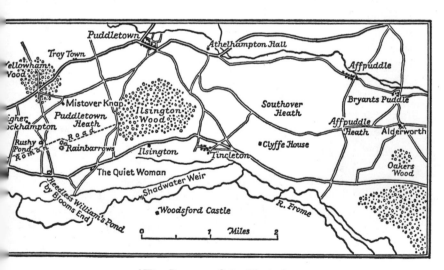

'*The Return of the Native*'
above: setting, from Hardy's map
below: country of its origin

Seasonal changes provide the most vivid contrast to the dominant gloom or darkness in July, when the heath, with its crimson heather 'fired' to scarlet, is 'gorgeous'. The most significant backgrounds, however, are more than seasonal, and harmonize with moods and events. After an ecstatic meeting with Eustacia, when 'All dark objects on the earth that lay towards the sun were overspread by a purple haze', the 'dead flat of the scenery overpowered' Clym, and 'gave him a sense of bare equality with, and no superiority to, a single living thing under the sun'. Awareness of antagonism between his mother and Eustacia had revived. It is felt even more strongly when he proceeds to Alderworth to prepare the home where he was to enjoy short-lived but supreme happiness in the July when Egdon was 'gorgeous'; he passes a fir and beech plantation where 'at every onset of the gale convulsive sounds came from the branches, as if pain were felt'. (*Here, incidentally, we have a foretaste of Housman's 'gale of life'.*)

Before Egdon's relative timelessness, man is insignificant, whether it is Clym in his Oedipus mood, or the Celtic and Roman civilizations; its superficial irregularities, originating in a far remoter period, are but the 'finger-touches of the last geological change'. It resists and absorbs civilizations, and endures 'unmoved', an 'untameable, Ishmaelitish thing', awaiting 'the final overthrow'.

'Slighted and enduring', in the sombre light of evening it is more in accord with the outlook of modern man than more beautiful scenes. In this characteristic mood, it reveals its 'great and particular glory'; and its countenance, like Clym's, is expressive of 'the view of life as a thing to be put up with'. 'The most thorough-going ascetic could feel that he had a natural right to wander on Egdon.'

To some its 'lonely face' might suggest 'tragical possibilities'. The storm was its lover, the wind its friend, and imminent darkness its ally. From time immemorial, man's protest against encroaching winter or darkness, deprivation and oppression, has found its ritualistic expression or symbol in fire. For Eustacia, Egdon was Hades. 'A true Tartarean dignity sat upon her brow', and her Promethean rebelliousness against destiny had its physical analogue in the bonfires which set in motion the opening and concluding events of the story, and which are her signal of protest and call for deliverance. She is the victim of Egdon; she rebels against the inevitable. Clym does otherwise. He tells her that he could 'rebel, in high Promethean fashion, against the gods and fate', but he is more philosophical and endures in the hope of doing good to his fellow-man.

For Eustacia, Egdon is a symbol of destiny to be rebelled against; for Clym, of a life to be endured with hope but not with overweening expectation. For the philosophical Hardy (whose recurrent views coincide with Clym's), it is an expression of almost timeless endurance against which the turmoil of a single man like Clym is a mere insignificance. It can be indifferent or cruel in the storms of winter or the torrid heat of summer. It can be intensely beautiful. It is like life; it reflects the moods and temperaments of individuals. It is not the same for Thomasin as it is for Clym or Eustacia, and it is not precisely the same for any one of these as it is for Hardy. He was capable of sharing and sympathizing with all these moods, but, more than any other, it expressed the inevitable, and was fraught with tragic possibilities.

All the incidents of the main story (omitting the epilogue) take place in a small area, and the number of actual localities which enter the novel under real or fictitious names is unusually small. The action is concentrated with greater regard for 'unity of place' than in any other of Hardy's novels; few places outside Egdon Heath, apart from Budmouth and Paris, are referred to, and their relevance to the central theme is obvious. It is worth noting that Wessex places in the immediate neighbourhood, such as Caster-bridge and Weatherbury, receive hardly a mention. The church, not to be confused with that at East Egdon where Clym and Eustacia are married, is unlocalized. It is two or three miles away for the inhabitants of Egdon Heath (II iv), and it has a gallery (II viii). Hardy may have had Stinsford or West Stafford in mind. The reference to Weatherbury (I iii) seems to rule out Puddletown.

After Henchard had made his final departure from Casterbridge, his wedding-present to Elizabeth-Jane and Farfrae was discovered; 'her heart softened towards the self-alienated man', and she and her husband inquired the way he had gone. 'They searched Egdon, but found no Henchard.' Later, in 'the neighbourhood of some extension of the heath to the north of Anglebury', they met Abel Whittle, and heard his account of Henchard's death. On their way they had skirted the north of Egdon Heath, where tumuli 'jutted roundly into the sky from the uplands, as though they were the full breasts of Diana Multimammia supinely extended there' (cf. *TL. 'By the Barrows'*).

Rhoda Brook lived near the southern edge of Egdon Heath. She accompanied Gertrude Lodge (the withering of whose arm she seems to have caused by a malignant spell beyond her control) across the heath to Conjuror Trendle's. Later, Gertrude visited the conjurer alone; he told her that she must lay her withered arm on the neck of a hanged man to effect a cure. When she journeyed to Casterbridge for this purpose, Gertrude rode across Egdon Heath to avoid publicity. The year was 1825, and most of the heath was open, with little cultivation and few enclosures. *Here (and again in the 1895 preface to* The Return of the Native) *Hardy suggests that Egdon Heath may have been the same 'which had witnessed the agony of the Wessex King Ina, presented to after-ages as Lear'.*

Tess walked over Egdon Heath to reach the Valley of the Great Dairies. One evening she accompanied Angel Clare as he drove with the milk to Wellbridge station. The meadows were remotely backed by 'the swarthy and abrupt slopes' of the heath, on which stood 'clumps and stretches of firs, whose notched tips appeared like battlemented towers crowning black-fronted castles of enchantment'.

When Caroline Aspent (Mrs Hipcroft) collapsed after dancing to his music at the Quiet Woman Inn, Ollamoor made off with 'little Carry'. Search was made on Egdon Heath just opposite, but concealment was too easy there on an autumn evening: 'Outside the house, on the other side of the highway, a mass of dark heath-land rose sullenly upward to its not easily accessible interior, a ravined plateau, whereon jutted into the sky, at the distance of a couple of miles, the fir-woods of Mistover backed by the Yalbury coppices – a place of Dantesque gloom at this hour, which would have afforded secure hiding for a battery of artillery, much less (*sic*) a man and a child.'

Local tradition maintained that the beacon-alarm was signalled to indicate that the French had landed in West Bay. Hardy seemed uncertain about the date. In The Trumpet-Major *he ascribes the landing to 1805, the year of Trafalgar. In the first edition of* Wessex Poems *he gave 1803 for 'The Alarm' (the MS. indicates 1804: Purdy, 100); later he altered it to 'Traditional'. In* The Dynasts *he gives 1805. The scene here, as in 'The Alarm', is Rainbarrows. Historical records show that this was the year when defensive measures in south Dorset reached their peak.*

'Domicilium'; *UGT.* v i; *HE.* i iii, xliv; *RN.* especially i i–iii, vi, vii, x; ii i–iii, v, vi; iii ii, v, vi; iv i–ii, v–viii; v ii, iii, v, vi, vii–ix; vi i, iv; *MC.* xlv; *WT.* 4; *TD.* xvi, xxi, xxx, lii, lv; *LLI.* 7; *WP.* 'The Alarm', 'A Meeting with

Despair' (*the MS. indicates Egdon Heath: Purdy*), 'The Slow Nature'; *PPP*. 'In Tenebris', iii; *D*. (1) II v; *TL*. 'By the Barrows' (for 'Diana Multimammia', cf. *MC*. above, and – on the chalk uplands – 'Cybele the Many-breasted', *TD*. xlii); *SC*. 'The Moth-Signal' (cf. *RN*. IV iv). *MV*. 'On a Heath' (see p. 439), 'Before Marching and After' (see p. 181); *LLE*. 'At Moonrise and Onwards'; *HS*. 'The Sheep-Boy' (*Kite Hill is south-west of Puddle-town; Pokeswell Hills are the downs near Poxwell*), 'The Paphian Ball'. See also references in the opening paragraph.

ELIZABETH-JANE (1). The daughter of Michael Henchard and Susan. When Henchard sold his wife at Weydon-Priors, she took Elizabeth-Jane with her and emigrated to Canada with Newson. The child died three months after the sale.   *MC*. i, xix

(2) It is part of the tragic irony of the story, and of Henchard's nemesis, that his affection for the second Elizabeth-Jane is rooted in the assumption that she was his daughter. He did not discover that she was Newson's daughter until after Susan's death.

On her first appearance she was about eighteen, 'completely possessed of that ephemeral precious essence youth, which was itself beauty'; she was devoted to her mother, and showed a strong respectability-complex. Accustomed to hard work, she did not hesitate to serve at the Three Mariners, where she felt her mother could ill afford to stay. She had learnt from experience and anxiety not to be light-hearted. She was reasonable in everything, and especially in her dress and appearance when she enjoyed relative affluence, after her mother's remarriage to Henchard. She possessed natural insight but lacked accomplishments, which she tried to gain by disciplined study, only to earn Henchard's ill-tempered disapproval after he had discovered that she was Newson's daughter. Before her death, Susan had done her simple best to bring Elizabeth and Farfrae together, but Henchard's jealousy and folly were such that he forbad their meeting. Though Henchard had informed her that she was his daughter before he learnt the truth, and chose not to undeceive her, he treated her with such impatience and disapproval after learning that she had demeaned herself by serving at the Three Mariners that she chose to live with the lady Lucetta, who had come to live at High-Place Hall. He had relented sufficiently, however, to allow Farfrae to renew his courtship, but the 'subtle-souled' girl knew intuitively how swift was the course of love between Lucetta and Farfrae. She endured stoically, isolated in her suffering, just as Henchard was at this time. 'She had learnt the lesson of renunciation, and was as familiar with the wreck of each day's wishes as with the diurnal setting of the sun.' When she knew that she had lost Farfrae to Lucetta, she left High-Place Hall and considered how she could earn an independent living. It was her lot to look after Henchard in his humiliation, to warn Farfrae of his threats, and to try to spare Lucetta the sight of the skimmington-ride. After Lucetta's death, she and her stepfather lived together for a period, and Henchard's affection for her grew until he could not bear to part with her. It was this that had prompted him to tell Newson his daughter was dead, and reawakened his jealous possessiveness when he discovered that Farfrae was courting her again. Newson's return completely unmanned him, and he left Casterbridge. Elizabeth and Farfrae were married, and Henchard returned in the hope of forgiveness, but Elizabeth upbraided him for having kept her from her father for five years. When she discovered his wedding-present, with the goldfinch starved in the cage in the garden where Henchard had left it, her heart softened and she could not rest until she had found him and reached reconciliation. It was too late. She lived with Farfrae in 'equable serenity', neither proud nor elated like Lucetta. She had reached a kind of wisdom of which her author approved. Like Hardy, she did not assume that life offered 'overmuch'. Hers were the 'Minerva-eyes of one "whose gestures" ' were ' "beamed with mind" '. Her tragedy is diminished by Henchard's, but it is persistent. (*To Hardy she was probably the most percipient and unexceptionable of his heroines.*) *MC.* iii ff.

ELM-CRANLYNCH (*named after Great Elm and Cranmore, near Frome, Somerset*). The home of Charles Phelipson. *GND.* 1

ELSENFORD. *Ilsington Farm on the south side of the road to Tincleton.*
The farmstead of Nicholas Long in the Froom valley, in the parish adjoining Froom-Everard. *CM.* 2

EMMELINE. The daughter of the Honourable and Reverend Mr Oldbourne, rector of the parish of Batton. She was attached to the curate, Alwyn Hill, but compelled to marry the Duke of Hamptonshire, who lived at Batton Castle. For her story, see pp. 61–2. *GND.* 9

EMMINSTER. *Beaminster, six miles north of Bridport.*
Angel Clare's father was the vicar of Emminster. Tess's memorable walk over the hills from Flintcomb-Ash to seek the support of Mr and

Mrs Clare (who were the kind of people not to refuse help had she persisted in her effort to see them) led ironically to her final disaster. They were out. On the way back she met Alec d'Urberville.

DBC (pp. 59–61); *TD.* xxv, xxxi, xxxiv, xxxix, xl, xliv, liii

ENCKWORTH COURT. *Encombe House, in a beautiful valley which runs down to the sea west of Swanage and St Alban's Head. Some of its features and history, however, were transferred from Kingston Maurward House at Stinsford; cf. HE. xxxviii and* KNAPWATER HOUSE.

The residence of Lord Mountclere and, ultimately, of the designing Ethelberta Petherwin (*née* Chickerel).

Old Mrs Chundle lived three miles away, and had never seen it.

HE. xxx–xxxii, *xxxviii*, xliv–xlvii, Sequel; *OMC* (p. 84)

ENDELSTOW. *Based on the village of St Juliot, Cornwall, where Hardy met his first wife, and probably named after St Endellion, a village twelve miles to the south-west. Hardy disguised the topography, and in 1919 expressed the wish that he had found time to correct it (Sydney Cockerell, Friends of a Lifetime; cf. the 1912 preface to* A Pair of Blue Eyes).

The description of Endelstow House (v) is of special interest, since it seems to indicate that Hardy and Miss Gifford had visited her father, a retired solicitor, at Kirland House near Bodmin before the summer of 1872. Much of it is drawn from Lanhydrock House; see plate facing p. 79. The first five chapters (the first instalment) of the novel were hurriedly completed before Hardy set out for Cornwall in August 1872 (Life, *91*).

In the novel there are two churches, that at West Endelstow, which was to be restored, and the other at East Endelstow, which contained the Luxellian family vault.

PBE. especially ii, iv, v, vi, xviii, xix, xxv–xxvii, xxxii, xl

ENDORFIELD, ELIZABETH. *The name was suggested by the witch of Endor, 1 Sam. xxviii.*

A Deep Body, locally thought to be a witch. Fancy Day took refuge in her house at Higher Mellstock (*Higher Bockhampton*) from a storm, and was given advice on how to make her father consent to her marrying Dick Dewy.   *UGT.* IV iii, iv

ENOCH. Geoffrey's Day's trapper.   *UGT.* II vi, IV ii, iv, v i

ESTMINSTER. *Yetminster, south-east of Yeovil.*

The story, relating to John Horsey (d. 1531) and his wife Elizabeth Turges of Melcombe, is based on Hutchins, iv 456. (Another version is to be found in MV. 'The Memorial Brass: 186–'.)   *LLE.* 'The Inscription'

ETHELBERTA. The daughter of a butler named Chickerel. She became a pupil-teacher, and then a governess in the house of Sir Ralph Petherwin. She looked the lady, 'skilfully perfected in manner, carriage, look, and accent'. At Solentsea, she met Christopher Julian, only to jilt him and marry Sir Ralph's son, who died soon after the marriage. Sir Ralph died shortly afterwards, and Lady Petherwin sent Ethelberta to Bonn to complete her education. She is seen on her return at Anglebury with her mother-in-law, and at her London house in Exonbury Crescent, which she occupied after Lady Petherwin's death (with her mother and brothers and sisters) in order to gain an income as a 'Professed Story-teller' at Mayfair Hall. She had written poems, which Lady Petherwin had thought scandalous when published; and a quarrel on this question led to Ethelberta's being cut off without a legacy. She had many admirers, including Mr Ladywell, a painter, and Mr Neigh. She would have married Mr Julian, if only he had been rich. She wanted someone who could provide for herself and family, and someone whom she could respect. Though she posed as a lady, she was always loyal to her family, and sometimes she could wish to be Berta Chickerel again 'and live in a green cottage' as she did when a child. Ultimately she consented to marry an old roué, Lord Mountclere, who skilfully parried all attempts to prevent the union. Ethelberta's managerial proclivities were soon shown; she took over the administration of the Enckworth estate, saved Mountclere from bankruptcy, and made him live a regular and respectable life. 'The Hand of Ethelberta' has a twofold implication.   *HE*

ETHLEEN.   *MV*. 'A Thought in Two Moods'

EVERARD, CHRISTINE. The daughter of the squire of Froom-Everard House. The local rector refused to marry her and Nicholas Long without her father's consent. Nicholas went abroad to improve his wealth and status, but in the meantime Christine married Mr Bellston, the nephew of the squire of Athelhall. He was cruel to her, and left her for foreign travel. When Nicholas returned, he was affluent and she was poor. They would have married had not news arrived, with Bellston's portmanteau, that her husband was returning. Years passed, and the lovers met, but Mr Bellston did not arrive. Many years later, Bellston's skeleton was found in the Froom behind Froom-Everard House. By this time Christine had lost the will to marry. *For the ending* ('*Is it worth while?*'), *compare the poem 'Long Plighted' (PPP).*   *CM*. 2

EVERARD, SQUIRE. He was agreeable to a marriage between Christine and Bellston. When he heard that she and Nicholas Long had attempted to marry, he urged them to marry, but with such resignation and evident disapproval that Nicholas decided he would go abroad and improve his fortune before returning to win his favour.   *CM.* 2

EVERDENE, BATHSHEBA. When Gabriel Oak met her at Norcombe Hill, she was a young and attractive woman, but suffering, he thought, from vanity. Nevertheless, he proposed to her, but she rejected him. Until she met Troy, she was proud of being a woman and had never thought seriously of marriage. 'Although she scarcely knew the divinity's name, Diana was the goddess whom Bathsheba instinctively adored.'

Oak met her again when he was seeking employment; she had taken over Weatherbury Upper Farm on the sudden death of her uncle, James Everdene. She needed a shepherd, and promptly accepted Oak's services after he had helped to extinguish the fire which threatened one of her ricks. At the Corn Exchange in Casterbridge she excited much comment, and it was the indifference of Farmer Boldwood which prompted her to send a valentine, with the most unfortunate consequences. Gabriel remonstrated against her behaviour when it was obvious that she had aroused Boldwood's interest, and was immediately dismissed. An emergency with the sheep made Bathsheba request his return.

Against her better judgment, she became infatuated with Sergeant Troy. She was so alarmed by the vague threats of the jealous Boldwood that she decided impulsively one night to drive off alone to Bath to warn Troy and sever connections with him. Admiration, fear of scandal from seeking out Troy in Bath, and the jealousy which he had succeeded in rousing, resulted, however, in her consenting to an immediate marriage. Events soon revealed his hollowness and his intention to pursue pleasure even if it meant her ruin. His perfidy was disclosed when jealous curiosity made Bathsheba open the coffin containing Fanny Robin and her child. Still she wished to cling to him, but Troy, overcome with contrition and a sense of his baseness, left her. He was presumed drowned, and Boldwood renewed his suit. Bathsheba kept postponing an engagement to which her heart could not consent. However, she promised to declare her decision at a Christmas party Boldwood held in her honour. Troy's sudden irruption and his seizure of Bathsheba's hand was too much for the overwrought Boldwood, who promptly shot him dead. Bathsheba took charge of her husband, had his body conveyed to her house, and prepared him, without assistance, for burial. 'She was of the stuff of which great men's mothers are made.' Afterwards she felt that life held nothing further for her. Nevertheless, when Oak talked of emigrating, she realized how much she had come to depend on him, and readily consented to marry him. Theirs was the love which grows up gradually 'in the interstices of . . . hard prosaic reality', the only love, Hardy adds, which is capable of being as 'strong as death'. *FMC*

EVERDENE, JAMES. Bathsheba's uncle, and tenant of Weatherbury Upper Farm. He was a good-hearted fellow, according to Jan Coggan, who was allowed to drink as much ale as he liked when he went to court his first wife at the farmhouse. Farmer Everdene died suddenly, and Bathsheba took over his farm; she refurnished the house, and dismissed the bailiff Pennyways for stealing. Everdene is mentioned twice in *The Mayor of Casterbridge*. *FMC*. viii, xv; *MC*. xvii, xxxi

EVERDENE, LEVI. Bathsheba's father. He lived in Casterbridge – ''a was a gentleman-tailor really, worth scores of pounds. And he became a very celebrated bankrupt two or three times.' He was inordinately fond of his wife, according to the gossips of Weatherbury – 'fond enough of her as his sweetheart'. It was said that he cured his roving heart by 'making her take off her wedding-ring and calling her by her maiden name' after the shop was shut. . . . 'And as soon as he could thoroughly fancy he was doing wrong and committing the seventh, 'a got to like her as well as ever . . .'. 'He used, too, to hold the money-plate at Let Your Light so Shine, and stand godfather to poor little come-by-chance children. . . .' In the newspaper announcement of his wedding to Bathsheba which Sergeant Troy handed Boldwood, her father's name is given as John Everdene. *FMC*. viii, xxxiv

EVERSHEAD. *Evershot, twelve miles north-west of Dorchester.*

On their journey to The Knap, Philip Hall and his family passed through Evershead, where he 'looked in' at the Sow-and-Acorn Inn (*The Acorn; see plate facing p. 398*) 'to see if old Mike still kept on there as usual.'

Among the friends whom Squire Dornell invited to his carousal at King's Hintock Court, in the absence of his wife and daughter, was the doctor from Evershead. Later, the squire sent his 'trusty servant' Tupcombe from Falls-Park to Evershead to find out what he could about Betty's marriage in London. Tupcombe obtained his information from a seat in the chimney-corner of the Sow-and-Acorn Inn.

On her way from Flintcomb-Ash to see Angel's parents at Emminster, Tess stopped to have breakfast at Evershead, 'not at the Sow-and-Acorn, for she avoided inns, but at a cottage by the church'. On her way back, she was amazed to see Alec d'Urberville preaching in a barn at Evershead.

Christopher Swetman's visitor at King's Hintock (traditionally assumed to be the Duke of Monmouth) left via Clammers Gate and took the road through King's Hintock Park to Evershead.

WT. 6; *GND.* 1; *TD.* xliv; *CM.* 10

EXETER. *For Hardy's visit, see Life, 364, 370; note also 404.*

MV. 'In a Museum'. See EXONBURY

EXON MOOR. *Exmoor, in north Devon, where Dunkery Beacon rises to a height of 1,707 feet.* *SC.* 'The Sacrilege'

EXONBURY. *Exeter, in south Devon.*

As there was no national (i.e. Church) school at Endelstow, Stephen Smith was sent to live with his uncle to attend a school near Exonbury. It was here that he first met Henry Knight. Later he was apprenticed to an architect in Exonbury.

For a period, John Loveday's regiment was moved from Budmouth to Exonbury Barracks. Anne Garland wrote to him there.

The main setting for the astonishing adventures of Margery Tucker is the Exe valley, north of Exonbury (*formerly the 'Swenn' valley, east of Casterbridge*), where she had hoped to attend the Yeomanry Ball in the Assembly Rooms before Baron von Xanten recommended a similar one at Lord Toneborough's. The military Review which she attended on some high ground just outside the city excited her jealousy, and contributed much towards her final acceptance of Jim Hayward as husband.

Grace Melbury's wedding-dress was made at Exonbury, and she hoped to escape there when she learned that her husband Fitzpiers was returning after his stay on the Continent with Mrs Charmond.

Mrs Frankland and her daughter taught music and dancing at Exonbury. Frances helped to decorate the churches at Easter and Christmas, was organist at one of them, and contributed 'to the testimonial of a silver broth-basin that was presented to the Reverend Mr Walker as a token of gratitude for his faithful and arduous intonations of six months as sub-precentor in the Cathedral'.

The towers of the Cathedral are the Exon Towers of 'The Carrier'. Sidwell Church is in Sidwell Street, Exeter, on the road which runs north-east towards Taunton. *PBE.* viii; *TM.* xxi, xxiv; *CM.* 12; *W.* xxiv, xl, xlii; *LLI.* 3; *WP.* 'My Cicely'; *HS.* 'The Carrier'

EXONBURY CRESCENT (LONDON). Here was the house which Ethelberta inherited for the remainder of its lease from Lady Petherwin, her mother-in-law. She soon contrived a scheme by which her family – all but her father, who was butler at the Doncastles' – could live there, without revealing her humble connections.

This part of the plot is a variant of a scheme Hardy's mother had put into effect before her marriage; see p. 29.

HE. x, xi, xvii–xix, xxii–xxiv, xxvi, xxviii–xxix, xxxvi

FAIRLAND. *Probably Higher Bockhampton (cf. the quotation below, the 'hermit-group of dwellings' in CM. 5, and Life, 99).*

The village next to Tollamore, where Egbert Mayne took lodgings 'such . . . as a hermit would desire' when he returned from London. Here Geraldine Allenville sought refuge to avoid her marriage with Lord Bretton. *ILH.* II 4–6

FAIRMILE HILL-TOP. *On the main-road, ten miles east of Exeter.*

TL. 'The Dear'

FAIRWAY, TIMOTHY. A turf-cutter on Egdon Heath. He lived at Blooms-End and was the local 'hair-cutter' on Sunday mornings. His references to the monument in Weatherbury church and the playing of Thomasin's father at Kingsbere church suggest not that he had attended church more frequently than most of the Egdon inhabitants but that he was very observant and an experienced story-teller. He was 'a firm-standing man of middle age, who kept each corner of his crescent-shaped mouth rigorously drawn back into his cheek, as if to do away with any suspicion of mirthfulness . . .'. *RN.* I iii,

v, ix; II iv, vi; III i, ii, iii, vii; IV vii; V vii, viii; VI i, iv

FALCON HOTEL, THE. At St Launce's (*Launceston, Cornwall*). Here Elfride Swancourt changed from equestrian to ordinary dress before travelling by train to London via Plymouth to marry Stephen Smith. The landlady was 'a distinguished-looking lady, with the demeanour of a duchess'. *PBE.* xi, xii, xxxvi

FALL, CONJUROR. For Henchard's visit to consult him about the weather, see p. 132. He lived somewhere to the west of Casterbridge. He was thought to be a good prophet at one time, but his reputation declined rapidly in later years; 'he's rotten as touchwood by now,' said Jonathan Kail. *MC.* xxvi; *TD.* xxi

FALLS-PARK. *The manor house of Mells Park, near Frome, Somerset, which belonged to the Horner family.*

The home of Squire Dornell, to which he was wont to retire after an altercation with his wife Susan of King's Hintock Court. She thought it an 'outlandish place', but its 'Palladian front, of the period of the first Charles, derived from its regular features a dignity which the great, many gabled, heterogeneous mansion of his wife could not eclipse'. The two residences were over twenty miles apart.   *GND.* 1

FALMOUTH. First news of the battle of Trafalgar came to Falmouth with dispatches brought by the schooner *Pickle*.

Susan Henchard lived here with Newson and their daughter Elizabeth-Jane after their stay in Canada. When news reached them of Newson's death at sea, Susan set off with her daughter to find her former husband, Michael Henchard.

Mr Heddegan had planned a honeymoon tour as far as Plymouth, but, after her shocking experiences at Pen-zephyr, Baptista was unable to travel beyond Falmouth.   *TM.* xxxv; *MC.* iv, xli; *CM.* 11

FARFRAE, DONALD. *The name indicates the wistfulness of a Scot, 'far frae hame'.*

A young Scot who happened to be travelling through Casterbridge on his way to America, where he would have more scope for his discoveries relating to the corn business. He was able to help Henchard in a crisis, and the Mayor took to him greatly. He needed friendship and an able manager for his corn business, and persuaded Farfrae to stay. The superiority of Farfrae's business methods and modern outlook were soon obvious, and all might have been well for Henchard but for the overpowering jealousy which certain incidents engendered. As a result, he not only dismissed Farfrae but refused to allow him to continue his courtship of Elizabeth-Jane. Farfrae was persuaded to stay in Casterbridge, and set up business on Durnover Hill, but he scrupulously avoided competition with Henchard, who ruined himself by rash speculation in the hope of ruining his rival. The two were rivals for Lucetta, and Henchard lost. Farfrae was not generous as a business man (Abel Whittle, for example, was paid a shilling a week less under him than under Henchard), but he did his best to help Henchard. Henchard was too proud to accept assistance, and preferred humiliation as a labourer in Farfrae's yard. By this time, Farfrae had taken over his business, his house, and Lucetta. To add to Henchard's gall, he quickly became Mayor and had the distinction of receiving the Royal visitor. At the point of extreme humiliation for the one, and extreme elevation for the other,

Henchard's enmity reached its climax and would have resulted in Farfrae's death, had Henchard's better nature not got the upper hand when he had Farfrae at his mercy. After the death of Lucetta, Henchard was schooled by experience and accepted the help which Farfrae as Mayor had always been disposed to give him. Farfrae accepted the loss of Lucetta philosophically: he had exchanged 'a looming misery for a simple sorrow . . . it was hard to believe that life with her would have been productive of further happiness'. When his friendship with Elizabeth-Jane was resumed, Henchard became even more intransigently opposed to losing her. She was his all; he had even deceived her father Newson to keep her. Newson's second return to Casterbridge removed Henchard and all opposition, and the marriage was quickly arranged. Farfrae's popularity had diminished as his success grew, but it may be assumed that he remained an astute and prosperous businessman.

Personally he was likeable and attractive, but his head seems to have developed at the expense of his heart, though he indulged in romantic songs and sentiments about his native land. When he is searching for Henchard on the heath, and when he hears of his death, his comments are quite inadequate. *Compared with Whittle he seems heartless. The suggestion of satire is confirmed by Hardy's comment towards the end of the novel, where we read that at his wedding festivities Farfrae gave 'strong expression to a song of his dear native country, that he loved so well as never to have revisited it'.*

He is introduced as young, handsome, romantic, and musical, exerting a great spell on Henchard. *In this role, he is David to Saul, as Hardy disclosed when he added in his 1912 revision that he was 'ruddy and of a fair countenance'* (cf. *1 Samuel xvi 12, and the Henchard–Saul parallelism in the novel*). MC. vi–ix, xii, xiv–xxvii, xxix–xlv

FARINGDON RUIN. *A gable end in the meadowland west of Came House is all that remains of the church which once stood here with its village. See plate facing p. 175.*

John Loveday was walking in the direction of Casterbridge when he met Anne Garland; they rambled on until they came to the ruin, in the middle of a field. Anne had at last realized the nobility of a brother who was ready to sacrifice her, and his own feelings, for the sake of his less deserving brother; but, however much she turned the conversation towards marriage ('Here where I sit must have been the altar . . .'), John pretended to be blind to her overtures and remained loyal to his brother.

Soon afterwards he left with his regiment and was killed in Spain.

TM. xxxviii

FARNFIELD. *Near Farnham, Surrey, and 'thirty or forty miles out of London in a south-westerly direction'*. See NEIGH.   *HE*. xxv, xxvi

'(LITTLE) FATHER TIME'. Jude's son was born in Australia after his parents had separated. He was brought up out there by Arabella's parents, and sent to England after her. She sent him immediately to Jude and Sue at Aldbrickham. 'He was Age masquerading as Juvenility' and doing it badly; 'his face took a back view over some great Atlantic of Time, and appeared to care not about what it saw.' He had known little love, and when he asked Sue if he could call her mother began to cry. Jude and Sue took him to their hearts; his face, Sue said, was like the tragic mask of Melpomene. He retained the nickname he had been given in Australia because he looked so old. When, at Christminster, Sue was worrying about where they would find rooms the next day, he said that she would have less trouble without him; he knew that she need not have had him, and decided in his logical way that he was a trouble wherever he was. She then told him why she was so worried: she was expecting another baby soon. It was more than he could bear. That night he hanged Sue's two children and himself. He left a piece of paper on which was written 'Done because we are too menny'. (He seems to bear the sin and grief of the whole world, and the death-scene and Hardy's comments remotely suggest the Crucifixion, to which 'the rashness of those parents' – *echoing Milton on the Fall* – may be related.) *The poem 'Midnight on the Great Western' raises certain questions. Did Hardy see such a boy himself, and was this experience the origin of Father Time in the novel? Or was the poem, like several others, the by-product of his fiction? The manner of the poem suggests an actual encounter, and the difference in time should be noted; in the novel the boy was travelling in the train which was due to arrive at Aldbrickham at 10 p.m.*

JO. v iii–vii, vi i, ii; *MV*. 'Midnight on the Great Western'

FAWLEY, MISS DRUSILLA. Jude's great-aunt, who ran a small bakery business at Marygreen. She was a 'tall, gaunt woman, who spoke tragically on the most trivial subject'. When Jude was at Christminster, she found that she was unable to leave her bed, and sold her business. Mrs Edlin came to live with her. So disastrous had been their parents' marriages that Miss Fawley advised Jude never to marry, and was opposed to Sue's marriage to Phillotson. She was most anxious that Jude should

not meet his cousin Sue at Christminster: the Fawleys were not made for
marriage, and their marriage would turn out worse than his marriage
with Arabella. Drusilla was ill for a long period, but died suddenly.

        JO. I i, ii, iv, vi, ix, xi; II i, ii, vi, vii; III viii, ix; IV ii
FAWLEY, JUDE. *The surname is identical with the name of the Berkshire
village where several of Hardy's ancestors had lived, the 'Marygreen' of
the novel. Of special interest is the fact that Jude's first surname was 'Head',
the name of Hardy's paternal grandmother, who lived there when she was
a girl; cf.* Life, *420. Whether 'Jude' has Scriptural significance is uncertain.*

    *According to Florence Hardy (letter to Lady Hoare, 30 July 1915),
Jude was drawn partly from the husband of Hardy's mother's sister at
Puddletown; he was 'a very clever man, and a good classical scholar'.*

Jude was handicapped from the start. His parents had quarrelled and
parted when he was a baby. His mother had drowned herself, and his
father then left for South Wessex. Jude was sent from Mellstock to live
with his great-aunt Drusilla Fawley at Marygreen, a gaunt woman with
little evident sweetness of disposition, though much pity for the boy, and
a tragic outlook on life. He was an 'idle young harlican', and it would have
been better, she told him in front of her neighbours, if 'Goddy-mighty'
had taken the 'poor useless boy' with his mother and father. Jude first
learned that he was in a world which had no place for charity from
Farmer Troutham; his next disillusionment came when, having faithfully performed his part of their bargain, he found that the quack-doctor
Vilbert had forgotten to purchase the grammars he needed for study.
He aimed at admission to Christminster, as his schoolmaster Mr Phillotson had done. He made prodigious progress at Latin and Greek by his
own unaided efforts, stealing every moment he could for study, even
when driving along roads and lanes to deliver Miss Fawley's bread. With
no one to whom he could turn for advice, he believed he could work as a
stone-mason while pursuing his studies at Christminster, and for this
reason he became apprenticed to a stone-mason at Alfredston. It was while
dreaming of Christminster and of becoming a bishop that he first
encountered Arabella Donn, and found that he was overpowered by something stronger than reason and will. His seduction followed, and, being
guileless and tender-hearted ('Never such a tender fool as Jude is if a
woman seems in trouble,' said Arabella later), he was soon tricked into
marriage, though he knew 'that Arabella was not worth a great deal as a

specimen of womankind'. He wished to commit suicide; fortunately, Arabella left him. But the marriage remained; he was 'caught in a gin which would cripple him . . . for the rest of a lifetime'. He thought he could 'battle with his evil star' and try Christminster. Here he worked as a stone-mason, fell in love with his cousin Sue Bridehead, and sought advice from colleges. All his appeals but one fell on deaf ears; he was told that he would do better to remain in his own 'sphere' and stick to his trade. (As he had not the time to study for a scholarship or exhibition, and was unable to pay for his education, the reply was not altogether unreasonable. Hardy's attack is not on Christminster but on the society responsible for keeping the doors of its universities virtually closed to poor scholars.) Jude's two Arch Enemies were his weakness for woman-kind and his impulse to strong liquor. He sought refuge in the latter, and reasoned that he had been guilty of self-seeking, a form of social unrest, the 'artificial product of civilization', which had no foundation in the nobler instincts. He therefore chose a humbler aim, to enter the Church as a licentiate and aspire to no more than a curacy. What better place to pursue his studies than a cathedral-city such as Melchester, where Sue was now at a training-college! He convinced himself that he could learn to love her 'as a friend and kinswoman'. When Sue discovered that he was married, she accepted Phillotson, and asked Jude to act as best man. Jude's self-deception continued, in reverse, when he sat up the same evening expecting Sue to return. He saw her at Shaston and Marygreen, and, finding 'the human was more powerful in him than the Divine', burnt all his religious books. Sue's marriage had proved a failure. Both heard 'the cry of a rabbit caught in a gin', and it symbolized the situation of each. 'Strange that his first aspiration – towards academical proficiency – had been checked by a woman, and that his second aspiration – to-wards apostleship – had also been checked by a woman. "Is it," he said, "that the women are to blame; or is it the artificial system of things, under which the normal sex-impulses are turned into devilish domestic gins and springes to noose and hold back those who want to progress?" '

The two lovers lived together at Aldbrickham and elsewhere, Sue deferring marriage even after both had secured divorce, because she was afraid that an 'iron contract' would extinguish tenderness. It was the fear that Jude would be drawn back to Arabella that led to its consumma-tion. Two children were born. People were scandalized at their relation-ship, and the result was that Jude found work hard to obtain or keep, and had to look for it in different parts of Wessex. At Kennetbridge, he was ill from putting up stonework for a music-hall at Quartershot. He still dreamed of Christminster, and went there with his family when he was able, embittered in soul: 'it was my poverty and not my will that consented to be beaten. It takes two or three generations to do what I tried to do in one; and my impulses – affections – vices perhaps they should be called – were too strong not to hamper a man without advantages; who should be as cold-blooded as a fish and as selfish as a pig to have a really good chance of being one of his country's worthies.' The death of her children seemed like retribution to Sue, and in her agony she felt she had to submit to the Church. Sue had only one husband in the sight of Heaven, and she returned to Phillotson. Jude was terrified at the thought of losing his 'guardian-angel', lest, like 'the pig that was washed' he turned back to his 'wallowing in the mire'. Sue, 'creed-drunk', was remarried to Phillotson; and Jude, 'gin-drunk', to Arabella. He was feverishly ill, but made a desperate effort to win back Sue by journeying to Marygreen. The effort was useless, and Jude submitted to the cold wind and rain by Ridge-way. He had lost the will to live, and died at Christminster, wishing he had never been born.

The character of Jude is far from complex. He is too full of charity and too much of an idealist to succeed in a world of self-seeking and harsh moral prejudices, and too easy a prey to self-deception to escape the snares of nature. At the end he has lost many illusions, but still deceives himself that his marriage to Sue is 'Nature's'; he is involved puppet-like ('my poor puppet', Hardy called him, Life, 272) in issues which are beyond resolution. His baulked Christminster aspirations are a subsidiary theme to that of sex and marriage, and the story is the framework for the perennial conflict between flesh and spirit and, even more, for the topical question of divorce.

One of the titles Hardy had in mind for Jude the Obscure *was* The Recalcitrants. *In the poem of this title, the 'pair' is Jude and Sue. Another poem, which was written while Hardy was working on the novel, recalls Jude, though it is about a glass-stainer.*   *JO; SC.* 'Wessex Heights' (*v. See 309n.*), 'The Recalcitrants'; *MV.* 'The Young Glass-Stainer'; *WW.* 'The Son's Portrait' (*cf.* i xi)

FELLMER, ALBERT. He was a young widower who lived with his mother at Narrobourne manor-house, and fell in love with Rosa Halborough, whom he married. Mrs Fellmer had been much impressed by the preaching of the new curate, Rosa's brother Joshua.   *LLI.* 4

FENNEL, MR and MRS. They lived at a lonely house called Higher Crowstairs on a grassy and furzy down not three miles from Casterbridge. Mr Fennel was a sheep-farmer, and his wife was the daughter of John Pitcher, a dairyman in a neighbouring vale. She was frugal, very anxious that the dances should not be too long at their christening-party for fear the guests should imbibe too much liquor, and very concerned when the second of the three uninvited strangers to arrive that evening helped himself plentifully to the mead.   *WT.* 1

FENSWORTH. *Letcombe Regis, between Letcombe Bassett and Wantage, Berkshire.*

Jude's mother and father parted where the road to Fensworth branches off, Drusilla Fawley told him. 'A gibbet once stood there not onconnected with our history.'

Arabella Donn persuaded her parents to go to the evening service at Fensworth in order to carry out her plans to secure Jude as a husband.

JO. I viii, xi

FERNELL HALL. *Embley House, near Romsey, Hampshire.*

It was the manorial house of the estate next to Deansleigh Park. The Contessa lived here a while in the hope that Sir Ashley Mottisfont would persude his wife Philippa to allow his natural daughter Dorothy to live with her. Philippa soon realized that Dorothy was the Contessa's daughter.

GND. 4

FIESOLE. *Near Florence. For Hardy's visit in 1887, see Life, 191–2.*

PPP. 'In the Old Theatre, Fiesole'

FITZPIERS, DR EDRED. *See* OAKBURY FITZPIERS.

A young, handsome doctor of aristocratic descent who had studied at Heidelberg and settled at Little Hintock, where he passed the time more in study and reading than in actual practice. He engaged in scientific experiments, had hopes of examining Grammer Oliver's unusually large brain when she was dead, and was devoted to metaphysics and poetry. Shelley appears to have been his favourite poet. He had too many interests to succeed, and was not a very practical man. 'In the course of a year his mind was accustomed to pass in a grand solar sweep throughout the zodiac of the intellectual heaven. Sometimes it was in the Ram, sometimes in the Bull; one month he would be immersed in alchemy, another in poesy; one month in the Twins of astrology and astronomy; then in the Crab of German literature and metaphysics.' For him the best list of virtues was Schleiermacher's: self-control, perseverance, wisdom, and love. He displayed none of them. He could resist neither Suke Damson nor Mrs Charmond. He believed that marriage was a mere civil contract, but consented to marry Grace Melbury at church to please her. When he met Mrs Charmond he felt that he had married beneath him. Yet, 'like others of his character, while despising Melbury and his station', he 'did not at all disdain to spend Melbury's money, or appropriate to his own use the horse which belonged to Melbury's daughter'. In short, he was a pleasure-seeking dilettante, in every way the antithesis of Giles Winterborne. He did not hesitate to go abroad to live with Mrs Charmond, and, after her death, he had no compunction in returning to Little Hintock and his wife. It is a mark of Grace Melbury's weakness that she accepted him. Her father had no illusions about their future.

W. i, iii, iv, vi, viii, xiv, xvi–xx, xxii–xl, xlii–xlviii

FLAXTON, MR. The parish clerk who began 'The History of the Hardcomes' while on his way with his wife and several other passengers in the carrier's van from Casterbridge to Longpuddle.

LLI. 8, Introduction, and prologue to (*b*)

FLINTCOMB-ASH. *Hardy's topography suggests that this was south of Church Hill, a chalky plateau north-east of Alton Pancras, with the 'summits' of Nettlecombe Tout to the east and Bulbarrow further away to the north-east. It was, in fact, first called 'Alton Ash Farm'. Hardy's map of Tess's 'wanderings' places it further east, however, almost south of Nettlecombe Tout.*

Flintcomb-Ash farm was 'a starve-acre place'. The desolate drabness of the fields where Tess toiled on these exposed heights with their 'myriads of loose white flints', the rigours of an unusually severe winter, and her victimization by Farmer Groby are in tragic accord with Tess's lot, separated from Angel Clare and afflicted by the renewed attentions of Alec d'Urberville.

Tess's suffering is emphasized by oblique references to larger forces in the universe: the cruelty of Nature (the blind, sleeping, or indifferent Mother of the poems; cf. pp. 174–5) as reflected in the long-range and close-up imagery of the Arctic birds, and of the First Cause, which works unconsciously like an automaton unaware of human suffering (cf. *The Dynasts*). Here it is hinted at in the threshing-machine, of which the engine acts as the. *primum mobile.* Tess endures the unremitting demands of 'the red tyrant' until she bleeds. General implications are linked with the particular as Tess is plagued by Alec d'Urberville. She lashes out against fate when she smites him with her glove, as she is to do again with fatal consequences. 'Once victim, always victim – that's the law!' she cries.

The contrasts between Flintcomb-Ash and Talbothays, in landscape and season, are obvious. In both phases of the novel, however, the narrative is enriched with overtones of meaning which reveal the artistry of a philosophical poet at his peak.

TD. xlii–xliv, xlv–xlix; WW. 'We Field-Women'

FLOWER, CAPTAIN. Coxswain of the Knollsea lifeboat. A 'sturdy sailor' with a stentorian voice, which he uses in the teeth of a storm to warn Captain Ounce of the *Spruce* not to bring his steamer close in. He knew the hazards of the bay from bitter experience, having had 'the two great ventures of his life . . . blown ashore and broken up within that very semicircle'. Ethelberta and 'her young relations' lodged for a while in his small cottage, where they were attended on by Mrs Flower, the captain assisting with dinner preparations. When she heard that Lord Mountclere was coming to Knollsea, Ethelberta decided instantly that they must move to the 'gayest house' that could be found; Captain Flower and his 'little cabin' must be 'things we have never known'. (*In this some personal humour may be detected; see* MASTERS.)   HE. xxxi, xxxvii, xliii

FLOWER-DE-LUCE. *The Fleur-de-Lis Inn at Cranborne.*

An inn at Chaseborough where Saturday evening frequenters from Pentridge danced and drank on fair-day.   *TD. x*

FLOY, MR. The coroner at the inquest on the assumed death of Mrs Manston in the fire at the Three Tranters Inn. It was held at the Rising Sun Inn. The witnesses were Abraham Brown of Hoxton, Joseph Chinney, Farmer Springrove, Mrs Fitler (chambermaid and wife of the ostler at the inn), Mrs Crickett, Mr Manston, Mr Flooks (agent of Lord Claydonfield at Chettlewood), and a surgeon. The verdict was accidental death.   *DR.* xi 2

FLYCHETT. *Lytchett Minster, five miles from Wareham on the road to Poole and Bournemouth.*

It was here that Christopher Julian had met Ethelberta, who had jilted him, while he was on holiday at Anglebury the summer before the story opens.

Here Sol, Ethelberta's brother, and the brother of Lord Mountclere stopped to have breakfast and change horses when they were hurriedly

driving across the heath in a storm to prevent the marriage of Lord
Mountclere and Ethelberta.   *HE*. ii, xliv

FONTHILL. *Fonthill Abbey, in south-west Wiltshire, built at the beginning
of the nineteenth century as a mansion in the grand Gothic style. (The
tower, which was 278 feet high, fell in 1825.)*

Jude suggested that Sue and he should go for an outing to Wardour
Castle and Fonthill the same afternoon. Sue decided on Wardour Castle,
as it was Corinthian in style.   *JO*. III ii

FONTOVER, MISS. A bespectacled old lady, who dressed like an abbess,
and one of the partners who owned the 'ecclesiastical establishment' in
which Sue Bridehead assisted and lodged. She was the daughter of a
clergyman in reduced circumstances, and, when he died, had boldly
taken over 'a little shop of church requisites' and developed its business
considerably. 'A dab at Ritual', she attended the 'ceremonial church' of
St Silas, and knew John Keble's *The Christian Year* by heart. Sue left
because Miss Fontover had deliberately smashed the two Greek statuettes
she had recently bought.   *JO*. II iii, iv, VI iii

FOUNTALL. *Wells, Somerset. It takes its name from the springs which well
from the Mendip Hills. For centuries it has been an ecclesiastical centre.
'Fountall' therefore is ambivalent, and probably, to some extent, ironical.*

Joshua Halborough was a student at Fountall Theological College, and
was much embarrassed when he saw his father with a gipsy-like woman
in the Cathedral Close. Later, Joshua's father was imprisoned at Fountall
for disorderly conduct.

Captain John Maumbry retired from the —th Hussars at Casterbridge
and proceeded to Fountall Theological College. He became a curate at
Durnover.   *LLI*. 4; *CM*. 1

FRANKLAND, FRANCES. The daughter of the unmarried Leonora
Frankland and Mr Millborne. Leonora left Toneborough, and she and
her daughter became teachers of music and dancing at Exonbury. After
twenty years' absence, Mr Millborne offered to marry her; only when
Leonora saw that this would enable her and Frances to give up teaching,
and thus improve her daughter's prospects of marriage, did she consent.
Frances was engaged to a young curate, the Reverend Percival Cope.
The engagement was nearly broken off when, in most unusual circumstances, he discovered that Frances was Mr Millborne's daughter. Mr
Millborne withdrew, after making it possible for mother and daughter to
live independently at a manor-house near Ivell (where Cope was a

Sherborne (Sherton) Castle ruins

Wolfeton House (the home of Lady Penelope)

*The Abbey gatehouse,
Cerne Abbas (Abbot's
Cernel)*

*Gateway to Stalbridge
House (Stapleford Park)*

curate), and the young couple were married. *LLI.* 3

FRANKLAND, LEONORA. She worked in a music-shop in Toneborough, and was promised marriage by Mr Millborne; but he left her when it was pointed out to him that the marriage would be to his disadvantage, and she had a daughter. Years later, mother and daughter taught music and dancing at Exonbury. Mr Millborne had remained a bachelor. When he proposed marriage, Leonora rejected him. He was a man of means, and pointed out that marriage would mean that she and Frances could give up teaching, and Frances's marriage prospects would thereby be enhanced. This argument prevailed; the marriage took place, and the Millbornes and Frances went to live in London. The discovery of Frances' paternity led almost, it seemed, to the end of her engagement, and to strained relations in the Millborne household. Mr Millborne found a manor-house near Ivell for his wife and daughter, left them the greater part of his income, and departed for the Continent. *LLI.* 3

FRAY, HENRY. *Like Hardy's uncle – also of 'Weatherbury' – he appears to have been christened 'Henery' (cf. Lois Deacon, Hardy's Grandmother, Betsy, and Her Family, Toucan Press, 1966).*

One of Bathsheba Everdene's farm-hands, and a member of the rustic group which provides comedy and chorus to the main action of *Far from the Madding Crowd*. 'He was a man of more than middle age, with eyebrows high up in his forehead, who laid it down that the law of the world was bad, with a long-suffering look through his listeners at the world alluded to, as it presented itself to his imagination.' He always signed his name 'Henery'. He imagined he ought to have been Miss Everdene's bailiff – 'I deserved that place,' wailed Henery, signifying wasted genius; ''twas to be, I suppose. Your lot is your lot, and scripture is nothing.' He had his 'great depths', and spoke with 'powerful words' when his pride was 'boiling wi' scarn'. *FMC.* viii, x, xv, xxi, xxii

FREDDY. The boy who objected to the catching and caging of birds by his father, left home without warning, took to sea, and was drowned one Christmastide when a hoy foundered at Durdle-Door.

HS. 'The Bird-Catcher's Boy'

FROOM. *The river Frome, which rises at Evershot (running through the farmyard with the barn where Alec d'Urberville preached) and flows through Maiden Newton, past Dorchester, below Lower Bockhampton, through 'the Valley of the Great Dairies', by Wool manor-house, and past Wareham to Poole Harbour.*

Near Dorchester, it flows immediately below the northern flank of Pummery or Poundbury Camp, round the north and eastern sides of the town, and through Fordington (which takes its Wessex name, Durnover, from the British name for the river, the 'Blackwater' of The Mayor of Casterbridge), *where it is joined by the Cerne river, which flows under Grey's Bridge (p. 344). See plates facing pp. 271, 302.*

Hardy sometimes calls it the Var, from its British name (see ANGLE-BURY). *See also* CHILLINGTON WOOD *aud* WHERRYBORNE.

UGT. I v; III iii; V ii; HE. i; MC. xvi, xix; CM. 2; TD. xvi, xxi, xxiii, xxiv, xxvii, xxix, xxxiv, xxxvii, xliii; WP. 'The Burghers', 'The Alarm', 'The Slow Nature'; PPP. 'The Milkmaid', 'The King's Experiment'; D. (1) II v; TL. 'At Casterbridge Fair' (ii), 'The Dead Quire', 'She Hears the Storm', 'Geographical Knowledge'; SC. 'Wessex Heights' (Is the ghost a spectre of the real or the fictitional, i.e. Tess? Cf. MV., 'The Head above the Fog', TD. xx, and the footnote, p. 309); LLE. 'A Sound in the Night'

FROOM-EVERARD HOUSE. *Stafford House, formerly known as Frome Everard – cf. Hutchins, ii 511–17 – on the southern side of the Frome river opposite Lower Bockhampton. The house, plantation, and weir are very much as described by Hardy. See plate facing p. 206.*

Christine, the daughter of the squire, and lover of the young farmer Nicholas Long, lived here. It was 'solidly built of stone in that never-to-be-surpassed style for the English country residence – the mullioned and transomed Elizabethan'. Behind the house was 'an extension of shrubberies and plantations along the banks of the Froom', by the waterfall or weir where Bellston was drowned.   CM. 2

FROOM-HILL BARROW. *A tumulus on Frome Hill, by which the road from Max Gate to Higher Bockhampton runs. It commands an extensive view, which includes Kingston Maurward House and Park, the Frome valley, the woods around Higher Bockhampton, and 'Egdon Heath'.*

WW. 'Seeing the Moon Rise'

FRY, AMOS. The principal of the labourers at Welland who provide some comic relief to the story of Swithin St Cleeve and Lady Constantine. He was known as Haymoss. Others in the main group are Sammy Blore, Nathaniel Chapman, and Hezekiah Biles. At the choir practice they display humour and character, to which the course of the story allows little development. *One comment on the lot of peasant labourers in*

Dorset should not pass unnoticed: 'I've not held out against the spectre o' starvation these five-and-twenty year on nine shillings a week, to be afeard of a walking vapour, sweet or savoury,' said Hezzy, when they were talking about what they assumed was the ghost of Sir Blount Constantine in his great-coat. Years earlier, Amos had been refused confirmation because, when the parson examined him on the articles of his belief, he had answered, at the instigation of Sir Blount, 'Women and wine'. *TT.* i, ii, xiii, xxii, xxiii, xli

FYANDER, DEBORAH. An old milker at Talbothays, whom Dairyman Crick rebuked for not washing her hands before milking; 'if the London folk only knowed of thee and thy slovenly ways, they'd swaller their milk and butter more mincing than they do a' ready; and that's saying a good deal'. *TD.* xx, xxi, xxvii

GALE, SIR JOHN. *Sir John Gage, the second husband of Lady Penelope Darcy of Wolfeton House.* *GND.* 8

GARLAND, ANNE. She lived with her mother at Overcombe Mill, and used to visit Oxwell Hall to read the newspaper to old Benjamin Derriman. Her mother's encouragement to marry his nephew Festus fell on deaf ears. She was quite indifferent to his advances, but narrowly escaped his clutches on more than one occasion. The trumpet-major, John Loveday, loved her unostentatiously, but she was more warmly disposed to his brother Bob of the merchant service, until he announced his forthcoming wedding to Matilda Johnson of Southampton. Bob's departure from Overcombe to serve on the *Victory* grieved her. She visited Portland Bill to see the ship pass on its way to Plymouth, and at Budmouth was approached and consoled by the King. When Bob, on his return to Portsmouth, lost his heart to someone else, she began to find much to admire in the steadfastness and self-abnegation of John, but her encouragement led only to a modest response and subsequently to a strange cooling, when the trumpet-major learned that Bob's hopes were still fixed on Anne. By the time John was due to leave England for Spain, she had forgiven Bob, and had promised to marry him in six months. Benjamin Derriman was just as fond of her as he was ill-disposed to his profligate nephew Festus. When a false invasion alarm was raised, and again when he suspected that Festus and Matilda Johnson were bent on stealing his hidden money, he brought his treasure-box to be hidden at the mill, his final trust being in Anne. He left her nearly all his property, including the neglected Oxwell Hall. *TM*

GARLAND, MRS MARTHA. Miller Day's apartments at Overcombe Mill had been divided, and in one part Mrs Garland lived with her daughter Anne. She was a widow, and her husband had been a landscape painter (Captain Hardy had one of his pictures). She hoped that Anne would marry Festus Derriman. She herself married Miller Loveday. *TM*

GAYMEAD. *Theale, west of Reading, Berkshire.*

Mr Twycott, who married his servant Sophy, was vicar here.

The coming of 'Father Time' to Aldbrickham, Jude and Sue's failure to marry at the registrar's office, and rumours that Jude had not defended himself in the divorce proceedings instituted by Phillotson against Sue and himself, created much gossip and scandal. Jude found it increasingly difficult to obtain work. He and Sue were busy re-lettering the Ten Commandments at a church near Aldbrickham, when they heard one of the onlookers say 'A strange pair to be painting the Two Tables!' Thereupon the church-warden told a story 'of a most immoral case that happened at the painting of the Commandments in a church out by Gaymead – which is quite within a walk of this one'. The workmen were too drunk to finish their work in readiness for Sunday – the next day – and sank senseless to the floor. A thunderstorm followed, during which they saw a dark figure with a curious foot finish their work. The next morning, when service began, it was noticed that all the 'Nots' had been left out. The Bishop had to reconsecrate the church. *LLI.* 2; *JO.* v vi

GAYTON, LAWYER. A lawyer of Bath, who wrote to Sir Ashley Mottisfont on behalf of the Italian contessa. *GND.* 4

GENOA. After his fruitless journeys to Nice and Monte Carlo to see Paula Power, George Somerset, unaware of the damage Dare's telegram to Miss Power from Monte Carlo had done him, went on to Genoa, only to find that she had moved on with her uncle and de Stancy to tour the Rhine valley. *L.* IV iv, v, v iii

Hardy did not visit the city until March 1887; cf. Life, *187.*

PPP. 'Genoa and the Mediterranean'

GEORGE. When sheep-farming at Norcombe Hill, Gabriel Oak had two dogs: George the elder, who 'had arrived at an age at which all superfluous barking was cynically avoided as a waste of breath', and George the younger, who chased Oak's flock over the brow of a chalk-pit, where Gabriel found them dead and dying, the dog above 'standing against the sky – dark and motionless as Napoleon at St. Helena'. George the younger 'was considered too good a workman to live'. *FMC.* iv, v

GEORGE III. He appears in several brief background scenes (in or near Budmouth) in *The Trumpet-Major*, all based on historical records. More memorable and moving is the scene where, after seeing the *Victory* with Bob Loveday on board disappear over the horizon, Anne Garland sat weeping and was approached by two gentlemen, one of whom proved to be the King, who asked kindly why she wept, and went away saying that he would remember the name of Robert Loveday.

On his way to Budmouth, George III stopped to change horses at Woodyates Inn (p. 514). One night he stopped at the King's Arms, Casterbridge, for the same purpose.

In 'A Committee-Man of "The Terror" ', we are told that George III and 'his royal Cwort' stayed at Budmouth 'every zummer since eighty-nine'.

In *The Trumpet-Major* the review of the troops on Bincombe Down took place in 1804. This may be no more than an author's licence. The review in *The Dynasts* is historical (July 1805).

Two scenes in which the King appears in *The Dynasts* are memorable: one in which he meets Pitt at Gloucester Lodge, Weymouth; the other at Windsor Castle, during his illness. Hardy generally presents him sympathetically.

> *TM*. xi–xiii, xxii, xxx, xxxiii, xxxiv; *MC*. xxxvii; *WT*. 3;
> *CM*. 8; *D*. (1) II iv, IV i, (2) VI v; *WW*. 'The Ballad of
> Love's Skeleton'. See BUDMOUTH

GEORGE V. *Hardy preferred not to accept the invitation to attend the Coronation in June 1911. See Life, 355.*   SC. 'The Coronation'

GERTRUDE, LADY. *Unidentified. There was a Lady Gertrude in the Grey family in the seventeenth century, but whether she was buried at Stinsford is not known.*

> *LLE*. 'Voices from Things Growing in a Churchyard'

GIFFORD, EVELYN. *She was Hardy's cousin by marriage, the daughter of the archdeacon who married Hardy and Emma Lavinia Gifford in London in September 1874. He held her in high regard. She was present at the Sheldonian Theatre when Hardy received his honorary degree of Doctor of Letters in January 1920, but died the following September* (Life, 101, 397–8, 407).   LLE. 'Evelyn G. of Christminster'

GILBERT. The husband of a fair 'vampire'. See WINGREEN.

GILES, OLIVER. This 'man of seventeen' bribed the musicians at the Fennels' christening-party to play as long as possible because he 'was enamoured of his partner, a fair girl of thirty-three rolling years'. Mrs Fennel, on the other hand, was very anxious not to have long dances, lest the guests should become too thirsty. *WT*. 1

GILLINGHAM, GEORGE. An old friend of Richard Phillotson. Both were headmasters; Gillingham's school was at Leddenton, not far from Phillotson's at Shaston. Phillotson sought his advice when his marriage to Sue proved a failure. Gillingham was more conventional in outlook than his friend, and did not think that it was a wise policy to release Sue. He attended Phillotson and Sue's second marriage at Marygreen.

JO. IV iii, iv, vi, VI iv, v

GLANVILLE, LOUIS. Lady Constantine's brother. He was in the diplomatic service, and became an attaché at Rio Janeiro (*sic*); but he grew tired of his life (and work, it may be assumed) out there, resigned his appointment, and came home suddenly. His main objective seemed to be Lady Constantine's marriage with a man of means, so that his own future could be provided for (*in this respect he recalls the more worthless Will Dare of* A Laodicean). The Bishop of Melchester's visit for the confirmation service at Welland seemed to have provided the opportunity. Lady Constantine's rejection of the Bishop and her interest in Swithin roused his suspicions, but he detected nothing of the reality, and came to the conclusion that Swithin was in love with Tabitha Lark. When Swithin had left to go abroad from Southampton, and Lady Constantine discovered she was with child, she told Louis everything and rushed to Southampton in order to marry Swithin publicly, since her private marriage had proved to be illegal. She was too late and unable to get in touch with Swithin, since she did not know to which country he had sailed first to continue his astronomical studies. Louis Glanville went to Melchester and told the Bishop his sister was in love with him, but that it was incumbent on him to make the first move. The ruse succeeded, but what happened to Louis after the marriage is not disclosed.

TT. xvi, xix–xxxii, xxxv–xxxix

GLASTON. *Glastonbury, Somerset.* *TL*. 'A Trampwoman's Tragedy'

GLIM, MR. Mr Swancourt's curate at Endelstow. *PBE*. xvii, xxiii

GOODENOUGH, MRS. The furmity-seller at Weydon-Priors Fair. It was in her tent that Henchard sold his wife Susan. Nearly twenty-one years later she was charged with indecent behaviour on the streets of Casterbridge. It happened that Henchard was on the bench when her case was tried. She remembered him, and told the court about the sale of his wife.

He denied nothing. She settled, it is not surprising to find, in the neighbourhood of Mixen Lane, and found solace at Peter's Finger.

MC. i, iii, xxvii–xxviii, xxxvi

GOODMAN, MRS. Paula Power's widow aunt, 'chaperon and adviser on practical matters'. She clearly had reservations about Captain de Stancy, and was sympathetic to George Somerset. She accompanied Paula on her Continental tours. *L.* I vi, viii,

xi–xv; II vii; III vii–xi; V ii, v, viii, xiii, xiv; VI i–iii

GOULD, HUMPHREY. A fashionable idler of Budmouth who was engaged to Phyllis Grove of Bincombe. He explained his long stay in Bath by saying that he had to look after his invalid father; in fact, he had secretly married 'a dear young belle'. *WT.* 3

GRADFIELD, MR. An architect at Budmouth Regis, for whom Owen Graye worked after the death of his father, Ambrose Graye.

DR. i 5, ii 1, 2, xii 4, xv

GRANSON, DR. The 'gentleman known as Dr Granson' lived at Castle Boterel (*Boscastle*). He was called in when Elfride Swancourt was overwrought after losing games of chess with Henry Knight; and again when Mrs Jethway was found buried under 'the ruinous heap of stones', which had formed the tower of West Endelstow church before it had been undermined by the 'restorers'. *PBE.* xviii, xxxiii

GRAYE, AMBROSE. A young architect, who fell from the scaffold round a church tower at Hocbridge and was killed. He was the father of Cytherea and Owen. Years earlier, he had fallen in love with Cytherea Bradleigh, a girl of nineteen or twenty, but they were 'divided eternally', he never knew why. The Bradleighs inherited the Knapwater estate from Cytherea's great-uncle on condition that they assumed his name. Cytherea became Miss Aldclyffe. When she discovered that Cytherea Graye was the daughter of the man she loved, she contrived her marriage to her illegitimate son Manston, not knowing that he was already married. *DR.* i 1–5, iii 1, v 3, xxi 3

GRAYE, CYTHEREA. The heroine of *Desperate Remedies*; see ALDCLYFFE; MANSTON, AENEAS; SPRINGROVE, EDWARD.

In some respects, her marriage to Manston foreshadows that of Tess to Alec d'Urberville. She marries for two reasons: she believes she has been deserted by the man she loves; and marriage to Manston can save her brother from poverty. So she consents passively: 'She felt as one in a boat without oars, drifting with closed eyes down a river – she knew not whither' (xii 6). In *Tess of the d'Urbervilles*, Angel Clare, returning too late, realizes 'that his original Tess had spiritually ceased to recognise the body before him as hers – allowing it to drift, like a corpse upon the current, in a direction dissociated from its living will' (lv).   DR

GRAYE, OWEN. Cytherea's brother. He was employed after his father's death in the same architect's office as Edward Springrove at Budmouth.

Later, he was indisposed for a long period as a result of lameness; it was his poverty, combined with Cytherea's belief that Edward Springrove had deserted her, which made Cytherea marry Manston.

When he recovered, he and his sister (after being saved from marriage with Manston, though the wedding-ceremony had taken place) settled at Tolchurch, where he superintended church restoration for Mr Gradfield.   *DR*. i–iii, v–vii, ix, xii–xviii, xx, xxi, Sequel

GREAT FOREST, THE. *The New Forest, Hampshire.*

GND. 4; *TD*. lvii–lviii; *TL*. 'A Trampwoman's Tragedy';
HS. 'Last Look round St. Martin's Fair'

GREAT HINTOCK. See the HINTOCKS.

GREAT PLAIN, THE. *Salisbury Plain.*

The 'figure against the moon' in 'Wessex Heights' is enigmatic. Was it reminiscential or fictional? The moon had set when Angel and Tess reached Stonehenge. See footnote, p. 309. TD. lviii; LLI. 5; SC. 'Wessex Heights'

GREBE, BARBARA. *Barbara Webb, wife of the fifth Earl of Shaftesbury.*

She eloped with Edmond Willowes. When he returned from Italy, horribly disfigured as the result of a theatre fire, she was so appalled that he left her and went abroad. Years later, concluding he was dead, she married Lord Uplandtowers, but remorse for failing her devoted Edmond (whose death had been confirmed) made her a rather indifferent wife, and her husband was resentful. When he discovered that she almost worshipped a statue of her former handsome husband, he treated her with such calculated and inhuman cruelty that she was terrified and became a clinging abject creature, completely submissive to his will. She bore him eleven children in nine years, and died in Florence, worn out in mind and body.   *GND*. 2

GREBE, SIR JOHN. He and Lady Grebe lived at Chene Manor (p. 275). They soon became reconciled to their daughter Barbara's marriage with Edmond Willowes, provided funds for him to travel a year on the Continent with a tutor, and a home at Yewsholt for the married couple when he returned from Italy.   *GND*. 2, 4

GREEN, ANTHONY. Lady Constantine's servant. He had married her maid Gloriana. 'But 'tis wearing work to hold out against the custom of the country, and the woman wanting 'ee to stand by her and save her from unborn shame; so, since common usage would have it, I let myself be carried away by opinion, and took her. Though she's never once thanked me for covering her confusion. . . . But, 'tis the way of the lost when safe, and I don't complain.'
TT. xiii, xvi, xvii, xix, xxi, xxiii, xxxvii–xxxviii

GREEN, MRS GLORIANA, Wife of Anthony Green, and Lady Constantine's maid. She accompanied her lady to Bath, when Lady Constantine had to reside there in order to qualify for her secret wedding with Swithin St Cleeve. The question what to do with Gloriana on the morning of the wedding-service solved itself, for Mrs Green heard that her child was ill, and was so upset at the thought of losing the 'tender deary, that made Anthony marry me, and thereby turned hisself from a little calamity to a little blessing' that she asked to return to Welland at once.
TT. xiii, xvii

GREEN, JOHN. The boatman at Port-Bredy harbour with whom Mrs Barnet and Mrs Downe went for a short sail round the cliff. The boat capsized, and Mrs Downe was carried out to sea and drowned. *WT.* 5

GREEN, PETER. He sang the song 'The Night of Trafalgar' at the Old Rooms Inn, Budmouth ('King George's Watering-Place'). *D.* (1) v vii

GREENHILL. *Woodbury Hill, east of Bere Regis. A great entertainment and sheep fair used to be held there annually in September. On 21 September 1873, while he was writing* Far from the Madding Crowd, *Hardy walked from Higher Bockhampton to Woodbury Hill Fair, more than ten miles away* (Life, 96). *According to Hutchins, Hardy's authority on Dorset antiquities, Woodbury Hill was a Roman camp, with a chantry or chapel on its west side.*

Joseph Poorgrass was taken there in the hope that it would cure his bashfulness: 'They took me to Greenhill Fair, and into the great gay jerry-go-nimble show, where there were women-folk riding round – standing upon horses, with hardly anything on but their smocks.'

On his return from the United States, Sergeant Troy found employment with a travelling circus, and took the hero's part in the play of 'Turpin's Ride to York'. Finding Bathsheba present for the performance at Greenhill, he disguised himself successfully, but the sight of his wife renewed his passion, and in seeking her at Boldwood's Christmas party he met his death.

Women used to 'run' for smocks and gown-pieces at Greenhill Fair. Timothy Fairways recalled the occasion when his wife returned from the fair with a gown-piece she had won, but very upset because Mr Yeobright, Thomasin's father, was taken ill as soon as he reached the fair-ground. He was taken home, but never recovered.

When Jack Durbeyfield heard that he was descended from the aristocratic d'Urbervilles, he told a boy named Fred to call at the Pure Drop Inn and order a horse and carriage to take him home. He asked the boy if he knew Kingsbere-sub-Greenhill (where the d'Urbervilles were buried in the family vault). The boy said he had been to Greenhill Fair. After Mr Durbeyfield's death, the family was evicted from their cottage at Marlott. In the waggon carrying their belongings they passed Greenhill, but at Kingsbere were told that the rooms they wanted had been let. As they were unable to find accommodation at Kingsbere, the driver would go no further, and their belongings were unloaded by the churchyard wall. The Durbeyfield family slept outside under the traceried window of the d'Urberville Aisle.

Nobody knew where Wat Ollamoor came from; some said his first appearance in the neighbourhood of Mellstock and Stickleford had been as fiddle-player in a show at Greenhill Fair.

The 'ancient hill' with 'the Pagan temple' of the poem 'The Well-Beloved' suggests Woodbury Hill rather than another location (cf. KINGSBERE). *FMC*. viii, 1; *RN*. I v; *TM*. xxvi; *TT*. xiii; *TD*. i, lii; *LLI*. 7; *D*. (1) II v; *PPP*. 'The Well-Beloved'

GREENSLEEVES, EVE. *'It was said her real name was Eve Trevillian or Trevelyan; and that she was the handsome mother of two or three illegitimate children, circa 1784–95' (Hardy's note). She was buried at Stinsford.* LLE. 'Voices from Things Growing in a Churchyard'

GREENWICH OBSERVATORY. *For Hardy's visit in connection with the writing of* Two on a Tower, *see* Life, *151. He practised a piece of honest deception.* TT. xxxii, xxxiii, xxxiv

GREY, SQUIRE AUDELEY. *One of the Grey family (cf. TD. xix) of the old manor-house at Kingston Maurward. He was buried at Stinsford.* LLE. 'Voices from Things Growing in a Churchyard'

GREY'S BRIDGE. *Commissioned by Lora Grey, the daughter of Audeley Grey (above). It is a stone bridge on the main road into Dorchester, just outside the town below Ten Hatches Weir; see plates facing p. 302. The old brick bridge (now rebuilt) over the Frome was at the entrance to Dorchester.*

Dick Dewy parted company with Mr Maybold here, after telling him of his forthcoming marriage to Fancy Day, and went on to Durnover Mill.

Fanny Robin, supported by improvised crutches on the last stage of her walk from Melchester, reached Grey's Bridge one Saturday evening in October. She was trying to reach Casterbridge Union, just before the birth of her child. A dog licked her cheek, and she made the rest of her way to her goal leaning on the dog, which was stoned away. Troy had seen her, and arranged to meet her at Grey's Bridge the following Monday morning. In the meantime Fanny had died in childbirth. When she did not appear at Grey's Bridge, Troy drove off to Budmouth races.

From the Bow (*the corner by St Peter's Church*) in the centre of Casterbridge, Bob Loveday saw the mail-coach rise over Grey's Bridge, a quarter of a mile away (*an understatement*). It did not bring the expected Matilda Johnson.

From Grey's Bridge, Henchard walked a short distance by the river, intending to commit suicide at Ten Hatches Weir. Here Elizabeth-Jane parted from him when he left Casterbridge after hearing that Newson had returned.

The two bridges described in *MC.* xxxii are referred to at the opening of 'A Few Crusted Characters'. The first, of brick, immediately at the lower or eastern end of High Street (not many yards from the White Hart Inn, where the carrier awaited his passengers) had just been reached, when the carrier realized that he had forgotten the curate of Longpuddle. Just beyond the second (*Grey's Bridge, 'about three hundred yards' out of town*), they turned off the main road along the road to Longpuddle (*Slyres Lane*). At the turning, they had to stop for another passenger, a stranger, who proved to be John Lackland; he had emigrated from Longpuddle with his parents and sister when he was a boy.

UGT. iv vii; *FMC.* xxxix, xl, xlv; *TM.* xvi; *MC.* xxxii, xxxviii, xl, xli, xliii; *LLI.* 8, Introduction; *CM.* 1 (cf. p. 264); *WP.* 'The Burghers'; *TL.* 'Bereft', 'At Casterbridge Fair' (vii); *MV.* 'Sitting on the Bridge'; *HS.* 'The Fight on Durnover Moor'

GREY'S WOOD. *North of the Dorchester–Puddletown road from Higher Bockhampton.*

Here Dick Dewy went nutting when he was tired of waiting for Fancy Day. He entered the wood by a winding path called Snail-Creep.

UGT. iv i

GRINHAM, MR. The former vicar of Mellstock. He was held in high repute because he did not put the parish to 'unnecessary trouble'.

The story that he was not worried because the font was cracked and would not hold water, and that he used to spit on his finger for christening, no doubt came from Fordington vicarage, where Hardy met Horace Moule. A predecessor of Horace's father never used water at christenings. He used to spit 'into his hand' (May O'Rourke, Thomas Hardy, Toucan Press, 1965).   *UGT.* II ii, IV iii

GROBY, FARMER. Before taking the 'starve-acre' farm at Flintcomb-Ash, he had been at Trantridge. At Casterbridge he had recognized Tess as 'Squire d'Urberville's friend', and made such an offensive remark that Angel had knocked him down. In retaliation, he worked Tess inhumanly at Flintcomb-Ash until Alec d'Urberville protested.

                                        TD. xxxiii, xli–xliii, xlvi–xlviii, liv

GROSVENOR HOTEL, THE. In Pimlico, London. Stephen Smith stayed here, on his second return from India, and found that Knight was staying at the same hotel. Their meeting revealed to Knight what wrong he had done Elfride, and revived the hopes of both lovers.   *PBE.* xxxvii–xxxix

GROVE, DR. The father of Phyllis Grove. He had been 'a professional man whose taste for lonely meditation over metaphysical questions had diminished his practice till it no longer paid him to keep it going; after which he had relinquished it and hired at a nominal rent the small, dilapidated, half farm half manor-house' at Bincombe.   *WT.* 3

GROVE, PHYLLIS. While Humphrey Gould, to whom she was engaged, was at Bath, she fell in love with the melancholy homesick Hussar Matthäus Tina of Saarbrück, and finally agreed to accompany him home when he deserted. They were to cross the Channel by boat with another deserter, Christoph Bless. When she was waiting to meet Matthäus for this venture, she saw Humphrey descend from a coach travelling to Budmouth, and overheard his remarks to a friend, which wrongly suggested that he was still her admirer. She decided that she could not leave him. The two deserters were shot, and buried behind the church at Bincombe. Phyllis tended their graves for the rest of her life. She died at the age of eighty-seven.   *WT.* 3

GROWER, MR. A magistrate and citizen of importance in Casterbridge. When Henchard failed in business, his greatest creditor was Grower. Grower, aided by Mr Blowbody, did his best to find out who was responsible for the disturbances occasioned by the skimmington-ride.

MC. xxix, xxxi, xxxvii, xxxix

HAGGARDON. *Eggardon Hill, five miles east-north-east of Bridport, and crowned with a prehistoric camp.*

It is 'the hill-fortress of Eggar'. *TM.* xxvi; *WP.* 'My Cicely'

HALBOROUGH, CORNELIUS. The younger of two ambitious brothers, who, by relentless ambition and application, made their way into the Church, in the face of great hardship and handicaps, chiefly their father, whose life they hesitated fatally to save when they were afraid that his presence at Narrobourne manor-house might wreck the prospect of their sister's marriage and their own advancement. After teaching, Cornelius succeeded his brother at Narrobourne. *LLI.* 4

HALBOROUGH, JOSHUA. The elder brother of Cornelius and the main driving-force in their ambitious careers. He attended Fountall Theological College and became curate at Narrobourne, where he set out to impress the manor-house family by his eloquent preaching, and promote the marriage of his sister and the squire. It was he who deliberately and fatally checked his brother's impulse to save their drunken father when, on his way to the manor-house – to be present at the wedding he might make impossible, they feared – he stumbled by a weir and was borne down by the stream. *LLI.* 4

HALBOROUGH, JOSHUA (senior). The father of Joshua, Cornelius and Rosa Halborough. He was a millwright whose business declined as he took to drink and dissipated the legacy which his wife had left for the university education of his sons. He was an embarrassment to the ambitious brothers, and especially to Joshua when he appeared with 'his strapping gipsy wife – if she were his wife', at Fountall Theological College. They persuaded him to go to Canada with her, but he soon returned unescorted, and was on his way to attend Rosa's marriage at Narrobourne when he was committed to prison for seven days for disorderly conduct at Ivell. On his release, he met the brothers on the way to Narrobourne, and insisted on going on to the squire's manor-house that evening. He threatened 'a hell of a row' if he were not allowed to give his daughter away to the squire. They saw him move and topple in the stream, as he was making his way across by a weir. Joshua held back his brother, and their father was drowned. His body was recovered from a culvert six months later, and remained unidentified. *LLI.* 4

HALBOROUGH, ROSA. Joshua borrowed money for his sister's education, and she was sent to boarding-schools at Sandbourne and Brussels. She visited him at Narrobourne, and attracted the attention of Albert Fellmer, the local squire, whom she married. Joshua realized that 'the physical gifts of nature to her might do more for them both [him and his brother] than nature's intellectual gifts to himself'. For that reason he allowed his father to drown. *LLI.* 4

HALL, HELENA. She was the daughter of a deceased naval officer, who had been brought up by her uncle, a solicitor, and had refused Darton in marriage. When she went out to Australia to marry Philip Hall, her uncle disinherited her. She returned to England with her dying husband and two children. Darton placed her orphaned boy in a Casterbridge school, and soon afterwards married her. But she had been severely tried, and was frail, 'and had it not been for the children Darton's house would have seemed but little brighter than it was before'. After less than a year and a half at Darton's farmhouse near Casterbridge, she died, leaving 'a tiny red infant in white wrappings'. *WT.* 6

HALL, PHILIP. The son of Mrs Hall at The Knap. He had emigrated to Australia. Helena, who had refused the wealthy farmer, Charles Darton, went out to join him there. They returned to The Knap in great destitution. Philip was in the last stages of consumption, and died on the night of his return. *WT.* 6

HALL, SALLY. She lived with her mother, a dairyman's widow, at The Knap near King's Hintock. 'Roseate good nature lit up her gaze; her features showed curves of decision and judgment, and she might have been regarded without much mistake as a warm-hearted, quick-spirited, handsome girl.' She refused several offers of marriage, including at least three from Charles Darton. See p. 69. *WT.* 6

HALWAY, MR. The auctioneer by whom articles belonging to Mrs Manston were sold when she left London for Carriford. *DR.* xvi 4

HAMBLEDON HILL. *A chalk hill in the Vale of Blackmoor east of Sturminster Newton and not far from the main line of hills overlooking the Vale from the south. While living at Sturminster Newton, Hardy was caught in a fog as he was taking a short cut from the neighbouring village of Shroton or Iverne Courtney, and all but lost among the earthworks on top of the hill* (Life, *116*).

Returning home by night from Flintcomb-Ash, on hearing of her mother's illness, Tess passed through Nuttlebury, and thought of the sleepers there 'undergoing a bracing process at the hands of sleep' until dawn, when 'a hint of pink nebulosity' would appear on Hambledon Hill.

TD. ii, 1

HAMMERSMITH. *On the Thames, west of Kensington.*

When Owen Graye missed the steamboat returning from Lulwind Cove to Budmouth, he spent the night at a railway gatehouse. The gateman had kept the inn at Hammersmith, London, when 'Jane Taylor' – the name by which Cytherea Bradleigh (Miss Aldclyffe) was known to the woman who had taken charge of her baby – arrived.

DR. iii 1, vi 1, xxi 3

HAMPSTEAD. *In 1920 Hardy joined the National Committee for acquiring Wentworth Place, where the poet had lived, as a Keats memorial* (*Life, 404*). *LLE.* 'At a House in Hampstead'

HAMPTON COURT. *A palace on the banks of the Thames near Twickenham, Middlesex. It was built by Wolsey, and presented to King Henry VIII in 1526. The 'straddling King' is Henry; 'his Minister' is Cardinal Wolsey.* *HS.* 'A Spellbound Palace'

HAMPTONSHIRE, DUKE OF. *Hamptonshire is the old name for Hampshire.*

He was impressive in appearance and lived at Batton Castle. Coarse and uncultivated, he was hardly the companion for Emmeline Oldbourne, whose beauty he found so captivating when she was seventeen that he insisted on marrying her. Emmeline found him jealous and cruel, and turned to the young curate Alwyn Hill, to whom she was attached, to take her with him to America. See pp. 61–2. The 'old Duke' (*GND.* 4) is a predecessor, probably the previous Duke of Hamptonshire.

While Jude lay dead and 'straight as an arrow' at Christminster, applause was heard from the (*Sheldonian*) Theatre, where honorary degrees were being conferred on another Duke of Hamptonshire and other 'illustrious gents of that sort'. Jude's old, superseded classical textbooks, 'roughened with stone-dust where he had been in the habit of catching them up for a few minutes between his labours, seemed to pale to a sickly cast at the sounds'. *GND.* 9; *JO.* VI xi

HANNAH. Mrs Martin's servant.

TT. ii, ix, x, xii, xvi, xxii, xxiv, xxxviii, xli

HANNER AND RAWLES. Solicitors for Swithin St Cleeve's paternal great-uncle, Dr Jocelyn St Cleeve. *TT.* xviii, xxxiv

HANNING, EMILY. Jealousy of Emily caused Joanna Phippard to marry the sailor Shadrac Jolliffe of Havenpool. Emily married a merchant widower named Mr Lester, and had two sons. Unlike Joanna, she was well-off. Joanna did not outlive her jealousy, and it was through emulating Emily's fortune that she lost her husband and two sons. When all hope of their return was lost, and Joanna could not afford to maintain her dwindling grocery business, Emily, after great difficulty, persuaded her to live in her house.   *LLI.* 6

HARDCOME, JAMES and STEPHEN. They were cousins, and small farmers at Climmerston near Longpuddle. James was engaged to Emily Darth and Stephen to Olive Pawle. At Tony Kytes's 'wedding-randy', each enjoyed dancing so much with the other's betrothed that they decided to change partners for life. After a year or two of marriage, they wondered if they had made the wrong choice. One fine summer day all four went to Budmouth-Regis. Stephen took Olive for a row in the bay, and they were both drowned. The marriage of James and Emily took place a year and a half later, and proved to be a happy one.

William Privett died in James Hardcome's meadow.   *LLI.* 8*b, c*

HARDMAN. The blacksmith at Nether-Moynton. He was caught by the Customs officers and compelled to make the requisitioned carts and horses fit for the road – after lynch-pins and shoes had been removed by the villagers – in order to transport the contraband spirits to Budmouth Custom-house.   *WT.* 7

HARDY, CAPTAIN. *He lived at Portisham, and was descended, like the Hardys of Higher Bockhampton, from the Hardys of Jersey who had settled in Dorset centuries earlier. After the battle of Trafalgar, he became Vice-admiral Sir Thomas Hardy. The monument erected to him in 1844 on Blackdown Hill, north-east of Portisham, is alluded to in* The Trumpet-Major, *xii. For his house, see plate facing p. 144.*

He was captain of Admiral Nelson's flag-ship, the *Victory*, at the battle of Trafalgar. As a result of his visit to the captain at Po'sham, Bob Loveday served on the ship and fought at Trafalgar. The captain was a bachelor of thirty-five, 'rather stout in build, with light eyes, bushy eyebrows, a square broad face, plenty of chin, and a mouth whose corners played between humour and grimness'.

When Nelson is dying, Captain Hardy's thoughts are 'all confused'. He recalls

> Old childish things at home, down Wessex way,
> In the snug village under Blackdon Hill
> Where I was born. The tumbling stream, the garden,

The placid look of the grey dial there,
Marking unconsciously this bloody hour,
And the red apples on my father's trees,
Just now full ripe.

TM. xxxiii–xxxv, xxxvii–xxxix; *D.* (1) iv, i, v ii, iv, vii

HARDY, EMMA LAVINIA (GIFFORD). *The romance of his early attachment to Emma Lavinia Gifford and their strained relations in subsequent years form the major irony of Hardy's life. There can be little doubt that his first wife suffered (like her father) from a sense of social superiority, and was subject to jealousy of Hardy's success and hallucinations which bordered on madness. 'Insanity' was a better word, Hardy told Vere H. Collins, with reference to the poem 'The Interloper'. She encouraged him to pursue his career as a professional writer, and, whatever their differences in later years, they travelled together a great deal. Her sudden death in 1912 removed all provocations; Hardy was filled with a sense of her loyalty and his neglect. All his old love revived. He went on penitential pilgrimages to the places where she had lived, and scores of reminiscential poems were written in which the author's love and remorse found cathartic expression.*

Emma Hardy's Some Recollections *provides the best account of their Cornish romance, and Hardy quoted from it at length in his* Life *(67–73). Little is known of their later relationships outside the poems. For analyses, the reader is referred to 'The Division' in Evelyn Hardy's* Thomas Hardy, A Critical Biography, *'Deep Division' and 'Magic Lights' in Carl Weber's* Hardy of Wessex, *and 'Hardy's Cornish Romance' in the latter's edition of* Hardy's Love Poems *(Macmillan, 1963).*

The arrangement which follows attempts no more than to relate the poems to the chronological order of the primary experiences which they convey.

1. *Early Years at Plymouth (poems evoked on reading* Some Recollections*):* SC. Places (stanzas i, ii; cf. PLYMOUTH), *MV.* During Wind and Rain (*cf.* Some Recollections, *5–6).*

2. *Hardy's First Visit to St Juliot:* LLE. 'A man was drawing near to me' (*for the places, see map, p. 352*), *MV.* The Wind's Prophecy (*the antithetical design suggests Hardy's inventiveness cf. pp. 436–7*) HS. Green Slates (Life, 75), *LLE.* A Duettist to Her Pianoforte (*see p. 370*), *MV.* At the Word 'Farewell', *SC.* A Week (Life, 74–5), *WP.* Ditty, *SC.* The Discovery.

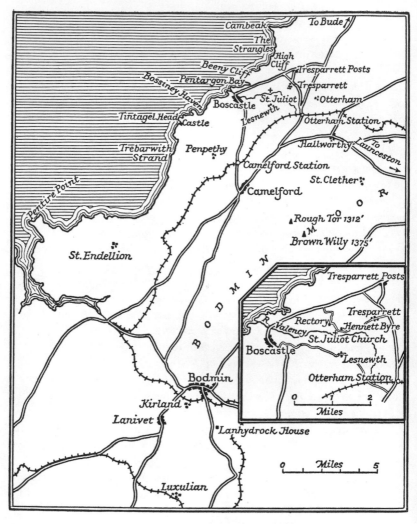

The Cornwall of Hardy's 'Lyonnesse'

Hardy, Emma Lavinia (Gifford)

3. *Subsequent Meetings: TL.* The Minute Before Meeting, *SC.* Under the Waterfall (Life, *71*), *TL.* In the Vaulted Way (*MS.* '*1870*'), *MV.* Love the Monopolist (*leaving Launceston*), *HS.* The Missed Train, *MV.* 'In the seventies', 'I rose and went to Rou'tor Town' (*written in the same stanza as 'When I set out for Lyonnesse', but in every way a contrasting piece. Row or Rough Tor is one of the two highest points on the Bodmin Moors. In 1872, Emma and Hardy stayed with her father, who lived near Bodmin. He disapproved of their proposed marriage, and later referred to Hardy as a base churl who had presumed to wish to marry into his family:* Hardy's Love Poems, *23. This explains the mood of the next poem*), Near Lanivet, 1872 (*south-west of Bodmin*), *SC.* The Place on the Map (*Beeny Cliff. For the 'weeks and weeks', see* Life, *91. The poem alludes to the problem of marrying without parental consent, the snobbish origin of which may be seen in the sub-title, 'A Poor Schoolmaster's Story', which accompanied the poem on its first publication in 1913*). *HS.* Midnight on Beechen, 187– (*Bath, 1873; see* Life, *93*).

4. *Early Years of Marriage: MV.* 'We sat at the window' (Life, *107*), *HS.* Once at Swanage, *MV.* Overlooking the River Stour (*at Sturminster Newton*), The Musical Box, On Sturminster Foot-Bridge.

5. *Outbreaks of 'Insanity': MV.* At the Piano, The Interloper (*recalls experiences in Cornwall, at Sturminster, in London or at some country mansion, and possibly at Max Gate*), The Man with a Past (*the three blows: insanity, separation, death; the one, separation*).

6. *The Division: PPP.* 'Between us now', *MV.* The Young Church-warden, The Chimes (*cf. MC. iv*), *HS.* Alike and Unlike (*MS.* 'She speaks'; *see* Life, *254*), *TL.* The Division, *SC.* Had you Wept, *MV.* The Wound, The Peace-Offering, *LLE.* Without, not Within Her, *HS.* When Dead (? *SC.* Wessex Heights; *cf. footnote, p. 309*).

7. *Last Years: MV.* Lines ('Show me again the time'), *LLE.* A Duettist to her Pianoforte (*see* HELEN CATHERINE HOLDER), *SC.* Lost Love, *MV.* The Last Performance (*see* Life, *359*), *SC.* The Walk, Your Last Drive.

8. *Her Death: SC.* The Going, Without Ceremony, *HS.* A Leaving (*the funeral*), *LLE.* End of the Year 1912.

9. *Her Grave at Stinsford: HS.* 'Not only I', *SC.* 'My spirit will not haunt the mound', *MV.* An Upbraiding, *SC.* Tolerance, Rain on a Grave, 'I found her out there', *MV.* An Anniversary, The Riddle, 'Something tapped', *LLE.* The Dream is – Which? *HS.* The Fading Rose, *LLE.* 'The curtains now are drawn', *SC.* The Voice, *MV.* Looking Across (*the graves of Hardy's father, mother, wife, and sister Mary*), *LLE.* 'If you had known'.

10. *Hardy's Pilgrimages: SC.* St Launce's Revisited, After a Journey, A Death-Day Recalled, *MV.* 'It never looks like summer', *SC.* At Castle Boterel, Places (*despite the footnote, the poem seems to have been composed at, or after a visit to, Boscastle; cf. stanza iii*), The Phantom Horsewoman, *HS.* Her Haunting-Ground (*the rectory garden, St Juliot*), *MV.* Where They Lived (*the rectory, St Juliot*), The Man who Forgot, *SC.* Where the Picnic Was, *LLE.* The West-of-Wessex Girl, The Marble-Streeted Town (*Plymouth*) The Seven Times (*for the first six, before Mrs Hardy's death, see pp. 6–7. If the title is taken literally, it agrees with the record of Hardy's six visits to St Juliot before his marriage. He seems to have forgotten his visit in October 1871 (see p. 7).*

11. *Her Memorial at St Juliot: LLE.* The Marble Tablet, *HS.* The Monument-Maker.

12. *Recollections: HS.* 'She opened the door', *MV.* Joys of Memory, *LLE.* The Old Gown, *MV.* Looking at a Picture on an Anniversary (*7 March, the day he first met Emma*), *LLE.* 'As 'twere tonight', A Woman Driving, *SC.* A Dream or No, Self-Unconscious, *HS.* Two Lips, *MV.* He Fears his Good Fortune, The Figure in the Scene, 'Why did I sketch?', *HS.* The Frozen Greenhouse, *MV.* The Young Churchwarden (*MS. 'At an evening service, August 14, 1870'. A note in Hardy's Prayer Book shows that the service was at Lesnewth, near St Juliot.*), *LLE.* A Wet August, *MV.* Quid Hic Agis? (*see Life, 157 and PBE. xix*), *LLE.* Where Three Roads Joined (*alludes to the deaths of Emma and her sister. MS. 'Tresparrett Posts'*), *LLE.* Fetching Her, *SC.* In Front of the Landscape (*stanzas vii and viii*), Beeny Cliff, *MV.* The Change (*recalling the week of Hardy's first visit to St Juliot, and Emma's first visit to London; see Some Recollections, 60*), *HS.* Days to Recollect, *LLE.* A Two Years' Idyll (*at Sturminster Newton; Life, 118*), *MV.* Old Excursions, On the Doorstep, Paths of a Former Time, *HS.* At a

Fashionable Dinner (*MS. shows 'Lavine' for 'Emleen'*), *SC.* Lament, A Circular, *LLE.* A Woman's Trust, Lonely Days, Read by Moonlight, *SC.* Tolerance, *MV.* 'I thought, my Heart, that you had healed', *HS.* When Oats were Reaped, *MV.* The Five Students (*'fair She; see p. 370*), The Coming of the End (*the 'journey of one day a week': visiting Hardy's parents*), The Clock of the Years, Everything Comes (*Max Gate*), *LLE.* Best Times, The Last Time, *SC.* A Poet. *See* STURMINSTER NEWTON.

13. *Living Bereaved: HS.* The Prospect, *LLE.* On a Discovered Curl of Hair, *MV.* The Shadow on the Stone (*Life, 233–4*), *LLE.* The Garden Seat, (?) The Little Old Table, The Selfsame Song, A Night in November, *SC.* In Front of the Landscape, The Haunter, His Visitor (*at Max Gate*), The Spell of the Rose, *MV.* Paths of a Former Time, He Prefers Her Earthly, *SC.* The Difference, *HS.* This Summer and Last, *MV.* The Tree and the Lady, *LLE.* By Henstridge Cross at the Year's End (*originally 'Mellstock Cross'*), *HS.* Ten Years Since, *LLE.* Penance, 'I look in her face', *MV.* Conjecture.

There are several other poems which may be related to Emma Hardy. Some are marginal, some disguised, e.g. *SC.* 'She charged me', *MV.* 'You were the sort that men forget', His Heart, By the Runic Stone (*with* A Pair of Blue Eyes *in mind?*), *LLE.* 'I was not he', The Chimes play 'Life's a Bumper', A Procession of Dead Days (*'third hour'?*), He Follows Himself, In a London Flat, *HS.* When Dead (*Emma speaking*).

HARDY, FLORENCE EMILY (DUGDALE). *Miss Dugdale lived at Enfield, and wrote children's books. She was introduced to Hardy by Mrs Henniker in 1904, and frequently stayed and helped at Max Gate during the later years of the first Mrs Hardy. When Hardy was completing* The Dynasts, *she made occasional visits to the British Museum to research for him. After the death of Mrs Hardy, she was invited to Max Gate to take charge, and save Hardy from intrusive visitors. They were married on 10 February 1914 at Enfield. She was thirty-five; he, seventy-three. Although the greater part of* The Life of Thomas Hardy *was prepared and written by Hardy himself, Florence played an important part in its preparation, and wrote the final chapters. Hardy's affection and gratitude are shown in his poems.*

TL. 'On the Departure Platform'; *SC.* 'After the Visit', 'To Meet, or Otherwise', 'A Poet'; *MV.* 'Conjecture',

'For life I had never cared greatly'; *LLE*. 'I sometimes Think', 'A Jog-trot Pair'

HARDY, JEMIMA. *Hardy's mother (1813–1904). As a writer, he owed much to her. She had 'an extraordinary store of local memories, reaching back to the days when the ancient ballads were everywhere heard at country feasts, in weaving shops, and at spinning-wheels'* (Life, 321). *These memories supplied many incidents in his books, Hardy told Hermann Lea. One of her ventures contributed to* The Hand of Ethelberta *(see p. 29). In his notebook, Hardy wrote: 'Mother's notion (and also mine) – that a figure stands in our van with arms uplifted, to knock us back from any pleasant prospect we indulge in as probable.' Her good taste in literature, he stated, was expressed in the books she selected for her children. There can be no doubt about her ambition for her son; when he was eight years old, she gave him Dryden's* Virgil, *Johnson's* Rasselas, *and* Paul and Virginia *(cf.* Life, *8, 13–14, 16, 18, 21–2, 25, 309, 321).*

> *PPP.* 'In Tenebris' (iii): *'She who upheld me'* on *'that loneliest of eves'* on Egdon Heath; *TL.* 'A Church Romance' (*her first sight of Hardy's father 'circa 1836'*), 'The Roman Road' (*on 'Egdon' Heath*), 'Night in the Old Home', 'After the Last Breath', 'She Hears the Storm' (? *after her husband's death*); *MV.* 'Looking Across' (*stanza ii*)

HARDY, MARY. *The novelist's sister (1841–1915). She and her younger sister Katherine (1856–1940) went to Salisbury Training College for teachers (see* MELCHESTER*), and taught at the Dorchester Girls' National School in Icen Way. Mary was headmistress there. She was a painter of no mean ability, as the portraits of her parents show, and a church-organist in more than one parish 'during all her active years'. She and Thomas were very close friends (see* Life, 371).

> *WP.* 'Middle-Age Enthusiasms'; *MV.* 'Conjecture', 'Logs on the Hearth', 'Molly Gone', 'Looking Across' (stanza iv), 'In the Garden'; *LLE.* 'Sacred to the Memory' (*words on the tombstone designed by Thomas Hardy*), 'The Sun's Last Look on the Country Girl'; *HS.* 'Paradox'

HARDY, MARY (HEAD). *Hardy's paternal grandmother (1772–1857), who lived with the family at Higher Bockhampton. She came from Fawley, the 'Marygreen' of* Jude the Obscure. *She and Hardy's grandfather were the first of three generations of Hardy's to live at Higher Bockhampton; the house had been built for 'Thomas Hardy the First' by his father John, and they occupied it in 1801. Hardy's grandmother's recollections made an indelible impression on the child Thomas Hardy the Third. They went back to her painful experiences as an orphan at Fawley; she could recall vividly just what she was doing when she heard that the King and Queen of France had been executed, and had good cause to remember the invasion scare in the south of England. She is the Molly of 'The Alarm' who was expecting a baby. The poem records the dilemma of Hardy's grandfather when he was a Volunteer.* When he observed the beacon burning on Rainbarrow, he decided by augury whether to proceed to the coast or return to his wife. He had left instructions that, should there be an invasion, his wife was to drive with the nurse to Kingsbere (*Bere Regis; cf. TM. xxvi*). *See* Life, 4 (*'Domicilium'*), 12, 215, 420.

WP. 'The Alarm'; TL. 'One We Knew'

HARDY, THOMAS. *'Thomas the First', Hardy's grandfather (1778– 1837), a builder, long associated with the Stinsford choir. As a violinist, he was recalled in William Dewy and Mr Yeobright. He was a Volunteer (a civilian trained to fight should the homeland be invaded) in 1803–5. See* Life, 8–13, 248, 250, 318.   RN. I v; WP. 'The Alarm'

HARDY, THOMAS. *'Thomas the Second', Hardy's father (1811–92); builder, farmer, and a leading member of the Stinsford string choir. See* Life, 10, 12–14, 19, 21, 23–4, 32–4, 96, 247–8, 250, 318, 444.

PPP. 'The Self-Unseeing'; TL. 'A Church Romance' ('*circa 1836*', Life, *14*), 'Night in the Old Home'; MV. 'To My Father's Violin', 'Looking Across' (stanza i); LLE. 'On One who Lived and Died where he was Born' (*Hardy's father did not die in November, but in other respects the poem is true.*)

HARDY, THOMAS. *The author (1840–1928). The extent to which he is reflected in his fiction is difficult to assess, and liable to exaggeration. Brief comments will be found elsewhere with reference to certain novels and characters. For his views, see pp. 167–83. The references below are restricted to recollections of early years, and some of the more personal poems. Others will be found under* HARDY, EMMA LAVINIA (GIFFORD), PHENA, LOUISA, *etc. See also* MAX GATE.

1. *Childhood:* 'Domicilium' (Life, *4*); PPP. 'The Self-Unseeing' (*written after his father's death; cf.* Life, *15*); TL. 'The Roman Road'.(cf. 'In Tenebris', iii); WW. 'Childhood among the Ferns' (*cf.* Life, *15–16 and JO. i ii*).

357

2. *Boyhood: TL.* 'The House of Hospitalities' (*identified as a neighbouring house 'by the well'; possibly the tranter's, cf.* Life, *92*), 'One We Knew' (see pp. 356–7); *MV.* 'Afternoon Service at Mellstock', 'Apostrophe to an Old Psalm Tune', 'At Middle-Field Gate in February' (*written c. 1889; cf.* Life, *223*), 'He Revisits his First School'.

3. *Early Manhood: TL.* 'Reminiscences of a Dancing Man'; *LLE.* 'A Young Man's Exhortation'; *MV.* 'In the Seventies', 'Great Things'; *HS.* 'Four in the Morning'.

4. *Later Years: PPP.* 'The Darkling Thrush', 'In Tenebris'; *TL.* 'Shut out that Moon', 'The Dead Man Walking' (*MS. '1896'*), 'He Abjures Love'; *SC.* 'In Front of the Landscape', 'The Ghost of the Past', 'Wessex Heights', 'Before and After Summer', 'Exeunt Omnes', 'A Poet'; *MV.* 'The Chimes', 'Old Furniture', 'Looking Across' (*the graves of his father, mother, wife, and sister Mary*), 'Who's in the next room?', 'Paying Calls', 'He Fears his Good Fortune', 'He Revisits his First School', 'Afterwards'; *LLE.* 'Penance', 'In the Small Hours', 'I was the midmost'; *WW.* 'A Poet's Thought', 'Seeing the Moon Rise', 'He never Expected Much', 'Not Known', 'He Resolves to Say No More'.

The date and circumstances of Hardy's invitation to the United States are not known. Other invitations followed; cf. Life, *331, 343, 385. Hardy was unable to accept any of them.*

In 1905, he received the honorary degree of LL.D. at Aberdeen University (Life, *323–4). Hardy told Vere H. Collins that the 'Queen' of the poem is Knowledge.*

> *PPP.* 'On an Invitation to the United States' (*the thought of the poem probably owes something to a passage which Hardy copied from Henry James's* Hawthorne; *see Purdy, 111*); *TL.* 'Aberdeen'

HARNHAM, MRS. *Hardy knew that Constable's picture of Salisbury* (*Melchester*) *Cathedral was painted from Harnham Hill* (Life, *388*). *The bridge over the Avon at Salisbury is called Harnham Bridge.*

Before marriage she was Miss Edith White and lived on the Great Mid-Wessex Plain (*Salisbury Plain*) not far from Anna's home. She married a rich wine-merchant in Melchester, but found she did not care for him. Anna came to Melchester as her servant; she taught her to speak well but found that Anna, who had not been to school, could make little progress with reading and writing. When the young barrister, Charles Bradford Raye, fell in love with Anna, Mrs Harnham replied to his letters, and soon found she was expressing a love which she could not feel for her husband. The barrister was enchanted, and it was only after marrying Anna that he discovered that 'in soul and spirit' he was bound to somebody else. *LLI.* 5

HARRIET. A duchess who lived at Shakeforest Towers near Marlbury Downs. She met her cousin Captain Ogbourne from Canada, at his request, by the Druid stones. The following night the Duke returned without warning, met Ogbourne there, accused him of dishonour, and murdered him. The Duchess never knew what had happened. *CM.* 7

HAVENPOOL. *Poole, Dorset; a port long engaged in 'the Newfoundland trade'.*

Sol and Lord Mountclere's brother drove through a 'drumming' storm over the heath from Sandbourne in a vain effort to stop the marriage of Ethelberta and the viscount. At one point they saw eyelets of light winking on the distance under 'a nebulous brow of pale haze'. This was 'the little town of Havenpool'.

Newson landed at Havenpool when he returned from Newfoundland.

St James's Church, and the Town Cellars, 'where the High Street joined the Quay', are associated with Shadrach Jolliffe, and the sad story of his wife. *See plate facing p. 463.*

According to the Havenpool marriage register, John Horseleigh, Knight, of Clyffton (*John Horsey of Clifton Maybank, near Yeovil*), married Edith, the widow of John Stocker, a Havenpool merchant, in 1539. No mention of this is to be found in the Horseleigh pedigree (*i.e. in Hutchins*, The History and Antiquities of the County of Dorset), and the explanation may be found in 'a strange local tradition' (see HORSE-LEIGH).

The Committee-man of 'The Terror' who arrived in Budmouth had travelled in a shabby stage-coach by a coastal by-route from Havenpool.

HE. xliv; *MC.* xli; *LLI.* 6; *CM.* 9; *CM.* 8;
LLE. 'The Chapel-Organist'; *WW.* 'The Mongrel'

HAVILL, MR. A Toneborough architect who built the unprepossessing Baptist chapel near Sleeping-Green. He had begun as a landscape gardener, then become a builder, and then a road contractor. He was a deacon at the chapel. On the verge of bankruptcy, he was anxious and ill-disposed towards his rival architect, George Somerset. Will Dare gained a hold over him, and had little difficulty in persuading him to gain access to Somerset's architectural plans and copy them. On Somerset's suggestion, the rival plans were sent to be judged by the R.I.B.A., who pronounced them 'singularly equal and singularly good'. As Havill was in debt, Miss Power was persuaded by Captain de Stancy to hand the work over to Havill. The deacon was overcome with compunction, on listening to a sermon preached by Mr Woodwell immediately after the death of Mrs Havill, and resigned his commission. When George Somerset resigned, he continued the work, only to find it did not extend far when de Stancy returned from the Continent, confident of his marriage with Miss Power and the return of Stancy Castle to the family which had owned it for so long. The work came to a sudden end when, all his hopes dashed, Dare set fire to the castle.

L. I viii–xi, xiv, xv; II i–vii; III iii, iv, xi; V xii; VI iv, v

HAWES, MRS. A widow with whom Sue Bridehead lodged when she was acting as pupil-teacher with Mr Phillotson at Lumsdon. *JO.* II v

HAWKSGATE. *Its location, like that of other places in the story (which remained uncollected and unadapted to Hardy's scheme of Wessex place-names), is vague; but the fact that Egbert Mayne walked across Tollamore Park on his way to school one morning suggests that it is not far from Stinsford, though it is described as 'a remote hamlet'. The school, like Fancy Day's, was undoubtedly suggested by the one at Lower Bock-hampton which Hardy attended. Tollamore House, like Knapwater House, is Kingston Maurward House.* *ILH.* I 3

HAYLOCK, MR. The Casterbridge butcher who supplied meat to Geoffrey Day, and to his daughter at the school house in Mellstock. The gamekeeper's visit to Haylock provides an amusing vignette. *UGT.* IV iv

HAYWARD, JIM. He was a lime-burner in business with his cousin Richard Vine, 'a widower of fifty odd years' with whom he lodged. He was young, with a fair, almost florid complexion. His trousers and waistcoat were of fustian and almost white, and he wore a jacket of old-fashioned blue West-of-England cloth. He was in love with Margery Tucker, but his suit did not prosper when she came under the spell of Baron von Xanten. Later he joined the Yeomanry. The flirtation which he pursued with Mrs Peach had the desired effect, thanks to the loyalty of the Baron. Some time after their secret marriage at the Baron's house, he and Margery settled down to a happy married life. *CM.* 12

HAZE, CUNNINGHAM. The chief constable for the Markton district.

Dare was three times in danger of being arrested by him.

L. II iv, V xi, xiv, VI v

HEARTALL, BOB. One of the Mellstock neighbours who was called in for the dance to celebrate the return of John Clark, Selina Paddock's 'intended' husband. *CM.* 5

HEDDEGAN, MR DAVID. He was a general merchant, who lived at Giant's Town in the Isles of Lyonesse and married Baptista Trewthen, not knowing that she had married and lost her husband by drowning two days previously. When she confessed, he was greatly relieved; he had not yet told her he was a widower and had four girls whom he wished her to educate. She had decided to marry because she disliked teaching. *CM.* 11

HEIDELBERG. *In describing Paula Power's visit to Heidelberg and other places in the Rhine Valley, Hardy recalled his own tour in 1876.*

Mrs Charmond had met Fitzpiers here when she was a girl and he was a medical student at Heidelberg. They recalled the two or three days 'spent in tender acquaintance on the romantic slopes above the Neckar' before her mother 'spirited' her away to Baden (cf. *L.* v vii and *Life*, 110).

L. v vi, vii; *W.* xxvi–xxvii

HELMSDALE, THE RIGHT REVEREND CUTHBERT, D.D. *The sly humour behind the story of the Bishop of Melchester (Salisbury) may have given Hardy a peculiar private satisfaction. It has long been held, though no evidence has yet appeared, that he applied for admission to Salisbury Theological College, and was rejected; see p. 167.*

Bishop Helmsdale of Melchester came to Welland to officiate at the confirmation service. He attended luncheon at Welland House and was fascinated by Lady Constantine, who had known him when she was a girl and he held the living of Puddle-sub-Mixen, in the neighbourhood (*a vague reference undoubtedly to one of the parishes in the Piddle valley north-west of Puddletown*). He proposed marriage, but she declined, as she was already secretly married to Swithin St Cleeve. The bishop was especially interested in Swithin's astronomical studies, as he had known his father at All Angels College. While at Welland for the confirmation visit, he went to Rings-Hill Speer to see Swithin's work, and detected a coral bracelet on his bed, and a movement behind the curtains. He did not, of course, suspect Lady Constantine. When she discovered that she was pregnant, and that it was impossible to get in touch with Swithin to marry him (her private marriage having proved to be illegal as soon as it was discovered that Sir Blount had died after it, and not long before as had been supposed), her brother Louis Glanville persuaded the Bishop that she was in love with him. In desperation, Lady Constantine accepted the Bishop's second offer of marriage. The marriage was not a happy one, and Lady Constantine's stay at the Bishop's palace at Melchester was short, the Bishop dying after a brief illness at the age of fifty-four.

TT. xxiii–xxix, xxxi–xxxiii, xxxvii, xxxix–xli

HENCHARD, MICHAEL. Henchard was an ambitious but frustrated hay-trusser, who was embittered in his worst moments at being encumbered with a wife and child. His wife became tired of his ill-temper and accepted her release when, in a drunken stupor, he offered her for sale at Weydon-Priors Fair and found she was snapped up by the sailor Newson. In penance, Henchard swore never to touch intoxicating liquor for another twenty-one years; he was twenty-one. Nineteen years later, his wife Susan returned with her daughter and found that the ex-haytrusser was Mayor of Casterbridge and a prosperous corn-merchant. He did not hesitate to remarry Susan, and did everything possible to make amends for his past folly. Susan thought that Newson had been drowned at sea, and Henchard assumed that Elizabeth-Jane was his daughter, and told her so after Susan's death, only to discover immediately afterwards that he had been deceived. 'His reinstation of her mother had been chiefly for the girl's sake', and 'the fruition of the whole scheme' had proved to be 'dust and ashes'. In his loneliness, he had turned to Farfrae, whom he had engaged as business-manager, much to his relief and profit, for friendship; but Farfrae's success, his open resistance to the threat to put Whittle to shame, and his apparent opposition in a bid for popularity created such overpowering jealousy in Henchard that he dismissed Farfrae and forbad him to continue a friendship that threatened to deprive him of Elizabeth-Jane. Farfrae set up in business at Durnover, and Henchard decided to crush him. Unlike Farfrae, he had no business acumen or method, and allowed superstitious respect for a local weather-prophet's forecast to influence his buying. So wild were his speculations that he was soon unable to pay his creditors; he was declared bankrupt, and lost his business, his house, and Lucetta (*q.v.*) to Farfrae. Eventually he humbled himself and worked in the yard where he had been master. When the twenty-one years of his pledge had expired, he took to drink once more, and threatened to do harm to Farfrae. His humiliation before the Royal visitor and at the hands of Farfrae, now the Mayor, made him decide to carry out his plan to fight to the death with his rival. When he had Farfrae at his mercy, he let him go and was ashamed of himself, just as at the critical juncture he could not divulge the contents of Lucetta's letters – he had promised to marry her, and she had come from Jersey and settled in Casterbridge for that purpose. The news of Lucetta's critical illness, after seeing the skimmington-ride, which was intended to spread a scandal about her past with Henchard, called forth his utmost exertions to make what reparations he could, but Farfrae distrusted him and ignored his appeal that he should return to his wife. The next morning, Newson called and made inquiries about his daughter Elizabeth-Jane. By this time, Henchard had come to realize that his happiness was bound up with Elizabeth-Jane, who regarded him as her father and had taken care of him in his degradation. He said that she was dead; Newson believed him and left. Henchard was so horrified at what he had done on the spur of the moment that he would have drowned himself at Ten Hatches Weir but for the sudden, apparently supernatural, appearance of himself in the water. (It was his effigy, which had been thrown into the river above Casterbridge after the skimmington.) He was a superstitious man and thought that Providence had interposed to save him. Elizabeth-Jane agreed to live with him and take care of him. They lived happily together, and ran a small seed-shop business until Henchard's fears that he would lose her were revived by Farfrae's renewal of courtship. Newson's return shattered Henchard's hopes, and he left Casterbridge, ashamed of his deception. He returned to Weydon-Priors as a hay-trusser, with no ambition but only the will to endure. He soon discovered that he was an outcast, and lost the will to live. His one hope was that he and Elizabeth could be reconciled, and he chose the occasion of her wedding with Farfrae to return to Casterbridge and see her, only to discover that she had not forgiven him for keeping her from her father for five years. He had given up ambition, and now was denied the love he sought so desperately. Abel Whittle, who could not forget the kindness Henchard had shown his mother, followed him as he left Casterbridge and tended him until his death. Elizabeth-Jane had discovered his wedding-present and relented; but she and Farfrae did not discover where Henchard had gone until just after his death.

The Henchard–Farfrae relationship has some important affinities with that of Saul and David, e.g. melancholy, ill-temper, fits of mad behaviour, jealousy, susceptibility to music. The visit to the soothsayer and the attempt to murder Farfrae also have their parallels in the life of Saul.

There are other overtones, especially of King Lear: *the initial folly, gradual redemption as a result of consequent suffering, happiness with Elizabeth (Cordelia), and the loyalty of the 'fool' Whittle on the heath (the edge of Egdon, which Hardy associated with King Lear; cf. the preface to RN).*
MC

HENCHARD, SUSAN. She lived with her sullen, frustrated, irritable, and ambitious husband, Michael Henchard, the hay-trusser, until, the worse for drink, he auctioned her at Weydon-Priors Fair. Her endurance had been overtaxed, and she welcomed release from him, and accompanied her purchaser, the sailor Newson, to Canada with her baby daughter Elizabeth-Jane, who soon afterwards died. Her simplicity was such that she assumed she was Newson's legal wife. A daughter was born to them, and also christened Elizabeth-Jane. They came to England and settled at Falmouth. Here Susan began to realize that her marriage had no legal sanction, and the result was that Newson returned to sea. When it was reported that he had been drowned, Susan with her eighteen-year-old daughter left Falmouth to find her husband Henchard. She found him Mayor of Casterbridge. By this time Susan was weak in health and spirits, but instinctively she sought to secure her daughter's future. After her remarriage, her main concern was to ensure Elizabeth-Jane's wedded happiness, and, in her simple-minded way, she endeavoured to bring her and Farfrae together. Her schemes were foiled by Henchard's wrong-headedness. Susan was too ill to enjoy the amenities which marriage with Henchard placed at her disposal, and she died about a year after their reunion. Her death is affectingly told by Mother Cuxsom.
MC. i–xiv, xviii–xix, xxviii, xli

HENDFORD HILL. *On the main road to the south in Yeovil* (Ivell), *Somerset.*
LLI. 4

HENNIKER, MRS. *The daughter of Lord Houghton. Her first novel was published in 1891. She was her brother's hostess in Dublin in May 1893, when the Hardys were their guests (see* Life, *254-5). The two authors met in London, Winchester and Salisbury. He collaborated with her in the writing of a short story, 'The Spectre of the Real', in the autumn of 1893, and continued to read her writings and offer critical advice. They corresponded from 1893 to 1922. Hardy's letters show that Sue Bridehead was drawn partly from Mrs Henniker. If Hardy was in love with her in the early part of their friendship he did not declare it, and she may not have been aware of it. The evidence of the poems is not conclusive. It was Florence Hardy who said that two of them were to be associated with Mrs Henniker: 'A Broken Appointment' (at the British Museum) and 'A Thunderstorm in Town'. Others attributed to her may have been misinterpreted, and it is often difficult to draw the line between fact and fiction.*

> *WP*. 'At an Inn'; *PPP*. 'A Broken Appointment'; *TL*. (?) 'The Division' (*Although this may have been written after Hardy met Mrs Henniker, the 'division' is surely that between him and his wife. It is more than the distance between London and Max Gate – which is just over a hundred miles. Hardy's letters – cf. Weber, Dearest Emmie – show that he was often in London when she was at home*). *SC*. 'A Thunderstorm in Town', 'Wessex Heights' (*'one rare fair woman'*), 'In Death Divided'; *MV*. 'He Wonders about Himself', (?) 'The Coming of the End' (*the whole poem seems clearly to be about Emma Lavinia Hardy: their meetings in Cornwall, Sturminster Newton, Max Gate; Emma's discontinuation of her visits with Hardy to his parents at Higher Bockhampton; her death*). *HS*. 'Come not; yet Come!', 'The Month's Calendar', 'Last Love-Word' (*more imaginary than real?*).

HENRY THE EIGHTH'S CASTLE. *Sandsfoot Castle, near Weymouth, overlooking Portland Harbour.* WB. I iii, iv, v; II iii; III iii, v

HENSTRIDGE CROSS. *North-west of Sturminster Newton. Hardy's note was intended to divert attention from the personal implications of the poem. It was first printed with the title 'By Mellstock Cross at the Year's End'. The general meaning seems to be: 'What's the use of anything? It is time civilisation made a new start.' The first verse alludes perhaps to Hardy's disillusionment and loss of faith in London; the second to his collateral ancestors who had once owned much property at Woolcombe (near Melbury Bubb) and Up Sydling (cf. Life, 5); the third to the death of his first wife; the fourth to the 1914–18 war.*

> LLE. 'By Henstridge Cross at the Year's End'

HERMITAGE. See the HINTOCKS, *and plate facing p. 303.*

HERVY, SIR WILLIAM. *Sir William Hervey, the third husband of Lady Darcy.* GND. 8

HEWBY, MR. The London architect to whom Mr Swancourt had written on the question of church restoration. Hewby sent Stephen Smith to make plans. PBE. i, ii, v, xiii, xviii

HEYMERE, MARIA. *In the 1906–7 pocket edition of the Wessex novels (Macmillan), Heymere House (not mentioned in the story) is shown about ten miles south-west of Bristol. Support for this is not found in Leland ('a fair maner-place' is one of his stock descriptive phrases) or in Hardy's location of Icenway House. See* ICENWAY.

For her story, see pp. 78–9. GND. 5

HICKS, JOHN. *The Dorchester architect with whom Hardy was articled as an apprentice before he went to London, and whom he helped with church-restoration at various times on his return. Hicks died in 1869. In 1911 Hardy went to Gloucester Cathedral to see how (according to tradition) the English style of Gothic architecture had begun; the poem on the subject was written with memories of John Hicks. Cf.* Life, *357.*

SC. 'The Abbey Mason'

HIGGINS, MRS. She lived at 3 Canley Passage, Hoxton, London. The description of her household is noteworthy for its Crabbe-like realism. She had bought Mrs Manston's workbox and pawned it. Edward Springrove retrieved it, and found that it contained incriminating evidence against Manston. *DR.* xvi 4, xvii 3

HIGH-STOY. *A wooded hill on the chalk downs south of Blackmoor Vale, and immediately to the west of Dogbury Gate, where the main Dorchester–Sherborne road crosses the range. The road down to 'Little Hintock' passes below High Stoy.*

W. i, xxiii, xxviii, xlii, xlv; *TD.* ii, xliv; *PPP.* 'The Lost Pyx', 'Doom and She' (*an MS. variant of the penultimate line reads* 'On High-Stoy Hill or Pilsdon Peak'); *HS.* 'Under High-Stoy Hill' (*the poem may have been occasioned by Hardy's last visit in August 1922:* Life, *417*).

HIGHAM, THEOPHILUS. A Scripture reader who officiated at the bogus marriage between Caroline and Charles de la Feste. He was an admirer of Caroline's sister Alicia. Charles had fallen in love with Alicia after his engagement to Caroline. After marrying Caroline at Alicia's insistence, he drowned himself. Years later, 'after a persistent wooing', Caroline was married to Theophilus Higham, who had become the fully ordained curate of the next parish to Wherryborne. *CM.* 3

HIGHER BOCKHAMPTON (*with special reference to Hardy's birthplace*). 'Domicilium' (*Life,* 4); *TL.* 'The House of Hospitalities' (p. 412), 'The Night of the Dance' (*Imaginary or recollected? The Hardys' house or the 'House of Hospitalities'? It recalls scenes in* Under the Greenwood Tree),

The church and the 'Pure Drop Inn' at Marnhull (Marlott)

Woolbridge (Wellbridge) Manor and the River Frome

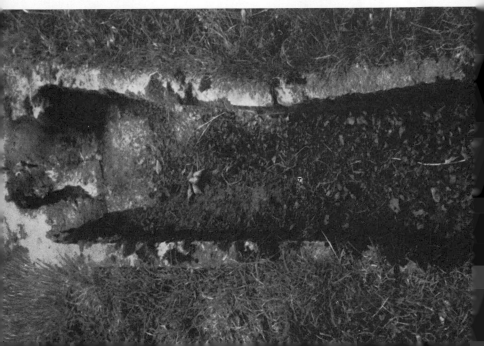

Left: The stone coffin, Bindon Abbey (see Wellbridge)

Right: Cross-in-Hand

'Night in the old Home'; *MV.* 'Old Furniture'; *LLE.* 'She did not turn'; (see p. 439); *HS.* 'A Bird-Scene at a Rural Dwelling', 'Four in the Morning'; *WW.* 'Concerning His Old Home', 'Silences'. *For TL.* 'She Hears the Storm', *see p. 356; for other references see* MELLSTOCK.

HIGHER CROWSTAIRS. A lonely house, occupied by Mr Fennel, a sheep-farmer, and his family, on a grassy furzy down, not three miles from Casterbridge (*and probably in the direction of the Piddle valley, since the third of the strangers to call on the evening of 28 March 182– had tramped from Blandford and was on his way to Dorchester. Large tracts of the country were then unenclosed. Hardy did not disclose its whereabouts, but agreed that it was somewhere to the north or north-east of Dorchester, since the hangman would come from Sherborne or Salisbury: Weber,* Hardy and the Lady from Madison Square, *Colby College Press, 1952, 85).*   *WT.* 1

HIGHRIDGE, MR. *The name suggests the High Church movement and Ridge Way (p. 457).*

The new curate at Marygreen, whom Jude heard praying with his great-aunt in the adjoining room when he arrived after being dismissed from his post at Christminster. Jude consulted him on entering the Church as a licentiate.   *JO.* II vii

HILL, ALWYN. Mr Oldbourne's curate at Batton. He was attached to Emmeline Oldbourne, but her father remained inexorable in his opposition, and 'soon the curate disappeared from the parish'. When Emmeline heard he was going to emigrate, she sent for him and implored him to take her to America and save her from the harsh treatment to which she was subjected by her husband, the Duke of Hamptonshire. Alwyn's principles were too strong for his heart, and he refused. He did not discover that she was on the *Western Glory* when he sailed to Boston, and that she had died on the voyage and he had officiated at her burial, until years later.   *GND.* 9

HILTON AND PIMM. Opticians in London, from whom Lady Constantine ordered an equatorial for the young astronomer Swithin St Cleeve.

TT. vii, viii

HINTOCKS, THE. *Woodland villages in the area which includes, to the west, the three Melburys north of Evershot, and Hermitage, Middlemarsh and Holnest further east. They are largely imaginary.*

They are mentioned in 'Interlopers at The Knap' (*King's Hintock is Melbury Osmond, and King's Hintock Court, Melbury House; see p. 381*),

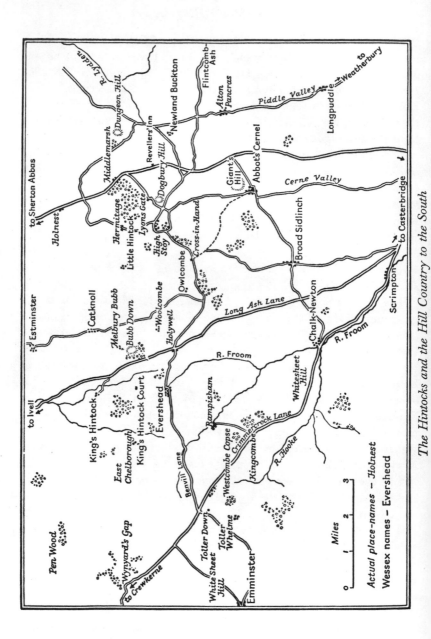

The Hintocks and the Hill Country to the South

Actual place-names — *Holnest*

Wessex names — *Evershead*

Miles
0 1 2 3

where we are told that the locality produced 'the best cider and cider-wine in all Wessex'. They are seen in the distance by Tess on her hill-route to Emminster, and by Angel Clare when he travels in the opposite direction in the hope of finding her at Flintcomb-Ash.

The Sergeant who fought at San Sebastian lived in the Hintock district. Patty Beech had lived at Hermitage. *The 'Horse' at Hintock Green is the White Horse Inn at Middlemarsh.*

LITTLE HINTOCK, *the setting for* The Woodlanders, *is an imaginary and composite village. It lay hidden in the landscape to the north of High Stoy and Bubb Down, not far from the Sherton Abbas road, and probably south-east of Hermitage. In May 1926 Hardy wrote* (Life, *432): 'it has features which were to be found fifty years ago in the hamlets of Hermitage, Middlemarsh, Lyons-Gate, Revels Inn, Holnest, Melbury Bubb, etc. . . . The topographers you mention as identifying the scene are merely guessers and are wrong. . . .' It is near 'Great Hintock' (see below).*

Charities were established at Little Hintock and other villages in the neighbourhood by the mother of the first Countess of Wessex.

GREAT HINTOCK *in* The Woodlanders *was Melbury Osmond ('King's Hintock'), but Hardy transferred it to the east in a later edition. See article by F. B. Pinion in* The Thomas Hardy Year Book, *Toucan Press, 1971.*

HINTOCK HOUSE (*W.* viii, xxiii, xxvi–xxvii, xxx, xxxii, xxxiv, xxxvi) *was drawn from Turnworth House, near Blandford Forum, and its situation 'in a hole', which was 'full of beauty'. The mansion no longer stands. See plate facing p. 303.*

MARSHCOMBE BOTTOM *and* MARSHWOOD (*W.* xxxv, xlv) *suggest Middlemarsh. See also* REVELLERS' INN (*W.* xxviii, xlv).

> *WT.* 6; *W. passim*; *GND.* 1; *TD.* xliv, liv; *WP.* 'San Sebastian'; *TL.* 'A Trampwoman's Tragedy', 'At Caster-bridge Fair' (v)

HINTON, ADELAIDE. The daughter of the retired editor of *The Caster-Bridge Chronicle*, who lived at Peakhill Cottage, Carriford. She had long been engaged to her cousin, the young architect Edward Springrove. Suddenly, just before the marriage of Manston and Cytherea Graye was due, it was announced that she had married Farmer Bollens.

> *DR.* viii 2; x 1, 4, 5; xiii 2

HIPCROFT, NED. A 'respectable mechanic' at Stickleford, who was engaged to Caroline Aspent; she refused him when she was under Mop Ollamoor's spell. He went to work in London, where he was engaged in the construction of the 1851 Exhibition. See pp. 92–3.   *LLI.* 7

HOBSON, SAM. A gardener at Gaymead Vicarage, who wished to marry the servant Sophy. However, the vicar, Mr Twycott, married her, and they went to London. When Sam heard that she was a widow, he became manager of a gardener's business near London in the hope of meeting her again. Sophy had been lamed for life, could take little exercise, and therefore slept poorly. She was in the habit of getting up at one o'clock in the morning to watch vehicles piled with vegetables proceeding to Covent Garden market (cf. *Life*, 7 July 1888). One morning she saw Sam, and they subsequently met. He proposed marriage; Sophy could help him to look after a master greengrocer's shop at Aldbrickham, which he wanted to take over. Her son Randolph would not allow her to marry a 'boor', and she pined away. She was buried at Aldbrickham, and Sam stood mourning as the funeral procession passed by.   *LLI.* 2

HOCBRIDGE. A Midland town where the young architect Ambrose Graye, father of Cytherea, was killed on 12 October 1863.   *DR.* i

HODGE, DRUMMER. A soldier killed in the Boer War. *Hardy's note on the poem when it was first published indicated that he was a native of a village near 'Casterbridge'.*   *PPP.* 'Drummer Hodge'.

HOLDER, HELEN CATHERINE (GIFFORD). *Wife of the Rev. Caddell Holder of St Juliot, and sister of Hardy's first wife. She died in December 1900. She had been a governess, and is probably the 'dark She' of the first poem; cf. Emma Hardy, Some Recollections, 36: 'My sister and I were very noticeable, she dark and I fair.'*

            MV. 'The Five Students'; *LLE.* 'A Duettist to her
            Pianoforte' (*Emma Hardy speaking; for the recollections,
                        see* Life, *75 – 'Elfin Call', etc.*)

HOLLOW-TURNER, THE. An anonymous neighbour of John Upjohn at Little Hintock. It was noticeable at Winterborne's Christmas party that he and Cawtree monopolized the new packs of cards for 'an interminable game of langterloo'.   *W.* iv, ix, x, xxiv, xxix, xlviii,

HOLMSTOKE. *Probably an imaginary or composite village drawn from East Holme, East Stoke, and Stokeford, west of Wareham.*

Farmer Lodge lived here with his young wife Gertrude until her tragic death.   *WT.* 4

HOLWAY, LUKE. His father, Sergeant Holway, had encouraged him, much against his will, to join the army. In India, under General Wellesley, he had been much discouraged and written a reproachful letter to his father. Sergeant Holway was a lonely widower, and the despondency the letter had thrown him into caused him to shoot himself. Christian interment was refused by the parson at Broad Sidlinch, and he was buried ignominiously at a crossroads. Luke returned from India, and arrived just after his father's burial and the singing of a carol over his grave by the Chalk-Newton choir on its Christmas rounds. He made arrangements with Mr Oldham, the rector of Chalk-Newton, for his re-burial there, ordered a tombstone, and left to fight in the Peninsular War. He won distinctions in many battles in Spain, and at Waterloo. When he returned, he found that his father was still buried at the cross-roads: it had been discovered that he had been buried with a stake through his body, and re-burial had therefore seemed out of the question. Luke rented a small cottage at Chalk-Newton, and lived a solitary life. When he heard the same carol at Christmas which he had heard over his father's grave at the crossroads, he went there and shot himself. *CM*. 4

HOLWORTH. The actual name of the hamlet (little more than a farm) through which Lizzy Newberry of Nether-Moynton passed one night, followed by Richard Stockdale, to warn the lugger carrying contraband spirits from Cherbourg (and lying off Ringsworth) that the activities of the suspect smugglers were being watched. *WT*. 7

HOMBURG. Marty South's letter to Fitzpiers had resulted in a quarrel between him and Mrs Charmond when they were living at or near Heidelberg. He had left her, and she had travelled to Homburg (*in the Saar*) in search of him. Here she met an earlier suitor, the Italianate stranger who had appeared at Little Hintock from South Carolina. After an altercation, the disappointed lover shot Mrs Charmond and then himself. *W*. xliii

HOOKHORN, PHILIP. He thought he saw William Privett looking pale and odd by Longpuddle Spring, a spot William had avoided ever since his only child had been drowned there. On inquiry, it was found that William had died two miles away at the very time when Hookhorn saw him. *LLI*. 8c

HOOPER, MRS. The landlady of Coburg House, Solentsea, where the Marchmills stayed for a summer holiday in the absence of Robert Trewe, the poet, who later committed suicide there. *LLI*. 1

HOOPER, SQUIRE. *The story is based on a passage in Hutchins (iii. 385) concerning Hooper of Boveridge, Cranborne, who died in 1795. He was ninety-four.* *WW*. 'Squire Hooper'

HOPKINS, HENRY.   *HS*. 'Inscriptions for a Peal of Eight Bells'
HORNIMAN MUSEUM (LONDON).   *LLE*. 'Haunting Fingers'
HORSELEIGH, SIR JOHN. *Sir John Horsey of Clifton Maybank near Yeovil. Hardy re-created a traditional story to explain an apparent discrepancy in his marriages as recorded in Hutchins (i. 50 and iv. 426–9).*

He found that he was illegally married to the daughter and heiress of Richard Phelipson of Montislope when it was was discovered that her husband, the rebel Decimus Strong, was still alive overseas. He married, on the advice of Henry VIII, Edith Stocker, the widow of a Havenpool merchant, but kept the marriage secret. Local tradition held that he visited her at Oozewood, where he was stabbed to death by her brother Roger, who believed that their relationship was immoral.   *CM*. 9

HOXTON. Mrs Manston lived here at the house of Abraham Brown, 41 Charles Square, Hoxton, London.   *DR*. xvi, xvii, xix

H.P. *Helen Paterson, the 'skilful illustrator' of Far From the Madding Crowd. During the progress of the story she married William Allingham, and Hardy married Emma Lavinia Gifford. The poem supplies what Hardy's Life omits (cf. pp. 100–1); 'those two almost simultaneous weddings would have been one but for a stupid blunder of God Almighty,' he wrote to Gosse in 1906 (Purdy, 220).*   *LLE*. 'The Opportunity'

HUETT, IZZ. One of the dairymaids at Talbothays who fell in love with Angel Clare. She controlled her feelings more than Marian or Retty Priddle, but was bitterly disappointed when Angel – after separating from Tess – withdrew his invitation that she should accompany him to Brazil. She 'had an ear' for 'pretty verses' at church, and could quote the Scriptures. She followed Marian to Flintcomb-Ash, and worked for Farmer Groby with Marian and Tess. In turn, she was followed by a lover, Amby Seedling. She and Marian wrote anonymously to Angel Clare, warning him of the danger to Tess from Alec d'Urberville.

TD. xxi–xxiii, xxv, xxix, xxxi, xxxii, xxxiv, xl, xli, xliii–xlv, xlvii, xlviii, lii

HUMPHREY (1). A furze-cutter on Egdon Heath, and 'a somewhat solemn young fellow'. He had not been to church for three years, 'for I'm so dead sleepy of a Sunday; and 'tis so terrible far to get there; and when you do get there 'tis such a mortal poor chance that you'll be chose for up above, when so many bain't, that I bide at home, and don't go at all'.

RN. I iii, v; II i, iv, vi; III i, ii; IV ii, vii; V i; VI iii, iv

(2) The miller at Cloton near Beaminster, and uncle of Agatha Pollin. He was a widower with four children; his aim was to marry Frances Lovill as soon as he could afford it, and emigrate to Australia. He owed old Farmer Lovill a lot of money, and hoped that his niece would clear him by consenting to marry the old man. DBC

HUNTWAY, MR. A former college friend of Ambrose Graye, who became a curate in Bloomsbury, London. While visiting him, Ambrose Graye met Cytherea Bradleigh (cf. ALDCLYFFE). DR. i 1, v 3

HURD, FANNY. *Fanny Hurden, a delicate child who went to school with Hardy* (Life, *413–14*).

LLE. 'Voices from Things Growing in a Churchyard'

HURST, MRS. Bathsheba Everdene's aunt. She had a small farm near Gabriel Oak's at Norcombe Hill. Gabriel first met Bathsheba while she was staying there. FMC. i, ii, iv, xlix

HURSTON, MRS. Postmistress at Tolchurch. DR. xvi 4

HYDE PARK. *Scenes in Hyde Park, London, in Hardy's early novels were probably drawn from* The Poor Man and the Lady. *The scene in Rotten Row which Alexander Macmillan admired appears in a modified form in* A Pair of Blue Eyes. ILH. ii 2, 3; PBE. xiv, xxxvii; HE. ix

ICENING WAY. *Hutchins was Hardy's authority for Roman roads in Dorset; the Via Iceniana or Ikenild (see* RIDGE-WAY) *took its name from the Iceni, the people of Norfolk, where it began. Below Woodyates (p. 514) it was called Ikling or Akling-dike (p. 459). In the Dorchester region it was called the Icening Way (a street in Dorchester is still named Icen Way); it continued south to the coast at Melcombe Regis or Weymouth.*

It is mentioned in 'A Tryst at an Ancient Earthwork', and it is the *Via* which Henchard watched with his telescope from the heights of Mai-Dun. In 'Her Death and After' (*WP*), a line in the first edition ran 'In the Field of Tombs, by the Via renowned', with reference to Dorchester cemetery on the Weymouth road.

RN. i; CM. 6; MC. xliii; WP. 'My Cicely'

ICENWAY, LORD. *In Hardy's map of Wessex, Icenway House appears to be Herriard House, south of Basingstoke. George Purefoy Jervoise (1770–1847) of Herriard House married Anna Maria Selina, daughter of Wadham Locke of Rowdeford House, Bromham, near Devizes, Wiltshire, and died without issue. How far the story is founded on fact, and whether Hardy's 'clues' were intentionally misleading, remain problems for research; see* HEYMERE *and p. 81*).

He married the widow Maria Heymere, and she left her uncle's home with her son to live at Icenway House (*ten miles from the* Via Iceniana, *which passed through Silchester*). Lord Icenway was 'a plain man, older than herself . . . a matter-of-fact nobleman, who spent the greater part of his time in field-sports and agriculture'. As he grew older, he became 'crustier and crustier', largely because Maria had not borne him a son and heir, as she had her former husband. *GND*. 5

ICKNIELD STREET. See RIDGE-WAY.

IDMOUTH. *Sidmouth, Devon.*

Baron von Xanten's yacht lay at anchor in the middle of an inlet near Idmouth. *CM*. 12

IKE. (1) The turnip-hoer whose saving of the Duchess of Southernshire's life eventually caused him to end his own. *HS*. 'The Turnip-Hoer'

(2) Ike and Job were tree-fellers in the New Forest.
WW. 'Throwing a Tree'

IKLING WAY. See the ROMAN ROAD.

INGPEN BEACON. *Inkpen Beacon, the highest* chalk *hill in England, south of Hungerford and the 'Marygreen' country of* Jude the Obscure).
SC. 'Wessex Heights'

ISEULT THE FAIR. Queen of Cornwall, generally known as Iseult of Ireland; 'the Fair' means 'the Beautiful'. She was dark. *QC*

ISEULT THE WHITEHANDED. Iseult of Brittany, the wife of Sir Tristram. *QC*

ISLE OF SLINGERS. See PORTLAND.

ISLE OF WIGHT. It was while sailing on a yacht and watching the effect of the choppy sea on their faces that the Rev. Percival Cope noticed a striking resemblance between Frances Frankland, to whom he was engaged, and Mr Millborne.

The poet Robert Trewe was staying on 'the Island opposite' Solentsea, while the Marchmills occupied his apartments at Mrs Hooper's. Mrs Marchmill crossed over to see the poet who lived so much in her imagination, but was disappointed. They never met. *LLI*. 3, 1

IVEL-CHESTER. *Ilchester, north of Yeovil.*

The trampwoman's sweetheart was hanged at the gaol for murdering 'jeering Johnny'. *TL*. 'A Trampwoman's Tragedy'

IVELL (IVEL). *Yeovil, Somerset.*

When she heard that her husband Fitzpiers was returning from the Continent, Grace Melbury left her home at Little Hintock with the intention of travelling to Ivell and on to Exonbury, where she could stay with a friend. She called at One-Chimney Hut to seek Winterborne's help, but the weather, his illness and death, and her own subsequent illness made it impossible for her to carry out her plan.

Joshua and Cornelius Halborough went to meet their father at the Castle Inn, Ivell. He was on his way from Fountall, where he had been imprisoned, and intent on attending his daughter Rosa's marriage.

Squire Dornell rode from Falls-Park to King's Hintock Court along 'dead level' country and through the town of Ivell.

To expedite the marriage of his daughter and Mr Cope, a curate at Ivell, Mr Millborne rented a manor-house near Ivell, left them most of his income, and departed for the Continent.

The girl who wished to be at home with 'dear daddee' when she came to her 'lonesome' house on windy Toller Down had lived at Ivel, where she was married that morning.

> *W.* xl, xlii; *LLI.* 4; *GND.* 1, 6, 7; *LLI.* 3; *WP.* 'San Sebastian'; *CM.* 5; *TL.* 'At Casterbridge Fair' (v), 'The Homecoming'; *HS.* 'Under High-Stoy Hill'

JACK. The story goes back to the period of William IV (1830–37), when Wessex people believed in the divination of 'white witches'. A young woman refused the advice of the white witch she consulted – to marry the gentleman who had sent her a ring and clothes for her wedding. She married a sailor named Jack, who advised her to wear the clothes and ring at her wedding, to save money. After the marriage, the figure of the gentleman appeared night after night and urged that she had married him. Eventually she left Jack, and was seen no more by the local inhabitants until his burial. A 'wealthy old lady' stood long by the grave, then stepped into her coach, never to return.

> *WW.* 'The Catching Ballet of the Wedding Clothes'

JACKSON, MRS. Owen and Cytherea Graye lodged with her at Budmouth.   *DR.* v 3

JACOBS, CAPTAIN. He was in charge of the excursion steamboat which ran from Budmouth to Lulwind Cove.   *DR.* ii 4

JAMES, GRANDFATHER. The father of Mrs Dewy. He visited the tranter's for the Christmas celebrations. He was a mason, and his clothing is well described (*probably from Hardy's observation of his father or one of his employees*).   *UGT.* i iii, viii, v i, ii

JANE. The dead wife of the carrier who thought she still sat beside him in his van. *HS.* 'The Carrier'

JENKINS, SIMPKINS. A colleague of Stephen Smith's in Hewby's London office, who wrote to say that his master was in 'a towering rage' because Stephen appeared to be spending too much time 'about the church sketches' at Endlestow. *PBE.* v

JENNY. *Hardy told Edmund Gosse that the poem was based on fact.*

The recollection of the wild times she had had in her youth with the King's Own Cavalry was too much for old Jenny. She stole from her husband's side to join in their ball at the Phoenix Inn (Casterbridge) and danced until past four in the morning. When she reached her door she had a heart-attack. She crept up to bed. Next morning her husband found that she had died. He did not know that she had been out. The King's Own Cavalry said nothing on the subject.

WP. 'The Dance at the Phoenix'

JERSEY. While in Jersey on business, Henchard had fallen in love with Lucetta. The scandal which arose from her unconventional conduct had worked on his conscience to such an extent that he had asked her to 'run the risk of Susan being alive' and marry him. Jopp had been in Jersey and knew enough of the affair to compromise Henchard. This he did when Lucetta's letters came into his hands.

Two soldiers of a German regiment which was stationed near Budmouth in 1801 deserted, and rowed across the Channel to Jersey, which they mistook for France. When they landed, they were handed over to the authorities and sent back to England, where they were shot.

Henri Leverre was the son of the Jersey gentleman whom Marcia Bencomb married. *DR.* xx; *MC.* xii, xviii, xxii, xxv, xxvi, xxxvi–xl; *WT.* 3; *WB.* III i, vi; *LLE.* 'The Contretemps'

JETHWAY, MRS GERTRUDE. Elfride Swancourt's evil genius. Her son Felix, a farmer, had died of consumption, but his widowed mother thought he had pined away for love of Elfride, and that she had encouraged him. She observed Elfride's return from London with Stephen Smith, and just before her death wrote a letter to Henry Knight divulging 'the scandal'. She was killed by the fall of the West Endelstow church tower, when it was undermined by the 'restorers'.

With each of her lovers, Stephen Smith and Henry Knight, Elfride figures in a 'Gothic' scene in which Felix Jethway's tomb is premonitory of death. *PBE.* viii, ix,

xii, xix, xxiv, xxv, xxviii-xxx, xxxii, xxxiii, xxxiv, xxxviii

JIM. While he sat in the Weatherbury stocks at eleven o'clock one night in 1850, he heard steps which indicated, he thought, that his Sophy was coming. It was his mother, who told him that Sophy had gone to Blooms-End dance, and that nobody cared for him as his mother did.

WW. 'In Weatherbury Stocks'

JINKS, DAIRYMAN. One of the group at the Lord-Quantock-Arms Inn, Markton, who discussed the wedding of Paula Power and George Somerset. He was 'an old gnarled character who wore a white fustian coat and yellow leggings; the only man in the room who never dressed up in dark clothes for marketing'. He doubted whether a marriage abroad would last. 'I thought it might be some new plan o' folks for leasing women now they be so plentiful, so as to get rid o' 'em when the men be tired o' 'em, and hev spent all their money.' *L.* VI iv

JOB, UNCLE. He was a sergeant in the 'Sixty-first foot' regiment which was stationed on the downs near Budmouth in 1804. One evening he accompanied his nephew Solomon Selby to watch the sheep at lambing-time above the Cove (*Lulworth*). They were disturbed by two Frenchmen, who were discussing a map, obviously preparatory to invasion. Uncle Job immediately recognized one of them as Bonaparte, and regretted that he had not brought his new-flinted firelock with him. *WT*. 2

JOE, WRESTLER. A gipsy who had won fame as a Cornish wrestler. He had been the rival of the narrator's brother for a gipsy beauty. In order to secure her, this brother had agreed, against his principles, to break into a cathedral (*Wells*) in order to win treasure which could be exchanged for jewellery. He had been caught and hanged at Toneborough. Before he started on this venture, he had made the narrator swear that if his love proved false to him, he was to take her life. She lived with Wrestler Joe, and the narrator caused her to drown. *SC*. 'The Sacrilege'

JOHN (1). The ostler, a 'little bow-legged old man', at the Red Lion Inn, Anglebury, who discussed Ethelberta and her mother-in-law with the old milkman Michael. *HE*. i, xliv

(2) 'Jeering Johnny', who was stabbed to death at Marshal's Elm Inn. *TL*. 'A Trampwoman's Tragedy'

(3) He and his wife Jane seem to be a common couple until the poem reveals how their son's worthlessness blighted their life. Perhaps the commonplace names were intended to suggest the commonness of the event. *TL*. 'John and Jane'

(4) The young man with the Mellstock choir who was shocked to

discover that the sweet young widow he hoped to marry had already married Giles Swetman. *TL.* 'The Rash Bride'

JOHN, SIR. *Sir John Horsey (d. 1531).* See ESTMINSTER.

JOHN, UNCLE. He was press-ganged while walking down Wapping High Street (*near London Docks*), and his parrot was neglected and died. According to his nephew's logic, therefore, Mr Pitt ('Billy') killed Uncle John's parrot. *D.* (1) v v

JOHNS, JAPHETH. A dairyman friend of Charles Darton, who rode with him to The Knap to act as groomsman at the wedding of Charles and Sally Hall. When Darton married the widowed Helena, he was very critical. Soon afterwards he moved to an area near the Hintocks. When Darton proposed to Sally a second time and was refused, he met Japheth on his way to The Knap for the same purpose. Japheth also was refused. Sally was happy to remain single. *WT.* 6

JOHNSON, MATILDA. An actress, with whom Bob Loveday of the merchant service promptly fell in love at Southampton. He wrote home to say that he had arranged for the wedding to take place at Overcombe so that his father should enjoy the wedding-feast. Her reputation, however, was such that John Loveday had no difficulty in persuading her to leave Overcombe immediately. She soon became acquainted with Festus Derriman, and was ready to help him in his designs on uncle Benjy's wealth. In order to leave the way clear for Bob, John pretended that he was not in love with Anne, but courting Matilda. She appeared in the play at Budmouth before the King (and Anne and Bob Loveday). Finally she married Festus Derriman.

TM. xiv–xix, xxii, xxv, xxx, xxxii, xxxiii, xxxvi–vii, xl, xli

JOLLICE, FARMER. A respectable but simple farmer, who was made drunk by a deserter from the Dragoons at Cheltenham and persuaded to change clothes with him. The deserter promptly decamped, and 'Farmer Jollice found himself in soldier's clothes, the money in his pockets gone, and, when he got to the stable, his horse gone too'. *LLI.* 8h

JOLLIFFE, SHADRACH. *The surname was suggested by that of a famous citizen of Poole, who captured a French privateer in the reign of William III.*

A sailor who returned to Havenpool, married Joanna Phippard, and started a small grocer's business. This was not very prosperous, and, in order to please his wife (who was intent on keeping up with her rival, Emily Hanning, who had married well and also had two boys) and secure a good education for her two sons, George and Jim, he went to sea again. He purchased a part-ownership in a brig and went off to join in 'the Newfoundland trade'. He returned triumphantly with three hundred guineas. It was not enough for his wife's jealous ambition. To make a greater profit, he set off with his sons on a second venture. They were lost at sea. *LLI*. 6

JONES, ANDREW. The architect for the house which Mr Barnet had built to please his wife at Port-Bredy. She insisted on naming it Château Ringdale. He also designed a tomb for Mrs Downe, but, to economize for his children, Mr Downe changed his plans until, ultimately, only a headstone was ordered. *WT*. 5

JONES, DR. An old doctor whose practice lay north of that of Fitzpiers at Little Hintock. As Fitzpiers fell into disfavour, it extended. He was called in to attend Grace Melbury.

W. iv, vi, xxv, xxxiv, xxxvii, xxxviii, xlii, xliv

JONES, MR. 'The reflective man in spectacles' who was one of the company which included Neigh and Ladywell at a dinner-party at Mr Doncastle's in London. The main subject of their conversation was Ethelberta's recently published poems. *HE*. vii

JOPP, JOSHUA. Henchard incurred Jopp's enmity when he did not wait to ratify what was virtually an agreement, but appointed Farfrae as his manager. For a while Jopp lived in poverty in Mixen Lane. He succeeded Farfrae, but was dismissed when Henchard's reckless buying and selling in opposition to Farfrae ruined him. It was strange that Henchard in his poverty went to live with Jopp, now living in a cottage by the Priory Mill, and that he asked him to return Lucetta's compromising letters to her. Jopp had been in Jersey, and knew too well that Henchard's relations with Lucetta there would create a scandal. He divulged the contents of the letters to the lower-class frequenters of Peter's Finger in Mixen Lane, and helped to organize the skimmington-ride which they thought Henchard and Lucetta's behaviour deserved. Lucetta had incurred his enmity when she refused to recommend him to Farfrae as a working partner. *MC*. vii, x, xxvi, xxxi, xxxii, xxxvi–xl, xlii

JOYCE, LAWYER. The town-clerk of Casterbridge. *MC*. xxxiv

JOYCE, MR. The butler at Wyndway House. *HE*. iv

JUDY. The mad woman who mourned over marriages and births, and rejoiced when babies died. *PPP*. 'Mad Judy'

JULIAN, CHRISTOPHER. A teacher of music, who lived with his sister

Faith at Sandbourne. He was attached to Ethelberta, and much admired by her sister Picotee. He set one of Ethelberta's poems to music, and stayed in London in the hope of winning her, with no reward other than the suspicion that Picotee was in love with him. Later, he became assistant organist at Melchester Cathedral. Like many others, he took part in vain efforts to prevent the marriage of Ethelberta to the aged and wily reprobate Lord Mountclere. The novel closes with prospects of happy marriage with Picotee and of his promotion to the post of chief organist at Melchester. *HE.* i–vi. viii, ix, xi–xiv, xvi–xxii, xxiv, xxxi, xxxv, xxxvii, xxxix, xl, xliv–xlvii, Sequel

JULIE-JANE. A 'girl of joy', who died with her babe in childbirth, and chose her bearers from her 'fancy-men'. *TL.* 'Julie-Jane'

KAIL, JONATHAN. An employee at Talbothays dairy farm, who brought Tess and Angel's luggage to Wool manor-house after their marriage, with the news that Retty Priddle had tried to drown herself. *TD.* xvii, xxi, xxii, xxxiv

KEINTON MANDEVILLE. See STURMINSTER NEWTON.

KENNETBRIDGE. *Newbury, on the River Kennet, Berkshire.*

Jude made a special visit from Melchester to Kennetbridge to see the composer of the hymn, 'The Foot of the Cross', only to find him soulless and materialistic. When they left Aldbrickham, he and Sue lived at Kennetbridge for a while. Jude was ill and made cakes in the shape of Christminster colleges; Arabella and Anny found Sue selling them at Kennetbridge spring fair. Jude was anxious to return to Christminster, and did so shortly afterwards with his family. Besides 'Father Time', there were now two other children, and a third was expected. *JO.* iii x, v vii viii

KIBBS, CAPTAIN. A distant relative of Jim Caro, Ann Avice's father. He was engaged in carrying stone from Portland to London. Pierston met him and his wife and Ann Avice on one of the London wharves. *WB.* ii v

KINGCOMB HILL. *Between Toller Down and Maiden Newton, above the Hooke valley.* *HS.* 'The Pat of Butter'

KING'S HINTOCK. *Melbury Osmond, a secluded village north of Melbury Park. Some of Hardy's maternal ancestors – the Swetmans – had lived at Townsend on the Park side (Life, 6). A doubtful tradition existed that the Duke of Monmouth sheltered there. See plate facing p. 494.*

It is 'a mile of two' from King's Hintock Court. The church was built

by Betty Dornell (*q.v.*). At one time the land around the village ('now owned by the Earl o' Wessex') belonged to the Paridelles, from whom Retty Priddle was descended.   *WT.* 6; *GND.* 1;
                              TD. xix, liv; *CM.* 10; *PPP.* 'Her Late Husband'

KING'S HINTOCK COURT. *Melbury House, near Melbury Sampford, north of Evershot. Portions of the house, which is situated in a large wooded park, belong to the fifteenth century. It belonged to Lord Ilchester, who was descended from Stephen Fox* (see REYNARD), *the husband of Elizabeth Horner* (DORNELL, BETTY). *He became the first Earl of Ilchester* (Betty became the first 'Countess of Wessex').

There is a story of the 'spirits of the Two Brothers who had fought and fallen, and had haunted King's Hintock Court a few miles off [from Little Hintock] till they were exorcised by a priest, and compelled to retreat to a swamp, whence they were returning to their old quarters at the Court at the rate of a cock's stride every New Year's Day, Old Style'.

Christopher Swetman's mysterious visitor (believed to be the Duke of Monmouth) left Townsend and 'disappeared through Clammers Gate [*the entrance to Melbury Park*] by the road that crosses King's Hintock Park to Evershead'.   *W.* iii, xix; *GND.* 1;
                              CM. 10; *TL.* 'Autumn in King's Hintock Park'

KING'S HINTOCK WOOD. See ONE-CHIMNEY HUT.

KING'S STAG. *A village in the Vale of Blackmoor, south-west of Sturminster Newton. The inn which is referred to in the first poem was burnt down at the end of the nineteenth century. The name recalls the semi-legendary story (cf. TD. ii) which gave the Vale the name of White Hart.*
                              TL. 'A Trampwoman's Tragedy'; *HS.* 'A Last Journey'

KINGSBERE. *This is Bere Regis, where King John often stayed. A portion of the manor estate eventually passed into the hands of the Turberville family, one of whose Norman ancestors came over at the time of the Norman Conquest. The church contains the Turberville Chapel. See plate facing p. 399.*

Flocks belonging to Bathsheba Everdene and Boldwood were driven through 'the decayed old town' on the way to Greenhill (*Woodbury Hill*) Sheep Fair.

Timothy Fairway recalled how Thomasin Yeobright's father used to walk over to Kingsbere and play the clarinet for part of the service to let Andrew Brown have 'a bit of a nap'. Immediately everyone in church felt there was 'a great soul' among them. Another Sunday he took his bass-viol, and played to such effect that the church windows rattled 'as if 'twere a thunderstorm'. Parson Williams seemed to say to himself 'O for such a man in our parish!'

When the smuggler Jim Owlett was shot in a skirmish with the Customs officers near Nether-Moynton, he was carried across the country to Kingsbere, and hidden in a barn till he recovered.

Civilians made preparations for evacuation to King's-Bere when the French invasion was expected in the summer of 1805 (*TM*; cf. *WP*. 'The Alarm'). A beacon stood ready to be lit on Kingsbere Hill (*Woodbury Hill*), we are told in *The Dynasts*.

John Durbeyfield was told by Parson Tringham that rows and rows of his ancestors lay in the vaults at Kingsbere-sub-Greenhill, with their effigies under Purbeck-marble canopies. For the Durbeyfield family (after John's death) the supreme irony fell when they were evicted: their chattels were set down by the church wall at Kingsbere, and they slept under the traceried window of the ancient d'Urbervilles.

The lover, who saw his 'very dream', the image of the well-beloved (cf. *WB*) by the Ikling Way, was walking at night to Kingsbere, where he was to be wedded next morning. *His route took him along the Ackling Dyke, the Roman road from Old Sarum (near Salisbury), and he was near 'the ancient hill and wood' when the vision appeared. Hardy read in Hutchins that there was a Roman camp and temple on Woodbury Hill. At one time, the scene was set at Jordan Hill, north of Weymouth Bay, where the remains of a Roman temple were thought to have been discovered in 1843.*

> FMC. l; *RN*. i v; *WT*. 7; *TM*. xxvi, xxvii; *TD*. i, xv, xvi, xix, xxxviii, xlix, li, lii, liv; *WP*. 'The Alarm'; *PPP*. 'The Well-Beloved'; *D*. (1) ii v (*Woodbury Hill*; *see p. 343*).

KINGSCREECH. *Kingston, south of Corfe Castle. The Wessex name is derived partly from Creech Barrow, 655 feet high, on the Purbeck Hills, four miles west of Corfe Castle.*

The parish on the outskirts of which old Mrs Chundle lived, two miles from Corvsgate Castle and three from Enckworth.   OMC

KINGSMORE, ARTHUR. The actor who married Lady Elfride Luxellian, Elfride's grandmother (*compare the story of Lady Susan, Life, 9, 163–4, 250*).   PBE. xxvi, xxvii

KINGSTON MAURWARD. *In the parish of Stinsford. The House is the principal setting for 'An Indiscretion in the Life of an Heiress' and*

Desperate Remedies (*see* TOLLAMORE *and* KNAPWATER HOUSE). *For the harvest-supper and dance to which Hardy was taken as a boy, see* Life, *18–20,* FMC. *xxxvi, and* HS. '*The Harvest-Supper*'. *See plate facing p. 15.* See CAROLINE (3).

Two poems were written in, or imagined from, Kingston Park, the first in the eweleaze across which Hardy had frequently walked from Stinsford to Higher Bockhampton; the 'garth' is Stinsford churchyard, and the poem alludes to the death of his parents, his first wife, and his sister Mary, all of whom were buried there. The second may be autobiographical; equally, it may be imaginary and related to the story of 'An Indiscretion in the Life of an Heiress'.

MV. 'An Anniversary', 'In Her Precincts'; HS. 'The Harvest-Supper'

KNAP, THE. Sally Hall lived there with her widowed mother. It was 'an old house with mullioned windows of Ham-hill stone, and chimneys of lavish solidity. It stood at the top of a slope beside King's-Hintock village-street, only a mile or two from King's-Hintock Court' (*i.e. Melbury Osmond, north of Melbury House*). *Its name suggests that it was situated on a hill.* WT. 6

KNAPWATER HOUSE. *Kingston Maurward House in the parish of Stinsford. The Wessex name describes its actual setting, on a hill beside a lake. Lora Grey, the last survivor of the Grey family which had lived in the old Tudor manor house nearby, married George Pitt (who was related to the William Pitt family) in the early part of the eighteenth century, and it was he who built the new manor house. Tradition has it that George III regretted that it was built of 'b-b-brick', and that the owner ruined himself by having it faced with stone in 1794. (Hardy transferred the story to Enckworth Court; cf. HE. xxxviii.)*

It was inherited by the Bradleigh family on condition they changed their name to Aldclyffe. Miss Aldclyffe left it to Cytherea Graye.

The old Tudor manor house, part of which Manston occupied, still stands, and has been restored recently. The Fane or Grecian temple where Miss Aldclyffe urged Cytherea to marry Manston overlooks the lake, and the water-wheel may still be seen. See plate facing p. 15.

Special references: DR. v 1, 2, vii 1, viii 4, xii 2, xix. It is 'the Manor' of UGT. i iv. See also TOLLAMORE.

KNIBBS, BECK. One of the two married dairywomen at Talbothays. She lived in one of the farm cottages and had 'woolly black hair and rolling

eyes'. The other was Frances, who was consumptive from the winter
damp of the 'water-meads'. *TD*. xxii, xxix

KNIGHT, HENRY. Formerly a Fellow of St Cyprian's College, Oxford,
he was a barrister, reviewer, and essayist. He had been Stephen Smith's
tutor by correspondence in Latin and Greek, and had written a scathing
review of Elfride Swancourt's romance, *The Court of King Arthur's
Castle*. He was introduced to the Swancourts in London by his aunt,
formerly Mrs Troyton, who had married Mr Swancourt. His rescue by
Elfride when in imminent peril of death on 'the Cliff without a Name'
(*Beeny, on Hardy's map of Wessex*) – just when Elfride had been looking
forward to Stephen's return from India – is the dramatic crux of the
principal story, and marks the beginning of his love for Elfride. He is
placed in situations parallel to (and physically identical with) previous
ones between Elfride and Stephen. Unguarded disclosures created a
growing jealousy in him, which became adamantine when he discovered
that she had eloped to London. Elfride did not defend herself, and he left
her. When she followed him to his chambers at Bede's Inn, London,
this simply provided further evidence to his jealous nature that she had
defied the 'proprieties' in the past. 'Knight's was a robust intellect, which
could escape outside the atmosphere of heart [cf. Angel Clare, in *Tess of
the d'Urbervilles*]. With him, truth seemed too clean and pure an abstraction to be so hopelessly churned in with error as practical persons find it.'
He left London for the Continent in the hope of forgetting Elfride. His
return coincided with Stephen's from India. When he discovered that he
had wronged Elfride, he hurried off, as Stephen did, with renewed hope.
The rivals met on the train, which, they later discovered, was taking the
coffined Elfride for interment at Endelstow. She had married Lord
Luxellian, and died of a miscarriage in London. When they saw Lord
Luxellian prostrate with grief across the coffin in the family vault, they
withdrew as intruders.

*Knight's character is in various ways a contrast to Stephen's, and is
closer in certain respects to that of Hardy when he visited St Juliot. He and
the Hardy of that period were of the same age, and physical characteristics
which are humorously referred to in chapter xiii may, to judge by a
photograph of Hardy in 1870, have been those of the author. The reading
of the lessons at Endelstow church (PBE. xix) is certainly autobiographical;
Hardy recalls reading the passage mentioned, 'a portion of the history of
Elijah', in the poem 'Quid Hic Agis?' (MV); cf. Life, 157. Knight's*

*character may in some ways have been suggested by Hardy's friend
Horace Moule, also an academic reviewer. Cf.* Life, *32-4, 77. See* ST
CLEATHER.   *PBE.* vii, viii, xiii, xiv, xvi–xxii, xxv, xxvii–xl

KNOLLINGWOOD HALL. *St Giles's House, Wimborne St Giles, near
Cranborne.*

The home of Lord Uplandtowers (*fifth Earl of Shaftesbury*). *GND.* 2

KNOLLSEA. *Swanage. The Hardys lived here in 1875-6, while he was
completing* The Hand of Ethelberta, *and heard many smuggling stories
from the captain in whose cottage they lodged:* Life, *107-8.*

Ethelberta decided on a holiday at Knollsea in order to obtain a copy
of the register of her aunt Charlotte's baptism from one of the nearby
parishes. Knollsea was a mere village. 'Everybody in the parish who was
not a boatman was a quarrier, unless he were the gentleman who owned
half the property and had been a quarryman, or the other gentleman
who owned the other half, and had been to sea.' For a while, until
alarmed by the news that Lord Mountclere was coming to stay there,
Ethelberta and Picotee lived in the small cottage of Captain Flower.
Knollsea was already becoming a resort, but its inhabitants were parochial
and regarded strangers with suspicion, although some wives had learned
to let lodgings. The storm at sea which prevented the landing of the
Spruce, and unsuccessful efforts to prevent the marriage of Ethelberta
and Lord Mountclere at Knollsea Church, provide some of the more
exciting scenes in the closing stages of the story.

Richard Stockdale, the temporary Wesleyan minister at the smuggling
village of Nether-Moynton, attended a commemoration service at
Knollsea.

The young barrister Charles Bradford Raye realized that his prospects
were ruined as he and Anna travelled to Knollsea for their honeymoon.

HE. xxix–xxxiii, xxxv–xxxvii, xxxix, xliii–xlv, xlvi,
Sequel; *WT.* 7; *LLI.* 5

KNOX, MILLER. *The story is based on a local tragedy at Puddletown,
where the mill building may still be found.*   *HS.* 'At the Mill'

KYTES, TONY. He had driven John Lackland and his family from Longpuddle to Casterbridge when they were emigrating, and sang 'The
Tailor's Breeches' (which Angel Clare found distasteful) in 'a religious
manner, as if it were a hymn'. For the story of this 'arch-deceiver', and
Milly Richards, Unity Sallet, and Hannah Jolliver, see pp. 85-6.

LLI. 8 Introduction, *a, b*

LACKLAND, JOHN. *The name indicates an uprooted person, with no land or country which is 'home' for him. White Lackington is part of 'Longpuddle'. See LLE. 'Welcome Home'.*

He emigrated with his parents and sister when he was a boy, and thirty-five years later, after the death of all three, he returned to Longpuddle, his birthplace, hoping to settle there for the remainder of his life. From Casterbridge he travelled to Longpuddle in the carrier's van, and it was his inquiries about people he had known which led to the telling of the stories in 'A Few Crusted Characters'. After a few days in Longpuddle, he disappeared, and did not return.

LLI. 8, Introduction; prologues to *a, b, c, d, f, g, h, i*; conclusion

LADYWELL, EUSTACE. An artist who saw Ethelberta at Wyndway House, and became her suitor in London. He had 'a Tussaud complexion' and 'high eyebrows arched like a girl's'. His family owned 'a good bit' of land 'out Aldbrickham way', Chickerel informed his designing daughter Ethelberta. Ladywell went to the coast near Knollsea to sketch and be near Ethelberta; by chance, he became a witness of her wedding.

HE. iii, iv, vii, xiii, xvi, xvii, xx, xxi, xxii, xxv, xxvii, xxxiv, xxxv, xlv

LALAGE. *The name of a local girl recalled Horace's ode,* I xxii, *which was the main inspiration for this dramatic love lyric.*   *MV.* 'Timing Her'

LAMBETH. Anne Seaway, who posed as Manston's wife, lived at 79 Addington Street, Lambeth, in South London.

When Christopher and Faith Julian arrived in London one winter's afternoon they saw 'from one of the river bridges snow-white scrolls of steam from the tall chimneys of Lambeth, rising against the livid sky behind, as if drawn in chalk on toned cardboard'.

Mr Cartlett, to whom Arabella had been married in Sydney, came to England 'to find her', and become landlord of the Three Horns, Lambeth, which was already doing a trade of £200 a month in that 'excellent, densely populated, gin-drinking neighbourhood'. He wanted her to help in the business, and remarried her after her divorce from Jude.

DR. xiv 3; *HE.* xi; *LLI.* 7; *JO.* III ix, V ii, iii, v

LAMBING CORNER. *Towards the upper end of Clatford Bottom in the Marlborough Downs, two miles west of Marlborough and north of the Bristol road. The downs are now arable, and the Devil's Den (the Devil's Door or 'Druidical trilithon') will be seen in a field on the left. On the other side of the road is Clatford Hall or 'Shakeforest Towers'.*   *CM.* 7

LAMBING-DOWN GATE. Joseph Poorgrass was lost here (*probably on one of the hills north of Puddletown*) and, finding the gate would not open, he knelt down and prayed. 'Well, when I got to Saying After Me, I rose from my knees and found the gate would open – yes, neighbours, the gate opened the same as ever.' *FMC*. viii

LANIVET. *Near Bodmin, Cornwall, where Emma Lavinia Gifford's father was living in 1872 when she and Hardy stayed with him. He is said to have disapproved of their marriage in no moderate terms (cf. MV. 'I rose, and went to Rou'tor Town', and SC. 'The Place on the Map'). This explains the 'crucifixion' of the poem.* *MV*. 'Near Lanivet, 1872'

LARK, MISS TABITHA. A happy and talented girl, the daughter of a dairyman at Welland. She used to read to Lady Constantine at Welland House, and was the church organist. At the confirmation service, Louis Glanville was quite certain that she and Swithin St Cleeve were in love; he concluded that the coral bracelet which the Bishop of Melchester had found at Swithin's observatory belonged to her, and, in consequence, Lady Constantine's intrigue with Swithin escaped detection. Tabitha studied music with great success in London, and played at concerts and oratorios. When the novel closes with the tragic death of Lady Constantine, there can be little doubt that Swithin's future is linked with hers; she was 'the single bright spot of colour and animation within the wide horizon'. *TT*. ii, vi, vii, xi, xxiv–xxv, xxvii–xxix, xxxiv, xli

LATIMER, WILL. *The actual name of such an officer, according to Hardy; he was buried at Osmington (J. V. Mardon, Thomas Hardy as a Musician, Toucan Press, 1964).*

A Customs officer from Budmouth who was in charge of the party which searched for smuggled liquor at Nether-Moynton. After a prolonged but successful search, he set out in the twilight with three of his assistants to transport the contraband tubs to Budmouth Custom-house. At Warm'ell Cross, they were set upon by twenty to thirty disguised men, who were engaged in this particular smuggling business, and tied to trees. *WT*.7

LAURA. The young lady who lived at 'Top o' Town' near the Casterbridge barracks and formed such idealized notions of military life that she thought that 'men-at-arms' were 'the only ones worthy of a woman's heart'. She married Captain John Maumbry (*q.v.*) *CM*. 1

LAURA, THE HONOURABLE. Daughter of Lord Quantock and secretly married to his nephew, Captain Northbrook. She eloped with an opera singer who called himself Signor Smittozzi. (See p. 64.)　　　*GND.* 10

LAUSANNE. *Not having Ruskin's 'aversion from the historian of the Decline and Fall', Hardy sat out until midnight on 27 June 1897, in the garden where Gibbon completed his monumental work exactly one hundred and ten years previously. See* Life, *293*.
　　　　　　PPP. 'Lausanne – In Gibbon's Old Garden: 11–12 p.m.'
LAUTMANN. Bandmaster of the —th Hussars.　　　　　　*CM.* 1
LAVINE. *Lavinia, i.e. Emma Lavinia, Hardy's first wife. The MS. shows that originally the poem read 'Emleen' (Purdy). This also suggests that the poem was based on some dinner at which Hardy and his first wife had been present.*　　　　　　*HS.* 'At a Fashionable Dinner'
LAWSON, SAM. Subject of a conversation at tranter Dewy's on Christmas Eve. A 'husbird' or rascal, who sold Reuben a faulty cider-cask. *UGT.* I ii
LEAF, THOMAS. A simple-minded member of the Mellstock choir, who laughed nervously, and said little, except on one occasion when he told a story which came to nothing. 'I never had no head, never! that's how it happened to happen, hee-hee!' His mother had twelve children, all of whom, except Thomas, died young. He is described as 'a human skeleton' in a smock-frock.　　　　　　*UGT.* I i–vi, II iii, iv, v i, ii
LEAT, ELIZABETH. The postmistress at Carriford and an intimate friend of Mrs Crickett, who told her about the discovery she had made in Manston's bed of 'a trailing brown hair, very little less than a yard long'. Mrs Leat stretched out 'towards the invisible object a narrow bony hand that would have been an unmitigated delight to the pencil of Carlo Crivelli'.
　　　　　　DR. ix 4, xii, 7, xv 3
LEDDENTON. *Gillingham, a town four miles north-west of Shaftesbury. The name derives from the River Lodden, 'a tributary of the Stour', which runs nearby.* George Gillingham (*whose name obviously derives from the place*) was the schoolmaster here, and an old friend of Richard Phillotson at Shaston.　　　　　　*JO.* IV iv
LEDLOW, DAME. Mrs Cuxsom recalled a party at 'old Dame Ledlow's' of Mellstock. She was farmer Shinar's aunt, and was called Toad-skin, 'because her face were so yaller and freckled'. 'Joan Dummett was took bad when we were coming home, and Jack Griggs was forced to carry her through the mud' but dropped her in Dairyman Sweetapple's cowbarton; 'we had to clane her gown wi' grass – never such a mess as 'a were in'.　　　　　　*MC.* xiii
LEDLOW, FARMER. The Mellstock choir were due to make their first

stop outside his house when they were carol-singing. From the church gallery, where they sat, they used to watch his wife count her money and reckon her week's marketing expenses during the First Lesson.

UGT. I iv, vi; *WP.* 'Friends Beyond'

LEE, 'MOTHER'. The trampwoman's friend. She died at Glaston.

TL. 'A Trampwoman's Tragedy'

LEGH, MR. 'A Wessex gentleman', who went out from Brussels to observe the fighting during the battle of Waterloo.   *D.* (3) VII v

LEIPZIG. The battle of Leipzig (1813), as described by Norbert in the Old Ship Inn, Casterbridge, was probably intended as part of a ballad sequence on Napoleonic campaigns (cf. *Life*, 106). In *The Dynasts*, the battle is presented in great detail; six stanzas from the poem are incorporated in two of the scenes.   *WP.* 'Leipzig'; *D.* (3) III i–v

LEVERRE, HENRI. Son of the 'Jersey gentleman' whom Marcia married after her father had refused to consent to her marriage with Jocelyn Pierston. After her husband's death, Marcia moved to Sandbourne, where Henri taught French. During her visit to the Isle of Slingers to discover what had happened to Jocelyn, Henri met Avice Pierston and fell in love with her. He came to see her just before her marriage to Jocelyn was due; he was ill and Avice felt she could not desert him. They eloped and were married in London.   *WB.* III v–viii

LEW-EVERARD. *The name is derived from Lewell Mill in the valley by the Frome river, and Frome Everard, the old name for Stafford House (see p. 336), and indicates West Stafford.*

After the marriage of Tess and Angel Clare, Marian and Retty Priddle walked to Lew-Everard, where they stopped to have a drink (*at the Wise Man?*), then went on to Three-armed Cross (*by Lower Lewell Farm?*), where they parted. Retty afterwards tried to drown herself in the 'Great Pool'. *See* SHADWATER WEIR.   *TD.* xxxiv

LEWELL, BILL. *For the name, see Lew-Everard (above).*

A farmhand at Talbothays.   *TD.* xxii

LEWGATE. *It was the name often suggested for Hardy's home at Higher Bockhampton during his lifetime, but never adopted. 'Lew' indicates sheltered; 'gate', a road or lane. The name was used for Upper Mellstock in the early editions of UGT. See plate facing p. 14.*

Tony Kytes settled at Lewgate, near Mellstock, after his marriage.

Caroline Aspent found that her companions at the Quiet Woman Inn were mostly people from neighbouring hamlets and farms – Bloom's

End, Mellstock, Lewgate, and elsewhere. *LLI.* 8, Introduction, and 7

LEWSDON HILL. *A high hill near Pilsdon Pen, north of Marshwood Vale in the west of Dorset.* *PPP.* 'Doom and She' (*an MS. variant of the penultimate line reads 'On Pilsdon Pen or Lewsdon Peak'*); *MV.* 'Molly Gone'; *HS.* 'At Wynard's Gap'

LICKPAN, ROBERT. Carrier and pig-killer at Endelstow. He drove Stephen Smith from the railway station at St Launce's on his first visit to Endelstow. He used to relate his grandfather's pig-killing joke, which always began, 'Bob will tell the weight of your pig, 'a b'lieve'. His grandfather was clever, but his uncle Levi 'cleverer'. *PBE.* ii, xi, xxiii

LIDDELL AND SCOTT. *Compilers of the standard Greek–English Lexicon.* *WW.* 'Liddell and Scott'

LITTLE HINTOCK. See the HINTOCKS.

LOCK, JUDGE BENJAMIN FOSSETT. *See Purdy, 245. He was born at Dorchester in 1847 and died at Bridlington, near Flamborough Head, in 1922.* *HS.* 'Nothing Matters Much'

LOCKHAM. See STUBB.

LODGE, FARMER. He was a rich farmer who lived at Holmstoke near Anglebury, and had abandoned Rhoda Brook and their illegitimate son to marry, years later, a young and attractive girl named Gertrude. Six years later, the son was hanged at Casterbridge gaol. Gertrude had made her way privately to the gaol to cure her withered arm. The shock of putting it to the hanged man's neck was aggravated by finding that her husband and Rhoda were present, and it was their son who had been executed. She collapsed and died shortly afterwards. Farmer Lodge gave up his farm, and bequeathed his estate to a reformatory for boys, subject to an annual payment to Rhoda Brook (which she refused to accept). He moved to the other side of the county, and lived in 'solitary lodgings' at Port-Bredy until his death two years later. *WT.* 4

LODGE, GERTRUDE. She was a pretty girl when she married Farmer Lodge of Holmstoke. Soon afterwards her left arm became discoloured, and began to shrink; eventually she went to Conjuror Trendle to find the cause. What she learned is not disclosed, but there is no doubt that Rhoda Brook, who was locally reputed to be a sorceress, was implicated. After consulting books of necromancy and trying all sorts of nostrums, she went again to 'the white wizard', who knew only one cure: she had to put her arm to the neck of a hanged man. She made arrangements to do so at Casterbridge gaol, only to find that her husband and Rhoda Brook were present, and that the young man whose neck she had touched was their son. The double shock was too much for her; she collapsed and died three days later.   *WT.* 4

LONDON. *Hardy lived in London from 1862 to 1867, and London scenes appeared frequently in his early novels. He knew 'every street and alley west of St. Paul's like a born Londoner, which he was often supposed to be'* (Life, 62). *In general, however, his impressions are from the outside; at best, those of a keen observer, with a satirical bent. The 'most important'* scenes in The Poor Man and the Lady *were set in London. The radical hero addressed a meeting of working-class men in Trafalgar Square; and a scene in Rotten Row impressed the publisher Alexander Macmillan, who thought it 'full of real power and insight'. Scenes and impressions were undoubtedly preserved in 'An Indiscretion in the Life of an Heiress'; others were adapted to the plots of* A Pair of Blue Eyes *and* The Hand of Ethelberta; *and one or two, possibly, to that of* Desperate Remedies.

The Hardys lived in London from 1878 to 1881. Afterwards he made frequent and sometimes prolonged visits to the capital almost every year. He kept a record of his impressions, in preparation for the time when he might be driven to write society novels. Glimpses are to be found in The Well-Beloved, *and many extracts in his* Life. *The most important were those which led him to regard the human race as subject to forces or tendencies, caught up in 'the wheel' (Life, 171) or behaving, not so much as individuals in the light of reason, but as members of a vast collective creature (Life, 131). This concept clearly explains much in the presentation and design of* The Dynasts.

Many references to London in Hardy's fiction are omitted because they have little or no significance. Others will be found under:
BEDE'S INN, BRITISH MUSEUM, CHEVRON SQUARE, CRIPPLEGATE CHURCH, EXONBURY CRESCENT, GREENWICH OBSERVATORY, GROSVENOR HOTEL, HAMMERSMITH, HAMPSTEAD, HAMPTON COURT, HORNIMAN MUSEUM, HOXTON, HYDE PARK, LAMBETH, MADAME TUSSAUD'S, MAYFAIR, OXFORD STREET, PADDINGTON STATION, PICCADILLY, ROYAL ACADEMY, ST PAUL'S, SURBITON, TOOTING, WARWICK STREET, WATERLOO STATION, WYKEHAM CHAMBERS.

In 'The Son's Veto', there are descriptions of the procession of waggons piled with vegetables for Covent Garden (cf. *Life*, 210), and of the

Thames towards St Paul's at sunrise, with impressions of the yearly public-school cricket match at Lord's.

Jocelyn Pierston accompanied Marcia Bencomb from the Isle of Slingers to London and was escorting her in a cab to her aunt's at Bayswater when he proposed to her and was accepted. They changed direction, therefore, went back to the Strand, and 'soon ensconced themselves in one of the venerable taverns of Covent Garden, a precinct which in those days was frequented by West-country people'. Jocelyn had rooms and a studio near Campden Hill; his friend, Alfred Somers, in Mellstock Gardens. Jocelyn met Mrs Pine-Avon at fashionable assemblies; she lived near Hamptonshire Square. Sometimes he walked to the wharves along the Thames, where building-stone from the Isle of Slingers was unloaded. In preparation for his marriage with Avice Pierston, he took a new house 'of the approved Kensington pattern' with 'a new studio at the back as large as a medieval barn'.

In *The Dynasts* there are scenes in the old House of Commons, a house of a lady of quality, before Lord Malmesbury's house in Spring Gardens, outside and in the Guildhall, at Bowling Green House, Putney (the death of Pitt), Fox's lodgings in Arlington Street, the Marchioness of Salisbury's, a club in St James's Street, Windsor Castle (*west of London*), Carlton House, Vauxhall Gardens, and the Opera House.

Some of Hardy's reminiscences as a dancing man at Almack's (or Willis's), Cremorne, and the Argyle Rooms (cf. *Life*. 34, 42–3, 123, 274) were 'drawn upon' in *The Poor Man and the Lady*.

> ILH. II 1–3; *DR.* vii 3, xvi 4; *PBE.* xii, xiii, xiv, xxix, xxxv, xxxvii–xxxix; *HE.* xvi, xvii, xviii, xx, xxii, xxiv, xxv; *L.* III v, vi; *GND.* 5; *LLI.* 3; *LLI.* 2; *WB.* I vi, II i–iii, v, xi, xii, III v, viii; *PPP.* 'At the War Office, London', 'A Wife in London', 'The Ruined Maid'; *D.* (1) I iii, v, IV vi, V v, VI viii; *D.* (2) I i, II iii, V iv, VI v, vi, vii; *D.* (3) II iv, IV viii, V v; *TL.* 'The Two Rosalinds', 'The Flirt's Tragedy', 'Reminiscences of a Dancing Man'; *MV.* 'The Statue of Liberty' (*Imaginary. See* Life, *214:* 'O richest City in the world! She knew the rules'*; *LLE.* 'In a London Flat'; *HS.* 'A Beauty's Soliloquy during her Honeymoon', 'Lady Vi'; *WW.* 'The Musing Maiden' (*composed at 16 Westbourne Park Villas in October 1866*). See other headings, p. 391.

LONG, LAWYER. A Casterbridge lawyer.   *FMC.* lii; *MC.* xxxvii

LONG, NICHOLAS. He and Christine Everard 'were excellently paired, the very twin halves of a perfect whole; and their love was pure'. As Christine's father did not approve of their marriage, Nicholas left his farm at Elsenford and went to America to make his fortune. (For the sequel, see EVERARD, CHRISTINE.)   *CM.* 2

LONG-ASH LANE. *Part of the old Roman road from Dorchester to Yeovil and Ilchester. It runs from Grimstone to Holywell.*

It was the road taken by the farmer Charles Darton on his way to The Knap. He rode this way three times to propose to Sally Hall.

Betty Dornell rode pillion behind her lover Charles Phelipson to escape Stephen Reynard. They proceeded along Long-Ash Lane and stopped at an inn because she was unwell. She had caught smallpox. Phelipson's alarm was so obviously self-centred that Betty indignantly insisted on returning home to King's Hintock Court.

Tess crossed Long-Ash Lane (*near Holywell*) on her way to Emminster. On the way back to Flintcomb-Ash, after passing Long-Ash Lane, she was overtaken by Alec d'Urberville, whom she had seen preaching in a barn at Evershead.

At the cross-roads where the road from Chalk-Newton to Broad Sidlinch cuts across Long-Ash Lane, Sergeant Holway, who had committed suicide as a result of the depression caused by his son's complaints that he had encouraged him to join the army against his will, was buried with a stake through his body. Years later, after serving with distinction in Spain and at Waterloo to restore his family's honour, his son Luke committed suicide at the same spot. The story is connected with the Chalk-Newton choir and carol-singing at Christmas.

WT. 6; *GND.* 1; *TD.* xliv, xlv; *CM.* 4

LONGPUDDLE. *The Wessex name was suggested by the long valley of the Piddle or Puddle river, which runs south from the chalk hills through the villages of Piddletrenthide and Piddlehinton to Puddletown. Longpuddle is Piddlehinton and beyond, i.e. in the direction of, possibly including, Piddletrenthide. It is sometimes called Upper Longpuddle to distinguish it from Weatherbury or Lower Longpuddle (FMC. vii, viii).*

When the Mellstock choir reached Upper Mellstock on Christmas Eve, they heard 'the faint sound of church bells ringing a Christmas peal . . . floating over upon the breeze from the direction of Longpuddle and

Weatherbury parishes on the other side of the hills' (Hardy recalled them in Venice; see *Life*, 193).

Against the French invasion, Longpuddle raised a volunteer force of sixty men under Captain Cunningham (cf. *WP*. 'The Alarm').

Most of the stories in 'A Few Crusted Characters' relate to Longpuddle, to which the passengers in Burthen's van were travelling (see pp. 85–9).

The Longpuddle choir was disbanded after a disgraceful performance in the church gallery. The players formed a good band. There were Nicholas Puddingcome, the leader, who played the first fiddle; Timothy Thomas, the bass-viol man; John Biles, the tenor fiddler; Daniel Hornhead, with the serpent; Robert Dowdle, with the clarionet; and Mr Nicks, with the oboe. They had been playing dance-music night after night at Christmas and were tired out. It was so cold in the church on the following Sunday that they imbibed hot brandy and beer to keep warm. The result was that they went to sleep during the sermon. When the parson announced the Evening Hymn, a boy named Levi Limpet, who sat in the gallery with the choir, nudged the leader. He started up but 'the church being so dark and his head so muddled', he thought he was at the party where they had played all the previous night, 'and away he went, bow and fiddle' at a popular jig, 'The Devil among the Tailors'. The rest of the choir joined in with vigour, and Nicholas, seeing nobody move, shouted 'Top couples cross hands!...' It was the end of the choir. Soon afterwards a barrel-organ that could play twenty-two psalm-tunes was installed.

Whatever the origin of the story, the choir was probably that of Puddletown; cf. Life, *10, 125. UGT.* I i, IV i; *FMC.* vii, viii, xxxii; *TM.* xxvii; *LLI.* 8; *HS.* 'The Sexton at Longpuddle'

LONGWAYS, SOLOMON. One of the working-class quidnuncs of Casterbridge. He was generally to be found in the company of Christopher Coney. He was a small old man, about seventy years of age, who was employed by Henchard, and frequently called at the Three Mariners for a 'warm-up'. Like Christopher Coney, he saw no reason why death should rob life of fourpence when money was scarce and throats were dry.

He was present at the burning of the effigy of Napoleon Bonaparte on Durnover Green.

MC. v, viii, xiii, xviii, xxxii, xxxvii, xxxix, xliii; *D.* (3) v vi

LORD-QUANTOCK-ARMS HOTEL. *The name suggests proximity to the Quantock Hills, Somerset.*

George Somerset stayed there while he was working on extensions to the neighbouring Stancy Castle.

L. I x, xii, xiii, xv; III vi–viii, x, xi; VI iv, v

LORNA. *The poem recalls* The Well-Beloved *but relates to an actual marriage in the family of Hardy's old friend, Bosworth Smith. Lorna the First died, and her disappointed suitor married her daughter Lorna eight years later.* *WW.* 'Lorna the Second'

LORNTON INN. *Horton Inn, on the road from Wimborne to Cranborne.*

It was 'the rendezvous of many a daring poacher for operations in the adjoining forest' (*Cranborne Chase, towards the end of the eighteenth century*). Here a chaise waited to take Barbara Grebe with her lover Edmond Willowes when she eloped at night.(L. Copse) *TT.* ii; *GND.* 2

LOUISA (LOUIE). *Louisa Harding, the daughter of a rich farmer at Stinsford, and about a year younger than Hardy. Hardy's youthful attachment to her led to his early obsession with the 'poor man and the lady' theme. Her family were socially superior, and made it clear that Louisa was not to encourage him. Hardy believed his affection was reciprocated, though the only words he dared to address to her were 'Good evening'. She was sent to a boarding-school at Weymouth, and Thomas went there Sunday after Sunday until he found the church she attended with her fellow-scholars. His one reward was 'a shy smile'* (Life, 26).

MV. 'Transformations'; *LLE.* 'The Passer-by'; *HS.* 'Louie' (*the 'elect one' is Emma Lavinia Hardy*); *WW.* 'To Louisa in the Lane'.

LOVEDAY, JOHN. Trumpet-major in the —th Dragoons, who were stationed near Overcombe when the French invasion was expected in 1804. He was the son of Miller Loveday of Overcombe Mill, and aged thirty-two. He fell in love with Anne Garland, but she clearly preferred his brother Bob, and he deferred to his brother's claims. He saved Bob from an indiscreet marriage with Matilda Johnson. When Bob lapsed from grace by falling in love with Caroline as soon as he returned from the battle of Trafalgar, John's ardour for Anne was more apparent. Unfortunately, he received a letter from Bob at the critical juncture telling him that the Portsmouth affair was over, and returned stolidly to the way of honour and self-renunciation, to Anne's annoyance. To clear the way for Bob, he pretended to be in love with Matilda Johnson, who was then at Budmouth. Bob discovered the truth, but the trumpet-major left with his regiment for Spain, where he was killed in action. *TM*

LOVEDAY, MILLER. The good-natured father of John and Robert Loveday. He lived at Overcombe Mill, married Mrs Garland, and became a local volunteer. His ancestors were corn-grinders 'whose history is lost in the mists of antiquity'. *TM*. ii–v, x–xi, xii, xiv–xxiv, xxvi, xxvii, xxviii, xxxii, xxxiii, xxxv, xxxvii, xxxix–xli

LOVEDAY, ROBERT. He was aged twenty-eight, and had been mate on the *Pewit* in the merchant service. Anne Garland remembered him with affection, but he was the proverbial suitor who was apt to fall in love, or imagine himself in love, with the first beautiful woman he met in port. At Southampton he fell in love with Matilda Johnson. Later, at Portsmouth, he fell in love with Caroline. Thanks to his brother John, his marriage to Matilda Johnson had been averted. He escaped being press-ganged at Overcombe Mill, and soon afterwards visited Captain Hardy at Po'sham to enlist in the navy. As a result he was wounded at the battle of Trafalgar. When Anne heard that she had been forgotten in favour of Caroline, she was more encouraging to John, but, just at the moment when John's suit was prospering, he heard that Bob had given up Caroline, and immediately cooled towards Anne. Bob had been made a lieutenant. When John left for Spain, where he was killed in battle, Bob announced that Anne had agreed to marry him in six months. Apart from his susceptibility, he was remarkable for his nautical metaphors. He was ready to renounce Anne to his worthier brother, when he discovered the truth; but he was much more light-hearted than the trumpet-major, and no doubt forgot his brother's claims as quickly as he had been in the habit of forgetting Anne. *TM*. (in particular) xiv–xix, xxii, xxix–xli (cf. xv and *HS*. 'The Rover Come Home'); *D*. (1) v vii

LOVILL, FARMER. The merry old farmer who outwitted Agatha Pollin, thanks to her 'adversary', Frances Lovill. *DBC*

LOVILL, FRANCES. 'The beauty of Cloton village, near Beaminster', who discovered that Agatha Pollin had stolen Oswald Winwood's affections from her. She married Agatha's uncle, Miller Humphrey (for whom, she was to discover, she had no affection), and worked to secure her revenge. *DBC*

LU, LADY. *HS*. 'The Caricature'

LUCETTA. She was the daughter of a rather reckless military officer, and lost both her parents when she was young. She lived in Jersey, tended Henchard while he was ill on a business visit to the island, and fell in love with him. Her conduct excited a great deal of comment, so much so that Henchard eventually agreed to marry her if she were prepared to run the risk of Susan's return. Susan did return, but, by the time of her death, Miss Lucetta Le Sueur had inherited a fortune from her widowed aunt. She took High-Place Hall, and engaged Elizabeth-Jane as her maid and companion in the hope that it would enable Henchard to call without exciting undue comment. Pride and pique on both sides conspired to the effect that it was not Henchard but Farfrae whom she saw first. He had come to see Elizabeth-Jane. Lucetta fell in love with him, and soon received the attentions of two men who were rivals not only in business but also in love. Ultimately, she promised to marry Henchard, but when she heard of the sale of his first wife (as a result of Mrs Goodenough's court disclosures) she immediately made arrangements to marry Farfrae at Port-Bredy. Henchard's business, personal life, and reputation all crashed within a very short period. In his bitterness, Henchard taunted Lucetta and threatened to compromise her by making known the contents of her letters to him. He could not do it, however, and handed them to Jopp to return to her. Lucetta was handsome but somewhat vain, and proud in the eyes of the humbler citizens of Casterbridge. She was affluent, and Casterbridge furniture, dresses, and ways were hardly elegant enough for her. She was elated by Farfrae's success, particularly on the day of the Royal visit when Farfrae as Mayor read the address of welcome to the 'Illustrious Personage'. Mastered by *Weltlust*, she had visions of her husband's knighthood. There were many besides Nance Mockridge who would have been delighted to see her 'toppered'. Jopp's disclosure of the contents of the letters she had written to Henchard from Jersey had immediately suggested a skimmington-ride, and the shock of its cruel exposure, when she was expecting a baby, resulted in her death.   *MC*. xii, xviii, xx–xxx, xxxii–xl, xlii

LULWIND COVE. *Lulworth, nine miles east of Weymouth; see plate facing p. 142.*

Owen and Cytherea Graye took an excursion by steamboat from Budmouth to Lulwind Cove. Sergeant Troy was thought to have been drowned there; and the bodies of Stephen Hardcome and his cousin's wife were cast ashore in Lullwind Bay (*sic*). It was here that Napoleon himself reconnoitred to invade England, according to popular tradition; and it was here that the poet John Keats came ashore on his voyage to Rome. It afforded an excellent place of concealment for smuggling. Eighty tubs, landed at Lullwind Cove (*sic*), were concealed near Egdon Heath in 1805, when the French invasion was expected (an allusion to the fact that Hardy's grandfather sometimes had up to eighty tubs of smuggled spirits concealed at Higher Bockhampton: Evelyn Hardy, *Thomas Hardy's Notebooks, 35*). *DR.* ii 4; *FMC.* xlvii, xlviii, l; *WT.* 7; *WT.* 2; *LLI.* 8*b*; *D.* (1) ii v; *LLE.* 'At Lulworth Cove a Century Back' (September 1920)

LUMSDON. *Cumnor, a village near Oxford.*

Sue Bridehead was a pupil-teacher at Mr Phillotson's school.

JO. ii iv, v, vii, vi vii

LUXELLIAN, LADY. Her two girls, the Honourable Kate and the Honourable Mary, were very fond of Elfride Swancourt. She was very delicate, 'a lady with skim-milky eyes and complexion, belonging to the "interesting" class of women, where that class merges in the sickly, her greatest pleasure being apparently to enjoy nothing'. Her death led to the two scenes in the family vault at East Endelstow church when workmen under John Smith prepared for her interment. Subsequently Lord Luxellian married Elfride for the sake of the children and grew very fond of her, but she too was doomed to die young. *PBE.* v, xiv, xxv–xxvii, xl

LUXELLIAN, SPENSER HUGO. *Named after a saint associated with Cornwall, particularly in the name of a village, Luxulian, east of Lostwithiel and not far from the original Endelstow House (see p. 319).*

Fifteenth Baron Luxellian. He lived at Endelstow House, and recommended Mr Hewby as architect for the restoration of West Endelstow church. His father was Lord George, the subject of some wry reminiscences in the Luxellian vault (xxvi). After the death of his first wife, he married Elfride Swancourt for the sake of his children. He was stricken with grief at her sudden death. *PBE.* ii, v, xiv, xxxiii, xl

LYONESSE, ISLES OF. *The Scilly Isles. See the next note.*

Mr Heddegan and the parents of Baptista Trewthen lived at Giant's Town, St Maria's (*Hugh Town, St Mary's, one of the Scilly Islands*).

CM. 11

LYONNESSE. *This romantic name, associated with Arthurian legend and the north coast of Cornwall, particularly Tintagel Castle, had been revived by Tennyson in his 'Morte d'Arthur' and Idylls of the King.*

Elfride's Swancourt's novel, *The Court of King Arthur's Castle*, is described as 'A Romance of Lyonnesse'. The name is associated with Hardy's first wife, and Iseult of Ireland (pp. 116–17).

PBE. xv; *SC.* 'When I set out for Lyonnesse', 'I found her out there'; *LLE.* 'Meditations on a Holiday'; *QC*

e Acorn Inn, and (below) *'the cottage by the church'*, *Evershot (Evershead)*

Bere Regis (Kingsbere) Church. The 'd'Urberville Window' is on the south (left) side of the Turberville Chapel

'The Caros' cottage, East Quarriers', Portland

MADAME TUSSAUD'S. *The wax-work exhibition chambers in London. An orchestra used to play there. The poem may have originated from Madame Tussaud's belief that her first fiddler had been the Dauphin, the son of Louis XVI.* MV. 'At Madame Tussaud's in Victorian Years'

MADEMOISELLE V—. A French emigrée, whose family had been sentenced to the guillotine. In 1802, when Monsieur B—, the man who had condemned her family to death, arrived, she was a governess at General Newbold's on the Esplanade at Budmouth. She and Monsieur B— were on the point of marriage, but after his departure, she returned to Mrs Newbold's as governess.   *CM.* 8

MAI-DUN CASTLE. *Maiden Castle, a vast prehistoric earthwork or fortress, surrounded with three ramparts, each about sixty feet high, to defend a whole community during a siege. It is situated on a hill two miles south-west of Dorchester. The best impression of this stronghold is given in the imaginary narrative of 'A Tryst at an Ancient Earthwork', where we are told that 'Mai-Dun' means 'The Castle of the Great Hill', said to be 'the Dunium of Ptolemy, the capital of the Durotriges, which eventually came into Roman occupation, and was finally deserted on their withdrawal from the island'.*

It was from Mai-Dun that Henchard observed the return of Newson along the *Via* or Icening Way.

   TM. xxvi (see STUBB); *CM.* 6; *MC.* xliii; *WP.* 'The
            Alarm', 'My Cicely'; *TL.* 'At Casterbridge Fair' (iii)

MAIL, MICHAEL. The second violin-player in the Mellstock choir. He experienced 'a friendly tie of some sort between music and eating', and had good reason to remember an auctioneer, to whom he nodded 'in a friendly way' as he was walking just below the King's Arms in Casterbridge. *He used to narrate the story of the Chalk-Newton choir (CM. 4), and he is the 'tenor' or 'tenor-viol' who narrates two of the poems.*

   UGT. I i–vi, viii, II ii–v; *LLI.* 7; *TL.* 'The Rash Bride',
   'The Dead Quire'; *MV.* 'The Choirmaster's Burial'; *LLE.*
   'The Country Wedding' (*at Puddletown*); *HS.* 'Winter
            Night in Woodland', 'The Paphian Ball'

MANSTON, AENEAS. The illegitimate son of Cytherea Aldclyffe, who had been deserted at the age of seventeen by her cousin, a 'wild officer' who went to India and died there. The child was named Manston after the widow who adopted him.

When Miss Aldclyffe discovered that Cytherea Graye was the daughter of the man she had subsequently fallen in love with, her plan was to make Manston her steward in the hope that he would marry Cytherea and both would inherit her estate. She did not know that he had married Eunice, 'a third-rate actress'. Manston came to Knapwater, and lived in the old manor-house. He was a handsome, sensual, and rather Satanic figure, apt to quote the Scriptures. Cytherea's first meeting took place in his rooms during a violent thunderstorm. To the accompaniment of thunder, lightning, and rain, he played the organ with 'full orchestral power' to such effect that she was completely overcome by it.

The story of the manslaughter of his wife Eunice, his marriage to Cytherea Graye, the rescue of Cytherea, the detection of Manston's guilt, and his ultimate arrest is cunningly contrived, but the whole truth is not revealed before his death in Casterbridge County Gaol; cf. xxi 1, 'Last Words'.

Hardy may have named him Aeneas and his mother Cytherea, after Virgil's hero and his mother Venus, as a clue to a relationship which was not disclosed until Miss Aldclyffe was dying. DR. vii ff.

MANSTON, EUNICE. She was born in Philadelphia. Manston had met her when she was an actress in Liverpool, and married her. She followed him from London to Carriford, where they quarrelled. Manston struck a blow which was fatal. He succeeded in making it appear that she had been burnt to death in the fire at the Three Tranters, where she had booked a room for the night on failing to meet Manston at Carriford Road Station. (For a succinct account of the whole story, see Manston's 'Last Words': xxi 1.) DR. ix–xi, xiii–xvi, xviii, xix, xxi

MARCHMILL, WILLIAM. He was a gunmaker in a Midland city, and his imaginative, day-dreaming wife Ella thought his outlook sordid and material. While she read poetry at Solentsea, and dreamt of the poet Robert Trewe, he was yachting. He was tall and long-featured, with a brown beard. 'He spoke in squarely shaped sentences, and was supremely satisfied with a condition of sublunary things which made weapons a necessity.' He was a kind and tolerant husband, though he was not interested in his wife's poetry, and paid little attention to her remarks about Robert Trewe, the poet she never met but whom she imagined she loved. She died, bearing her fourth child. Just before her death she began an apologetic explanation of her behaviour at Solentsea, saying how she imagined he had neglected her, how she looked for someone who would appreciate her more fully, rather than another lover. . . . Mr Marchmill was not the sort of person to be disturbed by 'retrospective jealousies', but two years later, when destroying papers 'before his second wife entered the house', he came across evidence which convinced him that his wife had been false to him. He was deceived by a 'known but inexplicable trick of Nature'. *LLI.* 1

MARIAN. *Hardy said she was 'one of the few portraits from life in his works'. She was a dairymaid, four years older than himself, whom he taught in the Sunday School at Stinsford. She could repeat the Scriptures with marvellous facility, 'though she was by no means a model of virtue in her love-affairs'* (Life, *25*).

One of Tess's fellow-dairymaids at Talbothays, and, like the rest of them, very much in love with Angel Clare. Her face was jolly and ruddy in complexion; her figure was decidedly plump. She tried to forget her disappointment in drink when Angel married Tess. Loyal and generous-minded, she helped Tess to find work at Flintcomb-Ash, and tried to save her from Alec d'Urberville. *TD.* xxi–xxiii, xxv, xxix, xxx, xxxi, xxxiii, xxxiv, xl, xliv, xlvii, xlviii, lii

MARK. King of Cornwall. *QC*

MARKTON. *Hardy's map of Wessex and a historical quotation relating to Stancy Castle indicate that this is Dunster, west of the Quantock Hills in Somerset. See, however, his 1912 postscript to the preface of the novel.*

A village near Stancy Castle, 'not far from the foot of its slopes'. George Somerset moved from 'the little inn at Sleeping-Green to a larger one at Markton', the Lord-Quantock-Arms Hotel, in order to plan the castle extensions. A 'tender episode between Somerset and Paula', which Dare must have witnessed, took place in the church. In the vestry, Dare outlined plans to Captain de Stancy whereby the captain (his father) should secure Paula Power and Stancy Castle by marriage, and thereby become the master of means which would enable him to support his son. The captain agreed to a game of cards and lost £10. More strikingly bizarre is a much later scene in the vestry, when Abner Power confronted Will Dare, and each in turn lifted a loaded revolver above the edge of the baize-covered table. *L.* I ii, x, xii, xiv; II iv, v, vi; III iv, vi–viii, xi; V xi; VI iv, v

MARLBURY DOWNS. *Marlborough Downs, Wiltshire.* *CM.* 7; *SC.* 'The Sacrilege'

MARLET. Alicia's mother and sister Caroline accepted an invitation to

stay with the Marlets at Versailles. While there, Caroline fell in love
with Charles de la Feste.   *CM.* 3

MARLOTT. *Marnhull, in the Vale of Blackmoor, between Stalbridge and
Shaftesbury. See plate facing p. 366.*

In the eighteenth century, Timothy Petrick acquired many estates,
including the manor at Stapleford (*Stalbridge*) where he lived, estates at
Marlott, estates near Sherton Abbas, nearly all the borough of Millpool,
and many properties near Ivell.

Here the Durbeyfields remained as 'liviers' until Tess's father died.
                    GND. 6; *TD.* i–vii, xii–xv, xxxviii, xlix–lii, liv

MARSHAL'S ELM. The inn at the top of the Poldon ridge (*the Polden
Hills, south of Glastonbury in Somerset*) where 'jeering Johnny' was
murdered by the trampwoman's 'fancy-man'.
                                  TL. 'A Trampwoman's Tragedy'

MARSHWOOD. *Marshwood Vale in west Dorset, north-west of Bridport.
It is overlooked by Pilsdon Pen and Lewsdon Hill to the north. (See also the
*HINTOCKS.) *TL.* 'A Trampwoman's Tragedy'; *HS.* 'At Wynard's Gap'

MARTHA. The nurse who tended Susan Henchard when she was dying,
and buried the pennies used for closing her eyes according to Susan's behest.
It was from her that Mrs Cuxsom learnt about Susan's death.   *MC.* xviii

MARTHA SARAH. A girl who lived in the village of Nether-Moynton,
and helped Mrs Lizzy Newberry, the smuggler, domestically. Her family
name is not disclosed.   *WT.* 7

MARTIN, MRS. The widow of Giles Martin, and grandmother of Swithin
St Cleeve, who lived with her at Welland Bottom.
                    TT. i, ii, ix, xvi, xxi, xxii, xxiv, xxxviii, xl, xli

MARTOCK MOOR. *West-north-west of Yeovil. The MS. indicates that
Durnover Moor was the actual or original scene. *HS.* 'On Martock Moor'

MARY. *The mother of Jesus.*
                    TL. 'Panthera'; *WW.* 'An Evening in Galilee'

MARYGREEN. *Named after Hardy's paternal grandmother Mary, and
the village green. Its original is Fawley, a small village with a Victorian
Gothic church in the hills south of Wantage, Berkshire. Some of
Hardy's ancestors were buried there. His father's mother, 'the gentle,
kindly grandmother who lived with the family at Bockhampton during
Hardy's childhood', lived there as an orphan for the first thirteen years of
her life, and her memories of it were so poignant that she never cared to
return* (Life, 420).

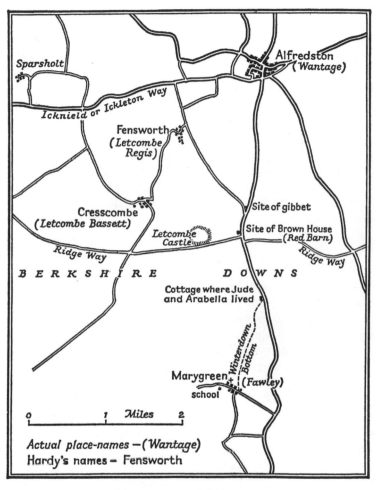

Marygreen and Ridge-way

Jude lived at Marygreen during his youth, with his great-aunt Drusilla Fawley. As a boy, he had worked on Mr Troutham's farm. He went back occasionally to see his aunt when she was ill. Her great friend and nurse was Mrs Edlin. Jude discovered that Sue was born there. After a checkered career, Phillotson returned to Marygreen as schoolmaster and was followed by his wife Sue. When Jude was lying ill with fever at Christminster, his wife Arabella promised to write to Sue asking her to come to see him. Rightly suspecting that Arabella had not sent the letter, Jude went to Marygreen, though he knew the journey might mean his death. Sue and he met her in the church, where they passionately declared their love for each other, though separated by marriages, one the result of gin, the other of creed-intoxication. *JO.* I i–vii;

II, vi, vii; III viii, ix; IV, ii, iii; V, v, viii, ix; VI iv, v, viii, ix MASTERS, MRS. *Probably the wife of the 'captain' with whom the Hardys lodged at Swanage; cf.* Life, *107–8,* HE. *xxxi, and* CAPTAIN FLOWER. *WW.* 'The Lodging-House Fuchsias' MAUMBRY, CAPTAIN JOHN. *His work during the cholera epidemic was based on that of the vicar of Fordington; cf.* Life, *390–1.*

While stationed at Casterbridge with the —th Hussars, he fell in love with Laura, who lived near the barracks and entertained romantic ideas about military life. They were married, and lived gaily, being leading figures at dinners, county balls, and theatrical performances. Great was Laura's disappointment when her husband decided to enter the Church, and he became the curate of Durnover, the most impoverished part of Casterbridge. Cholera broke out, and he found lodgings for her at Creston, near Budmouth. He met her twice a week in the open air – in order that she should not run the risk of infection – near where the highway from Casterbridge crosses Ridgeway. Still dreaming romantically of military life, she fell in love with Lt Vannicock, and decided to elope with him to Bristol, where his regiment was now stationed. On their way through Durnover in the evening gloom, they were diverted by the fires in Mixen Lane, where infested clothes were being burnt. There she saw her husband labouring to help his parishioners; he was ill, and she decided she could not leave him. He had fallen a victim of the pestilence, and died two days later. Vannicock returned from Bristol and offered to marry Mrs Maumbry, but she declined. Though there was now no 'material obstacle' to their union, there was 'the insistent shadow of that unconscious one; the thin figure of him, moving to and fro in front of the ghastly

furnace in the gloom of Durnover Moor'. Mrs Maumbry lived and died a
widow.   *CM.* 1

MAX GATE. *Hardy's house at Dorchester, on the Wareham Road, was
completed in 1885, and was called Max Gate to preserve a link with the
past. Not far away there had stood the cottage of the toll-gate keeper Mack,
and the place was long known as Mack's Gate. In D.* (1) II v, *Jems
Purchess, one of the beacon-keepers at Rainbarrows, notices the lantern at
Max Turnpike 'shining quite plain'.*

> *PPP.* 'An August Midnight'; *SC.* 'At Day-Close in Novem-
> ber', 'His Visitor', 'The Spell of the Rose', 'The Death of
> Regret' (*originally written about a cat strangled in a
> rabbit wire on Conquer Barrow and buried by a sycamore
> in the garden at Max Gate. In a letter to Lady Hoare,
> Florence Hardy stated that Hardy thought the poem 'too
> good for a cat' and made it apply to a person*), 'The Roman
> Gravemounds' (*Life*, 163); *MV.* 'The Photograph', 'The
> House of Silence', 'The Ageing House', 'Everything
> Comes' (*Life*, 173), 'On the Doorstep', 'The Shadow on
> the Stone' (*Life*, 233), 'A New Year's Eve in War Time';
> *LLE.* 'The Garden Seat', 'The Strange House'; *HS.*
> 'Nobody Comes', 'A Leaving'; *WW.* 'Evening Shadows',
> 'The Clasped Skeletons' (*both referring to Conquer Barrow*)

MAYBOLD, PARSON. The new vicar of Mellstock, whose proposal
tempted Fancy Day. He had new ideas, and was much more efficient
than his predecessor, Mr Grinham, though he was not held in high
favour by the choir, which was supplanted when the organ was installed
in Mellstock Church, to be played by Fancy Day. He did not 'take kindly
to the notion' that he should officiate at her wedding.

> *UGT.* I v, vi; II ii–v, vii, viii; IV v–vii; V i

MAYFAIR (LONDON). *HE.* xvi, xx, xxxvi; *MV.* 'At Mayfair Lodgings'
> (*the experience occurred 'off Piccadilly'*, Life, 267); *HS.*
> 'A Poor Man and a Lady' (*intended to preserve an episode in*
> The Poor Man and the Lady).

MAYNE, EGBERT. *The name is a modification of 'Will Strong', that of the
architect hero of* The Poor Man and the Lady. *G. W. Sherman* (Notes and
Queries, *September 1953*) *suggested that the name alludes to Sir Richard
Mayne, the Police Commissioner who took unusually strong measures to
preserve the peace at a working-class rally organized by the Reform*

League in 1866. *The offices of the Reform League were on the ground floor beneath Blomfield's, and Hardy was interested in its activities. He had heard J. S. Mill address a London crowd at an election* (Life, *330*), *and the hero of his first novel, Will Strong, addressed a working-class crowd of men in Trafalgar Square.*

Mayne was a schoolmaster, who fell in love with Geraldine Allenville, and proceeded to London to make his name as a writer (pp. 58–9). *ILH*

MELBURY, GEORGE. *The surname indicates the locality where he lived. See the* HINTOCKS.

A thriving timber-merchant of Little Hintock. 'He was a thin, slightly stooping figure, with a small nervous mouth, and a face cleanly shaven.' His body was rather stiff with over-exertion in handling heavy trees and timber in his youth. Though successful in business, he was over-anxious about his daughter, and had a habit of walking up and down, with bowed head, when he was undecided. The happiness and success of his only child Grace, the daughter of his first wife, who had died soon after her birth, were his main preoccupation. He was happily married to Lucy, but much troubled in conscience at winning his first wife from Giles Winterborne's father 'by a trick', and anxious to promote the marriage of Giles and Grace in reparation. He had given her the best education possible. Giles's Christmas party presented a grave dilemma: how could Melbury allow Grace, whom he wished to be a lady, to marry a humble country man? The prospect of marriage between Grace and Dr Fitzpiers, a man of aristocratic lineage, flattered him, but the marriage was only the beginning of his distress, as he discovered Fitzpiers's infidelities. The new divorce law raised his hopes, and removed all his objections to marriage with Giles. He did everything a solicitous father could in London to gain her divorce, only to discover that Fitzpiers's conduct had not been bad enough. He had no illusions about Grace's future when she and her husband were reunited. *W*

MELBURY, GRACE. The daughter of George Melbury, the timber-merchant of Little Hintock. Her mother died shortly after her birth, and Grace had developed so much affection for the nurse who replaced her that Melbury had married her for the child's sake. He spent a great deal on her education in the hope that it would promote her happiness and welfare. She was fair, slim, gentle, and rather indecisive. She continued to like Giles Winterborne, despite her genteel education and his social shortcomings, for she was not an ambitious girl. In marrying Fitzpiers she 'was borne along upon a stream of reasonings, arguments, and persuasions', chiefly her father's, 'supplemented, it must be added, by inclinations of her own at times'. She was soon disillusioned; their relationship was not founded on confidence or truth. It was not surprising that her heart returned to Giles. The 'veneer of artificiality which she had acquired at the fashionable schools' was 'thrown off, and she became the crude country girl of her latent early instincts. . . . Honesty, goodness, manliness, tenderness, devotion, for her existed only in their purity now in the breasts of unvarnished men; and here was one who had manifested such towards her from his youth up.' Never did she realize this quite to the full, as she did when his self-sacrifice was revealed to her at One-Chimney Hut. Yet such was her nature that she appeared to forget him, and her husband's hollowness, all too quickly. Fitzpiers had little difficulty in coming to a reconciliation with her, thanks to Timothy Tangs's man-trap. Grace's father had no illusions about her future (*cf.* Life, 220: *'the heroine is doomed to an unhappy life with an inconstant husband. I could not accentuate this strongly in the book, by reason of the conventions of the libraries, etc.'*). *W*

MELBURY, LUCY. The second Mrs Melbury, 'the first having died shortly after the birth of the timber-merchant's only child.' She had acted as nurse to the child, Grace, after her mother's death, 'and ultimately Melbury, in dread lest the only woman who cared for the girl should be induced to leave her, persuaded the mild Lucy to marry him'. She was of a placid, accommodating nature, ready to help in the preparations for Giles Winterborne's Christmas party, and creating no difficulties when Grace invited her to accompany her to the woods to observe what futurity had to offer the frisky maidens of Little Hintock on Midsummer Eve. She was ideally suited to her partner by temperament, very sympathetic, and anxious to allay his anxieties and distress, whether real or imaginary.

W. iii, iv, ix, x, xi, xx, xxii, xxiii, xxv, xxix, xxxiv, xxxv, xliii

MELCHESTER. *Salisbury. The cathedral with its tall steeple is described by Hardy as 'the most graceful architectural pile in England'. See plate facing p. 431. Other places of major interest to Hardy readers are the White Hart and Red Lion hotels, the Training College for teachers, and the church of St Thomas. The bridge over the Avon is known as Harnham Bridge. Bissett Hill is on the Blandford Forum road south of Coombe Bissett.*

Fanny Robin walked from Casterbridge to Melchester, when she found Sergeant Troy had gone there with the Eleventh Dragoon-

Guards. After a stay in another town near a military station, she returned to Melchester and 'picked up a living' as a seamstress. Then, just before the birth of her child was due, she set out to walk to Casterbridge Union.

Christopher Julian became assistant organist at the Cathedral, and, eventually, chief organist.

After his engagement to Ethelberta, the jealous old Lord Mountclere took her to Melchester to discover whether she was still in love with Mr Julian. They attended a concert at the Town Hall, where it was soon apparent that Picotee, not Ethelberta, loved him. Piqued by Lord Mountclere's behaviour, Ethelberta avoided him by entering the Red Lion Hotel with her sister, while Lord Mountclere waited at the White Hart in an adjoining street. In the Close, she met Julian and accompanied him into the Cathedral to hear him play, not perceiving 'an old gentleman who had crept into the mouldy place as stealthily as a worm into a skull'. It was Lord Mountclere, who implored her forgiveness for his suspicious behaviour. She promised to marry him. Walking in the city after tea, Julian saw Lord Mountclere buying Ethelberta a wedding-ring at an expensive jeweller's.

Louis Glanville had encouraged his sister Lady Constantine (for his own benefit) to think of marrying a person of affluence. The Bishop of Melchester had proposed to her. Louis learned that his sister had secretly married Swithin St Cleeve, thinking her husband had died in Africa. Realizing that the marriage was illegal, and knowing how desperate Lady Constantine was, since she was expecting a baby and was unable to communicate with Swithin, he visited the Bishop at Melchester, and informed him that his sister was ready to marry him but thought it undignified of her to make the offer. The ruse succeeded.

Henchard passed through Melchester on his last visit to Casterbridge to take Elizabeth-Jane a wedding present and 'ask forgiveness for his fraud'.

Susan Dornell met Stephen Reynard 'by accident' at the Red Lion while her mother was staying at the White Hart.

Sir John Grebe drove 'like a wild man' to Melchester in pursuit of his daughter Barbara, who had eloped with Edmund Willowes. 'But he soon saw that he was acting to no purpose; and by and by, discovering that the marriage had actually taken place', he gave up the idea of following them to London and returned to his house at Chene Manor.

The first marriage of Barbara came to a calamitous end as a result of Edmond's horrible disfigurement in a fire at Venice. She then married

Lord Uplandtowers, and his barbarous treatment of her hastened her death. Soon afterwards the Dean of Melchester preached a sermon upon 'the folly of indulgence in sensuous love for a handsome form merely', which was clearly a reflection on Barbara's attachment to Edmond Willowes.

After staying at Bramshurst Court in the New Forest, Tess and Angel Clare decided to walk north on the assumption that no search would be made for them in that direction. As they approached 'the steepled city of Melchester', he decided it was wise for Tess to rest in a clump of trees during the afternoon, and 'push onward under cover of darkness'. That night Tess slept at Stonehenge; in the early dawn she was arrested.

It was after a little transaction at Melchester fair that George Crookhill found it convenient to disguise himslf.

A young barrister, Charles Bradford Raye, while on the western circuit, stayed at Melchester during October and, after standing in the Close to gain a glimpse of the Cathedral in the darkness, passed out under 'the arched gateway', and walked on to the square to see what was happening at the noisy fair. Here he met Anna, who was living at Melchester with Mrs Harnham, and fell in love with her. The following day he walked with her out of the city to the earthworks of Old Melchester (*Old Sarum*).

After being a pupil-teacher with Mr Phillotson at Lumsdon, Sue Bridehead entered Melchester Normal School (*the Training College for teachers which Hardy's sisters attended*) as a Queen's Scholar. Jude found work as a stone-mason in the repairing of the Cathedral. Together they visited Wardour Castle, missed the train on the way back, and stayed the night at a shepherd's cottage. For this, Sue was ordered to solitary confinement for a week. She escaped through the window, struggled across the deep river at the bottom of the garden (*the River Avon*) and sought refuge at Jude's. She was engaged to Mr Phillotson and was married at St Thomas's Church (*the magnificence of its interior is significantly absent from the novel*), to which they drove with Jude as best man from the Red Lion. When Sue left Phillotson, she met Jude at Melchester, and they went to live at Aldbrickham.

The coach on which Mademoiselle V— travelled at night from Budmouth passed through Casterbridge and Shottsford, and stopped at the White Hart in Melchester. Here she alighted, to return to Budmouth, with the intention of marrying Monsieur B—. She did not know that he had travelled on the outside of the coach to London.

Two officers' wives, who had lost their way, were given the pass-word into Salamanca. It was 'Melchester Steeple'.

> *FMC.* x, xli; *HE.* xxiv, xxxix–xl, Sequel; *TT.* xxi, xxiv–xxviii, xxxi–xxxii, xxxvii–xxxix, xl, xli; *MC.* xliv; *GND.* 1, 2; *TD.* lviii; *LLI.* 8*h*, 5; *JO.* III i–viii, x, IV iv; *CM.* 8; *D.* (3) I ii. See also SALISBURY.

'MELIA.   *PPP.* 'The Ruined Maid'

MELLSTOCK. *Stinsford and the Bockhamptons. It consists of three 'hamlets': the first around the church and vicarage; the second, 'Lower Mellstock', with the school and post-office, more than half a mile to the east; the third, 'Upper Mellstock', a mile to the north-east of the church. These correspond to Stinsford, Lower Bockhampton, and Higher Bock-hampton. Between the church and Lower Bockhampton is Kingston Maur-ward House* (KNAPWATER HOUSE, *and* 'the Manor' *of* Under the Greenwood Tree). *A path from Church Lane continues a wooded or 'embowered' course below Kingston Maurward House to a bridge just below Lower Bockhampton. The road which runs in a northerly direction beyond the 'hamlet' of Lower Bockhampton and towards the Dorchester – Puddle-town (Casterbridge – Weatherbury) road is Bockhampton Lane. At Bockhampton Cross (Mellstock Cross) it intersects the Stinsford – Tincleton road (which runs east below 'Egdon Heath'); farther north it is known as Cuckoo Lane. Beyond the top of the hill, it is joined on the right by the lane from Higher Bockhampton, at the top of which the Hardys lived for over a century. The usual route of the Hardys to Stinsford led a short distance south along Cuckoo Lane, then along a lane to the right and across Kingston Maurward eweleaze, part of Kingston Park. It was 'on a stile leading to the eweleaze he had to cross on his way home' that Hardy read a damning review of* Desperate Remedies (Life, *84*).

Dick Dewy had been for a run down to the eweleaze and up Hollow Hill to Mellstock Cross when he was hailed by members of the choir on their way to his father's, before starting on their Christmas round of carol-singing.

Though rural features were generalized or minimized, the Stinsford–Bockhampton area provided the background for many scenes in Hardy's first two novels. The school occurs in the slight modification of the first which formed 'An Indiscretion in the Life of an Heiress'; it has the same origin as Fancy Day's. The church of 'An Indiscretion' and Desperate Remedies *is Mellstock church, though the name Mellstock was not used before* Under

The Heart of Wessex

411

the Greenwood Tree. *Old William Dewy, Reuben Dewy, Dick Dewy, and Michael Mail sat in the places occupied by Hardy's grandfather, his father, James Hardy, and James Dart respectively in the church gallery, and it was there that Hardy's mother first saw his father when he was playing in the Stinsford string choir (TL. 'A Church Romance'). The stories of the Mellstock players, or related by some of them, are legendary (e.g. 'The Dead Quire', 'The Paphian Ball' and 'The Grave by the Handpost). Their prowess is referred to in CM. 2, LLI. 8f, LLI. 7, and several poems.*

The first hill on the London road from Casterbridge to Weatherbury is Mellstock Hill. Fanny Robin descends this hill with the help of crutches until she collapses by Grey's Bridge. Later we see Farmer Boldwood mounting the hill from Weatherbury to give himself up at Casterbridge Gaol after shooting Troy. It was here that Lt Vannicock arranged for a fly to wait when he was planning to elope with Mrs Maumbry to Bristol. *See MC.* iv, xl, xliii

When Lucetta was critically ill as a result of the skimmington-ride, Henchard hurried off to warn Farfrae at the junction of Cuckoo Lane and the Weatherbury highway. Farfrae would not trust him, and drove on to Mellstock.

It was while they were on their way to Mellstock church that Angel Clare carried the milkmaids, including Tess, over the flooded road.

Jude Fawley spent his early years at Mellstock before going to live with his great-aunt at Marygreen, North Wessex.

Selina Paddock lived in a thatched cottage in a remote hamlet of Mellstock Parish. (*There can be no doubt that this was Higher Bockhampton.* The narrator says he had 'long been familiar' with the cottage; its garden str·tched down to '*the lane or street that ran through* a hermit-group of dwellings'. *Reference to the* Life (*p. 3*) *will show that the words in italics are substantially repeated with reference to the lane leading to Hardy's birthplace; and that other common characteristics are the communal well and bucket, the green gate, and brass-knockered door.* See FAIRLAND. *Like the 'House of Hospitalities' (p. 366) it is the 'house by the well' (Purdy, 140) and probably the same.*) The letter which indicated that Selina's former lover, and father of Johnny, had not been killed at the battle of Alma but was actually coming to see her just when she was preparing to marry Mr Miller was brought up from Lower Mellstock Post-office by one of the school children. *The post office at*

Lower Bockhampton still stands almost opposite the old school-house and school.

UGT; *FMC*. xl, liv; *MC*. ix, xiii, xxxviii–xl; *CM*. 2; *TD*. xvii, xxi, xxiii, xxxiii (?); *LLI*. *8b, f*; *LLI*. 7; *JO*. ɪ ii; *CM*. 4; *CM*. 1; *CM*. 5; *WP*. 'The Dance at the Phoenix', 'Friends Beyond'; *PPP*. 'Long Plighted', 'The Widow Betrothed' (*'the lodge' was originally 'Mellstock Lodge', i.e. Stinsford Lodge, at the entrance to the avenue leading from the Dorchester road to Stinsford House*); *D*. (3) ᴠ vi (Keeper Tricksey of Mellstock); *TL*. 'A Church Romance' (*cf.* Life, *13–14*), 'The Rash Bride' (*Hardy identified the scene at Higher Bockhampton; the Giles Swetman 'from Woolcombe way' may have been related to the Hardys*), 'The Dead Quire' (*the inn was at Lower Bockhampton; the path by the 'Froom' to the church has already been referred to; Moaning Hill is in a meadow, by which the track from the church proceeds, and takes its name from the sound of the wind among the trees which cover it; the Mead of Memories, which are associated with the choir, is the Churchyard to which the listener returns when the 'sad man' has finished his story*), 'By the Barrows', 'She Hears the Storm' (*at Higher Bockhampton, by Thorncombe wood*), 'A Wet Night' (*from Dorchester across Durnover Moor to Stinsford Hill and by Kingston Maurward eweleaze to Higher Bockhampton*), 'Geographical Knowledge' (*'Christina C—' was Mrs Coward, postmistress at Lower Bockhampton*), 'The Noble Lady's Tale' (*with reference to Lady Susan, who lived at Stinsford House, near the Church; cf.* Life, *9, 163 4, 250*); *SC*. 'His Visitor' (*the spirit of Emma Lavinia Hardy; for other poems associated with her grave at Stinsford, see p. 354*); *MV*. 'Afternoon Service at Mellstock' (*'swaying like trees' recalls Hardy's description of the congregation in the same church in his first novel (see* TOLLAMORE) *and in DR. xii 8*, 'At the Wicket-Gate' (*for 'the still meadows' by the church, compare 'the leaze' in 'The Dead Quire'. See p. 439*), 'An Anniversary' (*'the garth' is Stinsford churchyard*), 'Transformations' (*alluding to Louisa Harding, p. 395*),

'In Her Precincts', 'At Middle-Field Gate in February' (*originally* 'Middle-Hill' – *Purdy, 199. Bockhampton Lane, with boyhood recollections; cf.* Life, *223*); *LLE.* 'Voices from Things Growing in a Churchyard' (*cf. MV.* 'Transformations'), 'She did not turn' (*Higher Bockhampton* – *and Tryphena Sparks? See* PHENA), 'By Henstridge Cross at the Year's End' (*formerly 'Mellstock Cross'*); *HS.* 'Winter Night in Woodland' (*for the smuggling, see* LULWIND COVE), 'The Thing Unplanned'; *WW.* 'The Third Kissing-Gate' (*where the public footpath through the meadows, which starts not far from Grey's Bridge and proceeds below 'the gray garden-wall of Stinsford House', joins the path to Lower Bockhampton at the lower end of Church Lane*). See also HIGHER BOCK-HAMPTON, KNAPWATER HOUSE, and STINSFORD.

MELPORT. *Weymouth, formerly known as Melcombe Regis* ILH. 18

MENDIP HILLS. In north Somerset.

    TL. 'A Trampwoman's Tragedy'; *SC.* 'The Sacrilege' (*It took place at Wells Cathedral. The fair at Priddy, a Mendip village, was the most famous in that region*).

MENLOVE, MRS LOUIS. Lady Petherwin's maid, a flighty and spirited woman, who found employment with Mrs Doncastle at the London house where Mr Chickerel, Ethelberta's father, was butler. Joey, Ethelberta's young brother, fell in love with her, and great apprehension was caused lest he should disclose that Ethelberta (Mrs Petherwin) was of common stock. She discovered the secret, and reported to Tipman, the valet of Lord Mountclere, who duly reported it to his master. Lord Mountclere was not deterred.   HE. i, xxviii–xxix, xxxii–xxxiv, xlii

MEREDITH, GEORGE. *In 1869* ('Forty years back'), *when the novelist George Meredith was a reader for the publishers Chapman & Hall, he met Hardy for the first time, and gave him advice on his first novel* The Poor Man and the Lady. *In May 1909 Hardy was in London, and saw a poster announcing Meredith's death. He went on to his club, the Athenaeum, and wrote the memorial lines which were published in* The Times *a day or two later. Hardy succeeded Meredith as President of the Society of Authors. For other meetings and links, cf.* Life, *181, 263, 268, 304, 344.*   *TL.* 'George Meredith'

MERLIN. The magician. He speaks the Prologue and Epilogue.   *QC*

MICHAEL. An old milkman at Anglebury who exchanges remarks about Ethelberta with the ostler of the Red Lion. 'A man could make a meal between them eyes and chin – eh, hostler?' A 'good saying well spit out is a Christmas fire' to his 'withered heart'. *HE.* i, xliv

MIDDLETON ABBEY. *Milton Abbas. Most of the abbey buildings, and the village, were removed by the first Earl of Dorchester in the eighteenth century, to make way for a mansion by the Abbey Church.*

Mrs Charmond stayed here with a relative of her late husband, and was visited by Mrs Fitzpiers's husband.

'*The Doctor's Legend*' *(pp. 81–3) relates very closely to the history of Milton Abbas. It was bought by Joseph Damer of Came House, south of Dorchester. Hardy read about his character and his son John's suicide in Horace Walpole's Letters (cf. Life, 175, 237). John Damer married Ann Seymour Conway, a sculptress of distinction, in 1744, and died on 15 August 1776.*   *W.* xxvii, xxix; *DL*; *TD.* xlviii

MILAN. *The Hardys visited Milan in April 1887. Hardy afterwards thought that he conceived the Cathedral scene – Napoleon's coronation – for* The Dynasts *while he was on the roof* (Life, *195).

Alicia walked along the Via Alessandro Manzoni and entered the Galleria Vittorio Emanuele, where she caught sight of her sister Caroline and Charles de la Feste.   *CM.* 3; *D.* (1) I vi

MILD, MR. A lieutenant of Captain de Stancy's battery at Toneborough Barracks. Miss Paula Power agreed to play the part of the Princess of France in *Love's Labour's Lost* if he played the King of Navarre, her wooer. He was a diffident and unobjectionable young man, unlike de Stancy. By collusion, the captain took his place in the first performance. Miss Power sent for a professional actress to play her part, and the captain gave way to Mr. Mild in the second performance. *L.* III vi–viii, x

MILLBORNE, MR F. A bachelor of means, who was able to retire from banking in London and, though he had no inclination to marry, felt he must make amends to a woman with whom he had had a liaison twenty years earlier in Toneborough. She refused him, but eventually agreed to marry for the sake of her daughter's prospects. Her paternity was suspected, however, by her fiancé, and her marriage prospects seemed to be blighted. Millborne rented a manor-house near Ivell, where his daughter's fiancé, the Rev. Percival Cope, was curate, but, instead of accompanying his wife and daughter there, went abroad. At Brussels, he read with satisfaction that the marriage had taken place; he had come to think, like

Antigone, that, having performed an honourable rite, he had earned 'the reward of dishonourable laxity', and occasionally, as a result of excessive drinking, he had to be helped to his lodgings by his servant. *LLI.* 3

MILLER, BARTHOLOMEW. A master-wheelwright who was about to marry Selina Paddock, when 'her first intended husband' (and father of her son Johnny), Sergeant-Major John Clark, returned from the Crimean War. She had believed that he had been killed in battle. The sergeant-major died of a heart-attack on the evening of his arrival. Mr Miller was very fond of Johnny and Selina, and waited patiently for her to accept him. But she was content to remain 'John Clark's widow', and Mr Miller, finding it necessary to have someone else in the home now his mother was getting old, married a thriving dairyman's daughter who lived on the other side of Shottsford-Forum. *CM.* 5

MILLPOND ST JUDE'S. *If this is Milborne St Andrew, north-east of Puddletown, Hardy's directions are wrong, and perhaps deliberately so.*

Old Twills engaged the maltster in his earlier days eleven months at a time, 'to keep me from being chargeable to the parish if so be I was disabled'. Parson Tringham discovered that a family of d'Urbervilles had lived there. *FMC.* viii; *TD.* i

MILLPOOL. *Milborne Port, near Sherborne.*

Old Squire Petrick acquired nearly all the borough. *GND.* 6

MILLS. Employed by the vicar of Welland, Mr Torkingham. He cut short the choir-practice when he came with the message that Lady Constantine wished to consult the vicar about a letter she had just received. *TT.* ii

MILLS, BILL. The shepherd boy who was left in the hut at Lambing Corner on Marlbury Downs, and witnessed the principal events of the story. *CM.* 7

MILLY. The daughter of a woodman, and formerly the sweetheart of the parish clerk's son, whom Lady Caroline had secretly married. To remove the suspicions raised by the circumstances of his death, Lady Caroline induced her to announce that it was she who had married him secretly and removed his body to the door of his father's cottage in order to conceal the marriage from her parents. Milly not only told the story, but acted as his loving widow, and tended his grave with sincere affection. When Lady Caroline discovered that she was pregnant, she again enlisted Milly's aid to save her reputation. After a long absence, Milly returned to her home with a baby 'son'. The boy was educated at a grammar school, and joined the army, where he speedily rose to the rank of quartermaster. After the death of her second husband, the childless Marchioness of Stonehenge wished to claim her son. Milly insisted that he should decide. The son remained loyal to his 'mother', and the Marchioness died lonely, unloved, and broken-hearted. *GND.* 3

MISTOVER KNAP. *Approximately north of Blooms-End, from which the left-hand track led to that part of Mistover where Susan Nunsuch lived, and the middle track to Mistover Knap. In his own copy of* The Return of the Native, *Hardy vaguely identified Mistover as 'Troytown.' It must have been in the direction of Troy Town from Higher Bockhampton, for from it the Quiet Woman is to the south-east, and the intermediate Rain-barrow to the right. In 'The Fiddler of the Reels', 'the fir-woods of Mist-over' are seen above the heath and 'backed by the Yalbury coppices', i.e. Yellowham Wood.*

Captain Vye lived in a lonely house at Mistover Knap with his grand-daughter Eustacia. (To the west), three-eighths of a mile away, stood Susan Nunsuch's cottage and, a few yards further on, one other. These three habitations were all that remained of Mistover. *RN.* I iii, v, vi, viii, x, xi; II iii–v, vii; III iii, vi–viii; V, ii, iv–vi, vii; *LLI.* 7

MITCHELL, JOB. See COMFORT.

MOCKRIDGE, NANCE. A Casterbridge woman first seen by St Peter's church expressing her indignation that Henchard, the Mayor, should have sold 'growed wheat' to the bakers. 'I've been a wife, and I've been a mother, and I never see such unprincipled bread in Casterbridge as this before.' She worked in Henchard's yard, and revealed that Elizabeth-Jane had helped to serve customers at the Three Mariners. She was to be found there, and at Peter's Finger, with Mother Cuxsom. She looked forward to the 'skimmity-ride' in the hope of seeing Lucetta 'toppered'. *MC.* iv, xiii, xx, xxxvi, xxxvii, xxxix

MOLLY. A servant engaged by Miller Loveday, probably after his marriage with Mrs Garland. She attempted to drive Anne and Mrs Garland inland when it was thought the French had landed. *TM.* xxvi–xxviii, xxxii, xxxviii, xxxix

See also the two Mary Hardys (pp. 356–7).

MONEY, MARYANN. She was employed by Bathsheba Everdene, both domestically and on the farm. Her face was 'a circular disc, furrowed less by age than by long gazes of perplexity at distant objects. To think of her was to get good-humoured.' At the sheep-shearing, she was assisted by Temperance and Soberness Miller. *FMC.* vi, ix, xxii, xxx, xxxi, xxxii

MONKSBURY. *The name suggests Abbotsbury, but Abbotsbury appears as 'Abbotsea'.*

Jack Winter left Longpuddle parish to superintend a farm at Monksbury, and while there corresponded with Harriet Palmley.   *LLI.* 8*g*

MONMOUTH, DUKE OF. *An illegitimate and popular son of Charles II, who claimed succession to the throne and was defeated in 1685 at Sedgemoor in Somerset. He was captured at Shag's Heath, east of Wimborne Minster, and executed on Tower Hill, London. His supporters were dealt with ruthlessly by Judge Jeffreys. In Dorchester, the house where Jeffreys stayed in High Street for the trials (which are said to have taken place at the Antelope Hotel) may still be seen.*

MC. viii; *CM.* 10; *HS.* 'At Shag's Heath'

MONSIEUR B——. He had been a member of the Committee of Public Safety in Paris during the Revolution. He reached Budmouth in 1802, and lived in penury. There he was recognized by an emigrée, Mademoiselle V——, as the man who had sentenced her family to the guillotine. He fell in love with her. In England he was known as Monsieur G—— (see pp. 96–7).   *CM.* 8

MONTACUTE. *West of Yeovil, Somerset. The House is a magnificent Elizabethan mansion. The Crest is the neighbouring hill, from which Ham-hill stone is quarried.* See MONTISLOPE HOUSE.   *MV.* 'Molly Gone'

MONTE CARLO. See NICE.   *L.* IV iii–v, V i, iv, xii

MONTISLOPE HOUSE. *Montacute House, four miles west of Yeovil.*

Sir John Horseleigh found he was illegally married to the daughter and heiress of Richard Phelipson of Montislope.   *CM.* 9

MOON, MATTHEW. A labourer at Bathsheba's farm, 'a singular framework of clothes with nothing of consequence inside them'. He 'advanced with the toes in no definite direction forwards, but turned in or out as they chanced to swing'.   *FMC.* vi, x, xv, xix, xxi, xxxiii, xxxvi

MORE, JIMMY. When the landlord of the inn at Sleeping-Green was asked by George Somerset if there were many Baptists in the neighbourhood, he said there were more than usual, and gave as his reason that people turned Baptist 'to save the expense of a Christian burial for their children', and instanced a poor family in Long Lane – 'the husband used to smite for Jimmy More the blacksmith till 'a hurt his arm' – in which there would have been eleven children if they had not been lucky and buried five when they were three or four months old. They were buried at 'a shilling a head; whereas 'twould have cost a couple of pounds each if they'd been christened at church'. *L.* 1 iv

MOREFORD. *Moreton, east of Tincleton, in the Frome valley.*

LLI. 7; WP. 'The Slow Nature'

MORRIS, MRS. The housekeeper at Knapwater House.

DR. v 2–3, xv 3, xvii 3

MOTTISFONT, LADY. When Philippa, the daughter of Squire Okehall, married Sir Ashley Mottisfont, she adopted his illegitimate daughter Dorothy, and grew so fond of her that she was loth to part with her when the Contessa, now a widow, wished to reclaim her. When Dorothy was asked if she would prefer to live with the beautiful Contessa, she said she would, and Philippa allowed her to go. When, however, the Contessa was about to remarry, and wished to return her, the formerly over-submissive Philippa resisted steadfastly; she expected her own child, and Dorothy had to return to the cottage-woman who had looked after her when she was a baby. *GND.* 4

MOTTISFONT, SIR ASHLEY. *The name is from Mottisfont Priory, north of Romsey, Hampshire.*

He lived at Deansleigh Park (*Broadlands near Romsey*). He was a widower who had 'sowed his wild oats' with the Contessa, and was therefore anxious, when he married Philippa Okehall, that she should be interested in his daughter's welfare. When the Contessa returned to England, after the loss of her Italian husband, he was equally anxious that Dorothy should be allowed to live with her mother. The Contessa married a second time, and Sir Ashley hoped that Philippa would take Dorothy back. *GND.* 4

MOULE, HORACE. *One of Hardy's great friends and advisers, both at Dorchester and in London. He was the son of the Rev. H. Moule of Fordington, and a great classical scholar. Unfortunately, owing to his inability to pass in mathematics, he left both Oxford and Cambridge without a degree. Yet he won the Hulsean Prize at Cambridge for his work on Christian Oratory, which was published in 1859. He was awarded his B.A. in 1867, and his M.A. in 1873.*

When Hardy got to know him, in 1860 or 1861, he was just 'beginning practice as author and reviewer'. It has sometimes been assumed that Hardy's sombre cast of thought derived from Moule. What is certain is that Moule discussed modern thought with Hardy, and that Hardy followed The Saturday Review, *for which Moule wrote, particularly with reference to the controversy between science and Christian orthodoxy. Horace Moule lent him books, advised him on literary style, and encouraged him to write fiction, particularly when* Desperate Remedies *was attacked. He reviewed* Under the Greenwood Tree *and* A Pair of Blue Eyes.

His scholastic failure led to depression, and depression to drink. He committed suicide in 1873. Whether his career was 'the germ of Jude the Obscure' (Life, 208) *cannot be assessed. Hardy probably had him in mind to some extent when he created Knight (PBE). He is the 'dark He' of 'The Five Students' (Life, 405). 'Standing by the Mantelpiece' may* recall a meeting with Hardy not long before his death (Life, 93); 'Before My Friend Arrived' describes how Hardy sat by Ten Hatches Weir (p. 262) and sketched Moule's open grave as he looked across the meadows to Fordington Church. See* Life, *32–4, 84, 87, 93, 96.*

WP. 'A Confession to a Friend in Trouble'; *MV.* 'The Five Students'; *HS.* 'Before My Friend Arrived'; *WW.* 'Standing by the Mantelpiece (H.M.M., 1873)'

MOUNT LODGE. The residence of Baron von Xanten.   *CM.* 12

MOUNTCLERE, EDGAR. Brother of the viscount, Lord Mountclere. He kept a kennel of hounds at Mr Neigh's Farnfield estate near the grazing skeletons of horses 'waiting to be killed for their food'. He hoped to inherit his brother's Enckworth estate, and, with this in view, sought out Sol Chickerel on the premises of Messrs Nockett and Perch, builders and contractors (somewhere between the Thames and the Kensington squares), to stop the marriage of Ethelberta and Lord Mountclere. Their attempts by sea and land are part of the more farcical comedy with which the novel ends.   *HE.* xxv, xli, xlii–xlv

MOUNTCLERE, LORD. A viscount and owner of Enckworth Court; 'a wicked old man, they say'. When he made up his mind to marry Ethelberta, nothing could put him off, not even the information that she was the daughter of the butler Chickerel. He followed her to Rouen, took her to Melchester to discover whether she was attached to Christopher Julian, and gained her promise to marry him. Sly and observant, he foiled all attempts to prevent his marriage, but Ethelberta had the upper

---

* Purdy says that the person addressed is a woman; no evidence is given. It could have been Hardy. Lois Deacon, in *Providence and Mr Hardy*, Hutchinson, 1966, assumes the 'warmth' that grew 'without discouragement' to have been between Moule and Tryphena Sparks. The date 1873 seems to refer to the scene; Tryphena left London in 1871. An interesting parallel is drawn between the 'embitterment' of the poem and the estrangement between Knight and Smith (*PBE.* xxxvii–xxxviii).

hand finally, made him live a regular respectable life, and reorganized the administration of Enckworth Court. His face 'presented that combination of slyness and jocundity which we are accustomed to imagine of the canonical jolly-dogs in medieval tales. The gamesome Curate of Meudon might have supplied some parts of the countenance; cunning Friar Tuck the remainder. . . . Anybody could see that he . . . loved good company, warming drinks, nymph-like shapes. . . .' The discovery, immediately after her marriage, that the viscount had been keeping Miss Gruchette as 'Lady Mountclere' made Ethelberta determined to be mistress or leave. He had already dismissed Miss Gruchette, and the married couple were reconciled in the 'Petit Trianon of Enckworth Court'. *HE*. xiii, xxvii ff,

MOUSEHOLE. When Baptista Trewthen sailed from Pen-zephyr (*Penzance*) after the death of her husband Charles Stow, she watched 'Pen-zephyr and all its environing scenes' disappear behind Mousehole and St Clement's Isle. *CM*. 11

MYNTERNE, CONJUROR. The grandfather of Mr Crick, the dairyman at Talbothays, used to go to Conjuror Mynterne, out at Owlscombe, 'and a clever man 'a were'. (*Owlscombe is Batcombe, a village below the steep Batcombe Hill and Cross-in-Hand. Tradition held that Conjuror Mynterne was buried under the wall of the church; half of what was said to be his tomb was at one time to be seen protruding from the church towards the graveyard; cf. Life, 169*). *TD*. xxi

NAN. *TL*. 'The Husband's View'

NAN and NELL. They met to discover that they were in love with the same soldier, who had arranged to meet both in the same place.
LLE. 'A Military Appointment'

NANCY. *WW*. 'Henley Regatta'

NAPPER, MRS. One of the company at a house on the north side of Hyde Park who discussed Ethelberta's published verses. *HE*. ix

NARROBOURNE. *One of the Coker villages, south of Yeovil.*

A village near Ivell. Joshua Halborough was curate here; his brother Cornelius succeeded him. Their sister Rosa married the squire of Narrobourne House. *LLI*. 4

NEIGH, ALFRED. Mr Doncastle's nephew, and, like Ladywell, an admirer of Ethelberta. He was thirty-five, and of a phlegmatic temperament. His estate was at Farnfield, and Ethelberta thought it prudent to inspect it privately. She discovered that there was no mansion, only a park with horses in the last stage of decrepitude, waiting to be killed for the hounds belonging to Lord Mountclere's brother. Neigh's family had made a fortune as knackers and tanners. To Ethelberta he was 'handsome, grim-natured, rather wicked, and an indifferentist', and therefore attractive. She concluded that they were 'too nearly cattle of one colour for a confession on the matter of lineage to be well received by him', and looked elsewhere for a husband. Neigh continued his suit until he learned that she was engaged to Lord Mountclere, but did not give up hope apparently, since he gave the butler Chickerel a five-pound note to assist him in his efforts to prevent the marriage.

HE. vii, ix, xvi, xxi, xxv–xxxi, xxxiii–xxxv, xlii

NELL. One of the girls who danced with the Scotch-Greys in the barn (*at Kingston-Maurward; cf.* Life, *19–20*). The story of her compunction is in the ballad tradition. *HS.* 'The Harvest-Supper'

NEST COTTAGE. After being dismissed by Bathsheba, Gabriel Oak lived here a short time. Laban Tall rode across the fields to fetch him, at Bathsheba's request, when her sheep were dying from a surfeit of clover. The cottage was seen at the other side of the valley, 'a white spot . . . backed by blue firs'. Oak normally lived with the Coggans near Bathsheba's (viii, xxxii, xxxiv). It is not clear which is 'Oak's house' when Bathsheba visits him one evening to implore him not to emigrate (lvi).

FMC. xxi

NETHER-MOYNTON. *Owermoigne, six miles south-east of Dorchester.*

It appears as Nether Mynton, where Farmer Bollens lived, in *Desperate Remedies.* Jacob Noakes, the friend of Stubb (p. 484) and Festus Derriman, lived at Nether-Moynton Farm. Principally, it is the setting for the smuggling story, 'The Distracted Preacher'. There were many 'trimmers' in the parish, people who went to church in the morning and chapel in the evening; and among the devout were many smugglers.

DR. xiii 2; *WT.* 7; *TM.* ix, xxvi

NETHERHAY. *North-west of Broadwindsor (west Dorset).*

HS. 'The Pat of Butter'

NETTLECOMBE-TOUT. *A prominent hill, south-west of Bulbarrow, in 'that elevated dorsal line' of chalk hills which formed the southern boundary of the Vale of Blackmoor.*

After being deserted by Angel, Tess worked at Flintcomb-Ash farm, 'a starve-acre place' among the chalk hills near Nettlecombe-Tout.

TM. xii; *TD.* ii, iv, xlii

NEW FOREST. See GREAT FOREST.   *WW*. 'Throwing a Tree'.

NEWBERRY, MRS LIZZY. A pretty young widow (formerly Miss Simpkins), who lived with her mother at Nether-Moynton, and had a share in a smuggling business with her cousin Jim Owlett. Stockdale, a temporary Wesleyan minister, stayed with her, and the two fell in love; but Lizzy resisted every persuasion, including the offer of marriage, to give up her illicit trade. In this she actively helped Owlett, and was frequently away at night to give warnings to the carriers who transported tubs of spirits which were landed at such points as Ringsworth and Lulwind Cove. After Stockdale's departure she was wounded in an affray with Customs officers; the smugglers were caught; and her trade was gone. Her family had been smugglers for generations. She was now poor, and her mother was dead. Two years after his departure, the minister Richard Stockdale returned, proposed again, and was accepted. Lizzy took her duties as minister's wife in a Midland town seriously, and wrote a tract entitled 'Render under Caesar; or, The Repentant Villagers'. (*Hardy would have preferred an ending much closer to the reality: she married her smuggler cousin, and emigrated with him to Wisconsin.*)   *WT*. 7

NEWLAND BUCKTON. *Buckland Newton, near the chalk hills south-east of* The Woodlanders *country*.

When Fitzpiers was returning from Middleton Abbey, Darling stopped to drink at Lydden Spring (*the road from Milton Abbas crosses the Lydden river two miles west of Mappowder*), and he heard the church clock of Newland Buckton (*a mile away*) strike midnight.   *W*. xxix

NEWSON, RICHARD. His appearances are intermittent. He appeared in the furmity-seller's tent when Henchard was trying to auction his wife Susan, and bought her for five guineas. For a while they settled in Canada, where their daughter Elizabeth-Jane was born. They then stayed at Falmouth, but Susan began to worry about the legality of their marriage, and Newson returned to seafaring. He was presumed lost at sea on a voyage to Newfoundland. Newson escaped and lived in Newfoundland for a time, before returning to England to find Elizabeth-Jane. When Henchard told him that she was dead, he made no further inquiries, and left Casterbridge immediately. (*Hardy's inconsistency* – xxxvi, xli – *makes one wonder whether he witnessed* the skimmingtom-ride which he had expressed interest in on his arrival, and which he had helped financially to promote.) He harboured no resentment against Henchard for his deceit. The prospect of his daughter's marriage to Farfrae delighted him, and the wedding-festivities (in which he 'out-Farfraed Farfrae in saltatory intenseness') showed that he was a man who was ready to make the most of what pleasure life offered him. The sea was his abiding love, and he settled near it at Budmouth.　　　　　*MC.* i–iv, xix, xxxvi, xl–xlv

NICE (and MONTE CARLO). In order to weaken the ties between his niece and George Somerset, and in the hope that she would marry Captain de Stancy, Paula Power's uncle took her with Mrs Goodman and the captain on a European tour. Their first stay was at Nice, where George sent many personal and business communications, until, hearing no more from her, he decided to go and see her. He learned that the party had left the previous day for Monte Carlo. They stayed here one night, and Somerset just missed them. He went to the Casino out of curiosity, saw Dare gambling, and refused to lend him money. To vent his spite, and obtain the means to a fortune according to Moivre's *Doctrine of Chances*, Dare sent a telegram in Somerset's name to Miss Power, telling her he had lost everything and asking for £100. This was taken to Monte Carlo by Captain de Stancy. He was at the Pont-Neuf at the appointed time, only to meet Dare, and not the expected Somerset.

L. III xi, IV i–v, V i, iii

NINE-BARROW DOWN. *A ridge running in an easterly direction from Corfe Castle towards Swanage Bay.*

Ethelberta rode on a donkey from Knollsea along this ridge to attend the meeting of the Imperial Archaeological Association at Corvsgate Castle.　　　　　*HE.* xxxi

NINEMAN, CORPORAL. At his funeral in Casterbridge, Mr Penny heard the 'Dead March' for the first time (cf. p. 266).　　　*UGT.* I viii

NOAKES, JACOB. See STUBB.

NOBBS. Lady Constantine's coachman.　　　　　*TT.* i

NORBERT. An old man, said to be German, who told the story of the capture of Leipzig by the Allies in 1813. He sat with his audience in the Master-tradesmen's Parlour at the Old Ship Inn in Casterbridge.

WP. 'Leipzig'

NORCOMBE HILL. *We are told that it is 'not far from lonely Toller-Down', north-east of Beaminster. 'Through a spur of this hill ran the highway between Emminster and Chalk-Newton.' This suggests that it was north-east of Westcombe Copse. Tewnell Mill (the name at least) may have been suggested by Toller Whelme.*

It was here that Gabriel Oak lived in a hut during the lambing season,

and made the acquaintance of Bathsheba Everdene. The loss of his flock
meant that Farmer Oak had to seek employment elsewhere.

FMC. i–v, viii, xlix

NORMANDY. When the architect George Somerset was misrepresented
through the cunning of Dare, Paula Power lost interest in him, and he
resigned his commission to superintend the extensions at Stancy Castle.
Later he went on a holiday and architectural tour in Normandy. Paula
Power discovered she had wronged him. She postponed her marriage to
Sir William de Stancy, and set off to find the man she really loved. Before
finding him at Étretat, and making her peace with him, she visited
Cherbourg, Lisieux, St Jacques, Caen, and Havre. (*The Hardys had been
on holiday in Normandy in 1880; cf.* Life, *138–9.*)   *L.* V xii–VI iii

NORTHBROOK, CAPTAIN JAMES. Nephew of Lord Quantock, and
secretly married to his daughter, the Honourable Laura. See p. 64.

GND. 10

NOTTON. The clarionet-player in the Chalk-Newton choir.   *CM.* 4

NUNSUCH, JOHNNY. The son of Susan Nunsuch, and only 'a little boy'.
He was employed by Eustacia Vye to keep the bonfire burning
at Mistover Knap as a signal to Wildeve, and to listen for the 'flounce'
in the pond which indicated that he had arrived. Susan believed
that his subsequent indisposition was due to Eustacia's influence as a
witch.

Johnny met the exhausted Mrs Yeobright when she was beginning
her return journey from Alderworth to Blooms-End. She told him how
Eustacia had looked out of the window, and that she had been 'cast off
by her son'. Johnny fetched her water to drink from Oker's Pool. When
Clym recovered from the illness caused by the certainty that he was
responsible for his mother's death, he went to see Johnny at Susan's
cottage at Mistover, and there heard the evidence which precipitated the
final catastrophe.   *RN.* I vii, viii; IV vi, viii; V i, ii

NUNSUCH, SUSAN. She lived at Mistover, nor far from Captain Vye's.
A 'widespread woman whose stays creaked like shoes whenever she
stooped or turned', she was convinced that his granddaughter was a witch,
and that her son Johnny's ailments were caused by a spell she had cast
over him. To counteract this, she jabbed a needle into Eustacia's arm at
church. On the dark stormy night when Eustacia was wandering across
the heath to her death, she was busy preparing a wax image of Eustacia,
which she thrust through and through with pins, and melted over the

fire, as she repeated the Lord's Prayer backwards three times against her
enemy.   *RN.* I iii; III ii; IV vii, viii; V ii, vii

NUTTLEBURY. *Hazelbury Bryan, in the Blackmoor Vale, below Bulbarrow.*

When Angel was taking Tess home, after their abortive marriage, he
stopped ,at a point midway across the Vale, beyond Nuttlebury, saying
that if she intended to return to her mother's home he must leave her at
that point.

On hearing that her mother was ill, Tess left the farm at Flintcomb-
Ash immediately, though night had set in, walked over the uplands to
Bulbarrow and descended into the Vale of Blackmoor via Nuttlebury,
'every tree and tall hedge making the most of its presence', conjuring up
hunted harts, witches, and fairies 'that "whickered" at you'.

TD. xxxvii, 1

NYTTLETON, MR. Miss Aldclyffe's solicitor, of the firm of Nyttleton and
Tayling, Lincoln's Inn Fields, London. He gave sound advice on the
appointment of a steward, which Miss Aldclyffe rejected. *DR.* vii 2–5

OAK, GABRIEL. Until he lost his flock, he was a sheep-farmer at Norcombe Hill, where he met Bathsheba Everdene for the first time and was
impressed by her beauty and vanity. He could tell time by the stars, and
his solace was flute-playing. When seeking employment, after losing his
flock, he turned aside to put out a rick-fire, and was immediately
accepted as a shepherd by the farmer, Bathsheba herself. He is the central
character in great scenes, such as the sheep-shearing and the storm. A
man of supreme integrity, he could not flatter; he criticized Bathsheba for
her thoughtless conduct towards Farmer Boldwood and was immediately
dismissed. He was soon found to be indispensable and reinstated. He
saved Bathsheba's cornstacks from the storm after her marriage to Troy,
while her husband and the rest of the farm labourers were lying in a
drunken stupor in the barn after the harvest supper and dance. When
Boldwood lost interest in his farm through love of Bathsheba, Oak was
made overseer of his farm as well as Bathsheba's. When Troy and Boldwood were removed, and Oak was thinking of emigration, she appealed
to him to stay. The story ends with their marriage. Bathsheba had learnt
to respect, and admire, his stability, fortitude, unselfishness, and judgment in general matters. He is a foil to Troy: 'Troy's deformities lay deep
down from a woman's vision, whilst his embellishments were upon the
very surface, thus contrasting with homely Oak, whose defects were

patent to the blindest, and whose virtues were as metals in a mine.' *FMC*

OAKBURY FITZPIERS. *The name seems to have been suggested by Okeford Fitzpaine south-east of Sturminster Newton, but its fictitious location seems to be much nearer High Stoy.*

From High Stoy, Melbury points to his daughter Grace a hill rising out of the level of Blackmoor Vale 'like a great whale' (*Dungeon Hill*), and beyond it 'a particularly green sheltered bottom'. 'That's where Mr Fitzpiers's family were lords of the manor for I don't know how many hundred years, and there stands the village of Oakbury Fitzpiers.' On his mother's side, Fitzpiers was connected with the Lord Baxbys of Sherton. Melbury was therefore very flattered that Fitzpiers sought his daughter in marriage.   *W*. viii, xxiii

OAKER'S WOOD. *Eight miles east of Stinsford. See* RIMSMOOR POND.

Grandfather James recalled how a bridegroom had failed to appear for his wedding. He had been caught in a man-trap in Oaker's Wood. Three months passed before he recovered and the banns were re-published.

UGT. v i

O'FANAGAN, MRS TARA. A guest at Enckworth Court 'who had a gold-clamped tooth, which shone every now and then', and who asked Ethelberta to amuse the company by telling one of her stories. Ethelberta complied with a thinly disguised story of her life. Lord Mountclere realized it, but assured her that her lowly origin made no difference. 'Modern developments have shaken up the classes like peas in a hopper.'

HE. xxxviii

OGBOURNE, CAPT. FRED. He returned from Canada and requested his cousin, the Duchess of Shakeforest Towers, whom he had loved and still loved, to meet him one night by the Druid stones on Marlbury Downs. She could not understand his request, but met him there. The following night the Duke met him at the same spot, and murdered him.   *CM*. 7

OLDBOURNE, THE HON. AND REV. MR. He was the rector at Batton, and the father of Emmeline; 'a widower, over stiff and stern for a clergyman'. He regarded Emmeline's attachment to the young curate Alwyn Hill with disfavour, and no doubt was pleased when the Duke of Hamptonshire married her. See pp. 61–2.   *GND*. 9

OLDHAM, MR. The rector of Chalk-Newton, and brother to Lord Wessex. He was not opposed to the interment of Sergeant Holway in the churchyard at Chalk-Newton. (*Reference to Hutchins shows that Mr Oldham was Charles Redlynch Fox-Strangways, who died at Maiden*

Dictionary of People and Places

Newton, where he had been Rector for many years, in 1836. His brother was the Earl of Ilchester, of Melbury. See p. 381.)   CM. 4

OLIVER, GRAMMER. A spry old woman who did the housework and cooking at the Melburys'. She could not rest until the agreement which she had made with Dr Fitzpiers (and for which he had paid her £10), whereby he should have her skull when she died to examine its peculiarly large brain, had been cancelled. Before this worry made her ill, she had known no ailment. When her anxieties were relieved, she soon recovered and was out in the woods to watch the events of Midsummer Eve with Marty South. Her dialectal use of 'Ich' for the first person is of interest; cf. *Life*, 221.   *W*. iv, vi, xvii–xviii, xx, xliv

OLLAMOOR, WAT. Nobody knew where he came from, or where he went to. He lodged at Lower Mellstock, and was a veterinary surgeon in theory, and a musician, dandy, and 'company-man' in practice. To men he was unattractive; over young women he seemed to cast a spell, partly by his looks, more by his fiddling. Sometimes his hair was dressed in curls, a double row, running almost horizontally around his head. Hence his nickname, 'Mop'. His playing consisted almost entirely of country jigs, reels, and 'Favourite Quick Steps' of the eighteenth century. While fiddling, he invariably closed his eyes. Caroline Aspent of Stickleford fell under the spell of his music; whenever there was a dance in the neighbourhood at which he was the musician, she contrived to be present; whenever he passed through Stickleford to court a woman at Moreford, she was jealous. Gradually they became acquainted, and Mop 'could not resist a little by-play with her too easily hurt heart, as an interlude between his more serious lovemakings at Moreford'. She refused to marry her lover Ned Hipcroft, who went up to London. Four years or so later, she came up to London with a three-year-old daughter, in the hope that Ned would marry her. She said that Ollamoor had left soon after Ned. Soon Ned took to Ollamoor's daughter, 'little Carry', and married Caroline. After the wedding, they visited the Great Exhibition (*of 1851*), and Caroline thought she caught a glimpse of Mop there. One autumn they decided to return to Stickleford. Ned stayed behind in Casterbridge, making inquiries about employment, while Caroline walked on towards Stickleford with her daughter in the evening dusk. They paused at the Quiet Woman Inn for a rest and found a large company of local people assembled after an auction sale. Dancing began; the fiddler was Mop Ollamoor. Caroline had to dance to his music, but the reel was so long and

428

exhausting that she collapsed. Ned arrived, but Ollamoor disappeared with the child. The heath was searched unsuccessfully. Time passed, and nothing was heard of Ollamoor or 'little Carry', whose loss Ned Hipcroft grieved as if she were his child. Then it was rumoured that a fiddler and a girl resembling the pair had been seen at a fair in London. The Hipcrofts returned to London, where Ned spent his spare time looking for them in vain. It was generally thought that Carry and her father had emigrated to America. *LLI.* 7

ONE-CHIMNEY HUT. Giles Winterborne lived in this cottage in King's Hintock Wood towards Delborough (*on the west side of Melbury Park, between Melbury Osmond and Chelborough*) after being compelled to leave his house at Little Hintock. To escape from Fitzpiers, when he returned from the Continent, Grace Melbury walked some three or four miles west to seek Giles Winterborne's assistance, but was detained by rain. Outside, though she did not discover it until too late, Giles was lying ill under a poor shelter of hurdles and fern. He rapidly developed a fever and was past recovery when Fitzpiers arrived, at Grace's call, to give medical help. *W.* xl–xliii

OOZEWOOD. *Ringwood, on the Avon, fifteen miles south of Salisbury.*

Named after the 'fresh-water lagoon' which divided it from meadows and coppice. At the time of the story – the reign of Henry VIII – the surrounding woods were dense. Here Edith, the legal wife of Sir John Horseleigh, lived, and was visited secretly by her husband, at the house of a timber-dealer named Wall; and here Sir John was killed by her brother Roger, who believed that he was false, as he lived with wife and children at Clifton Horseleigh. *CM.* 9

OUNCE, CAPTAIN. In charge of the steamer *Spruce* which Sol and Edgar Mountclere boarded at Sandbourne for Knollsea. They were forced to turn back by the storm when they had managed to come in by Old-Harry Point and were almost in reach of the landing-stage. Captain Ounce was bringing a doctor to attend to his wife, and was thought to be attempting the well-nigh impossible for that reason. He had no reason to fear; his wife had given birth to a boy and was out of danger. *HE.* xliii–xliv

OVERCOMBE. *A village below Bincombe Down, though it was suggested mainly by Sutton Poyntz, further east, with its mill and pond. The mill bears some resemblance to that at Upwey, but it is largely imaginary. The church is that at Bincombe (cf. WT. 3).*

The mill-house had formerly been a manor house, and the residential portion was divided into two parts, one occupied by Mrs Garland and her daughter Anne, the other by Miller Loveday. On a neighbouring hill a beacon had been prepared to be lit if the French landed. (A panoramic view from the downs hereabouts is given in chap. xii.) *TM*

OWEN, REBEKAH. *An American admirer of Hardy's works, who settled in England and was frequently in touch with Hardy. See Carl J. Weber*, Hardy and the Lady from Madison Square, *Colby College Press, 1952. She and her sister were the 'good judges' who persuaded Hardy to restore the greater part of chap. xliv to* The Mayor of Casterbridge, *and her disapproval of* Jude the Obscure *is very probably the subject of the poem:*
WP. 'To a Lady'

OWLETT, JIM. A miller at Nether-Moynton, who conducted a smuggling business with the assistance of his widowed cousin, Mrs Lizzy Newberry, and hired men, many of them devout worshippers, in the neighbourhood. Tubs of smuggled spirits were hidden in various places, including the church and a pit in his orchard, over which grew an apple-tree in a square box. Eventually he was caught, after being badly wounded in an affray with Customs officers. He emigrated to Wisconsin. (*See Hardy's note of May 1912 at the end of the story.*) *WT.* 7; *CM.*5 (iv)

OXFORD. *Its actual name is sometimes used; elsewhere it is referred to as* Christminster (*q.v.*). *All Souls College, Oxford, suggested 'All Angels'.*
PBE. vii, viii, xiv; *TT.* xxv, xxvii; *LLI.* 2

OXFORD STREET (LONDON). *As seen on 4 July 1872.*
HS. 'Coming up Oxford Street: Evening'

OXWELL. *Poxwell, five miles north-east of Weymouth, see plate facing p. 174.*

At Oxwell Hall lived Squire Derriman, whose nephew Festus had designs on his hoarded wealth at the time of the expected French invasion. Anne Garland went there occasionally to read the newspaper to the old miser. On one occasion, after walking to a christening party in the adjoining parish of Springham (*Warmwell*), she was escorted back by the trumpet-major, and their way led past Oxwell Hall; to escape Festus and his revelling friends, Anne fled. When Squire Derriman died, it was found that he had left Anne nearly all his property, including Oxwell Hall 'with its muddy quadrangle, archways, mullioned windows, cracked battlements, and weed-grown garden'. *TM.* vi, viii, ix, xxiv, xxvi, xl

PADDINGTON. When Elfride arrived at Paddington station with Stephen, after their journey to London to be married secretly by licence, she lost

Sandsfoot (King Henry the Eighth's) Castle, south of Weymouth (see Portland)

Rufus (Red King's) Castle, Portland

Salisbury Cathedral and Close (see Melchester and Salisbury)

heart, Stephen gave way, and they rushed to another platform to catch the return train. On their last visit to Cornwall, Knight and Smith travelled on the same train from Paddington. Another traveller to the west of England from Paddington station was Mr Millborne.

PBE. xii, xxxix; *LLI.* 3

PADDOCK, JACOB. Father of Selina. *CM.* 5

PADDOCK, SELINA. She had borne a child to her 'first intended husband' John Clark, a corporal, who had to leave suddenly, before he could marry her, when the Crimean War broke out. She had been led to believe that he was killed in battle, and was on the point of marrying Mr Miller when news came that Sergeant-Major Clark was coming to see her. Overexertion in dancing on the evening of his arrival brought on a heart-attack from which he died. Selina insisted that she was Mrs Clark, and showed no inclination to marry Mr Miller, who ultimately married someone else. Selina then discovered that John Clark had married a woman in the north of England on his return from the Crimea, and left her. She understood why he had been so anxious for her to emigrate with him to New Zealand. *CM.* 5

PALMER, MR. He stood smoking by his garden door as the effigy of Napoleon Bonaparte was burnt on Durnover Green. When the news came that Napoleon, after his escape from Elba, had reached Paris, and King Louis had fled, he blew a cloud of smoke and spat perpendicularly, for the second time. 'Well, I'm d—. Dear me – dear me! The Lord's will be done,' he said. *D.* (3) v vi

PALMLEY, HARRIET. Niece of Mrs Palmley, the enemy of Mrs Winter. When she came from Exonbury to stay with her aunt, Mrs Winter's son fell in love with her. For the sequel, see WINTER. *LLI.* 8g

PANTHERA. *In support of the view that this Roman centurion might have been the father of Jesus, Hardy points to* Origen Contra Celsum, *the* Talmud, *Strauss, Haeckel, and other sources.* *TL.* 'Panthera';

and, by allusion, *WW.* 'An Evening in Galilee'

PARAMARIBO. *Dutch Guiana, South America.*

Maria Heymere sailed back to England on reaching Paramaribo. She had learnt that her husband Anderling had discovered his mistake in thinking that his first wife was dead. *GND.* 5

PARIS. *The Hardys made several visits to Paris, the first in 1874. One of Hardy's objects in visiting both Rouen and Paris seems to have been the noting of background scenes for* The Hand of Ethelberta (Life, *103*). *His*

431

plans were changed, however: Ethelberta decided to return to England from Rouen, when she learned that Lord Mountclere was also on his way to Paris.

Clym Yeobright described its attractions to Eustacia, to whom it appeared a dream-world in contrast to Egdon Heath. She was intending to escape to Paris when she was drowned.

George Somerset thought of Paula Power in Paris, and 'her drive past the Place de la Bastille to the Boulevard Mazas to take the train for Lyons'.

Many scenes in *The Dynasts* take place in Paris, the most important in the Tuileries Palace. They relate to the Napoleonic succession, the divorce of the Empress Josephine, the marriage of Napoleon and Marie Louise, and the birth of a son.

HE. xxxi–xxxiii; *RN.* esp. iii i, ii, iv, iv viii, v v; *L.* iv i;
D. (1) i ii, vi vii, (2) v i, ii, viii, vi iii, (3) i xii, iv ii

PAWLE, GRAMMER. For the effigy of Napoleon Bonaparte which was to be burned on Durnover Green, she gave Captain Meggs's old Sunday shirt, which she had saved for tinder-box 'linnit'. *D.* (3) v vi

PAWLE, OLIVE. She married James Hardcome, and was drowned (see p. 86). *LLL.* 8*b*

PEACH, MRS. A young, dark, and handsome widow – her husband had been captain of a ketch – who came to live with her father, the gardener at Mount Lodge. Jim Hayward flirted with her in order to stir up jealousy in Margery Tucker, and turn her mind from the fascinating Baron von Xanten. The plot succeeded. 'Mrs Peach vanished to Plymouth, and found another sailor, not without a reasonable complaint against Jim and Margery both that she had been unfairly used.' *CM.* 12

PEACH, WILL. During her husband's absence as a soldier, the wife had eventually been false to him:

There was Will Peach who plays the flute,
And Waywell with the dandy suit,
And Nobb, and Knight. . . . But she's been mute
As to the father's name.

WW. 'The War-Wife of Catknoll'

PEN WOOD. *Three miles north-east of Wynyard's Gap.*

HS. 'At Wynyard's Gap'

PENELOPE, LADY. *Lady Penelope Darcy. Wolfeton House near Dorchester became her home, as a result of her first marriage in the reign of James I. See plate facing p. 334.*

'Her beauty was so perfect, and her manner so entrancing, that suitors seemed to spring out of the ground wherever she went, a sufficient cause of anxiety' to the Countess, her widowed mother. The three who were most ardent were Sir George Drenghard, Sir John Gale, and Sir William Hervy. She said jokingly she would marry all three, and in course of time she did. She died the victim of a scandalous rumour that she had poisoned her second husband in order to marry Sir William.

GND. 8

PENNY, ROBERT. A bespectacled boot and shoe maker who sang in the Mellstock choir (*based on Robert Reason of Lower Bockhampton: cf.* Life, *92, 394, 428–9*). The pictures of Mrs Penny dancing with the tranter, and of how she sat up on Midsummer Eve and caught sight of her future husband are memorable. *See plate facing p. 46.*   *UGT.* i i–viii, ii ii, iv, v, v i, ii; *HS.* 'Winter Night in Woodland'

PENNYWAYS. The bailiff at Weatherbury Upper Farm who was dismissed by Bathsheba Everdene for stealing barley. He became Bathsheba's sworn enemy, and Troy, when he saw him at Greenhill Fair, decided to make use of him to re-establish himself at Weatherbury.

FMC. vii, viii, xxiii, l, lii

PENPETHY. *On the second day after his arrival at St Juliot, Hardy, the church-restorer, drove with Emma Lavinia Gifford and her sister to Tintagel and then on to Penpethy slate quarries, 'with a view to the church roofing'* (Life, *75*).   *HS.* 'Green Slates'

PEN-ZEPHYR. *Penzance, Cornwall.*

Here Baptista Trewthen missed the boat that was to take her home to marry Mr Heddegan. Here too she met Charles Stow, a former sweetheart, who persuaded her to marry him at Trufal. They intended to sail on the next boat to inform her parents; he decided to swim in the sea, and was drowned. When this was happening, Baptista was gazing at the outline of St Michael's Mount. She married Mr Heddegan as arranged, and spent the first stage of her honeymoon at Pen-zephyr. That night she lay between her two husbands – the body of Charles Stow lying in the next room.   *CM.* 11

PERCOMB, MR. The chief hairdresser in Sherton Abbas. 'He had the patronage of such county off-shoots as had been obliged to seek the shelter of small houses in that venerable town, of the local clergy, and so on; for some of whom he had made wigs, while others among them had compensated for neglecting him in their lifetime by patronizing him when they were dead, and letting him shave their corpses. On the strength of all this he had taken down his pole and called himself "Perruquier to the aristocracy".' His barber's shop and pole were in the back yard. He persuaded Marty South to sell her hair to adorn Mrs Charmond.

W. i, ii, v, xlviii

PETER, ST. *His denial (cf. Mark xiv 66–72):*

SC. 'In the Servants' Quarters'

PETHERWIN, ETHELBERTA. See ETHELBERTA.

PETHERWIN, LADY. She lived at Exonbury Crescent, London, but on the death of her husband she travelled with her widowed daughter-in-law, Ethelberta, and was first seen at Anglebury, then at Wyndway House and Rookington Park. She died in Switzerland.

She had quarrelled with Ethelberta over the publication of her poems, and dispossessed her, but while in Switzerland had forgiven her and written a letter to her brother asking him to transfer £20,000 of the £100,000 she had bequeathed him to Ethelberta. Before she could draw up a new will she died. The letter had no legal validity, and was ignored. Ethelberta was left with nothing but 'the fag-end of the lease of the town-house and the furniture in it'. *HE.* i, v, viii, x, xi, xiii, xxxiii

PETRICK, ANNETTA. *The wife of Peter Walter of Stalbridge House.*

Timothy Petrick, grandson of old Timothy Petrick, the lawyer who succeeded in amassing much property, had no social ambitions and married Annetta, a beautiful woman of middle-class estate. She died soon after the birth of her son, whom she had christened by the name of Rupert. Just before her death she confessed that he was the son of the Marquis of Christminster. Later her husband discovered that she was subject to a form of hallucination which made her believe that her dreams were realities. *GND.* 6

PETRICK, TIMOTHY. *Peter Walter of Stalbridge House, who died in 1745, at the age of eighty-three.*

A very astute lawyer who came into possession of many estates, including Stapleford Park, where he lived. He had no hesitation in altering his will to exclude 'the intruder' Rupert from his inheritance.

GND. 6

PETRICK, TIMOTHY. *Peter Walter of Stalbridge House. He died in 1753 (Hutchins, iii 671).*

Grandson of Timothy and brother of Edward. He married Annetta, and, on hearing that Rupert was the son of the Marquis of Christminster, had his grandfather's will altered to disinherit him. He grew fond of the boy, and indulged in hopes that his aristocratic qualities would give lustre to the Petrick family. For this reason he successfully altered his grandfather's will in Rupert's favour. When he discovered that his deceased wife had suffered from hallucinations, and that the Marquis of Christminster had been abroad during the whole of their married life, he was disappointed, particularly when he saw the more common features of his grandfather emerging in Rupert. From that time he treated him with growing antipathy. *GND.* 6

PEWIT, THE. The brig on which Bob Loveday was first mate in the merchant service. *TM.* v, xiv, xxx, xxxiii

PHELIPSON, CHARLES. He lived at Elm-Cranlynch, less than two miles from Falls-Park. His self-concern when Betty Dornell contracted smallpox to avoid Stephen Reynard ended their love, and he was 'packed off to sea by his parents'. *GND.* 1

PHELIPSON, RICHARD. *Richard Phelips of Montacute House near Yeovil.*

His daughter, the heiress of Montislope, was illegally married to Sir John Horseleigh in the reign of Henry VIII. *CM.* 9

PHENA. Very little was known about her until the publication of Lois Deacon's *Tryphena and Thomas Hardy* (Toucan Press, 1962) and the more highly documented and controversial *Providence and Mr Hardy* by Lois Deacon and Terry Coleman (Hutchinson, 1966). Unless much more comes to light, what is verifiable in Tryphena's relationship to Hardy is not very great, and its significance has been much overestimated. There is much that leaves room for conjecture, and even more which is inadmissible, in the 'evidence'.

Tryphena was Hardy's cousin (*Life*, 224); she was born at Puddletown in 1851, and at the age of eighteen proceeded, after a period as pupil-teacher in her home village, to Stockwell Training College for teachers, in London. In 1871, at the end of her course, she became headmistress of an elementary school for girls in Plymouth. In 1877 she married, and went to live at Topsham near Exeter, sometimes helping to serve at the bar of her husband's hotel. She had four children, and died in 1890, when the eldest of the children, a daughter, was eleven.

The daughter grew up believing that her mother had at one time been engaged to Hardy. In 1965, at the age of eighty-six and just before her death, she stated, when her mind was wandering and confused, and after repeated questioning on the subject, that a boy represented by a photograph in the family album was Hardy's son. Where her impressions came from, how much was real or imagined, to what extent, if any, she was susceptible to suggestion in her old age – these are questions which cannot be resolved. What seems most likely is that Tryphena talked of Hardy when he was becoming famous as a novelist, and said that she had often walked out with him. The mysterious boy, brought up by Tryphena's elder sister, may have been the extra-marital child of one or the other of them; of his paternity no clue has been traced. How Tryphena's daughter got the information, or formed the impression, that he was Hardy's son is left to conjecture. Her mother died when she was eleven years old.

Tryphena may have been engaged to Hardy (though *WP*. 'Ditty' suggests otherwise). There may be truth in the story that she sent back her engagement ring, and that Hardy presented it to Emma Lavinia Gifford. One thing is certain: looking back at the time of her death, Hardy regarded Tryphena as his 'lost prize' (she was not the only one he regretted not having married in preference to his first wife; see the note on H. P.). 'Thoughts of Phena' is the only poem which, from first to last, expresses his thoughts and feelings about her quite explicitly. There is nothing in the poem to suggest that Hardy had a guilt-complex. In view of the regret which he showed for the neglect of his first wife, it would seem likely that (when Tryphena died) he would have expressed remorse for any wrong he had done her, if such a wrong existed.

'Her Immortality' is a development of a thought expressed in the above poem. There can be little doubt of the authenticity of the past which it recalls, but the greater part of the poem is devoted to an exposition, with a pseudo-heroic flourish that borders on the ridiculous, of a contemporary view of survival after death which impressed Hardy when he read Pater in 1888 (see p. 169). One of the weaknesses of detective criticism is that it rarely assumes that a writer has an imagination; Hardy the novelist had shown that he could be highly inventive as well as imaginative. This is shown in 'My Cicely', a poem which appears to have been written with the underlying thought that Tryphena had demeaned herself in acting as a barmaid near Exonbury.

Inventiveness should certainly not be ruled out in reading 'The Wind's Prophecy'. This was conceived with reference to Hardy's first visit to St Juliot, in March 1870, when Tryphena was in London. He may have had her in mind, or some other woman. Tryphena's hair was not 'ebon'. The poem is antithetical throughout, for ironical emphasis. One suspects a great deal of exaggeration for the sake of effect. Whether Hardy was in love with Tryphena at this time is not known.

Lois Deacon's view is that they were lovers in the summer and autumn of 1867, after Hardy had given up his architectural work in London, and that they spent weeks and weeks together (the evidence for this is taken from a poem which recalls the time Hardy spent with Emma Lavinia Gifford in Cornwall in the late summer of 1870). A conjecture that Tryphena left home the following February to conceal the fact that she was bearing a child is based on one of Hardy's notes: 'In the February following a memorandum shows that he composed a lyric entitled "A Departure by Train", which has disappeared.' (*Life*, 57.) The general supposition must be based on the argument that, if Tryphena bore a child before proceeding to Stockwell Training College, the child was born and concealed in time for Tryphena to be engaged as a pupil-teacher long enough in 1868 and 1869 to work for the scholarship which was necessary for her to receive training as a teacher. The facts suggest that Hardy was far too busy to be involved in a long passionate courtship. He returned from London in July 1867, recovered from his illness in a few weeks, assisted the architect Hicks in various church-restoration projects, and finished the first draft of *The Poor Man and the Lady* by January 1868.

To support their reconstruction of Hardy's life at this critical phase, the authors of *Providence and Mr Hardy* contend that 'Neutral Tones' marks the end of the Tryphena episode and was written in 1871. It was written in London before friendship with Tryphena could have begun (*Life*, 54). 'At Rushy-Pond' has the same setting possibly, and it speaks of meeting there, 'in a secret year', a woman whom he had hoped to 'keep near' him. If the two poems are related – and the ending of 'At Rushy-Pond' suggests a link – it is difficult to see how they can refer to Tryphena, and one is left wondering whether they are real or imaginary in origin. If the second relates to Tryphena, the ending is significant:

> she withdrew thence, mirrored, and
> Her days dropped out of mine.

This does not accord with an engagement that lasted five years, continuing while Hardy paid court to Emma Lavinia Gifford from 1870 to 1874. A generalization in *The Hand of Ethelberta* (xxxvii), written in 1875, may be relevant here: 'Not the lovers who part in passion, but the lovers who part in friendship, are those who most frequently part for ever.'

In the 1895 preface to *Jude the Obscure*, Hardy wrote: 'The scheme was jotted down in 1890, from notes made in 1887 and onwards, some of the circumstances being suggested by the death of a woman in the former year.' This may well have been Tryphena (cf. *Life*, 224), and in this connection 'The Mound' (*WW*) is of interest. The poem seems to be wholly autobiographical. Here the girl

> crazed my mind by what she coolly told –
> The history of her undoing,
> (As I saw it), but she called 'comradeship',
> That bred in her no rueing;
> And saying she'd not be bound
> For life to one man, young, ripe-yeared, or old,
> Left me – an innocent simpleton to her viewing;
> For, though my accompt of years outscored her own,
> Hers had more hotly flown . . . .

(Lois Deacon suggests she was the 'comrade' of Horace Moule (q.v.), and quotes from 'Standing by the Mantelpiece'. He was twice Tryphena's age; Hardy was eleven years her senior.) If the girl of 'The Mound' was Tryphena (and the poem has sufficient in common with the recollections of 'Her Immortality' to make this at least a possibility), we can see one important resemblance between her and Sue Bridehead (there is little point in dwelling on the question of the paternity of Tryphena's supposititious son which the poem may appear to raise): neither believes in being tethered to a single man for life. Other obvious comparisons are the cousinship of the lovers, and the fact that Tryphena and Sue were pupil-teachers before attending training colleges. Tryphena is certainly not the epicene Sue, but the picture of Sue as a girl which Phillotson contemplates (*JO.* III vi) is similar to that of Tryphena in 1863 (see *Tryphena and Thomas Hardy*, 15). Another item of great interest derives probably from Hardy's visit to Topsham with his brother after Tryphena's funeral. There he met Tryphena's daughter, and subsequently criticized Nature's imperfections for not reproducing the mother in the child, just as Jude did when left to his reflections after the departure of the married Phillotson and Sue from Melchester (cf. 'To a Motherless Child' and *JO.* III viii. A similar thought, however, is to be found in 'At a Bridal', written in 1866 and included in *Wessex Poems.*)

On the question of 'Randy' and his paternity, it should be pointed out that there are greater mysteries in *Providence and Mr Hardy* than that of the relationship between Hardy and Tryphena. Why did Tryphena's sister marry at Puddletown, and immediately set off to live with Tryphena at Plymouth and subsequently at Topsham, never returning to her husband? The most objectionable child in all Hardy's fiction is named Randolph (*LLI*. 'The Son's Veto').

Fiction to consider:

1. The description of Fancy Day; her position as teacher; and the nutting episode. *UGT*. I vii; IV i
2. Part of the description repeated. *HE*. xxxiii
3. 'The Raffaelesque oval' of Lucy Savile's face, and her dark brown hair, parted in the middle, with thoughts of Tryphena in the sentiments of the story. *WT*. 5
4. See above for *Jude the Obscure*.
5. Avice Caro *WB*. II. iii

Poems to consider:

WP. My Cicely, Her Immortality, Unknowing, Thoughts of Phena (March 1890), To a Motherless Child, In a Eweleaze near Weatherbury (1890).

PPP. The Inconsistent.

TL. 'I Say I'll Seek Her'.

SC. Wessex Heights, vi; cf. *MV*. The Head above the Fog, and the footnote on p. 309.

MV. At the Wicket-Gate (*There is a family tradition that the parents of Hardy and Tryphena objected to their engagement because they were first cousins:* Dorset Evening Echo, *14 April 1967*), On a Heath (*The 'another looming' was 'a third person', Hardy told Vere H. Collins. This suggests that the meeting was not far removed in time from Hardy's first visit to Cornwall.* Her Love-Birds *cannot refer to Tryphena in Plymouth, which is 'the marble-streeted town' (see p. 444); the lover has journeyed 'citywards', i.e. to London.*

LLE. 'She did not turn'.

HS. At Rushy-Pond.

WW. The Mound, Standing by the Mantelpiece.

For 'The Wind's Prophecy', 'The Place on the Map', and 'The Five Students', see pp. 351, 353, and 370.

For 'Midnight on the Great Western', see p. 327.

If Tryphena turned from Hardy to Horace Moule while she was in London, an added significance may be seen in the epigraph of *PBE*. xxv. Its context in Psalm 55 (the Book of Common Prayer version) would be particularly apt:

'For it is not an open enemy, that hath done me this dishonour: for then I could have borne it. . . .
But it was even thou, my companion: my guide, and mine own familiar friend.'

If this supposition were true, it would explain the instability that marks the affections of some of Hardy's earlier heroines; it is most marked in Elfride, and there is a hint of it in Fancy Day.

The available evidence suggests that Tryphena completed her three years of pupil-teaching from the end of 1866 to the end of 1869, as was required for her admission to college at the minimum age of eighteen. Hardy's own marital problems may have been stressed by thoughts of 'Phena', when he heard of her death; but the part she was to contribute initially in the planning of *Jude the Obscure* changed considerably as a result of Hardy's friendship with Mrs Henniker in 1893.

PHILEMON, TIMOTHY TITUS. The Bishop of Bristol, whose greeting on the marriage licence (which was useless when Matilda Johnson had left) seemed 'beautiful' to Bob Loveday. 'Come to that, the old gentleman will greet thee like it again any day for a couple of guineas,' said the miller. *TM*. xxii

PHILLOTSON, RICHARD. A schoolmaster, whose departure from Mary-green to Christminster certainly sowed the seeds of Jude's strivings. He had hoped to graduate and enter the Church. When Jude reached Christ-minster, he discovered from his cousin Sue Bridehead that Phillotson was in charge of a school at Lumsdon. At this point, he was forty-five, thin-lipped, spare, and slightly stooping in his black frock coat. It was Jude who suggested that Sue should become his pupil-teacher when she left Miss Fontover's, and in fact arranged it with Phillotson. She was an apt pupil and won a Queen's Scholarship to Melchester Training College. She had allowed herself to become engaged to Phillotson, and their plan was to take a large double school in a great town, where they could make a good combined income, with Sue as head of the girls' school. In the meantime he had moved to a large school for boys at Shaston, and had resumed his old studies in Roman-Britannic antiquities. He visited Melchester, and discovered that Sue had left the Training College and that Jude was in love with her. Sue had learned that Jude was a married man; she became an assistant teacher in Phillotson's school in Shaston, and married him at Melchester, Jude acting as best man. The marriage proved a failure. Phillotson consulted his friend Gillingham at Leddenton, and did not accept his advice. His nobler 'instinct' prevailed, and he set Sue free, whatever the consequences. He was dismissed, and eventually went back to his old school at Marygreen at a much reduced salary. 'No man had ever suffered more inconvenience from his own charity, Christian or heathen, than Phillotson had done in letting Sue go. He had been knocked about from pillar to post at the hands of the virtuous almost beyond endurance,' yet his convictions on the rightness of his decision to release Sue had never been shaken. The loss of her children made Sue feel that she had sinned against God, that she must travel the road of self-abnegation, and submit to the Church and her solemnized marriage to Phillotson. She returned to Marygreen and Phillotson, was remarried, and drank her cup to the dregs. Jude died, thinking of Sue 'defiled'. *JO.* i i, iv; ii iv–vi; iii i, iv–vii; iv ii–vi, v i, viii; vi i, iv, v, ix

PHIPPARD, JOANNA. A Havenpool girl who married Shadrach Jolliffe mainly from jealousy of Emily Hanning. See p. 90.   *LLI.* 6

PHOEBE. When, after Susan's death, Henchard discovered that Elizabeth-Jane was not his daughter, he was very short-tempered with her; he thought she demeaned herself by doing jobs which the kitchen-maid Phoebe could have done, and by thanking the parlour-maid persistently.

MC. xx

PHYLLIS. The milkmaid whose thoughts are not on the scenery with which she seems to harmonize but on the gown she has ordered in the hope of winning Fred's attentions from 'that Other One'.

PPP. 'The Milkmaid'

PICCADILLY. Here Somers told his friend Jocelyn Pierston that he and Mrs Pine-Avon were to be married.

For the incident in the poem, cf. Life, *235.*

ILH. ii 2; *WB.* ii xiii; *LLE.* 'The Woman I Met'

PICOTEE. One of Ethelberta's younger sisters, 'an April-natured, pink-cheeked girl, with eyes that would have made any jeweller in England think of his trade'. She was a teacher at Sandbourne, but lived in the country 'two or three miles out'. She met Mr Julian on Sandbourne Moor and fell in love at first sight. When her family moved to Ethelberta's at Exonbury Crescent, she followed to act as her sister's maid. She was a witness at the private marriage of Lord Mountclere and her sister. In the end, she was engaged to be married to Mr Julian.

HE. ii, iii, v–vi, xii–xv, xvii–xx, xxii–xxv, xxviii–xxx, xxxvii, xxxix, xlv, xlvi, Sequel

PIERSTON, AVICE. Granddaughter of AVICE CARO. Her mother (to whom he had proposed twenty years earlier, and to whose mother he had been attached) hoped she would marry Jocelyn Pierston. He thought her 'the very She'. She was a governess at Sylvania Castle, lady-like, and finer in figure than her mother and grandmother. She agreed to marry Jocelyn, but the unexpected arrival of a young admirer, Henri Leverre, made her change her mind. She and Henri eloped, and were married in London. *WB.* III i–vi

PIERSTON, ISAAC. He and Avice's mother were married secretly. He was a quarryman on the Isle of Slingers but, not being on good terms with Anne Avice, went to work at Peter-Port (*St Peter Port*), Guernsey, returning just before Avice was born. The sculptor Jocelyn Pierston helped to set him up in business, but he was killed by accident in his quarry. *WB.* II vi, vii, xii, xiii; III i

PIERSTON, JOCELYN. A man of artistic temperament who was always in search of ideal beauty, and tried to express it in sculpture. He became famous and was an A.R.A. He was the son of a rich Portland stone-merchant. In love, he found the ideal form migratory and elusive. At the age of nine, he thought he had found it in Laura; later in Elsie, the daughter of Colonel Targe of Budmouth-Regis (he discovered that she was to marry Captain Popp in two days and proceed to India at once); thereafter in many forms and complexions. Returning to Portland (the Isle of Slingers) he found her in Avice Caro, a girl he had known in his early years. Her place was taken by Marcia Bencomb; then, by Mrs Pine-Avon. Twenty years later, when he heard of Avice's death, he returned to Portland, and thought he had found his ideal in her daughter Ann Avice; at length he discovered she was married. After her husband's death, she wrote to him, and he returned to Portland twenty years after his last visit. In her daughter, he discovered 'the very She', and they would have married, as her mother wished, had she not met a former lover, the young Henri Leverre, on the eve of the wedding. Finally he met Marcia again. She was a widow. Both were the victims of Time. They decided to marry, but Jocelyn had no illusions. He found no more beauty in art, and settled for a practical prosaic life on the Isle of Slingers, where he and Marcia were married. The Vision had vanished. (*Compare Hardy's view*: '*It is the incompleteness that is loved, when love is sterling and true.*': Life, *239*.)   *WB*

PIERSTON, MR. Jocelyn's father, a wealthy stone-merchant of East Quarriers on the Isle of Slingers. His chief rival in business was Marcia Bencomb's father. He died at Sandbourne, leaving Jocelyn £80,000.

WB. I i, iii, v, vi; II i

PILSDON. *Pilsdon Pen and Lewesdon Hill are each about 900 feet high, north of Marshwood Vale in West Dorset.*

*MS. variants of the penultimate line in the first poem are '*On High-Stoy Hill or Pilsdon Peak*' and '*On Pilsdon Pen or Lewsdon Peak*' (*Purdy, 112*).

PPP. 'Doom and She'; *SC.* 'Wessex Heights; *MV.* 'Molly Gone'; *HS.* 'At Wynyard's Gap'

PINE-AVON, MRS NICHOLA. Jocelyn Pierston met her at the Countess of Channelcliffe's and the Hon. Mrs Brightwalton's. She was a handsome widow. He thought he had found his ideal in her, but her interest waned and consequently her radiance was lost. (She had been led to believe he had married Marcia Bencomb.) It revived a little when he met her at Lady Iris Speedwell's, and again when he saw her on the Isle of Slingers, but no more, since it was now centred in Ann Avice Caro. Mrs Pine-Avon married Jocelyn's friend, Alfred Somers.   *WB.* II i–iii, vii, ix, x, xiii; III iv

PITCHER, JOHN. He and Charley Jake, the hedge-carpenter, and Elijah New, the parish-clerk, were the main male guests at the christening-party held at Higher Crowstairs by Mr and Mrs Fennel for their second daughter. For the dances Elijah New played the serpent, while a boy of twelve played the fiddle. John Pitcher was Mrs Fennel's father, and a dairyman in a neighbouring vale.   *WT.* 1

PITNEY, MRS. The wife of a squire, and Angel Clare's godmother. When she died she left jewellery for Mrs Clare to keep in trust for Angel's wife. She predicted a wonderful career for him.   *TD.* xxxiv

PITSTOCK. Festus Derriman meant to enjoy life and, in the view of Mrs Garland, had good prospects which she commended to her daughter Anne. 'He has given up the freehold farm his father held at Pitstock, and lives in independence on what the land brings him. And when

Farmer Derriman dies, he'll have all the old man's, for certain. He'll be
worth ten thousand pounds. . . .'   *TM*. viii

PLYMOUTH. *Emma Lavinia Gifford had spent the first eighteen years of
her life at Plymouth. See Emma Lavinia Hardy*, Some Recollections.
The poems relating to her were written after her death.

   *The 'Three Towns' are Plymouth, Stonehouse, and Devonport, which
were amalgamated in 1914. For the Hoe and St Andrew's Tower, see*
Some Recollections, *11–12.*

   *South of Plymouth, on the Cornish side of the Hamoaze water, is
Cremyll. Edgcumbe is the district around the neighbouring Mount
Edgcumbe.*

   Stephen Smith hoped to marry Elfride Swancourt secretly in Plymouth.
He discovered that the licence could be used only in his London parish.

   The *Western Glory* sailed from Plymouth. On board were Alwyn Hill
and, unknown to him, the Duchess of Hamptonshire.

   PBE. xi–xii, xxix, xxxix; *CM*. 12; *GND*. 9; *SC*. 'Places';
   MV. 'During Wind and Rain' (cf. *Some Recollections*, 5–6);
   LLE. 'The West-of-Wessex Girl' (cf. *Life*, 66), 'Lonely
      Days', 'The Second Night', 'The Marble-Streeted Town'

POLLIN, AGATHA. The girl who won Oswald Winwood's affections from
Frances Lovill, and was deprived of him in the end by her rival's guile.
She was tricked into marrying an old man on the day she expected to
marry Oswald, but pretended that she was happily married to spite her
enemy.   *DBC*

POORGRASS, JOSEPH. A very bashful man with a 'saintly profile', who
could not help blushing when he saw beautiful women like Bathsheba
Everdene, for whom he worked. He had been taken for a cure to Greenhill Fair, and engaged at the Women's Skittle Alley behind the Tailors'
Arms in Casterbridge, but it was of no avail. For the story of his fright in
Yalbury Wood, see p. 515. He read the Scriptures, and found victuals
and drink 'the gospel of the body, without which we perish, so to speak'.
Although he thought 'too much liquor is bad, and leads us to that horned
man in the smoky house', he allowed drink to get the better of him at the
harvest-supper, and at the Buck's Head, when he was taking the coffin
containing Fanny Robin and her child from Casterbridge to Weatherbury.
It afflicted him with 'a multiplying eye'.   *FMC*. vi, viii,
   x, xv, xix, xxi, xxii, xxiii, xxxiii, xli, xlii, l, li, lv, lvii

POPPLE, JIM. One of the spectators at the review of the troops on

Bincombe Down in July 1805 said that the possibility of the French invasion had made him take to drinking neat. For what good, he argued, had obeying his mother and refusing his allowance of rum done to Jim Popple? 'They say that a cannon-ball knocked poor Jim Popple's maw right up into the futtock-shrouds at the Nile, where 'a hung like a night-cap out to dry.' *D.* (1) II iv

PORT-BREDY. *Bridport, fifteen miles west of Dorchester, is actually named after the River Brit which runs south through the town. To the east lies the valley of the River Bride, formerly known as the Bredy (Hutchins), at the upper end of which are the villages of Little Bredy and Long Bredy. High up on the main road, half-way beween Bridport and Dorchester, and north of Long Bredy, stood the Hut Inn of a 'A Trampwoman's Tragedy'.*

Port-Bredy is the setting for the story of 'Fellow-Townsmen'. The town hall, St Mary's church where Mr Downe and Lucy Savile were married, the Black Bull Hotel where Mr Barnet stayed on his return, the Town Savings-Bank, the chapel erected on the site of Mr Barnet's old house (*at the upper end of South Street*) and such industries as flax manu-facture and rope-making are the principal local features which enter the story. A mile from the town between the cliffs was 'a little haven, seemingly a beginning made by Nature herself of a perfect harbour, which appealed to the passer-by as only requiring a little human industry to finish it and make it famous'. (*It is now West Port. The description is a paraphrase from Holinshed, as quoted by Hutchins, introduction, lxxix*).

When Mr Barnet returned to Port-Bredy after an absence of over twenty years, he found that 'a railway had invaded the town'.

On hearing that he had sold his first wife, Lucetta broke her promise to marry Henchard, and was married to Farfrae at Port-Bredy.

Melbury had invested in Port-Breedy (*sic*) Harbour bonds. 'We have a great stake in that harbour, you know, because I send off timber there.'

Farmer Lodge retired from his farm at Holmstoke, after the tragic death of his wife with the withered arm, and lived in solitary lodgings at Port-Bredy until his death two years later.

After Angel Clare had left her, Tess accepted dairy-work 'west of the River Brit' and near Port-Bredy, in order to be far away from both Talbothays and her home at Marlott, and also in the hope of meeting Clare's father at Emminster.

445

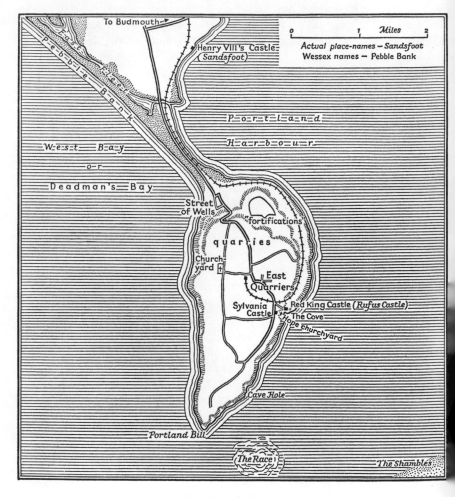

The Isle of Slingers

Andrey Satchel and Jane Vallens had intended going to Port Bredy (*sic*) for the day, after their wedding. Instead, they were locked up in the church tower at Scrimpton.

WT. 5; *MC.* xvi, xxviii–xxx; *W.* xii, xxxvi; *WT.* 4; *TD.* xli; *LLI.* 8*d*; *TL.* 'A Trampwoman's Tragedy'

PORTLAND. *A rocky peninsula, often called 'the Isle', projecting into the English Channel south of Weymouth. Its most southerly point is the Bill. Portland Harbour is to the north, and West Bay or 'Deadman's Bay' to the west. Behind this runs Chesil Beach for about eleven miles to Abbotsbury. East of Portland Bill is a dangerous shoal called the Shambles. Hardy called Portland the 'Gibraltar of Wessex'; more often 'the Isle of Slingers'.*

It is described by Knight to Elfride Swancourt, as they sail past on the coaster *Juliet* on their way to Plymouth.

A battery discharge in front of the King's residence at Budmouth announced the arrival of George III. This was answered by a salute from Portland Castle on the other side of Portland Harbour.

Anne Garland saw Portland in the evening gloom, 'lying like a whale on the sea'. When Bob Loveday sailed in the *Victory*, she set off for Portland Bill or Beal, in the hope of seeing the ship pass on its way to Plymouth. She was rowed across the Fleet – *a narrow strip of water between the mainland and Chesil Beach, not then bridged* – and from the Bill gazed at the area of the sea known as the Race, 'where two seas met to effect the destruction of such vessels as could not be mastered by one'. Later, with the aid of old James Cornick, whose son was on board, she was able to identify the *Victory* and watch it out of sight. It was as a result of the trumpet-major's care that she travelled in James Cornick's boat from Hope Cove (*Church Hope*) to Budmouth.

From Bincombe Down the view was extensive, 'commanding Portland – the Isle of Slingers – in front, and reaching to St Aldhelm's Head eastward, and almost to the Start on the west'.

Portland (*called 'Vindilia' by the Romans, and the Home of the Slingers – from its ancient form of defence*) is the setting for most scenes in *The Well-Beloved*. The three Avices, with whom Jocelyn Pierston fell in love, lived at East Quarriers (*Easton*). Here, for a while, he lived at Sylvania (*Pennsylvania*) Castle. Red King's or Bow-and-Arrow Castle (*Rufus Castle; see plate facing p. 430*) above the Cove (*Church Hope Cove*) is frequently mentioned. In old Hope Churchyard, where the church had long lain a ruin, Pierston kissed Avice (I ii). Street of Wells is *Fortune's*

Well (cf. the description in *TM*. xxxiv); Pebble-bank, *Chesil Bank*, connecting Portland to the mainland; Deadman's Bay, *West Bay*. The Beal (*or Bill*), the Race, and the Shambles are all mentioned.

Henry the Eighth's Castle (*Sandsfoot*) is on the mainland, south of Budmouth. *See plate facing p. 430.*

Hardy imagined that he heard, in the obscurity of night, by the Bill of 'the Isle by the Race', the whirring of wings as the spirits of those slain in the Boer War approached and alighted. They learned from one of their leaders who had gone ahead of them to what extent they were remembered at home. The disenchanted plunged into the Race; the rest continued their homeward way.

In *The Dynasts*, the Isle of Slingers is said to be 'like a floating snail', and reference is made to its 'bald grey brow' (cf. 'The Souls of the Slain'). The time was 1805, when the French invasion was anticipated. John Whiting expected it in Deadman's Bay, where Captain John Wordsworth's ship, the *Abergavenny*, was wrecked in February.

> *DBC*; *PBE*. xxix; *TM*. xi, xii, xxxi, xxxiv; *WT*. 3; *WB*;
> *PPP*. 'The Souls of the Slain'; *D*. (1) I i, II iv (scene), v,
> IV i (scene), V vii

PORTSMOUTH. Rather than be press-ganged, Bob Loveday volunteered for naval service. He was among the five hundred new hands who sailed from Budmouth to Portsmouth. Here he joined Captain Hardy's ship, the *Victory*, which sailed to Plymouth with Admiral Nelson on board. After the battle of Trafalgar, the *Victory* returned to Portsmouth, and then sailed to Sheerness for the public funeral of Lord Nelson at St Paul's Cathedral. Bob was one of the forty-eight seamen who walked two by two in the funeral procession. He seems to have been stationed at Portsmouth for some time afterwards, but little intelligence of him, apart from his falling in and out of love again, was received until John Loveday learned of his promotion to the rank of lieutenant.

> *TM*. xxxiii, xxxv, xxxvii–xxxviii; *TL*. 'Geographical Knowledge'

PO'SHAM. *Portisham, a village six miles north-west of Weymouth. See* BLACK'ON.

Bob Loveday, after escaping from the press-gang, visited Captain Hardy at his house (*see plate facing p. 174*), and requested to serve under him on the *Victory*. This request was later granted, with the result that Bob, formerly in the merchant service, was engaged on Admiral Nelson's flag-ship at the battle of Trafalgar.

It is 'the snug village under Blackdon Hill' of *The Dynasts*.

TM. xxxiii, xxxiv; *D.* (1) v iv

POWER, ABNER. He is introduced as a sinister-looking stranger. He seemed utterly un-English. His face was the colour of light porphyry, and 'pitted, puckered and seamed like a dried water-course'. He had 'the manner of a Dutchman, the face of a smelter, and the clothes of an inhabitant of Guiana'. He proved to be the brother of Paula's father, and soon persuaded her to accompany him on a European tour, in the hope of detaching her affections from George Somerset and raising the social status of the Powers through an alliance with the de Stancys. Despite his efforts, Captain de Stancy made no progress on the tour until Abner Power left suddenly with the injunction that Paula must on no account become engaged to the captain until he had investigated certain matters in England. He had learned that Dare was de Stancy's son and had been scheming to advance his father by marriage so that he could live at his expense. He met Dare at Markton Church after Sir William de Stancy's funeral. They confronted each other over the vestry table, but charge met counter-charge, and revolver, revolver. Abner Power was defeated. (Dare had discovered that Abner had been associated with a revolutionary political party in Europe, and had invented an explosive device for them. In the end he had grown disgusted with the group and become a reactionary. While he was tipping his 'combustible inventions' overboard into a certain lake, an explosion took place, as a result of which he was disfigured for life. He had escaped to Peru, where he was connected with the guano business. But he was still *wanted* by certain governments.) Abner Power wrote to his niece, informing her that business interests demanded his immediate presence in Peru.

L. III ix–xi; v i–v, vii, ix–xi, xiii

POWER, PAULA. *The surname alludes to the wealth of the new English industrial 'aristocracy'.*

The daughter of John Power, the great railway contractor who bought Stancy Castle. He was a staunch Baptist, and his dying wish was that she should bear public testimony to her faith by submitting to immersion in sight of the congregation. Paula tried to be dutiful, but could not face the ordeal. She was attracted to the architect George Somerset, and, realizing her ignorance, soon left the planning of Stancy Castle improvements and extensions to him. She believed that castles were to be held in trust for the nation. She visited Greece and Spain, and had a predilection for Greek forms and fitness, including gymnastics; nothing, however, could uproot her *prédilection d'artiste* for old castles and aristocratic lineages like that of the de Stancys. Whether her father would have allowed her to appear in *Love's Labour's Lost* even for charity is conjectural; the Baptist minister Mr Woodwell regarded this fall more in sorrow than in anger. How far her self-restraint with George Somerset, whom she loved, was due to temperament or to her *prédilection d'artiste* it is impossible to judge. It is George who expresses his feelings; and she who says that they are going to be 'practical young people'. In her letters to him from the Continent, she is indeed a Laodicean, 'neither cold nor hot'. When he is despondent, she can quote Marcus Aurelius: 'Be not perturbed.' Captain de Stancy was very persistent in his attachment when her uncle Abner Power took her away from Stancy Castle to the Continent in the hope that she would lose interest in Somerset and marry him, but he made no progress, even when his rival had been degraded by Dare's cunning, until – a surprising weakness in such a strong character – despite her uncle's warning, she suddenly agreed to become engaged to him on hearing that he had succeeded to the title of Sir William de Stancy. But for chance she would have married him. Her heart was with Somerset, and it is part of the 'ideal comedy' of the novel (cf. *Life*, 108, with reference to *The Hand of Ethelberta*) that she had to pursue him from place to place in Normandy, as he had pursued her from Nice to Carlsruhe, before she found him, and explained away all misunderstandings. They were married in Normandy. She is modern in many respects, especially in her technical and Hellenic outlook, but her closing words show that her predilections are not resolved: 'I wish my castle wasn't burnt, and I wish you were a de Stancy!' She is an unusual heroine in an unusual novel. *L*

PRESCOTT, MRS. The wife of one of the English officers at Salamanca. She found her husband lying dead after the battle, 'and in the dusk we bore them both away'. (*A note in the first edition of* The Dynasts *to the effect that Hardy had been unable to discover what happened to this unhappy lady and her children brought the reply from one of her descendants that she remarried, and lived and died at Venice.*) *D.* (3) I ii, iii

PRIDDLE, NANNY. A girl who was 'sick of the smallpox' and whom Betty Dornell deliberately kissed in order to avoid Stephen Reynard, whom she had formally married when she was a girl. She was in love with Charles Phelipson. The mild attack of smallpox which Betty suffered put both lovers to the proof with surprising results. *GND.* 1

PRIDDLE, RETTY. The Priddles were descendants of the aristocratic Paridelles who owned extensive estates in the King's Hintock area. Retty was a dairymaid at Talbothays, who fell in love with Angel Clare, and tried to drown herself when he married Tess. She was red-haired and slightly built (cf. *Life*, 202). *TD.* xix, xxi–xxiii, xxv, xxix, xxxi, xxxiii, xxxiv, xl

PRIVETT, BETTY. She was the wife of William Privett, who used to work for James Hardcome. Strange circumstances, in complete accordance with local superstitions, were related to his death (cf. pp. 133–4). Betty was certain he had gone out on Midsummer Night, and her suspicions and fears were confirmed when she met Nancy Wheedle and learned that she had been with others in the church porch at the time, to see the forms of those who were to die that year entering the church.

LLI. 8c; *HS.* 'Premonitions'

PROFITT, MR. The schoolmaster at Longpuddle, who told the story of 'Old Andrey's Experience as a Musician'.

LLI. 8, Introduction, and prologue to (e)

PROSPECT HOTEL. It stood near 'the wild north coast' of Lower Wessex (*east of Combe Martin*). *GND.* 10

PROWSE, CAPT. CECIL IRBY. *He was lost with his ship, the* Queen Mary, *at the Battle of Jutland, 31 May 1916. Hardy's interest arose from his friendship with H. G. B. Cowley (vicar of Stinsford, 1911–34) and his wife, who was Captain Prowse's sister.* *HS.* 'The Sea Fight'

PUMMERY (POMMERY). *The local name for the ancient earthworks of Poundbury Camp, which may have been occupied by the Romans. They are on a hill overlooking the Frome river, immediately to the north-west of Dorchester.* *MC.* xvi; *WP.* 'The Burghers', 'The Dance at the Phoenix', 'My Cicely'; *TL.* 'The Curate's Kindness'; *HS.* 'A Sheep Fair', 'The Fight on Durnover Moor'

PURCHESS, JAMES. The young beacon-keeper at Rainbarrows when the French were expected to land in 1805. His fellow keeper was an old man, John Whiting. *Hardy admits a slight disguise of names. Purchess may be the actual name (cf.* Life, *162 and* WHITING). *D.* (1) II v

PURE DROP, THE. An inn at Marlott. *See plate facing p. 366.* *TD.* i, ii, xxxviii

PYDEL VALE. *The valley of the Piddle or Trent river, with the villages of Piddlehinton and Piddletrenthide.* See LONGPUDDLE.

TL. 'A Sunday Morning Tragedy'

QUANTOCK, LORD. *Though his residence is not identified,* A Laodicean *suggests Dunster Castle. See* MARKTON.

Father of the Honourable Laura. *GND.* 10

QUARTERSHOT. *Aldershot.* Stoke-Barehills, we are told, stands at the centre of an imaginary triangle, with Aldbrickham, Wintoncester, and 'the important military station of Quartershot' for its three corners. At Kennetbridge Jude was ill through putting up the stone-work of a music-hall at Quartershot in the rain. *JO.* v v, vii

QUIET WOMAN, THE. *The original inn was called the Travellers' Rest (cf. LLE. 'Weathers'), and stood opposite Puddletown Heath on the Stinsford–Tincleton road. All that remains of it may be seen in one of the buildings of Duck Farm.*

After being an engineer at Budmouth, Damon Wildeve became the landlord of this inn. It was through winning a raffle at the Quiet Woman that Christian Cantle was tempted to gamble with the money he was charged to take to Thomasin and Clym. The inn sign 'represented the figure of a matron carrying her head under her arm'.

Mop Ollamoor disappeared from the inn with 'little Carry', after her mother had collapsed from dancing to his music.

RN. I iii, v; III vi–vii; v vi, viii, ix; *LLI.* 7

RACHEL. A girl of thirteen who helped Mrs Wildeve with the baby Eustacia. She borrowed Thomasin's gloves and lost one at the Maypole dancing. *RN.* v v, viii, VI ii, iv

RAINBARROWS. *Three tumuli (barrows or prehistoric burial mounds) on a high part of the heath backed by a plantation, only half a mile south-east of Hardy's birthplace. These form Rainbarrows; and the most prominent of the three is the Rainbarrow of The Return of the Native. There were no afforested areas or enclosures as there are today. The chalky heath was open, as described in 'The Withered Arm' (WT), with no other obstacles but furze and heather, white water-courses, natural steeps and declivities, and the conical pits which are a peculiar characteristic of the heath. The old tracks, including the Roman road which ran north of Rainbarrows, are now largely overgrown. Our first view of Rainbarrow is from the Tincleton Road, east of 'The Quiet Woman' inn.*

Diggory Venn saw the barrow on the hill like 'a wart on an Atlantean brow. . . . It formed the pole and axis of this heathery world.' Then he discerned the motionless figure of a woman above the barrow. 'Above the plain rose the hill, above the hill rose the barrow, and above the barrow rose the figure.' So we are introduced to Eustacia Vye, who dominates the novel. She disappeared to make way for the local inhabitants who arrived carrying bundles of furze for the Guy Fawkes Night celebrations. Rainbarrow stood more or less midway between Mistover Knap and the Quiet Woman, and there Eustacia met Wildeve and, later, Clym Yeobright. Here, too, after the death of Eustacia, Clym began his preaching career.

Rainbarrow was one of the beacon-hills when England was in danger of invasion during the Napoleonic War. Hardy remembered the 'heap of bricks and clods . . . which had formed the chimney and walls of the hut occupied by the beacon-keeper'. The names of two keepers are given with slight disguise in *The Dynasts* (see PURCHESS and WHITING). They were joined by Private Cantle of the Locals and his wife Keziar from Bloom's-End. The beacon at 'Black'on' in the west was seen burning, and the alarm – a false one – was raised. By the light of the Rainbarrow beacon, the purple rotundities of the heath showed like bronze, and 'the pits like the eye-sockets of a skull'. *The association of the last phrase shows an interesting re-shuffle of imagery in RN.* I *iii.*

In 'The Paphian Ball' (*the title alludes to the worship of Venus at Paphos in Cyprus*) the Mellstock choir saw Rainbarrow to the east against 'Clyffe-Clump's faint far-off crest' nearly three miles away.

> *RN.* I ii, iii, vi, ix; II vi, vii; III iv; V vii, viii; VI iv; *TM.* preface, xii, xxvi; *WP.* 'The Alarm'; *D.* (1) II v, (3) V vi; *TL.* 'By the Barrows'; *HS.* 'The Sheep-Boy', 'The Paphian Ball'

RANDLE, ANDREW. A stammering man. "A can cuss . . . but 'a can't speak a common speech to save his life.' A newcomer to Bathsheba's farm.   *FMC.* x

RAUNHAM, MR. The rector of Carriford, and a bachelor related to Miss Aldclyffe. He called to hear Joseph Chinney's story of Manston's illegal marriage to Cytherea Graye, and employed a detective to solve the mystery of Eunice Manston's disappearance.   *DR.* v 1, vii 1, xiii 5, xvi ff.

RAVENSBURY, JOHN. A school-friend of George Somerset, and a cousin of Charlotte and Captain de Stancy. He had, according to the captain, intended to be a parson, but had died in his youth.   *L.* I iii, iv, v; II iv

RAY, MR. A photographer at Markton, whom Charlotte de Stancy visited when she suspected Dare's vilification of George Somerset. He showed her some examples of photographic misrepresentation (e.g. the Pope the worse for liquor), and said he would not have known how they were produced but for Mr Dare, who did such things for his amusement.

L. v xiii

RAYE, CHARLES BRADFORD. The western circuit took this young barrister to Wintoncester, Melchester, and then further west. At Melchester, he saw a beautiful servant-girl named Anna at the fair, fell in love with her, and, having little legal business, was able to spend most of his time in her company; he won her 'body and soul' . . . (For the sequel, see ANNA.)

LLI. 5

REBEKAH. Rebekah assisted the Halls at The Knap in both dairy and house. Her house was 'a little "spit-and-dab" cabin leaning against the substantial stonework of Mrs Hall's taller erection'. Five years later, 'Rebekah, who had worn a cap when she had plenty of hair, had left it off now she had scarce any, because it was reported that caps were not fashionable.'

WT. 6

REDOUBTABLE, THE. During the battle of Trafalgar, Bob Loveday was injured by a grenade from the French ship *Redoutable*. He brought home several relics, including bullets from the French ship.

TM. xxxix; *D.* (1) v i, ii, iv

REDRUTIN. *Redruth, Cornwall.*

Here Baptista Trewthen attended the funeral of Charles Stow. *CM.* 11

REHAN, MISS ADA. *An actress whose presentation of the Shrew in Shakespeare's play Hardy admired. He was asked by his London friend Mrs Jeune (afterwards Lady St Helier) to write an appeal on behalf of her Holiday Fund for City (London) Children. He wrote the lines late at night at his club. They were read by Miss Rehan at the end of a performance of* As You Like It, *in which she was appearing in the part of Rosalind, at the Lyceum Theatre* (Life, *211, 228*).

WP. 'Lines'

RETTY. It was the custom in many villages to ring a wedding peal for an unmarried girl after her funeral. Retty's admirers (including Ned) rang her peal, while John filled in her grave. *The poem was recast from the first draft of 1868, in which the name was Hetty. HS.* 'Retty's Phases'

REVELLERS' INN. *Revels Inn, once a famous coach-inn on the old Bristol road via Dorchester and Sherborne, which kept to the hills above the modern main road through Cerne Abbas. The inn is now a farm-house; it stands half a mile south of the junction of these two roads near Middlemarsh.*

W. xxviii, xlv

REYNARD, STEPHEN. *Stephen Fox of Farley, near Salisbury, who married Elizabeth Horner in 1736, and became the first Earl of Ilchester.*

His home was near Melchester, and he was the suitor favoured by Mrs Dornell and opposed by Squire Dornell as their daughter's husband. Mrs Dornell settled the issue by taking Betty to London and arranging a secret marriage, when Betty was only twelve or thirteen. The two were not to live together until Betty was eighteen. In the meantime Stephen went abroad. He returned at the time agreed upon to live with Betty, and all the Squire's efforts to deter him were ineffectual. Betty deliberately contracted smallpox to avoid him, and left King's Hintock Court in the company of her lover Charles Phelipson, Squire Dornell's favourite. When he discovered that Betty was afflicted with smallpox, Phelipson's self-interest was so patent that she returned. Stephen showed no fears, and he and Betty lived happily together. He was made an earl, and Betty became Lady Ivell and the first Countess of Wessex.

GND. 1

RIDGEWAY. *The name generally denotes the old road which runs over the downs between Dorchester and Weymouth; see plate facing p. 495. It is sometimes used for the old road which runs east and west along these hills.*

After having tea at the Ship Inn, Dick Dewy and Fancy Day drove 'up the steep hill to the Ridgeway, and vanished in the direction of Mellstock'.

Anne Garland walked from Overcombe with her mother, Miller Loveday, and the trumpet-major, to the top of the Ridgeway on a summer night in 1804, to catch sight of George III and the Queen on their way to Gloucester Lodge, Budmouth. She was rewarded by seeing 'a profile reminding her of the current coin of the realm. . . . one old man said grimly that that sight of dusty old leather coaches was not worth waiting for.'

Phyllis Grove waited for Matthäus Tina, in the expectation of crossing the Channel with him by boat, near the highway to the south of Ridgeway. She saw her fiancé alight from a stage-coach and overheard a conversation between him and a friend which made her think he was still faithful to her. As a consequence, she told Matthäus she had changed her mind.

The Rev. John Maumbry found lodgings for his wife Laura at Creston when cholera broke out at Durnover. He met her twice a week 'near where the high road from town to town crosses the old Ridge-way [*sic*] at right angles'. In order that she might run no risk of infection, he insisted that they met in the open air, with a wall between them. Almost at the same spot, she saw Lt Vannicock approaching when he had

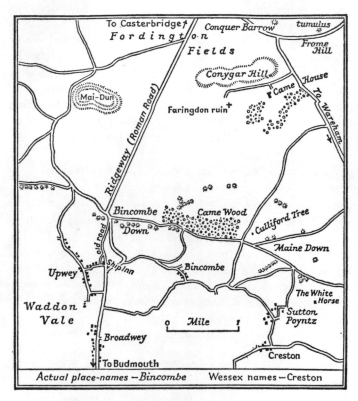

Around Ridgeway

come from Bristol to elope with her. Thinking that the rendezvous at such a point might be unlucky, she told him to go back to the milestone, where she would join him. They met at 'the milestone that stands on the north slope of the ridge, where the old and new roads diverge'.

ILH. I 8; *UGT.* III ii; *TM.* xi, xii; *WT.* 3; *CM.* 1; *WP.* 'The Alarm'; *D.* (1) I i, II v, IV i; *MV.* 'Great Things', 'Old Excursions'

RIDGE-WAY. *The old road running east and west along the hills south of Wantage, Berkshire. It is the Icknield Way of Saxon times; Icknield Street of the Roman era runs a few miles further north. Hardy states that the Ridge Way was 'the Icknield Street and original road through the district'. It crosses the route from Fawley to Wantage* (Marygreen to Alfredston) *at a point where the Red Barn used to stand. To the west, between 'Red Barn' and Letcombe Bassett, on the north side of the Ridge Way, is Letcombe Castle, 'the circular British earth-bank' to which Jude walked with Arabella.*   *JO.* I iii, vii, viii; V viii; VI viii

RIMSMOOR POND. *Not far south-west of 'Alderworth'. As the pond was dry, Johnny Nunsuch went to Oker's Pool* (in the direction of Oaker's Wood) *to find water for Mrs Yeobright.*   *RN.* IV vi

RING OF BELLS, THE. *There are still inns of this name in Dorset. The town may be Bridport, where there is an inn called the Five Bells.*

An inn which a whaler called at when he returned to settle in his native town, but which he left soon after his arrival, on hearing that his wife had been visited each week by a man. His wife heard of his arrival when she came out of church, fainted at the news, and waited all day for him. He never came, and she pined away. The visitor attended her funeral. Later it was discovered he was her father, who had deceived her mother and induced her to marry one in his service. This the wife knew, but had never divulged to her seaman husband.

WW. 'The Whaler's Wife'

RINGS-HILL SPEER. *Suggested by the obelisk memorial on Weatherbury Castle, a wooded hill ringed with earthworks, north of the road from Bere Regis to Tolpuddle. This setting for the novel is imagined further east, in the vicinity of the high tower in Charborough Park, four miles west of Wimbourne Minster.* See WELLAND.

The tower on the wooded hill above Welland Bottom – used by Swithin St Cleeve as an observatory – overlooked the field between it and the old Melchester road. Beyond lay Welland Park.   *TT*

RINGSWORTH. *The cliffs of Ringstead Bay, a few miles east of Wey-mouth Bay.*

It was when he had rowed across the north of Budmouth Bay and was opposite the cliffs of Ringsworth Shore that Edward Springrove expressed his love for Cytherea Graye.

Lizzy Newberry set fire to a bough of furze above the cliffs to warn the lugger carrying contraband spirits from Cherbourg that no landings were possible, as the Customs officers were on the alert that night.

DR. iii 2; *WT.* 7

RISING SUN, THE. An inn at Carriford where the inquest on the death of Mrs Manston was held, with Mr Floy as coroner.

It was here that Manston overheard a conversation on events which took place the night she was thought to have been burnt to death. He hurried off immediately. *DR.* xi 2, xiv 1, xxi 1

ROBIN, FANNY. A servant at Farmer Everdene's and, after his death, with Bathsheba Everdene. She left, trying to find Sergeant Troy, her lover, at Casterbridge barracks on the evening Gabriel Oak entered Weatherbury. Troy's regiment had left Casterbridge for Melchester. Fanny followed, and Troy would have married her at an unnamed town and military station 'many miles north of Weatherbury' had she arrived at the church in time. Unfortunately she mistook All Souls' church for All Saints'. She then 'picked up a living' as a seamstress in Melchester. When she was expecting her child she walked all the way to Casterbridge Union. In the last stages of her journey, she was completely exhausted. She made her way to Grey's Bridge with the aid of improvised crutches. A dog supported her from the bridge to the Union. Here she died in childbirth. She was due to be buried at Weatherbury, but Joseph Poorgrass, who was conveying her coffin, was persuaded to stay too long at the Buck's Head Inn. The coffin was left at Bathsheba's, only for Bathsheba (who had married Troy) to discover her husband's double perfidy. Troy's contrition was mocked at by fate, and for the first time in his life he despised himself. *FMC.* vii-xi, xv, xvi, xxxix-xlvi

ROGER. A sailor who returned to Havenpool in the *Primrose* about 1540, and found that his sister Edith's husband was dead, and that she had remarried and was living at Oozewood. When he traced her, and discovered that she had a baby and that her husband visited secretly, his suspicions were strong. He stayed at the Black Lamb Inn, and decided to keep watch for the husband's next visit and departure. By night he

followed him to his home at Clyfton Horseleigh near Ivell, and discovered that Edith's visitor was Sir John Horseleigh, and that he had a
wife and three children. He returned to Oozewood after a few days,
drinking heavily at Casterbridge on the way. When Sir John arrived, he
accused him; and a scuffle ensued in which Sir John was mortally
wounded. Before his death, Sir John vindicated himself. He had discovered that the husband of his first wife was alive abroad; Edith was his
legal wife, and married with the King's approval. Roger was never seen
in England again. *CM.* 9

ROLLIVER'S. An off-licence alehouse kept by Mrs Rolliver at Marlott;
'hence, as nobody could legally drink on the premises, the amount of
overt accommodation for consumers was strictly limited to a little board
about six inches wide and two yards long, fixed to the garden palings by
pieces of wire, so as to form a ledge'. As Rolliver's supplied a better 'brew'
than the Pure Drop Inn, local inhabitants resorted there in the evenings.
They met in a bedroom, the window curtained off by a great shawl.
When anyone unexpected was heard ascending the staircase, Mrs
Rolliver was always ready to explain that she was holding a party at her
own expense. *TD.* i, iii, iv, xiv, xxxviii

ROMAN ROAD, THE. *The Roman road, or Ackling Dyke, from Salisbury
to Dorchester crossed the heath not far south of Hardy's birthplace. It ran
past Rushy-Pond. It should be noted that the topography of Egdon Heath
in* The Return of the Native *does not conform to the geography of the
district in all respects. Hardy placed the Roman road further south than
it actually is. Diggory Venn was travelling along the Tincleton road from
Wareham* (Anglebury) *in the direction of 'The Quiet Woman' inn; according
to Hardy, many portions of its course overlaid 'an old vicinal way, which
branched from the great Western road of the Romans, the Via Iceniana, or
Ikenild Street, hard by'. In the novel and 'The Roman Road', it is compared to 'a parting-line' on a head of hair. Further east, in the direction of
Badbury Rings, it was known as the Ikling Way.* See ICENING WAY.

RN. I i–iv; *PPP.* 'The Well-Beloved'; *TL.* 'The Roman
Road'

ROME. *Hardy's impressions of Rome from his visit in April 1887 (cf.
Life, 188–9) are to be found in a series of poems and* The Well-Beloved.
*The dates below the titles of the poems indicate the time of the visit; some, if
not all, of the poems were written later.*

WB. III i; *PPP.* 'Rome: On the Palatine', 'Building a New

Street in the Ancient Quarter', 'The Vatican: Sala delle Muse', 'At the Pyramid of Cestius near the Graves of Shelley and Keats';   *LLE.* 'At a House in Hampstead'

RONDLEY, MRS. The name Eunice Manston assumed in Hoxton, and under which Anne Seaway wrote to Manston.   *DR.* xiv 3

ROOKINGTON PARK. *Suggested by Hurn (formerly Heron) Court and its wooded park, north-east of Bournemouth.*

'About three miles out of Sandbourne, in the opposite direction to' Wyndway House. Its park abounded with timber 'older and finer than that of any other spot in the neighbourhood'.

Ethelberta and her mother-in-law, Lady Petherwin, stayed there after being at Wyndway House. Christopher Julian walked there by moonlight, and surveyed 'the building that contained his old love'. He caught sight of another man, by the trunk of a tree, gazing as he had gazed, but did not recognize him as Ladywell until he met him in London. *HE.* v, viii

ROOK'S GATE. The cottage where Margery Tucker's grandmother and Edy, the woman who attended her, lived. It was four miles east of Silverthorn.   *CM.* 12

ROOTLE. A Budmouth dentist, 'who lived by such practices on the heads of the elderly' as 'the abstraction of some worn-out nether millstones within the cheek' of Mrs Garland (according to Miller Loveday). *TM.* xi

ROSE-ANN.   *TL.* 'Rose-Ann'

ROSY. She and Willy did not let their mother know how they had misbehaved. Now their mother is dead, they do what they will: 'Mother won't know.'   *TL.* 'Unrealized'

ROUEN. *One of Hardy's avowed purposes in visiting Rouen on his honeymoon in 1874 was to make notes for scenes in* The Hand of Ethelberta *(Life, 103). Its most impressive results may be seen in chap. xxxiv.*

Ethelberta's aunt Charlotte had married M. Moulin, who kept the Hôtel Beau Séjour in Rouen. Ethelberta spent a holiday with her, and was joined by her brothers Sol and Dan. She had crossed the Channel from Knollsea to Cherbourg on the steamer *Speedwell*, and noticed Lord Mountclere's yacht, the *Fawn*, crossing also. He travelled on the same train as Ethelberta to Rouen, and climbed to the parapets of the cathedral with her. Other suitors to follow were Neigh and Ladywell. *HE.* xxix–xxxv

ROU'TOR TOWN. *Bodmin, Cornwall, named after Row or Rough Tor, one of the highest points on Bodmin Moor. See p. 353.*

MV. 'I rose and went to Rou'tor Town'

ROY-TOWN. *Troy Town, a small hamlet on the Dorchester road, about a mile west of Puddletown. Its centre of interest was the old coach-inn, the Buck's Head (see p. 252).*

ROYAL ACADEMY, THE. Ethelberta took her brothers Sol and Dan to Burlington House, to see the portrait of her which had been painted by her admirer Ladywell.   *HE.* xxv; *LLE.* 'At the Royal Academy'

ROYAL INSTITUTE OF BRITISH ARCHITECTS, THE. *In 1863 Hardy received the R.I.B.A. prize medal for his essay (cf. p. 4) from Sir Gilbert Scott. In 1920 he was made an Honorary Fellow of the Institute.*

Miss Aldclyffe visited the Institute (*in Conduit Street, London*) to see if her son Aeneas Manston was a member; here she purloined an embossed envelope to complete her immediate plans.

As a result of Dare's machinations, the plans submitted by George Somerset and Mr Havill to the R.I.B.A. for the extensions to Stancy Castle were pronounced 'singularly equal'.   *DR.* vii 3; *L.* I xiv, II vi

RUSHY-POND. *On Puddletown Heath, a third of a mile south-east of Hardy's birthplace, and below Rainbarrow. Old roads met there, one following the Roman road a short distance, two others skirting the green valley in which lay Hardy's 'Blooms-End'. See Life, 202, and* PHENA.

On her way across Egdon Heath to Casterbridge, Gertrude Lodge passed by Rushy-Pond, which was then divided by a railing. In the distance she saw 'a white flat façade, denoting the entrance to the county jail', which was her destination.

(?) *WP.* 'Neutral Tones' (*written in London in 1867*); *WT.* 4; (?) *CM.* 2 (vi); *MV.* 'I said and sang her excellence' (*written by Rushy-Pond*); *HS.* 'At Rushy-Pond', 'The Paphian Ball'

RUSSIA. *Of the Russian scenes in* The Dynasts, *the most vivid relate to the French invasion and retreat. Hardy's gifts for transmitting keen visual and auditory effects in terse prose were never shown more effectively than in some of these scenes.*

D. (2) I vii, viii, V vii; (3) I, mosts cenes, especially ix and xi.

RYME, JOSEPH. He played the treble violin in Chalk-Newton church for forty-two years, and was advised by Robert Penny not to have clarinets in the choir.   *UGT.* I iv

ST ALDHELM'S (ST ALBAN'S) HEAD. *On this prominent headland, over 350 feet high, four miles south of Corfe Castle, a chapel was built in honour of St Aldhelm, first bishop of Sherborne (d. 709). Here a lamp was lit as a warning beacon to sailors. The headland is a feature in some of Hardy's panoramic views.*

> *TM.* xii, xxx; *WT.* 3; *D.* (1) IV i (scene); *HS.* 'Days to Recollect' (*recalling a visit Hardy made with his first wife, probably in 1875, when they were living in Swanage*)

ST CLEATHER. *St Clether, a village between Launceston and Camelford, about seven miles from St Juliot, Cornwall. Jealousy as a subject for fiction may have been prompted by Hardy's own experience* (*cf. p. 354, 'The Young Churchwarden'*). *It plays an important part in* A Pair of Blue Eyes (*cf. xxxviii ep. and the conclusion of the St Cleather poem*). *It seems less likely that this poem was founded on one of Mr Holder's stories* (Life, *155–6*), *and even less likely that it is autobiographical. The facts put forward in support of this view* (*that Emma Lavinia Gifford had a suitor at St Clether before his marriage in 1864*) *are unconvincing. Emma Hardy's* Some Recollections *does not indicate that she was in north Cornwall more than ten years before her marriage; in fact, she suggests only 'a few years'* (*39*). *SC.* 'The Face at the Casement'

ST CLEEVE, DR JOCELYN. Swithin's great-uncle was a misogynist bachelor who had amassed 'a fairly good professional fortune by a long and extensive medical practice' in a 'smoky, dreary, manufacturing town' in the north of England. On hearing of Swithin's astronomical pursuits, he had left him an annuity of £600, payment of which was to begin in his twenty-first year, and continue for life, on condition that he did not marry before he was twenty-five. *TT.* xviii, xxxiv–xxxv, xli

ST CLEEVE, REV. MR. Swithin's father. He was educated at All Angels (*All Souls, Oxford*), and became curate at Welland, where he (misguidedly, it was thought) married Farmer Martin's daughter, a delicate 'home-spun woman the toppermost folk wouldn't speak to', who did not live very long. St Cleeve was so annoyed by criticism of his marriage that he resigned his curacy. 'He took to farming straight away; and then 'a dropped down dead in a nor-west thunderstorm.' *TT.* i, ix, xxv–xxvii

ST CLEEVE, SWITHIN. *In the earlier pages the MS. gives 'Swithin Cleve', undoubtedly from Swithin Cleves, a seventeenth-century rector of Rampisham* (*north-west of Maiden Newton*), *which Hardy knew probably from 1859, when John Hicks was engaged in the restoration of its church* (*Purdy, 43, 293*).

He was an orphan who lived with his grandmother at Welland Bottom. He had been educated at Warborne Grammar School, and was an ardent

The Martyrs' Memorial (right), and the Sheldonian Theatre, Oxford (see Christminster)

Grove's Place, Shaftesbury (Shaston)

The Town Cellars, Poole (Havenpool)

astronomer. He pursued his observations with poor equipment at the top of Rings-Hill Speer. Lady Constantine became interested in his work, fell in love with him, and provided the equipment he needed. His ambition was to be no less than Astronomer Royal, 'the Copernicus of the stellar system'. He was young and handsome, with 'corn-coloured' hair. When he learned that his first important discovery had been forestalled by an American astronomer, he felt that life was not worth living. So preoccupied was he with stellar space, he did not realize for long how much he was in love with Lady Constantine. 'The alchemy which . . . transmuted an abstracted astronomer into an eager lover – and, must it be said? spoilt a promising young physicist to produce a commonplace inamorato – may be almost described as working its change in one short night.' They were secretly married in Bath; Swithin did not give Lady Constantine the information he had just learned, that by marrying before the age of twenty-five he was forfeiting an income of £600 a year. When it was discovered that Sir Blount Constantine had not died, as the lawyers assumed, before their marriage, they decided to marry publicly. When Lady Constantine discovered, however, what Swithin had forfeited for her sake, and how she had prejudiced his future, she was filled with compunction, and insisted that he should go abroad, as he had planned, to pursue his astronomical research, and not communicate with her, or return, before he was twenty-five. Soon after his departure she discovered that she was pregnant; when she found it impossible to communicate with him, she was desperate. Louis Glanville took advantage of the situation to inform the Bishop of Melchester that she was in love with him. Hardly knowing what to do for the best, she accepted the Bishop's renewed offer of marriage. Swithin was shocked at the news, but continued his studies at the Cape until they were completed. In the meantime he had learned that the Bishop had died, and that Lady Constantine was living again at Welland with her little boy. He had now fulfilled the terms of his agreement with his 'wife' Viviette, and returned to England to marry her. They met at the top of the tower, and Viviette knew that he was shocked by the change in her appearance which time had brought. When Swithin told her that he still loved her, and had come to marry her, her joy was too great and she died in his arms. 'He looked up for help. Nobody appeared in sight but Tabitha Lark, who was skirting the field with a bounding tread – the single bright spot of colour and animation within the wide horizon.' *TT*

The shock at the changes wrought by time in a loved and beautiful woman recalls Hardy's on seeing the idol of his boyhood and 'lady of his dreams', Julia Augusta Martin, in 1862; cf. 'Amabel' (WP) and Life, *41 and 102.*

SAINT GEORGE. *This traditional mummers' play, as described in* The Return of the Native, *had been seen by Hardy in his early years; cf.* Life, *411.* RN. II iv, v

ST JULIOT. *The parish, near Boscastle and the north coast of Cornwall, where Emma Lavinia Gifford lived with her sister and brother-in-law, the Reverend Caddell Holder, when Hardy visited the place in order to make plans for the restoration of the church (see* Life, v, *and Emma Hardy,* Some Recollections). *Hardy's first visit took place in March 1870. He and Emma were married in September 1874. In the meantime he had written* A Pair of Blue Eyes, *the setting of which, with a certain amount of topographical disguise – which he later wished he had found time to correct – was provided by St Juliot and neighbouring places along the coast and inland. For the poems connected with St Juliot, see pp. 351–3, 354.*

ST LAUNCE'S. *Launceston, Cornwall. Associated with Hardy's visits to St Juliot.*

The nearest railway-station to Endelstow, before the line was extended to Camelton, was at St Launce's. Stephen Smith's father left Endelstow to set up a building business there. PBE. ii, xi–xii, xxi, xxxv, xxxvi, xxxix; SC. 'St Launce's Revisited' (*after Mrs Hardy's death*); MV. 'Love the Monopolist' (*begun 1871*)

ST PAUL SC. 'In the British Museum' (*see p. 250*); HS. 'In St Paul's a While Ago' (MS. '*In St Paul's: 1869*').

ST PAUL'S CATHEDRAL. TM. xxxvii (*the funeral of Lord Nelson*); LLI. 2; MV. 'In a Whispering Gallery'; HS. 'In St Paul's a While Ago' (*see previous note*).

SAINWAY, MR. The curate of the Casterbridge chapel-of-ease which the —th Hussars attended. Captain Maumbry was so impressed by him that, much to his wife's chagrin, he decided to enter the Church. Some time before this decision was reached, when the friendship between the two men had lasted nearly a year, Mr Sainway was presented to a living in a densely populated town in the Midlands. Soon after his induction, he died of inflammation of the lungs. CM. 1

SALISBURY. *This cathedral city generally appears under the name of Melchester (cf. pp. 407–10). Hardy collaborated with the authoress Mrs*

*Henniker (cf. pp. 364–5), and met her occasionally in Salisbury; she is
'the one rare fair woman' of 'Wessex Heights'.*   *TL.* 'In a
    Cathedral City'; *SC.* 'Wessex Heights' (v, vii); *HS.* 'A
    Cathedral Façade at Midnight' (cf. *Life*, 295–6, 420)

SALLOWS, THE. The lovers Nicholas Long and Christine Bellston often
met and sat by the waterfall or weir, with its sarcastic hiss, in this
plantation below Froom-Everard House. *See plate fac ng p. 206.*   *CM.* 2

SAM. A turf-cutter on Egdon Heath.

          RN. I, iii, v; II i, iv; III i, ii, iii, vii; VI iv

SAMWAY, SAM. One of Boldwood's 'workfolk' who met Bathsheba's
farm labourers at Boldwood's Christmas party.   *FMC.* liii

SAN REMO. When de Stancy took the £100 to Monte Carlo for George
Somerset, as he thought, he met Dare, and guessed his intentions. He
would not hand over the money to Dare, and made inquiries for Somerset, to find that he had gone to San Remo. When he caught up with
Paula Power at Carlsruhe, Somerset told her that he had stayed two days
in Genoa, 'and some days at San Remo, and Mentone'. She was not
interested.   *L.* IV v; V i, iii, v

SANDBOURNE. *Bournemouth.* Here Christopher Julian lived, and taught
music. It was from Sandbourne that Sol Chickerel and Lord Mountclere's
brother attempted to reach Knollsea by sea to prevent Ethelberta's
marriage to Lord Mountclere. Afterwards she provided her father with
a smart villa at Sandbourne for his retirement.

Tess lived with Alec d'Urberville in a lodging-house called The Herons,
where she murdered him when Angel Clare returned. The hollow
stylishness of the life to which Tess tragically submitted is reflected in the
setting: 'An outlying eastern tract of the enormous Egdon Waste was
close at hand, yet on the very verge of that tawny piece of antiquity such
a glittering novelty as this pleasure city had chosen to spring up.'

Jocelyn Pierston's father died at Sandbourne. Here, after living in
Jersey, Marcia Bencomb, now Mrs Leverre, settled with her son Henri
Leverre, who taught French in one of the schools. When his mother
visited the Isle of Slingers to find out what had happened to Jocelyn,
Henri met Avice Pierston. She was sent to Sandbourne High School
(possibly the 'high-class school' where Rosa Halborough had been a
pupil), and prevailed upon her mother to let her take French lessons with
him. She married him, and settled in Sandbourne.

Before meeting Jude, Sue Bridehead had been friendly with a Christminster undergraduate, who lent her many books. He became a leader-writer for 'one of the great London dailies'. He was in love with Sue, but she was merely an intellectual companion – they shared a sitting-room in London for fifteen months and he was broken-hearted. After a period abroad, he went home to die, and Sue attended his funeral at Sandbourne.

HE. ii, iii, iv, xi, xviii, xliii, xliv, Sequel; *LLI*. 4; *TD*. xxxii, liv–lvii; *WB*. ii i; iii ii, v, vi, vii, viii; *JO*. iii iv, v vii

SARGENT, NETTY. She lived with her uncle at Longpuddle, and attracted the attention of Jasper Cliff. Jasper was more interested in her uncle's property than in Netty, however. This was held 'upon lives' (cf. p. 137), and when her uncle died it would revert to the squire unless a new agreement were drawn up. Old Mr Sargent did nothing about this until Netty told him that if there were no property there would be no husband for her. The agreement was drawn up, but before he could sign it her uncle died. Even so, Netty contrived to make the squire's steward think that he witnessed Mr Sargent sign the agreement. The property was retained, and Netty married Jasper Cliff, but he did not prove to be a satisfactory husband. *LLI*. 8*i*

SATCHEL, ANDREW ('ANDREY'). He was so tipsy when he appeared for his overdue marriage to Jane Vallens that Parson Toogood refused to perform the service. To make sure of him, Jane arranged that they should be locked in the tower of Scrimpton church until he was sober. The parson went hunting and forgot about them. They had to wait until the next morning. *LLI*. 8*d*

SATCHEL, OLD ANDREW. Andrey's father. In his youth, he joined the choir on its Christmas visit to the manor-house, posing as a fiddler, in order to enjoy a good supper afterwards in the servants' hall. He was detected and ejected by the squire's mother, but enjoyed the supper after all, thanks to the squire's wife. *LLI*. 8*e*

SAUNDERS, EZEKIEL. He and Thomas Wood had been clockmakers at Casterbridge. *UGT*. ii vi; v i

SAVILE, LUCY. The daughter of Lt Savile, who had died not long before the story opens. She lived on the way to Port-Bredy harbour. Mr Barnet had been in love with her, but they parted owing to a misunderstanding, and Mr Barnet married a superior lady who proved to be incompatible. He helped Lucy to gain a post as governess to Mr Downe's children soon after Mrs Downe was drowned. When Lucy announced her plan to go to India, Mr Downe was distressed at the prospect of losing her and proposed marriage. (For the sequel, see BARNET, GEORGE). *WT.* 5

SCHEVENINGEN. *For Hardy's visit and impressions, cf.* Life, *110, 120–1.*

'. . . human souls may find themselves in closer and closer harmony with external things wearing a sombreness distasteful to our race when it was young. The time seems near, if it has not actually arrived, when the chastened sublimity of a moor, a sea, or a mountain will be all of nature that is absolutely in keeping with the moods of the more thinking of mankind . . . and Heidelberg and Baden be passed unheeded as· he [the commonest tourist] hastens from the Alps to the sand-dunes of Scheveningen.'

Captain de Stancy thought that the place reflected 'the average mood of human life. I mean, if we strike the balance between our best moods and our worst we shall find our average condition to stand at about the same pitch in emotional colour as these sandy dunes and this grey scene do in landscape.' *RN.* i i; *L.* v ix

SCOTT-SIDDONS, MRS MARY FRANCES. *The great-granddaughter of Mrs Siddons. She made her London début as Rosalind in Shakespeare's* As You Like It *in April 1867.* *TL.* 'To an Impersonator of Rosalind'.

SCRIMPTON. *Frampton, near Maiden Newton. The Wessex name was suggested partly by the neighbouring village of Grimstone.*

Andrey Satchel and Jane Vallens were locked in the church tower, at her request, until he was sufficiently sober to be married.

The hunting parson of the story was suggested by the Reverend William Butler, a friend of the Prince Regent. He became vicar of Frampton in 1800 and died in 1843 (Hutchins, ii 305). *LLI.* 8d

SEAMORE, GRANNY. An old woman of Overcombe 'with wrinkled cheeks, who surveyed the earth and its inhabitants through the medium of brass-rimmed spectacles'. Indoors, she wore 'short' ones for reading the Collect and Gospel, darning, and catching fleas. Her 'long' ones were 'a beautiful pair for out o' doors'. *TM.* viii, xxvi

SEAWAY, ANNE. The woman who impersonated Mrs Manston, after Manston had killed his wife.

DR. xiv 2–4, xvii 3, xviii 1–3, xix 1–6, xxi 1

SEDGEMOOR. See MONMOUTH, DUKE OF.

TL. 'A Trampwoman's Tragedy'; *MV.* 'Molly Gone'

SEEDLING, AMBY. A labourer who was in love with Izz Huett at Talbothays, and found work at Flintcomb-Ash in order to be near her.

TD. xlv, xlix

SELBY, SOLOMON. He told the story of how when he was a boy he had gone one evening with his uncle Job to watch the sheep at lambing-time above the Cove (*Lulworth*), and had seen Napoleon. *WT*. 2

SHADWATER WEIR. *In the Frome meadows – the Talbothays country of Tess of the d'Urbervilles – more than a mile from its location in* The Return of the Native. *Although Hardy describes it as a ten-hatch weir, it has only nine hatches. In winter the river rushes through, and the pool is 'a boiling cauldron' (Hermann Lea). See plate facing p. 143.*

In his youth Hardy had witnessed the recovery of a body from the pool, and had first assumed it was that of a girl. It was from this incident that The Return of the Native *had developed (Gertrude Bugler, Personal Recollections of Thomas Hardy,* Toucan Press, 1962).

Here Eustacia Vye and Damon Wildeve were drowned. It is almost certainly the Great Pool in which Retty Priddle tried to drown herself after the marriage of Tess and Angel Clare. *RN*. v ix; *TD*. xxxiv

SHAKEFOREST TOWERS. *Clatford Hall, on the southern side of the London – Bristol road, a few miles west of Marlborough. The name was suggested by Savernake Forest. On the other side of the road is a track which leads to 'Lambing Corner' among the downs; the Devil's Den ('the Devil's Door' or 'Druidical trilithon') will be found on the left in what is now an arable field.* *CM*. 7

SHAKESPEARE. On the tercentenary of his death in 1916.
MV. 'To Shakespeare'

SHASTON. *The ancient hill-town of Shaftesbury. Originally it was known as Caer Pallador; more recently as Shaston, by which it is still known locally. It overlooks the Vale of Blackmoor.*

The Durbeyfields lived at Marlott, about six miles to the west-southwest in the Vale. Tess walked to Shaston, and then travelled by van to Chaseborough, when she made her visit to the 'd'Urbervilles' to seek employment.

When Sue escaped from Melchester Training College, she thought of staying with a sister of one of her student-friends who had a school near Shaston and had asked her to visit her. She married Mr Phillotson, who had moved to his native place Shaston from Lumsdon. He and Sue lived at Old-Grove Place (*see plate facing p. 463*), but her marriage was a failure and eventually Phillotson freed her.

'Grove's Place', the schools, and Trinity Church nearby, with its avenue of lime trees, are easily recognized. Other actual places mentioned

are Bimport Street and Abbey Walk. The 'old Church' where Jude thought of passing the time until he could return to Melchester is St Peter's, the only one of the twelve old churches left. Little remains of the Abbey, and 'Castle Green' is the only reminder that Shaston once had a castle.

TD. i–iii, v, vi, vii, liv; *JO.* III v, vi, x; IV i, iii, iv, vi; VI ix;

TL. 'The Vampirine Fair' (Shastonbury).

SHERBORNE. *If the family tradition relates to Hardy's maternal grandmother Elizabeth (Life, 6–7), it seems to be romanticized and unconfirmed by the date. Betty was a yeoman's daughter, but scarcely an 'heiress'. Perhaps one of the genealogical tables drawn up by Hardy holds the clue; it shows that Joseph Pitcher of Melbury Osmond, an ancestor on his maternal side, eloped with Miss Hellier of Kay, Yeovil, near Sherborne, in the eighteenth century.* HS. 'In Sherborne Abbey'

For other references to Sherborne, see SHERTON ABBAS and CASTLE.

SHERTON ABBAS. *Sherborne, a few miles north of 'the Hintocks'.*

It was the town most readily accessible to the people of Little Hintock. The hairdresser Percomb and the legal adviser Fred Beaucock, who accompanied Melbury to London to investigate the possibility of divorce proceedings for Grace, lived there. Giles Winterborne stood in the market-place with his apple-tree, trying, not very successfully, to attract customers, before accompanying Grace Melbury, who finished her schooling at Sherton, on her way home; he bought the docile white mare Darling for her at Sherton when he still had hopes of marrying her; much later, when her hopes of successful divorce proceedings against Fitzpiers had been raised, she walked with Winterborne in the Abbey, and had lunch with him at a cheap commercial inn, where Winterborne reflected sadly on his mistake in taking her to a place so different from the Earl of Wessex Hotel (*the Digby Hotel*), where he had seen her on her honeymoon with Fitzpiers. Mrs Charmond's rejected suitor, the 'Italianized American' from South Carolina, stayed a few days at Sherton in the hope of seeing Mrs Charmond at Hintock House; so too did Fitzpiers on returning from the Continent after the death of Mrs Charmond; and he and Grace were traced to the Earl of Wessex when they left Little Hintock to resume their married life.

The Abbey is designated 'the Abbey north of Blackmore Vale' in 'The Lost Pyx'. *W.* i, iv, v, xi, xxi,

xxiii, xxv, xxxvii, xxxviii, xlvi, xlviii; *PPP.* 'The Lost Pyx'

SHERTON CASTLE. *The 'original stronghold' of the Digby family at Sherborne. See plate facing p. 334.*

It was besieged during the Civil War. The last representative but one of the Horseleigh family was killed at the siege; the other was outlawed. Grace Melbury thought the castle ruins had been degraded by agricultural usage.   *W.* vi, xxiii; *GND.* 7; *CM.* 9

SHERTON TURNPIKE. A turnpike gate, kept by Dan Randall, 'the sleepiest man between here and London', on the main road from Caster-bridge to Sherton, just north of the junction with the road from Weather-bury. When Oak and Coggan reached the gate, they discovered that they had been following Bathsheba. She was on her way to Bath to meet Troy.
                                                    FMC. xxxii

SHINER, FARMER. *Hardy changed the name from 'Shinar' to 'Shiner'.*

He lived in 'a queer lump of a house' in Lower Mellstock, and did not welcome the carol-singers, though he was a churchwarden. He was Dick Dewy's rival for the hand of Fancy Day, and recommended that she should play the vicar's organ for the church services.

As 'Shinar', he is twice mentioned in *The Mayor of Casterbridge*. His aunt was old dame Ledlow, called 'Toadskin'. *See plate facing p. 46.*

                UGT. I v–viii, II iv–viii, III i–iv, IV ii, v ii; *MC.* xiii, xvii

SHIP, THE. *An inn which stands on the old section of the Ridgeway road just above its junction with the new, east of Upwey.*

Dick Dewy and Fancy Day stopped here for tea when they were driving back from Budmouth. It is the 'Old Ship', where the beacon-keepers, Corporal Tullidge and Simon Burden, often repaired to sit snugly 'in the settle' during 1804–5, when the French invasion was expected.   *UGT.* III ii; *TM.* xxvi

SHOCKERWICK HOUSE. *Four miles north-east of Bath, Somerset.*

It is generally assumed that Pitt was at Bath when he heard the news of the Allied defeat at Austerlitz. 'Tradition says that he was looking at a picture gallery when he heard the furious gallop of a horse. . . .' Hardy combines two scenes, the historic conclusion being transferred from Pitt's home, Bowling Green House, Putney, which he reached on 12 January 1806, ten days before his death (Lord Rosebery, *Pitt*, Macmillan, 1893, p. 256).   *D.* (1) VI vi

SHOTTSFORD (FORUM). *Blandford, a town eight miles north-east of Dorchester.*

After seeking employment in vain at Casterbridge hiring-fair, Gabriel

Oak set out for Shottsford, where another hiring-fair was due the next day. At Weatherbury he turned aside to help put out a rick-yard fire, and this led to his employment at Bathsheba's farm.

When Festus Derriman was invited in to join the company at Miller Loveday's party, he suggested that Anne should join him in yeomanry sprees at Casterbridge or Shottsford-Forum, where she would meet company more suited to her. 'The yeomanry are respected men, men of good substantial families, many farming their own land. . . .'

The prisoner who had escaped from Casterbridge Gaol and was the first of the intruders at the christening-party at Higher Crowstairs was Timothy Summers of Shottsford, a watchmaker who was condemned to be hanged for stealing a sheep to save his starving family in the 1820s. The third visitor, his brother, was also from Shottsford.

Henchard, on his last visit to Casterbridge, stopped at Shottsford for a night's rest; he bought clothing to improve his appearance, and a caged goldfinch to present to Elizabeth-Jane as a wedding-present next day.

When relations with her husband Fitzpiers were strained, Grace Melbury went to Shottsford to stay with an acquaintance. Melbury heard that his daughter was ill and went to visit her.

Nicholas Long left his home to make his fortune abroad, and made his way from Froom-Everard to the highway running north-easterly to Shottsford-Forum, where he awaited the coach that ran to Melchester and London.

Edmond Willowes, with whom Barbara Grebe eloped, lived there. His father, or grandfather, was 'the last of the old glass-painters in that place, where . . . the art lingered on when it had died out in every other part of England'.

> *FMC.* vi; *TM.* v; *WT.* 1; *MC.* xliv; *W.* iv, xxxiv, xxxv;
> *CM.* 2; *GND.* 2; *TD.* xlviii; *LLI.* 8*h*; *JO.* IV i; *CM.* 8

SHREWSBURY, EARL OF. *Hardy copied the story of the duel in which the Earl was killed by the second Duke of Buckingham at Cliveden in 1668 into his notebook (Purdy, 195).* *MV.* 'The Duel'

SIDWELL. See EXONBURY.

SILVERTHORN. *Silverton, in the Exe Valley, Devon. Originally Stickleford (q.v.).*

Margery Tucker's father kept a dairy-farm near the village. *CM.* 12

SIMPKINS, MRS. She lived with her daughter, the pretty young widow

Mrs Lizzy Newberry, at Nether-Moynton, and was obviously aware of Lizzy's nocturnal smuggling activities.   *WT*. 7

SLEEPING-GREEN. *The name for this imaginary village was taken from a place north of Wareham, Dorset.*

Near Stancy Castle. George Somerset, and Dare after him, stayed at the inn. Havill, Somerset's rival architect, was forced to spend the night there and share a twin-bedded room with Dare. While Dare was asleep, Havill's curiosity impelled him to look at the secret of his birth, which he found tattooed on his chest. The landlord was informative, and a man of decided views.   *L*. I ii, iv, v; II ii, iii, v; III ix; VI iv

SLOPES, THE. The modern red country-house near the Chase and Pentridge where Alec d'Urberville lived with his blind mother.

TD. v, viii, ix

SLYRE, LANE OF. *Slyres Lane, the road which turns left from the highway by Grey's Bridge and passes over Waterston Ridge on its way to Piddlehinton and Piddletrenthide. It is the road taken by the carrier's van from the White Hart, Casterbridge, to 'Longpuddle' (LLI. 8).*

The route followed by the soldier from Casterbridge Barracks about midnight is to Waterstone Ridge, about two miles along the Lane, *then right along Ridge Way about a mile (in the direction of Puddletown)*. There he met Agnette by the Sarsen stone (*in a pit in a meadow by Ridge Way Lane*), as he had done many times before they quarrelled twenty years earlier. He saw the sun rise, lighting up the landscape from Milton Woods (*Milborne Wood, east-north-east*) to Dole-Hill (*in the north*).

TL. 'The Revisitation'

SMALLBURY, JACOB. Son of the aged maltster at Warren's Malthouse, and one of Bathsheba Everdene's employees. He is 'a young man about sixty-five, with a semi-bald head' and a single tooth which stood 'prominent, like a milestone in a bank'. Father of William.

FMC. viii, x, xxiii, lvii

SMALLBURY, LIDDY. The maltster's great-granddaughter, and Bathsheba Everdene's maid. 'The beauty her features might have lacked in form was amply made up for by perfection of hue.' It was Liddy who light-heartedly suggested sending the valentine to Boldwood. Her married sister lived in woodland near Yalbury.

FMC. viii, ix, x, xii, xiii, xxx, xxxi, xxxiv, xli, xliii, xliv,
xlvi, xlviii, lii, liv, lvii

SMALLBURY, WILLIAM. Grandson of the old maltster; 'a child of forty, or thereabouts', with whiskers which 'were assuming a chinchilla shade here and there'; father of Liddy. He worked on Bathsheba's farm, and went to Casterbridge Barracks on Fanny Robin's behalf, only to find that Troy's regiment had moved to Melchester. (*Did Hardy confuse him and his father Jacob when he presented William 'bearing his one tooth before him'?*) *FMC*. vi, viii, x, xv, xxxvi, liii

SMITH. *Probably of the Stoke in Wessex, i.e. Stoke-sub-Hamdon near Yeovil, which was well known to Hardy for its Ham-Hill building-stone.*

HS. 'Epitaph on a Pessimist'

SMITH, JOHN. *Though Hardy's father was master-mason for the Kingston Maurward estate, as Stephen Smith's father was master-mason for Lord Luxellian, the likeness seems to end there (cf. Life, 73). The scene in which he and his workmen prepare for the interment of the first Lady Luxellian in the family vault at East Endelstow church was undoubtedly imagined (even to the extent of incorporating a version of the Lady Susan story, Life, 9) around the vault which Hardy's grandfather had constructed at Stinsford church. Stephen's humble origin gives rise to another variant on 'the poor man and the lady' theme.* The Smiths moved to St Launce's, where John set up a small building business, and discovered how important citizens, who had ignored them, were delighted to make their acquaintance when they discovered that their son was a famous architect.

PBE. iv, viii–x, xxiii–xxvii, xxxvi

SMITH, MRS MARIA. Wife of John, and mother of Stephen, the architect who won fame in India. She was undaunted by her social status, even to the point of talking to 'carriage people' who came to Lord Luxellian's 'without saying ma'am or sir to 'em'. She thought her son 'might go higher than a bankrupt pa'son's girl'. Her features expressed 'an argumentative commentary on the world in general'.

PBE. v, vii, viii, x, xxiii, xxxvi

SMITH, STEPHEN. An architect, and son of Lord Luxellian's master-mason, though this was unknown to Mr Swancourt, when Stephen arrived at Endelstow Rectory to prepare plans for Mr Newby on the restoration of the church. The parson assumed he had aristocratic connections with the Fitzmaurice Smiths of Caxbury Manor. He had learnt Latin and Greek by correspondence with Henry Knight when Knight was a Fellow at Oxford. He fell in love with Swancourt's daughter Elfride. All went well until Mr Swancourt discovered that he was of humble local origin. Elfride and Stephen decided to get married without his consent, but, on arrival in London, Elfride's resolution gave way, and they caught the next train back. In order to raise his status and chances of acceptance by Mr Swancourt, he took a well-paid post in India and eventually became famous. In the meantime he had returned to England, arriving at the juncture when Elfride saved Knight's life. When he discovered that Knight was in love with Elfride, he returned to India. Later the two rivals met in London; after an *éclaircissement*, each decided to set off at once by train to seek the hand of Elfride. They met on the train and discovered when they reached Camelton station that they had been accompanied by the splendid hearse bearing the body of the second Lady Luxellian – none other but Elfride – for interment in the Luxellian vault at East Endelstow church.

In his Life *(p. 73)* Hardy took pains to point out that the 'Adonis' of the story is not a self-portrait but an idealization of a pupil he met at Mr Hicks's office in Dorchester. He gave Stephen the surname of the London Professor of Architecture whom he assisted in designing schools for the London School Board in 1872 *(Life, 87–91).* PBE

SMITTOZZI, SIGNOR. A foreign-looking gentleman who spoke in 'native London-English' and was in fact the son of Mr and Mrs Smith 'in the vicinity of the City Road'. He was a baritone operatic singer, who eloped with the Honourable Laura, and, when challenged by her husband, pushed him over a chasm by a waterfall near Cliff-Martin, and escaped. *GND*. 10

SNEWSON, MRS. The second Mrs Swancourt's maid. She is introduced in London, when the Swancourts were staying at a hotel near Blackfriars Bridge and preparing to return to Cornwall via the English Channel and Plymouth. *PBE*. xxix

SNIFF, MISS VASHTI. One of the bridesmaids at Fancy Day's wedding, the others being Susan Dewy, Bessie Dewy, and Mercy Onmey.

UGT. v i, ii

SOLENTSEA. *Southsea, near Portsmouth. The Solent divides the mainland from the Isle of Wight.*

Here Christopher Julian fell in love with Ethelberta when she was a governess in the Petherwin family.

The Marchmills spent their summer holiday at Solentsea, while the poet Robert Trewe stayed on 'the Island opposite'. *HE*. ii; *LLI*. 1

SOMERS, ALFRED. A painter with a studio in Mellstock Gardens, London. He was the friend of Jocelyn Pierston, the sculptor, and married

Mrs Pine-Avon. When last seen, he is on the Budmouth Esplanade with wife and family – 'a middle-aged family man with spectacles', and 'a row of daughters tailing off to infancy, who at present added appreciably to the income of the bathing-machine women established along the sands'.

WB. I vi, vii, ix; II iii, ix, x, xiii; III iv

SOMERSET, GEORGE. A young architect, the son of the Royal Academician. While on a sketching holiday, he came to Stancy Castle, and became interested in plans for its development and even more in its owner, the attractive Paula Power. Owing to the dishonesty of Dare and Havill, and the latter's imminent bankruptcy, he did not obtain the commission for the castle extensions which Miss Power had virtually given him before he advised that competitive plans should be judged by the R.I.B.A. In his absence, Captain de Stancy, prompted by his illegitimate son Will Dare, did his best to engage her attentions. When Havill suddenly resigned his commission, Somerset continued his work at the castle; but the newly arrived Abner Power, favouring an alliance with the de Stancys, took Paula away for a tour on the Continent. When no further messages came from Paula, George went to Nice to find her, but was condemned to pursue her from place to place, always a stage behind, at Monte Carlo, for example. Here he refused to lend money to Dare. When he caught up with Paula at Carlsruhe, he was out of favour: Dare had sent a telegram in his name from Monte Carlo, stating that he had lost all his money at the gambling-table, and asking for more. The unfavourable impression Paula had formed of him was confirmed by the faked photograph which Dare allowed her to see. Somerset returned to England and resigned his work at Stancy Castle. If he had not met Charlotte de Stancy, when he was passing through Toneborough on his way to Normandy, Paula would have married Captain de Stancy. When she realized how George had been traduced, Paula set off without delay to find him in Normandy. At last they met, all misunderstandings were removed, and they were married before returning to England.   *L*

Apart from the interest he shows in architecture, George Somerset recalls the young architect Hardy in two ways: his interest in the arguments for and against Paedobaptism (cf. Life, 29–30) at Dorchester, and his intellectual interests in London, 'when poetry, theology, and the reorganization of society had seemed matters of more importance to him than a profession'.

SOMERSET, MR. Father of George Somerset, and an Academician.

L. III v; VI ii, iii

SORROW. The name given by Tess to her child when she christened it. A phrase in Genesis suggested the name; it is generally thought to be 'Benoni', which may have been read in translation 'Son of my sorrow' (xxxv 18); it may have been 'in sorrow thou shalt bring forth children' (iii 16). *TD*. xiv

SOUTH, JOHN. The father of Marty South. Owing to his illness, Marty had to cut spar-gads for Mr Melbury, and sell her hair. John South, as he lay ill in bed, developed an obsession that a tall elm immediately opposite his bedroom would be blown down and kill him. To relieve his fears, Giles Winterborne cut off the lower branches; as this was of no avail, he cut down the tree one night, on the advice of Dr Fitzpiers. The next morning, when the curtains were drawn, the old man sat up in bed and looked for the tree. The vacancy ahead of him was too great a shock for his nervous system; and nothing could restore him. By his death, the property which a member of the South family had leased from the lord of the manor three generations earlier became Mrs Charmond's, no agreement having been made for the extension of the tenure. One result of this was that Winterborne had to leave his home in Little Hintock and move to One-Chimney Hut near Delborough. *It can be argued that John South's death led to Winterborne's. Cf. 'liviers', p. 137.* *W*. ii, v, xii–xv

SOUTH, MARTY. The daughter of John South, on account of whose illness she toiled long hours, often far into the night, and sold her tresses of hair, her one pretension to beauty, to grace Mrs Charmond. She was young and slim; her face had 'the usual fulness of expression which is developed by a life of solitude', but 'the necessity of taking thought at a too early period of life had forced the provisional curves of her childhood's face to a premature finality'. When her father died, she had 'nothing more left on earth to lose, except a life which she did not over-value'. She did work for Melbury and occasionally for Giles Winterborne, whom she helped to plant trees. To her they seemed like human beings, ceasing to sigh only when lying down. She never told her love for Giles. When Grace was unhappy as a result of Fitzpiers's infatuation for Mrs Charmond, she did the only thing within her power to help. She wrote to Fitzpiers, revealing the origin of Mrs Charmond's beautiful hair. Marty's 'bullet reached its billet' in an unusual way. When Giles died she could claim him as hers. Grace had discovered that 'Marty South alone . . . had approximated to Winterborne's level of intelligent intercourse with Nature'. Marty intended to continue Giles's work with the cider-press, with Creedle to assist her. Her devotion to Giles never failed, like Grace's, and *her closing words over his grave reveal her as Hardy's true heroine. In her can be seen the Pauline virtues to which Hardy was to pay tribute in Tess and in his poetry: long-suffering, endurance, kindness, humility, and unfailing loyalty and devotion.*

Chap. viii – an afterthought, to judge by the MS. (Purdy) – should be read in conjunction with TL. 'The Pine Planters (Marty South's Reverie)'.

W. ii, iii, v, viii, ix, xii–xv, xvi, xix, xx, xxxiii, xxxiv, xliii, xliv, xlv, xlviii

SOUTHAMPTON. Here Edward Springrove saved Cytherea Graye from Manston when they were on their way to a honeymoon in Paris. *The scenes suggest a popular Victorian 'thriller'.*

Mr Swancourt was put ashore at Southampton because of illness on his return from London by the *Juliet* boat.

Bob Loveday met the actress Matilda Johnson here, promptly fell in love, and wrote to tell his father that he had arranged for the wedding to take place at Overcombe, so that his father should not miss the marriage-feast.

In order that he should not be debarred from a large annuity at the age of twenty-five, Lady Constantine insisted that Swithin St Cleeve should travel to further his astronomical career. She had discovered that their marriage was illegal, and, after his departure, that she was pregnant. She hurried to Southampton to marry him, but found that the *Occidental* on which he was to sail had just left the harbour. She had forbidden him to communicate with her, and nobody knew what place he was visiting first. He had, in fact, changed his plans, and left Southampton on another ship, for the Cape.

DR. xiii 6–10; *PBE.* xxix; *TM.* xiv–xv; *TT.* xxxvii–xxxviii; *CM.* 2; *GND.* 2; *GND.* 5; *PPP.* 'Embarcation', 'Departure', 'The Colonel's Soliloquy' (*Hardy saw the embarkation of troops for the Boer War at Southampton in 1899. 'The Going of the Battery' records a scene he witnessed at Dorchester*).

SOUTHERNSHIRE, DUCHESS OF.   *HS.* 'The Turnip-Hoer'

SOW-AND-ACORN. See EVERSHEAD.

SPADDLEHOLT FARM. Near Cresscombe. (*The name derives from two local villages, Chaddleworth, south-south-east of Fawley, and Sparsholt, west of Wantage.*)   *JO.* I viii

SPAIN. Reference is made to battles in the Peninsular War against Napoleon in *The Trumpet-Major*. In *The Dynasts*, the most interesting Spanish scenes relate to the escape of Godoy, 'The Prince of Peace', from the mob which invades his palace; stragglers in the retreat of the English to Coruña; and the battles of Coruña, Talavera, Albuera, Salamanca (*cf. HE. iv*), and Vitoria. *TM.* v, xii, xli; *D.*
(2) II ii; III i, ii, iii, iv; IV iv, v; VI iv, (3) I ii, iii, II i–iii etc.

SPEEDWELL, LADY IRIS. To Jocelyn Pierston, she was the brightest hostess in London. The first person he met when he went to dine with her was Mrs Pine-Avon, whose renewed interest in him was very obvious. His admiration might have revived had he not taken advantage of an opportunity during dinner to read a letter which informed him that Avice Caro was dead. The image of the Well-Beloved took him to 'his natal isle'. *WB.* II ii

SPINKS, ELIAS. A member of the Mellstock choir. A slow thinker, who occasionally expressed himself sententiously but was rather tongue-tied: 'Learning's a worthy thing, and ye've got it, Master Spinks.' He had once kept a night-school. *UGT.* I i, iii, iv, vi–viii, II ii–v

SPRINGROVE, EDWARD. *Though Hardy insisted that a fellow-assistant at Crickmay's office at Weymouth was his prototype, he is in some respects like Hardy. He was an architect and a poet who knew Shakespeare 'to the very dregs of the footnotes'. He was of 'rather humble origin'; the 'poor man and the lady' theme is introduced with a sentence ('The truly great stand upon no middle ledge; they are either famous or unknown') which occurs in 'An Indiscretion'. The boating scene which gives rise to these reflections is based on Hardy's experiences at Weymouth (Life, 63–4).*

Springrove left Carriford for London. Cytherea Graye, with whom he was in love, was told by Miss Aldclyffe that he was engaged to Miss Hinton. In order to help her brother, who was in desperate financial need because of prolonged illness, she consented to marry Manston. Miss Hinton's sudden marriage to Farmer Bollens freed Springrove; too late, however, to prevent the marriage of Cytherea and Manston. Springrove played the leading part in rescuing the heroine and in the arrest of Manston for the murder of his wife Eunice. He married Cytherea, who, as Manston's widow, inherited Miss Aldclyffe's estate. *DR*

SPRINGROVE, JOHN. Father of Edward. He was a small farmer and cider-maker, who kept the Three Tranters Inn at Carriford. Manston's wife Eunice had intended to stay at the inn the night it was burnt down.

DR. v 2, viii 3, x 2–3, 6, xi 1, xvi 3, xxi 1

STAGFOOT LANE. *Hartfoot Lane, a small village among the chalk hills between Nettlecombe Tout and Bulbarrow which overlook the Vale of Blackmoor.*

The antiquarian Tringham was the parson here. After their abortive marriage, Angel drove Tess the greater part of the way to her home at Marlott. They stopped at Stagfoot Lane for a rest.

Two of Mr Melbury's employees came from this village to make spars during the late autumn and winter.

An MS. note indicates that the Fox Inn, Stagfoot Lane, was the scene for 'The Man he Killed' (Purdy, 147).

TD. i, vii, xxxvii; *W.* iv; *TL.* 'The Man he Killed'

STAGG, JACK. One of the stone-masons with whom Jude worked on college repairs at Christminster.   *JO.* vi i, vii, xi

STANCY CASTLE. *Rather imaginary, though Hardy's map of Wessex identifies it as Dunster Castle, west of the Quantock Hills in Somerset. The excerpts from its history (*i xiii*) may be Hardy's invention. The name was suggested by the old Dunster family of Stanton or the neighbouring manor of Staunton. Hardy's 1912 postscript to the preface should warn topographers against too close an identification of either the castle or neighbouring places and features: Dunster Castle, after all, still stands.*

On a hill near Markton. Formerly the seat of the de Stancys. It was sold to a Mr Wilkins, who neglected it, and then bought by Mr Power. His daughter Paula inherited it, and had ambitious schemes for restoring and extending it. In the end, it was burnt down by Dare, and only the main walls were left standing. Paula and George Somerset, reconciled and married, agreed that a modern house should be built beside the ruin.   *L*

STANNER, SERGEANT. A member of a Foot Regiment, who was recruiting at Budmouth during the summer of 1805. He is seen there marching in front of his recruiting-party, with 'firm countenance, fiery poll, and rigid staring eyes', and with drawn sword; 'at intervals of two or three inches along its shining blade were impaled fluttering one-pound notes, to express the lavish bounty that was offered'. At Miller Loveday's party the previous year he sang verses on the improbability of Bonaparte's landing – 'Poor Stanner! In spite of his satire, he fell at the bloody battle of Albuera, a few years after this pleasantly spent summer at the Georgian watering-place. . . .' *The song was published in* Wessex Poems

479

under the title 'The Sergeant's Song'.   *TM.* v, xxx, xxxiv

STANNIDGE, MR. The landlord of the Three Mariners, Casterbridge. His wife was kind, but fat and lazy. On duty in the bar, she generally sat, 'corporeally motionless' but observant; in motion, she 'rolled'.

MC. vi–viii, xx, xxxiii, xliii

STAPLEFORD PARK. *Stalbridge House, Stalbridge, north Dorset. Only the Park wall and gateway survive. See plate facing p. 335.*

One of the estates which the cunning old lawyer Timothy Petrick acquired. Here he lived. His great-grandson nearly lost the inheritance as a result of his mother's hallucinations.   *GND.* 6

STEPHEN.   *HS.* 'One who Married above Him'

STEPHEN, LESLIE. *Climber, reviewer, critic, and editor of* The Cornhill,* *for which Hardy wrote* Far from the Madding Crowd *and* The Hand of Ethelberta. *As editor, he was anxious that Hardy should not offend his magazine-readers. The new scientific outlook made him an agnostic, and he chose Hardy to witness his renunciation of Holy Orders. See* Life, *36–7, 95–100, 103–4, 105–6, 108–9, 127–8, 171, 182, 293, 298. Hardy stated that Stephen's 'philosophy was to influence his own for many years, indeed, more than that of any other contemporary'.*   *SC.* 'The Schreckhorn'

STICKLEFORD. *The village of Tincleton, four miles east of Stinsford.*

After making a profit at reddle-dealing, Diggory Venn took a dairy-farm at Stickleford.

When Gertrude Lodge visited Casterbridge Gaol to cure her withered arm, she rode over Egdon Heath, avoiding the direct route through Stickleford.

Marian had intended marrying a dairyman at Stickleford until she met Angel Clare.

It was here that Caroline Aspent, who could not resist the dance music of the fiddler 'Mop' Ollamoor, lived.

RN. vi i; *WT.* 4; *TD.* xxiii; *LLI.* 7. See p. 68

STINSFORD. *Two miles east of Dorchester. It is generally referred to as 'Mellstock' (see pp. 410–14); also p. 354 and* TOLLAMORE. *Stinsford Hill is 'Mellstock Hill' (p. 412). The experience which gave rise to the poem occurred on 4 February 1894* (Life, 262).

LLE. 'On Stinsford Hill at Midnight'

STOCKDALE, RICHARD. A young Wesleyan minister who was sent to

---

* Cf. *SC.* 'The Jubilee of a Magazine' (*January 1910*).

Nether-Moynton temporarily, pending the arrival of the new minister. He fell in love with Mrs Lizzy Newberry, the pretty young widow with whom he lodged, only to discover that she was actively engaged in smuggling. His attempts to persuade her to give up a dangerous and illegal trade were useless; it was in her blood, as he might have seen from what he witnessed as he followed or accompanied her, on long nocturnal missions to the coast. Subsequently, he returned on a visit from the Midland town where he had settled, and discovered that the smugglers of Nether-Moynton and Chaldon had been caught in a shooting affray with the Preventives. Lizzy was now poor, and, having no reason to stay at Nether-Moynton, agreed to marry Stockdale. (*Such was the ending Hardy thought fit for his magazine readers. He would have preferred one close to the facts: she married her smuggler cousin and emigrated with him to Wisconsin.*) *WT.* 7

STOCKER, EDITH. The widow of John Stocker, a merchant of Havenpool in the reign of Henry VIII. When Sir John Horseleigh of Clyfton Horseleigh found that he was illegally married, he was encouraged to marry Edith secretly. He visited her at Oozewood in Upper Wessex. Her brother Roger discovered that Sir John had another wife, charged him with deception, and in the ensuing struggle stabbed him. Sir John died soon afterwards. Edith did not assert her legal claims, but retired to Havenpool. *CM.* 9

STOCKWOOL, GRAMMER. An old woman who came to live with Ann Avice Caro (Mrs Isaac Pierston) after her mother's death.

WB. II x, xii, xiii

STOCKWOOL, RUTH. The nurse who attended Mrs Pierston (the second Avice) when she was dying. *WB.* III vi

STOKE-BAREHILLS. *Basingstoke, Hampshire.* Jude and Sue took 'Father Time' to the Great Wessex Agricultural Show at this town. Other visitors included Mr and Mrs Cartlett, i.e. Arabella, who met her old friend Anny and the itinerant quack-doctor Vilbert.

JO. v v, vii; cf. CICELY

STONE, MRS. An intimate neighbour of the Paddock family at Mellstock.

CM. 5

STONEHENGE. *A prehistoric megalithic monument, eight miles north of Salisbury; once thought to have been a Druidic temple. It consisted originally of an outer circle of stones supporting a rim of horizontal stones; parallel to this ran an inner circle of smaller stones. Further within stood five trilithons, forming a horseshoe, with an inner horseshoe of smaller stones. In the centre was a flat stone, which was thought to have been an altar or Stone of Sacrifice. TM.* xxvi (simile); *TD.* lviii; *SC.* 'Channel Firing'

STONEHENGE, MARQUIS OF. Many years her senior, and for long her phlegmatic wooer, he married Lady Caroline and remained ignorant of her earlier romantic marriage and its less romantic consequences.

GND. 3

STOUR. *The main river in the Vale of Blackmoor.* As Phillotson left his friend Gillingham on his walk back from Leddenton to Shaston at night, 'no sound was audible but that of the purling tributaries of the Stour'.

JO. IV iv; *MV.* 'Overlooking the River Stour', 'On Sturminster Foot-Bridge'

STOURCASTLE. *Sturminster Newton (cf. p. 484) by the River Stour, where the Hardys lived from 1876 to 1878. Nothing is left of the castle, where King Alfred is said to have lived.*

The road south from Marlott led through it. Tess drove through Stourcastle before daybreak on her way to deliver beehives in Casterbridge. She passed through it on her way to Talbothays.

Sergeant Young of Stourcastle fought at Vitoria and Waterloo. It was a rustic from Stourcastle who went to see Napoleon burned on Durnover Green; he had heard that he was imprisoned at Casterbridge Gaol.

The MS. of the poem 'The To-be-Forgotten' (cf. 'His Immortality' and 'Her Immortality') indicates that it was written in, or with reference to, Stourcastle Churchyard' (Purdy, 114). *TD.* ii, iv, xvi; *PPP.* 'The To-be-Forgotten'; *D.* (3) II i, V vi

STOURTON TOWER. *King Alfred's Tower on Kingsettle Hill (850 feet), three miles north-west of Stourton, near Mere, Wiltshire. It marks the site where the Saxon King erected his standard against the Danes. It stands 160 feet high, and forms a prominent landmark from the Vale of Blackmoor.*

SC. 'Channel Firing' *(written in April 1914)*

STOW, CHARLES. He had attended the same Training College for teachers as Baptista Trewthen. At the end of a year, Baptista decided she would relinquish teaching for marriage, and was on her way home to the Isles of Lyonesse to marry a man she did not love, when, after discovering she had missed the boat at Pen-zephyr and had to wait three days for the next, she met her old sweetheart Charles Stow. When he heard she was to be married, he insisted that they should travel to Trufal and marry by licence. This they did. They then proposed to travel to Giant's Town to inform her parents. At Pen-zephyr, they found they had two hours to wait for the boat. Charles Stow decided to swim in the sea, and was drowned. Not daring to tell her parents, Baptista married Mr Heddegan, and found that they were to stay at Pen-zephyr for the first stage of their honeymoon. That night she lay between her two husbands, the body of Charles lying, as she had learned, in the neighbouring room. She contrived to attend his funeral at Redrutin. *CM.* 11

STRASSBURG (and the RHINE VALLEY). Paula Power travelled to Strassburg, Baden and the valley of the Murg, Carlsruhe (where George Somerset caught up with her party, and suffered a second disgrace in the eyes of Paula, thanks to the wiliness of Dare), Heidelberg and the Königsstuhl, Mainz, Coblenz, and Cologne. *How much this is based on the Hardy's visit in 1876 may be judged from Hardy's Life, p. 110.*

L. v i–ix; *W.* xxvii

STRATLEIGH. Bude, *'a small watering-place fourteen miles north' of St Juliot. The name was suggested by Stratton, a small ancient town near Bude.*

When Elfride Swancourt was preparing to elope, her father drove to Stratleigh to make his final marriage arrangements with the rich widow, Mrs Troyton. *PBE.* xi, xii

STRAW, DAVID. The stable-boy at the Red Lion Hotel, Anglebury. He came from Knollsea. *HE.* xliv

STREET OF WELLS. *Fortune's Well, Portland, the 'under-hill' townlet through which the road from the mainland runs to 'Top-o'-Hill' and on to 'the eastern village', Easton.*

TM. xxxiv; *WB.* I i–iii, II viii, ix, III ii, v, viii

STRONG, DECIMUS. He was married to the daughter of Richard Phelipson, heiress of Montislope. He joined in the revolt of the nobles against Henry VIII, and afterwards took refuge abroad. His wife, assuming he was dead, married Sir John Horseleigh. This marriage was found to be illegal when it was learned that Decimus was still alive. Sir John married Edith Stocker secretly, and was murdered in consequence by her brother. The widow Dame Horseleigh married a soldier of fortune from the Continent; according to tradition this was none other than Decimus Strong, 'who remarried her for appearance' sake only'. *CM.* 9

STROODEN, TIM. A 'mechanic' at Knapwater whom Miss Aldclyffe consulted on alterations to the old manor house to provide accommodation for Manston. He and his five journeymen carpenters watched the wedding of Cytherea Graye and Edward Springrove through the chancel windows. There were many others outside the church, including Dairyman Dodman and Christopher Runt, to see the bridal pair emerge.

DR. vii, 1, Sequel

STUBB. A farmer from Duddle Hole (*east of Lower Bockhampton?*), and friend of Festus Derriman. He was in the yeomanry, with Noakes of Nether-Moynton, and Brownjohn and Lockham, when Festus Derriman, having heard that the invasion alarm was false, rode up to them with drawn sword, boasting of the glorious deeds they would do that day against the French, and reminding them, with some sadistic satisfaction, of all the orgies they were to miss during the summer campaign: 'no bouncing health to our lady-loves in Oxwell Hall'; 'no rattling dinners at Stacie's Hotel' (Budmouth); 'no grinning-matches at Mai-dun Castle'; 'no thread-the-needle at Greenhill Fair'; 'no dancing on the green, Lockham, this year in the moonlight! You was tender upon that girl; gad, what will become o' her in the struggle?'   *TM*. ix, xxvi

STUBBERD. A Casterbridge constable.   *MC*. xxvii, xxviii, xxxix

STURMINSTER NEWTON. *See* STOURCASTLE. *The Hardys lived at 'Riverside Villa', overlooking the River Stour. Here he wrote the greater part of* The Return of the Native. *The poems were probably written after his visit to the house in 1916.*

When Hardy was leaving Sturminster, he wrote, on 18 March 1878, 'End of the Sturminster Newton idyll . . .'; later he added 'Our happiest time'. Cf. Life, *111–12, 117, 118–19, 373.*

> *MV*. 'Overlooking the River Stour', 'The Musical Box', 'On Sturminster Foot-Bridge' (*for the addition of 'Onomatopoeic', see* Life, *301, 390); LLE.* 'The Maid of Keinton Mandeville' (*in south Somerset, nearly twenty miles away. Sir Henry Bishop was the composer of 'Should he upbraid'; cf. PBE. iii and* Life, *118*), 'A Two-Years' Idyll'; *WW*. 'The Second Visit'

SUMMERS, TIMOTHY. A watch-maker of Shottsford, who stole a sheep in the 1820s to save his starving family, and was condemned in consequence to be hanged at Casterbridge Gaol. He escaped and asked for shelter one wild evening at Higher Crowstairs. See p. 66.   *WT*. 1

SURBITON. *A Surrey suburb in Greater London (south-west). The Hardys, after a short honeymoon on the Continent, lived at Surbiton during the winter of 1874–5.*   *HS*. 'A Light Snow-fall after Frost'

SUSAN, LADY. *Daughter of the first Earl of Ilchester* (cf. REYNARD), *she created a great scandal when she married the Irish actor William O'Brien in 1764. They lived at Stinsford House by the church, and were buried in a vault specially constructed for them by Thomas Hardy's grandfather. Thomas Hardy's father, when he was a boy-chorister in the gallery at Stinsford Church, used to see her, an old, lonely widow walking in the garden in a red cloak; cf.* Life. *9, 163–4, 250 and* PBE. *xxvi.*

WP. 'Friends Beyond'; TL. 'The Noble Lady's Tale'

SWANAGE. *The 'Knollsea' of Hardy's fiction (p. 385). The Hardys lived at Swanage during the autumn and winter of 1875–6. Here he finished* The Hand of Ethelberta, *which contains some interesting contemporary impressions of the place. He revisited it in 1892, 1908, and 1916. Durlston Head is a mile to the south of Swanage.* MV. 'The Sunshade'; HS. 'Once at Swanage', 'To a Sea-Cliff'

SWANCOURT, CHRISTOPHER. Rector of Endelstow, a widower and father of Elfride. With the assistance of William Worm, he had carried out church improvements. He encouraged Stephen Smith in his courtship of Elfride, assuming that he was of 'blue blood' – 'a very desirable colour, as the world goes' – but turned against him when he learned that he was the son of a local mason. Though related to the aristocratic Luxellians by his first marriage, he was only a 'poor gentleman' with few friends. He bettered himself by marrying a rich widow, Mrs Troyton. He was continually on the point of telling a story, but desisted, or pretended he must desist, because it was not appropriate to his company. 'All along the chimneypiece [of his study] were ranged bottles of horse, pig and cow medicines. . . .' A few books on some of the Pauline epistles 'just saved the character of the place'. His ecclesiastical duties alternated between the parish of West Endelstow (the church of St Agnes) and Lord Luxellian's estate (the church of St Eval) at East Endelstow. *PBE*

SWANCOURT, ELFRIDE. Granddaughter of Lady Elfride Luxellian, who eloped with the singer Arthur Kingsmore. Her mother had eloped with Mr Swancourt when he was a curate. At the time of receiving the young architect Stephen Smith at Endelstow Rectory, she had written *The Court of King Arthur's Castle*, a romance of Lyonnesse. She often wrote her father's sermons. She fell in love with Stephen, who was encouraged by her father. When he, for snobbish reasons, opposed their marriage, she eloped with Stephen to London, but lost heart immediately on arrival and returned. In the prolonged absence of Smith, she remained loyal to him. The saving of Knight's life was the turning-point in her life. She fell in love with him; but, prudish and suspicious of her past, he deserted her inhumanly. When Smith and Knight met again, Knight discovered that he had wronged Elfride. Each set off to Endelstow with renewed hope; but Elfride had married Lord Luxellian, and was dead.

PBE

SWANHILLS, LOT. A member of the Chalk-Newton choir.   *CM.* 4

SWEATLEY, TRANTER. Although she was in love with Tim Tankens, Barbree's uncle made her marry the tranter Sweatley. The bridegroom, celebrating his wedding, accidentally set fire to his house, and perished in the flames. Tim Tankens came to the rescue of Barbree, and married her.

This is a traditional Wessex story. The poem in which Hardy records it was written in 1866, and is notable for its use of dialect. See Life, *302.*

WP. 'The Bride-Night Fire'

SWETMAN, CHRISTOPHER. *One of Hardy's ancestors at Melbury Osmond. There was a tradition in the Swetman family that the Duke of Monmouth had sheltered at Swetman's house after the disastrous Battle of Sedgemoor. His daughters were Grace and Leonarde – the Grace and Leonard of the story; cf.* Life, *6. See plate facing p.494.*

SWETMAN, GILES. *Probably one of the same family. He came from near Woolcombe (where the Hardys had owned property for a long time; cf.* Life, *5, 214) in the region of the 'Hintocks'.*   *TL.* 'The Rash Bride'

SWINBURNE, ALGERNON CHARLES. *For Hardy's quotations from Swinburne, see p. 208. His love of Swinburne's poetry was neither short-lived nor uncritical. He could not forget the excitement caused in London in 1866 when* Poems and Ballads *appeared. Hardy was prevented from attending Swinburne's funeral, but visited his grave at Bonchurch near Ventnor in the Isle of Wight in March 1910. See* Life, *270–1, 325, 344–5, 349.*   *SC.* 'A Singer Asleep'; *HS.* 'A Refusal'

SYDLING. See BROAD SIDLINCH.

TABITHA. She looked sad on her wedding-day because the previous evening she had heard the man she was marrying (for the sake of the child she expected) express a preference for Carry.   '

LLE. 'The Wedding Morning'

TALBOTHAYS. A dairy farm in 'the Valley of the Great Dairies' – *the Frome valley between Puddletown Heath and West Stafford. The name derives from the farm owned by Hardy's father on the road east of West*

Stafford village. Some time after the death of both his parents at Higher Bockhampton, Hardy's brother Henry built a house there, and named it Talbothays. He lived there with his two sisters, Mary and Katherine. There can be no doubt that Hardy's familiarity with the neighbouring Frome valley stemmed from his boyhood days when he accompanied his father and other workmen to this farm, and wandered down to the river and rich meadows past Lewell Mill. For the origin of the name, see Life, *6.*

The farm was kept by Mr and Mrs Crick. Here, after her great sorrow, Tess spent her happiest days until she married Angel Clare.

TD. xv–xxxiii, xxxvii

TALL, LABAN. A young man employed at Bathsheba's farm. He had recently married, and was known as 'Susan Tall's husband' because he had 'no individuality worth mentioning'. His wife 'called herself five-and-twenty, looked thirty, passed as thirty-five, and was forty'. She never showed conjugal tenderness in public, like some newly married women. Her henpecked husband was 'as irrepressibly good-humoured under [her] ghastly snubs as a parliamentary candidate on the hustings'. Laban loved music: 'when there's tunes going on I seem as if hung in wires'. Even so, he dared not keep his wife waiting by staying at Warren's Malthouse to listen to Gabriel Oak's flute-playing. The thought that Gabriel might continue playing after he had left would make him melancholy. Laban was made parish-clerk, and suffered 'mortal terror at church on Sundays when he heard his lone voice among certain hard words of the Psalms, whither no man ventured to follow him'. (*Metrical psalms were sung as hymns.*)   *FMC.* viii, x, xxi, xxii, xxxvi, liii, lvii

TANGS, TIMOTHY (1). A bottom sawyer employed by Mr Melbury. He married Suke Damson, and set an ancient man-trap for Fitzpiers, whom he rightly suspected of being too interested in Suke, before they emigrated to New Zealand.   *W.* iv, xix, xx, xxiv, xxix, xlv–xlviii

(2) A top sawyer employed by Mr Melbury, and father of Timothy Tangs. He thought that his master was over-solicitous for Grace, and that he ought to have had a dozen children to 'bring him to reason'. Once, when taking a prohibited short-cut through the woods, old Timothy stopped above Hintock House to take a pinch of snuff, but, observing Mrs Charmond gazing at him from the staircase window, hastened to reach the top of the hollow in which the house stood, missed his footing, and rolled to the bottom.   *W.* iv, xii, xix, xxii, xxvii, xxix, xlvi

TANKENS, TIM. See SWEATLEY.

TANTRUM CLANGLEY. (*Suggesting a great deal of noise.*)

A tambourine player from this village, 'a place long celebrated for the skill of its inhabitants as performers on instruments of percussion', was invited to the festivities after the wedding of Dick Dewy and Fancy Day, 'under the greenwood tree' in Yalbury Wood. *UGT.* v ii

TARGAN. *Pentargon Bay, south of Beeny Cliff, Cornwall.*

PBE. v, vii; *SC.* 'After a Journey', 'A Death-Day Recalled'

TAYLOR, JANE. See HAMMERSMITH.

TEMPLEMAN, MRS. A banker's widow who lived at Bath and left her wealth to her niece Lucetta. *MC.* xviii, xxii

TETUPHENAY, T. The master of Biblioll College, who recommended that Jude should stick to his trade as a stone-mason. *JO.* II vi

THINN, JOHN. *HS.* 'Life and Death at Sunrise'

THIRDLY, PARSON. Of Weatherbury. He made arrangements for Fanny Robin's burial, and married Bathsheba and Gabriel Oak.

Gunnery practice just before the First World War awakened the dead. They thought it was the Day of Judgment; when Father Thirdly heard what was threatened, he said he wished he had 'stuck to pipes and beer' instead of preaching forty years.

FMC. viii, xxxiii, xlii, li, liv, lvii; *SC.* 'Channel Firing'

THOMAS, SIR. *Sir Thomas Strangways of Melbury House. See* KING'S HINTOCK COURT.

He told Christopher Swetman that the Duke of Monmouth had been executed at Tower Hill. *CM.* 10

THOMPSON, MRS EDITH. *She was hanged on 9 January 1923 for the murder of her husband. Her love-letters, many of which were published in the press at the time of her trial, made a great impression on Hardy and many others.* *HS.* 'On the Portrait of a Woman about to be Hanged'

THORNCOMBE. *The wood immediately south of Hardy's birthplace.*

TL. 'She Hears the Storm'

THREE TRANTERS INN. At Carriford. It was kept by Edward Springrove's father. Mrs Manston was thought to be staying there the night it was burnt down. *DR.* v 2, viii 3, x, xi 2, xviii 3, xxi 1

THROOPE CORNER. *At the crossroads south of Throop hamlet, and not far east of 'Alderworth'.*

Diggory Venn saw Wildeve escorting Eustacia to Throope Corner from the evening festivities at East Egdon, where, according to Thomasin, he had gone to buy a horse. 'I saw him . . . leading one home,' said Venn drily. 'A beauty, with a white face and a mane as black as night'.

RN. iv iii

TIMMS, MR. The lawyer at Southampton whose advice was sought on the illegal marriage of Manston and Cytherea Graye. *DR.* xiii 10

TINA, MATTHÄUS. A corporal in the German regiment of the York Hussars, which was stationed on Bincombe Down in 1801. His home was in Saarbrück. He was homesick, fell in love with Phyllis Grove, and persuaded her to accompany him and a fellow deserter across the Channel. At the last minute, she changed her mind. Matthäus and Christoph Bless travelled by boat from Budmouth to Jersey, and landed there, thinking they had reached France. They were handed over to the authorities, brought back to England, and shot before the German regiments on Bincombe Down as an example. Their bodies were buried behind the church at Bincombe. *WT.* 3

'TINKER TAYLOR'. One of Jude's drinking companions at Christminster. He was a bankrupt ecclesiastical ironmonger, 'who appeared to have been of a religious turn in earlier years, but was somewhat blasphemous now'. *JO.* II vii; III viii; VI i, vii

TINTAGEL. See DUNDAGEL. *QC*

TINTINHULL. *Four miles north-west of Yeovil.*

TL. 'The Flirt's Tragedy'; *LLE.* 'Vagg Hollow'

TIPMAN. Lord Mountclere's valet, who became engaged to the flighty Mrs Menlove, and to whom she imparted her discovery that Ethelberta was the daughter of the Chickerels. He passed on the information to his master. *HE.* xxxii, xlii

TITANIC, THE. *This magnificent liner collided with an iceberg on its first transatlantic crossing and sank with the loss of over 1,500 lives on 15 April 1912. The poem was first printed in a programme at Covent Garden to help the 'Titanic' Disaster Fund.* *SC.* 'The Convergence of the Twain'

TIVWORTHY. *Tiverton, a town in the Exe valley, Devon.*

The musician who recognized Margery Tucker as the young lady he saw dancing the polka at the Yeomanry ball given by Lord Toneborough was on his way to a fête at Tivworthy when he met her lover Jim. *CM.* 12

TOLCHURCH. *Tolpuddle, famous for its Trade Union 'martyrs', the 'six men of Dorset' (1836). Two miles east of Puddletown.*

Here Owen and Cytherea Graye lived for a while. He had just recovered from his long illness, and was engaged in supervising the restoration of the church for Mr Gradfield. Cytherea was recovering from the

489

shock of discovering that she had been married bigamously (so it appeared) to Manston. Manston was arrested for murder at their house.

DR. xv, xvii 3, xviii 2, xx

TOLLAMORE. *Hardy's first presentation of Stinsford, the 'Mellstock' of the Wessex novels. The school where Egbert Mayne taught when he was visited by Geraldine Allenville is the same as Fancy Day's school. Hardy was the first pupil to enter it in 1848* (Life, *16*). *It may still be seen in Lower Bockhampton.*

There is a reference to the gallery in the church (cf. MELLSTOCK). *The opening paragraph describing the swaying congregation as it sings is to be found in a slightly modified form in* Desperate Remedies (*xii 8*). *The most interesting feature of the church is the marble mural monument (well-known to Hardy at Stinsford) to the heroine's ancestors, with its 'winged skull and two cherubim'.*

For Tollamore House, the home of Squire Allenville, see KNAPWATER HOUSE. *The scene describing the laying of a foundation-stone for a tower or beacon in the Park is based on the experience of Arthur Blomfield, the architect for whom Hardy worked in London, when a memorial stone was laid at New Windsor by the Crown Princess of Germany (cf.* Life, *48*). ILH

TOLLER, RICHARD. The hautboy player in the Chalk-Newton choir.

CM. 4

TOLLER-DOWN. *Benvill Lane, the upper part of the road from Evershot, meets the Dorchester–Crewkerne road on the north side of this hill.*

Norcombe Hill is not far from 'lonely Toller-Down'.

FMC. ii; TL. 'The Homecoming'

TONEBOROUGH. *Taunton, the 'county-town' of Somerset, on the River Tone (mentioned in HS. 'Bags of Meat').*

Captain de Stancy's battery was stationed at Toneborough Barracks. The Hunt Ball, to which George Somerset made a hurried dash from London, was held at Toneborough. Miss Barbara Bell also made a hurried excursion, at Paula Power's call, and Somerset met her at Toneborough station. Much later, after he had been disgraced in Paula's estimation, Somerset was travelling by train via Toneborough when Charlotte de Stancy entered his compartment. Their conversation led to the postponement of the wedding between Paula and Sir William (Captain) de Stancy, and eventually to the reconciliation and marriage of Somerset and Paula.

Captain James Northbrook and the Honourable Laura were secretly wedded at St Mary's, Toneborough.

Mr Millborne was the son of a Toneborough solicitor. He became engaged to Leonora, an assistant in a music-shop, and deserted her.

> *L.* I v, viii; II iii, iv, v, vi; III iv, vi, x; V xii, xiii; *GND.* 10; *LLI.* 3; *WP.* 'The Dance at the Phoenix' (Tone); *SC.* 'The Sacrilege' (*the Vale of Taunton Deane, west of Taunton*)

TONEBOROUGH, LORD. The Yeomanry Ball to which Baron von Xanten took the dairymaid Margery Tucker was held at Lord Toneborough's.   *CM.* 12

TOOGOOD, PARSON BILLY. *For the 'truly delightful personage' who was the original of the ironically named Toogood, see Hardy's preface to the first edition of* Life's Little Ironies (*Orel,* Thomas Hardy's Personal Writings) *and* SCRIMPTON.

The bachelor parson of Scrimpton who could not resist a hunt. He had 'been in' at the death of three thousand foxes. He refused to perform the marriage service for Andrey Satchel and Jane Vallens, because Andrey was not sober, and promised to return in two hours. The bridal pair were locked in the tower at Jane's request; she was afraid she might never get Andrey to church again, and her condition was desperate. The parson was reminded of a hunt, and off he went with the clerk. The hunt extended to Waterston Ridge and Yalbury Wood, and it was not until the next morning that the locked-up couple were remembered. *LLI.* 8d

TOOTING. *In south London. The Hardys lived at 1 Arundel Terrace, Upper Tooting, from March 1878 to June 1881. The two poems in* Moments of Vision *present a mystery: the first relates to an incident that took place at Tooting (*Life, 124); *and an MS. note, 'January 1879', suggests that the second is related to it, though Purdy (197) states that 'elsewhere' Hardy identified the scene as Higher Bockhampton.*

> *SC.* 'Beyond the Last Lamp'; *MV.* 'A January Night', 'The Announcement'; *HS.* 'Snow in the Suburbs' (*originally 'Snow at Upper Tooting'*)

TOR-UPON-SEA. *Torquay, Devon.* Baptista Trewthen abandoned teaching at a nearby country school for a marriage of convenience.   *CM.* 11

TORKINGHAM, MR. The vicar of Welland.

> *TT.* ii–iv, ix, xi–xii, xiv, xxiii–xxvi, xli

TRACELEY, MISS. The principal of Melchester Training College (cf. WARDOUR CASTLE).   *JO.* III iii

TRAFALGAR, CAPE. *One of the Hardys was captain of the* Victory,

Admiral Nelson's flagship in the naval battle off Cape Trafalgar (1805).
                                                      TM. xxxv; *D.* (1) v i–iv

TRANTRIDGE. *Generally thought to be Pentridge, from its proximity to Cranborne, the 'Chaseborough' of Tess of the d'Urbervilles. There can be no doubt, however, that elsewhere it is Tarrant Hinton, on the main road from Salisbury to Blandford, and not far from the latter. It might seem more reasonable to assume that Hardy used the licence of fiction to locate Chaseborough much nearer to Trantridge than Cranborne is to Tarrant Hinton, rather than to deduce an inconsistency. Unfortunately, his map of Wessex does not support this view.*

At some distance from Trantridge, Alec d'Urberville lived with his blind mother at The Slopes.

George Crookhill and the deserter, whom he mistook for a farmer, and whose clothes and horse he stole, stayed the night at an inn in Trantridge.
                          TD. iv, v, viii–xii, xxvi, xxvii, xli, li; *LLI.* 8*h*

TREMBLE, THOMAS.   *HS.* 'Inscriptions for a Peal of Eight Bells'

TREMLETT, WILLIAM. He lived at Overcombe, and was a private in the Fencibles (a kind of Home Guard during the Napoleonic War). Some of the 'small beginnings of Fencible Tremlett's posterity', with representatives of the neighbouring houses of Cripplestraw, Comfort, Mitchell, Beach, and Snooks, followed Miller Loveday into his house to see his son Bob on his return from the merchant service.   *TM.* iv, v, xv, xxiii

TRENDLE, CONJUROR. He lived on Egdon Heath towards the end of the first quarter of the nineteenth century, and was a dealer in furze, turf, 'sharp sand', and other local products. As a conjurer or 'white wizard', he 'affected not to believe largely in his own powers'. When Farmer Lodge's wife Gertrude visited him to find why her left arm had withered, he emptied the white of an egg into a tumbler of water, and asked her what face or figure it suggested. She would not disclose to Rhoda Brook, who accompanied her, what she had learned. Finding no cure, Gertrude visited Trendle again, this time alone, and was told that there was no remedy but to lay the afflicted arm on the neck of a hanged man.

We hear of Conjuror Trendle's son 'in Egdon' (East Egdon?); 'he was nothing to what his father had been'.   *WT.* 4; *TD.* xxi

TREVES, SIR FREDERICK. *Treves was a Dorchester boy, who rose to be Sergeant-Surgeon to the Royal Family. He and Hardy were famous when they came to know each other. Both were Presidents of the Society of Dorset*

Men, Sir Frederick, 1904–7, and Hardy, 1907–9. *The last three lines of the original version of the poem* (*published in* The Times, *5 January 1924*) *appear on the* Treves *monument in Dorchester Cemetery* (*cf.* Life, *423–4*).

HS. 'In the Evening'

TREWE, ROBERT. Mrs Marchmill responded to his poetry so imaginatively that she thought she was in love with him. While she and her family occupied his rooms at Solentsea, he was staying on the Isle of Wight. They never met. He was a lonely, unhappy man, who yearned for womanly tenderness and devotion. His last book of verse was entitled 'Lyrics to a Woman Unknown'. They were inspired by the Idea (*which had affected the lives of Dr Fitzpiers and Jocelyn Pierston in different ways*) of the elusive, unattainable, perfect woman. A harsh review of his last volume was thought to have caused, in some measure, Robert Trewe's suicide at Mrs Hooper's. 'O, if he had only known of me!' cried Mrs Marchmill. (How surprised would he have been had he known that the child she conceived with his image in mind would bear his features!)

LLI. 1

TREWEN, MR. Bank-manager at St Launce's. The change of manner towards the Smiths when it was known that their son was famous is the subject of a humorous and satirical chapter. *PBE.* xxxvi

TREWTHEN, BAPTISTA. *Her name suggests a strict Nonconformist upbringing.*

In order to avoid teaching, she at last agreed to marry the elderly but rich Mr Heddegan, who lived near her parents at Giant's Town, St Maria's, one of the Isles of Lyonesse. At Pen-zephyr she met Charles Stow, a former sweetheart, who insisted on marrying her. He was drowned, and Baptista, on her honeymoon, lay between her two husbands, the one living, the other dead in the next room. When she told Mr Heddegan what had happened, he was relieved; he confessed that he was a widower, and had four girls. He had married her in order that she could attend to their education! *CM.* 11

TRICKSEY, KEEPER. A gamekeeper at Mellstock who generously emptied his powder-horn into a 'barm-bladder' to supply the heart for the effigy of Napoleon Bonaparte which was to be burnt at Durnover.

D. (3) v vi

TRINGHAM, PARSON. The antiquarian of Stagfoot Lane who discovered that John Durbeyfield was a descendant of the aristocratic d'Urbervilles. But for this revelation, it is most unlikely that Tess would ever have met

Alec d'Urberville. *TD*. i, iv, v, vii, xxxi, xxxv, l

TRISTRAM, SIR. The lover of Queen Iseult. *QC*

TROUTHAM, MR. The farmer at Marygreen who hired Jude to scare away the rooks in his cornfield (*by Winterdown Bottom*). He found that Jude had taken pity on the birds and let them eat his corn, gave him a thrashing (and sixpence for his day's work), and dismissed him. *JO*. i ii

TROY, FRANCIS. The son of a French governess and, presumably, of Lord Severn. Shortly before his birth, she married 'a poor medical man'. Troy was educated at Casterbridge Grammar School, and for a while was second clerk to a Casterbridge lawyer. Then he enlisted, and became a sergeant in the Eleventh Dragoon Guards. He fell in love with Fanny Robin, Bathsheba Everdene's servant. The regiment moved to Melchester, and then to a military station many miles north of Weatherbury. Here he would have married Fanny, who had followed him, had she not attended the wrong church. The dashing red sergeant came to Weatherbury; Bathsheba was infatuated with him, and married him in Bath. She discovered her mistake, and, by a strange sequence of events, his baseness towards Fanny Robin. Fanny's death revealed Troy's better nature temporarily. He was no longer the hero of his conceit, and left Bathsheba with a sense of his own ignominy. News spread that he had been drowned at Lulwind Cove; he had in fact been picked up by a vessel, on which he sailed to the United States, where he taught swordsmanship, fencing, gymnastics, and pugilism. He returned to England, and joined a travelling circus, taking the leading role in the play of *Dick Turpin*. At Greenhill Fair, he saw Bathsheba again, and decided to claim her as his wife. He made a dramatic entrance at Boldwood's Christmas party. When he seized Bathsheba, Boldwood, whose mind had long been unhinged by his jealous passion for Bathsheba, grabbed a gun, and shot his rival dead. *FMC*. vii ff.

TROYTON, MRS CHARLOTTE. A rich widow of West Endelstow, whom the widower Mr Swancourt married. She had an income of £3500 a year. On his marriage, after a brief stay in their new house in Kensington, Mr Swancourt and Elfride left the rectory to settle at The Crags, where Mrs Troyton had been living. It commanded a view of the (*Valency*) valley to the sea at Castle Boterel (*Boscastle*). She was Henry Knight's aunt. *PBE*. viii, xi, xii, xiv–xx, xxix, xl

TRUFAL. *Truro, Cornwall.* Baptista Trewthen and Charles Stow were married here by licence. *CM*. 11

Townsend, Melbury Osmond, scene of 'The Duke's Reappearance'. Sketch by Emma Hardy, 1887

Ridgeway, with Weymouth (Budmouth) and Portland in the distance. Sketch by Thomas Hardy for 'The Alarm' (WP). See Thomas Hardy ('Thomas the First') and Ridgeway

Fordington (Durnover) Church from the Green

TUBBER, ALDERMAN. A good-natured friend of Henchard, when the latter was Mayor of Casterbridge. *MC.* xvi, xxxvii

TUCKER, DAIRYMAN. The short-tempered father of Margery. *CM.* 12

TUCKER, MARGERY. The dairymaid of Silverthorn Dairy-house who fell under the spell of Baron von Xanten, and eventually married Jim Hayward. *CM.* 12

TULLIDGE, CORPORAL. Friend and neighbour of old Simon Burden. He was on 'the shady side of fifty', and hard of hearing; he wore a hat over a red cotton handkerchief, which was wound several times round his head to conceal the injuries sustained at the siege of Valenciennes 'in July, Ninety-three'. His left arm had been 'knocked to a pummy', and he took delight in twisting it to make the bones crunch for the satisfaction of his listeners. He and Simon mistook a light on the beach for a signal of the French invasion, and spread the alarm by lighting the beacon beside which they had watched night after night.
TM. iv, v, xii, xxvi, xxxv; *WP.* 'Valenciennes'

TUPCOMBE. Squire Dornell's confidential servant and travelling-companion. *GND.* 1

TWILLS, MRS. After leaving Casterbridge, Sergeant Troy's regiment went on to Melchester and then, presumably, to 'a certain town and military station, many miles north of Weatherbury'. Fanny Robin followed, and stayed with Mrs Twills in North Street. *FMC.* xi

TWINK, CHRISTOPHER. The master-thatcher who told the stories of 'Andrey Satchel and the Parson and Clerk' and 'Absent-Mindedness in a Parish Choir', while travelling to Longpuddle in Mr Burthen's carrier-van. Mr Burthen told Lackland that his tales would bear pruning.
LLI. 8, Introduction, prologues to (*d*) and (*f*), (*i*)

TWINKLEY. A parish near Endelstow with a strong dissenting element, of which Mr Swancourt strongly disapproved. However objectionable, it was 'nothing to how it is in the parish of Sinnerton'. *PBE.* iv

TWYCOTT, MR. The vicar of Gaymead who married Sophy, his servant, found that he had 'committed social suicide' in consequence, and therefore exchanged livings with an acquaintance in south London. Here he died, leaving his wife with a boy named Randolph. *LLI.* 2

TWYCOTT, RANDOLPH. His mother, the widow Sophy, spared no expense in his education. He proceeded from a public school to Oxford, but education 'ousted his humanity'. Even as a boy he was insufferable (to a detached observer), conscious of his mother's social inferiority, and of solecisms in her speech. She wished to marry an old admirer, Sam Hobson, who used to be the gardener at Gaymead Vicarage. The son opposed this to the end, and made her swear before cross and altar that she would never marry him. She pined away, and was buried at Aldbrickham. As the funeral procession passed, a middle-aged man stood in mourning by a large fruiterer's shop; it was Sam. From the mourning coach, 'a young smooth-shaven priest in a high waistcoat looked black as a cloud at the shopkeeper'. This was Randolph Twycott. *LLI.* 2

TWYCOTT, SOPHY. While tending the widower Mr Twycott at Gaymead Vicarage, she slipped as she was descending the stairs with a tray. She was never able to walk again, and for this reason decided she must leave. The vicar found he could not part with her, and married her. Their son was Randolph (q.v.). *LLI.* 2

'UNCLE JIM'. A stonemason whom Jude knew at Christminster.

JO. II vii

'UNCLE JOE'. A stonemason with whom Jude worked at Christminster. He attended the liquor celebration which Arabella and her father arranged to mark her second wedding to Jude. *JO.* II iv, vii; VI i, vii

UNITY. The cook at Endelstow Rectory. She married Martin Cannister, the sexton, and left Mr Swancourt's for the Welcome Home Inn, where she told the rival lovers, Stephen Smith and Henry Knight, how Elfride Swancourt had married Lord Luxellian and died. *PBE.* iv, vii, ix, xl

UPJOHN, JOHN. Melbury's 'regular' employee, in contradistinction to itinerant or seasonal workers in his timber business. He claimed to know the five 'climates' of courtship. *W.* iv, xix, xxii, xxix, xxxiv, xlviii

UPLANDTOWERS, LORD. *The fifth Earl of Shaftesbury, who married Barbara Webb in 1786.*

He lived at Knollingwood Hall and was intent upon marrying Barbara Grebe of Chene Manor, ten miles away along the new Melchester–Havenpool turnpike road. She eloped, however, with Edmond Willowes. When Lord Uplandtowers married Barbara, he found that she was still in love with her first husband, and that her devotion to him was perpetuated by a beautiful statue of him which had been sent from Pisa. The strategy he employed to cure her was as sadistic as it was effective, and typical of his 'cynical doggedness'. His severity on the bench towards poachers, smugglers, and turnip-stealers was notorious. *GND.* 2

UPWAY. *Upwey, between Dorchester and Weymouth.*

A boy played a tune for a handcuffed convict (*who was being taken back to Portland?*) until the train came in. Suddenly, 'with grimful glee', the convict sang: 'This life so free/Is the thing for me!'

LLE. 'At the Railway Station, Upway'

VAGG HOLLOW. *A marshy spot on the Fosse Way, the old Roman road south-west of Ilchester in south Somerset; cf. Life, 314.*

LLE. 'Vagg Hollow'

VALENCIENNES. See TULLIDGE.

VALLENCY. *The Valency river south of St Juliot, Cornwall; see map, 352*

SC. 'A Dream or No', 'A Death-Day Recalled'

VALLENS, JANE. See SATCHEL, ANDREW.

VANNICOCK, LIEUTENANT. He was stationed at Budmouth infantry barracks with his regiment, the —st Foot. When Mrs Maumbry took lodgings at Creston during the cholera plague at Durnover, she decided to play the part of heroine, with Vannicock as the hero, in a play that was produced to raise funds for the suffering people of Durnover. Later they decided to elope. See pp. 98–9.   *CM.* 1

VAR. *The British name for the Frome ('Froom') river. See pp. 335–6.*

VATT, ALDERMAN. He was a neighbour of Farfrae in Corn Street, Casterbridge, and called to announce the death of the Mayor, Dr Chalk-field. He offered to nominate Farfrae as his successor.   *MC.* xxxiv

VENICE. *Hardy visited Venice in April 1887; cf. Life, 192–5.*

Here Alicia and her father overtook Caroline. Charles de la Feste stayed at a hotel on the Riva degli Schiavoni *(where the Hardys stayed; Life, 195)*. The scene of most interest occurs in the Church of the Frari.

CM. 3; *TL.* 'The Flirt's Tragedy'

VENN, DIGGORY. *Professor J. O. Bailey suggests that the name Diggory comes from the expression 'to work like diggory', which he equates with 'to work like the devil'. This harmonizes with his Mephistophelean theme. As, however, Diggory is providential, the name may suggest merely that he is unresting in vigilance. Professor Bailey also suggests that Venn (not an uncommon name in south-west England) means 'fen'; Diggory appears like a will o' the wisp. His supernatural powers may be discounted; his dramatic dicing-luck is romantically probable in its setting, and has all the elements of the traditionally popular or ballad narrative.*

He had been a dairy-farmer, but for some reason (cf. I ix) he had become one of the fast-disappearing class of reddlemen who supplied farmers with reddle or 'redding' to mark their sheep for sales at fairs. Before the invasion scare had supplied Wessex mothers with the more terrifying image of Bonaparte, they had for generations threatened their children with 'The reddleman is coming for you!' No wonder little Jimmy Nunsuch was frightened at night when he saw Diggory Venn, blood-coloured from reddle dust, darning his stocking by the light of his stove. Diggory was gentlemanly, however. He had long been an admirer of Thomasin, but Mrs Yeobright had frowned on the marriage because reddlemen were shunned. He seems to appear uncannily whenever her need is critical. He brought Thomasin home after her ill-fated visit to Anglebury to marry Wildeve, and used various resources to keep Wildeve from Eustacia and bring about his marriage to Thomasin. Had he been more concerned for his own interests and less for Thomasin's, there is little doubt that he would have married her himself. The marriage accomplished, Diggory was seen no more in the neighbourhood for many months. He returned in time to win back the hundred guineas Wildeve had won from Christian Cantle and hand them, as he thought, to their rightful owner Thomasin. The fact that Clym did not receive his share immediately led to the misunderstanding between Mrs Yeobright and Eustacia, which was the initial cause of the final rift between Eustacia and Clym. When Eustacia's friendship with Wildeve was renewed, Venn took the law into his hands to keep Wildeve away from her. Thomasin suspected Wildeve's designs on the dark stormy night when Eustacia decided to escape to Paris via Budmouth. She took her baby to Blooms-End to consult Clym, and then decided to return home. On the way, she met Venn in the darkness, and he accompanied her, carrying Eustacia Wildeve. The movement of a light over Shadwater Weir convinced him that someone had fallen in, and he hurried off, just in time to save Clym, but too late to save Eustacia and Wildeve.

Hardy did not originally intend a happy ending to the novel. The reddleman was 'to have disappeared mysteriously from the heath, nobody knew whither'. He became a dairy-farmer at Stickleford, and married Thomasin.

RN. I, ii–iv, viii–xi; II vii, viii; III vii–viii; IV i, iii, iv; V ii, viii, ix; VI i–iv

VESPASIAN. *Romans under the Emperor Vespasian defeated the Durotriges at Mai-Dun. Archaeological discoveries bearing on this battle may be seen in the Dorset County Museum.* CM. 6; GND, conclusion

VI, LADY. A satirical sketch. HS. 'Lady Vi'

VICTORIA, QUEEN. *Written a few days after her death.*
PPP. 'V.R. 1819–1901'

VICTORY, THE. Captain Hardy's ship, and Admiral Nelson's flagship at the battle of Trafalgar. Serving on board were Bob Loveday and Jim Cornick. Anne Garland and Jim's father watched it from Portland Bill, as it sailed towards Plymouth with the frigate *Euryalus*.

> *TM.* xxxiii–xxxv, xxxvii–xxxix; *D.* (1) v i–iv

VILBERT, 'PHYSICIAN'. An itinerant quack-doctor whom Jude had seen selling a pot of coloured lard to an old woman as a certain cure for a bad leg, at the price of one guinea.

He agreed to obtain Latin and Greek grammar books for Jude if he advertised his celebrated pills, but promptly forgot his side of the bargain. At the Great Wessex Agricultural Show he sold Arabella a love philtre to win back Jude. He attended Jude when he was ill at Christminster, but his interest was mainly in Arabella. Arabella, with an eye to the main chance, went off with him to the regatta immediately after Jude's death.

> *JO.* I iv, ix, x; V v; VI x, xi

VINEY, DAIRYMAN. His farm lay in the direction of Blooms-End from Lower Mellstock. $\qquad$ *UGT.* IV iv; V i

VOSS, THOMAS. *His was the only real name in* Under the Greenwood Tree (Life, *92; cf. also 214*). *He was buried in Stinsford churchyard.*

He was left at the tranter's to prepare hot mead and bread and cheese for the Mellstock choir to partake of in the church belfry on their Christmas Eve rounds. $\qquad$ *UGT.* I iv, v; *LLE* 'Voices from Things Growing in a Churchyard'; *HS.* 'Winter Night in Woodland'

VYE, CAPTAIN. Grandfather of Eustacia, with whom he lived at Mistover Knap on Egdon Heath, after retiring from the Royal Navy. He was 'white-headed as a mountain'. When his supplies of rum were exhausted, he would go to the Quiet Woman, where he was often seen 'standing with his back to the fire, grog in hand', telling 'remarkable stories' of the 'seven years under the water-line of his ship', the *Triumph*, on which he had seen men 'with their legs and arms blown to Jericho' in the Napoleonic War. He could not understand why Eustacia married Clym Yeobright and – when the marriage failed – said he had always been against it.

> *RN.* I ii, vi, x, xi; II i, vii; V iv, v, vii–ix

VYE, EUSTACIA. *Hardy found the name Eustacia in Hutchins (i 456); see* Life, *117.*

A girl of nineteen, she lived with her grandfather Captain Vye at Mistover Knap. She was the daughter of a Corfiote bandmaster at Budmouth, and well educated. When her parents died she was taken from this fashionable seaside resort to live a lonely life on Egdon, from the boredom of which there was little escape but reading and dreams of a glamorous life at Budmouth or elsewhere. Wildeve was her one real distraction, and it is hardly surprising that she used the bonfire signal again to renew their meetings when she heard he had returned unmarried from Anglebury.

She was a voluptuous creature; a whole winter did not contain darkness enough to form the shadow of her hair; her eyes were 'pagan' and 'full of nocturnal mysteries'. She was 'the raw material of a divinity'. The darkness in which she is introduced on Rainbarrow is in harmony with her lot. Egdon was her Hades; the bonfire, a parallel to her Promethean 'rebelliousness'. Her disposition, however, was to 'let events fall out as they might sooner than wrestle hard to direct them'. The first sound we hear from her is 'a lengthened sighing' that harmonizes with the sounds of the heath. She yearned for sunny afternoons on an esplanade, with military bands, officers, and gallants. She idealized Wildeve 'for want of a better object'. 'Her high gods were William the Conqueror, Strafford, and Napoleon Buonaparte.' The telescope and hour-glass which she often carried suggest 'the desire of something afar', and the sense that the time for enjoyment is slipping away. Clym's return from Paris was 'like a man coming from heaven'. When he spoke to her, her perfervid imagination produced 'a cycle of visions'. The captain suggested that reading had filled her head with too much 'romantic nonsense'. She wanted 'life – music, poetry, passion, war, and all the beating and pulsing that is going on in the great arteries of the world'. In a moment of tragic decision, shortly before her death, she regretted that Wildeve was not Saul or Bonaparte! Before Clym's return to his native heath, she lived in a wilderness, and desired love 'as one in a desert would be thankful for brackish water'. All that Egdon offered was the 'pond' associated with Wildeve. When she realized that Clym did not intend to return to Paris, her moon of love was eclipsed.

Happiness in marriage with him – when the July sun fired the crimson heather to scarlet, and 'the heath was gorgeous' – did not last long. She tired of the dullness of life with a man who by turns studied and took to furze-cutting for a living, and soon renewed her meetings with Wildeve. She had resented what seemed to her the ignoble implications of Mrs Yeobright's asking whether she had received money from Wildeve, and swore she would never see her again. Wildeve came with the intention of telling her of the fortune he had unexpectedly inherited, just when Mrs Yeobright was reaching Alderworth to seek a reconciliation with Clym and Eustacia. Hearing Clym utter 'Mother', Eustacia assumed he had opened the door to her, and promptly saw Wildeve out another way. But Clym, worried about the rift with his mother, had been talking in his sleep. Mrs Yeobright went away and died on the return journey, completely exhausted and bitter at heart. She had seen Clym enter the house ahead of her and Eustacia look out at the window when she knocked.

It was while Clym was recovering from the illness consequent on his mother's death and his sense of guilt that his suspicions were awakened against Eustacia. His inquiries led him to think that she was both a 'murderess' and adulteress. Eustacia bore his false accusations and fury with dignity and without any attempt at self-exoneration, but at last broke down and left him. She returned to her grandfather's and was tempted to think of suicide when she saw his pistols. Charley, suspecting her intention, hid them. She recovered, and decided to take advantage of Wildeve's offer to help her to Paris. The night she chose for her departure was wild, dark, and stormy. Eustacia was lost on the heath, and in great distress as she tried to make her way to her rendezvous. She fell into the swirling flood below Shadwater Weir and was drowned. *Many readers have assumed that she committed suicide, and Clym, in his self-condemnation for the death of the two women he had loved, did not appear to rule out the possibility. Hardy's clues indicate that Eustacia quickly recovered from the temptation which came to her at her grandfather's, that she was looking forward to her escape from Egdon, and that when she found that resistance was useless in the vortex of the pool, she resigned herself to fate, as was customary with her. She lay 'still in death. . . . The expression of her finely carved mouth was pleasant. . . . Eternal rigidity had seized upon it in a momentary transition between fervour and resignation.'* RN

WACE, MRS. A widow who lived in a village near Tor-upon-Sea. She let rooms to the young teacher Baptista Trewthen. *CM*. 11

WADDON VALE. *South of the chalk hills which run west from Ridgeway to Portisham.* Seen on a gloomy day. *PPP.* 'The Lacking Sense'

WAKE, MRS. The wife of the farmer who tenanted Froom-Everard House and allowed Christine to keep what rooms she wanted. She helped to prepare the supper on the eve of Christine's expected wedding to Nicholas Long. *CM.* 2

WALCHEREN. '*A marshy island at the mouth of the Scheldt.*' *A brief scene fully evokes the tragic waste of an ill-judged and futile military enterprise.* *D.* (2) IV viii

WALKINGHAME. *The author of the arithmetic book which Hardy used at his first school* (Life, *16*).

The eight books which constituted Gabriel Oak's library included Walkinghame, *Paradise Lost, The Pilgrim's Progress,* and *Robinson Crusoe.* *FMC.* viii; *MV.* 'He Revisits his First School'

WALLIS, SUSAN. She called very late one night at Mrs Lizzy Newberry's for mustard 'to make a plaster with, as her father was taken very ill on the chest'. *WT.* 7

WARBORNE. *Wimborne Minster, north of Poole, See pp. 510–11.*

The railway station plays a part of some importance in *Two on a Tower.* Swithin St Cleeve was educated at Warborne Grammar School.

Lord Uplandtowers passed through Warborne on his way from Knollingwood Hall to attend a ball at Chene Manor, the home of Barbara Grebe. *TT.* i, xvi, xviii–xx, xxiii, xxviii, xxxii, xxxvii–xxxix, xli; *GND.* 2

WARDLAW, MR. Miss Power's London lawyer. *L.* V xiii, xiv; VI i, iii

WARDOUR CASTLE. *Five miles north-east of Shaftesbury.*

Sue went to the Normal School or Training College for teachers at Melchester, after serving as a pupil-teacher with Mr Phillotson at Lumsdon; and Jude, who was now studying to enter the Church, followed her. He proposed an excursion to Wardour Castle and Fonthill. Sue chose Wardour Castle because it was Corinthian in style. Jude was very much interested in 'the devotional pictures by Del Sarto, Guido Reni, Spagnoletto, Sassoferrato, Carlo Dolci, and others'; Sue was more interested in a Lely or Reynolds. They decided to walk across 'the high country to the north' and return to Melchester from another station, but they missed the train, and were compelled to stay at a shepherd's cottage for the night. For this misdemeanour Sue was condemned to solitary confinement at college for a week. She escaped through the window, struggled through the deep river at the back of the Normal School, and took refuge at Jude's lodgings. *JO.* III ii, iii

WARM'ELL CROSS. *Cross-roads, where the road from Warmwell meets the old turnpike road from Dorchester to Wareham (cf.* MAX GATE).

Here the Budmouth Customs officers, who were conveying the smuggled liquor they had seized at Nether-Moynton, were set upon in the twilight and tied to trees.

WT. 7; *LLE*. 'At Lulworth Cove a Century Back'

WARREN'S MALTHOUSE. *An old type of 'public house' (which made its own brew) at Puddletown. It has long since disappeared. It was probably named after its first owner.*

The building was simple in structure, consisting of one stone-flagged room with a kiln and a thatched roof surmounted by a louvred wooden lantern, from which the vapour caused by heating the liquor escaped. Its owner or tenant, the ancient maltster, often slept there. (It was the meeting-place for the local gossips.) Here Gabriel Oak met him, his son Jacob Smallbury ('a young man about sixty-five'), his grandson William Smallbury ('a child of forty, or thereabouts'), and several others, mainly labourers on Bathsheba's farm. With them, he drank cider from the 'God-forgive-me', a tall two-handled mug, cracked, charred, and encrusted on the outside with ashes 'accidentally wetted with cider and baked hard'. *FMC*. vii, viii, xv

WARWICK STREET. The London address of the architect Edward Springrove. *DR*. xvi 3

WATERLOO. *Hardy talked to many veterans of the battle of Waterloo, 1815; cf. footnotes to D. (3) VII v, viii, and p. 284. He made two visits to the battlefield (Life, 110, 284), and on each occasion spent time in Brussels trying to locate the scene of the Duchess of Richmond's ball on the eve of the battle. RN*. III i *(autobiographical?)*; *TM*. xii; *L*. v ix; *CM*. 4; *WP*. 'The Peasant's Confession'; *D*. (3) VI, VII

WATERLOO STATION, LONDON. *The description of the train journey (LLI. 7) from Dorchester to Waterloo Station is probably based on Hardy's recollections of a similar journey about 1848 (Life, 17). Third-class passengers travelled in 'open trucks'. DR*. xvi 4; *HE*. xxv; *LLI*. 5, 7

WATERSTON RIDGE. *The highest point along the Lane of Slyre (p. 472), overlooking the Piddle valley. LLI*. 8d; *TL*. 'The Revisitation'

WAYWARD, JOHN. A joiner presented his wife with a workbox, which he had made from a piece of oak left over from John Wayward's coffin. When he told her, she turned pale, as if she had not only known John but also the cause of his death. *SC*. 'The Workbox'

WAYWOOD, JOHN. *TL*. 'At Casterbridge Fair' (v)

WEATHERBURY. *Puddletown, about five miles north-east of Dorchester. It takes its name from Weatherbury or Weatherby Castle, further east, which suggested the setting for* Two on a Tower *(cf.* RINGS-HILL SPEER

503

and WP. 'My Cicely'). For the Stinsford, Puddletown, and Maiden Newton choirs, see Life, 10. Weatherbury is the setting for the main action of Far from the Madding Crowd. *'Warren's Malthouse' disappeared many years ago. Bathsheba's house is drawn to some extent from Waterston House; and that of the great barn at Weatherbury Upper Farm from the tithe-barn at Cerne Abbas (see* ABBOT'S CERNEL *and plates facing pp. 79, 110, 111). The original of Boldwood's farm is Druce Farm; the house was built in 1867. The stocks stood in the square near St Mary's Church. The gargoyles, the fine Jacobean gallery where the choir used to play, and the chapel containing effigies of the Martins of Athelhampton are the most interesting features of the church. Hardy's cousin, Tryphena Sparks, lived in the village, near 'Mill-tail-Shallow' (cf. HS 'At the Mill').*

UGT. I i (*cf. Life, 193*), iv; V i; *FMC*; *RN.* I iii ('the cross-legged soldier that have had his arm knocked away by the school-children'; *cf. LLE.* 'The Children and Sir Name-less'), V iv; *MC.* ix, xxxviii–xl, xlv; *TD.* xvi, xxxvii; *LLI.* 8*b*; *WP.* 'In a Eweleaze near Weatherbury' (*probably recalling Tryphena Sparks; see p. 435–40*); *LLE.* 'The Country Wedding'; *HS.* 'A Last Journey'; *WW.* 'In Weatherbury Stocks'. (For *LLI.* 8*f*, see pp. 393, 394.)

WEEDY, GAD. Farmer Springrove's assistant, and a bell-ringer at Carriford church. *DR.* viii 3, Sequel

WEIR HOUSE, THE. A little square building, near some hatches and a weir on Sandbourne Heath, where two sportsmen were sheltering one wet afternoon when they saw Picotee walking along the road in the hope of meeting Mr Julian again. One of the men was Mr Ladywell, who was a guest at Wyndway House. *HE.* iii

WELLAND. *Although Hardy's map of Wessex indicates that the village is located in or near Charborough Park, five miles west of Wimborne Minster, the setting for* Two on a Tower *is composite, and the village must be regarded as imaginary. The tower is not that of Charborough Park, or in the same direction. To reach it, Lady Constantine left the park, crossed the old Melchester Road, and walked across a field to Rings-Hill. The Speer or tower was suggested by the obelisk (or 'spire') on the wooded top of Weatherbury Castle, a hill, the upper part of which is ringed with earth-works, seven miles to the west; see plate facing p. 207.*

The village was so scattered that separate choir-practices were held in homes in different parts of the parish, e.g. old Mrs Martin's at Welland

Bottom, below Rings-Hill, The church was near Welland House, the residence of Lady Constantine. Old village cottages had been demolished to extend the park, leaving the church 'to stand there alone, like a standard without an army' (*much as Stinsford Church is isolated from its parishioners by Kingston Park. The demolition of the village refers to Charborough Park, however; cf. Hutchins, iii 497.*)   *TT*

WELLBRIDGE. *Wool, formerly known as Woolbridge, about ten miles east of Dorchester on the road to Wareham. The railway runs on the southern side of the river Frome. On the northern side, across the five-arched Elizabethan stone bridge, stands the 'Caroline' manor-house which belonged to the Turberville family. Replicas of the fading portraits of the two Turberville ladies may be seen in the County Museum at Dorchester. A quarter of a mile or so from the manor-house are the remains of Bindon Abbey, where the open stone coffin may be seen by the north wall of the chancel. The flour-mill may be seen through the trees by the stream on the northern side of the Abbey site. See plates facing pp. 366, 367.*

Tess and Angel were to have spent their honeymoon at the manor-house. They stayed there a short while, but Angel's love was reduced to ashes by her revelation of the past, after he had confessed his 'fall'. He could not forgive her as she forgave him. His love was dead, as is reflected in the sleep-walking scene, in which he carries her and lays her in the open stone coffin.   *TD.* i, xxx, xxxii, xxxiv–xxxvii

'WESSEX'. *Hardy's dog (cf. Life, 434–5).*

HS. 'A Popular Personage at Home'; *WW.* 'Dead "Wessex" the Dog to the Household'

WESSEX, EARL OF. The first Earl and Countess of Wessex are the subject of the first story in *A Group of Noble Dames*. Their successors are mentioned in the fourth. The family acquired extensive property. 'Yalbury Wood', where Geoffrey Day was head gamekeeper, is described as one of his 'outlying estates' (see DORNELL, BETTY and SUSAN). A hotel at Sherton Abbas was named after one of the Earls.   *UGT.* II vi,
W. xxv, xxxviii, xlvii, xlviii; *GND.* 1, 4; *TD.* xix

WESSEX FIELD AND ANTIQUARIAN CLUB, A. *Hardy became a member of the Dorset Natural History and Antiquarian Field Club while he was living at Wimborne (Blunden). The County Museum at Dorchester, which is the setting for their imaginary conference, was opened in 1884.*

It held a two-day conference in a town museum. On the afternoon of the first day, rain made a proposed excursion impossible, and the historian produced the manuscript of 'The First Countess of Wessex' and read it. The old surgeon then related 'Barbara of the House of Grebe', which he thought 'perhaps a little too professional'. The story suggested that of 'The Marchioness of Stonehenge' to the rural dean, who began with a recommendation of Robert South's sermons; this led the sentimental member to relate the story which is entitled 'Lady Mottisfont', though the child Dorothy emerges as the central point of interest. This story closed the afternoon session.

After dinner, several members met to hear more stories. The churchwarden, 'now thoroughly primed', told the story of Lady Icenway. This suggested that of Squire Petrick's lady (related by the retired crimson-faced maltster), and so one story led to another. The colonel told a story of the Civil War ('Anna, Lady Baxby'); the man of family, a story relating to several distinguished families ('The Lady Penelope'); the quiet gentleman, 'The Duchess of Hamptonshire'; and the Spark, 'The Honourable Laura'. *GND*

WESTCOMBE. *The town is mentioned to underline the class differences between Geraldine Allenville and Egbert Mayne.* She could not understand why he thought it took about two hours to reach it; he had assumed she meant by foot. The period was 1848. *ILH*. 1 7

WESTERN GLORY, THE. The ship on which Alwyn Hill sailed from Plymouth to America. He did not know that Emmeline, the Duchess of Hamptonshire, with whom he had been in love, was also on board, and that she had died at sea and he had officiated at the funeral, until he returned to England to see her. *GND*. 9

WESTMINSTER, DEAN OF. He refused the plea, signed by Hardy and other writers and statesmen, that a commemorative tablet to Byron be placed in Poets' Corner on the centenary of his death (1924).

HS. 'A Refusal'

WEYDON-PRIORS. *Weyhill, west of Andover in Hampshire, famous for its centuries-old fair, which was held mainly for the selling of sheep. By tradition, the principal day of the fair falls on, or as near as possible to 10 October. In* The Mayor of Casterbridge *it is held in September.*

It was here, after drinking heavily at the tent of the furmity-seller, Mrs Goodenough, that Henchard sold his wife for five guineas to Newson.

Lord Icenway, whose main interests were field-sports, had fortunately gone 'to do a little cocking and ratting out by Weydon Priors' when Lady Icenway returned from Southampton, where she had met Anderling.

506

MC. i–iii, xxviii, xliv; *GND.* 5; *HS.* 'A Last Journey'

WEYMOUTH. *While Hardy was at Weymouth, working for Mr Crick-may, from the summer of 1869 to February 1870, he wrote several poems which have Weymouth for their setting. 'The Contretemps' appears to have been written, or re-written, much later.* TL. 'Her Father', 'At Waking', 'The Dawn after the Dance' (cf. 'Her Father'); *MV.* 'At a Seaside Town in 1869' (*see* Life, *63*); *LLE.* 'The Contretemps'; *HS.* 'On the Esplanade', 'Singing Lovers' (*MS. 'in 1869'*), 'The Harbour Bridge'

Weymouth is mentioned in Hardy's first short story, 'Destiny and a Blue Cloak', and in 'Great Things'. It is 'the town by the sea' in 'Molly Gone'. See BUDMOUTH. *DBC; MV.* 'Great Things', Molly Gone'

WHEELER, CAPTAIN. When Alwyn Hill returned to England and heard that the former Duchess of Hamptonshire had run away with the curate (himself) and sailed to America, he went to Plymouth to find out what had happened to her. He saw Captain Wheeler, who had commanded the *Western Glory*, on which he had sailed to Boston. *GND.* 9

WHERRYBORNE. Alicia's father was the rector of Wherryborne. When Charles de la Feste, who had become engaged to Alicia's sister Caroline while she was staying at Versailles, visited the rectory, he fell in love with Alicia. They walked in Wherryborne Wood. After marrying Caroline, for the sake of honour, Charles drowned himself in the pool by a weir in the nearby meadows. (*The setting is reminiscent of the Frome Valley.*) *CM.* 3

WHITE HORSE, THE. An equestrian figure of George III cut out on the chalk hill above Overcombe. It was said to cover an acre. The trumpet-major took Ann to see 'forty navvies at work removing the dark sod so as to lay bare the chalk beneath'. John, out of deference to the prior claims of his brother Bob – who was now a free man again, after giving up his Caroline – did not display his former ardour, and allowed Anne to pace up and down the figure while he 'remained all the time in a melancholy attitude within the rowel of his Majesty's right spur'. *It seems an anachronism for Hardy to write about 'White Horse Hill' earlier in the novel. See plate facing p. 175.* TM. xxxvii–xxxviii (cf. viii)

WHITESHEET. *The hill to the west of Maiden Newton, on the main Crewkerne road which passes over Toller Down.* MV. 'Molly Gone'

WHITING, JOHN. *His actual surname; cf. Evelyn Hardy,* Hardy's Notebooks, *34*.

The old beacon-keeper at Rainbarrows at the time when the French were expected to land (August 1805).   *D.* (1) II v

WHIT'SHEET HILL. Gusts blow from *White Sheet Hill, above Bea-minster*, over Toller Down to Benvill Lane.   *TL.* 'The Homecoming'

WHITTLE, ABEL. A lean 'round-shouldered, blinking young man of nineteen or twenty, whose mouth fell ajar at the slightest provocation, seemingly because there was no chin to support it'. He worked for Henchard, who kept his old mother provided with coals and snuff throughout the winter. Unfortunately, he was in the habit of oversleeping. In his fury that Whittle had not arrived punctually at four o'clock one morning to accompany his wagons to Blackmoor Vale, Henchard hauled him out of bed and would have made him travel without his breeches if Farfrae had not resisted such madness. When Farfrae took over Henchard's business, Whittle stayed on, although he had to work harder and was paid a shilling a week less. It was fear of Henchard, he said, that had made his hair so thin. Whittle remembered Henchard's kindness to his mother, and looked at the ex-mayor with pitying eyes when he saw him working for Farfrae. He watched him leave Caster-bridge on the night of Elizabeth-Jane's wedding, thought he looked 'low and faltering', and insisted on accompanying him. He attended Henchard until his death. Henchard regarded him as a fool, but (*like the fool in* King Lear) he was the only one to help his master in his last distress. *His account of Henchard's death provides a tragic ending which is perhaps the most moving in all Hardy's fiction. (It is worth noting that the two most moving scenes in the book are expressed in an apparently artless way by unlettered people; the other is that of the death of Susan Henchard as narrated by Mother Cuxsom.)*

MC. xv, xxxi, xxxii, xxxiii, xxxviii–xxxix, xlv

WILDEVE, DAMON. An engineer who had been employed at Bud-mouth before becoming landlord of the Quiet Woman Inn on the margin of Egdon Heath. 'Altogether he was one in whom no man would have seen anything to admire, and in whom no woman would have seen anything to dislike' (Mrs Yeobright was an exception). His move-ment was 'the pantomimic expression of a lady-killing career'. He ad-mitted his 'inflammability', and said that it was responsible for his change of occupation from engineering to innkeeping. He had been friendly with Eustacia Vye, and Mrs Yeobright's dislike of him was so strong that she objected in church to his marriage with her niece Thomasin. Ultimately she consented, and Wildeve arranged to be married by licence at Budmouth. Thomasin preferred a place where she was not known. They therefore went to Anglebury, only to discover that the licence was not valid there. Eustacia's bonfire, which had been the signal for a rendezvous the previous year, was interpreted as another by Wildeve, and he responded; but Clym's return from Paris revived Eustacia's hopes of escaping from the tedium of Egdon Heath to the gay life of a city. Her consequent indifference, coupled with hints from Mrs Yeobright that her niece had another eligible suitor (Diggory Venn), precipitated Wildeve's marriage with Thomasin. When Eustacia realized after marrying Clym that her dream was not likely to be fulfilled, she was drawn to Wildeve again. His association with her was the mainspring of tragic misunderstandings and the catastrophe set in motion by Mrs Yeobright's death. When Eustacia left her husband she asked Wildeve to help by taking her to Budmouth on her way to Paris. There can be no doubt that, had Eustacia consented, he would have deserted Thomasin in the hope of living with her in Paris. His attempt to save Eustacia, when all was in readiness for flight on the dark and stormy night of 6 November, a year and a day after the opening of the story, led to his death. He had inherited a fortune from his uncle in Wisconsin, and had intended to settle in Casterbridge with Thomasin. 'To be yearning for the difficult, to be weary of that offered; to care for the remote, to dislike the near; it was Wildeve's nature always. This is the true mark of the man of sentiment. . . . He might have been called the Rousseau of Egdon.'

> *RN.* I, iii–vii, ix–xi; II i, ii, v–viii; III iii, vi–viii; IV i, iii, iv, vi, viii; V i–iii, v–ix

WILDEVE, EUSTACIA CLEMENTINE. The daughter of Damon Wildeve and Thomasin. On the night of 6 November, when Wildeve was preparing to drive Eustacia to Budmouth, Thomasin carried the child through the storm to Blooms-End, to find out from Clym where Eustacia was. Clym's suspicions were aroused, and he left. Thomasin, in her anxiety to know what was happening, decided to return with her infant to the Quiet Woman Inn. She was helped on the way by Diggory Venn.

The news that a girl had been born to Thomasin and that her name was to be Eustacia reached Clym just after his wife Eustacia left him.

> *RN.* V iii, v, viii; VI i, ii, iii, iv

WILDWAY, JOHN. A shoemaker who had courted Mrs Penny before she met Mr Penny – also a shoemaker – one Midsummer Eve. *UGT.* I viii

WILKINS, MR. Charlotte's father, Sir William de Stancy, had sold Stancy Castle to Mr Wilkins. He became blind soon after buying it, and never lived there. As a result, the castle and its pictures suffered neglect. *L.* I iv

WILLIAM. (1) A boy employed by the landlord of the Prospect Hotel. When visitors arrived unexpectedly out of season, he came in from the yard, 'scrubbed himself up, dragged his disused jacket from its box, polished the buttons with his sleeve, and appeared civilized in the hall'. He is later referred to as 'the hundred plated buttons'. *GND.* 10

(2) Commander of the Parliamentarian army besieging Sherton Castle, which was held by his sister, Lady Digby, in the absence of her husband, who was raising forces for the king. William urged her to leave, but she refused. He had to withdraw when General Lord Baxby's forces appeared. *GND.* 7

WILLIAMS, MRS. Comparatively a stranger at Marygreen. She shopped at Miss Fawley's. *JO.* I ii

WILLOWES, EDMOND. A handsome young man, with whom Barbara Grebe eloped. Though the match was a disappointing one for them, her parents soon grew reconciled to it, and provided funds for him to travel in Italy with a tutor. He was horribly burnt and disfigured in a fire at a theatre in Venice. On his return, Barbara was so appalled by his appearance that he decided to go abroad in the hope that she would accept him at the end of a year. He died six months later. *GND.* 2

WILLS, BILLY. A Casterbridge glazier, who often spent his evenings at the Three Mariners ('as every passer knew') with Smart the shoemaker, Buzzford the general dealer, 'and others of a secondary set of worthies', of a grade somewhat below that of the diners at the King's Arms'. *MC.* vi, viii, xliii

WILSON. One for whom beauty was not merely physical and subject to time. Whatever friends might think, or hint, about Fanny as she aged, she was still beautiful to him. (*The poem was suggested by an epigram of Strato in J. W. Mackail's* Select Epigrams from the Greek Anthology.) *WW.* 'Faithful Wilson'

WILTON, PARSON. In a dispute with Mr Torkingham, Haymoss (Amos) Fry said that he had known music ever since Luke Sneap broke his new fiddle bow at Parson Wilton's wedding, when the choir sang 'His wife, like a fair fertile vine, her lovely fruit shall bring', and the young bride turned as red as a rose. *TT.* ii

WIMBORNE MINSTER. *Hardy lived in this small ancient town (the 'Warborne' of his fiction) from 1881 to 1883. 'The Levelled Churchyard' was written in 1882, and the MS. adds* '(W — e Minster)' – *Purdy, 115; cf. Hardy's* 'Memories of Church Restoration'.

PPP. 'The Levelled Churchyard'; *MV.* 'Copying Architecture in an Old Minster', 'The Pedestrian' (*Hardy identified the scene as Coll-Hill, i.e. Cole Hill, near Wimborne*); *HS.* 'Bags of Meat' (*MS. 'Wimborne'*)

WINDWHISTLE INN, THE. *Hardy's note explains why he found it 'high and dry'. It stands on a high spine of hills west of Crewkerne.*

TL. 'A Trampwoman's Tragedy'

WINDY BEAK. The second cliff in height to 'the Cliff without a Name' (cf. BEENY) along the coast near Endelstow.

Here Elfride lost the ear-ring when she was with Stephen Smith. It was found during her next visit with the jealous and prying Henry Knight. PBE. vii, xxxi

WINGREEN. *A high hill, south-east of Shaftesbury, in the chalk downs north of Cranborne Chase. To the west lies Melbury Down. The Manor Court is likely to have been suggested by Rushmore, near Tollard Royal, which Hardy visited in 1895* (Life, 269). *Nearby is a view up the 'nether Coomb' to Wingreen.* TD. viii; *TL.* 'The Vampirine Fair'

WINTER, JACK. The rivalry in good looks of two unmarried Longpuddle women was not decreased when one won Mr Winter from the other and married him. Years later, the disappointed rival married Mr Palmley. Each wife was left a widow with an only son. Mrs Winter was well-off; and Mrs Palmley was poor, and therefore allowed Mrs Winter to take charge of her boy. Unfortunately he was terrified by 'something' that 'came out from behind a tree' in Yalbury Wood, lost his reason, and died. Mrs Palmley did not forgive Mrs Winter.

Soon afterwards Mrs Palmley was joined by her niece Harriet, an educated girl from Exonbury with whom Jack Winter fell in love. While superintending a farm at Monksbury, he corresponded with her. She was proud; his illiteracy irritated her; and soon she rejected him. Jack lost his ambition, returned home, and asked Harriet to return his letters. She refused. He broke into Mrs Palmley's house one night, and carried away the workbox in which he knew they were kept. Next morning he started burning the letters, but when he reached the last he found that the box contained several guineas. He had been watched, however, by two constables, and was arrested. At the trial, Harriet, who could have saved him, was absent. Mrs Palmley gave evidence. Jack Winter was convicted, and hanged at Casterbridge. *For some of the details of the execution, see the story told Hardy by his father: Newman Flower, Just* as it Happened *(Cassell, 1950) p. 92.* LLI. 8g

WINTERBORNE, GILES. *Giles and Grace are common names in the pedigree of the Strangways family, who for centuries lived at Melbury House, near the Hintock country; see* KING'S HINTOCK COURT.

He lived at Little Hintock, and his main business was in the apple and cider trade. When he was free, he helped Melbury, planting trees or preparing timber for the market. Marty South loved him silently, but he was in love with Grace Melbury. Her father would have promoted their marriage but for his qualms about its suitability for a daughter who had been expensively educated. When Giles lost his house and Fitzpiers began to court Grace, all Melbury's resolutions to right the wrong he had done Winterborne's father crumbled, so dazzling was the lure of aristocratic connections. Giles felt the loss of Grace deeply, but smothered his emotions. 'He was one of those silent, unobtrusive beings who want little from others in the way of favour or condescension'; 'like Hamlet's friend', *and Hardy's father* (Life, *248*), he bore himself 'As one, in suffering all, that suffers nothing'. Grace's unhappy marriage made her appreciate more than ever before the honesty, goodness, manliness, tenderness, and devotion which he had manifested towards her from her youth up. For her they existed now only in the breasts of 'unvarnished men' such as he. Unlike Grace and her father, he took nothing for granted when they were optimistic about her divorce, and refused to encourage Grace's hopes of marriage with him. *Like Hardy, he had learned that life offers, to deny.* 'When the sun shines flat on the north front of Sherton Abbey – that's when my happiness will come to me!' Exposure to the elements and lack of amenities at One-Chimney Hut had weakened Giles physically. By relinquishing his cottage for her comfort, when she fled from Fitzpiers, he sacrificed his life. 'The purity of his nature, his freedom from the grosser passions, his scrupulous delicacy, had never been fully understood by Grace till this strange self-sacrifice in lonely juxtaposition to her own person was revealed.' After his death, 'she found that she had never understood Giles as Marty had done. Marty South alone, of all the women in Hintock and the world, had approximated to Winterborne's level of intelligent intercourse with Nature.' It was Marty alone who remained true to him at the end: 'But no, no, my love, I can never forget 'ee; for you was a good man, and did good things!' *W*

WINTONCESTER. *Winchester.*

The Bishop officiated at the wedding of Sir Ashley Mottisfont and Philippa Okehall in Wintoncester Cathedral. Some interesting reflections, characteristic of the speaker, are made on the Cathedral by the sentimental member of the club in introducing his story.

Tess was executed at the County Gaol.

Charles Raye was educated at Wintoncester School.

The two schoolmasters, Phillotson and Gillingham, had been friends at school and at Wintoncester Training College.

Hermann Lea stated that 'At an Inn' was written at the George Inn, Winchester; Purdy, that the poem 'is, perhaps, to be associated with Mrs Henniker' (see pp. 364-5). GND. 4; TD. lix; LLI. 5; JO. IV iv, *WP.* 'At an Inn'; *SC.* 'The Abbey Mason' (Winton)

WINWOOD, OSWALD. The young man who mistook Agatha Pollin for Frances Lovill, lost his heart to her, went to India, and came back to marry her, only to find that he had lost her. Unknown to him, Frances had secured her revenge. *DBC*

WOODSFORD CASTLE. *A fourteenth-century manor house, which has been carefully restored (cf. Life, 27), and is now a farm-house. It stands by the main road, two miles east of West Stafford, and not far from 'Shadwater Weir'. What truth there is in Hardy's story is not known.*

LLE. 'A Sound in the Night'

WOODWELL, MR. *'Among the few portraits of actual persons in Hardy's novels, that of the Baptist minister in* A Laodicean *is one – being a recognizable drawing of Perkins the father as he appeared to Hardy at this time, though the incidents are invented.' See* Life, 29–30.

Baptist minister at the chapel built by Paula's father near Sleeping-Green. He was a preacher of fiery eloquence and conviction, with a devastating battery of texts against pro-Paedobaptist arguments. When Paula refused to follow her deceased father's wishes that she should submit herself to public Baptist immersion, he preached a spontaneous sermon on the Laodicean temperament, 'all the more vigorous perhaps from the limitation of mind and language under which the speaker laboured'. Paula did not take offence, for he was a kindly man, and very charitable to the poor. Another example of 'the fervid minister's rhetoric' was given on the Sunday evening after Mrs Havill's death; Mr Havill was so overcome by remorse for his dishonesty in preparing his plans for the additions to Stancy Castle that he resigned the commission immediately. Mr Woodwell disapproved of theatricals, and was astonished that Paula Power could 'associate with people who show contempt for their Maker's intentions by flippantly assuming other characters than those in which He created them'.   *L* I ii, vi–viii, xii; III iv, xi; VI v

WOODYATES INN. *Once a splendid coach-inn, eleven miles west of Salisbury on the London–Dorchester–Weymouth road* (*cf.* Life, *388*). *The red-brick buildings, including the stables around the coach-yard, were to be seen until 1967, when the site was cleared.*

George III was due to change horses here on his way to Weymouth.

TM. xi; *LLI.* 8*h*

WOOLFREY, MR. A draper in High Street, Casterbridge, from whom Henchard made sundry purchases to welcome the Royal visitor.

MC. xxxvii

WORM, WILLIAM. Mr Swancourt's servant; 'a poor wambling man', who had noises in his head 'like people frying fish'. He left the parson to take charge of a turnpike gate; as a result, he saw less of his friends, 'coming to church o' Sundays not being my duty now, as 'twas in a parson's family, you see'.

His wife Barbara was about twice his size; she was 'a wide-faced, comfortable-looking woman, with a wart upon her cheek, bearing a small tuft of hair in its centre'.   *PBE.* ii, iv, vii, xxiii, xxvi

WYGMORE, ABBOT. *The abbot who was responsible* (*according to tradition*) *for the new style of Gothic architecture, the Perpendicular, in the south transept of Gloucester Cathedral. He died in 1337. Abbots Staunton and Horton succeeded him.*   *SC.* 'The Abbey Mason'

WYKEHAM CHAMBERS. *In Spring Gardens, London.*

When Miss Aldclyffe was trying to secure the appointment of her son Aeneas Manston to the stewardship of the Knapwater estate, she assumed that he was still a bachelor, as he was still living in 'chambers'. *DR.* vii 3

WYLLS-NECK. *The highest point in the Quantock Hills, between Taunton and the Bristol Channel.*   *SC.* 'Wessex Heights'

WYNDWAY HOUSE. *Largely imaginary, though its setting near* '*a sheet of embayed sea*' *may have been suggested by that of Upton House, north-west of Poole and east of Lytchett Minster.*

Here, thanks to the designing but mistaken Ethelberta, Christopher Julian was suddenly invited to play at a dance. He was accompanied by his sister Faith.   *HE.* iv–v

WYNYARD'S GAP. *Here the road from Toller Down descends steeply towards the valley, beyond which lies Crewkerne. At the crossroads, below the steepest part of the descent, stands the inn.* TL. 'A Trampwoman's Tragedy'; *MV.* 'Molly Gone'; *HS.* 'At Wynyard's Gap'

XANTEN, BARON VON. *No ordinary mortal but an embodiment of psychological, possibly satanic powers,* which exerted a magnetic force on Margery Tucker. She saved him from utter despondency, and he rewarded her by taking her to a grand ball. Although at one point tempted to sail away with her, he appears to be a model of propriety. *It is as if the prince of darkness had turned gentleman.* His main business, after discovering that Margery had given up her wedding with Jim Hayward in response to his call, was to ensure that the two settled happily. Despite the difficulties which had arisen, he was successful. He was ill, and once at the point of death. Whether he died after Margery's marriage or just disappeared from Lower Wessex was never discovered. *CM.* 12

YALBURY. *'Geoffrey Day's parish' in the early edition of* Under the Greenwood Tree. *An imaginary village near Troy Town (p. 461).*

Here Fancy Day and Dick Dewy were married.

UGT. v i; *FMC.* x, xxxi, lvii

YALBURY HILL, YALBURY WOOD. *Yellowham Wood (see p. 516), between Puddletown and Dorchester. The road down the long slope of Yellowham Hill intersects the wood. Below this hill is 'Yalbury Bottom'.*

Geoffrey Day was the keeper of Yalbury Wood. *His cottage ('remodelled', according to Hermann Lea) may be found on the northern side of the road, with 'the greenwood tree' behind it. The copses between which the newly married Dick Dewy and Fancy Day passed in the tranter's 'excellent new spring-cart' extend from Grey's Wood to Higher Bockhampton. See plate facing p. 47.*

Gabriel Oak walked by Yalbury Wood on his way from Casterbridge to Shottsford, when he was seeking employment.

Joseph Poorgrass, who had been working late at Yalbury Bottom, and had taken a drop of drink, lost himself in Yalbury Wood, and cried 'Man-a-lost'. An owl happened to be crying 'Whoo-whoo-whoo!', and Poorgrass answered, all in a tremble, 'Joseph Poorgrass of Weatherbury, sir'.

Bathsheba's maid Liddy was allowed a week's holiday to stay with her sister, who lived in a hazel copse near Yalbury. Bathsheba was on her way to visit her when she saw Farmer Boldwood, whose love she had aroused by her thoughtless valentine, advancing over Yalbury Hill. The interview made her fear for the life of his rival, Sergeant Troy.

Here, as the sea fogs enveloped Yalbury Great Wood to saturation, Joseph Poorgrass drove with the coffin enclosing Fanny Robin and her child from Casterbridge Union to Weatherbury.

The story of the poacher Charl, who was beaten by the keeper's wife in Yalbury Wood, is of interest (*MC*. xxxvi). When he tried to intercept Farfrae late at night with the message that his wife was critically ill, Henchard waited in Yalbury Bottom. The slow wind made its moan among the masses of spruce and larch until he heard Farfrae's gig approaching. Henchard then hurried back to the junction of Cuckoo Lane and the highway to stop Farfrae as he slowed down to turn towards Mellstock. Henchard's effort was in vain. The same moan was heard among the same larches when Henchard made his last unhappy visit to Casterbridge.

Mrs Palmley's son, who was Mrs Winter's charge, was making his way through Yalbury Wood when 'something came out from behind a tree and frightened him into fits'. He never recovered, and soon afterwards died.

Yalbury Brow in 'At the Mill' is the top of Yellowham Hill. The tragedy took place at Puddletown.   *UGT*. I iv; II vi;
        IV ii; V i, ii; *FMC*. vi, viii, xxxi, xxxix, xlii, liv, lv;
        MC. xxxvi, xl, xliv; *LLI*. 8d, g; *LLI*. 7; HS. 'At the Mill'
YARBOROUGH, LADY. *See Life, 264*.   *MV*. 'The Pink Frock'
YELLOWHAM. *Yellowham Wood and its vicinity. For its location, see*
YALBURY WOOD.
        PPP. 'The Mother Mourns', 'Long Plighted', 'The Comet
        at Yell'ham' (*Hardy remembered seeing it in 1858 or 1859.*
        It was Encke's Comet, October 1858 – Weber, Hardy of
        Wessex, *133*). *TL*. 'Geographical Knowledge', 'Yell'ham
        Wood's Story'; *SC*. 'Wessex Heights' (*see footnote, p. 309*);
        MV. 'Old Excursions'; *LLE*. 'The Milestone by the
                Rabbit-burrow'; *HS*. 'Ice on the Highway'
YEO. *A Somerset river which flows through Yeovil, and then west by 'sad Sedge-Moor', to join the River Parrett.*
        WP. 'The Dance at the Phoenix'; *TL*. 'A Trampwoman's
                Tragedy'; *HS*. 'At Wynyard's Gap', 'The Pat of Butter'
YEOBRIGHT, CLEMENT (CLYM). Mrs Yeobright's son. As a boy he had learned to love Egdon Heath. He went to school early, and was a lad 'of whom something was expected'. He worked in Budmouth and

London (*in some ways he was like Hardy*), and then became engaged in a diamond business in Paris. In the end it seemed a mere vanity, 'flashy' and 'effeminate', and he returned to his native heath, much against his mother's wishes. He is compared to John the Baptist and St Paul. He saw the world 'groaning and travailing in pain' (*as Jude Fawley did*), and decided to study in order to educate and improve the lot of his fellow-men. Their superstitions and prejudices made him wonder whether his hopes were premature, but he was too much of an idealist or 'ameliorist' to be deterred. He believed in 'plain living' and 'high thinking'. His countenance was marked with thought; it expressed the 'view of life as a thing to be put up with'. It was strange and tragically ironical that he should fall in love with, and marry, Eustacia Vye, for whom the Heath was Hades, and the glamour of life in Paris her objective in marrying. When he became a furze-cutter, she despised him and resumed her flirtation with the 'inflammable' Wildeve. Clym would rather live on Egdon Heath than anywhere else in the world. ('The most thorough-going ascetic could feel that he had a natural right to wander on Egdon'.) He suffered agonies over the death of his mother; and the certainty that his neglect was the cause of her death haunted him so much that he broke down mentally and physically. Before he had recovered from his illness, his suspicions were inflamed into almost ungovernable fury against a wife whom the evidence he had heard convicted of 'murder' and adultery. His mother had warned Eustacia that, though 'gentle as a child', he could be 'as hard as steel'. In a paroxysm of fury he accused Eustacia. She bore his false accusations with dignity, and left him, never to return. Her drowning made him feel that he was responsible for the death of the two women he had loved most.

Subsequently he took to itinerant open-air preaching and lecturing, but not with unqualified success. The time was not ripe. 'But everywhere he was kindly received, for the story of his life had become generally known.'   *RN.* II i, vi; III i–viii; IV i, ii, v–viii; V i, iii; VI iii, iv

YEOBRIGHT, MR. Thomasin's father. See KINGSBERE. *Hardy acknowledged that the description of his playing the bass-viol in Kingsbere church was a humorous exaggeration of the traditions concerning his grandfather 'as locum-tenens' (Life, 12).*   *RN.* I v

YEOBRIGHT, MRS. *Her disappointment when Clym gives up his career may have been based on that of Hardy's mother when he gave up architecture.*

She was a middle-aged widow who lived with her niece Thomasin at Blooms-End. Her husband had been a small farmer ('as rough as a hedge', according to Captain Vye), but she was a curate's daughter and had 'dreamt of doing better things'. She was superior to the unlettered inhabitants of Egdon Heath, and her outlook was such that at times 'she seemed to be regarding issues from a Nebo denied to others around'. She seems to have been a woman who had made up her mind rather inflexibly, and thought more than she was accustomed to speak. She felt strongly, and was rather quick to take offence (if, once again, Captain Vye can be trusted). Disappointment in life made her ambitious for Clym and Thomasin. She had hoped that they would become 'man and wife'. In both she was to be disappointed, and her disappointment was to reach its tragic climax with her death. For Thomasin she hoped marriage would bring social and professional status. Diggory Venn did not meet her requirements, and she disapproved of Wildeve because he was anything but a 'saint'. She was upset when Clym abjured the flashy business life of Paris to settle on Egdon Heath, but this was nothing compared with her unhappiness when she saw that her son was falling in love with Eustacia Vye. His 'steady opposition and persistence in going wrong' almost broke her heart: 'O Thomasin, he was so good as a little boy – so tender and kind'. 'Well, well! and life too will be over soon', she murmured as she heard the distant bells proclaim that the wedding service at East Egdon church was over. Her efforts to bring about a reconciliation, after the quarrel with Eustacia over the guineas which had gone astray, are the last act in a tragic drama which is accentuated by the long and pitiless walk across the heath in a torrid sun, and her apparent rejection by her son. She dies exhausted and comfortless, her last thoughts with him. *She is one of Hardy's most convincing dramatic presentations. Eustacia has great imaginative appeal, but she does not stir such deep and lasting sympathy.*   *RN.* I ii–v,

ix, xi; II ii, iii, vi, viii; III ii–vii; IV i, ii, v–viii; V i, ii

YEOBRIGHT, THOMASIN. Presumably Thomasin had lived with her father until his sudden death. She had gone to live with her aunt Mrs Yeobright at Blooms-End. She was slight in build; her face fair, sweet and honest; her hair wavy and chestnut. When she was herself, she had a happy temperament, and was very much at home on Egdon Heath. She was 'a dimant' in the opinion of Timothy Fairway. There can be little doubt that she was not wholly indifferent to her first suitor, Diggory

Venn; but she rejected him out of respect for her aunt, who hoped she would marry a professional man. She fell in love with Damon Wildeve, the landlord of the Quiet Woman Inn, but her aunt publicly forbad the banns of marriage in church after discovering that the ex-Budmouth engineer was no 'saint'. Thomasin did not change her mind, however, and Mrs Yeobright at length consented to the marriage. To avoid further publicity and gossip, Thomasin insisted on a quiet marriage miles away from West Egdon. She preferred Anglebury to Budmouth, to discover that the marriage licence was valid only in Budmouth where Wildeve had obtained it. To escape further scandal, Thomasin insisted on returning to Blooms-End alone, but she had met Diggory Venn in her distress, and he brought her home in his reddle-van. But for Diggory's gallantry and cunning, the marriage might never have taken place, as Wildeve, immediately on his return, renewed his meetings with the flirtatious Eustacia Vye. After her marriage with Wildeve, Thomasin lived at the Quiet Woman. Precisely at the time when Clym's marriage with Eustacia was disrupted, a daughter was born to her, and, ironically, named Eustacia Clementine. Wildeve inherited a fortune and, had he not been involved again with Eustacia, he and Thomasin would have moved to Casterbridge. After Wildeve's death, Thomasin married Diggory and moved to his dairy-farm at Stickleford.   *RN.* I ii–v, ix–xi; II ii, vi–viii; III vi, vii, viii; IV viii; V i, iii, viii, ix; VI i–iv

YEWSHOLT LODGE. *Farrs House, a mile and a half to the west of Wimborne.*

The house which 'her kind-hearted father' prepared for Barbara Grebe to reside in when her husband returned from Italy. It was 'a cottage built in the form of a mansion, having a central hall with a gallery running round it, and rooms no bigger than closets to support this introduction'. It stood on a solitary slope surrounded by trees. *GND.* 2

YORE, DR. He read a paper on Corvsgate Castle at the meeting there of the Imperial Archaeological Association. As he warmed to his subject, his face was 'no longer criticized as a rugged boulder, a dried fig, an oak carving, or a walnut shell, but became blotted out like a mountain top in a shining haze by the nebulous pictures conjured by his tale'. *HE.* xxxi

YORK HUSSARS, THE. A regiment of the King's German Legion who were quartered near Overcombe. When Anne Garland saw 'how triumphantly other handsome girls of the neighbourhood walked by on the gorgeous arms of Lieutenant Knockheelmann, Cornet Flitzenhart, and

Captain Klaspenkissen, of the thrilling York Hussars . . . she was filled with a sense of her own loneliness'.

A spectator at George III's review of the troops on Bincombe Down in July 1805 pointed out the York Hussars, and added that they were 'the same regiment the two young Germans belonged to who were shot here four years ago'. *TM.* i–iii, x; *WT.* 3; *D.* (1) ii iv

ZERMATT. *At Zermatt, one night in the summer of 1897, Hardy could see from his hotel window 'where the Matterhorn was by the absence of stars within its outline. . . . He meant to make a poem of the strange feeling implanted by this black silhouette . . . but never did, so far as is known.' However, he wrote another on the 'terrible accident' on its summit which had 'so impressed him at the time of its occurrence', thirty-two years before* (Life, *264, 294*). *PPP.* 'Zermatt: To the Matterhorn'

Glossary

There are three main classes of words: dialect, literary (e.g. archaic and Shakespearian), and words of foreign derivation (chiefly French).

a-croupied, crouched, squatting

anighst, almost

arrant, errand, mission

a-scram, shrunken, withered.

ashleaf (or *ashtop*), a variety of potato

asile, refuge, haven, retreat

axe, axle

ayless, always

azew, go (of cows), dry up

ba'dy, wicked

bagnet, bayonet, stab

bain't, are not

ballet, ballad, song

ballyrag, scold, abuse violently

bandy, bent stick

banging, bang-up, fine, smart

barley-mow, stack of barley

barrow-pig, gelt pig, hog

barton, farm-yard

beater, an old type of watch with a loud tick

beneaped, vapid, left high and dry

biffins, red winter apples

biggen, grow big (with child)

bitter weed, mischief-maker

bivering, with chattering teeth, shaking with cold

black-hearts, whortleberries

blade, fellow

blinking, contemptible, poor

blooth, bloom, blossom

blow up, scold, reprimand

blow-hard, boaster, blusterer

blue-vinnied, mouldy (lit. of a kind of cheese which turns blue when it becomes mouldy)

boam, (vb. intrans.) trail

bobbin, string and attachment fastened to the latch (for opening a door)

bolt, sift, refine (flour)

borus-snorus, bold or outspoken without fear of consequences or people's opinions

bouncer, very great one

brandise, a three-legged iron stand for supporting a pan or kettle, brandiron

brave, fine, capital

breath-shotten, breathless, exhausted

brimbles, brambles, blackberry briars

bruckle, brittle, unstable

521

bruckle het (or *hit*), misfortune, failure, mistake

brume, fog, mist

buffer, simpleton

burn, stream, brook

Byss, (lit. bottom, foundation) Fundamental or First Cause

caddle, quandary, entanglement

call home (in church), to have the banns of marriage published

cappel-faced, with a white face dappled with red

cast, divine, interpret

cerule, azure, heavenlike

cess, impose a tax or levy

'ch, I (used only by Grammer Oliver in *The Woodlanders.* The old Anglo-Saxon form was dying out rapidly in Hardy's day; cf. *Life,* 221)

chainey, china

chammer. See *chimmer*

chaps, cheeks

charactery, expression, features (lit. letters, writing)

chaw, (n.) bite, mouthful; (vb.) eat; *chaw high,* have superior tastes

chevy, pursue

chick, child

chiel, child

chimley, open fireplace

chimley-tun, chimney-stack

chimmer, bedroom, chamber

chimp, produce offspring (a *chimp* is a young shoot)

chine, cleft or ravine; the meat adjoining the backbone of an animal.

chips-in-porridge, person of no importance

chitlings, chitterlings, the smaller intestines (usually of a pig) dressed and fried for food

church-hatch, churchyard gate

church-hay, churchyard

cit, citizen

clam, clog, to be (or make) sticky

clane, clean

climm, climb

clink off, make off, run away

clipse, embrace, clasp

clitch, crook of arm or leg

clown, rustic

coats, skirt, petticoat

cock, a conical heap, as in *haycock*

cohue, people of conventional views

coil, trouble, turmoil

cole, coll, embrace

coming-on, responsive

con, read, study

coomb, deep valley or hollow on the side of a hill, combe

cot, cottage

coz, dear

crabs, crab-apples

craters, creatures

creeping up, growing up, life

criddled, curdled

crimp, seize, arrest (press-gang)

crock, pot, 'a bulging iron pot' (Barnes)

crooping, crouching, squatting down

crope, crept

croud, lit. fiddle

crumby, plump, luscious

cuckoo-father, cuckolder, the lover who is guilty of cuckoldry. From the cuckoo, which lays its eggs in another bird's nest.

cue, intimation

culpet, culprit

cwoffer, coffer, chest

cyme, cyma (arch.), cornice mould-
    ing

dab, expert, (an) adept
daddle, dandle, idle
dand, dandy
dang, damn
daps, likeness, image
darkle, (sat) in the dark (cf. *darkling*,
    in the dark)
daze, damn
deedy, earnest, serious, intent
dew-bit, a 'snap' or 'bite' before
    breakfast
dibs, an old game of 'toss and catch'
    played with pebbles or the
    knuckle-bones of sheep
dip, dip-candle, a candle made by
    dipping a wick into melted tallow
doff, take off
doggery, roguery
don, put on (dress); cf. *doff*
dorp, hamlet or village, thorp
douce, sweet, pleasant
dra'ats, draughts, strong gusts of wind
draw-latching, *draw-latcheting*, lazy,
    spineless
draw up (a clock or watch), wind up
dree, suffering, what has to be
    endured; three
drong, lane between walls or hedges,
    alley
droudged, drudged
drough, through
dumble, *dumbledore*, humble-bee
Dumpy level, kind of spirit-level
dunderheaded, stupid
durn, door-post

easting, turning to face the east end
    of the church (for example, to
    recite the Creed)

'ee, you
een, eyes (cf. *eyne*)
effets, newts
emmet, ant
en, him, it
er, he
eweleaze, down or meadow stocked
    with sheep
eyne, eyes

fairing, gift, (orig. bought or given
    at a fair)
fall, autumn, a woman's veil
fancy-man, lover, sweetheart
fantocine, puppet
fare, farrow, litter
farrel, cover or binding of a book
fay, faith; prosper, succeed
fell, cruel; skin
felon, whitlow, inflamed sore
fence, keep or ward off; plans for
    defence
fend hands, take guard
fendless, against which defence is
    impossible
fess, proud, eager, active, strong
fidgets, matters of trifling concern
fineless, endless
fleed, flew
flick-flack, trippingly, without
    pause; thoughtless talk
flounce, (n.) flop (e.g. caused by
    something dropped or flung into
    water); (vb.) make a heavy splash
flummery, nonsense, humbug
fondly, foolishly
footy, mean, base
foreshades, is foreshadowed
fuddle, tipple, booze
fugle, (vb.) direct
full-buff, suddenly, face to face
fulth, fullness, amplitude

gaberlunzie, wandering beggar (Scottish)
gaffer, master, 'old man'
gallicrow, scarecrow
gallied, worried, alarmed, scared
gammer, old woman
gam'ster, fortune-seeker
garth, churchyard, enclosure (as for home and garden)
gawkhammer, gaping fool; idiotic
gied, gave, given
gipsying, picnic, open-air festivities
glane, leer, sneer
glum, gloom
glutch, swallow, gulp, make a gurgling noise in the throat
glutchpipe, throat
goodman, husband, master of the house
grammer, grandmother
grandfer, grandfather
greggles, wild hyacinths
griddle, grill, broil on a gridiron
griff, (n.) claw, grip
griffin, variety of apple
grintern, granary compartment
gristing, flour from corn which is gleaned
grizzel, grizzle, turn anything grey; (adj.) grey
gwine, going

hacker, utter with chattering teeth
hag-rid, hag-rode, afflicted with nightmares, bewitched
haggler, dealer or middle man, higgler
halter-path, bridle-path
hang-fair, public execution, hanging-fair
hapeth, halfpennyworth
hapless, luckless

harlican, wretch, rascal, good-for-nothing
harnet, hornet
hatch, small gate
haw, enclosure or field adjoining a house
hawk, clear the throat violently
heft, weight
hele, pour out
hell-and-skimmer, 'blazes'
hent, hint
het, gulp down, 'knock back' (lit. hit, knock); hot, heat
het across, to strike across, take a short cut across
hit, turn, direct one's course; cause to be 'smitten' with love
ho, long, pine for, care
hob-and-nob, be on friendly terms
hobbed, hobnailed
hobble, troublesome business, predicament, problem
homely, plain-speaking, unpolished, plain
hontish, haughty
horn, publish, proclaim, blare
horn up, (of dilemmas) occur, arise (cf. 'the horns of a dilemma')
huddied, hidden
huff, scold, reprimand
huffle, blow unsteadily or in gusts
humour, dampness
hurdle-sauls, stakes to which hurdles are fastened
husbird, 'hore's-bird, rascal, 'bastard'
hussif'ry, housekeeping, housewifery

idden, is not
incarn, assume bodily form
indemn, indemnify
inkle, hint at, give an inkling of

Glossary

interlune, period between the old moon and the new
intermell, intermixture
intervolve, (n.) intertwining
inutile, useless, futile

jack-o'clock, figure which strikes a clock-bell mechanically, and is metaphorically associated with
These flesh-hinged mannikins Its hand upwinds
To click-clack off Its preadjusted laws
jack-o'-lent, numskull (a puppet stuffed with straw, at which cudgels were thrown in old Lenten recreational observances)
Jack-straw, common fellow
jaw, lecture, reprimand
jee, gee, a word of command to a horse, generally to move forward or faster, sometimes to turn right
jerry-go-nimble, circus
jim-cracks, gimcracks (in the old sense of mechanical contrivances)
jinks, frolics, pranks
jints, joints
jonnick, honest, agreeable, jolly
jown, damn
Jumping-jack, Jumping-jill, toy figure (of man, woman) which is manipulated by strings
jumps, (n.) stays
junk, lump, chunk
junketing, feasting, merrymaking

keacorn, windpipe, throat
ken, know (Scottish)
kennel, gutter
kex, dry hollow stalk (of cow parsnip)
kick up Bob's-a-dying, make a great to-do or fuss

kimberlin, foreigner, stranger (to Portland)
kip, keep
knap, hillock, a low hill
knee-naps, leather pads worn over the knees by thatchers
knock in, eat, consume
knop, bud, projection

lackaday, careless, indifferent
lacune, empty space
laiter, (vb.) search
lamiger, cripple
lammicken, lammocken, ungainly, slouching, clumsy
lanch, lanchet. See *lynchet*
langterloo, old form of the game of loo
larry, noisy celebration, excitement, disturbance, lark
lave, bale, draw water
leaze, a meadow for grazing (and therefore left unmown)
leazings, bundles of gleaned corn
leer, leery, empty, hungry, exhausted, faint
lerret, boat for heavy seas
lew, lewth, shelter from the wind
liefer, rather
limber, limberish, lacking resistance, frail, weak
linhay, lean-to building, shed
linnit, lint
lirruping, lazy, slovenly
livier. See p. 137
list, thick layer of inedible bread; (vb.) wish, desire
lock, bundle, quantity
lumper, stumble
lynchet, strip of uncultivated land in a ploughed field, flinty outcrop
lynes, loins

malkin, damp rag for cleaning the oven

mammet, doll, puppet (cf. *mommet*)

mampus, crowd

man-jack (*every*), every individual man

mandy, saucy, cheeky

mangling, the process of being decided or settled

manse, mansion

maphrotight, hermaphrodite

marnels, marbles

martel. See *mortal*

maul down, lift down

mawn-basket, wicker basket, hamper

med. See *mid*

meetinger, chapel-goer, Nonconformist

mete, (vb.) measure

metheglin, spiced mead

mid, may, might

miff, slight quarrel, 'tiff'

mill-tail, stream below water-mill

minney, minnow

mischty, mischief

mixen, manure, manure-heap

mizzel, vanish, take oneself off

modden, must not

moil, toil, drudgery, turmoil

mollyish, soft, yielding, weak

mollyhorning, gallivanting

mommet, odd figure, laughing-stock, guy

mops and brooms, (*to be all*), to be out of sorts, upset

mortal, extremely great, mighty; individual, single

mossel, bit, morsel

moue, make grimaces at

mouster, be stirring or on the move

mumbudgeting, without notice, taking by surprise

mumm, play a part (as in mumming)

nab, seize

nabs, clever, pretentious fellow

name it all, damn it all

nammet, mid-morning or early afternoon meal in the fields

nater, nature

nath, puffin (Cornish)

'nation, damnation

navarchy, Commander(s) of the fleet

neat(s), oxen

nesh, delicate, sickly

ness, promontory

night-rail, night-dress

nipperkin, small measure of liquor

nitch, bundle of sticks, faggot

nobble, hobble, potter

nonce, occasion, the present

nott, hornless

nunch, lunch

nunnywatch, fix, predicament (looking like a ninny from not knowing what to do)

on-end, ready, set

oneyer, unusual person, 'fine person' (generally used sarcastically)

ooser, oozer, a grotesque mask with opening jaws, surmounted by a cow's horns and hair

orchet, orchard

out-set, set out, present

outshade, outline the purpose of

outstep, out-of-the-way

overget, overtake

overlook, cast an evil eye on

over-right, opposite

paean, (vb.) hymn

parle, talk, conversation

peckled, pickled
pent, enclosed, buried
philosopheme, philosophizing
pinion, the hipped end of a building (a sloping roof instead of the gable)
pinner, apron and bib
pitch one's nitch, set down one's load or whatever is being carried over one's shoulder
plain, complain
plim, (vb.) rise, swell
poll, head of hair
pomace, *pommy*, apples crushed to pulp in cider-making
poppett, dear, doll (a term of endearment to a child)
poppling, bubbling, brewing (of a plot)
pot-housey, vulgar, characteristic of the ale-house
projick, prodigy, project
pucker, confusion, agitation
pulsion, the action of driving or impelling
pummy. See *pommy*
purblinking, stupid
pyle, a baker's shovel with a long handle for inserting loaves in the oven or taking them out

quag, mess
quarrenden, a red early apple
quat, squat, stoop
queue, follow, dog
quick, quicken, give life to

racket, exciting occasion
rackety, noisy, boisterous
rackless, careless, heedless, reckless
raffle, three throws which are all the same (in dicing)
raft, upset

rafting, rousing
rames, skeleton, carcase, remains
randy, *randyvoo*, party, celebration, merrymaking, drunken carousal, disturbance
rantipole, noisy
ratch, extend, stretch
rathe, soon, early
rathe-ripes, apples which ripen early
rawmil, (lit. raw milk) made from unskimmed milk
re'ch, reach (yachting)
reck, (vb.) care
rendlewood, oak off which the bark has been stripped
rithe (or *rathe*), fast
rock, to clean (probably remove incrustations)
rout, party
rozum, quaint saying, oddity, queer person; (vb.) work away at
rummer, large drinking-glass

sappy, simpleton
sartin, certain
scammish, rough, awkward, unrefined
scantling, small piece, remnant
scath, harm, loss, misfortune
scathe, (vb.) damage
sconced, hidden, screened
scram, emaciated, withered, puny, contemptible
screw, worn-out or broken-down horse
scrimped up, screwed up
scrimping, economizing
scroff, rubbish, odds and ends, refuse (cf. *shroff*)
scrub, insignificant person
seed, (vb.) saw, seen
seed-lips, baskets or boxes in which

corn was carried for sowing by
hand
sengreen, houseleek
sereward, towards decay (cf. 'the
sere and yellow leaf')
shail, shuffle, drag the feet
shalloon, light woollen dress
sheen, shine
shrammed, numbed, stiff with cold
shroff. See *scroff*
shroud, lop off the side-branches
sich, such
skellington, skeleton
skimmer-cake, cake baked on a metal
skimming-ladle
skimmer your pate, beat your head
with a skimming ladle
skimmington-ride, skimmity-ride, 'a
kind of matrimonial lynch law or
pillory intended for those in a
lower class of life who, in certain
glaring particulars, may have
transgressed their marital duties'
(J. S. Udal, *Dorsetshire Folk-
Lore*). The name may have
originated from the skimming-
ladle which was used to beat the
effigies of the offenders in the
public procession.
skit, restive horse
skiver, fasten with a skewer
slack, impudence, cheek
slack-twisted, spineless, shiftless
slat, (n.) splintering
slent, shattered
slittering, skipping, always on the
move
slummocky, dirty, slovenly
smack-and-coddle, kiss-and-cuddle
snacks, go s. with someone, share any
thing, marry
snap, a hasty meal

snapper, a sudden fall (e.g. of rain)
sniche, stingy, grasping, avaricious
snoach, snuffle, snore
snock, knock, crash
snoff, snuff of a candle
sock, sigh loudly (cf. *sough*)
solve, to cause (one's) dissolution
sommat, sommit, something
spatterdashes, leggings, gaiters
spet, spit
sprawl, energy, activity
squail, fling, throw
squat, strike, flatten, crush
staddle, framework (supported by
staddle-stones) on which corn was
stacked
stand-to, (adj.), stubborn; (vb.) come
round, have some sense
stap, step
stillicide, dripping of water
stooded, stationary
stoor, to-do, crisis, disturbance
strakes, sections of iron which form
the rim of a wheel
strappen, strapping, well-built
strawmote, single straw
strent, slit, rent
stud, quandary, 'brown study'
stumpy, heavy-footed
stunpole, stunpoll, blockhead
stuns, put the s. upon, check, hamper
subtrude, steal in or under
sumple, soft, supple
swealed, burnt, scorched
swingel, cudgel, flail
swipes, weak beer

tacker-haired, wiry-black-haired
tailing, light or inferior corn
tale, number
tallet, loft
tardle, entanglement

taters, taties, potatoes
tear-brass, rowdy, boisterous
teave, (vb.) toil, struggle
teen, (n.) sorrow
teuny, weak, undersized
thik, this, that
thill, in the shafts
thimble-and-button, 'thimble and bodkin', a term of contempt (first used with reference to the Parliamentarian Army during the Civil War)
thirtingill, wrong-headed, perverse
thirtover, contrary, cross, obstinate
three-cunning, secretive, knowing
thrid, make one's way through the intricacies or windings of (lit. thread)
thrums, flower-tufts (ivy)
tickle, touch-and-go, a ticklish situation
tidden, it isn't
tidetimes, holidays (coinciding with Church feasts and fairs)
tilt, canopy for a cart or waggon
tine, close
ting, make a ringing noise with a shovel or warming-pan and large key to induce the bees to swarm
tisty-tosty, round like a ball
tole, entice, draw
Tom-rig, common woman
topper, something hard to beat or outdo
tops, upper, turned over part of riding-boots
touse, mauling, dislocation
tout, hill (e.g. Nettlecombe Tout. The word meant a look-out.)
trading o't, going, journeying
traipse, walk aimlessly or listlessly
trangleys, toys and playthings, bits or apparatus

trant, trade as a tranter
tranter, a common carrier, one whose business was to transport goods for other people
traps, articles, belongings
treen, trees
trendle, large circular bowl for making dough
trimming, great, excellent
tristful, sad
twanking, twanky, mournful, sighful, peevish
twit, twyte, tease, taunt, reproach

unbe, unknow, unsee, (do) not exist, know, see
un'rayed, undressed
unreave, unravel, fray
unshent, unashamed, not disgraced
unweeting, unaware, unconscious
upclomb, arose (climbed up)
uppingstock, stone or steps for mounting a horse
use-money, interest on money

vair, grey and white fur from squirrels (for lining)
vamp, (vb.) tramp, walk; foot of stocking or sock, sole of a shoe
vanned, winged
varden, farthing
varmits, vermin, objectionable things or persons
vawardly, in the vanguard
vell, ('vell or mark'), trace, sign
vill, village, mansion
vinger, finger
vinnied. See *blue-vinnied*
vitty, fitting, just so, proper
vlankers, outflying flakes of fire, 'red embers and sparks'
vlee, (n.), fly, carriage; (vb.) fly, flee
vlock, flock

voidless, unavoidable
volk, folk
voot, foot

walm, (lit. boil, seethe) rise, well up
wamble, walk unsteadily or shakily, totter
wanzing, wasting away, decaying
weasand, throat, windpipe
weedery, clothing, dress (arch. 'weeds')—usually indicative of mourning
weet, know
weird, of destiny
wherrit, worry
whicker, snigger, giggle
whilom, formerly
whimmed, carried away by a whim
whindling, dwindling, declining, wasting away
white witch, white wizard (generally known as conjurer) a person who claimed magical curative powers, and to whom superstitious people turned when they were ill or physically afflicted
whop and slap at, proceed energetically with
wide-awake, cute
wight, person, man
wimble, (vb.) twist bands for hay-trussing; (n.) instrument for so doing
windling. See *whindling*
windrow, line into which hay or corn used to be raked by hand during the drying period
wisht, sad, mournful
wist, knew
wistlessness, unawareness
withwind, withywind, bindweed
withy, willow
woak, oak
wold, old
woll, wool, will
won, dwell
wont, custom
wot, know
wring-house, shed or building to house the cider-press
wuld, old

yean, (vb.) lamb
yclept, called, named

zeed, (vb.) saw
zell, sell
zid, saw
zot, (vb.) *sat*
zull, plough (sull)
zwailing, swaying from side to side

Hardy's Manuscripts

Several of the early MSS. were lost or destroyed. In 1911 Hardy handed over to Sydney Cockerell all those in his possession for distribution to 'any museums that would care to possess one' (*Life*, 356); 'the cupboard which contained the MSS. is now agreeably empty,' he wrote. Certain drafts and numerous individual poems are excluded from the list.

A Changed Man
  1. 'A Changed Man'. Berg Collection, New York Public Library
  4. 'The Grave by the Handpost'. Halsted B. Vander-Poel, Rome
  6. 'A Tryst at an Ancient Earthwork'. University of Texas
  7. 'What the Shepherd Saw'. Untraced (sold in 1955)
  8. 'A Committee-Man of "The Terror" '. Berg Collection
  9. 'Master John Horseleigh, Knight'. University of Texas
  10. 'The Duke's Reappearance'. University of Texas
  12. 'The Romantic Adventures of a Milkmaid'. Pierpont Morgan Library, New York
The Dynasts. The British Museum
'The Doctor's Legend'. Berg Collection
The Famous Tragedy of the Queen of Cornwall. Dorset County Museum
Far from the Madding Crowd (found in London in 1918, and sold in aid of the Red Cross Fund). Edwin Thorne, New York.
A Group of Noble Dames (seven of the stories only: the six written for *The Graphic*, and 'Lady Penelope'). Library of Congress, Washington.
Human Shows. Yale University Library
Jude the Obscure. The Fitzwilliam Museum, Cambridge
Late Lyrics and Earlier. Dorset County Museum
Life's Little Ironies
  1. 'An Imaginative Woman'. Aberdeen University Library

2. 'The Son's Veto'. Bodmer Collection, Switzerland
3. 'For Conscience' Sake'. Manchester University Library
4. 'A Tragedy of Two Ambitions'. The John Rylands Library, Manchester
5. 'On the Western Circuit'. The Central Library, Manchester
8. 'A Few Crusted Characters' (a rough and incomplete draft with the original title of 'Wessex Folk'). Berg Collection

The Mayor of Casterbridge. Dorset County Museum
Moments of Vision. Magdalene College, Cambridge
'Old Mrs Chundle'. Dorset County Museum
A Pair of Blue Eyes (incomplete; see Purdy, 10–11). Berg Collection
Poems of the Past and the Present. The Bodleian Library, Oxford
The Return of the Native. University College Library, Dublin
Tess of the d'Urbervilles. The British Museum
Time's Laughingstocks. The Fitzwilliam Museum, Cambridge
The Trumpet-Major. The Royal Library, Windsor Castle
Two on a Tower. The Houghton Library, Harvard University
Satires of Circumstance. Dorset County Museum
Under the Greenwood Tree. Dorset County Museum
Wessex Poems. The Museum and Art Gallery, Birmingham
Wessex Tales

1. 'The Three Strangers'. Berg Collection
3. 'The Melancholy Hussar'. The Huntington Library, California

Winter Words. Queen's College, Oxford
The Woodlanders. Dorset County Museum

Select Bibliography

The Works of Thomas Hardy

Prose Fiction and Drama

The Wessex edition, Macmillan, London, is the only one which contains Hardy's final revisions. It consists of fourteen novels, four volumes of short stories, *The Dynasts*, and *The Famous Tragedy of the Queen of Cornwall*.

An Indiscretion in the Life of an Heiress, ed. Carl J. Weber, Russell & Russell, New York, 1965.

Poetry

Eight volumes of Hardy's poetry were published. They are all contained in *The Collected Poems of Thomas Hardy*, 4th ed., Macmillan, London, 1930.

Miscellaneous Prose

Harold Orel, *Thomas Hardy's Personal Writings*, University of Kansas Press, 1966; Macmillan, 1967.

A valuable collection, which includes, among many other items, 'How I Built Myself a House', 'The Dorsetshire Labourer', 'The Profitable Reading of Fiction', 'Candour' in English Fiction', 'The Science of Fiction', 'Memories of Church Restoration', the article on Maumbury Ring, writings on the poetry of William Barnes, Hardy's defence of the dramatic form of *The Dynasts*, and all the prefaces to his works, including the General Preface of 1912. The great advantage of having these in a single volume is obvious. The collection is supplemented by notes on Hardy's less important contributions and articles, and the annotation is excellent.

Evelyn Hardy, *Thomas Hardy's Notebooks*, Hogarth Press, 1955.
The first notebook contains several interesting items; much of the second
is incorporated in Hardy's *Life*.

Letters

Most remain unpublished, and an edition seems overdue. Carl J. Weber
has edited two volumes, the first rather miscellaneous:
Letters of Thomas Hardy, Colby College Press, 1954.
'*Dearest Emmie*': *Thomas Hardy's Letters to his First Wife*, Macmillan,
1963.

Bibliography

R. L. Purdy, *Thomas Hardy, A Bibliographical Study*, Oxford University
    Press, 1954.
This is likely to remain the standard work of reference, and an invaluable
source-book. 'The book has become, one might almost say, a biography
of Hardy in bibliographical form.' It includes information on composition, serial issues, editions, and revisions; notes on many poems as well
as contributions to books, periodicals, and newspapers from 1856 to 1928;
and, with other appendices, a summary of the Hardy–Tinsley correspondence, six letters to Leslie Stephen on *Far from the Madding Crowd*,
a note on Tillotson and Son and their 'newspaper fiction bureau', and
another on Hardy's friendship with the Hon. Mrs Arthur Henniker.

Biography

Florence Emily Hardy, *The Life of Thomas Hardy 1840–1928*, Mac-
    millan 1962; St. Martin's Press, 1962.
It was first published in two volumes: *The Early Life of Thomas Hardy*,
and *The Later Years of Thomas Hardy*. Almost the whole of this work
was prepared by Hardy himself. It has been criticized for its omissions;
but, as Hardy had revealed most of his personal life in his poems, this
rather conventional depreciation is hardly warranted. Hardy was moved

to prepare this record by inaccurate statements and impressions in the work of two writers (F. A. Hedgcock and Ernest Brennecke). His *Life* is based on notes and letters which he kept systematically for many years; they serve to make this 'autobiography' unusually reliable and indispensable. Altogether, few writers have revealed so much about themselves and their thought.

Clive Holland, *Thomas Hardy*, *O.M.*, Herbert Jenkins, 1933.
A useful introduction. It is drawn very largely from Hardy's *Life*. The topographical information is rather sketchy. Occasional reminiscences, statements by Hardy, and items such as Hardy's clues to Christminster provide evidence which is not available elsewhere.

W. R. Rutland, *Thomas Hardy*, Blackie, 1938.
It is unfortunate that this excellent biography, which goes deeper into the life and thought of Hardy than any other, is no longer in print. One could wish it longer. Extracts suggest that many unpublished letters would be of biographical and critical value. The writer's attitude is at times a trifle conventional; two topographical details (notably one on Sturminster Bridge) are erroneous, and the interpretation of 'In Tenebris' is puzzling; but the work in general shows scholarship and judgment of unusual distinction.

There are two studies of Hardy, by Evelyn Hardy and Carl J. Weber, in which biography plays an important part. See pp. 543 and 548.

Emma Hardy, *Some Recollections*, ed. Evelyn Hardy and Robert Gittings, Oxford University Press, 1961.
This brief work (completed in January 1911) is important for the light it throws on Hardy's Cornish romance and on some of the poems he wrote after the author's death. Hardy quotes from it in his *Life*, 67–73. Two statements in *Some Recollections* have a bearing on the differences between the novelist and his first wife:

My home was a most intellectual one and not only so but one of exquisite home-training and refinement – alas the difference the loss of these amenities and gentlenesses has made to me!

I have had various experiences, interesting some, sad others . . . but all showing that an Unseen Power of great benevolence directs my ways. . . .

Topography

Hermann Lea, *Thomas Hardy's Wessex*, Macmillan, 1913.
This is the most reliable guide, though it contains a few improbable conjectures. It follows Hardy's classification of the novels and short stories in the General Preface:

> Novels of Character and Environment
> Romances and Fantasies
> Novels of Ingenuity,

includes *The Dynasts*, and ends with *Time's Laughingstocks* (1909).

Wessex Folklore

Ruth Firor, *Folkways in Thomas Hardy*, University of Pennsylvania
  Press, 1931.
Invaluable for superstitions, premonitions, divination, witchcraft, folk-medicine, weather-lore, seasonal rites, sports and pastimes, folk-songs, mumming, folk-wit, folk-law, prehistoric and pagan survivals, medieval legends and Napoleonana; and almost undeviatingly true to Hardy.

J. S. Udal, *Dorsetshire Folk-Lore*, Stephen Austin & Sons, Hertford, 1922.
A less comprehensive work, but much of it is very closely related to Hardy's writings.

Essays, Mainly Critical

(The critical essays are recommended for critical consideration.)

J. O. Bailey, 'Hardy's "Mephistophelian Visitants" ', *Publications of the
  Modern Language Association*, lxi, December 1946.
Emma Clifford, 'Thomas Hardy and the Historians', *Studies in Philology*,
  lvi, 1959. (This relates to *The Dynasts*.)

D. A. Dyke, 'A Modern Oedipus, *The Mayor of Casterbridge*', *Essays in Criticism*, ii, April 1952.

Robert B. Heilman, 'Hardy's Sue Bridehead', *Nineteenth-Century Fiction*, 1965–66.

C. Day Lewis, 'The Lyrical Poetry of Thomas Hardy', *Proceedings of the Royal Academy*, 1951.

Julian Moynahan, '*The Mayor of Casterbridge* and the Old Testament's First Book of Samuel', *Publications of the Modern Language Association*, lxxi, March 1956.

Alastair Smart, 'Pictorial Imagery in the Novels of Thomas Hardy', *Review of English Studies*, 1961.

The Southern Review, Summer 1940.

The essays in this centennial issue vary considerably in style and value. Blackmur cannot be ignored, and Auden and Leavis have important things to say, on Hardy's poetry; Delmore Schwartz, on his poetry and beliefs; and Bonamy Dobrée, on *The Dynasts*. Morton Zabel writes impressively on Hardy's artistic dilemma in an age of uncertainty and transition; Katherine Anne Porter makes a spirited and reasoned rejoinder to Eliot's notorious criticism; Donald Davidson writes well on the novels and balladry; Jacques Barzun strikes the right note in opposing the view that Hardy was a realist or naturalist rather than 'a poet miscast as a novelist'; and Arthur Mizener provides one of the better criticisms of *Jude the Obscure*. Herbert Muller sees dangers in some modern critical approaches to Hardy.

Modern Fiction Studies, vi, Autumn 1960.

This Thomas Hardy number contains articles on *The Mayor of Casterbridge, The Return of the Native*, 'Hardy's Gurgoyles', *Jude the Obscure*, and *The Woodlanders*, with a selected checklist of critical works and essays. The essays by John Paterson on the 'poetics' of *The Return of the Native* and by Frederick McDowell on 'the symbolical use of image and contrast' in *Jude the Obscure* are particularly illuminating.

Hardy, A Collection of Critical Essays, ed. A. J. Guerard, Prentice-Hall, 1963.

In addition to four essays from the centennial number of *The Southern Review*, this selection contains extracts from D. H. Lawrence's *Study of Thomas Hardy*, a chapter on *The Dynasts* from *The Pattern of Hardy's*

Poetry by Samuel Hynes, Dorothy Van Ghent's essay on *Tess of the d'Urbervilles*, John Paterson on *The Mayor of Casterbridge* as tragedy, Alvarez on *Jude the Obscure*, John Holloway on 'the major fiction', Guerard on 'The Women of the Novels' (from *Thomas Hardy, The Novels and Stories*), and an interesting essay by David Perkins on 'Hardy and the Poetry of Isolation'.

Critical Works

Abercrombie, Lascelles, *Thomas Hardy*, Secker, 1912.
He sees the deeper forces at work in Hardy, but his grand generalizations can be misleading. One result, for example, is that Gabriel Oak, Diggory Venn, and Giles Winterborne are seen as brothers, so identical that they are 'beyond the accomplishment of human generation'. The distinction between the 'dramatic' and 'epic' novels is a rather uncritical simplification. It is not just 'the will to enjoy' which is baulked by Fate in *Tess*, nor is it true that 'the will to enjoy' in *Jude* becomes 'the will to power'. The Christminster theme is subordinated to the marriage question, and in the end it is 'the will to enjoy' which is baulked. Abercrombie is more interested in the broader issues than in the detail; Angel Clare is 'the only one of Hardy's characters who is genuinely odious', and Arabella 'in a rough classification' is comparable to Marty South, we are told. For him, Hardy's great qualities require expatiation rather than concentration. Hence, probably, his rather summary discussion of the poems, and his greater success with *The Dynasts*. He is one of the few critics who present its vision, its rich multiplicity, and its formal artistry in the brief span of a chapter. In only one respect has he proved to be wrong: 'it is scarcely to be supposed that a thing so vivid and great in its imagination . . . can long miss common acknowledgment as one of the most momentous achievements of modern literature'. There is much truth and depth of perception in Abercrombie, but he should be read very critically.

Bailey, J. O., *Thomas Hardy and the Cosmic Mind: A New Reading of 'The Dynasts'*, University of North Carolina Press, 1956.
Its main purpose 'is to examine Hardy's drama, particularly in the light of his perusal of Eduard von Hartmann's *Philosophy of the Unconscious*. Consideration of this book as an informing force in Hardy's own philoso-

phy leads to an examination of his interest in psychic phenomena, to a
new interpretation of the Spirits in his drama, to reconsideration of the
Immanent Will as Mind, to definition of Hardy's evolutionary meliorism,
and to understanding his treatment of Napoleon as servant of his Will.'
The question of Hardy's preliminary indebtedness to Robert Buchanan's
The Drama of Kings and Schopenhauer is also discussed. The work is
thorough and compact. The evidence is compendious and illuminating,
though there is no absolute proof that Hartmann's thought was causative
rather than coincidental, and Hardy's use of psychic phenomena may
sometimes have no more than a technical significance. Some detailed
conclusions seem to be drawn without sufficient regard for context;
comments, for example, by the Spirit Ironic are occasionally presented
as if they were detached reflections on the Immanent Will, whereas they
reflect only moods occasioned by events. The optimism of Hardy's conclusion may be exaggerated. The work is scholarly, and should not be
neglected by those interested in Hardy's thought.

Beach, J. W., *The Technique of Thomas Hardy*, University of Chicago
Press, 1922; Russell & Russell, New York, 1962.
As a study of structure in Hardy's novels, this work is disappointing. It
presents certain aspects of the stories (e.g. ingenuity of plot in *Desperate
Remedies*, irony in *A Pair of Blue Eyes*, dramatic tensions in *The Return
of the Native*), but the labelling convenience has its drawbacks, as may
be felt when *The Woodlanders* is classified as 'chronicle'. Readers should
be on their guard when they find reference to the *King's* visit in *The
Mayor of Casterbridge*, or discover that Eustacia, 'seeing no way out . . .
leaps* into the black pool of the *millrace*'. The plot of *Far from the
Madding Crowd* was not sold to Hardy. The first impression of this study
is that, as criticism, it does not go very deep; at the end, one is impressed
by the author's wisdom in his discussion of determinism, fate, chance, and
natural consequence in Hardy. He enters into the spirit of *The Well-
Beloved* far more fully and sympathetically than many critics, and writes
admirably on Henchard, Tess, and Jude. With certain reservations, this
book is recommended as one of the best general surveys of the novels.

Blunden, Edmund, *Thomas Hardy*, Macmillan, 1942.
This is a biographical criticism which shows wisdom and scholarship. It
never goes astray through critical obliquities of thought or the influence
of fashionable cults. Of special interest are the numerous quotations from

contemporary reviews and records which contribute cumulatively to impressions of Hardy, his writings, and the reading public. The first publication which bore Hardy's name on its title-page was *A Pair of Blue Eyes*, and not *Far from the Madding Crowd*. Blunden's discernment is clear in the discussion of Hardy's prose and poetry, and Hardy's weaknesses are not overlooked. The clue to his success is that from first to last he was 'a student' of life.

Brown, Douglas, *Thomas Hardy*, Longmans, Green, 1954.
The plight of the agricultural labourer in Dorset and its relation to some of the Wessex novels is a special feature of this work. It leads to some biased interpretations and the labelling of *Under the Greenwood Tree* as 'an agricultural story'. Ballad elements and the influence of balladry – a more conventional theme – are also overplayed. Brown's intensive criticism has left little room for the discussion of several novels, and *The Dynasts* is virtually excluded. The criticism is sensitive but sometimes over-subtilized, and not always adequately expressed; occasionally Hardy's poetry, we read, 'is immersed in the athletic sensation of the "moment" '. In stating that Hardy as a novelist 'evidences a continual uncertainty about the interests, the expectations, the likely response of his readers', the author takes us much nearer the heart of the problem than do most critics. The work contains some unusually discriminating criticism, particularly of the poetry. One or two factual errors should be removed.

Carpenter, Richard C., *Thomas Hardy*, Twayne Publishers, 1964.
This provides a general survey of Hardy's works for the student. It is readable, eminently informed, rather eclectic, but generally judicious and rewarding. The mythic bias is noticeable.

Cecil, Lord David, *Hardy the Novelist*, Constable, 1943.
The treatment is rather general, but well illustrated and linked with some wide and profound analyses of the significance of Nature and Fate (involving character and chance) in Hardy's novels. Cecil emphasizes the importance of visualization in Hardy's presentation, his film-director technique, and his imagination as a dramatic poet. He is more successful with the rustics of Hardy's choruses than with other characters; Henchard, Tess, and Jude are inadequately presented, and Sue is seen as 'the old-fashioned Hardy heroine'. An inconsistency in Cecil's reading of

Hardy's Fate shows itself when he comes to the defence of the 'unfortunate clergy and dons' of *Jude the Obscure*; in describing them as 'puppets' who were not responsible for their errors, he overlooks Hardy's purpose and philosophy, which did not rule out a 'modicum of free will' (except in times of stress) and the growth of human percipience. Preoccupation with the *incongruous* Aeschylean phrase at the end of *Tess* leads to the view that the unconscious Will in Hardy assumes the form of 'an Aeschylean fury'. A variety of critical lapses marks the closing stages of this work, which recovers to assert that, though Hardy rejected Christian theology, he was 'one of the most Christian spirits that ever lived'.

Chase, Mary Ellen, *Thomas Hardy, from Serial to Novel*, University of Minnesota Press, 1927; Russell & Russell, New York, 1964.
This study of Hardy's changes from serial to novel form is limited to *The Mayor of Casterbridge*, *Tess of the d'Urbervilles*, and *Jude the Obscure*. The work is admirably systematic and lucid, and includes reference to some changes in later editions.

Chew, Samuel C., *Thomas Hardy, Poet and Novelist*, Knopf, rev., 1928; reissued Russell & Russell, 1964.
The work may be recommended as a general introduction, but it needs to be read critically. It deals in generalizations rather than in detailed criticism, and may be described as a series of short essays or lightning tours. Some of the generalizations are facile: Hardy's women are all of one type, essentially Cyrenaics, differing only in degree; he seeks to show how closely akin men are. The assumption that the same Conjuror Trendle appears in 'The Withered Arm' and *Tess*, and that therefore the period and the general locality of the two stories are about the same, is surprising. And how true is it that, as night draws on, the tales told in *A Group of Noble Dames* become darker in tone?

Child, Harold, *Thomas Hardy*, Nisbet, rev., 1925.
This introductory work is admirably written, and presents a clear account of Hardy's philosophy and his artistic purpose. Within the limitations imposed by the length of the work, the novels are handled deftly, and *The Dynasts* appreciatively. One or two factual errors may be noticed.

Duffin, H. C., *Thomas Hardy*, Manchester University Press, 1916; 3rd ed., with further revisions and additions, 1937.

The third edition opens with a running commentary on the novels in chronological order. Studies of various aspects of the novels follow, with critical analyses of *The Dynasts* and the poems. A great deal of penetrating criticism may be found in this lengthy study, which is cumulative rather than constructive. Occasionally, the author betrays a lack of judgment and restraint. His anti-feminism is too marked to influence the unbiased reader.

Eliot, T. S., *After Strange Gods*, Faber, 1934.

Eliot's remarks are not lengthy, but they are sufficiently weighty and damning to require comment. He wishes he knew more of modern novelists, and shows a very limited knowledge of Hardy, finding him 'unhampered' by ideas or the desire to please a large public. Hardy 'always' wrote 'very badly', and it was in consequence of his self-absorption that he made a great deal of landscape. His characters come to life only in 'emotional paroxysms'. Eliot finds 'a world of pure Evil' in 'Barbara of the House of Grebe', and concludes that it was written 'solely to provide a satisfaction for some morbid emotion'. How far the story was based on historical research or imagination is not known, but Hardy's motive in presenting it was his horror at man's inhumanity to woman, one of his avowed themes. Eliot's attitude is that of a Grand Inquisitor; he deplores heterodoxy, and translates the horror which the story rouses into the *diabolical* operating through Hardy. A firm and reasoned rejoinder came from Katherine Anne Porter; it is included in *The Southern Review*, Summer 1940.

Elliott, A. P., *Fatalism in the Works of Thomas Hardy*, Philadelphia 1935; reissued Russell & Russell, 1966.

'It is interested only in a general way with the man as a philosopher. Its chief concern is with Hardy the artist, and with an analysis of his art in its relation to Fate as an artistic motif.' What is said on Hardy as a philosopher is much more acceptable than many of the detailed and general judgments in the 'analysis of his art in its relation to Fate'.

Guerard, A. J., *Thomas Hardy, the Novels and Stories*, Harvard University Press and Oxford University Press, 1949.

A vigorous and penetrating book which undermines a number of critical clichés (e.g. that Hardy regretted the passing of the old agricultural order, and that the philosophy of *The Dynasts* cast its long shadow anticipatively over the novels). Repeatedly it pays tribute to Hardy's imaginative genius. Grotesque and supernatural incidents are gathered somewhat indiscriminately to show the powerlessness of man against the unpredictable. Many of these simply originated from local history and superstitions, and were the obvious materials for arresting stories. Guerard restores the balance when he emphasizes that Hardy's 'anti-realism' was aesthetic rather than metaphysical, and that his 'psychological curiosity was melodramatic, the curiosity of a teller of tales'. In the analysis of some of the characters, his insight is profoundly illuminating, but the classification of Hardy's women leads to superficial and dangerous appraisals. The dubious conclusion is reached that the secret of Hardy's popularity is that 'things not men are to blame' and that '*everybody* is good enough'. 'Good and evil seemed irrelevant in such an indifferent universe; he wanted people to be happy.' Some minor conclusions may occasion surprise: *The Mayor of Casterbridge* is nearly a hundred pages too long (they include chapters xxxvi to xl); Diggory Venn obstinately refuses to live, and few can be expected to love him – he has more in common with 'the criminal voyeur' such as William Dare than we like to think; George Somerset is the most convincing of Hardy's 'intellectuals'; and the sleep-walking of Angel Clare is 'of course a major scar on the surface of a great book'. This book measures up to Hardy's greatness in a variety of ways, and takes the study of his fiction a long way forward. Perhaps it could go further still if the view were not held that Hardy 'stumbled' into greatness as a novelist.

Hardy, Evelyn, *Thomas Hardy, a Critical Biography*, Hogarth Press, 1954; reissued Russell & Russell, 1970.
This work is enriched by extensive original research; many details are not to be found elsewhere. The presentation of Hardy's earlier years, and the chapter on the estrangement between him and his first wife, are of special interest. The biography is sounder than the criticism; it is surely a misjudgment, for example, to hold that Tess is 'the victim of her own strong sensuality'. Critical thought tends to be associative, and is more valuable when imagery is under consideration. Analysis of *The Dynasts* is more comprehensive, and has much to offer.

Hawkins, Desmond, *Thomas Hardy*, Arthur Barker, 1950.
An eminently readable and urbane study of the novels. It is too discursive, especially in the earlier chapters, to be recommended as an introduction and too general to provide much intensive criticism. Too often Hardy's

works are dealt with expeditiously as if they were bagatelles. We are told that he may have abandoned novel-writing because he was weak in devising plots and characters. The author finds it difficult to distinguish between Gabriel Oak and Giles Winterborne, and makes occasional errors which suggest that criticism can become too detached. The last chapter may persuade readers of this series of rather distant surveys that Hardy is worth close attention.

Holloway, J., *The Victorian Sage*, Macmillan, 1953.
The essay on Hardy is limited to the novels. It shows the relatedness of things in time and space, and of man and nature. The attempt to reveal society as a microcosm of nature seems inconclusive. Figurative description is taken continually as the reflection of philosophical thought. The complex of causation which Hardy's novels illustrate, often with ironical effects, is an acceptable – and even commonplace – view of life in a scientific era; but to adduce proof of causation is not a proof of determinism in the philosophical sense, as Holloway argues. He concludes that Hardy presents 'a determined system of things' which 'controls human affairs without regard for human wishes'. Hardy, as he insisted in a cancelled preface to *A Pair of Blue Eyes*, was just as interested in the influence of character on events as on circumstances affecting destiny. This implies the existence of degrees of will and choice. Another conclusion drawn from Hardy's novels is that '*it is right to live naturally*'. Whatever general impressions some of the more pastoral stories may appear to provide, Hardy's views of Nature were certainly not romantic; they were far too complex for any such conclusion to be drawn. The corollary that 'to adapt one's self to one's traditional situation is good' can be controverted from several novels, especially *Tess of the d'Urbervilles*. Swithin was not made unhappy because he was a successful astronomer, and Jude was not wrong in aspiring to Christminster. The essay contains many illuminating details, but its general tendency and conclusions require many qualifications.

Howe, Irving, *Thomas Hardy*, The Macmillan Co., New York, 1967; Weidenfeld & Nicolson, 1968.
One of the most important of the general critical surveys.

Hynes, Samuel, *The Pattern of Hardy's Poetry*, University of North Carolina Press, 1961.
The work is scholarly and stimulating. It does not overlook Hardy's

poetical shortcomings. Several poems are sensitively and imaginatively analysed, and new light is thrown on Hardy's imagery. The range and depth of the criticism are admirable, especially with reference to *The Dynasts*, but schematization, one suspects, is over-assimilative. The thesis that 'the antinomial pattern' is generally a trustworthy one as a criterion of judgment is strikingly presented, but it does not seem to be the obvious key, for example, to the discrepancy between the language of the human characters and the style of the Spirits in *The Dynasts*. The first was geared to human speech, actual or probable; it is variable, not 'monotonic', though often dulled and flattened by Hardy's limitations as a writer of blank verse. Only in the comments of the principal Spirits did Hardy express himself, and it is there that the main conflict or antinomy exists.

Johnson, Lionel, *The Art of Thomas Hardy*, John Lane, 1894; new ed., 1923.
A rewarding critic for those who have the time and patience to wait for the relevant in a discursive series of literary essays. For him Wessex is a 'living palimpsest'; he unfolds its historicity and variety. He shows genuine appreciation of Hardy's form and style, and the principal qualities that endow him with greatness. Evocations of Hardy's characters follow.

Lawrence, D. H., *Study of Thomas Hardy*. The complete text is to be found in *Phoenix*, Heinemann, 1936; reprinted 1961.
The study of Hardy was merely incidental to the larger theme which Lawrence developed in his horrified reaction to the outbreak of the First World War. 'What colossal idiocy, this war. Out of sheer rage I've begun my book about Thomas Hardy. It will be about anything but Thomas Hardy, I'm afraid – queer stuff – but not bad.' Lawrence takes and re-creates from Hardy no more than will serve his purpose. This is simply to show that the Law (or nature) and Love must be reconciled by the Holy Spirit. The Law is found strongest in women, and Love in men. In Hardy they conflict, and the result is Death.

The tragedy of Hardy's characters is that when they break out of 'the comparative imprisonment of the established convention' or bourgeois morality into the wilderness of life they die. It is the one theme of the Wessex novels; even Fancy Day will regret lost opportunities, and Dick Dewy 'will probably have a bad time of it'. The vast unwritten morality of nature 'would have bidden Eustacia fight Clym for his own soul, and

Tess take and claim Angel . . . would have bidden Jude and Sue endure for very honour's sake . . .'. Hardy's *prédilection d'artiste* was for the 'aristocratic' or non-bourgeois person, but his moral sense was so bourgeois that the exceptional had to die. His first show of sympathy was for Eustacia; his last for Jude and Sue. Among the passionate aristocrats we find Alec d'Urberville and Arabella. The undistinguished bourgeois usually succeeds; if he fails, 'he has flowers on his grave': A lack of 'sternness', 'a hesitating between life and public opinion . . . diminishes the Wessex novels from the rank of pure tragedy'. By abstracting or creating qualities in Hardy's characters which suit his dialectic, Lawrence makes everything syllogistically plain. His finest analysis is reserved for Sue Bridehead. He insists that Jude and Sue were not shunned because they defied the conventions, but because people were instinctively aware that their marriage was unnatural or sinful.

Lerner, L., and Holmstrom, J., *Thomas Hardy and his Readers*, Bodley Head, 1968.
Most of this selection of contemporary reviews is devoted to *Far from the Madding Crowd, Tess of the d'Urbervilles*, and *Jude the Obscure*. Altogether, eight novels are represented: *Desperate Remedies* and the seven which have retained their popularity in recent years.

McDowall, Arthur, *Thomas Hardy*, Faber, 1931.
The work is devoted to the novels, *The Dynasts*, and the poems. The tragic scope of the novels, their comedy, style, and characters are discussed, but Hardy's Nature demands a deeper and more extensive treatment than it receives. Though written on rather ample and general lines, this study is characterized by sound judgment and sensitive awareness. Valuable comparisons of Hardy and other writers are introduced. The writer's fidelity to tone, texture, and atmosphere is revealed throughout; one can only regret that more space was not devoted to critical analysis at various points.

Morrell, Roy, *Thomas Hardy: the Will and the Way*, University of Malaya Press, 1965.
This is refreshing criticism because it challenges many stale judgments inherited from the critics, and insists on a faithful reading of Hardy. His characters are not helpless puppets in the hands of Fate; they are presented with choice and the making of decisions. Some, like Oak, Farfrae,

and Wellington, are practical and use knowledge and initiative to adapt themselves; others, like Henchard, are more stupid though non-acquiescent; some, like Giles Winterborne or Tess, are too acquiescent. In this sense, character, like circumstance, is part of fate, but the principle of choice or free will is not excluded. Hardy could not have been a 'meliorist' if he had been an out-and-out determinist. The book consists largely of articles and papers. This leads to much reiteration, but ample compensation for this is found in the vigour, clarity, and cogency of the argument. Some of the more detailed criticism (of symbolical passages, for example) is less convincing.

Orel, Harold, *Thomas Hardy's Epic-Drama: A Study of 'The Dynasts'*, University of Kansas Press, 1963.
In the preface it is stated that Hardy vehemently declared on several occasions that *The Dynasts* should be judged on artistic grounds. The book is scholarly, and sketches in masterly style the developments which made Hardy turn from prose fiction to poetry and *The Dynasts* (though more should be said on the Immanent Will in the poetry which preceded *The Dynasts*). The bulk of the criticism is rather too heavily biased in the direction of Burke and the sublime, *Paradise Lost*, the *Iliad*, and Hardy's views on war. The problem is not eased through regarding Napoleon as the hero of the drama, or assuming that Hardy's attitude to war in general is the only relevant criterion to assess this aspect of *The Dynasts*. Hardy wrote not only poems on war but patriotic poems in time of war; his sympathies are against Napoleon, and admiration is implicit in his presentation of certain war-leaders and gallant troops and soldiers, despite the horrible carnage and suffering. Numerous observations in this study provide a welcome counterpoise to the lack of fervour in many critics for a work which is undeservedly neglected, and make one wish that the author had devoted more time to a critical assessment of the work as a whole.

Paterson, John, *The Making of 'The Return of the Native'*, University of California Press, 1960.
This analysis of the textual changes which a re-orientation of the course of the novel involved after the earlier chapters had been written, and of subsequent changes in the novel as a whole, goes far to show that Hardy did not always regard novel-writing as 'journeyman' work, as well as to

disprove the common view that he worked closely to preconceived plots. Hardy's first conception of Eustacia is adumbrated; she was certainly presented less sympathetically, but not as demonically as the author attempts to prove. Her transformation to a romantic heroine constitutes the most remarkable of the many changes which this novel underwent. Other modifications affected Wildeve and Clym Yeobright in particular. The movement towards the creation of a classical framework of reference, and stylistic changes, especially in imagery, which continually emphasize the hostility of Nature and Fate (symbolized in Egdon Heath), are impressively illustrated. It is significant that, though in the 1895 edition Hardy went so far as to suggest illicit relations between Eustacia and Wildeve at the opening, second thoughts prevailed; it was one thing to challenge public opinion, but another to weaken respect for a Promethean heroine by making her fall soul and body to a man she despised. The conclusiveness of this study is questionable at certain points.

Rutland, W. R., *Thomas Hardy, a Study of his Writings and their Background*, Blackwell, 1938; reprinted Russell & Russell, 1962.
This stands out among the critical books on Hardy by virtue of its scholarship and original research. The researches centred in *The Poor Man and the Lady* and Hardy's historical reading for *The Dynasts* are of special value. Rutland gives an excellent account of the climate of Victorian England when Christianity was under attack. His critical views are often sound, but sometimes sweepingly reactionary, especially with reference to *Tess of the d'Urbervilles* and *Jude the Obscure*. Even so, his book has much to offer scholarly readers.

Stewart, J. I. M., *Eight Modern Writers*, Oxford University Press, 1963.
The essay is written with breadth of vision and masterly compactness. So much is concentrated in this study, including outlines of important novels, that it provides an excellent introduction or summing-up for the mature reader. A few details may be questioned: does Tess become Alec's mistress before she returns home, and is it accurate to regard the Will as *malevolent*? Hardy's novels, his poetry, and *The Dynasts* receive attention. A very helpful bibliography is provided.

Weber, Carl, *Hardy of Wessex*, Columbia University Press, and Routledge & Kegan Paul, 1965.
This is the best of the literary (rather than critical) biographies of Hardy. It is eminently readable, scholarly, and comprehensive. Room is found

for many of the important discoveries which the author has made during years of devoted first-hand research. There is little that he has overlooked in the field of Hardy scholarship. This work gives more information on the history of Hardy's publications than any other of its kind. Some of the biographical facts have been found in Hardy's unpublished letters. Topographical details are sometimes only approximate. The story of Martha Brown (repeated from the earlier edition) is unverified; she lived at Broadwindsor in west Dorset.

Webster, H. C., *On a Darkling Plain*, University of Chicago Press, 1947; reprinted, 1964.

This work presents a clear picture of the intellectual background which changed Hardy's outlook. Certain aspects of the new scientific mode of thinking are applied as criteria to evaluate the novels. The analysis, novel by novel, in terms of natural selection, chance, circumstance, and determinism, tends by sub-division and cumulation to reduce the critical effect. The limitations and dangers of this approach are recognized in the 1964 preface: 'I feel that I write of the novels too often as though they were illustrations of Hardy's philosophy rather than *his dramatization of his search for a philosophy.*' Hardy's thought and its development with reference to the novels is of the highest importance, and it is primarily for this reason that this succinct and scholarly work has much to offer.

Wing, George, *Hardy*, Oliver & Boyd, 1963.
The work is brief but intensive. It includes close impressions of Hardy's work in all its forms, and finds space for assessments of some important works on Hardy. The approach is neither too solemn nor too finical. The author is critically tolerant, and can find something to appreciate in neglected novels. His style is vigorous, though it tends to exaggerate sex and 'savagery' in Hardy's stories. It is perhaps surprising to find *The Trumpet-Major* among the 'inner' novels with *Far from the Madding Crowd*, *The Return of the Native*, and *The Woodlanders*.

(A supplementary selection follows)

Bibliographical Supplement

Texts

Poems of Thomas Hardy, a selection with introduction and notes by T. R.M. Creighton, Macmillan, 1974.

The New Wessex Edition of the Novels, with introductions and notes (hardback and paperback), Macmillan, 1974-76

The Complete Poems, with introduction and notes by James Gibson, Macmillan, 1976.

The Short Stories (including previously uncollected), with introduction and notes by F. B. Pinion, Macmillan, 1977.

Bibliography

(ed.) A. E. Dyson, *The English Novel: Select Bibliographical Guides* (a descriptive chapter with classified lists by F. B. Pinion), Oxford University Press, 1974.

Biography and letters

F. E. Halliday, *Thomas Hardy, His Life and Work*, Bath, 1972. (edd.) Evelyn Hardy and F. B. Pinion, *One Rare Fair Woman*, Macmillan and the University of Miami Press, 1972. Letters of Thomas Hardy to Florence Henniker from 1893 to 1922, some of the earliest throwing important light on the final developments in the plot of *Jude the Obscure*.

Robert Gittings, *Young Thomas Hardy*, Heinemann, 1975. All future biographers of Hardy will be indebted to the immense research behind this book. It reflects a current bias here and there, and is sometimes romantic.

Timothy O'Sullivan, *Thomas Hardy, An Illustrated Biography*, Macmillan, 1975 and St. Martin's Press, 1976. Very informative, and handsomely illustrated.

Bibliographical Supplement

Topography

D. Kay-Robinson, *Hardy's Wessex Reappraised*, David and Charles, 1972. Very thorough, on a regional basis.

Essays (mainly critical)

(ed.) R. G. Cox, *Thomas Hardy, The Critical Heritage*, Longman, 1970. A most interesting collection of contemporary reviews of Hardy's works as they appeared, with some of the earlier critical essays, and a valuable introduction.

(ed.) Margaret Drabble, *The Genius of Thomas Hardy*, Weidenfeld and Nicolson, 1976. A most uneven collection, with a few important contributions and a rash resurrection of unverified and unverifiable biography.

(ed.) F. B. Pinion, *Thomas Hardy and the Modern World*, The Thomas Hardy Society Ltd, Dorchester, 1974. Like the next volume, this consists of papers given by recognized Hardy scholars at a Summer School organized by the Society.

(ed.) F. B. Pinion, *Budmouth Essays on Thomas Hardy*, The Thomas Hardy Society Ltd, 1976.

Critical Works

1. General:

Jean Brooks, *Thomas Hardy, The Poetic Structure*, Paul Elek, 1971. Intensive, with an existentialist slant.

Ian Gregor, *The Great Web, The Form of Hardy's Major Fiction*, Faber and Faber, and Crane, Russak, 1974. A close study of the six major tragic novels.

Desmond Hawkins', Hardy, *Novelist, and Poet*, David and Charles, and Barnes & Noble, 1976.

Dale Kramer, *Thomas Hardy, The Forms of Tragedy*, Wayne State University Press and Macmillan, 1975.

J. Hillis Miller, *Thomas Hardy, Distance and Desire*, Harvard University Press, 1970. Brilliantly written, with many fine observations, though some of its assumptions and conclusions would have astonished Hardy.

Michael Millgate, *Thomas Hardy, His Career as a Novelist*, The Bodley Head, 1971. Scholarly in background knowledge and the reading of the novels.

Harold Orel, *The Final Years of Thomas Hardy, 1912-28*, Macmillan and the University Press of Kansas, 1976.
Special emphasis is given to Hardy's writings and thought.
F. R. Southerington, *Hardy's Vision of Man*, Chatto and Windus, 1971.
J. I. M. Stewart, *Thomas Hardy, A Critical Biography*, Longman, 1971.
More valuable critically than biographically, and very readable.
Penelope Vigar, *The Novels of Thomas Hardy, Illusion and Reality*, Athlone Press, 1974.

2. Poetry:

J. O. Bailey, *The Poetry of Thomas Hardy*, University of North Carolina Press, 1970.
A valuable reference book for the discriminating reader, it gives an immense amount of background and explanatory material on all the poems and on Hardy's two dramatic works.
K. Marsden, *The Poems of Thomas Hardy*, Athlone Press, 1969.
One of the soundest studies of Hardy's poetry.
Tom Paulin, *Thomas Hardy, The Poetry of Perception*, Macmillan, 1975, and Rowman & Littlefield, 1976.
Original and illuminating.
F. B. Pinion, *A Commentary on the Poems of Thomas Hardy*, Macmillan, and Barnes & Noble, 1976.
Elucidatory background for nearly all the poems, showing relationships among them and with Hardy's work and thought generally, with some textual notes.
Paul Zietlow, *Moments of Vision, The Poetry of Thomas Hardy*, Harvard University Press, 1974.
A study of *Wessex Poems* and, in categories, of selections from the remainder of Hardy's verse.

3. More Specialized Studies:

J. T. Laird, *The Shaping of 'Tess of the d'Urbervilles'*, Oxford University Press, 1975.
R. J. White, *Thomas Hardy and History*, Macmillan and Barnes & Noble, 1974.
Merryn Williams, *Thomas Hardy and Rural England*, Macmillan

and Columbia University Press, 1972.
Background, with studies of seven of Hardy's novels in relation to
it and to some contemporary fiction.
W. F. Wright, *The Shaping of 'The Dynasts'*, University of
Nebraska Press, 1967.

Index

Index

cider-making, 44, 140–1
Collins, Wilkie, 17
conjurers (white wizards or witches), 72, 131–2, 324, 375, 421, 492
Crabbe, George, 125, 202, 366
Crickmay, G. R., 6, 17, 252, 478, 507
crowd, the (and automatic behaviour), 103, 391

Defoe, Daniel, 16, 58, 206
Desperate Remedies, 6, 16, 17–19, 33, 36, 47, 153, 155
'Destiny and a Blue Cloak', 59–61
Dickens, Charles, 5, 22, 30
'Doctor's Legend, The', 81–3, 209, 415
Donne, John, 126
Dorchester, 1, 2, 3, 4, 5, 9, 12, 14, 40, 43, 69, 191, 235, 259–70, 336, 356, 405, 418
Dorset County Museum, 14, 268, 498, 505, 531, 532
Dorset Natural History and Antiquarian Field Club, 9, 70, 505
'Dorsetshire Labourer, The', 9, 137–40, 533
Dynasts, The, 10, 11–12, 13, 34, 39, 101–15, 117, 120, 124, 127, 160, 172, 180, 181, 182, 201, 209–10, 391, 533, 536, 538–9, 543, 545, 547, 548

Edward VII, 12, 312
Eliot, George, 8, 18, 19, 27, 29, 39, 41, 206–7
emigration, 136–7
Encke's Comet, 516

Famous Tragedy of the Queen of Cornwall, The, 13, 116–17
Far from the Madding Crowd, 7, 8, 26–8, 33, 44, 154
fiction, Hardy's views on, 143–51
First Cause (or Immanent Will), the, 41, 45–6, 48–9, 53–4, 103, 109, 110, 161, 169, 175–8, 332

Fordington, 3, 7, 14, 98, 309–11, 336, 346, 419–20
frost and the 'universal harshness', 1, 124, 165, 182, 332–3

Galsworthy, John, 179
garden symbolism, 158, 165, 166
General Preface to the Novels and Poems, 204, 210, 217, 223, 533, 536
George V, 339
ghostly visitants, 155–6, 158–9
Gibbon, Edward, 11, 388
Gifford, Evelyn, 280, 339
Gosse, (Sir) Edmund, 8, 39, 180, 203, 248, 372, 376
Goethe, 107, 153, 156, 157
Gothic elements, 19, 25, 37–8, 121, 153–6, 212
Group of Noble Dames, A, 9, 10, 80–1, 94, 130, 541; the stories, 61–2, 64, 75–80
Grove, Mrs (Lady), 228

Hand of Ethelberta, The, 8, 16, 28–31, 32, 61
Harding, Louisa, 3, 395
Hardy, Captain (Admiral Sir Thomas), 1, 35, 102, 112, 242, 350–1, 448–9
Hardy, Emma Lavinia (Gifford), 6, 7–8, 9, 10–11, 12–13, 22, 23, 24, 116, 128, 132, 176, 191, 239, 305, 319, 351–5, 365, 383, 387, 388, 433, 439, 440, 444, 462, 464, 535
Hardy, Florence Emily (Dugdale), 13, 15, 29, 52, 83, 103, 116, 188, 309 n., 328, 355–6, 365, 534
Hardy, Henry (brother), 7, 13, 487
Hardy, Katherine (sister), 4, 13, 356, 487
Hardy, Jemima (mother), 1, 2, 12, 29, 31, 97, 131, 356, 383, 517
Hardy, Mary (paternal grandmother, *née* Head), 1, 20, 31, 101, 131, 190, 247, 328, 356–7, 402

555

Moule, Henry J., 83
Moule, Horace, 3–4, 6, 7, 52, 309, 311, 385, 419–20, 438, 440
mumming, 2, 31, 117, 464
music, church, 141; in Hardy's writings, 188–93; the Hardys and, 2, 3, 20–1, 187–8, 190, 191, 192, 412, 517

nature, 1, 19, 21, 27, 31, 33, 34, 44, 48, 49, 50, 53, 56, 57, 74, 105, 125, 144, 150, 162, 163, 165–6, 172–6, 182, 314, 332
'negative beauty of tragic tone', 125, 144, 314, 467
non-rational elements in Hardy, 158–61

'Old Mrs Chundle', 83–5
'Our Exploits at West Poley', 100
Owen, Rebekah, 81, 91, 293, 430
Oxford, 4, 13, 52, 92, 278–80, 339, 430, 532

painters, influence and recollections of, 5, 19, 48, 143, 144, 193–200, 212
Pair of Blue Eyes, A, 7, 16, 23–6, 154, 185, 191, 440, 462
Pater, Walter, 33, 169, 436
Paterson, Helen, 372
pessimism and 'meliorism', 178–80, 547
poaching and man-traps, 135–6
Poems of the Past and the Present, 11, 121, 127
poetry, Hardy's, 118–29
political views, 5, 6, 15, 30, 180–1, 405–6
Poor Man and the Lady, The, 5, 6, 15–17, 18, 20, 23–4, 30, 43, 58–9, 180, 391, 548
poor man and lady theme, 23–4, 29, 43, 58–9, 72, 172, 244, 353, 395, 462–3, 473, 478, 506

'Profitable Reading of Fiction, The', 146–8, 533

Return of the Native, The, 8, 18, 19, 31–4, 38, 39, 40, 45, 68, 131, 156–7, 162, 170–1, 184, 185, 312–15, 468, 539, 547–8
Richardson, Samuel, 148, 158 n.
'Romantic Adventures of a Milkmaid, The', 66–8, 153, 157, 158
rural life, 135, 137, 141, 173

St Juliot, 6–7, 13, 23–4, 319, 351–5, 433, 464
Salisbury, 4, 185, 356, 358, 361, 407–10, 464–5
Satires of Circumstance, 13
Schopenhauer, 106, 107, 175, 539
'Science of Fiction, The', 143, 148–149, 533
scientific thought, effect on Hardy, 4, 5–6, 25, 34, 39, 106, 108, 120, 121, 125, 126, 144, 165, 168, 176, 179, 218
Scott, Sir Walter, 4, 25, 41, 152, 205, 211–13
Scott-Siddons, Mrs Mary Frances, 467
Shakespeare, 4, 9, 22, 25, 39, 41, 48, 109, 114, 146, 147, 151, 157, 163, 165, 215–17, 364, 468, 512
Shelley, 4, 16, 25, 45, 50, 56, 107–8, 126, 153, 164, 165, 169, 178, 180, 182, 213–14
Shrewsbury, Earl of, 471
skimmington-rides, 42, 135
Smith, T. Roger, 7, 474
smuggling, 1, 62–3, 142, 385, 397–398, 414, 423, 430
social satire, 15, 16, 29–30, 172
society novels, 11, 28, 50, 143, 148
Sophocles, 42, 44, 208
Sparks, Tryphena, 5–6, 21, 52, 53, 120–1, 160, 280–1, 414, 420 n., 435–40, 504
Stephen, Leslie, 8, 26, 29, 32, 35, 118, 120, 121, 480, 534

Index

Stinsford, 1, 2, 14, 25, 187, 246,
258, 301, 339, 344, 360, 382, 383,
395, 410–14, 451, 480, 485, 490,
499
superstitions, 86–7, 122, 131–4,
141, 152, 158–9, 160, 212, 536, 543
Susan, Lady (Fox-Strangways), 25,
75, 473, 485
Swanage, 8, 30, 142, 244, 385, 404,
462, 485
Swetman, Elizabeth (Hardy's
maternal grandmother), 29, 469
Swinburne, Charles Algernon, 4–5,
5–6, 12, 54, 116, 126, 208, 486
symbolism, 25, 27, 31, 32, 33, 34,
35, 48–9, 55–6, 162–6, 281, 332,
500

Tennyson, Alfred (Lord), 8, 26, 49,
116, 126, 157, 208–9
Terry, Ellen, 50
Tess of the d'Urbervilles, 3, 9–10,
18, 19, 24, 33, 46–9, 51, 53, 68,
105, 108, 125, 138, 140, 150, 158,
163–5, 167–8, 171–2, 173–4, 185,
538, 541
'Thieves Who Couldn't Help
Sneezing, The', 100
'things rank and gross in nature',
165–6
Thompson, Edith, 488
time (as a theme), 34, 40, 50, 51, 73,
119, 121, 130, 142, 170–2, 230,
241, 286, 463–4
Time's Laughingstocks, 12
tragedy, Hardy on, 143–5

Trumpet-Major, The, 8, 34–6, 37,
74, 101, 102, 120, 339
Two on a Tower, 9, 38–40, 51, 159,
171

Under the Greenwood Tree, 7, 16,
20–23, 24, 26, 43, 132, 163
United States, the, 12, 36, 61, 136,
358, 494

Victorian reading public, the, 32,
35, 43, 46–7, 52–3, 149–51
Virgil, 2, 16, 109, 209, 400

Walpole, Horace, 108, 209–10, 415
war, 13, 105–6, 181–2
Webster, John, 34, 204
Well-Beloved, The, 10, 11, 45, 49–
51, 121, 135, 153, 185, 539
Wessex Poems, 11, 120–1
Wessex Tales, 73; the stories, 62–4,
65–6, 68–9, 71–2, 74–5
Weymouth, 6, 17, 19, 35, 60,
252–5, 507
Wimborne Minster, 9, 39, 68, 510–
511
Winchester, 364, 513
Winter Words, 14, 120
witchcraft, 131, 132
Woodlanders, The, 9, 12, 22, 43–6,
50, 52, 125, 155, 162, 172, 173,
184
Wordsworth, 83, 121, 126, 144,
172, 214–15, 289

Yarborough, Lady, 516

558